A NEW
INTRODUCTION
TO
PHILOSOPHY

A NEW INTRODUCTION TO PHILOSOPHY

STEVEN M. CAHN

New York University

‏ܐ‏

HARPER & ROW, PUBLISHERS
New York, Evanston, San Francisco, London

A NEW INTRODUCTION TO PHILOSOPHY

Copyright © 1971 by Steven M. Cahn

FIRST EDITION

Standard Book Number: 06–041141–4

Library of Congress Catalog Card Number: 75–151329

To the memory of my uncle

MORTON BAUM

אדם אחד מאלף מצאתי

"One man among a thousand have I found"
—*Ecclesiastes,* VII, 28

CONTENTS

PREFACE

Teachers of philosophy are all aware of the difficulties inherent in an introductory philosophy course. A single-authored text can be well organized and clear, but it necessarily presents one man's views, whereas one of the most fascinating aspects of philosophy is the diverse ways in which different philosophers approach the same problem. A book of readings illustrates this diversity, but students find it difficult to grasp the relationships between the readings and often lose sight of the basic problems with which the readings are concerned.

This book attempts a new approach to the teaching of introductory philosophy by combining a single-authored text with closely related readings, a combination that utilizes the best of these two approaches while minimizing the weaknesses each possesses when used in isolation from the other. The text is simple and provides a framework within which the readings can be understood and related to each other. The readings illustrate the diversity of philosophical perspectives alluded to in the text and thus place the text in its proper light.

ACKNOWLEDGMENTS

At virtually every stage in the writing of this book, I have been aware of how much I owe to those who have contributed to my own philosophical education: to Richard Taylor, who taught me the love of wisdom and whose innumerable kindnesses I shall never be able to repay; to Ernest Nagel, who introduced me to philosophy and who gave freely of his time to provide the encouragement that led me to pursue philosophical inquiry; to my former teachers, Justus Buchler, Arthur Danto, Charles Frankel, and Sidney Morgenbesser, each of whom has generously aided me whenever I have been in need of help; to Sidney Hook, who was never formally my teacher, but whose writings have been a constant source of inspiration to me; to my colleagues, John O'Connor, James Rachels, and Garrett Vander Veer, with whom I have spent so many fruitful and enjoyable hours; and to Frank Tillman, who has befriended me in countless ways.

It was Professor Tillman who first discussed the idea for this book with me, and he has aided me at every stage of the work. Earlier drafts of the book were also read by Professor Rachels, Professor Taylor, and my close friend Ronald Bettauer, and I deeply appreciate their valuable suggestions. I also wish to thank Mr. James Clark, my editor at Harper & Row, for his advice and encouragement.

I cannot conclude without acknowledging the special contribution which was made to this work by my brother Victor. He read every single page of every draft, bringing his literary skills to my aid time and time again. The reader can be grateful to him for whatever clarity the book possesses. I am grateful to him for so much more.

A NEW
INTRODUCTION
TO
PHILOSOPHY

INTRODUCTION

Philosophy is a subject about which most people know very little. It is reputed to be abstruse, dark, and obscure, a mysterious combination of psychology, theology, and astrology. Philosophers are thought to be men of great wisdom, though their wisdom, oddly enough, is considered of no practical value. To some nonphilosophers the supposed impracticality of philosophy is reason enough to disregard or denigrate it, but to others it is precisely the supposed separation between philosophy and the everyday problems of life that is most appealing. Such individuals may regret that they do not have the time to philosophize, and they may envy those who do.

Often an appeal is made to philosophy when a discussion touches on matters that are highly complex and obscure. "That's too deep for us; let's leave it for the philosophers." Reference is also made to philosophy when an expert is asked for his deepest thoughts about his area of expertise. "Mayor, what's your philosophy of government?" or "Coach, what's your philosophy of football?" Finally, one may ask a close friend or a member of one's family, "What's your philosophy of life?" This is thought to be a question of enormous profundity, and one that philosophers ponder endlessly.

The aura surrounding philosophy is in part due to the fact that this subject is almost never studied below the college level. Elementary and secondary school students study mathematics, literature, and history, but not philosophy. It would be thought foolish even to suggest that ten-year-olds study philosophy, for it seems obvious that a young person does not have a philosophy of life, or if he claims to have such a thing, his views are surely too immature to concern adults.

It is only at college that the opportunity is presented to study philosophy. Many students avoid the subject because it is reputedly difficult. They feel that they do not think clearly or deeply enough to understand what will be discussed. Other students welcome the opportunity to study philosophy, for they have thought a great deal about life and wish to learn what others have said about this subject.

But many of these students undergo a severe disappointment. They are surprised and frustrated to find that philosophers spend little, if any, time discussing the subjects they are thought to discuss. What they actually discuss seems quite technical, often boring, and difficult to master. Philosophers appear oblivious to those vital issues that were supposed to occupy their attention, and they seemingly concern themselves with manipulating meaningless symbols, making useless distinctions between words, and imagining improbable examples to refute insignificant claims.

It must be admitted that philosophers have done little to alleviate the misunderstandings that surround their enterprise. Their writings are generally technical and difficult to understand. Philosophers rarely contribute to widely known periodicals, and when they do, they engage in literary criticism or social commentary, not philosophy. Most people have never read even a single article that is considered by professional philosophers to be a significant contribution to the field. It is no wonder then that philosophy remains a subject virtually unknown to the general reader.

Why, to put it bluntly, do philosophers do such a poor job of public relations? Do they believe their work to be a waste of time? If so, why do they bother with it? If philosophy is important, why cannot its importance be explained to those who do not specialize in the subject?

Some philosophers consider such questions unworthy of response. To these individuals the study of philosophy is its own justification. Any other justification demeans the subject. If a nonphilosopher does not understand the issues that concern philosophers, that is just too bad. His questions simply indicate his ignorance and lack of appreciation for the subtleties of the human mind.

Other philosophers discount the importance of what they do. They consider philosophy an intellectual game, somewhat more complex than bridge or chess. That they are paid to philosophize and to teach others to philosophize is an unwarranted stroke of luck. They discount all attempts to give significance to philosophical inquiry, for they consider this mere rationalization.

I believe that the time is long overdue to dispel the misconceptions surrounding philosophy. The study of philosophy is simply too important to remain the province of a chosen few. Every person who wishes to think and act intelligently needs to understand the methods and accomplishments of philosophy. The fact that much philosophy is technical is no reason why the insights of philosophy cannot be made accessible to the nonphilosopher. That there are such insights is a fact which ought to be acknowledged by anyone who surveys the history of the subject. Many of these insights are directly applicable to such vital areas of human concern as morality, politics, religion, and education, and any inquiry that is able to shed light on such crucial subjects is surely of the greatest practical significance.

It is my aim in this book to break through the clouds of confusion that surround discussions of the nature and significance of philosophical inquiry. Philosophy has made and will continue to make major contributions to the life of man, and an understanding and appreciation of these contributions will enrich the life of each member of society.

PART I

WHAT IS PHILOSOPHY?

Chapter 1

THE CHALLENGES OF PHILOSOPHY

The study of philosophy is unlike the study of any other subject. We need not memorize dates, formulas, or rules. No field work is necessary and no technical equipment required. The only prerequisite is an inquiring mind.

All of us from time to time engage in serious discussion of matters which are of the greatest concern to us. When we are challenged to defend our religious beliefs, our moral and political commitments, or our educational ideals, we feel impelled to meet this challenge with all the intellectual resources at our command. We rely upon our knowledge of history and the various sciences. We appeal to widely accepted ethical standards. We cite the views of experts and quote from classic texts. On some occasions such tactics suffice to settle the question at hand. But at other times the authorities upon which we depend are themselves subject to dispute. Our opponent may refuse to recognize the ethical standards to which we appeal or the experts whom we cite. History, he may say, is always biased, for it reflects the prejudices of the historian, and scientific knowledge is never reliable, for it is constantly changing. Suddenly the very foundations of our beliefs are shaken. We feel unsure of ourselves. So long as our opponent recognizes the sources of knowledge to which we appeal, the dispute may be resolved simply by checking in the library. But what if he questions these authorities upon which we rely? Is there any way we can defend our position?

At such a time philosophical techniques are essential. What exactly do we mean by "philosophical"? Or, more precisely, what do we mean by "philosophy"?

The word "philosophy" is of Greek origin and literally means "the love of wisdom." However, this definition hardly serves to differentiate philosophy from other inquiries, for we might rightfully ask what sort of wisdom it is that philosophers love. Historians love the study of human events, and scientists love the study of the natural world. What sort of study do philosophers love?

Philosophical inquiry began in the Greek colony of Miletus about 600 B.C. Throughout its history we can distinguish two different, though related, approaches. These I shall call "analytical philosophy" and "speculative philosophy." Analytical philosophy has been a prevalent mode of philosophizing ever since the time of Socrates (ca. 470–399 B.C.). Although virtually every philosopher of note has engaged to some degree in analytical philosophy, it was not until the beginning of the twentieth century that this type of philosophy took on its distinct identity. Under the influence of its leading proponents, G. E. Moore (1873–1958), Bertrand Russell (1872–1970), and Ludwig Wittgenstein (1889–1951), analytical philosophy has been a powerful influence in the development of contemporary thought.

The analytical philosopher is, as his name implies, an analyst. But he is not an analyst in the same sense, for example, as is a scientist. The scientist is an inquirer who seeks to explain systematically the world in which we live. In order to carry out this task effectively, he engages in carefully controlled observation and experimentation, often utilizing various technical equipment. The analytical philosopher, on the other hand, has a different aim. He seeks to discover the nature of and justification for the basic principles that underlie scientific inquiry. In other words, when the analytical philosopher views science, he concerns himself with certain fundamental presuppositions of scientific inquiry. He attempts to clarify the methodological principles employed, perhaps unknowingly, by a scientist.

For example, it has often been claimed that science rests on the principle of determinism, the thesis that every event which occurs has some cause that accounts for the occurrence of the event. Suppose a scientist, when asked to explain the occurrence of a particular event, were to reply that no such explanation could possibly be given since the event in question had no cause. Would not such a reply be scientific heresy, a repudiation of the scientific enterprise itself? This question brings to the fore important philosophical issues. What exactly is it for one event to cause another? Is it a scientific law that every event has a cause? What, in fact, is a scientific law? How does it differ from a scientific theory? How are such laws and theories proven to be true? Has determinism been proven to be true or has it been assumed to be true? There is a sense in which science can proceed in its task without answers to all of these questions. Nevertheless, if we are fully to understand what the scientist is doing and to evaluate his work properly, it is necessary to employ the tools of analytical philosophy in order to answer satisfactorily questions such as these. And it is such questions that belong to that field of analytical philosophy known as philosophy of science.

Analytical philosophy, however, is not limited to analyzing the methodological principles of scientific inquiry. Each of the other major areas of human inquiry has its own basic principles that need clarification and justification.

Consider, for example, moral inquiry. Suppose an individual declares that all wars are immoral. What exactly is the meaning of his statement? Is he stating a fact or merely expressing his personal opinion? Is there any way of determining whether his view is right or wrong? If some other individual takes an opposing view, is there any method of resolving their disagreement? Such questions lie in that field of analytical philosophy referred to as metaethics. Metaethics is not concerned with how a man ought to live his life or what his moral views ought to be. Just as philosophy of science is not itself a part of science, so metaethics is not itself a part of moral inquiry. If we claim that moral disagreements can be resolved, we do not thereby defend or oppose the claim that all wars are immoral. We simply acknowledge that the question is decidable. Just as philosophy of science seeks to discover the nature of and justification for the basic principles that underlie scientific inquiry, so metaethics seeks to discover the nature of and justification for the basic principles that underlie moral inquiry.

Similarly, each of the other major areas of human inquiry gives rise to other major fields of analytical philosophy. History, mathematics, theology, psychology, political theory, educational theory, legal theory, linguistics, and art criticism give rise in turn to philosophy of history, philosophy of mathematics, philosophy of religion, philosophy of mind, political philosophy, philosophy of education, philosophy of law, philosophy of language, and philosophy of art (or, as it is sometimes called, aesthetics). Each of these fields of analytical philosophy bears the same relation to its central area as philosophy of science bears to science and metaethics bears to moral inquiry.

Moreover, each of these fields of philosophy has certain basic principles which underlie its particular inquiry. Such principles are, for example, that material objects exist, that people perceive material objects, and that people differ in important respects from mere objects. However, even these seemingly obvious principles are themselves the subject of philosophical investigation. It is the investigation of the nature of and justification for such principles that gives rise to the two fundamental fields of analytical philosophy, metaphysics and epistemology. In other words, metaphysics and epistemology underlie all the other branches of analytical philosophy, for it is in these two fields that we discuss the most fundamental questions possible. Metaphysics, the study of basic features of all existing things, concerns itself with such questions as the relation between a man's mind and his body, the possible incompatibility of determinism and man's free will, and the nature of space and time. Epistemology, the theory of knowledge, concerns itself with such issues as the nature of perception, the relationship between knowledge and belief, and alternative theories of truth.

This rapid survey of analytical philosophy is a mere sketch of a complex and stimulating branch of inquiry. The only way to thoroughly understand its nature is to consider in depth some of its central concerns, and we shall soon begin to do so. For the moment all we need is a general sense of the direction in which we are headed.

It is now time to consider the second branch of inquiry that has occupied the attention of philosophers throughout the centuries. This branch, which I have referred to as "speculative philosophy," moves in an opposite direction from analytical philosophy. Whereas analytical philosophy is concerned with the analysis of the foundations of knowledge, speculative philosophy concerns itself with the synthesis of that knowledge into a world view. Such a world view is based on the results of all human inquiries and involves a systematic presentation of the ultimate nature of the world and the proper place of man and his activities within the world. Speculative philosophy is a description not only of how things are but also how men ought to live their lives and what their moral values ought to be. Speculative philosophy thus involves two elements foreign to analytical philosophy: first, the attempt to synthesize all knowledge so as to create a single, all-embracing view of reality; secondly, the formulation of a unified system of religious, moral, and artistic values.

Speculative philosophy, just as analytical philosophy, is composed of various fields, and these fields correspond to the fields of analytical philosophy. In other words, the fields of philosophy, for example, philosophy of art, philosophy of religion, philosophy of science, etc., actually possess two branches, an analytical branch and a speculative branch. Each of these branches, however, approaches the same subject matter in a quite different manner. Art, religion, and science, for instance, are studied by speculative philosophy not in order to analyze their fundamental principles but in order to understand the role that each of these activities plays in human life. What leads men to engage in these activities? Do these different enterprises complement or conflict with one another? Which of them in the long run is the most important to the life of man? Answers to these questions depend upon our knowledge of such subjects as psychology, sociology, and anthropology, as well as upon our whole system of values. It is precisely the need to take these factors into consideration that distinguishes the speculative branch of philosophy from the analytical.

One simple way to illustrate the distinct approaches of these two branches is to contrast the topics of inquiry considered by each branch when the same field of philosophy is under consideration. Take, for instance, philosophy of art. One influential work in analytical philosophy of art contains such chapter titles as "The Analysis of a Visual Design," "Structure and Texture in Music," "The Interpretation of Literature," and "The Nature of Critical Argument."[1] One important work in speculative philosophy of art contains such chapter titles as "Art as the Expression of Subjectivity," "Art as the Joint Revelation of Self and World," "Language as Articulation of Human Being," and "The Spiritual Truth of Art."[2] The differences between these approaches are quite apparent.

In many respects speculative philosophy may strike one as far more interesting than analytical philosophy. Questions regarding the proper aims of education, the role of the arts in society, the correct ethical standards, and the place of man in the universe are matters of concern to all, whereas questions regarding the foundations of scientific or historical inquiry may seem dry and unimportant. It would be a serious mistake, however, to assume that one may bypass analytical philosophy and jump immediately into speculative philosophy.

[1] Monroe C. Beardsley, *Aesthetics: Problems in the Philosophy of Criticism* (New York: Harcourt Brace Jovanovich, 1958).

[2] Albert Hofstadter, *Truth and Art* (New York: Columbia University Press, 1965).

We are not in a position to formulate a sound world view without having carefully studied the foundations of knowledge, for how are we to decide what knowledge to synthesize without appraising the worth of competing claims to knowledge? Nor are we in a position to form a sound system of values without having thoroughly investigated the standards by which these values are justified, for deciding intelligently between conflicting value systems necessitates the adoption of standards for decision.

Thus, speculative philosophy presupposes analytical philosophy, and, indeed, virtually all those thinkers who have made significant contributions to speculative philosophy have also made contributions to analytical philosophy. This is not to say that philosophers must limit themselves to analytical philosophy. Many philosophers of the first rank from Plato (427–347 B.C.) to John Dewey (1859–1952) have not restricted themselves in this way, and we are fortunate that they did not. But there is no shortcut to sound speculative philosophy which bypasses the detailed work of analytical philosophy. A comprehensive view of the nature of philosophy therefore requires understanding of both these branches.

Our discussion of the scope of philosophical inquiry is now complete. The challenges confronting us are clear. As the contemporary American philosopher Sidney Hook (1902–   ) has written, "At the very least, the philosopher should make men critically aware of their fundamental commitments and the consequences of their commitments. At his best, he projects a vision of human excellence, of what men may become, rooted in a firm knowledge of the limiting conditions of nature, and a sober assessment of the possibilities of the development open to men in an unfinished universe."[3]

To possess philosophical understanding is one mark of a wise man. Such a man cannot be intimidated by dogmatic statements, and he is prepared to strive against those who would control his thoughts. The study of philosophy thus serves as a bulwark against mental servitude and provides the framework within which we can think and act intelligently.

---

[3] Sidney Hook, *The Quest for Being* (New York: St. Martin's Press, 1961), p. viii.

Chapter 2

THE TOOLS OF PHILOSOPHY

It is a simple matter to assert a belief. To defend a belief is far more difficult. Yet if a belief is not defended adequately, there is no reason to accept it. Just because someone says that something is true does not prove that it is true. Suppose Smith says that Mark Twain was born in 1835 and Jones denies this claim. If saying that something is true proved that it was true, then Smith is right in saying that Mark Twain was born in 1835 and Jones is right in his denial—an obviously absurd situation. No matter how loudly or forcefully a belief is asserted, its mere assertion is no reason for us to accept it.

Under what conditions, then, ought we to accept a belief? We normally expect and ought to require that a statement offered for our consideration be supported by evidence. Each time that we cite certain evidence in support of a particular statement, we are presenting an argument. The evidence we cite is the premise or premises of the argument, and the statement we defend is the conclusion of the argument. Not all arguments, however, are valid ones, and not all valid arguments are sound ones. We ought to accept a belief only when that belief is supported by an argument that is both valid and sound. It is thus crucial to be able to distinguish between valid and invalid arguments as well as between sound and unsound ones.

A. LOGIC

Logic is the field of inquiry that distinguishes between valid and invalid arguments. It was Aristotle (384–322 B.C.) who first formalized the fundamental principles of logic, but it is in the last hundred years that the introduction of mathematical methods into logic has greatly increased both its power and its range of application. Although logic is not, strictly speaking, a part of philosophy, it is often considered as such, for logic provides philosophers with essential tools of their trade. There is no use in presenting arguments if we cannot distinguish valid from invalid ones.

A valid argument is an argument in which the premises imply the conclusion. Here are two examples of valid arguments.

a. All United States Senators must be at least thirty years old.
   Mr. White is a United States Senator.
   Therefore, Mr. White is at least thirty years old.
b. The capital of Massachusetts is Springfield.
   There are no banks in the capital of Massachusetts.
   Therefore, there are no banks in Springfield.

Both these arguments are valid, for if we affirm the premises, we must affirm the conclusions. We would contradict ourselves if we affirmed the premises and yet denied the conclusions.

This is not to say that the conclusions of these arguments are true. Truth and validity are two very different things. Although arguments (a) and (b) are both valid, the conclusion of (b) is false and the conclusion of (a) may well be false. A valid argument need not have true premises or a true conclusion. A valid argument is simply one in which the conclusion necessarily follows from the premises. Validity is thus a relationship between the premises and the conclusion of an argument. It is a relationship that holds regardless of the truth or falsity of premises or conclusion.

A valid argument may have (1) true premises and a true conclusion, (2) false premises and a true conclusion, or (3) false premises and a false conclusion. Example (a) illustrates the first possibility (assuming that Mr. White is a Senator); example (a) also illustrates the second possibility (assuming that Mr. White is not a Senator but is at least thirty years old); and example (b) illustrates the third possibility. In all these cases the conclusion follows necessarily from the premises. A valid argument, however, cannot have true premises and a false conclusion, for a valid argument is such that *if* the premises are true, then the conclusion must be true.

It should be apparent now that we ought not to accept every belief which is supported by a valid argument. Such a belief might be false if one or more of the premises of the argument are false. What we ought to accept is a belief which is supported by a valid argument with true premises. Such an argument is referred to as a "sound argument." We may accept a belief supported by a sound argument, for such a belief must be true. It must be true since it follows from a valid argument with true premises, and if the premises of a valid argument are true, the conclusion must be true.

How can we tell if an argument is valid? The general principle is this: An argument is valid if the assertion of the premises and the denial of the conclusion together involve a contradiction. Logic is the tool that enables us to determine in every case whether such a contradiction arises. Logic is not concerned with whether the premises or conclusion of an argument are true; what is of concern is whether *if* the premises are true, then the conclusion must be true.

Since the validity of an argument depends upon whether one can assert the premises and deny the conclusion without contradiction, it is important to understand just what a contradiction is. Two statements are contradictory if the truth of either one guarantees the falsity of the other, and the falsity of either one guarantees the truth of the other. In other words, two statements are contradictory if both cannot be true and both cannot be false. For example, the following two statements are contradictory:

c.   All triangles have three sides.
d.   Some triangles do not have three sides.

If (c) is true, then (d) is false. If (c) is false, then (d) is true. If (d) is true, then (c) is false. If (d) is false, then (c) is true.

If you know that a particular statement is true, then you can be certain that its contradictory is false. If you know that a particular statement is false, then you can be certain that its contradictory is true. It is thus important to know whether one statement is the contradictory of another, for if two statements are contradictory, knowing whether one is true or false enables you to know whether the other is true or false.

It is easy, however, to think that two statements are contradictory when, in fact, they are not. Consider the following two statements:

e. All crows are black.
f. No crows are black.

These two statements are not contradictory. Remember that two state-ments are contradictory only if the truth of one guarantees the falsity of the other, and vice versa. The truth of (e) guarantees the falsity of (f), but the falsity of (e) does not guarantee the truth of (f). If it is false that all crows are black, it does not necessarily follow that no crows are black. Perhaps some crows are black and some are not. In that case both (e) and (f) are false. But if two statements are contradictory, they cannot both be false. Thus (e) and (f) are not contradictory statements.

There is a name, however, for the logical relationship between (e) and (f). These two statements are said to be contraries. Two statements are contrary if both may be false, though both cannot be true. It may be false that all crows are black and false that no crows are black, but it cannot be true that all crows are black and also true that no crows are black. These two statements are thus contraries.

It is vital to distinguish between statements which are contradictory and those which are contrary, for if we confuse the two, as we are prone to do, our reasoning will go astray. If you erroneously believe that state-ments (e) and (f) are contradictories rather than contraries, you will erroneously believe that by showing (e) to be false, you will have shown (f) to be true. But as a matter of fact both (e) and (f) may be false, for these are contraries, not contradictories.

Since we do not discuss the pigmentation of crows very often, consider a more interesting example of this type of logical error.

Smith: There's not an honest politician in the country.
Jones: I disagree. I think Adams, Brown, and Crawford are honest poli-ticians.
Smith: So, you think all politicians are honest. What about Dexter?

Our friend Smith has confused contrary statements with contradictory ones. Jones denies that all politicians are dishonest. He does not thereby commit himself to the view that all politicians are honest. What he does commit himself to is the view that some politicians are not dishonest. The contradictory of "All politicians are dishonest" is "Some politicians are not dishonest." "No politicians are dishonest" is not the contradictory but the contrary of "All politicians are dishonest." Although this confusion of contradictory and contrary statements is relatively easy to spot, it is one that is committed quite often in everyday discussion.

The fact that logic is of great use to us in ordinary conversation should not be surprising, for we all wish to avoid contradicting ourselves. To assert and deny a statement is to say nothing at all. Suppose you ask someone where the nearest hotel is located. He replies, "There is a hotel across the street, and there is no hotel across the street." Such an answer is worthless. You know no more about the location of the nearest hotel than you did before you heard his answer, for he has yet to say anything that makes sense.

He has failed to abide by the most fundamental principle of logic, the law of contradiction. According to this law, no statement can be both true and false. If any statement is true, it cannot also be false. If it is false, it cannot also be true. In order to utilize this principle of logic properly, we must keep in mind that it applies only to statements that are understood in the context of time, place, and person. For instance, the statement "I am cold" may be true now but false an hour from now, or true outside but false inside, or true if uttered by me but false if uttered by you. These are not exceptions to the law of contradiction but merely point out the need to understand statements within their proper context.

Just as the sign of a valid argument is that one cannot assert the premises and deny the conclusion without contradiction, so the sign of an invalid argument is that one *can* assert the premises and deny the conclusion without contradiction. An invalid argument is also referred to as a fallacious argument, an argument that contains a fallacy. Although there are innumerable types of fallacies, certain types recur constantly in common discourse and deserve special attention. The ability to avoid these fallacies in our own thinking and to recognize them when committed by others is a major step forward in increasing philosophical skill.

Perhaps the simplest of all fallacies is the so-called argument *ad hominem* (Latin: "to the man"). To argue *ad hominem* is to argue against a man instead of against the argument he is presenting. You are arguing *ad hominem* if you refuse to accept a particular argument because the person who is presenting it is uneducated, or poor, or un-American, or too highly educated, or too rich, or too patriotic, or is, for any reason, imagined to be unqualified to hold an opinion. An argument is sound only if it is valid and the premises are true, and this is the case no matter in what circumstances or by whom it is presented. When a person reports on what he himself has observed, we may wish to question his competence as a witness due to his poor eyesight or his prejudices. But whether an argument is sound has nothing to do with a man's eyesight or his prejudices. A sound argument is sound no matter who presents it, and an unsound argument is unsound no matter who presents it. It is thus fallacious to argue that "Since Martin was born before 1940, we needn't pay any attention to what he says." When, where, or in what circumstances Martin was born is irrelevant to the soundness of the arguments he presents for our consideration.

A second type of fallacy is the so-called appeal to authority. This fallacy is virtually the exact reverse of the argument *ad hominem*. To argue *ad hominem* is to argue against a man instead of against the argument he is presenting. To argue by appealing to authority is to argue in support of a man instead of in support of the argument he is presenting. You are appealing to authority if you accept an argument simply because the person who is presenting it is famous, or powerful, or a good speaker, or under thirty, or over thirty, or is, for any reason, imagined to be especially qualified to hold an opinion. Again, whether an argument is sound has nothing to do with who presents it. It is true that if a person is a recognized expert in a particular field, his opinions regarding matters in his special field of expertise do carry extra weight. However, it must be kept in mind that even an expert must ultimately be able to defend his views with sound arguments. It is only if he can do so that he is acknowledged as an expert by those who are competent in his field.

A special form of the appeal to authority involves an appeal to the large number of people who hold a particular belief: "That must be a good argument, since everyone accepts it." But no matter how many people believe that an argument is sound, their opinions alone do not make it sound. An argument is sound only if it is valid and the premises are true. The popularity of an argument and the soundness of an argument are two very different things. The fact that everyone at one time believed that the earth was flat did not prove that the earth was flat.

A third type of fallacy, a more complex sort than we have previously discussed, results from the confusion of what are termed "necessary" and "sufficient" conditions.

One state of affairs, *A*, is a necessary condition for another state of affairs, *B*, if *B* cannot occur without *A* occurring. For instance, in the United States a person must be at least eighteen years old before he is entitled to vote. His being eighteen is a necessary condition for his voting legally, for he cannot vote legally unless he is at least eighteen.

One state of affairs, *C*, is a sufficient condition for another state of affairs, *D*, if the occurrence of *C* ensures the occurrence of *D*. For instance, if one candidate in an American Presidential election receives three hundred electoral votes, that is a sufficient condition for his election. This is simply another way of saying that receiving three hundred electoral votes ensures a Presidential candidate's election.

It is important to recognize that just because *A* is a necessary condition for *B*, it does not follow that *A* is a sufficient condition for *B*. Similarly, just because *C* is a sufficient condition for *D*, it does not follow that *C* is a necessary condition for *D*. Though a person's being eighteen is a necessary condition for his voting legally, it does not follow that his being eighteen ensures that he votes legally, for he may fail to register or not be interested in exercising his constitutional rights. Similarly, while receiving three hundred electoral votes is sufficient for a Presidential candidate's election, it is not necessary for him to receive three hundred votes. He may receive fewer than three hundred and still be elected, or he may receive more than three hundred and be elected.

Although we ordinarily do not use the terms "necessary" and "sufficient," we often confuse these concepts. For example, consider the following conversation:

Smith: If you wish to be a concert pianist, you must begin practicing at a very early age.
Jones: That's not true. I know many people who started practicing at a very early age and are not good enough to be concert pianists.

Jones believes that his evidence refutes Smith's statement. In other words, Jones believes that if we accept the premise that many people who start practicing at a very early age are not good enough to be concert pianists, we are led to the conclusion that you do not have to begin practicing at a very early age in order to be a concert pianist. But Jones' argument is fallacious. He has confused necessary and sufficient conditions. Smith asserted that practicing at a very early age is a necessary condition for being a concert pianist. Jones' evidence implies that practicing at a very early age is not sufficient for being a concert pianist. But Smith did not say that it was sufficient. He only said that it was necessary.

Since this type of fallacy is a bit tricky and is also very common, it might be well to consider an additional example.

Smith: Anyone who has graduated from college is educated.
Jones: That's ridiculous. My friend Johnson is highly educated, and he didn't even go to college.

Once again Jones believes that his evidence refutes Smith's statement. Jones believes that since his friend Johnson is highly educated and did not attend college, it follows that not all persons who graduate from college need be educated. But once again Jones' argument is fallacious, for he has again confused necessary and sufficient conditions. Smith asserted that graduating from college is a sufficient condition for a person's being educated. Jones' evidence implies that graduating from college is not a necessary condition for being educated. But Smith did not say that it was necessary. He only said that it was sufficient. In order to refute Smith's view, what is required is not a case of an individual who is educated though he did not attend college. What is required is a case of an individual who is not educated even though he did graduate from college. For if there were such a case, then graduating from college would not be, as Smith claimed, a sufficient condition for being educated, for graduating from college would not ensure that a person was educated.

It would be possible to present many other types of fallacies, and in the course of the book we shall take note of some of them. At this point what is especially important to keep in mind is the general principle that enables us to spot invalid arguments: An argument is invalid if one can assert the premises and deny the conclusion without contradiction.

We have thus far been concerned with distinguishing valid arguments from invalid ones. As you may recall, however, we ought not to accept every belief that is supported by a valid argument, for such a belief might be false if one or more of the premises of the argument are false. What we ought to accept is a belief supported by a sound argument, that is, a valid argument with true premises. The obvious question now is this: How can we tell if the premises of an argument are true? It is to this question that we turn next.

B. CLARITY

The first step in determining whether a statement is true is to understand what the statement means. This principle may appear elementary, but it cannot be overemphasized. On innumerable occasions when people disagree, their disagreement is due solely to the fact that one person does not understand what the other is saying. We often rush headlong into an argument without knowing just what we are arguing about.

Consider the following example:

Smith: The United States is not a democracy. The citizens go to the polls only once a year. They do not have an opportunity to vote on the crucial issues that affect their lives.

Jones: Of course the United States is a democracy. The citizens have freedom of speech, freedom of religion, and freedom of assembly. The country's leaders are elected by the people.

We can imagine this particular dispute continuing for many hours, and, indeed, it seems doomed to do so unless Smith or Jones possesses the philosophical sophistication to ask one key question: What do we mean by the word "democracy"? Smith understands the word "democracy" to mean a form of government in which all citizens vote on all issues. Jones understands the word "democracy" to mean a system of government in which minority rights are protected and the leaders govern with the consent of the governed. It is clear that Smith and Jones are using the crucial term "democracy" in two different ways, and so long as this ambiguity remains, their discussion can make no progress.

It might seem that in order to resolve their disagreement about the United States Smith and Jones need to determine which one of them has defined the word "democracy" correctly. But to make this decision is, in fact, not very important. To understand why we must carefully examine how words are defined and how we can distinguish between proper and improper definitions.

To define a word is to state the necessary and sufficient conditions for its use. For example, the definition of "quadrilateral" is "a plane figure of four sides and four angles." For something to be a quadrilateral it is both necessary for it to be a plane figure of four sides and four angles and sufficient for it to be a plane figure of four sides and four angles. In other words, nothing can be a quadrilateral which is not a plane figure of four sides and four angles, and anything must be a quadrilateral which is a plane figure of four sides and four angles.

All definitions are of two types: nominal and real. A nominal definition is an arbitrary stipulation that a particular word is to be given a particular meaning. For instance, we might invent a word such as "brillig" and stipulate that it was to mean "four o'clock in the afternoon."[1] Such invention is the origin of many scientific terms such as "neutron" or "einsteinium." Or we might take an accepted English word such as "glory" and stipulate that it was to mean "a nice knock-down argument."[2] Such

---

[1] This example and the following one are taken from Lewis Carroll's *Through the Looking Glass*. This book, as well as *Alice's Adventures in Wonderland*, contains innumerable philosophical allusions. Carroll was himself a logician of some note, and these two marvelous books reflect his strong philosophical interest. An excellent edition of these books is *The Annotated Alice*, ed. Martin Gardner (Cleveland: The World Publishing Co., 1960).

[2] ". . . There's glory for you!" said Humpty Dumpty.
"I don't know what you mean by 'glory,' " Alice said.
Humpty Dumpty smiled contemptuously. "Of course you don't—till I tell you. I meant 'there's a nice knock-down argument for you!' "
"But 'glory' doesn't mean 'a nice knock-down argument,' " Alice objected.
"When *I* use a word," Humpty Dumpty said, in rather a scornful tone, "it means just what I choose it to mean—neither more nor less."
"The question is," said Alice, "whether you *can* make words mean so many different things."
"The question is," said Humpty Dumpty, "which is to be master—that's all."
(*The Annotated Alice*, pp. 268–269.)

a stipulation would, of course, be a departure from common English usage and might well be confusing to those who were not aware of the special
way in which the word was being used. However, such stipulation is not
erroneous. It may be justified by its convenience, as it often is in our legal
system, for example, in which terms such as "infant" or "assignment" are
used in quite different ways from the ways in which we ordinarily use
them.

Normally, however, we do not take the time or effort to create and
explain our own nominal definitions. Rather, we adopt the nominal definitions that have been accepted by most speakers of our language, the
definitions that can be found by consulting a dictionary. An English
dictionary, for instance, is a vast collection of nominal definitions that are
utilized by the overwhelming majority of speakers of the English language.
The definition of "quadrilateral" quoted above is one example of such a
commonly accepted nominal definition. There is nothing philosophically
mysterious about such definitions; they are simply linguistic conventions
which have developed over a period of many centuries.

When we speak of someone's misusing a word, what we mean is that
without indicating otherwise he has departed from standard English
usage. Such a departure does not necessarily invalidate the point he intends to make, for, if challenged, he may just rephrase his claim according to standard usage or state explicitly how he is using his terms.
However, as this is a rather laborious and often confusing process, we
prefer to converse with individuals who are willing, in general, to adopt
our usual linguistic conventions.

It is important at this point to recognize the difference between the meaning of a word and the specific things to which the word refers. The
meaning of a word, technically called the word's "intension,"[3] is the necessary and sufficient conditions for the word's use. For instance, the intension of the word "dog," according to Webster, is "a carnivorous
domesticated mammal type of the family *Canidae.*" The specific things to
which the word "dog" refers, technically called the word's "extension,"
are Rin Tin Tin, Lassie, Fala, your pet dog, and every other dog.

Note that two words or phrases may have different intensions but the
same extension. In other words, two words or phrases may have different
meanings and yet refer to the same things. For example, the phrase
"person who served as President of the United States in 1910" has a
totally different meaning from the phrase "person who served as Chief
Justice of the United States Supreme Court in 1925." Yet both phrases

---

3 This is not to be confused with the word "intention," meaning "purpose."

refer to the same individual, William Howard Taft. Similarly, the phrases "rational being" and "being capable of laughter" have different meanings but refer to the same animal, namely, man. When two words or phrases refer to the same things, they are said to be extensionally equivalent. As we have seen, however, two phrases that are extensionally equivalent need not have the same meaning. If they do have the same meaning they are said to be synonymous.

The distinction between a word's intension and extension becomes significant when we distinguish between nominal definitions and real definitions. The nominal definition of a word is that word's intension. After we decide upon a word's intension, we can proceed to investigate its extension, that is, the specific things to which it refers. Whether something is part of a word's extension depends upon whether it meets the necessary and sufficient conditions that determine the word's intension, that is, its meaning.

Suppose, however, that we are presented with a number of individual things and are asked to provide the characteristics that all of these things have in common and that are possessed by nothing else. In other words, we are asked to provide the necessary and sufficient conditions for membership in this particular class of things. A statement of these necessary and sufficient conditions is a real definition. For instance, if we are asked to define "religion," we are surely not being asked to create an arbitrary definition for this important term. Nor are we being asked for a definition that necessarily can be found in a dictionary, for a dictionary definition may not capture precisely the necessary and sufficient conditions that characterize the class which includes, among others, Hinduism, Buddhism, Confucianism, Shinto, Zoroastrianism, Judaism, Christianity, and Islam. A real definition of "religion" would have to provide us with a set of characteristics possessed by all of these genuinely accepted religions and yet not possessed by anything that is not generally accepted as a religion, such as the Democratic Party or the Freemasons. Whether such a real definition of "religion" can be provided is a controversial matter that need not concern us at this point.

What is vital to note is that we can speak of a real definition as true or false. A true real definition of "religion" would present the necessary and sufficient conditions that characterize all those organizations generally accepted as religions. A real definition could be shown to be true by pointing out that the necessary and sufficient conditions that it presented effectively differentiated between all those organizations generally accepted as religions and all those not accepted as religions. Any proposed real definition that failed to meet this test might be said to be a false real definition. If, for instance, "religion" were defined as "conviction of the existence of a personal supreme being," reference to Hinduism, Buddhism, and Confucianism would show this definition to be incorrect.

In formulating a nominal definition we are bound only by the criterion of convenience. Nominal definitions are neither true nor false; they are only more or less useful. In formulating a real definition, on the other hand, we are bound by factual consideration. If a real definition does not properly delimit the class of things with which it is concerned, the definition is false. If it does properly delimit this class, the definition is true.

It is of the utmost importance to know whether a proposed definition is put forth as a nominal definition or as a real definition. If a proposed definition is unusual and is put forth as a nominal definition, we may wish to point out that it does not conform to normal English usage or that it may tend to confuse the discussion. However, we can accept without worry this nominal definition, for it is a mere stipulation as to how we are going to use our words. If, on the contrary, a proposed definition is put forth as a real definition, we should refuse to accept it until we are convinced that this definition accurately characterizes a predetermined group of items. To agree to an erroneous real definition would be to agree to what is false.

Most writers do not bother to explain whether the definitions they put forth are nominal or real, so that it is often up to the reader to make this decision and to respond accordingly. Consider, for example, the opening sentence of *Dynamics of Faith* by the noted theologian, Paul Tillich: "Faith is the state of being ultimately concerned."[4] Leaving aside the question of what is meant by "being ultimately concerned," the sophisticated reader must ask, is Tillich presenting a nominal definition of "faith" or a real definition of "faith"? If this is a nominal definition, we may express some surprise at it, since this is not what we normally mean by "faith." However, there is no harm in accepting Tillich's definition of this term and agreeing to use it as he suggests. If this definition is presented as a real definition, however, we will be dubious about it and await whatever evidence Tillich can muster in support of his definition. Such evidence would consist in pointing out how all the usual instances we refer to as instances of faith are, in fact, instances of being ultimately concerned. Without such evidence his definition is unacceptable.

Such an approach to Tillich's book may seem to be an excessively critical one, but the philosophically sophisticated thinker is a critical thinker—not critical in the sense of being antagonistic, but critical in the

---

4   Paul Tillich, *Dynamics of Faith* (New York: Harper & Row, 1957), p. 1.

sense of being alert to the complexities of argument. Open-mindedness is indeed a virtue, but, as John Dewey pointed out, "Open-mindedness is not the same as empty-mindedness. To hang out a sign saying 'Come right in; there is no one at home' is not the equivalent of hospitality."[5]

Bearing in mind the distinction between nominal and real definitions, we are ready to reconsider the short dialogue at the opening of this chapter between Smith and Jones regarding the question of whether the United States is a democracy. Assuming Smith and Jones were philosophically alert, their discussion might have proceeded as follows:

Smith: The United States is not a democracy. The citizens go to the polls only once a year. They do not have an opportunity to vote on the crucial issues that affect their lives.

Jones: Of course the United States is a democracy. The citizens have freedom of speech, freedom of religion, and freedom of assembly. The country's leaders are elected by the people.

Smith: What do you mean by the word "democracy"?

Jones: I am using the word "democracy" to mean a form of government in which minority rights are protected and the leaders govern with the consent of the governed.

Smith: I will accept your definition for the sake of argument. What we disagree about then is whether democracy, as we are using that term, is the best form of government. I prefer a form of government in which all citizens vote on all issues. For the sake of argument I will term the form of government I prefer a "plebocracy." The real question between us is whether democracy or plebocracy is the better form of government.

The disagreement between Smith and Jones is not resolved, but it has become far clearer. Smith accepts Jones' definition of "democracy" as a nominal definition and creates his own nominal definition to designate the form of government he prefers. The issue between Smith and Jones is, as previously noted, not a matter of which one of them has defined the word "democracy" correctly. The real definition of "democracy" is not in dispute, for neither individual has challenged the other to present the necessary and sufficient conditions that characterize such sometime democratic societies as Athens, England, or Switzerland. The issue between Smith and Jones is far deeper than a verbal disagreement; it is an issue

---

[5] John Dewey, *Democracy and Education* (New York: The Macmillan Company, 1963), pp. 175–176.

about the relative merits of various forms of government. By agreeing to nominal definitions, a neutral procedure that does not prejudice the issue, they have avoided a semantic dispute and delved right into the heart of the matter.

One pitfall to avoid in formulating definitions deserves special mention. The word to be defined must not appear in the definition itself. For example, it would be useless to define "quadrilateral" as "anything that has a quadrilateral shape." Such a definition is useless, because if the term "quadrilateral" is not understood, neither is the term "quadrilateral shape." With such a definition we merely go around in circles without achieving any clarity.

A final word of caution regarding the use of nominal definitions is now in order. Many words have strong connotations that tend to affect their literal meaning. There is a great deal of difference between calling someone "an unmarried older woman" and calling her "an old maid." Nevertheless, these terms have the same meaning. A familiar tactic of debaters is to adopt unusual nominal definitions of terms that already possess emotional connotations. It is then hoped that the connotation remains, although the familiar meaning of the word is changed. For example, a political party may call itself the "Freedom and Equality Party." This label may have nothing to do with the party's platform, but it is hoped that the positive connotations of these words will present the party in a favorable light. Similarly, you might be tempted to term your opposition as "reactionaries," and when asked what you mean by that term, reply simply that you use the term "reactionary" to refer to anyone who disapproves of the changes advocated by the party in power. It might seem harmless to accept this as a nominal definition, but if an opponent of the party in power were to accept this nominal definition, he would be forced to refer to himself as a reactionary and admit that those in power were not reactionaries. Such a definition might be just too much for him to swallow. The connotation of the term "reactionary" is too strong to allow it to be used in a neutral fashion. Novel nominal definitions of such terms with strong connotations are referred to as "persuasive definitions."[6] A persuasive definition, like any nominal definition, is not erroneous. Nevertheless, persuasive definitions are best avoided, for under the guise of adopting neutral terminology, such definitions stir up emotion and shed more darkness than light.

At the beginning of this section it was said that the first step in deter-

---

[6] This term was coined by Charles L. Stevenson in his article "Persuasive Definitions," *Mind, 47* (1938), reprinted in his book *Facts and Values* (New Haven: Yale University Press, 1963).

mining whether a statement is true is to understand what the statement means. The most effective way of understanding what a statement means is to clarify the meanings of the crucial words in the statement. Such clarification is essential to clear thinking and is of great importance in carrying on an intelligent discussion. Perhaps the importance of such clarification can best be illustrated by a brief anecdote.

Several years ago during a summer vacation I met a young man of college age who very much enjoyed engaging in political discussions. During the summer he made the acquaintance of two men who were as committed to conservatism as he was to liberalism. Unfortunately for him, these two conservatives seemed to win every argument he had with them. Toward the close of the summer he came to me in disgust late one evening and related how he had just lost another argument. He assumed that, being a philosopher, I knew how to win arguments, and he asked me how he could win at least one argument from these two conservatives so as to end the summer on a positive note. I suggested that we review the argument he had just lost in order to see where he might have gone wrong. No sooner had he told me how his opponents had begun the argument than I asked him to clarify the meanings of some of the key terms they had been using. He was unable to do so, and he suddenly realized that he ought to have asked them the same questions I had asked him. That night he went to bed swearing vengeance.

As it happened he was taking a course in political science with these two conservatives. The next day in class the instructor began by asking the students to give their opinions regarding a recent foreign policy decision of the United States. My friend spoke in opposition to this particular policy and was immediately attacked by one of his opponents for "defending communism." Armed with his previous evening's lesson, my friend replied, "What do you mean by 'communism'?" To his everlasting delight his two opponents spent the rest of the class disagreeing violently with each other about the nature of communism.

There is no panacea for intellectual confusion. But I suggest one powerful drug: clarity. If you use crucial terms without clarifying what they mean and rush into an argument before you take the time to clarify what you are arguing about, you may just find that you are not arguing about anything at all.

C. SCIENTIFIC METHOD

To understand what a statement means is the first step, but only the first step, in determining whether the statement is true, for we may know what a statement means and yet not know whether it is true. What exactly does it mean for a statement to be true? The difference between truth and falsehood was expressed concisely by Aristotle: "To say of what is that it is not, or of what is not that it is, is false, while to say of what is that it is, and of what is not that it is not, is true."[7] But although this general statement tells us what truth is, it does not tell us how to determine whether a particular statement is true, and that is the vital information we are seeking. In order to achieve our end, we shall have to draw some important distinctions.

There are two types of statements: analytic and synthetic. An analytic statement is one that is true or false simply by virtue of the meanings of the words in the statement. The following are examples of analytic statements:

g.   All tall men are tall.
h.   That bachelor is unmarried.

Anyone who understands the meanings of the words in these statements knows that the statements are true. To deny that all tall men are tall would be to contradict oneself, for the denial of this statement amounts to asserting that some men who are tall are not tall, which is a contradiction. Similarly, to deny that a bachelor is unmarried would be to contradict oneself, for the denial of this statement amounts to asserting that an unmarried man is not unmarried, which is also a contradiction.

Any statement that is not analytic is synthetic. A synthetic statement is one that is not true or false simply by virtue of the meanings of the words in the statement. The following are examples of synthetic statements:

i.   The population of India exceeds 500,000,000.
j.   Charles Darwin and Abraham Lincoln were both born on February 12, 1809.

Understanding the meanings of the words in these statements is not sufficient for knowing whether the statements are true. No contradiction is involved in denying either of these statements, although it is possible that either one is false.

As there are two types of statements, so there are two types of methods of determining whether statements are true. To determine the truth of a statement by *a priori* methods is to determine its truth without consideration of factual evidence. To determine the truth of a statement by *a*

---

[7]   Aristotle, *Metaphysics,* trans. W. D. Ross, in *The Basic Works of Aristotle,* ed. Richard McKeon (New York: Random House, Inc., 1941), 1011*b*, 26–28.

posteriori methods is to determine its truth with the use of factual evidence.

In order to clarify the difference between a priori and a posteriori methods, let us consider statements (g), (h), (i), and (j). We know (g) to be true without any appeal to empirical evidence, that is, without any appeal to the way the world is. No facts about the world have the least relevance to the truth of (g), for we know it to be true regardless of how many men there are in the world, how tall most men are, the height of the tallest man, or any other factual information. Since no facts, interesting though they may be, have anything to do with the truth of (g), it is said to be known a priori to be true. The situation is the same for (h). We know (h) to be true without any appeal to empirical evidence, for no facts about the world affect the truth of this statement. The average age of bachelors or the percentage of men who are bachelors have nothing whatever to do with the truth of (h). Once we know its meaning, we know a priori that it is true.

On the other hand, the truth of (i) is dependent upon the number of persons who happen to live in India. Only by considering the factual evidence can we determine the truth of this statement. Its truth or falsity is thus said to be known a posteriori. The same is true for (j). Since (j) states a fact about the world, we must consider the factual evidence in order to determine whether (j) is true. In other words, we must determine the truth of (j) by a posteriori methods.

We are now in a position to return to the question of how we determine whether statements are true. If the statement is analytic, we can determine its truth a priori in the following manner: The statement is true if its negation (that is, its contradictory) is a contradiction; the statement is false if it itself is a contradiction. For example, "All tall men are tall" is true, for its negation, "Some tall men are not tall," is a contradiction. Such a true analytic statement is sometimes referred to as a "tautology." "No tall men are tall" is false, for it is a contradiction. By this simple a priori method that relies solely on principles of logic, we can determine the truth or falsity of any analytic statement.

But what if the statement in question is synthetic? How can we determine its truth or falsity in that case? It would appear that the truth of synthetic statements cannot be determined by purely a priori methods, for a synthetic statement is neither one that is contradictory nor one whose negation is contradictory. Synthetic statements assert something about the way the world is, and so we must utilize some a posteriori method in order to determine whether the facts are as the statement claims them to be.

There is such an a posteriori method available to us, a method that has provided mankind with vast amounts of factual information. This method is self-corrective and has proven to be highly reliable. Furthermore, it does not run contrary to common sense but, instead, refines and systematizes our common-sense beliefs. This method is known as the "scientific method."

The scientific method of determining whether a statement is true consists of four steps: (1) formulating the statement clearly; (2) working out the implications of the statement; (3) performing controlled experiments to verify whether these implications hold; (4) observing the consequences of these experiments and, as a result, accepting or rejecting the statement. Stated in this abstract way, of course, the scientific method may sound strange and formidable. But an example should serve to reveal how familiar and accessible this method actually is.

Suppose we wish to know whether a particular disease is caused by a specific type of mosquito. Obviously, one implication of this hypothesis is that if individuals are exposed to this type of mosquito they will develop the disease, whereas if they are quarantined so as not to come into contact with this type of mosquito, they will not develop the disease. We perform an experiment to determine whether these implications hold by exposing some individuals to this type of mosquito and quarantining others. We then observe the consequences of this experiment. If those who have been exposed develop the disease and those who have been quarantined do not, we have strong evidence that this type of mosquito is the cause of the disease. If those who have been exposed do not develop the disease or those who have been quarantined do develop the disease, we reject the statement that the disease is caused by this type of mosquito.

This simple example of the scientific method is based on the experiences of Dr. Walter Reed, who, in similar fashion, discovered the cause of yellow fever. The example reveals a number of interesting and significant features of the scientific method of inquiry. First, this method recognizes no authority but the authority of experimental consequences. No matter how forcefully or how loudly some factual claim is asserted to be true, this assertion does not prove the claim to be true. Proof comes only through unbiased, objective testing procedures. Second, this method requires imagination and creativity, for no statement can be tested without devising suitable experimental conditions, and the determination of both the statement to be tested and the conditions under which it can be effectively tested rests upon the inventiveness of the experimenter. Third, this method is applicable whenever and wherever there is dispute about facts. No supposed fact is beyond the test of scientific method.

One further aspect of the scientific method requires special attention.

Since we determine the truth of factual claims by experimentation, and there is no end to the number of possible experimental situations, it follows that no single statement of fact ever achieves absolute certainty. This is no reason to despair, however, for the very high probabilities that the scientific method provides are superior to the results of all other methods and serve for all practical purposes. In addition, it is the infinite number of experimental situations that accounts for the self-corrective nature of the scientific method. A falsehood that has passed many tests may still be corrected by additional testing.

In the case of the disease supposedly caused by mosquitoes, it is possible, though extremely unlikely, that all those individuals who were exposed to the mosquitoes and subsequently developed the disease did so as a result of another factor, such as the temperature of the room in which they were sleeping. Similarly, it is possible, though extremely unlikely, that all those individuals who were not exposed to the mosquitoes and subsequently did not develop the disease, did so as a result of this same temperature factor. Although both of these hypotheses are possible, they appear highly unlikely, and the strength of the scientific method of inquiry is that each such hypothesis is open to experimental test.

Because there are an indefinite number of such hypotheses, weird though many may seem, it is not possible to check all hypotheses, although we can check any specific one that is proposed. Furthermore, we can continue to check the hypothesis that seems most probable, and, with each additional test, this hypothesis becomes more and more probable. If, after the elimination of a particular type of mosquito, the disease in question is not contracted by any one of thousands or millions of individuals, we can be virtually certain that the disease is caused by such mosquitoes.

After a certain point the distinction between high probability and certainty becomes negligible. Just where this point lies is an issue in that part of philosophy of science known as inductive logic or the logic of confirmation. (This logic is in contrast to the sort of logic, discussed earlier in the chapter, which is technically known as deductive logic.) Inductive logic is concerned with arguments in which the premises render the conclusion probable, although the argument is not strictly valid. Here is an example of such an argument:

k. All swans that have been observed have been white.
    Therefore, all swans are white.

The premise of this argument does provide strong evidence for the conclusion, although it is possible to affirm the premise and deny the conclusion without contradiction. It is possible, but improbable, that although we have observed numerous white swans, somewhere there is a nonwhite swan. Determining the precise degree to which the premises of an argument such as (k) render the conclusion probable is a central task of inductive logic.

Because the scientific method is such a powerful tool of inquiry, it has come under strong attack from those who fear the consequences of its use. We shall proceed, therefore, to consider some of the most common of these attacks.

It is often said that we ought not to employ the scientific method because so much of life is not scientific. How is it possible for us to be scientific about such deep human feelings as love, kindness, or despair? What sense does it make to speak of music, painting, or poetry as scientific?

But these questions reveal a total misunderstanding of the nature of the scientific method. The scientific method is a method of acquiring factual information. To be scientific is to use this method when you wish to dispel your ignorance regarding certain facts. If you are not in a situation in which you wish to acquire information, there is no point in referring to the scientific method. Clouds, trees, love, painting, and light bulbs are neither scientific nor unscientific. If, however, you claim that due to the shape of the clouds, the height of the trees, the depth of your love, the colors of the painting, or the lucky number on your light bulb, you know that your car will not run out of gas, this claim is unscientific. Those who hold beliefs without regard to the scientific method of inquiry have no monopoly on human feelings or aesthetic appreciation. They simply do not utilize the most reliable method available for ascertaining facts.

A second criticism of the scientific method is that although this method of inquiry may be effective in the laboratory, it is ineffective in the usual situations of life. Scientists may use this method to uncover truths about the chemical structure of various compounds, but the average man cannot go through life engaged in laboratory research.

This criticism, like the first, reveals a basic misunderstanding of the scientific method. Although it is undoubtedly true that science has made amazing strides through the use of the scientific method of inquiry, it does not follow that we need laboratories in order to use this method. The four steps of the scientific method are equally effective in everyday contexts.

Suppose we wish to know whether a particular movie is being shown this evening at the local cinema. We do not just guess or flip a coin. Rather, we look at the movie listings in today's newspaper. If we analyze this simple situation, we can see that it embodies in elementary form the basic steps of the scientific method of inquiry. First, we formulate clearly the statement we wish to test; in this case the statement is that a particular movie is being shown this evening at the local cinema. Second, we work out the implications of this statement; in this case one implication is that today's newspaper will indicate that the movie is being shown. Third, we perform an experiment to verify whether this implication holds; in this case our experiment consists of carefully looking at today's newspaper. Fourth, we observe the consequences of the experiment, and, as a result, we accept or reject the statement; in this case positive information from today's newspaper gives us reason to affirm that the movie is being shown, while negative information from the newspaper gives us reason to deny that the movie is being shown.

What I have described in very simplified terms is not an exotic procedure. It is precisely what we expect people to do in such circumstances. As I said earlier, the scientific method is not opposed to common sense but is just a refinement and systematization of common sense. The man who employs the scientific method need not be a laboratory scientist. He simply follows that method of inquiry which is most reliable, a method utilized by scientists just because of its reliability.

The third and final criticism of the scientific method that we shall consider emphasizes the admitted fact that the scientific method of inquiry does not work in every instance. It is possible, though highly improbable, that the cinema which we choose after careful reasoning is not showing the movie we wish to see. It is also possible that a cinema which we choose on sheer impulse is showing the movie we wish to see. The critic of the scientific method points to situations such as these in an effort to convince us to abandon the method.

But we should not be persuaded by such examples. The scientific method of inquiry was not presented as an infallible method of ascertaining the truth. Indeed, by its own procedures it disclaims infallibility, for why would an infallible method need to be self-correcting? However, to admit that a method is fallible is not to declare it unworkable. All that is claimed for the scientific method of inquiry is that it is more reliable than any other method that has been proposed. Proponents of the scientific method may be said to have issued a challenge to proponents of any other method: Show us a more reliable method than ours, and we shall relinquish ours and adopt yours. But this challenge has never been successfully met. Whatever the facts to be determined—whether it be the distance to the moon, the proper procedures for farming, or the most effective way to build a safe bridge—no other method of inquiry has proven to be as reliable as the scientific method. It is true that on rare occasions we may be more successful by guesswork, intuition, or superstition. But for every time that such methods work and the scientific method fails, there are innumerable times that such methods fail and the scientific method works. Furthermore, whereas such methods can lead us astray time after time, the scientific method possesses its built-in mechanism of self-correction.

In summary, then, the scientific method, although not infallible, is the most reliable method available for determining whether a factual statement is true. As Morris R. Cohen (1880–1947) and Ernest Nagel (1901–   ), two outstanding philosophers of science, noted some years ago, "None of the precautions of scientific method prevent human life from being an adventure, and no scientific investigator knows whether he will reach his goal. But scientific method does enable large numbers to walk with surer step."[8]

We set out at the beginning of this chapter to determine under what conditions it is reasonable to accept a belief. In order to achieve our aim, it was necessary to distinguish between valid and invalid arguments as well as between sound and unsound arguments. Both these tasks are now completed. Logic enables us to distinguish valid arguments from invalid ones. Sound arguments are distinguished from unsound ones by the truth of the premises. We can determine the truth of an analytic premise by the use of an a priori method that relies solely on principles of logic, and we can determine the truth of a synthetic premise by the use of the scientific method. Thus, a reasonable or rational person is simply one who tests his beliefs by the canons of logic and scientific method and acts in accordance with beliefs confirmed by these canons.

The only tools required by the philosopher are those required by any reasonable person. And so with these tools in our grasp, we are now equipped to handle the crucial philosophical problems that confront us. The first one we shall consider is of vital concern to jurists, psychologists, historians, religious thinkers, and all those who are interested in the nature of man. This is the problem of free will.

---

[8]   Morris R. Cohen and Ernest Nagel, *An Introduction to Logic and Scientific Method* (New York: Harcourt Brace Jovanovich, 1934), p. 402.

PART II

FREE WILL

Chapter 3

DETERMINISM

In 1924 the American people were horrified by a senseless crime of extraordinary brutality. The defendants were eighteen-year-old Nathan Leopold and seventeen-year-old Richard Loeb. They were the sons of Chicago millionaires, brilliant students who had led seemingly idyllic lives. Leopold was the youngest graduate in the history of the University of Chicago, and Loeb was the youngest graduate in the history of the University of Michigan. Suddenly they were accused of the kidnapping and vicious murder of fourteen-year-old Bobby Franks, a cousin of Loeb's. Before the trial even began Leopold and Loeb both confessed. From all across the country there arose a great outcry for the execution of the confessed murderers.

The lawyer who agreed to defend them was Clarence Darrow, the outstanding defense attorney of his time. Since Leopold and Loeb had already confessed, Darrow's only chance was to explain their actions in such a way that his clients could escape the death penalty. He was forced to argue that Leopold and Loeb were not morally responsible for what they had done, that they were not to be blamed for their actions. How could he possibly defend such an incredible position?

Darrow's defense was a landmark in the history of criminal law. He argued that the actions of his clients were a direct and necessary result of hereditary and environmental forces beyond their control.[1] Leopold suffered from a glandular disease that left him depressed and moody. He was a homosexual, a young man originally shy with girls, who had been sent to an all-girls school in an effort to cure this shyness and had come out with deep psychic scars from which he never recovered. His parents instilled in him the belief that his wealth absolved him of any responsibility toward others. Pathologically inferior, because of his diminutive size, and pathologically superior, because of his wealth, he became an acute schizophrenic.

Loeb suffered from a nervous disorder that caused fainting spells. He had a very unhappy childhood and often thought of committing suicide. He was under the control of a domineering governess and was forced to lie and cheat in order to deceive her. His wealth led him to believe that he was superior to all those around him, and he developed a fascination for crime, an activity in which he could demonstrate his superiority. By the time he reached college he had become an acute psychotic.

In his final plea Darrow recounted these facts and many others. His central theme was that Leopold and Loeb were in the grip of powers beyond their control. They themselves were victims.

> I do not know what it was that made these boys do this mad act, but I do know there is a reason for it. I know they did not beget themselves. I know that any one of an infinite number of causes reaching back to the beginning might be working out in these boys' minds, whom you are asked to hang in malice and in hatred and in injustice, because someone in the past has sinned against them. . . .
>
> What had this boy to do with it? He was not his own father; he was not his own mother; he was not his own grandparents. All of this was handed to him. He did not surround himself with governesses and wealth. He did not make himself. And yet he is to be compelled to pay.[2]

Darrow's plea was successful. Leopold and Loeb escaped execution and were sentenced to life imprisonment. Although they had committed

---

[1] The facts that follow are to be found in Irving Stone's *Clarence Darrow for the Defense* (Garden City, N.Y.: Garden City Publishing Co., Inc., 1943), pp. 384–391.

[2] *Attorney for the Damned,* ed. Arthur Weinberg (New York: Simon and Schuster, Inc., 1957), pp. 37, 65.

crimes and were legally responsible for their actions, the judge believed that they were not morally responsible for what they had done. They were not to blame, for they had not acted out of their own free will.

The line of argument which Darrow utilized in the Leopold-Loeb case is of the utmost importance, for if his argument is sound, then it would seem that not only were Leopold and Loeb not to blame for what they had done, but no man is ever to blame for any of his actions. As Darrow himself put it, "We are all helpless."[3] But is Darrow's argument sound? This is the crucial philosophical issue we shall investigate in this chapter.

We recall that an argument is sound if the conclusion necessarily follows from the premises, and the premises are true. What are the premises and what is the conclusion of Darrow's argument? We can formalize his argument as follows:

Premise 1: No action is free if it must occur.
Premise 2: In the case of every event that occurs, there are antecedent conditions, known or unknown, that ensure that the event will occur.
Conclusion: Therefore no action is free.

Premise (1) provides an explication of what is meant by a free action. An individual's action is free if it is within his power to perform the action and it is within his power not to perform the action. In other words, a person's action is free if it is up to him whether he performs it. If circumstances are such that a man either *must* perform a certain action or *must not* perform the action, then that action is not a free one.

Premise (2) is the thesis known as determinism. This thesis can be stated in a number of ways. In its simplest form it is the view that every event that occurs has some cause that accounts for the occurrence of the event. In a more picturesque version, determinism is the view that if there were a being who knew at any time the position of every particle in the universe and all the forces acting upon each particle, that being could predict with absolute certainty every future event. It should be made perfectly clear that this version of determinism does not require that such a being actually exist. The being is imagined solely in order to provide a graphic illustration of what the world would be like if determinism were true.

Darrow's conclusion, which is supposed to follow from premises (1) and (2), is that no man has free will. A man has free will if he is free with regard to at least some actions. Clearly, no man is free with regard to

---

[3] *Ibid.*, p. 37.

all actions, since, for example, no man is free to jump from the earth to the moon. But the doctrine of free will was never supposed to apply to all human actions. So long as any human action is free, man is said to have free will. What Darrow's argument purports to prove is that no human action that ever has been performed or ever will be performed is a free one.

Is Darrow's argument a valid one? In other words, does the conclusion of his argument necessarily follow from the premises? If premise (2) is true, then every event that occurs must occur, for its occurrence is ensured by antecedent conditions. Since every action is an event, it follows from premise (2) that every action that occurs must occur. But, according to premise (1), no action is free if it must occur. Thus, if premises (1) and (2) are true, it follows that no action is free—and that is the conclusion of Darrow's argument. Thus, his argument is valid.

Does this mean that we must accept the conclusion of Darrow's argument and admit that no men are free? Not at all, for as we saw in Chapter 2, a valid argument may have a false conclusion. We need accept the conclusion of a valid argument only if the premises of the argument are true. The crucial question is: Are the premises of Darrow's argument true?

Hard determinism is the view that premises (1) and (2) of Darrow's argument are both true. In other words, a hard determinist believes that determinism is true and that, as a consequence of this, no man has free will.[4] To defend his view that determinism is true, a hard determinist points to the fact that in the case of any event that occurs, we all assume that there is a causal explanation that accounts for the occurrence of that event. For example, suppose you feel a pain in your arm, and you go to a doctor to find out what is causing this pain. He examines the arm carefully, considers the matter, and informs you that the pain in your arm has no cause, either physical or psychological. It is, he suggests, an uncaused pain. Upon hearing this diagnosis you would no doubt switch doctors. It is possible that your doctor does not know what is causing the pain in your arm, but surely something is causing it. If nothing were causing the pain, there would be no pain. But there is a pain, so there must be a cause for it. And this same line of reasoning applies whether the event to be explained is a loud noise, a change in the weather, or an individual's action. If there were no cause for it, why would it occur?

---

[4]   The expressions "hard determinism" and "soft determinism" were coined by William James (1842–1909) in his essay "The Dilemma of Determinism," reprinted in *Essays on Faith and Morals* (Cleveland and New York: The World Publishing Company, 1962).

We may be inclined to accept the hard determinist's argument in regard to the vast majority of events and yet believe that human actions cannot be subsumed under the principle of determinism. Although there are causal explanations for rocks falling and birds flying, human beings are far more complex than rocks and birds. The hard determinist may be correct with regard to mere physical occurrences, but is his principle tenable when he applies it to human actions?

The hard determinist is prepared for this objection. He asks us to consider a specific example of a human action, for instance, your decision to read this book. You may think that your decision was uncaused, but did you not wish to acquire information about philosophy? Your desire for this information together with your belief that this book contained such information caused you to read this book. Just as physical forces cause rocks and birds to do things, so your wants, wishes, and desires cause you to do things.

If you doubt that this is true, the hard determinist says, consider how accurately we can predict people's actions. There is a surprising amount of uniformity in men's behavior. When we read novels or see plays, we expect to understand what motivates the characters to do what they do. An author who does not provide us with understandable characters is charged with poor characterization. The similarity of men's reactions to the human condition also accounts for the popularity of the incisive psychological insights of a writer such as François de La Rochefoucauld, the French aphorist. We read one of his maxims, for instance, "When our integrity declines, our taste does also,"[5] and nod our heads with approval. But what are we agreeing to except a generalization about the human psyche? Of course, it is not possible to predict men's behavior with absolute certainty, but this, the hard determinist tells us, is because each individual is influenced by a unique combination of hereditary and environmental factors. Just as each rock is slightly different from every other rock and each bird is somewhat different from every other bird, so men too differ from each other in various ways. But just as rocks and birds are part of a deterministic chain of causes and effects, so men also are part of such a chain. Just as a rock falls because it breaks off from a cliff, so men act because of their desires and beliefs. And just as a rock has no control over the wind that causes it to break off, so a man has no control over the desires and beliefs that cause him to act. None of us has any more control over his desires and beliefs than Leopold and Loeb had

[5] *The Maxims of La Rochefoucauld,* trans. Louis Kronenberger (New York: Random House, 1959), #379.

over theirs. If you can control your desire for food and your friend cannot, this is because your will is of the sort that can control your desire and your friend's will is of a sort that cannot. But the fact that your will is of one sort and your friend's will is of another is not itself something that either one of you can control. As one contemporary philosopher has written, "If we *can* overcome the effects of early environment, the ability to do so is itself a product of the early environment. We did not give ourselves this ability; and if we lack it we cannot be blamed for not having it."[6]

It is usual at this point for an antideterminist to call attention to recent developments in physics that have been interpreted by some thinkers as a refutation of determinism. Work in quantum mechanics has led some to claim, on the basis of Heisenberg's principle of uncertainty and von Neumann's theorem, that certain subatomic events are uncaused and inherently unpredictable, and that the principle of determinism has thus been proved false on the subatomic level. Things are not nearly so simple, however, as the antideterminist suggests. To begin with, there are wide differences of opinion among physicists and philosophers of science as to the correct interpretation of experimental results in quantum mechanics. Some investigators are of the opinion that determinism has not been refuted, that the events in question can be understood in causal terms.[7] In any case, even if certain subatomic events are uncaused, this has little relevance for human freedom, since the events with which we are concerned in discussing such freedom are not events on the subatomic level, and indeterminism on the subatomic level is entirely compatible with the universal causation of events on the much larger level of bodily events.

Let us now summarize the viewpoint of hard determinism. According to this view, determinism is true and no man has free will. To defend the claim that determinism is true, the hard determinist points out that every event that occurs must be caused to occur, for if it was not caused to occur, why would it occur? Your present actions are events caused by your desires and beliefs. These desires and beliefs are in turn caused by your previous desires and beliefs, and so on back to hereditary and environmental factors. Your present actions are part of a causal chain that extends back far before your birth, and each link of the chain determines the succeeding link in the chain. Since you surely have no

6 John Hospers, "What Means This Freedom?," *Determinism and Freedom in the Age of Modern Science,* ed. Sidney Hook (New York: Collier Books, 1961), p. 138.

7 For a detailed discussion of the philosophical implications of quantum mechanics, see Ernest Nagel's classic book, *The Structure of Science* (New York: Harcourt Brace Jovanovich, 1961), chapter 10.

control over links of the chain that occurred before your birth, and these earlier links necessitate the later links, it follows that you have no control over your present actions. In short, you do not have free will.

The hard determinist's argument does seem plausible. Nevertheless, most of us do not find it convincing. The reason for this is that the argument leads to a conclusion we find unacceptable. What are we to do when faced by plausible premises that lead to an unacceptable conclusion? This is a surprisingly common situation in philosophical inquiry and deserves our careful attention.

Let us imagine a valid argument that has two premises and a conclusion. Suppose we are not sure whether the premises are true, but we are certain that the conclusion is false. Would we accept the conclusion of such an argument? Certainly not. Since the argument is valid and we are certain that the conclusion is false, we realize that one of the premises must be false. Recall that a valid argument is one in which the truth of the premises ensures the truth of the conclusion. To put it another way, a valid argument is one in which the falsity of the conclusion ensures the falsity of at least one of the premises. If the conclusion could be false and the premises true, we would not have a valid argument.

In order for a valid argument to be convincing, the truth of the premises must be more certain than the falsity of the conclusion. If we are not sure of the truth of the premises but we are sure of the falsity of the conclusion, the fact that the argument is valid simply alerts us to the fact that one of the premises is false.

For instance, suppose that someone claims that life exists on Jupiter, and that since such life wishes to communicate with people on earth, it is sending out electrical impulses that our scientific equipment can pick up. It follows from this that we should be receiving electrical impulses from Jupiter. Let us grant the validity of this argument, although we are not sure about the truth of the premises. However, all available scientific evidence confirms that no electrical impulses are being received from Jupiter. Here is a case in which there is more evidence in support of the falsity of the conclusion than in support of the truth of the premises. Thus, we would reply to this argument intended to prove that we are receiving electrical impulses from Jupiter by simply asserting that since the denial of the conclusion is more certain than the premises, we deny both the conclusion and at least one of the premises.

Any statement can be the conclusion of a valid argument if one adopts suitable premises. The difficulty is to find premises that yield the desired conclusion and are more certain than the denial of that conclusion. Obviously, the premises also have to be more certain than the affirmation of the conclusion, or else we are proving on weak evidence what we already know to be the case. This explains, incidentally, why we become flustered when we are asked by a shallow thinker to prove that we exist, or to prove that the chair in front of us exists, or to prove that the world exists. Each of these statements is so certain that it is not possible to find premises that are more certain than these statements. But this is no reason to reject these statements. Quite to the contrary, it is the very reason to accept them. The only reason the statements cannot be proven is that they are more certain than any other statements, and thus cannot sensibly be proven on the basis of these other, less certain statements. The best reply to the captious challenge "Prove that you exist," is "Tell me what premises you would accept with which such a proof could be constructed." All proofs require premises, and no matter what premises your challenger suggests, if he doubts your existence, why does he not doubt his proposed premises? It is absurd to attempt to prove statements whose acceptance is so vital for human life on the basis of other statements that are less secure than these vital statements themselves.

We return now to the argument of the hard determinist. He has argued that since premises (1) and (2) are true, so is the conclusion. Our tendency, and that of most philosophers, is to argue that since the conclusion is false, so is premise (1) or (2). Soft determinism is the view that the conclusion is false because premise (1) is false. In other words, a soft determinist believes both that determinism is true and that man has free will. As a consequence of this, he believes that an action may be free even if it is causally necessitated by antecedent conditions beyond the agent's control. Although this view may not appear immediately plausible, it has been defended by many great philosophers, including Thomas Hobbes (1588–1679), David Hume (1711–1776), and John Stuart Mill (1806–1873).

One important tool that is employed, explicitly or implicitly, by soft determinists in defense of their position is the paradigm-case argument. Since this type of argument is useful in many philosophical contexts, it deserves our careful attention. We shall begin by considering a classic instance in which this type of argument can be successfully employed.

When we study physics we are surprised to learn that solid physical objects are composed of sparsely scattered, minute particles. This fact may lead us to believe that objects we normally regard as solid are, in fact, not solid at all. This belief was forcefully expressed by Sir Arthur Eddington, the noted physicist, who wrote that a "plank has no solidity of substance. To step on it is like stepping on a swarm of flies."[8]

---

[8] A. S. Eddington, *The Nature of the Physical World* (New York: The Macmillan Company, 1928), p. 342.

Eddington's view that a normal plank is not solid was forcefully attacked by the British philosopher, L. Susan Stebbing (1885–1943). She
pointed out that the word "solid" derives its meaning from examples such
as planks.

> For "solid" just is the word we use to describe a certain respect in
> which a plank of wood resembles a block of marble, a piece of
> paper, and a cricket ball, and in which each of these differs from a
> sponge, from the interior of a soap-bubble, and from the holes in a
> net. . . . The point is that the common usage of language enables
> us to attribute a meaning to the phrase "a solid plank"; but there is
> no common usage of language that provides a meaning for the word
> "solid" that would make sense to say that the plank on which I
> stand is not *solid*.[9]

In other words, a plank is a paradigm case of solidity. Anyone who claims
that a plank is not solid does not know how the word "solid" is used in
the English language. It should be clear that in utilizing the paradigm-case
argument, Miss Stebbing is not criticizing Eddington's scientific views.
What she is criticizing is the manner in which he interprets these views.

We might anticipate the way in which soft determinists utilize the
paradigm-case argument. They are faced by the hard determinist's claim
that no human action is free. The soft determinist responds to this claim
by pointing to a paradigm case of a free action, for instance, a person's
walking down the street. They stipulate that the person in this example is
not under the influence of drugs, is not attached to any ropes, is not
sleepwalking, etc. In short, we are asked to consider a perfectly normal,
everyday instance of a person walking down the street. That, says the soft
determinist, is a paradigm case of a free action. It is to be distinguished
from cases in which a person *is* under the influence of drugs, or *is*
attached to ropes, or *is* sleepwalking, etc. These are not cases of free
actions, or at best they are problematic cases. The case the soft determinist cites is not such a problematic case. It is a perfectly clear case of a
free act. According to the soft determinist, anyone who claims that this is
not a case of a free action does not know how the word "free" is used in
the English language. Thus, man does have free will, for there are perfectly clear cases in which men act freely.

If we ask to know the necessary and sufficient conditions for a free
action, the soft determinist is prepared to tell us. According to him, an
action is free if the agent who performs it wishes to perform it and could,
if he wished, not perform it. A man whose arm is forcibly raised is not
free, for he did not wish to raise his arm. A man in jail is also not free,

---

9 L. Susan Stebbing, *Philosophy and the Physicists* (New York: Dover Pub-
lications, Inc., 1958), pp. 51–52.

even if he wishes to be in jail, for if he wished to leave, he could not do so. A man is free only if the action he performs is one that he wishes to perform, *and* is such that if he wished not to perform it, he would not have to perform it.

Soft determinists hasten to point out that if we define freedom correctly, that is, as they have suggested, there is no incompatibility between freedom and determinism. Consider some particular act that is free in the sense explicated by the soft determinist. That act may well be one link in a causal chain extending far back beyond the agent's birth. Nevertheless, the agent is free with regard to that action, for he wishes to perform it, and if he did not wish to perform it, he would not have to. This is entirely consistent with supposing that his wish is ultimately a result of hereditary and environmental factors over which he has no control. That there are such factors is, according to the soft determinist, irrelevant to the question of whether the action is free. I may be walking down a particular street because of my desire to buy a coat and my belief that this street will lead me to an excellent clothing store. This desire and belief may themselves be caused in any number of interesting ways. Nevertheless, since I desire to talk down this street and could walk down some other street if I so desired, it follows that I am freely walking down this street. Thus, the soft determinist affirms both free will and determinism, and claims to have reconciled these two seemingly opposed doctrines.

Soft determinism is certainly an inviting doctrine. It allows us to maintain our belief in free will along with our belief that every event has a cause. Unfortunately, soft determinism is open to serious objections. Although there are those philosophers who have not been persuaded by these objections to abandon soft determinism, many others find these objections to be insurmountable and, consequently, find the soft determinist's position untenable.

The most fundamental problem for soft determinists is that the definition of freedom they propose does not seem in accordance with the ordinary way in which we use that term. It is important to realize that soft determinists and hard determinists have offered two very different definition of freedom. According to a hard determinist, an act is free if it is within the agent's power to perform the action and it is within his power not to perform the action. According to a soft determinist, an act is free if it is such that if we wish to perform it, we may, and if we wish not to perform it, we also may. To see how different these definitions are, consider the case of a man who has been hypnotized. Under hypnosis, he rolls up the leg of his pants as if to cross a stream. Is his action free? According to the hard determinist, his action is not free, for it is not within his power not to roll up the leg of his pants. According to the soft determinist's definition of freedom, his action is free, for he desires to perform it, and if he did not desire to, he would not have to. But we would not say that a man under hypnosis is a free man. Therefore, the soft determinist's definition of freedom is unsatisfactory.

We might be inclined to believe that this objection to soft determinism is unfair, since in the case of a hypnotized man, his desires are not his own but are controlled by the hypnotist. However, the force of this objection to soft determinism lies in the realization that the soft determinist does not pay sufficient attention to the question of whether a man's wishes or desires are themselves within his control. The hard determinist is willing to grant that an action is free only if it is entirely up to the agent whether he performs it. In order for an action to be entirely up to the agent, he must have control over what he wishes or desires. If he does not, his desires can be controlled by a hypnotist, a brainwasher, his parents, his heredity, his environment, etc., and he is thus not free. Soft determinism fails to take such possibilities seriously, for according to soft determinism, a man may be free even if his desires are not within his control. So long as he is acting according to his desires and could act differently if his desires were different, he is, according to the soft determinists, free. But could his desires have been different? That is the crucial question. If his desires could not have been different, then he could not act in any other way than the way he does act. And that is the description of an unfree man, not a free man.

By not considering the various ways in which a man's desires can be controlled by external forces beyond his control, soft determinists present a definition of freedom that does not accord with our normal use of that term. Of course, a soft determinist may claim that he is simply providing his own nominal definition of "free," and that, therefore, we have no right to object to his analysis. But we are interested in the concept of freedom that is relevant to questions of moral responsibility, and any concept of freedom that leads us to consider hypnotized or brainwashed individuals morally responsible for their actions is not the concept with which we are concerned. Soft determinists may use words as they wish, but after they choose their nominal definitions, they will still be faced with the objection that what we call freedom is incompatible with determinism, and it is our concept of freedom that is a necessary condition for ascribing moral responsibility to an agent.

In defending his view the soft determinist appealed to the case of a person walking down the street as a paradigm case of a free action. But although the paradigm-case argument is effective when used properly, there is good reason to believe that the soft determinist has not used it properly. To see where he has gone wrong, let us consider a clear misuse of the paradigm-case argument.

Suppose we traveled to a land in which the inhabitants believed that every woman who was born on February 29 was a witch, and that every witch had the power to cause a drought. If we refused to believe that any woman was a witch, the philosophically knowledgeable inhabitants might try to convince us that indeed there were witches by appealing to the paradigm-case argument. Here, they might say, is a woman born on February 29. She is a clear case of what we call a witch. If you claim that no women are witches, you simply do not know how to speak our language properly.

What would we say in response to this argument? How does this appeal to a paradigm case differ from Miss Stebbing's appeal to a plank as a paradigm case of solidity? The appeal to a plank as a paradigm case of solidity is an appeal to an indisputable case. No one doubts that a plank that can hold sizable weight is solid. On the other hand, the appeal to a woman born on February 29 as a paradigm case of a witch is surely disputable, for until such a woman has demonstrated her supposedly supernatural powers, there seems no reason to accept the view that she is a witch.

Is the soft determinist appealing to an indisputable case when he appeals to a person's walking down the street as a paradigm case of free action? Not at all, for as we saw in the Leopold-Loeb case, we can easily be led to believe that such an apparently free action is not, in fact, free. By appealing to a disputable example as a paradigm case, the soft determinist begs the question, that is, he assumes what he is supposed to be proving. What he is supposed to be proving is that actions such as walking down the street are examples of free actions. To simply assert that such an action is free is to pay no attention to the hard determinist's argument that purports to prove that such an action is not free. No example can be used as a paradigm case if the example is itself questionable, and clearly the soft determinist's example of a free action is questionable since, as Darrow proved, people can easily be led to assert that the action is not free. Thus, it seems that soft determinism is not a correct view.

The hard determinist argues that since premises (1) and (2) of Darrow's argument are true, so is the conclusion. The soft determinist argues that premise (1) is false. If the soft determinist's view is not correct, then the only way to avoid hard determinism and its claim that no man is free is to argue that premise (2) is false. And that is the view known as libertarianism.

The libertarian agrees with the hard determinist that no action is free if it must occur. For the libertarian as well as for the hard determinist, a man is free with regard to a particular action only if it is within his power to perform the action and it is within his power not to perform the action. But are men ever free? The hard determinist believes that men are never free, since in the case of every action there are antecedent conditions, known or unknown, ensuring that the action will occur. The libertarian finds this conclusion unacceptable, since he is certain that men are free. But he believes that it is impossible to reject premise (1) of Darrow's argument. His only recourse, therefore, is to reject premise (2). As Sherlock Holmes noted, "When you have eliminated the impossible, whatever remains, *however improbable,* must be the truth. . . ."[10] The libertarian thus denies that every event has a cause.

But why is the libertarian so certain that men sometimes act freely? In order to understand his view, consider an ordinary example of a simple human action—for instance, raising your hand at a meeting in order to catch the speaker's attention. If you are attending a lecture and the time comes for questions from the audience, you believe that it is within your power to raise your hand and that it is also within your power not to raise your hand. The choice is up to you. Nothing forces you to ask a question, and nothing prevents you from asking one. What could be more obvious than this? But if this description of the situation is accurate, then hard determinism is incorrect, for you are free with regard to the act of raising your hand. And there are innumerable examples of free actions that seem equally incontrovertible. Suppose you are walking home and have the choice of two convenient routes. It seems perfectly clear that you could take either of these routes. In fact, some days you choose one, and other days you choose the other. How could anyone seriously believe that it is not up to you which route you choose to take? To make the libertarian's point even more forcefully, try this little experiment. Hold up your arm and move it first to the right and then to the left. If the hard determinist is correct, then it was not possible just now when you held up your arm for you to move it first to the left and then to the right. According to the hard determinist, what you did was the only thing that you could have done, conditions being what they were. But it seems obvious that you could have moved your arm first to the left and then to the right, rather than first to the right and then to the left. Therefore, the hard determinist is in error, and you do have free will.

---

[10]   Sir Arthur Conan Doyle, "The Sign of Four," in *The Complete Sherlock Holmes* (New York: Doubleday & Company, Inc., 1953), vol. I, p. 118.

The libertarian never tires of presenting examples of this sort, for it is the heart of his position that such examples are conclusive evidence for man's free will. And, indeed, we do normally accept these examples as conclusive. We assume on most occasions that we are free with regard to our actions, and, moreover, we assume that other persons are free with regard to their actions. If a friend agrees to meet us at six o'clock for dinner and arrives an hour late claiming to have lost track of the time, we blame him for his tardiness, for we assume that he had it within his power to keep track of the time. All he had to do was glance at his watch, and assuming that no special circumstances were involved, he had it within his power to glance at his watch. He was simply negligent and deserves to be blamed for his negligence, for he could have acted conscientiously. But to believe that he could have acted in a way other than the way he did act is to believe that he was free.

How do hard determinists respond to examples such as these? They request us to examine in greater detail the situations we have described. Consider the case of our friend who arrives an hour late for dinner. We assume that he is to blame for his actions, but the hard determinist points out to us that there is some reason why our friend was late; some motive impelled him to be late. Perhaps he was more interested in finishing his work at the office than in arriving on time for his dinner appointment. But why was he more interested in finishing his work than in arriving on time? Perhaps because his parents instilled in him the importance of work but not the importance of promptness. Whatever the reason for his lateness, says the hard determinist, it is obvious that the motive that caused him to arrive late was stronger than the motive that impelled him to arrive on time. He acted as he did because his strongest motive prevailed. Which of his motives was the strongest, however, was not something over which he had any control. Therefore, he was not free.

The hard determinist's reply may seem persuasive. How can we deny that a man is always caused to act by his strongest motive? But there is something highly misleading about this claim, and it is crucial that we examine it with great care. The first step in analyzing the thesis that a man is always caused to act by his strongest motive is to realize that the thesis is immune from refutation. No matter what example of a human action is considered, a defender of this thesis could argue that the person's action was a direct result of his strongest motive. If a person goes for a swim, it must be due to the fact that his strongest motive is the motive to take a swim. If he decides to forego the swim and read a book instead, then his strongest motive is to read a book. How do we know in this latter case that his motive to read a book is stronger than his motive to take a swim? Because, in fact, he read a book and did not take a swim. This line of argument seems impervious to criticism. But, paradoxically, it is the very fact that the thesis seems undeniable that ought to give rise to our suspicions. No statement of fact is absolutely certain, especially one that is a universal generalization applying to an indefinite number of cases. How can it be so undeniable that every action that ever has occurred or ever will occur is the result of the agent's strongest motive? There are so many types of actions, so many different agents, and so many different situations; how could the explanation of every action be expressible in such a simplistic formulation?

The answer to this question is that, contrary to appearances, the claim that a man is always caused to act by his strongest motive is not a factual claim at all. It is a mere tautology. To see this, all we need to do is to ask what is meant by the phrase "the strongest motive." How can we identify a man's strongest motive? The only possible answer seems to be that the strongest motive is the motive that prevails, the motive that causes the man to act. But if the strongest motive is the motive causing the man to act, what force is there in the claim that the motive causing a man to act is the one that causes him to act? This is an analytic statement, one that is true solely by virtue of the meanings of the words in the statement. But analytic statements give us no information about the world. They do not provide us with insight into men's actions or motives. They can be known to be true a priori just because the way the world is has nothing to do with their truth. That is why they are immune from empirical refutation. They are just redundancies.

Thus, the claim that a man always acts in accord with his strongest motive, far from providing us with a deep insight into human motivation, provides us with no insight at all. To know that a man acts for the reason that he acts is to know nothing at all about the human psyche. A tautology, masked as a factual statement, has led us astray. This happens surprisingly often in discussions, and it is important for us to be on guard against such a masquerade. Indeed, before we have concluded our philosophical inquiry, we shall uncover a number of other statements that purport to be factual and yet are, in truth, nothing but tautologies. The surest way to spot such statements is to examine carefully the meanings of the words we use. Here, as elsewhere, there is no substitute for clarity.

We have seen that the hard determinist has not succeeded in his attempt to overturn the examples of free actions presented by the libertarian. However, the hard determinist has yet another argument to offer against the libertarian's position. If the libertarian is correct in his claim that when a person acts freely nothing causes him to act as he does, then, says the hard determinist, a free act is an inexplicable occurrence. To act freely is to act in a random, chaotic, unintelligible fashion, for if nothing causes a person to perform an action, why would he perform it? Consequently, the hard determinist claims, we cannot hold men morally blameworthy for their actions, for their actions are inexplicable. If a person is driving a car and suddenly finds himself turning the wheel to the right, we can hardly blame him if an accident occurs, for what he does is beyond his control. He just acted without rhyme or reason.

Thus, it would seem that the libertarian is caught in a dilemma. Either he accepts the fact that men are caused to do what they do and he is thus forced to relinquish the notion that men are morally responsible for their actions, or he must accept the fact that men's actions are inexplicable and he is led to the same conclusion, that men are not morally responsible for their actions. Is there any way that the libertarian can escape this dilemma?

Indeed there is. In order to understand fully the libertarian's reply, let us consider a man who is walking toward a telephone booth. Suppose we want an explanation of this man's action. We are told that he is walking toward the telephone booth in order to place a call to his stock broker. The man has decided to buy some stock and wishes his broker to place the appropriate order. With this explanation in hand we now know why this individual is walking toward the telephone booth. Although we may be interested in learning more about the man or his choice of stocks, we do have a complete explanation of his present action. We know exactly why he is acting as he does. There seems nothing random, chaotic, inexplicable, or unintelligible about his action. However, and this is the libertarian's essential point, we have not yet inquired what is causing the man to do what he does. In fact, it is entirely possible that nothing is causing him to do what he does. What we do know is the *reason* for the man's action. We know his purpose, his intention, what he is trying to achieve by his action. But knowing this, says the libertarian, is very different from knowing the cause of the man's action, if there is one.

In short, the libertarian's reply to the dilemma posed by the hard determinist is that human actions can be understood in a perfectly clear fashion without any appeal to the cause of the actions. We need not be forced to choose between considering actions as caused and considering them as inexplicable, for there is a third alternative, namely, considering them as purposeful. What the libertarian claims is that to explain actions in this third way is not to explain them in either of the first two ways. To know the purpose of a man's action is not to know its cause, for there may not be one, and it is not to leave the action unexplained. It is to explain it in an entirely satisfactory, although not causal, manner. The libertarian thus escapes the hard determinist's dilemma, for we *can* understand the action of a person who is not caused to do what he does. We understand it in terms of his purposes.

We are now in a position to contrast the libertarian's description of a human action with the determinist's description of the same action. Let the action in question be that of a person's raising his arm to adjust his television set. A determinist would say that the person was caused to raise his arm by his desire to adjust the set and his belief that he could effectively carry out this adjustment by turning the set's dials. A libertarian would say simply that the person raised his arm in order to adjust the set.

In contrasting these two descriptions, it is important to note that the libertarian is explaining human actions very differently from the way in which any of us would explain the movements of rocks or rivers. If we speak of a rock's purpose in falling off a cliff or a river's purpose in flowing south, we do so only in a metaphorical way, for we assume that rocks and rivers have no purposes of their own but are caused to do whatever they do. Strictly speaking, a rock does not fall in order to hit the ground, and a river does not flow in order to reach the south. But the libertarian is not speaking metaphorically when he says that a man acts in order to achieve his purpose. The libertarian considers his statement to be literally true. Not even the most complex of machines can act in just the way that a man can act. A machine can break down and fail to operate, but only a man can protest and stop work on purpose.

Is the libertarian's view correct? No one really knows the answer to that question. But we can say this much: If he is correct, then human beings are often morally responsible for their actions. They deserve praise when they act admirably, and they deserve blame when they act reprehensibly. Darrow may have been correct in arguing that Leopold and Loeb were not acting freely, but if the libertarian is right, then the burden of proof lay with Darrow. He had to show that the actions of these boys, unlike the actions of most other people, were not free. Whether he showed this, of course, is a question that lies beyond our immediate concern.

But what if the libertarian is not correct? What if all human actions are caused by antecedent conditions, known or unknown, which ensure their occurrence? In that case it would seem that no one is morally responsible for his actions. But it is vital to note that the fact that no man is morally responsible for his actions does not imply that men ought not to be held legally responsible for their actions. Just as a mad dog that endangers us must be taken from our midst to ensure our safety, so people who endanger us must also be taken from our midst to ensure our safety. There is nothing irrational about isolating mad dogs even though they are not morally responsible for their behavior, and there is nothing irrational about isolating disturbed people even though they are not morally responsible for their behavior. Thus, even in a world in which no man was morally responsible for his actions, we would have a legal system, law courts, criminals, and prisons. Remember that Darrow's eloquence did not free his clients, and, indeed, he would not have wanted them to be freed. Although he did not blame them for their actions, he certainly did not want their actions to be repeated. To Darrow, Leopold and Loeb were sick men who needed the same care as any sick person with a contagious disease. A world without freedom is not a world in which everything is taken to be acceptable. It is a world in which everything is understood to be necessary.

Chapter 4

FATALISM

As if our examination of the concept of free will were not already complicated enough, there is yet another aspect of the subject which requires our attention. It is possible to argue that no man has free will without relying on the principle of determinism. Instead of using the premise that every event has a cause to reach the conclusion that no man has free will, some thinkers have claimed to reach this same conclusion using as a premise nothing more than a basic law of logic. This claim is referred to as fatalism. Because the fatalist utilizes only a principle of logic, he is thus in one way a more dangerous opponent for the defender of free will than is the determinist: Although we can deny the principle of determinism without absurdity, we cannot deny a principle of logic without denying reason itself. Thus, if the fatalist can construct a valid argument whose premise is an unassailable law of logic and whose conclusion is the denial of man's free will, defenders of free will will be forced to relinquish their position. Can the fatalist construct such an argument? That is the question we shall now consider.

The law of logic utilized by the fatalist in his argument is the fundamental logical principle known as the law of excluded middle. According to this law, every statement must be either true or false. If a statement is not true, then it must be false. If it is not false, then it must be true. To take a simple example, it is either true or false that Benjamin Franklin signed the Declaration of Independence. If it is not true that he signed, then it is false that he signed. If it is not false that he signed, then it is true that he signed. Of course, you may not know whether Benjamin Franklin signed the Declaration of Independence. But even if no one knew whether he signed, either he did sign or he did not sign. That much is certain. Stated in this way, the law of excluded middle may appear to be such an elementary and unexceptionable principle that it is hardly necessary to formulate it at all. Nevertheless, the fatalist seizes upon this seemingly innocuous principle and employs it in an apparently devastating manner.

In order to understand the fatalist's argument, let us consider any future human action. Suppose the action we consider is your raising your right arm five minutes from now. The fatalist's argument is designed to show that you are not free with regard to raising your right arm five minutes from now. In other words, either you must raise your right arm five minutes from now or you cannot raise your right arm five minutes from now. And not only does the fatalist claim that it is not up to you whether you raise your right arm five minutes from now, but he also proposes to prove this claim in four easy steps:

1. Either it is true that you will raise your right arm five minutes from now or it is false that you will raise your right arm five minutes from now.
2. If it is true that you will raise your right arm five minutes from now, then there is nothing you can do to avoid raising your right arm five minutes from now.
3. If it is false that you will raise your right arm five minutes from now, then there is nothing you can do to enable you to raise your right arm five minutes from now.
4. Therefore, either you must raise your right arm five minutes from now or you cannot raise your right arm five minutes from now. In either case, you are not free with regard to raising your right arm five minutes from now.

And the fatalist can employ this same form of argument no matter what action or event you substitute for the act of raising your right arm five minutes from now. Let the action in question be that of a man setting foot on the planet Venus in the year 2100. Either it is true that this act will occur or it is false that this act will occur. If it is true that this act will occur, then there is nothing anyone can do to prevent it. If it is false that this act will occur, then there is nothing anyone can do to bring it about. In either case, the act is not a free one, for an act is free only if it is within someone's power to bring it about and it is within someone's power to prevent it. Of course, no one knows whether a man will set foot on the planet Venus in the year 2100, but our present ignorance is entirely irrelevant to the fatalist's argument. Although we do not know whether the event in question will occur, we do know that either it will occur or it will not occur. And that fact alone, according to the fatalist, is sufficient to prove that we have no control over the event. In short, our destiny is in the hands of fate.

One way to understand clearly the fatalist's position is to realize that the fatalist views the future as most of us view the past. As we look back on the past we may regret that certain events occurred, but we can do nothing now to undo or "prevent" the occurrence of any event that did, in fact, occur. Similarly, we can do nothing now to bring about the occurrence in the past of any event that did not, in fact, occur. The fatalist argues that we should adopt an analogous attitude toward the future. As we look ahead, we may hope that certain events will occur, but, according to the fatalist, we can do nothing now to prevent the occurrence of any event that will, in fact, occur. Similarly, according to the fatalist, we can do nothing now to bring about the occurrence in the future of any event that will not, in fact, occur. In brief, what the fatalist claims is that we can do no more about the future than we can about the past.

This is, indeed, a sorry picture of human life. According to fatalism we are all powerless to change our destinies. We *can* only do what we *shall* do, and what we shall do is not up to us. Is there any way to avoid this fatalistic conclusion?

Some philosophers reply to the fatalist in the following manner. Fatalism, as they understand it, implies that no matter what a person does, the result of his actions will be the same. What is fated to happen will happen regardless of anything anyone might do. But, these philosophers argue, just because it is true that an event will occur, it does not follow that the event will occur no matter what anyone does. For example, if it is true that a man who is presently unmarried will be divorced next year, it does not follow that he will be divorced whether or not he gets married. For if a man is not married, he cannot be divorced. Therefore, contrary to what the fatalist seems to claim, a man does have some control over the future, for if he does not get married he cannot be divorced.

But this reply to fatalism misses the mark by misrepresenting the fatalist's position. The fatalist does not claim that if it is true that an event will occur, then that event will occur no matter what other events occur previously. What the fatalist claims is that if it is true that an event will occur, then that event will occur despite what anyone is actually able to do. A man will not be divorced if he never marries, but if it is true that he will be divorced then it is also true that he will be married.

To consider another example, some philosophers have supposed that the fatalist claims that learning how to swim is a useless precaution against drowning, since if it is true that you are going to drown, then nothing you can do will prevent your drowning, while if it is false that you are going to drown, then there is no need to take precautions against drowning. This, however, is not the fatalist's position. The fatalist admits that your learning how to swim may save you from drowning. What the fatalist claims is that if your learning how to swim saves you from drowning, then it was fated to save you. According to fatalism, you have no choice as to whether you will drown, and you have no choice as to whether you will learn how to swim. But this is not to deny that learning how to swim may save you from drowning. It may, and if it does, it was fated to do so.

Since this attack on fatalism is unsuccessful, other philosophers have tried a different approach. They argue that steps (2) and (3) of the fatalist's argument are incorrect. According to these philosophers, even if it is true that an event *will* occur, it does not follow that the event *must* occur. If it is true that a man will raise his right arm five minutes from now, then it is still within his power not to perform this action. He *can* refrain from performing it, though, in fact, he will not. If it is true that an event will occur, it follows that no one *will* prevent it. It does not follow that no one *can* prevent it.

Although this answer to fatalism has convinced many thinkers, it does not seem quite satisfactory, for the very same argument being employed against the fatalist supposedly to prove that we have control over future events can be employed in turn by the fatalist supposedly to prove the absurd view that we have control over past events. Suppose, for instance, that it is false that a man attended a particular lecture yesterday. Today he is asked to read the notes he took at yesterday's lecture. Of course, he cannot do so. But, the fatalist points out, suppose someone were to say that he *could* do so—it's just that he won't. That would be an obvious error, for a man not only *will* not read notes that were never taken, he cannot. Similarly, the fatalist argues, if it is true that a man will be in New York at 1:00 P.M. tomorrow, then he cannot be in London at 12:59 P.M. tomorrow. Imagine that someone were to say that he *could* do so, but that he won't. That, too, is an obvious error, for a man not only *will* not be in London at 12:59 P.M. if he is in New York at 1:00 P.M., he cannot be. Thus, says the fatalist, steps (2) and (3) are correct, for the argument that has been presented to show that we have control over the future would have the absurd consequence of showing that we also have control over the past. Since it clearly does not prove the latter claim, it does not prove the former claim either.

Is the fatalist's position then impregnable? Is there no way to avoid his dire conclusion? Indeed, there is such a way, but this involves a modification of the law of excluded middle, a modification, incidentally, that appears to have been envisoned by Aristotle, who first formalized this law. Although we can say with regard to most statements that if they are not true then they are false, and if they are not false then they are true, this is not the case with regard to all statements. The exceptions are statements about future events whose occurrence is up to us. Such statements are neither true nor false. However, they become true or false when it is no longer up to us whether the events in question occur.

To make this point clearer, let us consider a specific example of such a statement. Suppose we borrow Aristotle's classic example: "A sea fight will occur tomorrow." Since under normal conditions it is up to us whether there will be a sea fight tomorrow, it is not now true that there will be a sea fight tomorrow and it is not now false that there will be a sea fight tomorrow. We may speak of the statement as "indeterminate." Tomorrow, however, the statement will become true or false, depending upon what we decide to do. It is important to realize that it is not just our ignorance regarding tomorrow's events that leads us to say that the statement is indeterminate, for we are also ignorant regarding many events that occurred millions of years ago. Statements about the occurrence of such past events, however, *are* either true or false, since it is not up to us whether these events occurred. However, it *is* up to us whether certain events occur in the future, and it is for this reason that statements affirming or denying their occurrence are indeterminate. It cannot be true that an event whose occurrence is up to us will occur, for we may decide to prevent it. It also cannot be false that an event whose occurrence is up to us will not occur, for we may decide to bring it about. Whether it is true or false that the event occurs depends upon us, and so it is not yet either true or false that it will occur.

The fatalist's argument is thus unsound, for premise (1) is not acceptable as it applies to statements about future events whose occurrence is up to us. If it is true that you will raise your right arm five minutes from now, then the fatalist is correct that there is nothing you can do to avoid raising your right arm five minutes from now. Similarly, if it is false that you will raise your right arm five minutes from now, then the fatalist is also correct that there is nothing you can do to enable you to raise your right arm five minutes from now. But where the fatalist's argument goes awry is in its assumption that either it is true that you will raise your right arm in five minutes or it is false that you will raise your right arm in five minutes. For, in fact, it is not true now that you will perform this action, and it is not false now that you will perform this action. It is indeterminate now whether you will perform this action, for your performing it depends upon what you decide to do, and what you decide to do is up to you. Thus, the fatalist's argument fails, and we can maintain a belief in man's free will without fear of the fatalist's threat.

Before concluding this section it is interesting to note that the fatalist's argument has long been of serious concern to religious thinkers. They have discussed this same problem with one additional modification: Instead of considering the implications of the law of excluded middle for man's free will, they have been concerned with the implication of God's omniscience for man's free will. To see how similar these two issues are, we can transform the fatalist's argument into a religious context with one simple substitution. According to our Western religious tradition, God is considered to be omniscient, that is, He knows everything that is the case. If a statement is true, then God knows that it is true. If a statement is false, then God knows that it is false. Therefore, instead of speaking of statements as true, let us speak of statements as items of God's knowledge. The fatalist's argument will then read as follows:

1. Either God knows that you will raise your right arm five minutes from now or God knows that you will not raise your right arm five minutes from now.
2. If God knows that you will raise your right arm five minutes from now, then there is nothing you can do to avoid raising your right arm five minutes from now.
3. If God knows that you will not raise your right arm five minutes from now, then there is nothing you can do to enable you to raise your right arm five minutes from now.
4. Therefore, either you must raise your right arm five minutes from now or you cannot raise your right arm five minutes from now. In either case, you are not free with regard to raising your right arm five minutes from now.

Arguments of this sort have greatly troubled religious thinkers for centuries, since many of these thinkers have wished to believe both that God is omniscient and that man has free will. Can both these beliefs be maintained without contradiction?

As a consequence of our previous discussion, you may anticipate correctly that there is a way to reconcile these two beliefs. This way was first suggested by the Jewish medieval philosopher, Levi ben Gersom (known as Gersonides). Gersonides (1288–1344) adopted the Aristotelian view that a statement about a future event whose occurrence is up to us is neither true nor false. Gersonides then reasoned that although God is omniscient, He cannot know what is not the case, and it is not the case that you will raise your right arm five minutes from now and it is not the case that you will not raise your right arm five minutes from now. If God knew that you were going to raise your right arm five minutes from now, then He would be in error, for it is not true that you will raise your right arm five minutes from now. Similarly, if God knew that you were *not* going to raise your right arm five minutes from now, then He also would be in error, for it is not true that you will not raise your right arm five minutes from now. But since God is omniscient, He is never in error. He knows only what is the case. But what is the case is that it is indeterminate whether you will raise your right arm five minutes from now. So that is what God knows. He knows that what you are going to do is up to you. That is all He knows, but, then again, that is all there is to know. In this way Gersonides was able to claim both that God is omniscient and that man has free will.[1]

Of course, in bringing into our discussion the concept of God, we have opened up all sorts of questions pertaining to the existence of God, the attributes of God, and the nature of religious belief. These complex topics lead us into an entirely new area of philosophical inquiry, and to this area, known as philosophy of religion, we now turn.

---

[1] For further discussion of the issues raised in this chapter, see my book *Fate, Logic, and Time* (New Haven: Yale University Press, 1967).

PART III

PHILOSOPHY OF RELIGION

Chapter 5

DOES GOD EXIST?

One may take various positions in answer to the question "Does God exist?" Theism is the belief that God does exist. Atheism is the belief that God does not exist. Agnosticism is the belief that there is not sufficient evidence available to decide whether God exists. But which of these positions is the correct one?

The first step in answering this question is to determine just what is meant by the term "God." This term has been used in various ways, ranging from the Greek concept of the Olympian gods to John Dewey's concept of the *"active* relation between ideal and actual."[1] However, we shall adopt the more usual view, common to many religious believers, that the term "God" refers to an all-good, all-powerful, eternal Creator of the world. The question then is this: Does a Being so described exist?

---

[1]   John Dewey, *A Common Faith* (New Haven: Yale University Press, 1934), p. 51.

A. THE APPEAL TO REASON

There are several proofs that have been put forth to defend the claim that such a Being does exist. One of the best known of these proofs is the cosmological argument. According to this argument, everything that exists is caused to exist by something else. For example, a house is caused to exist by its builder, and rain is caused to exist by certain meteorological conditions. But if everything that exists is caused to exist by something else, then the world itself must be caused to exist by something else. This "something else" is what we call God.

Although the cosmological argument may have a certain initial plausibility, careful consideration has led virtually all contemporary philosophers to reject it. The major difficulty with this argument is that if everything that exists is caused to exist by something else, then the cause of the world's existence is itself caused to exist by something else. But in that case the cause of the world's existence cannot be identified as God, for God is an all-powerful, eternal Being who does not depend upon anything else for His existence. A defender of the cosmological argument might try to surmount this difficulty by claiming that the cause of the world's existence is not caused to exist by something else but is self-caused, that is, the reason for its existence lies within itself. However, if the defender of the cosmological argument is willing to admit the possibility that something is self-caused, his argument crumbles, for if the cause of the world's existence can be self-caused, why cannot the world be self-caused? In that case there would be no need to postulate an external cause of the world's existence, for this cause was postulated to explain the existence of the world, and if the reason for the world's existence lies within itself, then no further explanation of its existence is necessary.

As a last-ditch attempt to salvage the cosmological argument, one might argue simply that something must have started everything, and that this "something" is God. But, even if we grant the claim that something must have started everything (and we could question this claim by appealing to the entirely acceptable mathematical notion of an infinite series), it hardly follows from the fact that something started everything that this "something" is all-good, all-powerful, or eternal. Perhaps this first cause is evil, or perhaps it passed out of existence soon after getting things rolling. No such possibilities are excluded by the cosmological argument, and so this argument does not prove the existence of God.

A second classic proof for the existence of God is the ontological argument. This argument, which was defended by such eminent philoso-phers as René Descartes (1596–1650), Baruch Spinoza (1632–1677), and Gottfried Leibniz (1646–1716), is still the subject of much discus-sion. The distinguishing feature of this argument is its a priori character, that is, the argument makes no appeal to empirical evidence. Rather, it purports to show that the very nature of God implies His existence.

There are various versions of the ontological argument, but the basic structure of all these versions is the same. God is defined as a Being who possesses every perfection. It is then pointed out that existence is a perfec-tion, for it is more perfect to exist than not to exist. Thus, since God possesses every perfection and existence is a perfection, it follows that God exists.

Despite the fact that this argument has been defended in highly in-genious ways, it is open to at least one devastating criticism. This criticism was stated succinctly by Immanuel Kant (1724–1804), who argued that existence is not an attribute. What he meant by this claim is that the definition of a thing remains the same whether the thing exists or not. For example, our definition of a unicorn would not be altered if we happened to discover a living unicorn, just as our definition of a whooping crane would not be altered if whooping cranes happened to become extinct. In other words, whether there are any unicorns or whooping cranes does not affect the meaning of the terms "unicorn" and "whooping crane."

To understand this point more clearly, try a little experiment. First imagine a ferocious tiger. Now imagine a ferocious tiger that exists. It is evident that there is nothing more to imagine in the second case than there is in the first case. The reason for this is that our concept of a ferocious tiger remains the same whether or not any ferocious tigers actually exist.

Applying Kant's insight directly to the ontological argument, we can now see why the argument is unsound. Since the definition of a thing remains the same whether the thing exists or not, it follows that the definition of God remains the same whether He exists or not. Thus, existence cannot be part of the definition of God. God may be defined as a Being who possesses all perfection, but existence is not one of these perfections, since existence is no attribute at all. To say that something exists is not to ascribe a perfection to the thing but to describe a fact about the world. What we mean by the term "God" is one matter; whether God exists is an entirely different matter. The ontological argu-ment confuses these two matters and thereby goes awry.

Even if the ontological argument were sound, though, it is probable that few people would be led to believe in the existence of God as a result of considering this argument. It is simply too abstruse to appeal to a wide audience. However, the next argument we shall consider, the teleological argument, does not share this difficulty. The argument is easy to understand and highly persuasive.

Defenders of the teleological argument begin by asking us to look around at the world in which we live. They point out that the world possesses a highly ordered structure, just like an extraordinarily complex machine. Each part of the machine is adjusted to all the other parts with wondrous precision, and the more we investigate the workings of our world, the more we are amazed at our discoveries of its intricate patterns. For instance, the human eye, which so many of us take for granted, is a mechanism of such enormous complexity that its design is breathtaking. But, say the defenders of the teleological argument, a design requires a designer. The magnificent order of our world cannot be a result of pure chance but must be the work of a Supreme Mind responsible for the order. This Supreme Mind is what we refer to as God.

Although the teleological argument has undoubtedly convinced many people, most philosophers agree that the argument suffers from several fatal flaws. First, let us note that it is not at all surprising that our world exhibits an order, since any world must exhibit an order of some sort. Were you to drop ten coins on the floor in the most random fashion, they would still exhibit *some* order. An order, therefore, does not imply an orderer. If we use the term "design" to mean "a consciously established order," then it is true that a design implies a designer. But the question is this: Does our world exhibit mere order or a design?

If the world were just like a machine, as the teleological argument asserts, then, since a machine has a design and a designer, so would the world. But is it so obvious that the world is just like a machine? In his classic book *Dialogues Concerning Natural Religion,* David Hume argues that our experience is too limited for us to accept such an analogy. Hume notes that although the world bears some slight resemblance to a machine, the world is also similar to an animal in that "[a] continual circulation of matter in it produces no disorder; a continual waste in every part is incessantly repaired; the closest sympathy is perceived throughout the entire system; and each part or member, in performing its proper offices, operates both to its own preservation and to that of the whole."[2] Hume further points out that the world is also somewhat like a vegetable, since neither has sense organs or brains, though both exhibit

---

2 David Hume, *Dialogues Concerning Natural Religion* (New York: Hafner Publishing Co., 1948), p. 42.

life and movement. But whereas any machine requires a designer of the machine, we see that animals and vegetables come into being in very different ways from machines. Hume, however, does not intend to prove that the world actually came into being as an animal or vegetable does. Rather, he wishes to show that the world is not *sufficiently* like an animal, a vegetable, or a machine to permit us to draw reasonable conclusions from such weak analogies.

But if we cannot draw an analogy between the world and a machine, the teleological argument collapses, for we then have no reason to believe that the world exhibits a design rather than an order. For this reason defenders of the teleological argument are likely to insist that, contrary to what Hume says, we *can* draw a reasonable analogy between the world and a machine. Surprising as it may seem, however, even if we grant this rather dubious analogy, the teleological argument does not succeed. Hume himself demonstrated this fact by provisionally accepting the analogy and then bringing to light some of its less obvious implications.

Let us grant, he says, that like effects prove like causes. In that case, if the world is like a machine, the cause of the world is like the cause of a machine. Machines are usually built after many trials; so the world was probably built after many trials. Machines are usually built by many workers; so the world was probably built by many deities. Those who build machines are often inexperienced, careless, or foolish; so the gods too may be inexperienced, careless, or foolish. As Hume suggests, perhaps this world "was only the first rude essay of some infant deity, who afterwards abandoned it, ashamed of his lame performance." Or perhaps "it is the work only of some dependent, inferior deity, and is the object of derision to his superiors." It might even be "the production of old age and dotage in some superannuated diety, and ever since his death has run on at adventures, from the first impulse and active force which it received from him."[3] Hume's point in suggesting such possibilities is that even if we grant an analogy between the world and a machine and agree that the world was designed in the way that a machine is designed, we are not committed to the view that the world's design is due to one all-good, all-powerful, eternal Designer. In other words, even if we grant the dubious analogy upon which the teleological argument rests, we are not thereby committed to the existence of God.

Although the teleological argument does call our attention to the order in the universe, the argument does not succeed in proving that this order was consciously established by a Supreme Designer, for, as Hume sug-

---

[3] *Ibid.,* p. 41.

gests, this order may well be a natural outcome of changes inherent in the world itself. The world may go through innumerable structural changes until a stable pattern is reached, and the existence of such complex phenomena as the human eye may be a result of the process of natural selection whereby those forms of life that cannot adjust to their environment die out and those forms of life that can adjust survive. This explanation of the type of order the universe exhibits seems perfectly adequate and requires no recourse to the hypothesis of a Supreme Designer. Furthermore, this explanation finds confirmation in developments of biology since the time of Darwin. These developments are a further blow to the teleological argument, for they demonstrate that the argument's basic assumption, that the world is designed, is not merely an unsupported hypothesis; it is also an unnecessary hypothesis.

Our attack upon the theological argument may appear conclusive, but some proponents of the argument have attempted to construct one last line of defense. They argue that it is not just the fact that the world exhibits an order which leads to the conclusion that God exists. Rather, it is, as George Berkeley (1685–1753) put it, the "surprising magnificence, beauty, and perfection" of the order which leads to this conclusion.[4] In other words, such a perfect world as the one in which we live could not possibly be either the work of an inferior deity or the outcome of impersonal natural processes, since neither could be expected to create a flawless world. Only an all-good, all-powerful Creator could have produced such a masterpiece, and, therefore, the existence of such a world proves the existence of God.

This defense of the teleological argument, however, rests upon the highly dubious premise that the world is perfect. As a matter of fact, the evidence against this view is overwhelming. Just consider droughts, floods, famines, hurricanes, tornadoes, earthquakes, and the innumerable varieties of disease that plague the life of man. Is it a perfect world in which babies are born deformed, small children are bitten by rats, and young people die from leukemia? And what of the evils men cause each other? The savageries of war, the indignities of slavery, and the torments of injustice and treachery extend far beyond the limits of our imagination. In short, the human condition is of such a nature that, as Hume observed, "The man of a delicate, refined temper, by being so much more alive than the rest of the world, is only so much more unhappy."[5]

We need not go on for too long describing the ills of our world before

---

[4] George Berkeley, *A Treatise Concerning the Principles of Human Knowledge* (New York: The Liberal Arts Press, Inc., 1957), p. 97.

[5] Hume, p. 65.

the teleological argument loses its last vestige of plausibility. But human misery poses a serious problem for the theist even if he abandons the teleological argument, for why should there be evil in the world if, as theism affirms, the world was created by an all-good, all-powerful Being? A being who is all-good would do everything within his power to abolish evil. A being who is all-powerful would have it within his power to abolish evil. Therefore, if there were an all-good and all-powerful Being, there would be no evil. But there is evil. Thus, it would seem that there is no being who is all-good and all-powerful. Hence, God does not exist.

Up until this point those who do *not* believe in the existence of God have been on the defensive as they have attempted to refute arguments that purport to prove the existence of God. But now it is those who *do* believe in the existence of God who are on the defensive, for they must answer the classic challenge to theism known as "the problem of evil": How is it possible for evil to exist in a world created by an all-good, all-powerful Being?

There have been numerous attempts to find a solution to the problem of evil. The most promising of these attempts begins by distinguishing two types of evil: moral evil and physical evil. Moral evils are those for which men are responsible, evils such as murder, theft, and oppression. Physical evils are those for which men are not responsible, evils that result from such natural phenomena as typhoons, locusts, and viruses. Having distinguished these two types of evil, each is justified in a different way.

Moral evils are justified by the hypothesis that God has given man free will. The gift of free will means that man has it within his power to do both good and evil. Which he does is up to him. God could have ensured that men always act rightly, but if He had done this, He would have had to take away man's free will, since a man who *must* act rightly is not free. It is true that God is all-powerful, but this fact does not imply that God can perform an act whose description is contradictory, for such an act is no act at all. For example, since it makes no sense to speak of a square circle, so it is no limitation on God's ability that He cannot draw a square circle. Similarly, it is no limitation on God's ability that He cannot create free men who must always do what is right, for, by definition, a free man is one who does not always have to do what is right. God, therefore, had to choose between creating beings who always did what was right and creating beings who were free to do both right and wrong. In His wisdom He chose the latter, since it constituted the greater good. Thus, all moral evils are justified since they are necessary concomitants of the best possible world that God could have created, namely, a world in which men have free will.

Physical evils are justified in one of two ways. According to one hypothesis, physical evils provide the opportunity for human beings to develop their moral qualities. If the world were a paradise without hardships and dangers, it would not be possible for people to acquire the inner strength of character that comes only from standing firm in the face of difficulties. On this view the world was not intended as a pleasure palace but as an arena in which men grapple with their weaknesses and in so doing acquire the strength that will serve them well in some future life. A second way to justify physical evil involves the traditional figure of the devil. According to this hypothesis, physical evils are caused by the free actions of the devil, who has been granted the freedom to bring about these evils for the same reason that human beings have been granted the freedom to commit moral evils, namely, it is a greater good for beings to be free than for them to perform right actions involuntarily.

Does this two-pronged reply to the problem of evil succeed in blunting its force? To some extent it does. Those who pose the problem of evil claim that it is logically impossible that an all-good, all-powerful Being would permit the existence of evil. But, as it turns out, it is possible under certain circumstances that an all-good, all-powerful Being would have to allow evil to exist, for if this evil were a necessary component of the best possible world, then a being who wished to bring about the best possible world would have to utilize that evil which was necessary to the achievement of his goal. Thus, there is no contradiction involved in asserting that a world containing evil was created by an all-good, all-powerful Being.

But the fact that no contradiction is involved in this assertion is no reason to believe that the assertion is true. There is no contradiction involved in asserting that you will live to be one hundred fifty years old, but the absence of contradiction does not imply that this assertion is true. Thus, we are still faced by the following question: Is there any reason to believe that we live in the best possible world and that all the evils we face are necessary for the existence of this world? The answer to this crucial question appears to be clearly negative. The explanations of evil presented above may be logically possible, but they are highly implausible. What evidence is there that there is such a being as the devil? What evidence is there that there is any future life? What evidence is there that the world would not be better without the horrors of bubonic plague? What evidence is there that the free will of a Hitler achieved greater good than would have been achieved by his performing right actions involuntarily? The hypothesis that all the evil in the world is a necessary part of this best of all possible worlds is not contradictory; nevertheless, it is about as unlikely as any hypothesis could be. But, if this is not the best of all possible worlds, then it could not have been created by an all-good, all-powerful Being.

Thus, although the problem of evil does not show theism to be an impossible view, it shows it to be a highly improbable one. If the theist can produce any other evidence in favor of his position, he may be able to increase its plausibility, but unless he can produce such evidence, the reasonable conclusion seems to be that there is no God.

The force of this conclusion can be clearly seen in the following story that is told about the renowned British philosopher Bertrand Russell. Russell, an atheist, was once asked what his reaction would be if, after death, he found himself in the presence of God. Russell replied that this possibility was extremely unlikely. But, his questioner persisted, "What would you say to God if, contrary to all that you believe, it turned out that God did exist?" Russell replied, "I would tell Him that He should have given me more evidence."

It is possible that this is the best of all worlds and that the evils in it only heighten the good, but it is also possible that this is the worst of all worlds and that the goods in it only heighten the evil. It is possible that the world was created by God, but it is also possible, as Russell once ironically suggested, that the world "was made by the devil at a moment when God was not looking."[6] It is possible that those who believe in the existence of God despite the lack of evidence may be rewarded in the hereafter for their faith, but it is also possible that those who do not believe in the existence of God will be rewarded in the hereafter for their intellectual honesty. These are all possibilities, but, in fact, we have no reason to accept any of them. We live in a world in which there is some good and some evil. We have the power to increase the good and decrease the evil, but we also have the power to increase the evil and decrease the good. There seems no reason either to rely on God or to fear the devil. The only beings we need rely on or fear are ourselves.

B. THE APPEAL TO FAITH

The conclusion at which we have arrived has been accepted by the majority of philosophers since the time of Hume and Kant, but there are those persons who have maintained a belief in the existence of God despite the fact that the available evidence supports the opposing belief. Often such persons defend their belief by arguing that the existence of God is a matter of faith, not of reason. In other words, although reason does not provide evidence to support belief in the existence of God, this

---

[6] Bertrand Russell, *Why I Am Not a Christian* (New York: Simon and Schuster, Inc., 1957), p. 12.

fact does not invalidate a person's faith that God exists. We may know of no plausible way to reconcile the existence of evil with the existence of an all-good, all-powerful Being, but the man of faith assures us that the ways of God are mysterious, and that despite the fact that our limited minds are unable to solve the problem of evil, there is no doubt that God in His infinite wisdom could provide the solution.

Although this appeal to faith in order to justify belief in the existence of God is a common strategy, it is entirely inadequate. To begin with, our decision to determine the truth of empirical statements by the scientific method was not an arbitrary one. We chose the scientific method because of its high reliability and its self-corrective nature. The method of faith, however, is neither reliable nor self-corrective. We would not decide whether a road is safe, whether a vaccine is effective, or whether a particular economic policy achieves its goals by appeals to faith. Why then should we appeal to faith in order to decide whether God exists?

Faith in a statement does not prove that the statement is true. If it did, then if one individual had faith that a statement was true and another individual had faith that the contradictory statement was true, it would follow that the statement and its contradictory would both be true—which is impossible. That a man has faith in some statement is a fact about him; it is not a proof of the statement. As we noted earlier, no matter how many people believe that the earth is flat, it does not follow that the earth is flat.

Furthermore, the appeal to faith in order to defend theism is not merely inadequate. Taken seriously, this appeal to faith destroys the very meaningfulness of the theistic position, for a statement that one accepts no matter what evidence to the contrary is presented is, if not a tautology, a statement with no meaning at all. In order to understand this crucial insight, consider the following situation.

Suppose you wish to discover the present whereabouts of a friend named Peterson. You hire an investigator, and after some weeks he informs you that Peterson is in Paris. You go to Paris, but to your surprise you learn that Peterson has never been in Paris; as it turns out he has been staying in London. You accuse the investigator of incompetence, but he replies that when he told you that Peterson was in Paris, he meant only that Peterson was near Paris, and so your discovery does not contradict his statement. Imagine that this investigator is next asked to locate a certain person named Robinson, and the investigator reports that Robinson is in Paris. However, as it turns out, Robinson has never been in Paris but is finally found in Buenos Aires. When a complaint is raised, the investigator again replies that the evidence does not contradict his statement, since Buenos Aires is not that far from Paris. Suppose that every time this investigator is asked to locate someone, he always reports that the individual is in Paris, even if the individual is thousands of miles away or actually died years before. And suppose that each time the investigator is accused of incompetence, he replies that the evidence does not conflict with his statement, since his statement was not meant to rule out the possibility of such evidence. In that case, whenever you are told, on the basis of this investigator's report, that an individual is in Paris, you will pay no attention whatever to this supposed information, for coming from this investigator such "information" is no information at all. Being compatible with every situation, the information is of no use in distinguishing one situation from another. Thus, although under normal circumstances the claim that an individual is in Paris is a meaningful one, this investigator has utilized this claim in such a way as to render it meaningless.

Some theists treat the claim that God exists in precisely the same way that this investigator utilizes the claim that an individual is in Paris. Whatever facts are brought to light, be it the facts of evolution or facts surrounding the tragedies of human life, these theists reply that their faith in the existence of God is compatible with all these facts. Their faith, they say, would be steadfast in the face of any facts at all. But then what is it in which they have faith?

A person may have faith that his candidate for President will be elected, but on election night he learns whether his faith has been misplaced. What sense would it make for a person to announce that his faith will be steadfast, no matter what the outcome of the election? It may appear to be a weakness in one's faith that it can be mistaken, but, quite to the contrary, it is a weakness in one's faith if it cannot be mistaken, since a faith that cannot be contradicted by facts is not a meaningful faith. To believe one fact is to disbelieve other facts. For instance, if I believe that my radio works well, I do not believe that it will go on and off uncontrollably. If it begins to do so, I no longer believe that it works well. But if belief in one fact involves disbelief in other facts, then belief in the existence of God, if it is to be a meaningful belief, must involve disbelief in other facts. It cannot be compatible with all facts.

The man of faith, however, claims that his belief in the existence of God *is* compatible with all facts. This is an unfortunate claim, since it follows from this claim that his belief is meaningless. This is not to deny that his belief may provide him with psychological support, but then a belief that ghosts do not haunt his house may also provide him with such support. It does not follow from the fact that a belief is psychologically helpful that it makes any sense, and although believing what is senseless may be temporarily comforting, for those who take their beliefs seriously enough to act upon them, believing what is senseless may well be disastrous (witness the sick man who waits for God to cure his illness).

The theist thus faces what appears to be an insoluble dilemma. Either he admits that his belief in the existence of God is open to refutation, in which case the existence of evil appears to provide such a refutation; or he denies that his belief in the existence of God is open to refutation, in which case his belief loses meaning. In other words, what the theist asserts is either wrong or meaningless.

The line of argument we have followed in our discussion of the existence of God is not universally accepted, but it has received quite wide acceptance. Indeed, it is this line of argument that lies behind the so-called "Death of God" movement in contemporary theology. Those who support this movement find the analysis presented above totally convincing. They do not conclude from this, as the popular title of their movement suggests, that God has died, for if there ever were a God, an eternal Being, then He could not die. Rather, the "Death of God" theologians believe that our traditional concept of God is dead, for God, defined as the all-good, all-powerful, eternal Creator of the world, never did exist. What these theologians call for is a new concept of religion in which the old concept of God has no place. In the next chapter we shall examine such a possibility.

Chapter 6

THEISM AND
RELIGIOUS COMMITMENT

In order to understand recent developments in religion, it is vital to distinguish between belief in the existence of God and belief in the efficacy of religion. This distinction is too often overlooked, as, for example, in magazine surveys that supposedly determine whether religion is in decline by determining what percentage of people believe in the existence of God. Two assumptions clearly underlie such surveys: (1) if a person believes in the existence of God, then he must be religious; (2) if a person does not believe in the existence of God, then he cannot be religious. Both these assumptions are widely accepted, but both are false.

A. GOD WITHOUT RELIGION*

Suppose we assume, contrary to what most philosophers believe, that the three traditional proofs for the existence of God, the cosmological, the

---

* Part of this section originally appeared in the *American Philosophical Quarterly,* vol. 6 (April, 1969), as a segment of my article, "The Irrelevance to Religion of Philosophic Proofs for the Existence of God."

ontological, and the teleological, are all sound. In short, let us grant that an all-good, all-powerful, eternal Creator of the world does exist. What implications can be drawn from this fact that would be of relevance to human life? In other words, what difference would it make in men's lives if God existed?

Perhaps some men would feel more secure in the knowledge that the universe had been planned by an all-good Being. Others, perhaps, would feel insecure, realizing the extent to which their very existence depended upon the will of this Being. In any case, most men, either out of fear or respect, would wish to act in accordance with the moral code advocated by this Being.

Note, however, that the proofs for the existence of God provide us with no hint whatever as to which actions God wishes us to perform, or what we ought to do so as to please or obey Him. We may affirm that God is all-good, and yet have no way of knowing what the highest moral standards are. All we may be sure of is that whatever these standards may be, God always acts in accordance with them. One might assume that God would have implanted the correct moral standards in men's minds, but this seems doubtful in view of the wide variance in men's moral standards. It is not known which of these numerous standards, if any, is the correct one, and no appeal to a proof for the existence of God will cast the least light upon the matter.

For example, assuming that it can be proven that God exists, is murder immoral? One might argue that since God created man, it is immoral to murder, since it is immoral to destroy what God in His infinite wisdom and goodness has created. This argument fails on several grounds, however. First, if God created man, He also created germs, viruses, disease-carrying rats, and man-eating sharks. Does it follow from the fact that God created these things that they ought not to be eliminated? Secondly, if God arranged for men to live, He also arranged for men to die. Does it follow from this that by committing murder we are assisting the work of God? Thirdly, if God created man, He provided him with the mental and physical capacity to commit murder. Does it follow from this that God wishes men to commit murder? None of these arguments is valid, for all of them involve the fallacy of deducing value judgments from purely factual premises. No such deduction is valid, and, thus, any moral principle is consistent with the existence of God.

The fact that the proofs of God's existence afford no means of distinguishing good from evil has the consequence that no man can be sure of how to obey God and do what is best in His eyes. One may hope that his actions are in accord with God's standards, but no test is available to check on this. Some seemingly good men suffer great ills, and some seemingly evil men achieve great happiness. Perhaps in a future life these things are rectified, but we have no way of ascertaining which men are ultimately rewarded and which are ultimately punished.

One can imagine that if a group of men believed in God's existence, they would be most anxious to learn His will, and, consequently, they would tend to rely upon those individuals who claimed to know the will of God. Diviners, seers, and priests would be in a position of great influence. No doubt competition between them would be severe, for no man could be sure which of these oracles to believe. An oracle might claim that as a sign of his special status God had granted him the power to perform miracles, but since any supposedly miraculous event is in principle explicable by some known or unknown laws of nature, no man could distinguish the genuine prophet from the fraud.

It is clear that the situation described here is paralleled by a stage in the actual development of religion. What men wanted at this stage was some way to find out the will of God. Individual prophets might gain a substantial following, but prophets died and their vital powers died with them. What was needed on practical grounds was a permanent record of God's will as revealed to His special prophet. And this need was eventually met by the writing of holy books, books in which God's will was revealed in a permanent fashion.

But there was more than one such book. Indeed, there were many. Which was to be believed? Which moral code was to be followed? Which prayers were to be recited? Which rituals were to be performed? Proofs for the existence of God are silent upon these crucial matters.

There is only one possible avenue to God's will. One must undergo a personal experience in which one senses the presence of God and apprehends which of the putative holy books is the genuine one. But it is most important not to be deceived in this experience. One must be absolutely certain that it is God whose presence one is experiencing and whose will one is apprehending. In other words, one must undergo a self-validating experience, one that carries its own guarantee of infallibility.

If one undergoes what he believes to be such an experience, he then is certain which holy book is the genuine one, and consequently he knows which actions, prayers, and rituals God wishes him to engage in. In short, he knows whether to accept any particular religion. But notice that if it is not possible to undergo such a self-validating experience, then it is not possible to learn God's will; and if it is not possible to learn God's will, then, even if God exists, there is no reason to accept one religion rather than another or, indeed, to accept any religion at all. Perhaps God does not wish us to belong to any religious organization. Who can know? Thus, whether belief in the existence of God leads to acceptance of a particular religion depends entirely upon whether it is possible for anyone to undergo a self-validating experience.

But, in fact, the whole notion of a self-validating experience is a mistaken one. No experience is itself conclusive evidence for an assertion about the cause of that experience. The fact that an individual in the desert believes that he is seeing an oasis does not imply that there actually is an oasis there. Similarly, the fact that an individual believes that he has experienced the Divine and has learned His will does not imply either that God exists or that this individual has learned God's will. Persons undoubtedly have experiences they believe to be experiences of the Divine, just as persons in the desert undoubtedly have experiences they believe to be experiences of an oasis. But we must subject the factual claims that arise from such experiences to the tests of rational inquiry, inquiry under controlled experimental conditions confirmed by impartial observers.

If we forego this method of testing factual claims, there is no limit to the absurdities that result. For example, one person may claim to have experienced the will of God and to have discovered that God wishes him to climb a particular mountain. Another person claims to have experienced the will of God and to have discovered that God wishes no one to climb mountains. To accept both these claims leads to contradiction, but if we do not utilize our reason, how can we intelligently decide which, if either, of these claims is to be accepted? Both persons may describe their experiences in equally vivid terms, and both may assert that their experiences possessed extraordinary intensity. But the intensity with which one holds a given view has nothing to do with whether the view is correct. Falsehoods can be held every bit as tenaciously as truths. The only reliable way to distinguish truth from falsity is by the use of reason, whether the truths in question concern chemistry, sociology, or theology. As Sidney Hook has written: "Whether an actual angel speaks to me in my beatific vision or whether I only dreamed he spoke, the *truth* of what he says can only be tested in the same way as I test what my neighbor says to me. For even my neighbor may claim to be a messenger of the Lord."[1]

Theistic religions, those that depend upon belief in the existence of God, are only defensible if claims about the will of God can be tested under controlled conditions. But no such test has ever been accepted by proponents of theistic religion, since they wish to protect their beliefs by considering them to be compatible with any possible evidence. As should

---

[1] Sidney Hook, *The Quest for Being* (New York: St. Martin's Press, 1961), pp. 130–131.

be clear by now, however, protecting beliefs in this way is much like protecting ice cream by keeping it in one's pocket. Soon there is nothing left to protect.

The claim that we ought to perform a certain ritual or engage in a particular action because God wishes us to do so is met directly by the response: How would you know if God did not wish us to perform that ritual or engage in that action? If this question is answered by an appeal to the contents of a holy book, one can ask how this book is known to express God's will. If the reply to this question is that the book is known to express God's will because it was written by individuals who had experienced God's will, one can request evidence that the individuals in question actually did experience God's will and did not merely *think* that they had experienced God's will. In other words, one can inquire why the claims of these individuals are to be accepted while the competing claims of other individuals with similar experiences are to be rejected. There seems no other reply to this query except an appeal to faith, but as we have seen, such a "defense" is, in effect, no more than unconditional surrender.

It is thus possible that an individual might believe that God exists and yet, since he does not accept the validity of any person's supposedly self-validating experience, his belief in the existence of God would provide him with no reason to adhere to any religion. In short, such an individual would be best described as an irreligious theist, a description that is certainly unusual, but nonetheless accurate.

B. RELIGION WITHOUT GOD

Some years ago at Columbia College I took a course that surveyed the masterpieces of Western literature from the Greek age to modern times. One day just before class a Japanese friend complained to me about the difficulty of that day's reading assignment, which happened to be selections from the Bible. "I just can't keep in mind all those small details," he said. "How can we be expected to remember the names of the first man and woman, or the guy who built the ark, or the fellow who received those commandments?" My first reaction to this complaint was one of astonishment, but it soon occurred to me that names such as Adam and Eve, Noah, and Moses were as strange to my friend as names from his religious heritage would have been to me. I had forgotten that for many of the world's peoples the Bible is simply a book, just like *Don Quixote* or a Dostoevsky novel. It may be appreciated for beauties of language and thought, but it has no special religious significance.

We tend to assume that all religions are just like the one we happen to know best, but this assumption may easily mislead us. For example, many Christians believe that all religions place heavy emphasis on the afterlife, although, in fact, the central concern of Judaism is life in this world, not the next. Similarly, many Christians and Jews believe that a person who is religious must believe in the existence of God. They are surprised to learn that Jainism, Theravada Buddhism, and certain schools of Hinduism deny the existence of a Supreme Creator of the world.

The concept of a nontheistic religion may appear contradictory, but, indeed, no contradiction is involved. It is the assumption that all religions are like Catholicism, Protestantism, or Orthodox Judaism, which leads us to believe that all religions are committed to the existence of a Supreme Creator of the world. And this assumption is fostered by those who oppose religion, for these opponents of religion realize that if they can convince us that all religions are theistic, then the arguments that prove that we cannot learn the will of God will also prove that all religions are unacceptable. But if there are religions that do not depend upon their adherents' belief in the existence of God, that is, if there are nontheistic religions, then the arguments against theistic religion will not prove that all religions are unacceptable.

To see one way in which a nontheistic religion can arise, recall our previous conclusion that since it is not possible for a person to undergo a self-validating experience, adherence to a particular theistic religion is unreasonable. Having no adherence to a theistic religion, however, does not imply that one does not still face the serious moral dilemmas inherent in life. How are these dilemmas to be solved? To believe that God exists is of no avail, for one cannot learn His will. Therefore, a person must use his own judgment. But this need not be solely an individual effort. One may join others in a communal effort to propound and promulgate a moral code. Such a group may have its own distinctive prayers and rituals emphasizing various aspects of the group's beliefs.

Such a nontheistic religious organization does not depend upon its members' belief in the existence of God, for such a belief is irrelevant to the religious aims and activities of the group. If a proof for the existence of God is shown to be sound, it has no implications for an adherent of nontheistic religion, for such a proof does not provide him with any information that he can utilize in his religious practice. If, on the contrary, proofs for the existence of God are shown to be unsound, no doubt is cast on the nontheist's religious views, since these views have been formulated independently of a belief in the existence of God.

The concept of a nontheistic religion may still appear strange, however, for how is it possible for an individual to perform rituals, utter prayers, and commit himself to moral standards unless he believes in the existence of God? But this objection rests upon a number of questionable assumptions, and it is these assumptions that have been the target of recent attacks by those thinkers who are dissatisfied with theistic religion and yet wish to preserve what they take to be the advantages of religious belief and activity. In order to achieve their aim, these thinkers must defend the position that ritual, prayer, and morality can all be understood in a nontheistic context. Can such a position be adequately defended? That is the crucial question to which we now turn.

Let us begin with the concept of ritual. A ritual is a prescribed, symbolic action. In the case of religion, the ritual is prescribed by the religious authorities, and the act symbolizes some aspect of religious belief. Those who find the beliefs of theistic religion to be unreasonable or the authorities of theistic religion to be unacceptable may come to consider any ritual irrational. But, although particular rituals may be based on irrational beliefs, there is nothing irrational about ritual as such.

Consider the simple act of two men shaking hands when they meet. This act is a ritual, prescribed by our society and symbolic of the individuals' mutual respect. There is nothing irrational about this act. Of course, if men shook hands in order to ward off evil demons, then shaking hands would be irrational. But that is not the reason that men shake hands. The ritual has no connection with God or demons but indicates the attitude one man has toward another.

It might be assumed that the ritual of handshaking escapes irrationality only because the ritual is not prescribed by any specific authority and is not part of an elaborate ceremony. But to see that this assumption is false, consider the graduation ceremony at a college. The graduates and faculty all wear peculiar hats and robes, and the participants stand and sit at appropriate times throughout the ceremony. However, there is nothing irrational about this ceremony. Indeed, the ceremonies of graduation day, far from being irrational, are symbolic of commitment to the process of education and the life of reason.

At first glance it may appear that rituals are comparatively insignificant features of our lives, but the more one considers the matter, the more it becomes apparent that rituals are a pervasive and treasured aspect of human experience. Who would want to eliminate the festivities associated with holidays such as Independence Day and Thanksgiving? What would college football be without songs, cheers, flags, and the innumerable other symbolic features surrounding the game? And even society's dropouts, who disdain popular rituals, proceed to establish their own distinctive rituals, ranging from characteristic habits of dress to the widespread use of drugs, all symbolic of the rejection of traditional society and its values.

The religious man, like all others, searches for an appropriate means of emphasizing his commitment to a group and its values. Rituals provide him with such a means. It is true that theistic religion has often infused its rituals with superstition, but nonreligious rituals can be equally as superstitious as religious ones. For example, most Americans view the Fourth of July as an occasion on which they can express pride in their country's heritage. With this purpose in mind, the holiday is one of great significance. However, if it were thought that the singing of the fourth verse of "The Star-Spangled Banner" four times on the Fourth of July would protect our country against future disasters, then the original meaning of the holiday would soon be lost in a maze of superstition.

A nonthesitic religion need not utilize ritual in such a superstitious manner, for it does not perform rituals in order to please a benevolent deity or appease an angry one. Rather, nontheistic religion views ritual, as one writer has put it, as "the enhancement of life through the dramatization of great ideals."[2] If a group places great stress on justice or freedom, why should it not utilize ritual in order to emphasize these goals? Such a use of ritual serves to solidify the group and to strengthen its devotion to its expressed purposes. And these purposes are strengthened all the more if the ritual in question has the force of tradition, having been performed by many generations who have belonged to the same group and have struggled to achieve the same goals. Ritual so conceived is not a form of superstition; rather, it is a reasonable means of strengthening religious commitment and is as useful to nontheistic religion as it is to theistic religion.

Having considered the role of ritual in a nontheistic religion, let us next turn to the concept of prayer. It might be thought that nontheistic religion could have no use for prayer, since prayer is addressed to God and proponents of nontheistic religion do not believe in the existence of God. But this objection oversimplifies the concept of prayer, focusing attention on one type of prayer while neglecting an equally important but different sort of prayer.

Theistic religion makes extensive use of petitionary prayer, prayer that petitions God for various favors. These favors may range all the way from the personal happiness of the petitioner to the general welfare of all society. But petitionary prayer rests upon two assumptions that are highly

---

2 Jack J. Cohen, *The Case for Religious Naturalism* (New York: The Reconstructionist Press, 1958), p. 150.

doubtful: (1) God is listening to our prayers, and (2) God answers our prayers. We have cast serious doubt on both these assumptions, and the second seems especially unreasonable in view of the fact that so many prayers utttered by persons of the highest moral character are unanswered. In any case, it is clear that petitionary prayer has no place in a nontheistic religion.

However, not all prayers are prayers of petition. There are also prayers of meditation. These prayers are not directed to any divine being and are not requests for the granting of favors. Rather, these prayers provide the opportunity for persons to rethink their ultimate commitments and rededicate themselves to live up to their ideals. Such prayers may take the form of silent devotion or may involve oral repetition of certain central texts. Just as Americans repeat the Pledge of Allegiance and reread the Gettysburg Address, so adherents of nontheistic religion repeat the statement of their ideals and reread the documents that embody their traditional beliefs.

It is true that theistic religions, to the extent that they utilize prayers of meditation, tend to treat these prayers irrationally, by supposing that if the prayers are not uttered a precise number of times under certain specified conditions, then the prayers lose all value. But there is no need to view prayer in this way. Rather, as one author has written, prayer "permits the bringing before the mind of a world of thought which in most people must inevitably be absent during the occupations of ordinary life: . . . it is the means by which the mind may fix itself upon this or that noble or beautiful or awe-inspiring idea, and so grow to it and come to realise it more fully."[3]

Such a use of prayer may be enhanced by song, instrumental music, and various types of symbolism. These elements, fused together, provide the means for adherents of nontheistic religion to engage in religious services akin to those engaged in by adherents of theistic religion. The difference between these two services is that those who attend the latter services come to express their trust in God, while those who attend the former services come to express their trust in man.

We have so far discussed how ritual and prayer can be utilized in nontheistic religion, but one crucial point still remains in doubt. We have referred to nontheists who commit themselves to certain moral ideals. But can those who do not believe in the existence of God commit themselves to moral principles, or is the acceptance of moral principles dependent

---

[3] Julian Huxley, *Religion Without Revelation* (New York: American Library, 1957), p. 141.

upon acceptance of the existence of God? It is sometimes assumed that atheists are necessarily immoral, for their denial of the existence of God leaves them free to act without fear of Divine punishment. This assumption, however, is seriously in error.

The refutation of the view that morality must rest upon theism was provided by Socrates (c. 470–399 B.C.), the Athenian who lived and died for the ideals of philosophical inquiry. Socrates asked the following question: Are actions right because God says they are right, or does God say actions are right because they are right? This question is not a verbal trick; on the contrary, it poses a serious dilemma for theists. Socrates was inquiring whether actions are right due to God's fiat or whether God is Himself subject to moral standards. If actions are right due to God's command, then anything God commands is right, even if He should command torture or murder. But if one accepts this view, then it makes no sense to say that God Himself is good, for since the good is whatever God commands, to say that God commands rightly is just to say that He commands as He commands, which is a tautology. This approach makes a mockery of morality, for might does not make right, even if the might is the infinite might of God. To act morally is not to act out of fear of punishment; it is not to act as one is commanded to act. Rather, it is to act as one ought to act. And how one ought to act is not dependent upon anyone's power, even if the power be Divine.

Thus, actions are not right because God commands them; on the contrary, God commands them because they are right. But in that case, what is right is independent of what God commands, for what He commands must conform with an independent standard in order to be right. Since one could act in accordance with this independent standard without believing in the existence of God, it follows that morality does not rest upon theism. Consequently, nontheists can be highly moral (as well as immoral) persons, and theists can be highly immoral (as well as moral) persons. This conclusion should come as no surprise to anyone who has contrasted the life of Buddha, an atheist, with the life of Torquemada, the monk who organized the Spanish Inquisition.

We have now seen that nontheistic religion is a genuine possibility, since it is reasonable for an individual to perform rituals, utter prayers, and commit himself to moral principles without believing in the existence of God. And this insight provides the key to understanding the most recent developments in religion, for there are indeed many religious believers who wish to maintain their belief in the efficacy of religion without maintaining a belief in the existence of an all-good, all-powerful, eternal

Creator of the world. Some of those who wish to follow such a policy and who do not have allegiance to an established religion have developed their own religious viewpoint which has come to be known as religious humanism.[4] There are others, however, who wish to follow such a nontheistic, religious policy while maintaining allegiance to an established religious tradition. Those who wish to adhere in this way to Christianity are referred to as "Death of God" theologians.[5] Those who wish to adhere in this way to Judaism have developed what is known as Reconstructionist Judaism.[6]

Although evaluation of these specific movements lies beyond our present concern, it is vital to note that each of these places heavy stress on the importance of accepting particular ethical values. And this fact raises a highly controversial issue, for there are those individuals who claim that one's choice of ethical values is essentially arbitrary, that is, there is no rational way to decide between competing ethical viewpoints. If such a claim were true, then not only would nontheistic religion be undermined, but so, it might seem, would our entire social fabric. For how could society function if there were no reasonable method of resolving ethical disputes? In order to pursue these matters in detail, however, we must move beyond philosophy of religion into another area of philosophical inquiry, and so it is to this area, known as ethics, that we turn next.

---

[4]   See, for example, Julian Huxley, *Religion Without Revelation.*

[5]   See, for example, John H. T. Robinson, *Honest to God* (Philadelphia: The Westminster Press, 1963).

[6]   See, for example, Mordecai M. Kaplan, *Judaism as a Civilization* (New York: Schocken Books, 1967). Both Kaplan and Robinson choose to reinterpret the term "God" rather than to deny that they are theists.

PART IV
ETHICS

Chapter 7

MORAL JUDGMENTS

We live in an age beset by a mood of moral uncertainty. Even those moral principles held most tenaciously by previous generations are being challenged from every quarter. Indeed, we are urged more and more frequently and with more and more seriousness to abandon all moral standards, since, it is claimed, the adoption of any such standard is an infringement upon our personal freedom. In the face of such ethical anarchy, is there any way to justify belief in a moral order?

There are those who claim that it is possible to justify such a belief, for just as there are scientific truths, so there are moral truths. Just as it is true that water freezes at 0° C. and boils at 100° C., so murder is wrong and honesty is right. Just as laws of nature are true at any time and at any place, so moral laws are true for any person in any situation. According to those who maintain such analogies, the only difference between factual statements and moral judgments is that whereas the truth of factual statements is tested by an appeal to scientific method, the truth of moral judgments is tested by an appeal to that moral sense that every human being possesses. Faced with an instance of unmitigated cruelty, for example, must not every person acknowledge that this cruelty is evil? As the Scottish philosopher Thomas Reid (1710–1796) argued: "Every man in his senses believes his eyes, his ears, and his other senses. . . . And he has the same reason, and, indeed, is under the same necessity of believing the clear and unbiased dictates of his conscience, with regard to what is honourable and what is base."[1]

But this theory runs into trouble when it is noted that the dictates of one person's conscience may differ greatly from the dictates of another person's conscience. For example, one person's conscience may dictate that capital punishment is immoral, while a second person's conscience may dictate that capital punishment is not immoral. How can we reasonably decide between these incompatible ethical views? It might be argued that one of these persons possesses an unbiased conscience while the other person's conscience is a biased one. But how are we to decide whose conscience is the unbiased one? Each of us could appeal to our own conscience to decide the matter, but perhaps our own conscience is biased. We could take a poll and determine which ethical view was accepted by the majority of people, but the majority of people may possess biased consciences. There thus seems no way to distinguish a biased conscience from an unbiased one without first deciding whether capital punishment is immoral, but this would be a circular procedure that would only bring us back to the original question of whether capital punishment is immoral. The appeal to conscience, therefore, appears to be a pointless maneuver.

Faced with this apparent dead end, there are those who argue that the reason the appeal to conscience leads us astray is that it assumes that there is a right and a wrong, that is, that moral judgments are either true or false. But this assumption, it is claimed, is erroneous, for moral judgments are merely expressions of individual preferences. According to this view, to assert that capital punishment is moral is merely to express your preference for capital punishment; to assert that capital punishment is immoral is merely to express your preference for the abolition of capital punishment. Just as there is no point arguing about whether red or blue is a better color, so there is no point arguing about whether capital punishment is moral or immoral, for in both cases all that is involved is an expression of personal feelings. Thus, on this view there are no moral truths; there are only moral preferences. Some people prefer honesty,

---

1   Thomas Reid, *Essays on the Active Powers of the Human Mind* (Cambridge, Massachusetts: The M.I.T. Press, 1969), p. 237.

while others prefer dishonesty. Both views are equally tenable, for there is no reasonable method of deciding between opposing moral sentiments.

But this theory suffers from a major flaw, for, in fact, we do convince people that they are maintaining incorrect moral positions, and we do so by presenting reasons in behalf of our view. We do not argue about whether red or blue is a better color, for such a discussion would clearly be silly. But we do argue about whether capital punishment ought to be abolished, and sometimes people change their views as a result of such discussion. So it would seem that moral judgments are not just emotional outpourings but are either true or false. This view, however, seems to take us back again to the first theory, a theory whose difficulties have already been noted. We thus seem to be stymied in our attempt to understand the nature of moral judgments.

In order to break through this impasse, let us consider some value judgments that are not moral judgments. It may come as a surprise to realize that there are such nonmoral, value judgments, but the words "good" and "bad" often function in contexts that have nothing to do with morality. Consider "a good meal" or "the bad reception on your television set." Perhaps if we can discover how the terms "good" and "bad" function in such nonmoral contexts, we shall discover some clue as to the use of these terms in moral contexts.

Suppose, for instance, that you are a member of an organization that participates in a softball league. You are told by your friend Ferguson that a fellow named Benson is an excellent ballplayer. You ask Benson to join your team and he is happy to do so. But Benson turns out to be woefully inadequate. He drops balls thrown to him, he lets ground balls go through his legs, and every time he comes to bat he strikes out. You tell Ferguson that his recommendation of Benson was a mistake. Either Ferguson does not know what a good ballplayer is or someone has misled him about Benson's capabilities, for it is obvious that Benson is not a good player.

Now notice that when you say that Benson is not a good player there is nothing necessarily emotional or unclear about what you are saying. You are not just expressing your preference nor are you appealing to the dictates of your conscience. To say that Benson is not a good ballplayer is just to say that Benson hits poorly and fields inadequately. To defend your view all you need do is point to Benson's batting and fielding averages. Although there may be some disagreement as to whether a player who bats .250 and commits a number of errors is a good player, there is no doubt whatever that an individual who bats .100 and commits errors in every game is not a good player, while an individual who bats

.400 and hardly ever commits an error is a good player. In other words, the distinction between good players and bad players is a clear one, despite the possibility of borderline cases, just as the distinction between bald men and hirsute men is a clear one, despite the possibility of border-line cases.

Notice also that it would be senseless to say that although Benson hits well and fields well, he still lacks one attribute essential to an all-star, namely, goodness, because if Benson could hit well and field well, then he would be a good softball player. Goodness is not another attribute besides these abilities. It is simply a shorthand way of referring to these abilities.

Suppose next that when you tell Ferguson that Benson is not a good player, Ferguson replies that you are mistaken, for he has seen Benson play in practice and in practice Benson hits the ball over the fence and fields flawlessly. How would you reply to Ferguson? You would not say that since value judgments are just matters of preference, there is no reasonable method of deciding whether Benson is a good player. Nor would you appeal to Ferguson's conscience in an effort to convince him of your point of view. All you need do to convince Ferguson that he is mistaken is to explain that sometimes an individual performs well in practice but plays badly in actual games. To defend your claim, you would simply point out that in the first ten games of the season, Benson batted .075 and committed twenty-two errors. Ferguson would no doubt be amazed at these statistics, but he would surely agree that although Benson is impressive in practice, he is not a good player under game con-ditions. Here then we have a clear example of a disagreement about a value judgment that is resolved by an appeal to the facts.

But what if Ferguson is not so cooperative? Suppose that he does not agree that a good ballplayer is one who, under game conditions, hits and fields well. Suppose he claims instead that a good ballplayer is one who *looks* good when he plays, that is, one who is handsome, graceful, and appealing to the opposite sex. Assuming that Benson possesses these characteristics, he is, according to Ferguson, a good ballplayer.

No doubt Ferguson's position would be quite exasperating, but how could you answer him? Your disagreement may appear irresolvable, but it would be a mistake simply to assume that it is. The criteria of a good ballplayer that you have chosen are not arbitrary, and, in order to reply intelligently to Ferguson, you need to reflect on the reasons that led you to choose your criteria.

You play softball in order to win. A good player is one who would aid you in achieving your goal. Players who look good might not aid you in winning; players who hit and field well would aid you in winning. There-fore, you consider a player good if he hits and fields well.

If Ferguson plays softball in order to win and he thinks that players who look good win more often than players who hit and field well, then you can resolve your disagreement by appealing to the record books. Here again would be an example of a disagreement in values that could be resolved by an appeal to the facts. If, on the other hand, Ferguson plays softball in order to gain popularity, then it is quite possible that players who look good will be of greater aid to him than players who hit and field well. In that case, in order to resolve your disagreement, you would have to continue the discussion and try to determine whether your disparate goals are a means to some further end that you have in common. If so, your disagreement would be resolvable by deciding the factual question as to the most effective means of achieving that end. If you could not find such a common end, then you could find no reasonable way to resolve your disagreement.

There is no need to prolong this example, for the crucial points are already clear. First, although the word "good" is always used as a term of commendation, the criteria for its use vary, depending upon the context. Good apples, good radios, and good ballplayers are good for different reasons. Second, the criteria we choose for the word "good" depend in each context upon our aims or purposes. If I play softball in order to win, then I consider a good player to be one who would help me to achieve that end. Third, if two people disagree about whether something is good but agree upon the criteria for goodness, then their disagreement is a factual one which ought to be resolved in the way that all factual matters ought to be resolved, namely, by the application of scientific method. For instance, if you and Ferguson agree that a good ballplayer is one who hits and fields well but you disagree as to whether Benson is a good ballplayer, then the way to resolve your disagreement is to check Benson's batting and fielding averages. Fourth, if two people disagree about the criteria for goodness but agree upon the ends they wish to achieve, then their disagreement is also a factual one. For example, if both you and Ferguson agree that you play softball to win but disagree as to what type of players win the most games, your disagreement can be resolved by checking the record books. Fifth and finally, if two people disagree about the goals they wish to achieve, then their disagreement can be rationally resolved only by further reflection on the reasons that led them to choose their respective goals. If they chose their opposing goals in order to achieve some further end upon which they can agree, then once against their disagreement is a factual one that can be resolved by determining how that end can be most effectively achieved. If they have no further end in common, then their disagreement will not yield to rational resolution.

We have now seen how value terms function in nonmoral contexts. Do they function similarly in moral contexts? Let us consider a typical moral dispute and observe the pattern of argument.

Suppose Thorndike and Williams, citizens of the country of Freedonia, become embroiled in a dispute as to whether Freedonia ought to attack the country of Sylvania.[2] Thorndike argues that Freedonia ought to attack Sylvania, since Sylvania is committed to the conquest of Freedonia and will soon possess the necessary armaments to carry out this conquest. Williams, however, claims that it would be immoral for Freedonia to initiate all of the horrors of war, and that, in any case, Freedonia can successfully defend itself from Sylvania's attack.

Faced with this dispute it would be a mistake simply to assume that since it is a moral dispute, it is therefore irresolvable. Before we can reach a reasonable conclusion regarding the status of the dispute, a good deal of careful analysis is necessary.

The first step in analyzing a moral dispute is to determine whether the disputants disagree about the most effective means of achieving agreed-upon ends or about which ends ought to be achieved. If Thorndike and Williams agree that Freedonia should defend itself and retain its independence while not inflicting unnecessary suffering upon other countries, then what Thorndike and Williams disagree about is the most effective means of achieving these ends. Thorndike believes that Freedonia's independence is in grave danger due to the military might of Sylvania, but Williams does not share this fear. Thus, Thorndike believes that for Freedonia to attack Sylvania would inflict unnecessary suffering on Sylvania's citizens and would therefore be immoral, while Williams believes that in view of Sylvania's threat to Freedonia an attack is necessary for Freedonia's survival and is thus morally justifiable. In this case the decision as to whether Freedonia should attack Sylvania, bomb its cities, knock out its supply line, and kill many of its citizens—a decision with enormous moral implications—depends upon factual considerations.

In other words, the moral disagreement between Thorndike and Williams is reducible to a factual disagreement. That such a reduction can be carried out does not imply that there is any simple means of resolving the dispute, for many factual disputes are extremely complex. Scientific disputes, for example, are factual, but scientific progress is not necessarily quickly or easily achieved. Nevertheless, to reduce a moral dispute to a factual one is an important step, for such a reduction permits the moral dispute to be handled with the same tool that is so useful in solving

---

[2] The names of the countries are borrowed from the Marx Brothers' classic film *Duck Soup*.

factual disputes: scientific method. Moral disputes that can be reduced to factual ones are thus no more matters of personal preference or individual conscience than are disputes regarding the exact distance to the moon, the proper procedures for farming, or the most efficient way to build a safe bridge.

But what if Thorndike and Williams do not agree that Freedonia should retain its independence? Suppose that while Thorndike believes that a good policy for the citizens of Freedonia is one that ensures the independence of their country, Williams believes that the government of Freedonia is immoral, since it denies its citizens basic freedoms. He believes that a good policy for the citizens of Freedonia is one that aids the government of Sylvania and that, therefore, the citizens of Freedonia ought not to attack Sylvania.

Here then we are faced with a situation in which Thorndike and Williams are using the phrase "a good policy" in different ways. Does this disagreement in terminology imply that their dispute is irresolvable? Not necessarily, for again we must determine whether the disputants disagree about the most effective means of achieving agreed-upon ends or whether they disagree as to which ends ought to be achieved. If we assume that Thorndike and Williams agree that a government that guarantees freedom of speech, freedom of assembly, freedom of the press, and freedom of religion is morally preferable to one that does not, then their ethical disagreement as to whether the citizens of Freedonia ought to go to war is reducible to the factual disagreement as to whether the citizens of Freedonia lack basic freedoms possessed by the citizens of Sylvania. If the political situation is as Thorndike supposes, then Williams would agree that it would be morally defensible for the citizens of Freedonia to go to war. If the political situation is not as Thorndike supposes, then he would agree that it would be morally indefensible for the citizens of Freedonia to go to war. But the nature of the political situation is not a matter of personal preference or individual conscience; it is a matter of fact that is most effectively determined by rational inquiry.

Of course, it is possible that Thorndike and Williams do not agree that a government ought to guarantee freedom of speech, freedom of assembly, freedom of the press, and freedom of religion. Thorndike may hold this view, but Williams may believe that a government ought to guarantee other freedoms, for instance, freedom from military service. If Thorndike and Williams disagreed in this way, would there be any rational way to resolve their disagreement? By now the pattern of possible resolution should be clear. If Thorndike and Williams agree upon the ends for which governments are established, then their ethical disagreement as to what sort of governmental authority is morally justifiable can be reduced to a factual disagreement as to how these ends can be most effectively achieved. If Thorndike and Williams do not have any further ends in common, then their disagreement will not yield to rational resolution.

We are now in a position to formulate the general principles that govern the rational resolution of moral disagreements. To the extent that moral disagreements are disagreements about the most effective means of achieving agreed-upon ends, they are reducible to factual disagreements and can thus be rationally resolved. In those cases in which there is disagreement about the ends to be achieved, the possibility of rational resolution of the disagreement requires agreement regarding the achievement of further ends to which the disputed ends are merely means. To the extent that such further ends can be agreed upon, moral disagreements are reducible to factual disagreements and can thus be rationally resolved. If further ends cannot be agreed upon, moral disagreements will not yield to rational resolution.

Before considering the implications of these principles for the establishment of a moral order, it is interesting to note the connection between these principles and the popular maxim that "the ends do not justify the means." Although it is possible to interpret this maxim in such a way as to make it defensible, taken literally the maxim is false, for whenever one's means can be justified, they can be justified only by one's ends.

To see this point clearly, consider an individual, whom we shall refer to as "Speedy," whose principal aim in life is to win a particular automobile race. All other aims he possesses are subordinate to this one. Assume that as this particular automobile race nears its conclusion, an accident occurs. A car overturns and its driver is left sprawled on the track directly in the path of Speedy's oncoming car. If Speedy slows down to avoid running over the injured driver, he will lose the race. Faced with the choice between killing the injured driver or slowing down and losing the race, Speedy decides to continue ahead at full speed.

No doubt his decision is deplorable. But is it deplorable because ends cannot justify means? Not at all. Speedy's ends, if we accepted them, would justify his means. His principal aim is to win the race, and if we accepted the view that it is right for an individual to subordinate all other aims to this one, then we would accept the fact that any action Speedy had to take in order to win the race would be justified. But we do not find his ends acceptable. We are committed to the value of human life, and we place this value far above the value of winning a race. Thus, we would not have done what Speedy did, for we reject his ends.

Contrast Speedy with a physician who advises a patient to undergo a series of painful injections in order to avoid a possibly fatal disease. The physician expresses his regret to the patient that these injections are necessary, for one of a physician's aims is to alleviate pain. But we would agree with the physician that the injections are justified by the ends they will achieve. Indeed, how else could the injections be justified? These two examples differ only in that in the physician's case the ends are acceptable, while in Speedy's case the ends are unacceptable. In both cases the ends, if acceptable, would justify the means that led to those ends.

How then is it possible to interpret the maxim "the ends do not justify the means" in a defensible manner? In appealing to this maxim we may intend to point out that an individual's action is not justified because it promotes some of his ends while preventing the achievement of other ends that are more important to him. For instance, if Speedy desired not only the end of winning the race but also, as a more important end, the promoting of human well-being, then his ends, taken as whole, would not justify the action he took, because in achieving one end he would prevent the achievement of other more important ends. In short, his ends would justify means opposed to the means he actually chose.

We might also appeal to the maxim that the ends do not justify the means in order to point out that an individual's ends are unacceptable, and that, therefore, any means that achieve those ends are themselves unacceptable. For instance, since Speedy's ends are unacceptable, so are the means he employs to achieve those ends. However, were one to accept his ends, they would justify the means he utilized.

The upshot of this discussion is a reemphasis of our previous conclusion that the rational resolution of moral disagreements depends upon the disputants agreeing at some point upon the ends to be achieved. If such agreement is reached, then the ends will justify the means that lead most effectively to these ends, and since the question as to the most efficient means of achieving agreed-upon ends is a factual question, agreement upon ends permits moral disagreements to be resolved by the scientific method, the most reliable method available for determining the truth of factual statements.

We are thus led to the following crucial question: What are the chances that disputants in a moral disagreement will agree at some point upon the ends to be achieved? At first glance it might appear to be an extraordinary stroke of luck if disputants in a moral disagreement did agree upon the ends to be achieved, but more careful consideration shows that there is very strong reason to believe that such agreement can be reached. The basis for such agreement lies in the fact that human beings all desire happiness and depend upon the cooperation of other people in order to achieve this goal. As one contemporary philosopher has put it:

> We cannot conceive of a being like ourselves, who desires his own happiness, and the happiness of his family and friends (if not the happiness of the whole of mankind), who needs the company of his fellows, who is easily injured by their hostile acts, and who cannot continue to exist unless they co-operate with him—we cannot conceive of a being such as this approving of promise-breaking, dishonesty, and deliberate callousness to the interests of others.[3]

In short, all human beings are dependent upon others, and, therefore, all human beings approve of those rules that facilitate cooperation among people.

A person who rejects such rules, who favors persecution and cruelty for its own sake, is hardly a person at all. In any case, we must guard ourselves against such a character, for he is a threat to all of us. It is interesting to note in this connection that no political leader has ever come to power by promising his followers that if he gains control he will eventually bring about a golden age characterized by increased hatred, violence, and oppression. Even the worst of dictators must mouth the usual moral sentiments if he is to gain any support. It is thus doubtful that disputants in a moral disagreement would not agree at some point upon the ends to be achieved, and it is for this reason that it is probable that any moral disagreement can be reduced to a factual disagreement and resolved by the scientific method.

Of course, it is possible that there are occasions upon which disputants in a moral disagreement cannot agree at any point upon the ends to be achieved. How can we know in any particular case that such an impasse has been reached? The only way to find out that such an impasse exists is to analyze the moral dispute, determining in the case of every end proposed by both disputants the reasons they provide in defense of their proposed ends. As we have seen, we may suppose that each end that is proposed will be defended as a means to some further end. So long as an end is defended in this way, the analysis must continue in order to determine whether there is agreement upon these further ends. But at some point in the analysis conflicting ends may be proposed for which no reasons are offered. In other words, one individual may declare something to be good and when asked to defend this claim, he may reply, "Well, it just *is* good," or "Well, I just prefer it." Let us refer to such moral judgments, ones put forth and not defended by any reasons, as "funda-

---

[3] Jonathan Harrison, "Empiricism in Ethics," *The Philosophical Quarterly,* vol. 2 (1952), p. 306.

mental moral judgments." If conflicting fundamental moral judgments are reached, then the dispute will not yield to rational resolution.

Having arrived at such fundamental moral judgments, we have now come full circle and are returning to the question with which we began this chapter, the question as to whether moral judgments are analogous to factual statements or whether they are merely expressions of personal preference. Yet there are several reasons why this question does not seem nearly as crucial now as it did earlier. First, we have seen that the question is only applicable to a very small class of moral judgments, namely, fundamental moral judgments, and these judgments are very rarely—if ever—reached in actual moral disputes. All other moral judgments are statements of effective means to preferred ends, and as such they are capable of testing by the scientific method. Second, we have seen that if no agreement upon ends can be reached prior to arriving at fundamental moral judgments, the dispute is quite hopeless. A person, for example, who favors persecution and cruelty is not a person whom it pays to face in debate, although we would do well not to turn our backs on him. Third and finally, since fundamental moral judgments are not defended by reasons, there is little to choose between interpreting such a judgment as a matter of ethical intuition or as a matter of personal preference. Neither interpretation leaves open the possibility of rationally resolving conflicts between such judgments, since there is no use arguing about judgments that are not rationally defended.

Thus, the claim which has been propounded by many philosophers that fundamental moral judgments are merely matters of personal preference turns out not to have the anarchic consequences some thinkers have supposed. Regardless of how one analyzes fundamental moral judgments, the vast majority of moral disagreements—and virtually all those that are significant—remain open to rational resolution.

Before we conclude this chapter, one further point should be clarified. In discussing the nature of moral judgments, no use has been made of the terms "objective" and "subjective," and there is good reason for this omission. Although it is common for people to claim either that moral judgments are objective or that they are subjective, it is not clear exactly what these supposedly opposing claims are intended to mean.

What exactly is a subjective statement? Is it (1) a statement about what the speaker himself thinks: for example, I think that Gilbert and Sullivan wrote fourteen comic operas? Or is it (2) a statement about what any person thinks: for example, my brother thinks that Wagner wrote *The Ring of the Nibelung*? Or is it (3) a statement about what the speaker feels: for example, I feel sick? Or is it (4) a statement about what any person feels: for example, my friend feels sick? Or is it (5) a value judgment: for example, Benson is not a good softball player? Or is it (6) an emotional statement: for example, I love you? Or is it (7) a prejudiced statement: for example, all Italian men are handsome? Or is it (8) a statement that is true at one time and place but false at another: for example, it is raining here? Or is it (9) a statement that is true relative to one group but false relative to another: for example, Nelson is a tall man (which is true relative to the members of the general population but false relative to the members of a professional basketball team)? Or is it (10) any statement that at present cannot be proven or disproven: for example, there is life in another galazy?

There is no need to continue this list of possibilities, for it is apparent that to ask the seemingly simple question, "Are moral judgments objective or subjective?" is to ask a highly ambiguous question. It is also a very misleading question, since it assumes that moral judgments are all of one sort, whereas we have seen that a fundamental moral judgment is quite different from other moral judgments. In short, the best reply to the question, "Are moral judgments subjective?" is the answer, "I don't know what you mean by 'subjective,' but the vast majority of moral disagreements, and virtually all those that are significant, are open to rational resolution."

Chapter 8

MORAL STANDARDS

In the previous chapter it was suggested that the common lot of all men leads ultimately to their agreement upon the ends they wish to achieve and hence to the possibility of their rationally resolving moral disagreements. As we have seen, however, reaching agreement upon ends in specific moral disputes can be a long and arduous process, for when we actually become embroiled in moral disagreements, the issues at stake can be so complex and of such deep concern to us that it is difficult to think clearly about them. This difficulty has led many thinkers to try to discover a single moral principle which, if we adhered to it in any situation, would provide us with the best possible chance of achieving all our agreed-upon ends. All other moral principles would be subordinate to this one, comprehensive moral principle, and we could thus turn to it to guide us in the resolution of any moral disagreement. But is it possible to formulate such a supreme moral principle? That is the question now confronting us.

It might seem that we do not have far to look in order to find such a principle, for, it might be claimed, the principle in question is none other than the familiar adage known as the Golden Rule. This principle, common to various religious traditions, has both a positive and a negative formulation. The positive formulation, attributed to Jesus, is: ". . . whatever you wish that men would do to you, do so to them. . . ."[1] The negative formulation, which appeared 500 years earlier, is attributed to Confucius and was later proposed by the Jewish sage Hillel. The latter put it as follows: "What is hateful to you, do not to your neighbor. . . ."[2] Is either of these the comprehensive moral principle for which we are searching? Recall that what we are looking for is a principle we could adhere to in any situation which would provide us with the best possible chance of achieving our agreed-upon ends. In other words, if a proposed principle implies a course of action that in any situation does not maximize the probability of our achieving our agreed-upon ends, that principle is not the one for which we are searching. Of course, there are many moral principles to which we all might subscribe but which do not provide guidance in every situation. For instance, "Thou shalt not murder" is a principle upon which we all might agree, but it does not guide us when we must decide whether or not to lie. The comprehensive moral principle for which we are looking is comprehensive just because it does provide guidance in all moral situations. In short, we are searching for a principle that is always applicable and never leads us astray. Is the Golden Rule such a principle?

Let us first consider the positive formulation of this maxim. Undoubtedly, there are numerous instances in which we ought to treat others as we would wish them to treat us. For instance, we ought to go to the aid of an injured person, just as we would wish that person to come to our aid if we were injured. However, were we to follow this adage in all situations, the results would be unfortunate. To begin with, consider a person who derives pleasure from being hurt by others. Were he to act according to the principle in question, he would consider it his duty to hurt other people, thereby doing to them what he wishes them to do to him. Similarly, consider a person who enjoys receiving telephone calls, even calls from people he does not know. Were he to act according to the principle in question, he would consider it his duty to telephone everyone, thereby treating everyone as he wishes to be treated. These are but a few of the unfortunate implications that would follow from rigorous adherence to

1 *The Holy Bible: Revised Standard Version* (New York: Thomas Nelson & Sons, 1952), Matthew 7:12.

2 *The Babylonian Talmud* (London: The Soncino Press, 1938), Shabbath, 31a.

the positive formulation of the Golden Rule. Indeed, strictly speaking, it would be impossible to follow this principle in every situation, for there are so many things we would wish others to do for us, that we would never have time to do all of these things for everyone else. As the philosopher Walter Kaufmann (1921–) has noted, ". . . anyone who tried to live up to Jesus' rule would become an insufferable nuisance."[3]

Then perhaps the negative formulation of the Golden Rule is more satisfactory, for this formulation does not imply that one has innumerable duties toward all of humanity. Neither does it imply that masochists ought to inflict pain on other people, nor that those who enjoy receiving telephone calls ought to call everyone else. However, although the negative formulation does not require these actions, neither does it forbid them. The negative formulation enjoins us not to do to others what is hateful to ourselves, but pain is not hateful to the masochist and innumerable telephone calls are not hateful to the telephone enthusiast. Thus, the negative formulation would not prohibit such people from performing actions that hurt or annoy others. But surely one ought not to perform such actions. Thus, the negative formulation of the Golden Rule, although superior in this sense to the positive formulation, is not the comprehensive moral principle for which we are searching, since it does not prohibit actions that ought to be prohibited; the principle for which we are searching both requires us to perform all the actions we ought to perform and forbids us from performing any action we ought not to perform.

It begins to appear as if the task we have set ourselves is insuperable, since no principle can fulfill the proposed requirements. But before jumping to this conclusion, we ought to consider carefully two intriguing principles, each of which has been thought by some notable philosophers to be the supreme moral principle.

One of these principles was originally put forth by the German philosopher Immanuel Kant. It was Kant's view that the moral worth of an action is to be judged not by the consequences of the action but by the nature of the maxim (the principle) that motivates the action. Thus, right actions are not necessarily those with favorable consequences but those which are performed in accordance with the right maxims. But what are the right maxims? According to Kant, any acceptable maxim must be applicable to every person at any time, that is, it must admit of no exceptions. Kant thus believed that a maxim is acceptable if and only if it

---

[3] Walter Kaufmann, *The Faith of a Heretic* (New York: Doubleday & Company, Inc., 1963), p. 212.

can be a universal law. In other words, you should act only on that maxim that can be universalized without contradiction.

To see just what Kant had in mind, let us consider a specific example he used to illustrate his view. Suppose you need to borrow some money, and the money will only be lent to you if you promise to pay it back. However, you realize that you will not be able to pay it back. Is it permissible for you to promise to pay back the money, knowing that you will not keep your promise? Kant proposed that the way to determine whether such an action is permissible is to universalize the maxim in question and see whether it leads to contradiction. The maxim in question is: Whenever I am short of money, I will borrow it, promising to pay it back even if I know that I will not do so. Can this maxim be universalized without contradiction? Kant argued that it cannot.

> For the universality of a law which says that anyone who believes himself to be in need could promise what he pleased with the intention of not fulfilling it would make the promise itself and the end to be accomplished by it impossible; no one would believe what was promised to him but would only laugh at any such assertion as vain pretense.[4]

In short, to make promises with no intention of keeping them would lead to the destruction of the practice of promising. Thus, since the maxim in question cannot be universalized without contradiction, it is not a morally acceptable maxim and, consequently, any action motivated by that maxim is immoral. According to Kant, then, the supreme moral principle is the following: "Act only according to that maxim by which you can at the same time will that it should become a universal law."[5]

Is Kant's principle the one for which we have been searching? Unfortunately, the principle does not meet the requirements we have proposed, for it prohibits some actions that ought to be permitted. Although we might agree that the maxim of making insincere promises cannot be universalized, we can easily imagine cases in which a person ought to make a promise that he has no intention of keeping. Suppose, for example, that you and your family will starve to death unless you obtain food immediately, and a very wealthy man offers to provide the food if you will promise to repay him within one day. Surely we would say, contrary to Kant's principle, that under these circumstances you ought to act upon a maxim that cannot be universalized and make a promise you

---

4 Immanuel Kant, *Foundations of the Metaphysics of Morals,* trans. Lewis White Beck (New York: The Liberal Arts Press, Inc., 1959), p. 40.

5 *Ibid.,* p. 39.

have no intention of keeping. Furthermore, Kant's insistence that maxims admit of no exceptions is such an excessively rigid position that it leads him not only to affirm judgments that are morally repugnant but also to affirm judgments that are inconsistent, for in some cases maxims conflict, and adherence to one involves the violation of another. This is the case in the preceding example, for were you to adhere to the maxim of never making insincere promises, you would violate another maxim affirmed by Kant, the maxim of aiding those who are in distress. Kant argues that both these maxims admit of no exceptions, but since it is impossible to adhere to both in every case, the rigidity of Kant's position leads to a contradiction.

Perhaps Kant's principle goes astray because it concentrates exclusively on the maxim that motivates an action and fails to take into account the actual consequences of the action. So let us consider, instead, a principle that does take the consequences of an action into account, the supreme moral principle defended by the English philosopher John Stuart Mill (1806–1873). Mill was a leading spokesman for the ethical position known as utilitarianism. According to this view, an action is right in so far as it promotes the happiness of mankind; it is wrong in so far as it promotes the unhappiness of mankind. By the term "happiness" Mill means pleasure and the absence of pain. By the term "mankind" he means all persons, each valued equally. So, the supreme moral principle according to Mill is: Act in such a way as to produce the greatest pleasure for the greatest number of people, each person's pleasure counting equally.

This principle avoids the pitfalls of Kant's view, for whereas Kant admitted no exceptions to moral rules and was thus led to condemn insincere promises that saved human lives, the utilitarian principle is flexible enough to allow for exceptions to rules when those exceptions would produce greater happiness for mankind than would strict adherence to the rules. Although a utilitarian would agree, for example, that it is usually wrong to make insincere promises, for such promises generally cause more pain than pleasure, he would still maintain that in some cases, such as that of the starving man and his family, an insincere promise is morally justifiable, for in such a case the insincere promise leads to greater happiness for mankind than would the alternative course of action.

The flexibility of the utilitarian principle is undoubtedly an advantage over the rigidity of the Kantian principle, but the utilitarian principle is, in fact, too flexible, for it sanctions actions that ought to be prohibited. Consider, for example, the inhabitants of a city who each week abduct a stranger and place him in an arena to wrestle a lion. When the inhabitants of the city are asked how they can possibly justify this practice, they point out that although the stranger suffers much pain, the thousands of spectators obtain greater pleasure from this form of entertainment than they do from any other. Thus, even after the pain of the stranger is subtracted from the pleasure of the spectators, the spectacle results in far greater pleasure than does any other activity. So, the inhabitants of the city argue, since the spectacle maximizes pleasure, it is justified on utilitarian grounds. At this point it becomes clear that the utilitarian principle sometimes justifies activities that ought not to be justified. And, as it happens, it is possible to construct innumerable other cases along similar lines that illustrate the laxity of the utilitarian principle. The sheriff who hangs an innocent man in order to satisfy the vengeance of the townspeople may maximize pleasure, but he nevertheless acts immorally. Similarly, the teacher who agrees with his students' views in order to curry their favor may maximize pleasure, but he is not acting responsibly.

In an effort to salvage the utilitarian principle, one might argue that not all pleasures are of equal quality; for example, the pleasure of spectators at a lion arena is less valuable than the pleasure of spectators at a piano recital. As Mill put it, "It is better to be a human being dissatisfied than a pig satisfied; better to be Socrates dissatisfied than a fool satisfied. And if the fool, or the pig, are of a different opinion, it is because they only know their own sides of the question. The other party to the comparison knows both sides."[6]

But this seems a dubious move to make, for there are no doubt quite a few individuals, knowing both sides of the question, who would prefer to witness a struggle between man and lion rather than a struggle between man and keyboard. And even if there were only one knowledgeable individual who had such taste, why should his view be disregarded? Of course, one could argue that attendance at a piano recital develops sensitivity whereas attendance at a lion arena dulls sensitivity, but to argue in this way is to abandon utilitarianism, for, according to utilitarianism, actions are good to the extent that they produce pleasure, not to the extent that they produce sensitivity. Thus, it seems that there is no way to salvage the utilitarian principle, for the principle is simply too lax and does not prohibit all the actions that ought to be prohibited.

With the failure of the Kantian and utilitarian principles to meet the requirements for a supreme moral principle, it may appear that our search for such a principle has been fruitless. But just as it is possible to learn a

---

6   John Stuart Mill, *Utilitarianism* (New York: The Liberal Arts Press, Inc., 1957), p. 14.

great deal from a scientific experiment that fails to confirm a particular hypothesis, so it is possible to learn a great deal from a philosophical inquiry that shows certain claims to be false.

Even if there is no supreme moral principle, a conclusion that has been suggested by our examination of the most likely possibilities, still our search for such a principle has uncovered a fundamental feature of morality we might otherwise have overlooked. The positive and negative formulations of the Golden Rule, the Kantian principle, and the utilitarian principle all stress one crucial fact: To be a moral person one must be sensitive and responsive to the feelings of all other persons. This is the insight that motivates not only the Biblical injunction to treat others as we wish to be treated but also the utilitarian insistence that each person's happiness is to count no more and no less than another's. And this insight is also central to Kant's view, a point he made explicit by claiming that his supreme moral principle could be reformulated as follows: "Act so that you treat humanity, whether in your own person or in that of another, always as an end and never as a means only."[7] Whether we speak of treating other people as ends, or of counting their happiness equally, or of treating them as we wish to be treated, the basic insight is the same: To act morally is to act not only out of concern for oneself but also out of concern for all others. This insight is not itself a supreme moral principle, for by itself it is not specific enough either to require us to perform all the actions we ought to perform or to forbid us from performing all the actions we ought not to perform. But considering the range and complexity of human situations, it is quite understandable that no single moral principle can provide specific guidance in all instances. What we can hope for, however, and what we have found is a key to understanding the basis of all moral obligation. As we have seen, such obligation arises when we are concerned enough about others to have an interest in satisfying their desires as well as our own. And it is this concern that leads us to distinguish between what is in our own interest to do and what we ought to do.

At this point it may seem that the conclusion we have reached regarding the basis of moral obligation is in conflict with a claim put forth in the previous chapter. There it was argued that an individual's realization that he is dependent upon others will lead him to approve of those rules that facilitate cooperation among people, while here it is argued that moral obligation arises from a genuine care for other persons. But these two claims are not inconsistent. Indeed, their juxtaposition emphasizes the

---

7   Kant, p. 47.

important distinction between doing what is moral and being a moral person. The moral person performs moral actions because he possesses a genuine interest in others and wishes to satisfy their desires as well as his own. A person who is not motivated by such considerations may still perform moral actions, but he performs them because he believes that it is in his own interest to do so. In other words, the moral person does not merely do what is moral; he does what is moral out of moral considerations. In the previous chapter we were concerned only with the resolution of moral disagreements, and, hence, it was sufficient at that point to indicate that men can be brought to agreement upon ends if they realize what is in their own interest. In this chapter we are concerned not only with the resolution of moral disagreements but also with the motivation of moral agents. Hence the need arises to introduce altruistic considerations.

But the introduction of such considerations gives rise to a crucial problem, for it is sometimes claimed that no person ever acts altruistically. According to this theory, often referred to as egoism, all human actions are motivated by selfishness. In other words, on this view every individual acts solely in an attempt to increase his own pleasure, and a person is kind to others only if he believes that this kindness will eventually redound to his own benefit. If egoism is correct, then no person is ever a moral agent, for no one ever acts out of altruistic considerations. But is egoism correct?

In the face of the egoist's challenge, our immediate response is to bring forth cases in which it seems obvious that a person has acted in an unselfish manner. For example, we might call the egoist's attention to a doctor who has devoted his entire life to serving the poor. This doctor, we may suppose, lives among the poor and has no interest whatever in publicizing his work. His only interest lies in improving the lot of his fellow men. Thus, the actions of this doctor would seem to provide a clear refutation of the egoist's thesis.

But the egoist is prepared for such examples. He replies that although this doctor appears to be acting altruistically, he is in fact acting selfishly, for he just happens to be the sort of person who derives great pleasure from ministering to others, and were he to forego this activity he would be far less happy. Thus, argues the egoist, the doctor is just as selfish as all the rest of us, but whereas most of us enjoy owning cars and attending parties, the doctor enjoys living a simple life and providing medical aid to the poor. All of us act out of a desire to maximize our enjoyment, but since we enjoy different things, we act in different ways. Nevertheless, the underlying motive for all our actions is the same, namely, the desire to increase our own pleasure.

The philosophically unsophisticated thinker may be impressed by the egoist's argument and may try to imagine some more complicated example the egoist cannot handle so easily. But the egoist will be able to handle every example, for in every case he will simply assert that since the person in question has chosen to act in a particular way, he must have wanted to act in this way, and since he is acting as he wants to act, he is acting to fulfill his own desires. And if he is acting to fulfill his own desires, is he not acting selfishly?

The egoist's line of argument will work in every possible case, but, paradoxically, that is just what is wrong with it. For, as we have seen in previous chapters, a factual claim must be open to possible refutation. Since the assertion of one fact involves the denial of other facts, a claim that is compatible with all possible facts is not itself a factual claim but is, at best, a tautology. And that is the case with the egoist's claim. He argues that a man is selfish if he acts to fulfill his own desires. But how can we identify what a man desires? According to the egoist, a man desires to do whatever he chooses to do. In that case, however, to say that a man chooses to act as he desires to act is to say that he chooses to act as he chooses to act, which is a tautology. If we call a man selfish because he chooses to act as he chooses to act, then, of course, every man acts selfishly, but this is obviously a misuse of the word "selfish." As the British philosopher P. H. Nowell-Smith (1914–) notes, "To be selfish is not to do what one wants to do or enjoys doing, but to be hostile or indifferent to the welfare of others."[8] In other words, an unselfish person cares about the welfare of others, whereas a selfish person does not. The tautology that all men choose to act as they choose to act does not obliterate the distinction between an unselfish man and a selfish man, no matter how the egoist distorts the usual meaning of words. Thus, the egoist's challenge to morality fails.

Although it is now clear that a man can act altruistically, still, it might be asked why should he do so? In other words, granted that in general it is in a person's own interest to do what is moral, is there any reason for him to do what is moral when it is not in his own interest to do so?

This final question rests upon two dubious assumptions. First, the question seems to assume that men act only out of self-interest. But, quite to the contrary, men often act out of compassion for others, a fact attested to both by extraordinary examples, such as that of the soldier who intentionally falls upon a grenade to save the lives of his comrades, as well as by far more common examples, such as the vast number of

---

8   P. H. Nowell-Smith, *Ethics* (Baltimore: Penguin Books, 1954), pp. 142–143.

contributions given each year to various charities. There is thus no need to prove that moral action is always in one's self-interest, for virtually all of us are moved not only by egoistic considerations but also by altruistic ones.

The second dubious assumption that underlies the question as to why we ought to forsake self-interest when it conflicts with morality is the assumption that there are occasions when a person knows that to act morally is to act against his own best interest. But are there such occasions? An immoral action may appear at first glance to be in one's own interest, but, as Hume noted, "Knaves, with all their pretended cunning and abilities, [are] betrayed by their own maxims; and while they purpose to cheat with moderation and secrecy, a tempting incident occurs—nature is frail—and they give in to the snare, whence they can never extricate themselves without a total loss of reputation and the forfeiture of all future trust and confidence with mankind."[9] In short, immoral action is always a threat to one's self-interest, and rarely, if ever, can this threat be minimized to the extent that it is in one's interest to risk such an action.

But what if someone knowingly wishes to take such a risk and is not moved by any altruistic considerations? Can we reason further with him? There seems nothing more to say in this case except to recall the words of La Rochefoucauld: "To virtue's credit we must confess that our greatest misfortunes are brought about by vice."[10] Thus, when sympathy is missing, morality rests solely upon practicality.

We have now completed our examination of the nature of moral judgments and the basis of moral obligation. However, we have not yet considered some of the most crucial of all ethical issues, namely, those involved in political and educational decisions. Since these issues depend upon special sorts of considerations, they are treated in a separate area of philosophical inquiry, one referred to as social philosophy, and it is in this area that we shall conclude our philosophical investigations.

---

9   David Hume, *An Enquiry Concerning the Principles of Morals* (New York: The Liberal Arts Press, 1957), p. 103.

10   *The Maxims of La Rochefoucauld,* #183.

PART V

SOCIAL PHILOSOPHY

Chapter 9

POLITICS

Throughout history men have sought an ideal system of social organization. Some have envisioned the ideal society as one in which each member possesses total freedom, where the individual is responsible to no one but himself. Others have imagined their utopia as highly ordered, a social structure in which all are assigned roles and are taught to fulfill them for the good of the society. Considering the enormous range of competing political theories and the great variety of possible societal models, how can we reasonably decide which is to be preferred?

In order to answer this question let us imagine a situation in which a group of people have full opportunity to choose their own social system. Suppose, for example, that one thousand persons, survivors of a shipwreck, have taken refuge on a deserted island. Believing that there is little chance of their being rescued, they decide to settle down and make the best of their situation. Assuming these people differ widely in age and background, what sort of social arrangement should they adopt?

It might be suggested that they already possess the best form of social arrangement, namely, anarchy. It may seem paradoxical to speak of anarchy as a form of social arrangement, since anarchy is, by definition, a state of society without law, government, or any formal organization at all. However, just as we may arrange a sequence of numbers in random order, so a group may arrange to live without any form of governmental authority.

It is easy to see why the thought of such an arrangement might at first appeal to some of the islanders, for each person desires to be as free as possible, and anarchy appears to be an arrangement that allows each individual total freedom. We might even imagine one of the islanders named Anderson addressing the group as follows: "Government is the source of evil, for government imposes its will on people and prevents them from living as they wish. Let us live a totally free life, a life without government, a life in which no man interferes with another and each is thus enabled to achieve his own happiness."

Anderson's line of reasoning may seem convincing, but it is, in fact, seriously defective, for it involves a misunderstanding of the nature of freedom. It is not possible for everyone to be ensured total freedom, for granting freedom to one individual involves placing restraints on other individuals. If you possess freedom of speech, then those who may wish to prevent you from speaking are not free to do so. Similarly, if you are granted the right to privacy, those who may wish to prevent you from exercising this right are not permitted to do as they wish. In short, ensuring one person's freedom requires limiting other people's freedom. To those who cry, "Freedom to the People," the best reply is, "Which freedoms to which people?"

Anderson views government as the source of evil, but without any authority to protect the freedom of individuals, no individual's freedom is safe. Even the strongest of men is no match for one hundred others who set out to prevent him from doing as he wishes. Of course, it is possible to imagine a society in which it just so happens that no one wishes to do anything anyone else wishes to prevent him from doing. Such an angelic society would have no need of government, but the islanders have no reason to believe that their compatriots are angels. Thus, they require some type of authority that will ensure that disputes are settled in an equitable manner and that no individual or group of individuals takes unfair advantage of others. Without such authority no freedoms would be secure, and each person would quite understandably live in fear of his fellows. Such a life would be, as Thomas Hobbes wrote, "solitary, poor, nasty, brutish, and short."[1]

---

[1] Thomas Hobbes, *Leviathan* (Cleveland and New York: Meridian Books, 1963), p. 143.

Anderson fears that any government must impose its will on people and prevent them from living as they wish, but there is no reason why a government must do so. On the contrary, a good government is precisely one that protects crucial freedoms and thereby provides the framework within which each person is sufficiently secure to seek happiness in his own way. Of course, the possibility of good government is easy to speak of but difficult to realize. Indeed, some governments are so bad that they are even worse than no government at all. But the islanders would prefer the best possible social system, and since we may suppose that most of them recognize the errors in Anderson's line of reasoning and realize that good government is preferable to no government, they must next decide which form of government they ought to adopt.

The choice that confronts them is essentially threefold. They may adopt monarchy, the rule of one person; oligarchy, the rule of a few persons; or democracy, the rule of all persons. Let us consider each of these possibilities in turn.

Monarchy was the form of government favored by Hobbes. He pointed out that "a monarch cannot disagree with himself, out of envy, or interest; but an assembly may; and that to such a height, as may produce a civil war."[2] Monarchy thus avoids the possibility of dissension within the government and increases efficiency, for the monarch is able to pursue a consistent line of policy without the need to compromise with those who disagree with him.

It must be admitted that the simplicity of monarchal government does possess a certain attractiveness, especially if one imagines himself as the monarch. Therein, however, lies the catch, for who is to be the monarch? We can, of course, hypothesize some all-good, all-knowing individual who will always choose to perform the best possible actions, and we can then crown him as our monarch, thereby ensuring ourselves the best possible government. But, unfortunately, the islanders have no reason to believe that such a divine individual resides among them. Therefore, they would have to choose the most knowledgeable, most benevolent person in their group and crown him instead.

Such an arrangement, however, seems quite unsatisfactory for a number of reasons. To begin with, how are the islanders to decide who among them is most knowledgeable and most benevolent? It is possible to imagine various theoretical schemes for making such a decision effectively, but even if any such scheme were practical—which is highly doubtful—still no scheme is infallible, and the islanders might choose wrongly. This is a dangerous possibility indeed, for the pages of history

---

2 *Ibid.,* p. 189.

have been bloodied by numerous monarchs who exercised the divine right of kings in a less than divine manner. But even if the islanders did choose the most knowledgeable and most benevolent among them as their monarch, his knowledge and benevolence might be quite limited, for the most knowledgeable and most benevolent individual among a thousand or even a million might lack much knowledge and much benevolence. Finally, even if the islanders' choice were a person of exceptional knowledge and goodness, what assurance is there that he would continue to act wisely after he had been crowned as monarch? Rulers tend to lose touch with the ruled, and even the best-intentioned of rulers finds it difficult to remain sensitive to the needs and desires of those he rules. As the English historian Lord Action (1834–1902) noted, "Power tends to corrupt; absolute power corrupts absolutely."

Thus, although it is theoretically possible to hypothesize a monarch who would provide the islanders with the best possible government, it is in practice virtually impossible for them to find such an individual and immensely dangerous for them to choose any other. Granted that monarchal government may be efficient, still there is more to good government than efficiency. Mussolini, it may be remembered, made the trains run on time.

Assuming, then, that our islanders are unimpressed with monarchy, let us suppose that they next consider the merits of oligarchy. Oligarchy, the rule of the few, was the form of government favored by Plato in his *Republic*. Plato proposed a form of government in which the rulers would be philosophers, that is, lovers of wisdom. Since Plato believed that a person who knows what is good will do what is good, he supposed that the ideal rulers would be those who had been taught what is best and who would, consequently, act for the best.

Plato was in error in believing that those who know what is good will do what is good, for there are numerous exceptions to that principle—the smoker who knows that it is best for him to stop smoking but continues to do so anyway, or the student who knows that it is best for him to study but nevertheless spends his time talking with friends.[3] But the fact that a person sometimes acts contrary to what he believes only serves as a warning that the rulers of an oligarchy should be selected not only on the basis of their knowledge but also on the basis of their benevolence.

---

[3] Readers who are tempted to defend Plato's principle against these apparent exceptions, claiming that it is obvious that a man must always act in accordance with what he believes to be for the best, are urged to recall how two structurally similar claims, namely, "a man always acts in accord with his strongest motive" and "a man always acts to fulfill his own desires," were shown in previous chapters to be either falsehoods or tautologies masquerading as factual claims.

Does an oligarchy, such as that proposed by Plato, avoid any of the problems that beset monarchy? There is at least one respect in which an oligarchy is superior to a monarchy. When one person controls all the power, there is no way to offset his mistakes, but when power is divided among a few people, one ruler's mistake can be offset by a decision of the other rulers. But this advantage of oligarchy may be somewhat neutralized by the fact that an increase in the number of rulers involves a corresponding decrease in the efficiency of the government. As Hobbes noted, a single ruler cannot disagree with himself. Several rulers, however, may waste a great deal of time and effort disagreeing with each other and reversing each other's policies.

In any case, although the merits of oligarchy may outweigh those of monarchy, the disadvantages of oligarchy seem almost as great as those of monarchy. An oligarchy, like a monarchy, depends for its effectiveness upon the knowledge and benevolence of its rulers. Thus, once more the islanders are faced with the crucial and inordinately difficult problem of deciding who among them is most knowledgeable and most benevolent. Again the islanders might easily choose wrongly and would thereby doom themselves to a life of misery, for a few tyrants can be almost as insufferable as one. But even if the islanders do choose the most knowledgeable and benevolent among them, and even if the individuals chosen are truly exceptional, what assurance is there that this group of rulers may not eventually be corrupted? Plato himself feared that unworthy rulers of his society would come to be dominated by the motives of ambition or wealth and would, consequently, bring about the decline of his ideal state. And so long as all power is concentrated in the hands of a few, that few may eventually abuse their power and the many will suffer the consequences. Since none of the islanders knows in advance whether he will be one of the many or one of the few, oligarchy will not be much more attractive than was monarchy. The dictatorship of the Communist Party has little to recommend it over the dictatorship of Stalin.

As neither monarchy nor oligarchy satisfy the islanders, the only remaining possibility is democracy. The democratic form of government rests upon the view, clearly stated by John Dewey, that "no man or limited set of men is wise enough or good enough to rule others without their consent . . . that all those who are affected by social institutions must have a share in producing and managing them."[4] In a democracy political power is not limited to any one individual or any single group of individuals. Instead, power is divided equally among all adult members of

---

[4] *Intelligence in the Modern World: John Dewey's Philosophy,* ed. Joseph Ratner (New York: The Modern Library, 1939), p. 401.

society, and decisions are made in accordance with the will of the majority.

Democracy has at least two important advantages over both monarchy and oligarchy. First, by placing power in the hands of all the people, democracy forestalls the possibility that a small, ruling minority may tyrannize the majority. Members of a democracy do not have to make the difficult, dangerous, and unalterable decision as to who among them is most knowledgeable and most benevolent. Second, although monarchs or oligarchs may possess greater expertise in certain technical matters than do other individuals, each member of a society possesses special knowledge regarding his own problems, interests, and goals. As Dewey noted, "The individuals of the submerged mass may not be very wise. But there is one thing they are wiser about than anybody else can be, and that is where the shoe pinches, the troubles they suffer from."[5] Only the democratic system ensures that each individual's self-knowledge is taken into account in the governmental process.

The advantages of democracy are obtained at a price, however, for, as we have seen previously, the greater the number of rulers, the greater the amount of inefficiency. Anyone who has ever attended a large meeting conducted in accordance with parliamentary procedure knows the frustration of observing even the most innocuous of motions subjected to endless haggling. As a general rule, the more people who are involved in making a decision, the more people there are who must be satisfied; the more people there are who must be satisfied, the more compromises there must be. And it is the need for compromise that prevents any single individual from achieving his ends, directly and without distraction.

But it would be shortsighted to view compromise as merely a stumbling block to progress, for compromise is also a valuable safeguard against extremism. The need to explain one's position to others, to defend it against objections, and to modify it in order to gain majority support, restrains any individual from single-mindedly pursuing a mistaken policy until it turns into a disaster for all. Democracy does not maximize efficiency, but efficiency may sometimes have a high price. Consider the cost of the excellent superhighways of Nazi Germany.

It thus appears that there is a very strong case for democracy, as against monarchy and oligarchy, and we may assume that the islanders appreciate the merits of the case and, consequently, decide to adopt the democratic form of government. In carrying out their decision, however, the islanders must exercise great care, for the proper functioning of

---

[5] *Ibid.,* p. 402.

democracy requires the protection of certain crucial civil liberties. Indeed, to disregard these liberties leads inevitably to the collapse of democracy.

To understand why this is so, let us recall that democracy is a form of government in which decisions are made in accordance with the will of the majority. What the majority wills is determined by a vote in which each person is free to cast his ballot as he wishes. But in order for a person to vote freely, he must be free in arriving at his decision. In other words, to control the process by which decisions are arrived at is, in effect, to control the voting process itself. It is for this reason that democracy protects the right of each person to speak freely, to write freely, and to assemble freely. In a democracy every point of view is entitled to a hearing, since everyone has a right to hear all sides of all issues. No man or idea is beyond criticism no matter how popular the man or idea may be. As John Stuart Mill, a staunch defender of civil liberties, wrote, "If all mankind were of one opinion, and only one person were of the contrary opinion, mankind would be no more justified in silencing that one person, than he, if he had the power, would be justified in silencing mankind."[6] The pride of a democracy is its open marketplace of ideas, for the clatter in the market is the sound of freedom. When that sound is silenced, the voice of the people is silenced, and without the voice of the people there can be no democracy.

Of course, it is far easier to recognize the importance of our own civil liberties than to defend the civil liberties of those with whom we disagree. But the free expression of opinion is always of value, even to those who most strongly oppose the opinion expressed. For, in Mill's words, "If the opinion is right they are deprived of the opportunity of exchanging error for truth: if wrong, they lose, what is almost as great a benefit, the clearer perception of truth, produced by its collision with error."[7] We can never be certain that the opinion we oppose is false opinion; to presume otherwise is to presume our own infallibility. But even if the opinion we oppose is incorrect, its mere expression leads us to rethink our own view and reconsider the grounds of our belief. And such a reexamination of our ideas in the light of criticism prevents us from becoming mere dogmatists, blindly clinging to views we cannot defend and may not even understand. As Mill put it. "He who knows only his own side of the case, knows little of that."[8]

The important role of civil liberties in a democracy is now clear, and

---

[6] John Stuart Mill, *On Liberty* (New York: The Liberal Press, 1956), p. 21.

[7] *Ibid.*, p. 21.

[8] *Ibid.*, p. 45.

we may suppose that the democratic government established by the islanders safeguards these liberties. Nevertheless, we should not assume that the islanders have resolved all their political problems, for when a democracy actually begins to function, two critical complications arise. The success of a democracy depends in great part upon how well its citizens respond to these complications.

The first is that intelligent decisions about governmental matters require more time and effort than most members of society are willing or able to afford. If a farmer, a shopkeeper, or a doctor had to study in depth all of the wide variety of issues that confront the government, he would be unable to effectively pursue his individual calling, a situation that would not only be unfair to him but would also be disturbing to all those who depend upon his services.

It is in order to avoid this situation that absolute democracy, in which all citizens vote on all issues, is usually transformed into representative democracy, in which duly elected representatives of all citizens decide governmental matters. But this transformation has its dangers, for if the representatives are, in fact, not duly elected or are not responsive to the will of the people, representative democracy will collapse into oligarchy, the rule of the few. To prevent such a collapse, a representative democracy must hold free elections at fixed intervals, so that the populace may indicate its approval or disapproval of public officials and their policies. A supposed democracy in which free elections have been suspended and public officials are beyond recall is, in fact, no democracy at all. In a representative democracy a public official is not a ruler; he is a representative of the people, and if he loses the people's confidence, he must relinquish his office.

But there will always be those officials who scorn the democratic process and who attempt to seize governmental power from the people. These potential tyrants endeavor to undermine democracy by alternately cajoling and threatening their fellow citizens. And if the members of a democracy exhibit indifference and cowardice in the face of this pressure, their democracy will soon crumble, for a democracy of sheep will not be a democracy for very long. Therefore, it is incumbent upon all those who prize democracy to have the concern and the courage to stand up to their representatives and remind them who is the boss. Democracy safeguards freedom, but democrats must safeguard democracy, for as it is said, "Eternal vigilance is the price of liberty."

Let us next turn to the second crucial complication that arises when democracy begins to function. It is the essence of the democratic system that decisions are made in accordance with the will of the majority. But, given the wide diversity of interests involved, few decisions will be unanimous, and so almost every single action taken by a democracy will be thought by some of its members to be mistaken. This fact may not seem particularly troublesome so long as you imagine yourself to be in the majority on every decision, but what if on some occasion you are in the minority? What do you do when the majority of citizens oppose your viewpoint?

The obvious course of action is to try to convince those who disagree with you that they are mistaken. Since a democracy protects the right of every citizen to speak freely, to write freely, and to assemble freely, the government itself guarantees that you may express your viewpoint to all who wish to listen, that you may publish whatever materials you deem relevant, and that you may meet with those who agree with you and discuss how to win over others to your side.

Sometimes your efforts will succeed, and the democracy will reverse its decision in accordance with your view. Other times, however, your efforts will not succeed, and despite your attempts to influence public opinion, the democracy will not reverse its decision. But such situations are to be expected, for if everyone always agreed about everything, there would be no need for government in the first place. Democracy is a method of deciding conflicts of interest, and since most decisions in a democracy are not unanimous, virtually every decision will be passed by a majority over the opposition of a minority. Consequently, each individual may at times find himself in such a minority.

Nevertheless, it is most frustrating to be outvoted, and this frustration of the minority is a grave danger to a democracy, for those who cannot get their way at the polls may be tempted to carry their fight to the streets. But if the minority gives in to this temptation and attempts to override the will of the majority by sheer force, democracy breaks down and anarchy ensues.

To understand why this breakdown occurs, remember that each individual in a democracy agrees to abide by majority rule on the provision that all other individuals agree to do likewise, for if all members of the democracy agree to abide by majority rule, then each citizen is ensured that when he is in the majority, the majority view will prevail. But if some undemocratic individuals refuse to abide by majority rule when they are in the minority, other individuals will have no reason to abide by majority rule when these undemocratic individuals are in the majority. The basis of democracy is the agreement that all decisions will be made in accordance with the will of the majority. If that agreement is breached by some individuals, others cannot be expected to carry out their end of the bargain, and so democracy collapses, bringing about the anarchic situation vividly described by Hobbes as the "war of every man, against every man."[9] In such a state one need not abide by the will of the majority, but as we saw previously, in such a state no freedoms are protected and no individual is secure. In short, the frustration of being outvoted by a majority is replaced by the fear of being attacked by a mob.[10]

Thus, if a democracy is to survive, those who find themselves in the minority on any particular issue must exercise self-restraint and not allow their defeat at the polls to undermine their commitment to the democratic process. But the principle of abiding by majority rule may lead to a serious dilemma, even for those most committed to democracy, for how is an individual to respond if the government passes legislation that requires him to act contrary to his basic moral principles? Should he adhere to democratic procedure and act contrary to his principles? Or should he adhere to his principles and act contrary to democratic procedure?

At first glance there appears to be no satisfactory way out of this dilemma, for if an individual chooses to adhere to democratic procedure and act contrary to his principles, he thereby abandons his own ethical standards and becomes a moral marionette, pulled about by forces beyond his control. If, on the other hand, an individual chooses to adhere to his principles and act contrary to democratic procedure, he thereby becomes an enemy of democracy whose actions lead the society toward anarchy. This dilemma is, indeed, a difficult one for democrats, but there is a possible course of action that avoids the unsatisfactory implications of both alternatives. And it is this course of action that is generally referred to as civil disobedience.

A person who commits civil disobedience adheres to his principles and refuses to act as the government requires, but he willingly accepts the legal punishment for his behavior and, by so doing, indicates to his fellow citizens his respect for democratic procedure. This respect for democratic procedure is further emphasized by carefully limiting civil disobedience in three ways. First, acts of civil disobedience are always nonviolent, for if a member of the minority attempts by force to impose his will upon the majority, he thereby abandons the democratic process. Second, those who commit civil disobedience obey all laws except the one against which they are protesting, for to engage in widespread disruption of the social order

9   Hobbes, p. 145.

10   It is conceivable, though highly unlikely, that a democracy could be so evil that even anarchy would be preferable. If such a situation, however improbable, were to occur, revolution in a democracy would be justifiable.

is to display total disregard for the will of the majority. Third, those who resort to civil disobedience do so only upon those rare instances in which they are required to act contrary to their *basic* moral principles. An individual must decide for himself which moral principles he values most highly, but if he simply disobeys any law he believes to be immoral, then he has no right to claim that he is a democrat who abides by majority rule.

Thus, civil disobedience provides the means by which an individual can retain his commitment to democracy while acting contrary to the will of the majority. But if this means is utilized too often or without regard to its other limitations, civil disobedience turns into mere lawlessness, and democracy collapses into anarchy. As the contemporary American philosopher Charles Frankel (1917–   ) has written, "Acting on conscience is a fine thing; but a complete conscience ought to engage in some conscientious consideration of the consequences of acting on conscience."[11]

At the beginning of this chapter we began a search for the most effective form of social arrangement. The problem was stated in terms of a decision facing inhabitants of an island; however, the same problem faces inhabitants of any land, whether large or small, populous or sparsely inhabited, for the potential evils of tyranny and the potential benefits of democracy remain the same even if the populace numbers five billion and the land be as large as the earth itself.

But, as we have seen, the success of a democracy depends in great part upon the intelligence, the courageousness, and the fairmindedness of its citizens. And this fact raises a critical problem, for how can the members of a democracy ensure that its citizens possess the necessary understanding and capability to reap the greatest possible benefits from the democratic process while at the same time protecting that process from those potential tyrants and anarchists who would wish to destroy it? The solution to this problem lies in matters of educational policy, and so in order to complete our discussion of social philosophy, we must examine crucial issues regarding the proper aims and methods of education.

---

11   Charles Frankel, *Education at the Barricades* (New York: W. W. Norton & Company, 1968), p. 67.

Chapter 10

EDUCATION

Education is the acquisition of knowledge, skills, and values. But what is the knowledge, what are the skills, and what are the values that ought to be acquired? These questions are clearly of the utmost importance, for their answers form the foundation upon which a person builds his life. No man, however, is an isolated being. Each man's life is intertwined with the lives of many others, and, as we have seen, when men live together it is to their advantage to form a democratic society. But the welfare of a democratic society depends ultimately upon decisions made by all members of the community, and a proper education is the key to making wise decisions. What specifically constitutes a proper education for the citizens of a democracy? That is the crucial question now confronting us.

In a democracy each individual's education should be of equal concern, for all citizens participate in the decision-making process. A democracy that neglects the education of some of its members will pay a dear price, for the enemies of freedom feed upon ignorance, fear, and prejudice. Thus, if an individual should complain that his democracy is providing too much education for too many people, he thereby reveals his ignorance about the very nature of democracy. There is no such thing as too much education in a democracy; too little education, however, and there may soon be no democracy.

Equal concern for each person's education means providing each person with appropriate educational opportunities; it does not mean providing each person with exactly the same education. Individuals differ in their capacities and interests; what stimulates one individual may stultify another. A democracy should recognize such individual differences and should show equal consideration for all persons by enabling each to enjoy his own distinctive growth, for, as John Stuart Mill pointed out, "In proportion to the development to his individuality, each person becomes more valuable to himself, and is therefore capable of being more valuable to others."[1]

But just as it is important to recognize the need for individuality within a democracy, so it is important to recognize the need for all members of a democracy to possess certain characteristics in common. Indeed, an examination of the most important of these characteristics will disclose the essential elements of a proper education for free men in a free society.

Let us begin such an examination by noting the obvious fact that all members of a democracy should be able to read, write, and speak effectively. An individual who is unable either to understand others or to make himself understood is not only hindered in his personal growth but also cannot fully participate in the free exchange of ideas so vital to the democratic process. A command of language is indispensable for such an exchange, and so it is of vital importance for members of a democracy to acquire linguistic facility.

Also of vital importance to members of a democracy is an understanding of public issues, for how can a citizen participate intelligently in the discussion of an issue he does not understand? Furthermore, how can he intelligently evaluate the decisions of his representatives if he is unable to comprehend the complexities of the questions they are deciding? But public issues in a democracy cover an enormous range of topics. Indeed, every action taken by the government is a subject for public discussion, and such actions typically involve social, political, economic, scientific, and historical factors. Consider, for example, some of the most critical issues that confront the world today: overpopulation, poverty, pollution, racial conflict, ideological conflict, the dangers of nuclear warfare, and the possible benefits of space research. How can these issues even be

---

1 John Stuart Mill, *On Liberty* (New York: The Liberal Press, 1956), p. 76.

intelligently discussed by those who are ignorant regarding the physical structure of the world, the forces that shape society, or the ideas and events that form the background of present crises? Thus, knowledge in the areas of science and social studies is essential for all those who are called upon to think about public issues, and in a democracy such thinking is required of everyone, for although elected representatives must carry the major burden of formulating and implementing governmental policies, each citizen has both the right and the duty to evaluate and try to influence the decisions of his government.

But knowledge in the areas of science and social studies requires familiarity with the fundamental concepts and techniques of mathematics, since not only do mathematical notions play a crucial role in the natural sciences, but they are also playing an ever-increasing role in the social sciences. Furthermore, apart from its use in other areas of study, mathematics is itself an invaluable aid in the handling of everyday affairs, for, as the British philosopher and mathematician Alfred North Whitehead (1861–1947) noted: "Through and through the world is infected with quantity. To talk sense, is to talk in quantities. It is no use saying that the nation is large,—How Large? It is no use saying that radium is scarce,—How Scarce? You cannot evade quantity."[2]

It is not enough, however, to know the results of inquiry in science and social studies; one must also understand the methods of inquiry that have produced these results. No amount of knowledge brings intelligence, unless one also possesses the power of critical thinking. To think critically is to think in accord with the canons of logic and scientific method, and such thinking provides needed protection against the lure of simplistic dogmas which, while appearing attractive, threaten to cut the lifeline of reason and stifle the intellect. A member of a democracy who cannot spot a fallacious argument or recognize relevant evidence for a hypothesis is defenseless against those who would twist the facts to suit their own purposes.

There is yet another characteristic that should be possessed by all members of a democracy: sensitivity to aesthetic experience. Such experience is, to use John Dewey's words, "a manifestation, a record and celebration of the life of a civilization, a means of promoting its development, and is also the ultimate judgment upon the quality of a civilization."[3] An appreciation and understanding of literature, art, and music

---

2 Alfred North Whitehead, *The Aims of Education and Other Essays* (New York: The New American Library, n.d.), p. 19.

3 John Dewey, *Art as Experience* (New York: Minton, Balch & Co., 1934), p. 326.

enriches the imagination, refines the sensibilities, deepens feelings, and provides increased awareness of the world in which we live. It should never be forgotten that in a society of aesthetic illiterates it is not only the quality of art that suffers but also the quality of life.

Now that we have almost completed our examination of the essential elements of education within a democracy, it is clear that such an education must not be limited to training individuals in occupational skills, for no matter what occupation a member of a democracy may choose, he is called upon to take part in decisions of public policy, and so his education must be broad enough to enable him to make such decisions wisely. Among the Romans such a broad education was permitted only to freemen (in Latin: *liberi*), and so this sort of education is today appropriately referred to as a "liberal education."

It would be a serious mistake, however to assume that liberal education and vocational education have nothing in common. Such a view confuses vocational education with mere job-training. Animals are broken in and trained; men ought to be enlightened and educated, for an individual who does not understand the aims of his actions is unable to adjust those actions in the face of changing conditions, and he is, therefore, stymied by a world in flux. To perform almost any job intelligently requires the power of critical thinking as well as some intellectual perspective. Thus, a member of a democracy who is unable to reason and who lacks orientation to the world about him will be a failure both as a citizen and as a worker.

At this point it would be well to consider a question about liberal education that has recently been widely discussed. The question is usually put this way: "Is a liberal education really relevant?"

How you respond to this question is a good test of your philosophical skill. There are those who will immediately proceed to answer the question, declaring either that "Obviously a liberal education is really relevant" or that "Of course a liberal education is really not relevant." But to answer in either of these ways is a mistake, for the first thing to note about the question is that it is ambiguous and unclear. Trying to answer such a confused question without first clarifying what it means is as pointless as trying to decide the quickest way to get some place without knowing where you are trying to get.

The philosophically sophisticated thinker, instead of blindly rushing to decide whether a liberal education is "really relevant," begins by attempting to understand what is meant by the crucial phrase, "really relevant." The word "really" is one of those terms that were so aptly described by the influential English philosopher J. L. Austin (1911–1960) as "snakes in the linguistic grass." Such a term, according to Austin, is used "without caution or definition or any limit, until it becomes, first perhaps obscurely metaphorical, but ultimately meaningless."[4] In the question "Is a liberal education really relevant?" the word "really" has no function at all, except perhaps to suggest subtly that the questioner is a deeper thinker than others who have discussed the same issue. The way in which the entire question is phrased, however, belies that suggestion.

We have now reduced the question "Is a liberal education really relevant?" to the question "Is a liberal education relevant?" Obviously, the next step is to clarify the meaning of the word "relevant." Those who are on the lookout for snaky words should have no trouble spotting this one, for nowadays the word "relevant" seems to wriggle into every conceivable context, although it rarely possesses any clear-cut sense. The only practical way to deal with a word of this sort is to distinguish its various possible meanings and then consider how each of these different meanings would affect the sense of the question we are examining.

Sometimes the word "relevant" is used to mean "topical." In this sense a study is relevant just in case it deals with current matters. Thus, a course in Greek tragedy or the history of the United States would not be relevant, whereas a course dealing with today's avant-garde dramatists or the current racial conflict in America would be relevant. Using the word "relevant" in this sense, however, there is no reason why all or most of a liberal education should be relevant. To think otherwise is to confuse what is topical with what is timely. The plays of Sophocles were topical only during the golden age of Athens, but they are timely in every age, for they never lose their power to enrich human experience and deepen our response to life. Slaves in America were freed by 1865, but an understanding of the sort of lives they lived prior to that time is crucial to an understanding of racial problems in the United States today. To confine a liberal education to what is topical would exclude much material that is of value to all members of a democracy. Therefore, if "relevant" is taken to be synonymous with "topical," relevance should not be a criterion for deciding what ought to be included in a liberal education.

However, the word "relevant" is not always used in this sense. Sometimes it is used in such a way that any subject of study is relevant so long

---

4 J. L. Austin, *Sense and Sensibilia* (Oxford: The Clarendon Press, 1962), p. 15. For those who are interested in the study of other snaky words (a study that might properly be called "verbal ophiology"), I suggest the following especially venomous specimens: objective, subjective, natural, absolute, relative, pragmatic, and existential. Those who handle these words do so at their own risk.

as it is concerned with the nature, origin, or solution of the fundamental social, political, intellectual, or moral problems of our time. In this sense a liberal education *should* be relevant, for the very purpose of such an education is to enable citizens of a free society to make wise decisions about the problems that confront them.

But in order to apply this notion of "relevance" without distortion, it is necessary to clarify its potentially misleading aspects. First, not every problem of our time is a fundamental problem. An education that fails to analyze the nature of capitalism but concentrates instead upon devising plans to increase sales in a local store will not provide the intellectual perspective required to understand economic decisions taken by the government. Of course, it might be useful to examine capitalism from the standpoint of a local storeowner, but it is important not to concentrate so heavily upon this individual case as to lose sight of the broader picture that a liberal education ought to provide. Second, there are subject matters and skills which, although not directly related to any specific contemporary problems, are nevertheless crucial to a liberal education, since they form the basis for an intelligent approach to all problems. As we have seen, without linguistic and mathematical facility, the power of critical thinking, and aesthetic sensitivity, it would not be possible to deal adequately with the fundamental problems of our time. Third, concentration upon present issues may result in a failure to recognize how inextricably the present is tied to the past and how much can be learned about the present through a study of the past. Dewey put this point very well when he noted that "knowledge of the past is the key to understanding the present" and that "the way to get insight into any complex product is to trace the process of its making,—to follow it through the successive stages of its growth."[5] The urgencies of present concerns should not mislead us into believing that it is a waste of time to consider what has occurred in the past, for in order to know where you are going, it is advantageous to know where you have been. With these three clarifications in mind, and remembering how the term "relevant" is being used in this context, we can safely say that the liberal education we have described is and should be relevant.

Our examination of the word "relevant" is not yet completed, however, for there is yet another sense in which that term is sometimes used, namely, as a synonym for "interesting." In this sense a subject of study is relevant to a person just in case he happens to find it interesting, and a

---

[5] John Dewey, *Democracy and Education* (New York: The Macmillan Company, 1963), p. 214.

subject that is relevant to one may not be relevant to another, for not all persons are interested in the same subjects. Using the term "relevant" in this way, is a liberal education relevant? No doubt to some people it is and to others it is not. But should an individual's education be restricted to what he finds relevant?

There is one way to ensure that people are always interested in what they are being taught and that is to teach them only what they are interested in. In other words, if a person is interested in history but not in science, then he is taught history and not science. And if he is not interested in all of history but only in the history of the American cowboy, then he is taught that history and nothing else. Such an education would unquestionably be relevant, that is, interesting, but it would not achieve the aim of a liberal education, for it would not properly equip members of a democracy to carry out their obligations as citizens in a free society. And this aim is not an arbitrary one, for, as we have seen, the success of a democracy ultimately depends upon the education of its citizens, and it is in each person's interest to live within an enlightened, democratic society. Thus, education should not be restricted to what an individual happens to find relevant, for mastery of certain knowledge and skills is indispensable to all members of a democracy, whether or not they are interested in acquiring such mastery.

It would be a serious mistake, however, to assume that because an individual's education should not be restricted to what he finds interesting, that it therefore makes no difference to the quality of his education whether he is interested in what he is learning. An interested, attentive learner unquestionably derives far greater benefit from his education than does a learner who is bored and inattentive. But we have already seen that it would be a major error to interest the learner by teaching him only what he is interested in. How then should the interest of the learner be aroused and maintained?

There are basically two possible answers to this critical question. One answer, which might appropriately be labeled the view of "traditional education," is that the learner's interest should be engaged by the external pressures of reward and punishment. The other answer, which is the fundamental principle of what has come to be known as "progressive education," is that the learner's interest should be engaged by presenting material in such a way that it connects with the learner's own experience, with his own aims and purposes; the material itself thereby becomes the learner's personal concern. Dewey distinguished these two methods of engaging interest by posing the following question regarding the learner's experience: "Is the experience a personal thing of such a nature as inherently to stimulate and direct observation of the connections involved, and to lead to inference and its testing? Or is it imposed from without, and is the pupil's problem simply to meet the external requirements?"[6]

To engage the learner's interest through the promise of reward and the threat of punishment involves an obvious danger, for if the learner's interest in the material to be learned remains dependent upon external factors, then when these factors disappear, so will the learner's interest, and he will thus fail to develop a most important characteristic, the desire to continue learning. In so far as possible, therefore, it is advantageous to focus the learner's interest directly on the material itself. But it is not at all easy to accomplish this goal, and finding the means of doing so is one of the most important and most difficult challenges facing any teacher. Indeed, this challenge is so demanding that one is tempted to escape it by falling back upon the device of allowing the learner's interest to dictate the material he is taught. But to succumb to this temptation is, as we have seen, a fatal blunder. Every attempt should be made to render the content of a liberal education relevant, that is, interesting, but to do so by abandoning the proper content of a liberal education is to repair the ship by sinking it.

By this point it should be clear that it is foolish to reply to the question, "Is a liberal education really relevant?" without first carefully clarifying what the question means. Those who glibly answer such turbid questions display not intellectual brilliance but philosophical naiveté. He who hesitates may not be lost; he may just be thinking.

It is now time to return to our examination of the essential elements of education within a democracy, for we omitted from our previous discussion one final aspect of such an education. In addition to linguistic and mathematical facility, knowledge in the areas of science and social studies, the power of critical thinking, and a sensitivity to aesthetic experience, there is one further element requisite to a liberal education, and that is a knowledge of human values.

Aristotle recognized long ago that virtue is of two kinds, what he termed "moral virtue" and what he termed "intellectual virtue." Moral virtue, which we might call "goodness of character," is formed by habit. One becomes good by doing good. For example, repeated acts of justice

---

[6] *Ibid.*, p. 155. Dewey, whose ideas were the major force in the development of progressive education, strongly criticized progressive educators for misinterpreting and misapplying his philosophy of education. See his short but powerful book *Experience and Education* (New York: The Macmillan Company, 1963), reprinted in its entirety in *The Philosophical Foundations of Education,* ed. Steven M. Cahn (New York: Harper & Row, 1970).

and self-control result in a just, self-controlled person. Such a person not only performs just and self-controlled actions but does so, in Aristotle's words, "from a firm and unchangeable character."[7]

Intellectual virtue is what we might refer to as "wisdom." In a narrow sense of this term, a wise man is one who is a good judge of value. He can distinguish what is of worth from what is merely costly. He possesses discernment, discretion, and an abundance of that most precious of qualities: common sense. Wisdom, in this sense, is acquired partly as a result of habit, partly as a result of teaching, and perhaps partly, as the ancient Greeks would have said, as a gift of the gods.

But in a broader sense a wise man is one who possesses intellectual perspective, who is familiar with both the foundations of knowledge and its heights, who can analyze the fundamental principles of thought and action while maintaining a view of the world that encompasses all reality—both what is and what ought to be. Such wisdom is of inestimable value to members of a free society, for it enables them to stand firm in the face of intellectual challenge and to hold fast against those who would first entrap the minds of free men and then enslave their bodies. The path to wisdom, in this sense, lies in the study of philosophy, which thus serves as the capstone of a liberal education.

Having now concluded our examination of education within a democracy, we have come to the end of this introduction to philosophy. Hopefully the mystery of the subject is gone while its fascination remains, for although the challenges of philosophical inquiry are unparalleled, so are its rewards.

---

[7] Aristotle, *Nicomachean Ethics,* trans. Martin Ostwald (New York: The Bobbs-Merrill Company, Inc., 1962), 1105a, 34.

SELECTED
READINGS

PART I

WHAT IS PHILOSOPHY?

C. D. Broad was, until his retirement, Knightbridge Professor of Moral Philosophy at Trinity College, Cambridge.

C. D. Broad

THE NATURE OF PHILOSOPHY

I shall devote this introductory chapter to stating what I think Philosophy is about, and why the other sciences are important to it and it is important to the other sciences. A very large number of scientists will begin such a book as this with the strong conviction that Philosophy is mainly moonshine, and with the gravest doubts as to whether it has anything of the slightest importance to tell them. I do not think that this view of Philosophy is true, or I should not waste my time and cheat my students by trying to teach it. But I do think that such a view is highly plausible, and that the proceedings of many philosophers have given the general public some excuse for its unfavourable opinion of Philosophy. I shall therefore begin by stating the case against Philosophy as strongly as I can, and shall then try to show that, in spite of all objections, it really is a definite science with a distinct subject-matter. I shall try to show that it

Reprinted from *Scientific Thought* (London: Routledge and Kegan Paul Ltd., 1923), by permission of the publisher.

really does advance and that it is related to the special sciences in such a way that the co-operation of philosophers and scientists is of the utmost benefit to the studies of both.

I think that an intelligent scientist would put his case against Philosophy somewhat as follows. He would say: "Philosophers discuss such subjects as the existence of God, the immortality of the soul, and the freedom of the will. They spin out of their minds fanciful theories, which can neither be supported nor refuted by experiment. No two philosophers agree, and no progress is made. Philosophers are still discussing with great heat the same questions that they discussed in Greece thousands of years ago. What a poor show does this make when compared with mathematics or any of the natural sciences! Here there is continual steady progress; the discoveries of one age are accepted by the next, and become the basis for further advances in knowledge. There is controversy indeed, but it is fruitful controversy which advances the science and ends in definite agreement; it is not the aimless wandering in a circle to which Philosophy is condemned. Does this not very strongly suggest that Philosophy is either a mere playing with words, or that, if it has a genuine subject-matter, this is beyond the reach of human intelligence?"

Our scientist might still further strengthen his case by reflecting on the past history of Philosophy and on the method by which it is commonly taught to students. He will remind us that most of the present sciences started by being mixed up with Philosophy, that so long as they kept this connexion they remained misty and vague, and that as soon as their fundamental principles began to be discovered they cut their disreputable associate, wedded the experimental method, and settled down to the steady production of a strapping family of established truths. Mechanics is a case in point. So long as it was mixed up with Philosophy it made no progress; when the true laws of motion were discovered by the experiments and reasoning of Galileo it ceased to be part of Philosophy and began to develop into a seperate science. Does this not suggest that the subject-matter of Philosophy is just that ever-diminishing fragment of the universe in which the scientist has not yet discovered laws, and where we have therefore to put up with guesses? Are not such guesses the best that Philosophy has to offer; and will they not be swept aside as soon as some man of genius, like Galileo or Dalton or Faraday, sets the subject on the sure path of science?

Should our scientist talk to students of Philosophy and ask what happens at their lectures, his objections will most likely be strengthened. The answer may take the classical form: "He tells us what everyone knows in language that no one can understand." But, even if the answer be not so unfavourable as this, it is not unlikely to take the form: "We hear about the views of Plato and Kant and Berkeley on such subjects as the reality of the external world and the immortality of the soul." Now the scientist will at once contrast this with the method of teaching in his own subject, and will be inclined to say, if *e.g.* he be a chemist: "We learn what *are* the laws of chemical combination and the structure of the Benzene nucleus, we do not worry our heads as to what exactly Dalton thought or Kekule said. If philosophers really know anything about the reality of the external world why do they not say straightforwardly that it is real or unreal, and prove it? The fact that they apparently prefer to discuss the divergent views of a collection of eminent 'back-numbers' on the question strongly suggests that they know that there is no means of answering it, and that nothing better than groundless personal opinions can be offered."

I have put these objections as strongly as I can, and I now propose to see just how much there is in them. First, as to the alleged unprogressive character of Philosophy. This is, I think, an illusion; but it is a very natural one. Let us take the question of the reality of the external world as an example. Common-sense says that chairs and tables exist independently of whether anyone happens to perceive them or not. We study Berkeley and find him claiming to prove that such things can only exist so long as they are perceived by someone. Later on we read some modern realist, like Alexander, and we are told that Berkeley was wrong, and that chairs and tables can and do exist unperceived. We seem merely to have got back to where we started from, and to have wasted our time. But this is not really so, for two reasons. (i) What we believe at the end of the process and what we believed at the beginning are by no means the same, although we express the two beliefs by the same form of words. The original belief of common-sense was vague, crude and unanalysed. Berkeley's arguments have forced us to recognise a number of distinctions and to define much more clearly what we mean by the statement that chairs and tables exist unperceived. What we find is that the original crude belief of common-sense consisted of a number of different beliefs, mixed up with each other. Some of these may be true and others false. Berkeley's arguments really do refute or throw grave doubt on some of them, but they leave others standing. Now it may be that those which are left are enough to constitute a belief in the independent reality of external objects. If so this final belief in the reality of the external world is much clearer and subtler than the *verbally* similar belief with which we began. It has been purified of irrelevant factors, and is no longer a vague mass of different beliefs mixed up with each other.

(ii) Not only will our final belief differ in content from our original one, it will also differ in certainty. Our original belief was merely instinctive, and was at the mercy of any sceptical critic who chose to cast doubts on it. Berkeley has played this part. Our final belief is that part or that modification of our original one that has managed to survive his criticisms. This does not of course *prove* that it is true; there may be other objections to it. But, at any rate, a belief that has stood the criticisms of an acute and subtle thinker, like Berkeley, is much more likely to be true than a merely instinctive belief which has never been criticised by ourselves or anyone else. Thus the process which at first sight seemed to be merely circular has not really been so. And it has certainly not been useless; for it has enabled us to replace a vague belief by a clear and analysed one, and a merely instinctive belief by one that has passed through the fire of criticism.

The above example will suggest to us a part at least of what Philosophy is really about. Common-sense constantly makes use of a number of concepts, in terms of which it interprets its experience. It talks of *things* of various kinds; it says that they have *places* and *dates,* that they *change,* and that changes in one *cause* changes in others, and so on. Thus it makes constant use of such concepts or categories as thinghood, space, time, change, cause, etc. Science takes over these concepts from common-sense with but slight modification, and uses them in its work. Now we can and do *use* concepts without having any very clear idea of their meaning or their mutual relations. I do not of course suggest that to the ordinary man the words *substance, cause, change,* etc., are mere meaningless noises, like *Jabberwock* or *Snark.* It is clear that we mean something, and something different in each case, by such words. If we did not we could not use them consistently, and it is obvious that on the whole we do consistently apply and withhold such names. But it is possible to apply concepts more or less successfully when one has only a very confused idea as to their meaning. No man confuses place with date, and for practical purposes any two men agree as a rule in the places that they assign to a given object. Nevertheless, if you ask them what exactly they mean by *place* and *date,* they will be puzzled to tell you.

Now the most fundamental task of Philosophy is to take the concepts that we daily use in common life and science, to analyse them, and thus to determine their precise meanings and their mutual relations. Evidently this is an important duty. In the first place, clear and accurate knowledge of anything is an advance on a mere hazy general familiarity with it. Moreover, in the absence of clear knowledge of the meanings and relations of the concepts that we use, we are certain sooner or later to apply them wrongly or to meet with exceptional cases where we are puzzled as to how to apply them at all. For instance, we all agree pretty well as to the place of a certain pin which we are looking at. But suppose we go on to ask: "Where is the image of that pin in a certain mirror; and is it in this place (whatever it may be) in precisely the sense in which the pin itself is in *its* place?" We shall find the question a very puzzling one, and there will be no hope of answering it until we have carefully analysed what we mean by *being in a place*.

Again, this task of clearing up the meanings and determining the relations of fundamental concepts is not performed to any extent by any other science. Chemistry *uses* the notion of substance, geometry that of space, and mechanics that of motion. But they assume that you already know what is meant by *substance* and *space* and *motion*. So you do in a vague way; and it is not their business to enter, more than is necessary for their own special purposes, into the meaning and relations of these concepts as such. Of course the special sciences do in some measure clear up the meanings of the concepts that they use. A chemist, with his distinction between elements and compounds and his laws of combination, has a clearer idea of substance than an ordinary layman. But the special sciences only discuss the meanings of their concepts so far as this is needful for their own special purposes. Such discussion is incidental to them, whilst it is of the essence of Philosophy, which deals with such questions for their own sake. Whenever a scientist begins to discuss the concepts of his science in this thorough and disinterested way we begin to say that he is studying, not so much Chemistry or Physics, as the *Philosophy* of Chemistry or Physics. It will therefore perhaps be agreed that, in the above sense of Philosophy, there is both room and need for such a study, and that there is no special reason to fear that it will be beyond the compass of human faculties.

At this point a criticism may be made which had better be met at once. It may be said: "By your own admission the task of Philosophy is purely verbal; it consists entirely of discussions about the meanings of words." This criticism is of course absolutely wide of the mark. When we say that Philosophy tries to clear up the meanings of concepts we do not mean that it is simply concerned to substitute some long phrase for some familiar word. Any analysis, when once it has been made, is naturally *expressed* in words; but so too is any other discovery. When Cantor gave his definition of Continuity, the final result of his work was expressed by saying that you can substitute for the word "continuous" such and such a verbal phrase. But the essential part of the work was to find out exactly what properties are present in objects when we predicate continuity of them, and what properties are absent when we refuse to predicate continuity. This was evidently not a question of words but of things and their properties.

Philosophy has another and closely connected task. We not only make continual use of vague and unanalysed concepts. We have also a number of uncriticised beliefs, which we constantly assume in ordinary life and in the sciences. We constantly assume, *e.g.* that every event has a cause, that nature obeys uniform laws, that we live in a world of objects whose existence and behaviour are independent of our knowledge of them, and so on. Now science takes over these beliefs without criticism from common-sense, and simply works with them. We know by experience, however, that beliefs which are very strongly held may be mere prejudices. . . . Is it not possible that we believe that nature as a whole will always act uniformly simply because the part of nature in which the human race has lived has happened to act so up to the present? All such beliefs then, however deeply rooted, call for criticism. The first duty of Philosophy is to state them clearly; and this can only be done when we have analysed and defined the concepts that they involve. Until you know exactly what you mean by *change* and *cause* you cannot know what is meant by the statement that *every change has a cause*. And not much weight can be attached to a person's most passionate beliefs if he does not know what precisely he is passionately believing. The next duty of Philosophy is to test such beliefs; and this can only be done by resolutely and honestly exposing them to every objection that one can think of oneself or find in the writings of others. We ought only to go on believing a proposition if, at the end of this process, we still find it impossible to doubt it. Even then of course it may not be true, but we have at least done our best.

These two branches of Philosophy—the analysis and definition of our fundamental concepts, and the clear statement and resolute criticism of our fundamental beliefs—I call *Critical Philosophy*. It is obviously a necessary and a possible task, and it is not performed by any other science. The other sciences *use* the concepts and *assume* the beliefs; Critical Philosophy tries to analyse the former and to criticise the latter. Thus, so long as science and Critical Philosophy keep to their own spheres, there is no possibility of conflict between them, since their subject-matter is quite different. Philosophy claims to analyse the general concepts of substance and cause, *e.g.;* it does not claim to tell us about particular substances, like gold, or about particular laws of causation, as that *aqua regia* dissolves gold. Chemistry, on the other hand, tells us a great deal about the various kinds of substances in the world, and how changes in one cause changes in another. But it does not profess to analyse the general concepts of substance or causation, or to consider what right we have to assume that every event has a cause.

It should now be clear why the method of Philosophy is so different from that of the natural sciences. Experiments are not made, because they would be utterly useless. If you want to find out how one substance behaves in presence of another you naturally put the two together, vary the conditions, and note the results. But no experiment will clear up your ideas as to the meaning of *cause* in general or of *substance* in general. Again, all conclusions from experiments rest on some of those very assumptions which it is the business of Philosophy to state clearly and to criticise. The experimenter assumes that nature obeys uniform laws, and that similar results will follow always and everywhere from sufficiently similar conditions. This is one of the assumptions that Philosophy wants to consider critically. The method of Philosophy thus resembles that of pure mathematics, at least in the respect that neither has any use for experiment.

There is, however, a very important difference. In pure mathematics we start either from axioms which no one questions, or from premises which are quite explicitly assumed merely as hypotheses; and our main interest is to deduce remote consequences. Now most of the tacit assumptions of ordinary life and of natural science claim to be true and not merely to be hypotheses, and at the same time they are found to be neither clear nor self-evident when critically reflected upon. Most mathematical axioms are very simple and clear, whilst most other propositions which men strongly believe are highly complex and confused. Philosophy is mainly concerned, not with remote conclusions, but with the analysis and appraisement of the original premises. For this purpose analytical power and a certain kind of insight are necessary, and the mathematical method is not of much use.

Now there is another kind of Philosophy; and, as this is more exciting, it is what laymen generally understand by the name. This is what I call *Speculative Philosophy*. It has a different object, is pursued by a different method, and leads to results of a different degree of certainty from Critical Philosophy. Its object is to take over the results of the various sciences, to add to them the results of the religious and ethical experiences of mankind, and then to reflect upon the whole. The hope is that, by this means, we may be able to reach some general conclusions as to the nature of the Universe, and as to our position and prospects in it.

There are several points to be noted about Speculative Philosophy. (i) If it is to be of the slightest use it must presuppose Critical Philosophy. It is useless to take over masses of uncriticised detail from the sciences and from the ethical and religious experiences of men. We do not know what they mean, or what degree of certainty they possess till they have been clarified and appraised by Critical Philosophy. It is thus quite possible that the time for Speculative Philosophy has not yet come; for Critical Philosophy may not have advanced far enough to supply it with a firm basis. In the past people have tended to rush on to Speculative Philosophy, because of its greater practical interest. The result has been the production of elaborate systems which may quite fairly be described as moonshine. The discredit which the general public quite rightly attaches to these hasty attempts at Speculative Philosophy is reflected back on Critical Philosophy, and Philosophy as a whole thus falls into undeserved disrepute.

(ii) At the best Speculative Philosophy can only consist of more or less happy guesses, made on a very slender basis. There is no hope of its reaching the certainty which some parts of Critical Philosophy might quite well attain. Now speculative philosophers as a class have been the most dogmatic of men. They have been more certain of everything than they had a right to be of anything.

(iii) A man's final view of the Universe as a whole, and of the position and prospects of himself and his fellows, is peculiarly liable to be biased by his hopes and fears, his likes and dislikes, and his judgments of value. One's Speculative Philosophy tends to be influenced to an altogether undue extent by the state of one's liver and the amount of one's bank-balance. No doubt livers and bank-balances have their place in the Universe, and no view of it which fails to give them their due weight is ultimately satisfactory. But their due weight is considerably less than their influence on Speculative Philosophy might lead one to suspect. But, if we bear this in mind and try our hardest to be "ethically neutral," we are rather liable to go to the other extreme and entertain a theory of the Universe which renders the existence of our judgments of value unintelligible.

A large part of Critical Philosophy is almost exempt from this source of error. Our analysis of truth and falsehood, or of the nature of judgment, is not very likely to be influenced by our hopes and fears. Yet even here there is a slight danger of intellectual dishonesty. We sometimes do our Critical Philosophy, with half an eye on our Speculative Philosophy, and accept or reject beliefs, or analyse concepts in a certain way, because we feel that this will fit in better than any alternative with the view of Reality as a whole that we happen to like.

(iv) Nevertheless, if Speculative Philosophy remembers its limitations, it is of value to scientists, in its methods, if not in its results. The reason is this. In all the sciences except Psychology we deal with objects and their changes, and leave out of account as far as possible the mind which observes them. In Psychology, on the other hand, we deal with minds and their processes, and leave out of account as far as possible the objects that we get to know by means of them. A man who confines himself to either of these subjects is likely therefore to get a very one-sided view of the world. The pure natural scientist is liable to forget that minds exist, and that if it were not for them he could neither know nor act on physical objects. The pure psychologist is inclined to forget that the main business of minds is to know and act upon objects; that they are most intimately connected with certain portions of matter; and that they have apparently arisen gradually in a world which at one time contained nothing but matter. Materialism is the characteristic speculative philosophy of the pure natural scientist, and subjective idealism that of the pure psychologist. To the scientist subjective idealism seems a fairy tale, and to the psychologist materialism seems sheer lunacy. Both are right in their criticisms, but neither sees the weakness of his own position. The truth is that both these doctrines commit the fallacy of over-simplification; and we can hardly avoid falling into some form of this unless at some time we make a resolute attempt to think *synoptically* of all the facts. Our *results* may be trivial; but the *process* will at least remind us of the extreme complexity of the world, and teach us to reject any cheap and easy philosophical theory. . . .

Morris R. Cohen (1880–1947) was Professor of Philosophy at City College, New York. Ernest Nagel was for many years John Dewey Professor of Philosophy at Columbia University.

Morris R. Cohen and Ernest Nagel

THE NATURE OF LOGIC

LOGIC AND THE WEIGHT OF EVIDENCE

Most of our daily activities are carried on without reflection, and it seldom occurs to us to question that which generally passes as true. We cannot, however, always remain in a state of unquestioned belief. For our habitual attitudes are frequently challenged by unexpected changes in our environment, if they are not challenged by our own curiosity or by the inquisitiveness of others.

Let us suppose the reader to be seated at his table some late afternoon. The gathering darkness is making his reading difficult. Ordinarily he would turn on the electric light near him and continue with his work. But on this

Abridged from *An Introduction to Logic and Scientific Method* by Morris R. Cohen and Ernest Nagel, copyright, 1934, by Routledge and Kegan Paul, and by Harcourt Brace Jovanovich, Inc.; renewed, 1962, by Ernest Nagel and Leonora Cohen Rosenfield. Reprinted by permission of the publishers.

occasion, we suppose, the Shade of Socrates suddenly appears to the busy reader, just as his hand is on the switch, and asks him to please tell what he is doing. The reader has stout nerves, and quickly recovering from his surprise, explains: "I wish to put on the light, and this is the switch. Since your day . . ." "Yes, yes," we can imagine the Shade to interrupt, "I know all about your modern methods and theories of lighting. You needn't take time to tell me about *that*. But I do wish you would tell me how you know that it is the electric switch you were just pointing to." The reader's temper may by this time have been thoroughly ruffled, and after an embarrassed silence, he may reply with pained surprise and some asperity: "Can't you see, Socrates?"—and turn on the light.

What is of interest to us in this imaginary dialogue is that a doubt, however slight, might be raised in the reader's mind about a proposition. *This is the electric switch,* which had previously been accepted without question; and that the doubt might be resolved by claiming that any evidence besides *seeing* was superfluous. There are other propositions for which it would be difficult to find any evidence other than a direct seeing, hearing, touching, or smelling. *It is half-past eleven on my watch; My forehead is hot to the touch; This rose I am smelling has a fine fragrance; The shoes I have on are uncomfortable; That is a loud noise.* These are examples of propositions on account of which most of us would lose our tempers if we were pressed to give reasons why we believed them to be true.

Not all propositions, however, are regarded as so obvious. If the Shade should accost the reader entering the office of a life insurance company, and ask him what he is about, the reader might perhaps say: "I am going to buy a life insurance policy." Should the reader be pressed for his motives, a possible answer might be: "I shall die some day, and I wish to provide for my dependents." If Socrates should now demand why the reader believes in the truth of the proposition *I shall die some day,* the answer will no longer be, "Can't you see?" For we cannot literally see our own future death. But a little reflection may suggest the following reply: "All living creatures, O Socrates, must perish some day, and since I too am a living creature, I too shall die some day."

There are propositions, therefore, which we believe to be true because we can find some *other* propositions of whose truth we have no doubt and which we think will serve as *evidence* for the disputed proposition. *The sun is approximately ninety-three million miles away; Caesar crossed the Rubicon; There will be an eclipse of the sun next year in North America; The sum of the angles of a triangle is equal to two right angles.* These are a few propositions in whose truth we may believe because we think others, if not we ourselves, can find supporting propositions for them.

The distinction between propositions which are believed without grounds other than direct observation or apprehension and propositions which are believed because other propositions can be found to serve as evidence for them, cannot always be drawn very sharply. We sometimes believe a proposition to be true partly because we can make direct observations and partly because we can find supporting propositions. If we drop two rocks of unequal weight from the same height at the same time, we believe the proposition, *The two rocks strike the ground at the same time*, not only because we *see* that they do, but because we know a *reason* why they should do so. Moreover, many propositions whose truth seems very clear to us are in fact false. For we often see what we expect to see rather than that which actually happens. Many remarkable advances in knowledge have resulted from our questioning the truth of propositions which we previously regarded as "self-evident." And a critical study of human beliefs reveals how much "interpretation" is present in what at first sight seems like "immediate knowledge." But it is not necessary for our present purpose to settle the question as to what propositions, if any, can be known to be true "immediately."

All that we now require is the recognition of the general need of evidence for what we or others believe or question. In scientific or historic research, in courts of law, and in making up our minds as to all sorts of practical issues, we are constantly called upon to pass on diverse considerations offered in support of various propositions at issue. Sometimes we find such considerations to be irrelevant and to constitute no evidence at all, even though we have no doubt as to their truth, while other propositions we regard as conclusive or demonstrative proof of a point at issue. Between these two extremes we have situations in which there is some testimony or circumstance that points to a given conclusion but is not sufficient to exclude some alternative possibility. For most occasions we are satisfied with a preponderance of evidence, that is, if there is more evidence in favor of a proposition than against it; but in some cases, for example, when as jurymen we pass on the guilt of one accused of a crime, we are required to act affirmatively only if there is no reasonable doubt left, that is, no doubt which a "reasonably" prudent man would act on in the course of his affairs.

Logic may be said to be concerned with the question of the adequacy or probative value of different kinds of evidence. Traditionally, however, it has devoted itself in the main to the study of what constitutes proof, that is, complete or conclusive evidence. . . .

CONCLUSIVE EVIDENCE OR PROOF

Let us consider the proposition *There are at least two persons in New York City who have the same number of hairs on thier heads,* and let us symbolize it by q. How could its truth be established? An obvious way would be to find two individuals who actually do have the same number of hairs. But this would require an extremely laborious process of examining the scalps of perhaps six million people. It is not a feasible method practically. We may be able to show, however, that the proposition q follows from or is necessitated by other propositions whose truth can be established more easily. In that event, we could *argue* for the truth of the proposition q, in virtue of its being *implied* by the others, and in virtue of the established truth of the propositions offered as evidence. Let us try this method.

Suppose it were known by an actual count that there are five thousand barber shops in New York City. Would the proposition *There are five thousand barber shops in New York City* be satisfactory evidence for q? The reader will doubtless reply, "Nonsense! What has the number of barber shops to do with there being two persons with an identical number of scalp hairs?" In this way the reader expresses the judgment (based on previous knowledge) that the number of barber shops is no evidence at all for the equality in the number of hairs. Not all propositions are *relevant,* even if true, to the truth of a proposition in question.

Let us now consider the proposition *The number of inhabitants in New York City is greater than the number of hairs that any one of its inhabitants has on his head.* We shall denote this proposition by p. Is the truth of p sufficient to establish the truth of q? The reader might be inclined to dismiss p, just as he dismissed the information about the number of barber shops, as irrelevant. But this would be a mistake. We can show that if p is true, q must be true also. Thus suppose, taking small numbers for purposes of illustration, that the greatest number of hairs that any inhabitant of New York City has is fifty, and that there are fifty-one people living in New York City, no one of whom is completely bald. Let us assign a number to each inhabitant corresponding to the number of hairs that he has. Then the first person will have one hair, the second person two hairs, and so on, until we reach the fiftieth person, who will have, at most, fifty hairs. There is one inhabitant left and, since we have assumed that no person has more than fifty hairs, he will necessarily have a number of hairs that is the same as that possessed by one of the other fifty persons. The argument is perfectly general, as a little reflection shows, and does not depend on the number fifty we have selected as the maximum number of hairs. We may, therefore, conclude that our proposition *p, The number of inhabitants in New York City is greater than the number of hairs that any one of its inhabitants has on his head,* implies proposition *q, There are at least two persons in New York who have the same number of hairs on their heads.* The two propositions have been shown to be so related that it is impossible for the first (called the *evidence* or *premise*) to be true, and the second (called the *conclusion* or *that which is to be proved*) to be false.

Other instances of conclusive evidence can be multiplied indefinitely. Thus we can prove that a missing individual is dead by showing that he sailed on a boat destroyed at sea by an explosion that prevented anyone from being saved. So we can prove that our neighbor, Mr. Brown, has no right to vote by showing that he is not yet twenty-one years of age and that the law prohibits such individuals from voting.

Mathematics is, of course, a field in which proof is essential. A distinction, however, must be noted in this respect between applied and pure mathematics. In the former, as in the examples already mentioned, we assume that certain propositions, for example, the laws of mechanics, are *true;* and we prove the *truth* of other propositions by showing that they necessarily follow or are mathematically deducible from those assumed. In pure mathematics, on the other hand, we restrict ourselves to demonstrating that our primary assumptions necessarily imply or entail the theorems which are deduced from them, and ignore the question whether our conclusions as well as our axioms or postulates are in fact true.

It might be of some advantage to use the word "proof" for the former procedure (by which we conclude a proposition to be *true*), and to designate by "deduction" or "demonstration" the procedure which only establishes an *implication* or *necessary connection* between a premise and its conclusion irrespective of the truth or falsity of either. Such a terminology would permit us to say that a proposition is *proved* when, and only when, a premise *implies* that proposition and that premise is itself *true*. But so habitual is the usage which speaks of "proving" theorems in pure mathematics that it would be vain to try to abolish it. It is therefore safer to continue to speak of "proof" in pure mathematics, but to recognize that what we prove there are always implications, that is, that *if* certain propositions are true, certain others must be true. And this, after all, is the phase of all proof in which logic is primarily interested.

In all cases, then, of complete evidence or proof the conclusion is implied by the premises, and the reasoning or inference from the latter to the former is called *deductive*. We *infer* one proposition from another *validly* only if there is an objective relation of *implication* between the first proposition and the second. Hence, it is essential to distinguish *inference*, which is a temporal process, from *implication*, which is an objective relation between propositions. An implication may hold even if we do not know how to infer one proposition from another. Thus an inference to be valid requires that there be an implication between propositions. On the other hand, the being of an implication does not depend upon the occurrence of the psychological process of inferring.

THE NATURE OF LOGICAL IMPLICATION

In every attempt at a complete proof of propositions of practical importance we thus find two questions involved:

1. Are the propositions offered as evidence true?
2. Are the conclusions so related to the evidence or premises that the former necessarily follow from and may thus be properly deduced from the latter?

The first question raises what is called a factual or material issue; and the answer to it cannot be assigned entirely to logic without making the latter include all the sciences and all common knowledge. Logic as a distinctive science is concerned only with the second question—with the relation of *implication* between propositions. Thus the specific task of logic is the study of the conditions under which one proposition necessarily follows and may therefore be deduced from one or more others, regardless of whether the latter are in fact true.

As any number of propositions can be combined into one, every instance of implication or logical sequence can be said to hold between two propositions, which might be most accurately designated as the *implacating* and the *implied*,[1] but are generally called *antecedent* and *consequent*, as well as *premise* and *conclusion*. We must, however, note that in using the terms "antecedent" and "consequent," or the expression, "It logically follows," we are referring to an abstract relation which, like that between whole and part, does not directly refer to any temporal succession. The logical consequences of a proposition are not phenomena which follow it in time, but are rather parts of its meaning. While our

---

[1] In grammar they are known as the *protasis* and *apodosis* of a subjunctive sentence.

apprehension of premises sometimes precedes that of their conclusion, it is also true that we often first think of the conclusion and then find premises which imply it.

Let us consider this relation of implication a little more closely.

LOGICAL IMPLICATION DOES NOT DEPEND ON THE
TRUTH OF OUR PREMISES

The specific logical relation of implication may hold (1) between false propositions or (2) between a false and a true one, and (3) may fail to hold between true propositions.

1. Consider the argument *If Sparta was a democracy and no democracy has any kings, it follows that Sparta had no king.* The falsity of the proposition, *Sparta was a democracy,* does not prevent it from having certain implications nor from determining definite logical consequences.

No argument is more common in daily life than that which draws the logical implications of hypotheses contrary to fact. If there were no death there would be no cemeteries, funeral orations, and so on. All our regrets are based on drawing the consequences of propositions asserting what might have been but did not in fact happen.

> Had we never loved sae kindly,
> Had we never loved sae blindly,
> Never met or never parted,
> We had ne'er been broken-hearted!

It is a great error to suppose, as many have unthinkingly done, that in the reasoning we call scientific we proceed only from facts or propositions that are true. This view ignores the necessity for deduction from false hypotheses. In science as well as in practical choices, we are constantly confronted with alternative hypotheses which cannot all be true. Is the phenomenon of burning to be explained by the emission of a substance called phlogiston or by the combination with one called oxygen? Does magnetism act at a distance like gravitation, or does it, like sound, require a medium? We generally decide between such conflicting propositions by deducing the consequences of each and ruling out as false that hypothesis which leads to false conclusions, that is, to results which do not prevail in the field of observable fact. If false hypotheses had no logical consequences we should not thus be able to test their falsity.

That a proposition has definite logical consequences even if it is false follows also from the fact that these logical consequences or implications are part of its meaning. And we must know the meaning of a proposition before we can tell whether it is true. But in all cases (whether a proposition is true or false) the test as to whether there is a logical implication between one proposition and another is the impossibility of the former being true and the latter being false.

2. There is a widespread impression to the effect that false premises must logically lead to propositions that are false. This is a serious error, probably due to a thoughtless confusion with the true principle that if the consequences are false the premises must be false. But that true consequences may be implied by (or logically follow from) false premises can be seen from the following simple examples:

If all Mexicans are citizens of the United States and all Virginians are Mexicans, it logically follows that all Virginians are citizens of the United States. If all porpoises are fishes and all fishes are aquatic vertebrates, it necessarily follows that porpoises are aquatic vertebrates. (The same conclusion follows if all porpoises are mollusks and all mollusks are aquatic vertebrates.) For again the relation between the antecedents and the consequents is such as to rule out the possibility of the former being true and the latter at the same time false.

Of course if a premise is false, the conclusion is *not proved* to be true even though the conclusion is implied by the premise. But it is of the utmost importance to realize that a proposition is not necessarily false, or proved to be so, if an argument in its favor is seen to rest on falsehood. A good cause may have bad reasons offered in its behalf.

3. We have already seen that the proposition *There are five thousand barber shops in New York City,* even if true, is irrelevant to and cannot prove or logically imply the proposition *There are at least two persons in New York City who have the same number of hairs on their heads.* Let us, however, take an instance in which the absence of logical connection or implication is perhaps not so obvious. Does the proposition *Perfect beings can live together without law and men are not perfect* imply *Men cannot live together without law?* Reflection shows that nothing in the premise rules out the *possibility* of there being men who, though not perfect, live together without law. We may be able, on other grounds, to prove that our conclusion is true, but the evidence here offered is not sufficient. There is no necessary connection shown between it and that which is to be proved.

LOGICAL IMPLICATION IS FORMAL

The fact that the logical implications of a proposition are the same whether it happens to be true or not, and that the validity of such implications is tested by the *impossibility* of the premise being true and its consequences false, is closely connected with what is called the formal nature of logic.

What do we mean by *formal?* The reader has doubtless had occasion to fill out some official blank, say an application for some position, a lease, a draft, or an income-tax return. In all these cases the unfilled document is clearly not itself an application, lease, draft, or tax return; but every one of these when completed is characterized by conforming to the pattern and provisions of its appropriate blank form. For the latter embodies the character or fixed order which all such transactions must have if they are to be valid. A form is, in general, something in which a number of different objects or operations agree (though they differ in other respects), so that the objects may be varied and yet the form remain the same. Thus any social ceremony or act which diverse individuals must perform in the same way if they occupy a given position or office, is said to be formal. Similarly, logical implication is formal in the sense that it holds between all propositions, no matter how diverse, provided they stand to each other in certain relations. Consider any of the foregoing instances of proof, such as *Brown is a minor; all minors are ineligible to vote; therefore Brown is ineligible to vote.* The implication here does not depend on any peculiarity of Brown other than the fact that he is a minor. If any other person is substituted for Brown the argument will still be valid. We can indicate this truth by writing X *is a minor, all minors are ineligible to vote, therefore* X *is ineligible to vote,* where X stands for anyone of an indefinitely large class. Reflection shows that we can also replace the word "minor" with any other term, say, "felon," "foreigner," without invalidating the argument. Thus if X *is a* Y, *and all* Y's *are ineligible to vote, then* X *is ineligible to vote,* no matter what we substitute for Y. We can now take the third step and realize that the logical implication is not only independent of the specific character of the objects denoted by X and Y, but that the term "ineligible to vote" might be replaced by anything else (*provided it is the same in premise and conclusion*). Thus we get the formula: *If* X *is* Y *and all* Y's *are* Z's *then* X *is* Z is true in all cases no matter what $X, Y,$ and Z denote. On the other hand it would be an error to assert that if *All Parisians are Europeans and all Frenchmen are Europeans,* it follows that *All Parisians are Frenchmen.* For if in the generalized form of this argument, *All* X's *are* Y's, *and all* Z's *are* Y's, *therefore all* X's *are* Z's, we substitute "Belgians" for "Parisians," we get an argument in which the premises are true but the conclusion false. Similarly we can assert the implication that *If Socrates is older than Democritus and Democritus is older than Protagoras, then Socrates is older than Protagoras.* For this will hold no matter what persons are substituted for these three, provided we keep the form, X *is older than* Y *and* Y *is older than* Z implies X *is older than* Z. On the other hand, from the proposition: A *is to the right of* B, *and* B *is to the right of* C, it does not necessarily follow that A *is to the right of* C. For if three men are sitting in a circle *A* can be said to be to the left of *C* even though he is to the right of *B* and the latter to the right of *C*. It is the object of logical study to consider more detailed rules for distinguishing valid from invalid forms of argument. What we need to note at present is that the correctness of any assertion of implication between propositions depends upon their form or structure. If any form can be filled by premises which are true and conclusions which are false, that form is invalid, and the assertion of an implication in any such case is incorrect.

* * *

Like any other science, logic aims at attaining truth in its own special field and is not primarily concerned with the values or uses to which these truths can be put. Bad men may be logically consistent. But correct inference is such a pervasive and essential part of the process of attaining truth (which process in its developed form we call *scientific method*) that . . . we may note some of the ways in which formal, deductive logic aids us in arriving at true propositions.

1. It is obvious that it is often difficult, if not impossible, to determine the truth of a proposition directly, but relatively easy to establish the truth of another proposition from which the one at issue can be deduced. Thus we have observed how difficult it would be to show by actual count that there are at least two people in New York City who have exactly the same number of scalp hairs. But it is fairly easy to show that the number of inhabitants in New York City exceeds the maximum number of hairs on a human head. For the study of the physiology of hair follicles, as well as random samplings of human heads, enables us to establish that there are not more than five thousand hairs to a square centimeter. Anthropological measurements lead to the conclusion that the maximum area of the human scalp is much under one thousand square centimeters. We may conclude, therefore, that no human being has more than five million scalp hairs. And since the population of New York City is close to seven million, there must be more inhabitants in New York City than any human head has hairs. It follows, in virtue of our previous demonstration, that there must be at least two individuals in that city who are precisely alike in the number of hairs on their heads.

2. Many of our beliefs are formed to meet particular problems, and we are often shocked to find these beliefs inconsistent with one another. But they can be integrated, and their bearings on one another made clear, by exploring deductively their mutual relations. Thus it is deductive reason-

ing which enables us to discover the incompatibility between the following propositions: *Promise-breakers are untrustworthy; Wine-drinkers are very communicative; A man who keeps his promises is honest; No teetotalers are pawnbrokers; All communicative persons are trustworthy; Some pawnbrokers are dishonest.*

3. Deductive reasoning enables us to discover what it is to which we must, in consistency, commit ourselves if we accept certain propositions. Thus if we admit that two straight lines cannot inclose an area, as well as some other familiar geometric propositions, we must also admit, as we soon discover, that the sum of the angles of any triangle cannot be greater than two right angles. The full meaning of what it is we believe is discovered by us when we examine deductively the connections between the diverse propositions which we consider. For the propositions which we may be inclined to accept almost without question may have implications altogether surprising to us and requiring us to modify our hasty acceptance of them as premises.

In pointing out these uses of deductive inference, it is not denied that men may and do successfully employ it without any previous theoretical study of logic, just as men learn to walk without studying physiology. But a study of physiology is certainly valuable in preparing plans for training runners. Any competent electrician can adjust our electric lights, but we think it necessary that an engineer who has to deal with new and complicated problems of electricity should be trained in theoretical physics. A theoretical science is the basis of any rational technique. In this way logic, as a theoretical study of the kinds and limitations of different inferences, enables us to formulate and partially mechanize the processes employed in successful inquiry. Actual attainment of truth depends, of course, upon individual skill and habit, but a careful study of logical principles helps us to form and perfect techniques for procuring and weighing evidence.

Logic cannot guarantee useful or even true propositions dealing with matters of fact, any more than the cutler will issue a guarantee with the surgeon's knife he manufactures that operations performed with it will be successful. However, in offering tribute to the great surgeon we must not fail to give proper due to the quality of the knife he wields. So a logical method which refines and perfects intellectual tools can never be a substitute for the great masters who wield them; none the less it is true that perfect tools are a part of the necessary conditions for mastery.

*L. Susan Stebbing (1885–1943) was Professor of
Philosophy at Bedford College, London.*

L. Susan Stebbing

TAKING ADVANTAGE
OF OUR STUPIDITY

I wish . . . to draw a distinction between . . . 'twisted thinking' and
. . . 'using crooked arguments.' My thinking is twisted when I believe
that I am thinking effectively and have discovered sound reasons for my
conclusion but am mistaken in this belief. The twist may be due to my
supposing that I am in possession of all the relevant information, but in
fact I am not. It may be due to my failure to see that my argument is
invalid. It may be due to my inability to rid myself of some habit of
thought that keeps my mind in blinkers. When I use a crooked argument I
am in a quite different frame of mind. Then *I* am trying to persuade *you*
to accept a conclusion, although I know that I have not offered you
reasonable grounds for its acceptance. I try to persuade you by a trick,
that is, by some dishonest device calculated to impress you.

This distinction between twisted thinking and using crooked arguments

Reprinted from L. Susan Stebbing, *Thinking to Some Purpose* (London:
Penguin Books Ltd., 1939), by permission of the publisher.

can be very sharply drawn by me at the moment, since I am thinking of two very sharply distinguishable mental attitudes. But it is not always possible for me to know whether I am using a crooked argument or whether I am the victim of twisted thinking. In trying to think out some problem which concerns me deeply it is very easy to slip from one attitude to the other. This is what we must expect to be the case if thinking involves our whole personality. . . . Since I may find it difficult at times to know when I have slipped into a crooked argument, I must admit that it may be impossible for me to be sure when *you* are using a crooked argument and are not the victim of twisted thinking. This difficulty should be borne in mind. We are only too ready to accuse those who disagree with us of being 'scoundrels,' 'lying jades,' 'ignorant fellows,' and so on. Even when we are convinced, after due reflection, that the other man's argument is crooked, we may sometimes need to admit, 'Perhaps he[1] is stupid and not dishonest.' Certainly many of the arguments presented to us must be regarded as evidence that the speaker is either 'stupid though honest' or 'dishonest and cunning.' If the latter, then he deserves to be shown up; if the former, then he needs our pity. In both cases it is desirable he should be refuted. But *quis custodes custodiet?* Our anxiety to refute must be so controlled that the refutation is neither dishonest nor stupid.

. . . I shall examine some very common forms of crooked arguments. You are fortunate if you have never been tempted to use any one of them. I doubt whether I can say as much for myself. . . .

[I]n considering the devices used in crooked arguments, it is not possible to proceed in an orderly manner. These devices are so numerous that we cannot hope to enumerate them all; they are so illogical that it is difficult to find a principle that would enable us to give a neat list. No importance is to be attached to the order in which I deal with these devices. . . .

The attempt to establish a conclusion by appealing to selected instances is a common device of dishonest disputants. Its success depends either upon our want of attention or upon our ignorance that a selection has been made. The former defect we can remedy if we will; the latter defect is not so easily avoided. We can, however, develop the habit of noticing the form of the argument, and be ready to press the speaker to show us whether his selected instances are in fact representative, i.e. fair samples. A disputant who uses this device lays himself open to the possibility of

---

1 Here, and elsewhere in this chapter, 'he' covers 'she' in accordance with convention.

being dishonestly refuted by an opponent who selects other, but conflicting, instances. Thus, for example, two people may argue whether the thirty-mile speed limit in built-up areas has been an effective measure in reducing the number of road accidents. One man may cite instances in which the accident was admittedly due to fast driving. The other may reply by citing instances in which an accident was averted just because the car shot by so rapidly. (This answer may surprise some readers, as it did surprise me. I quote it from a conversation I had with a man who was addicted to driving at sixty to seventy miles an hour, but had not himself ever been involved in an accident.) By selecting instances and counter-instances, neither disputant can establish his point. There is an appropriate method for obtaining a reasonable answer to the original question. The first step is to collect statistical data from reports of road accidents; the second step requires a careful statistical analysis of the conditions that are most prevalent in cases of road accidents. An analysis of these conditions might suffice to establish the conclusion that a speed limit does (or does not, as the case may be) *tend* to diminish the number of accidents. No arm-chair discussion could contribute anything of importance for establishing this conclusion. You have probably heard discussions on this topic in which people who are normally sensible make wild assertions with regard to *the* cause of road accidents. Such assertions proceed from prejudice or from a failure to take into account relevant data such as, for instance, that not all drivers of cars are as expert or as courteous as the speaker, and that many pedestrians are careless or foolhardy or ill-adjusted to the conditions of modern road traffic. I assume that it is admitted that there are various causes of road accidents. This being so, it is tempting to use crooked arguments and only too easy to slip into twisted thinking on this topic. The disputant who has been maintaining that the enforcement of a speed limit 'would not help to reduce the number of road accidents' can easily appeal to cases where neither of the two cars involved in a collision has been travelling at over 30 m.p.h. This selection of instances does nothing to disprove the moderate statement that the imposition of a speed limit in built-up areas *tends* to reduce the number of accidents. Nor does it contribute to establishing his own extreme position that *no* accidents are due to driving at high speeds. An unwary and prejudiced opponent, instead of pointing this out, may retort, 'So you think that all accidents are due to inefficient driving,' and thus lay himself open to the reply, 'No, I think that most accidents are due to inefficient driving, such as giving wrong signals or no signals at all, but none are due to high speeds.' This leaves the argument where it began.

I remember that just after the speed limit had been reimposed, one of my guests, who had driven from a town just over fifty miles away, was complaining bitterly of 'the utter idiocy of these 30-mile limits.' I, not being a motorist, inquired whether it was not worth while to try them in order to see if the number of accidents would be reduced. He replied, 'Oh, well, if you want us all to crawl about at 5 m.p.h., then no doubt there wouldn't be any accidents, barring the old women who step off the pavement sideways in front of the car.' Now, I was not defending any such reduction in speed, but the remark was no doubt intended as a diversion; first by substituting for my statement one that I had not made and could not perhaps defend, and secondly, by suggesting to our hearers that I had made a ridiculous proposal.

Diversion from the point at issue is a source of much fallacious thinking and the secret of much crooked arguing. It is difficult to keep to the point. The difficulty may be the intellectual difficulty of keeping the main point fairly in mind despite complexity of details. Resolute hard thinking is our only remedy. In carrying on a discussion with other people we may allow ourselves to be diverted if our opponent succeeds in making us look ridiculous, with or without justification. On such occasions it is important that we should keep our tempers. An angry man is not likely to argue effectively, still less to think clearly. There are exceptions to this statement. An angry man may be put on his mettle and stimulated to rapid thinking. I am inclined to think, however, that this is not usually the case. If a prejudice which we hold as peculiarly dear, or 'sacred' to us, is attacked, and we find ourselves unable to refute the attack and equally unable to surrender the prejudice, then our wisest course is to admit that some things that we hold to be true by authority, or by inward conviction, are beyond the reach of argument. In such a case argument is powerless both for defence and attack. I suspect that most people have some convictions belonging to this class. Some bitter and fruitless controversy might be avoided if we could bring ourselves to acknowledge that this is so.

There are some forms of diversion that could hardly be used other than dishonestly. For instance, if the speaker says that not all is well with our public school education, his opponent may reply: 'So you are an advocate of sending your boys to these namby-pamby crank schools, are you?' The original speaker must refuse to accept this diversion, pointing out that his moderate statement does not entail either the travesty of it presented by his opponent, or even the denial that our public schools are better than any other schools in the country; the assertion was merely that they are not as good as they conceivably might be. It is, I think, surprising how often this trick occurs. To admit that there is anything to criticize in, say, our marriage laws may be distorted into the contention that we don't believe in marriage at all. To recognize that there are some things that are better done in the United States than in this country may be regarded as equivalent to denying that *anything* is better done here than in the United States. The attitude of mind that makes such distortion possible is perhaps expressed in the slogan: 'My country, right or wrong.' . . .

An examination of the correspondence on some disputable topic, carried on through several issues of a newspaper, shows how easy it is to wander from the point. The topic of fox-hunting is still discussed in the correspondence columns. It is a matter about which people feel keenly. I wonder sometimes whether either side ever converts one of the other side. For it is a question in which people 'take sides.' Those who have hunted from their youth up, who know the exhilaration of hunting and the delight of a good seat, are naturally enough disinclined to ask whether there are any sound reasons against this sport. Those who have had no experience of hunting may be too ready to condemn it without considering whether there is, perhaps, something to be said in favour of it. A fresh batch of letters on this topic appeared in the *Manchester Guardian,* between the dates November 30th and December 10th, 1937. The arguments I am going to discuss are taken from this correspondence.

Two main objections had been made against fox-hunting: (1) that it was an extremely cruel sport, (2) that it involved much damage to farmers, both because foxes, preserved for the hunt, are destructive to chickens, and because the cross-country run often involved damage to the farmer's fences and land.

There are, it would seem, two ways of meeting these objections: either by refuting them or by admitting them but urging in defence that there are advantages to offset these evils. With regard to the first objection, it has frequently been maintained that 'foxes enjoy the hunt.' This amounts to a simple denial of the disputant's contention that fox-hunting is cruel, so that unless evidence be offered in support of it, the reply is a *petitio principii,* i.e. it assumes the point in dispute. Recent defenders of the sport seem to admit that it is cruel. One correspondent makes merry with the suggestion that the 'antis' must have had conversations with a fox in order to know what the feelings of a hunted fox are. He argues that to hunt foxes is to follow 'Nature's way,' whereas to exterminate them (in the interests of the farmer's poultry) is to adopt a method fostered by an anthropomorphic way of regarding animals. This argument involves an undue assumption, since artificial means are admittedly used to prevent the escape of the fox. He replies to the objection that fox-hunting damages the property of farmers by the argument that the loss to the farmers is small in amount compared with the 'annual turnover' in the fox industry. This correspondent's reply to the objections brought by 'the antis' amounts, then, to admitting that the sport is cruel, but not as cruel as is supposed, and that it is 'Nature's way'; whilst, he urges, the farmers' loss is the huntsmen's gain. But he is not content with these considerations, which are certainly relevant whether justifiable or not. He suggests further that 'the antis' are like the Puritans (according to Macaulay) who 'objected to bear-baiting, not because it gave pain to the bears, but because it gave pleasure to the spectators.' This accusation, even if true, is irrelevant to the point at issue, for the point is whether pain is felt by the fox. It is as crooked an argument as that often urged (but not by any of these correspondents) by 'the pros,' that those who condemn fox-hunting have 'no guts.' The point of such accusations is to cast unpleasant aspersions against the arguer whilst ignoring his argument.

The device of reiterating what has not been denied and ignoring what has been asserted has been painfully evident, from time to time, in discussions concerning the private manufacture of armaments. I do not think anyone is likely to deny that this is a topic of great political importance, whatever may be the right decision. This topic has again been brought to the notice of the House of Commons in speeches made by the Opposition during the recent Budget debates.[2] The mounting profits of armament firms were commented upon both by Sir Archibald Sinclair and by Mr. Stokes. (The latter had also raised the question on March 7th.) I shall select two replies, made on different occasions and in different years, to the contention that the private manufacture of armaments creates conditions that make war more likely.

On March 27th, 1935, Lord Marley protested:

> There are a great many officers who go from important positions in the Services to the private employment of these armament firms. I have a long list here, which I do not propose to read out, of officers holding most important and responsible positions in the Admiralty, the War Office, and the Air Ministry who have left these important positions, dealing with the Ordnance Department and with the purchase of arms and munitions, and have stepped straight into lucrative positions in private armament firms.[3]

To this Lord Halifax replied:

> I do not profess to any professional knowledge, but having perhaps some little knowledge of human nature, I do not suppose myself that people who trade in armaments are very much better or

---

2 *The Times,* April 27th, 1938.

3 This quotation, and the two following quotations, are taken from *Inquest on Peace,* pp. 73, 74.

very much worse than any other ordinary business men, and I do not suppose that business men are very much better or very much worse than many politicians.

This reply does not meet the difficulty raised by Lord Marley, although it was offered as doing so. First, Lord Halifax seems to rely upon prestige suggestion. He is a well-known and much respected and, no doubt, widely travelled man; he claims to have 'some little knowledge of human nature' whilst not professing to 'professional knowledge.' This is an obvious trick. Secondly, he indulges in a remarkably obvious diversion to an irrelevant conclusion. The point was not at all whether those who trade in armaments were 'better or worse' than 'ordinary business men,' nor whether these are 'better or worse' than 'many politicians.' Lord Halifax's statements on both these points may be true; they are certainly totally irrelevant. The point at issue was that armament trading is *not* an 'ordinary business,' so that peculiar safeguards might be necessary. That Lord Halifax was aware of the point, but failed to meet it, is shown in his comparison of those 'who trade in armaments' with 'other *ordinary* business men.'

The same failure to see, or at least to reply to, the point was evident in a speech made by Sir John Simon, in the House of Commons, on November 22nd, 1934. He said:

> It would be very unjust to armament firms and to those responsible people connected with them, to imply that there is something in their business which essentially makes undesirable methods their practice. . . .

This again is a flagrant example of failing to keep to the point and of deliberately ignoring the point in dispute. Both Lord Halifax and Sir John Simon are content to make vague statements suggesting that *unjust* accusations have been made, whereas the contention was that these accusations are *true*. Neither of them met the contention that there are certain trades (such as the opium traffic, or the white slave traffic) which are not ordinary trades and out of which it is undesirable that private persons should be allowed to make profits.

The device of 'abusing the plaintiff's attorney' when no case can be put up by the defence is recognized as a dishonest trick. Perhaps it sometimes works. A prosecuting counsel might influence a jury by speaking of the accused man as a scoundrel because the crime of which he is accused (but not yet found guilty) is an atrocious crime. Stated thus baldly, the device would be, I hope, too obvious to mislead any jurors. It can, however, be made to work if the suggestion that the accused man is a scoundrel be conveyed by subtle implications. Lord Halifax and Sir John

Simon seem to me to have used this device, but on the side of the defendant, and not with any considerable degree of subtlety.

An example of another device for taking advantage of our stupidity is also provided by the Armaments Inquiry. The following account is given in the *Press Reports:*

> When Sir Charles Graven[4] was being questioned by Sir Philip Gibbs yesterday, he said Messrs. Vickers' trade was not particularly dangerous.
>
> *Sir Philip:* You do not think that your wares are any more dangerous or obnoxious than boxes of chocolates or sugar candy?— No, or novels.
>
> *Sir Philip:* You don't think it is more dangerous to export these fancy goods to foreign countries than, say, children's crackers?
>
> *Sir Charles:* Well, I nearly lost an eye with a Christmas cracker, but never with a gun.

It is difficult to believe that these replies were intended to be serious. There is an obvious diversion from the point under the guise of a contemptuous joke. At least, I think it must have been meant for a joke, although it is certainly a poor one. There is a further crooked argument. The hearer might willingly assent to the suggestion that someone might 'nearly lose an eye with a Christmas cracker' although he has never been in danger from a gun. Crackers, however, are not made for this purpose, whereas armaments are made solely for the purpose of killing and wounding people and destroying buildings. But it is *armaments* that are being discussed. I hardly think this crooked argument could deceive anyone.

I shall conclude . . . by setting out an argument that contains a considerable number of fallacious modes of reasoning and twisted thinking. I have constructed this argument for the purpose of illustrating these defects. The argument has been 'made up' by me much in the way in which a patchwork quilt is made by connecting together various pieces brought together from different sources. I do not think that any one speaker would combine in so comparatively short a speech so many dishonest devices or exhibit so many forms of twisted thinking. On the other hand, every argument that appears in this 'speech' has been used by someone or other in the course of the prolonged controversy concerning Women's Suffrage. My imaginary speaker will quote some passages from the speech made by Sir F. E. Smith (afterwards Lord Birkenhead) in moving the rejection of the Conciliation Bill, introduced to the House of Commons by Mr. Shackleton in 1910.[5] In the context in which these

---

[4] Sir Charles Craven is a director of Vickers-Armstrong, Ltd.

[5] These quotations are taken from the report of Sir F. E. Smith's speech, given in *The Times,* July 13th, 1910.

passages are now forced (by me) to appear, they have undoubtedly a twist that is more obvious, and perhaps more vicious, than in the original. In my opinion Sir F. E. Smith's speech was a masterpiece, regarded from the point of winning over the undecided to agreement with him.

For the purpose of examining this imaginary speech, I shall adopt the device . . . of affixing small letters to those statements upon which I shall subsequently comment.

> 'It has been truly said by Mrs. Humphry Ward that "the political ignorance of women is irreparable and is imposed by Nature."(a) Women are incapable of forming a sound judgment on important political affairs. But it is not only the right, it is, I submit, also the duty of every voter to judge soundly and wisely of those matters that are put before him. It has been said that women have a right to exercise the parliamentary vote. But, as Sir F. E. Smith has wisely said: "No one has an abstract right of that kind. The theory that there is such a right is as dead as Rousseau. The vote is given on approved public grounds to such citizens as in the opinion of the State are likely to exercise it for the benefit of the whole community.(b) If women have a right to vote, they have the right everywhere, including priest-ridden Italy and our great Eastern dependencies.(c) Supposing that our Indian fellow-subjects ever are enfranchised, the operation must include, not the men only, but the unillumined zenanas." How frightful would it be even to contemplate the enfranchisement of 'the unillumined zenanas.' (d) Yet, if we give the vote to women in this country we cannot stop short of enfranchising the most ignorant women in our Europe. The women in this country have no need for a vote. Sir Frederick Smith challenged the House of Commons to cite one case 'where the advocates of a woman's grievance have come to the House and said, "I have established this grievance, and I ask the House to remedy it,"' and have failed to get it remedied.(e)
>
> If women are given the Parlimentary vote, it might happen that women combined with a minority of men should attempt to impose their views upon an actual majority of men. This would be intolerable. Women will vote together and there will be a regiment of women indeed. But the power behind the vote is force; it is by force that the law is made effective. What part can women play in the exercise of this most necessary sanction of law? No part at all. Make no mistake. Those who are working for the enfranchisement of women will not stop with the parlimentary vote. They will press for complete equality between the sexes; they will not stop short of demanding that women should sit in the House of Commons. Indeed, as Mr. Gladstone so clearly saw, "The capacity to sit in the House of Commons logically and practically draws in its train the capacity to fill every office in the States."(f) That a woman should be a Cabinet Minister is too horrible to contemplate. Women have the feminine graces. Let us reserve for men the masculine part.(g)
>
> 'To quote one more from the powerful speech of Sir Frederick

Smith: "We are told that it is no answer to say that women voters might be ignorant—that men voters are ignorant too. That is the most crude application of the doctrine of political homœopathy to which I have ever listened. I do not assent to the gloomy view held as to the capacity of the male voter."(h) Here Sir Frederick Smith put his finger on the true answer. Women have not the capacity of men.(g) Women are women and men are men whatever be their class or rank or country.(g) It is a shameful thing that women should attempt to usurp the powers and perform the duties entrusted by Nature to men and to men alone.(i) Let them content themselves with the noble work some of them are performing so well of influencing their men to judge concerning the gravest political questions of the day. A woman's sphere is her home. There she can represent her political views to her husband and his friends; there she can play her part by exercising sweet feminine influence without sullying herself by entering into the strife and turmoil of practical politics. To be the power behind the throne is better than to be seated uneasily upon the throne itself.(j) Let me once again repeat the words of Sir Frederick Smith. "I do not," he said, "wish to decry the claim of women to intellectual distinction. I have never . . . founded myself on some assumed intellectual inferiority of women. I do not believe it; but I venture to say that the sum total of human happiness, knowledge, and achievement would be almost unaffected if—I take the most distinguished names—Sappho had never sung, if Joan of Arc had never fought, if Siddons had never played, and if George Eliot had never written, and that, at the same time, if the true functions of womanhood had not been faithfully discharged throughout the Ages, the very existence of the race and the tenderest and most sacred influences which animate mankind would have disappeared." These are weighty words. You are asked to support a movement that will prevent the true functions of womanhood, and threaten the very existence of the human race.(k) When I reflect upon the consequences that would ensue upon the enfranchisement of women I am filled with dismay. I detest this proposal.(l) Every right-thinking person, be it man or woman, agrees with me.(m) The alternatives are clear: Either you give the vote to women and destroy the sanctity of the home, or you reject this most iniquitous proposal and preserve that which every Englishman holds dear.'(n)

It is not difficult to detect the absurdities in this speech, nor to discern the contradictions in it. I have indeed put them together for this purpose.

(a) This statement is a good example of potted thinking; it has the effect of a slogan, and conceals, I fancy, much begging of the question. The statement immediately following it is a repetition with variation in the wording. This is by no means a dishonest device. As we have already seen, it may be necessary for a speaker to repeat his points, lest his hearers be slow to take them in. It is, however, wise not to slip into the habit of supposing that every new statement advances the argument.

(b) The claim that women have a right to the franchise is not equivalent to the claim that they have an 'abstract right.' On the contrary, the claim was based upon the need for women, in their own interests, to be enfranchised, and it was justified on the ground that women were not more politically incompetent than men. Accordingly, the assertion that 'the vote is given on approved public grounds to such citizens as in the opinion of the State are likely to exercise it for the benefit of the whole community' involves a deliberate disregard of the point at issue. It asserts what had not been denied.

(c) This involves an extension of the opponent's contention, which may have been a legitimate extension, but it derives its force here from the irrelevant denial of 'an abstract right.'

(d) An appeal to emotion that is not, in itself, unjustifiable in a speech. But the appeal depends upon representing the zenanas as 'unillumined,' whereas the original contention was that *all* women were politically incompetent.

(e) Simple denial of the point at issue, combined with another irrelevant conclusion. In point of fact, advocates of a woman's grievance were proposing that the grievance should be removed. Sir F. E. Smith, failing to see that their lack of a parliamentary vote was a grievance, replied, in effect, to the women that *other* grievances of theirs had always been remedied.

(f) This is indeed a logical conclusion. This point was made by Sir F. E. Smith as well. It is an effective argument against the proposal to enfranchise women, provided it be admitted that women are not fitted to be Members of Parliament.

(g) A diversion from the point at issue, which was no doubt all the more effective for being a mere tautology. The same diversion is made twice more in rapid succession. In all three cases the hearers are intended to get the impression that the speaker's opponents are contesting the indisputable fact that women are not men. The point at issue is whether the differences between women and men are relevant to the 'exercise of the vote.'

(h) This is a straightforward expression of personal opinion. If the hearers accept it as in any way supporting the speaker's contention, they should do so only in so far as they recognize that he is in a position to have expert knowledge of the matter in dispute.

(i) This is a flagrant begging of the question, reinforced by an appeal to what is in accordance with Nature.

(j) The inconsistency of the last two statements with the contention that 'women are politically incompetent' is so obvious that I should not have included it in this 'speech,' were it not for the fact that exactly this inconsistency was repeated again and again both by men and by women anti-suffragists.

(k) An extreme extension of the opponent's contention, combined with the false suggestion that it has already been agreed what are the 'true functions of womanhood' and what exactly is incompatible with the exercise of them.

(l) Again a perfectly legitimate expression of personal feeling.

(m) But this legitimate expression of personal feeling is at once regarded as evidence that everyone else will have the same feeling unless he (or she) is not 'right thinking.'

(n) A dishonest conjunction of the two exclusive alternatives—either give or not give, the vote—with two other alternatives that are not necessarily conjoined with the first pair. To assume that they are thus conjoined is to beg the question.

To protect ourselves from these tricks we must be constantly on the alert; the cost of thinking effectively is a difficult vigilance.

Charles Sanders Peirce (1839–1914) was the American philosopher who founded the philosophical movement known as pragmatism.

Charles Sanders Peirce

THE FIXATION OF BELIEF

We generally know when we wish to ask a question and when we wish to pronounce a judgment, for there is a dissimilarity between the sensation of doubting and that of believing.

But this is not all which distinguishes doubt from belief. There is a practical difference. Our beliefs guide our desires and shape our actions. The Assassins, or followers of the Old Man of the Mountain, used to rush into death at his least command, because they believed that obedience to him would insure everlasting felicity. Had they doubted this, they would not have acted as they did. So it is with every belief, according to its degree. The feeling of believing is a more or less sure indication of there being established in our nature some habit which will determine our actions. Doubt never has such an effect.

Reprinted by permission of the publishers from Charles Hartshorne & Paul Weiss, eds. *Collected Papers of Charles Sanders Peirce,* Vol. V, Cambridge, Mass.: The Belknap Press of Harvard University Press, Copyright, 1934, 1962, by the President and Fellows of Harvard College.

Nor must we overlook a third point of difference. Doubt is an uneasy and dissatisfied state from which we struggle to free ourselves and pass into the state of belief, while the latter is a calm and satisfactory state which we do not wish to avoid, or to change to a belief in anything else. On the contrary, we cling tenaciously, not merely to believing, but to believing just what we do believe.

Thus, both doubt and belief have positive effects upon us, though very different ones. Belief does not make us act at once, but puts us into such a condition that we shall behave in some certain way, when the occasion arises. Doubt has not the least such active effect, but stimulates us to inquiry until it is destroyed. This reminds us of the irritation of a nerve and the reflex action produced thereby; while for the analogue of belief, in the nervous system, we must look to what are called nervous associations—for example, to that habit of the nerves in consequence of which the smell of a peach will make the mouth water.

The irritation of doubt causes a struggle to attain a state of belief. I shall term this struggle *Inquiry,* though it must be admitted that this is sometimes not a very apt designation.

The irritation of doubt is the only immediate motive for the struggle to attain belief. It is certainly best for us that our beliefs should be such as may truly guide our actions so as to satisfy our desires; and this reflection will make us reject every belief which does not seem to have been so formed as to insure this result. But it will only do so by creating a doubt in the place of that belief. With the doubt, therefore, the struggle begins, and with the cessation of doubt it ends. Hence, the sole object of inquiry is the settlement of opinion. We may fancy that this is not enough for us, and that we seek, not merely an opinion, but a true opinion. But put this fancy to the test, and it proves groundless; for as soon as a firm belief is reached we are entirely satisfied, whether the belief be true or false. And it is clear that nothing out of the sphere of our knowledge can be our object, for nothing which does not affect the mind can be the motive for mental effort. The most that can be maintained is, that we seek for a belief that we shall *think* to be true. But we think each one of our beliefs to be true, and, indeed, it is mere tautology to say so.

That the settlement of opinion is the sole end of inquiry is a very important proposition. It sweeps away, at once, various vague and erroneous conceptions of proof. A few of these may be noticed here.

1. Some philosophers have imagined that to start an inquiry it was only necessary to utter a question whether orally or by setting it down upon paper, and have even recommended us to begin our studies with questioning everything! But the mere putting of a proposition into the interroga-

tive form does not stimulate the mind to any struggle after belief. There must be a real and living doubt, and without this all discussion is idle.

2. It is a very common idea that a demonstration must rest on some ultimate and absolutely indubitable propositions. These, according to one school, are first principles of a general nature; according to another, are first sensations. But, in point of fact, an inquiry, to have that completely satisfactory result called demonstration, has only to start with propositions perfectly free from all actual doubt. If the premises are not in fact doubted at all, they cannot be more satisfactory than they are.

3. Some people seem to love to argue a point after all the world is fully convinced of it. But no further advance can be made. When doubt ceases, mental action on the subject comes to an end; and, if it did go on, it would be without a purpose.

If the settlement of opinion is the sole object of inquiry, and if belief is of the nature of a habit, why should we not attain the desired end, by taking as answer to a question any we may fancy, and constantly reiterating it to ourselves, dwelling on all which may conduce to that belief, and learning to turn with contempt and hatred from anything that might disturb it? This simple and direct method is really pursued by many men. I remember once being entreated not to read a certain newspaper lest it might change my opinion upon free-trade. "Lest I might be entrapped by its fallacies and misstatements," was the form of expression. "You are not," my friend said, "a special student of political economy. You might, therefore, easily be deceived by fallacious arguments upon the subject. You might, then, if you read this paper, be led to believe in protection. But you admit that free-trade is the true doctrine; and you do not wish to believe what is not true." I have often known this system to be deliberately adopted. Still oftener, the instinctive dislike of an undecided state of mind, exaggerated into a vague dread of doubt, makes men cling spasmodically to the views they already take. The man feels that, if he only holds to his belief without wavering, it will be entirely satisfactory. Nor can it be denied that a steady and immovable faith yields great peace of mind. It may, indeed, give rise to inconveniences, as if a man should resolutely continue to believe that fire would not burn him, or that he would be eternally damned if he received his *ingesta* otherwise than through a stomach pump. But then the man who adopts this method will not allow that its inconveniences are greater than its advantages. He will say, "I hold steadfastly to the truth, and the truth is always wholesome." And in many cases it may very well be that the pleasure he derives from his calm faith overbalances any inconveniences resulting from its deceptive character. Thus, if it be true that death is annihilation, then the man who believes that he will certainly go straight to heaven when he dies, provided he have fulfilled certain simple observances in this life, has a cheap pleasure which will not be followed by the least disappointment. A similar consideration seems to have weight with many persons in religious topics, for we frequently hear it said, "Oh, I could not believe so-and-so, because I should be wretched if I did." When an ostrich buries its head in the sand as danger approaches, it very likely takes the happiest course. It hides the danger, and then calmly says there is no danger; and, if it feels perfectly sure there is none, why should it raise its head to see? A man may go through life, systematically keeping out of view all that might cause a change in his opinions, and if he only succeeds—basing his method, as he does, on two fundamental psychological laws—I do not see what can be said against his doing so. It would be an egotistical impertinence to object that his procedure is irrational, for that only amounts to saying that his method of settling belief is not ours. He does not propose to himself to be rational, and, indeed, will often talk with scorn of man's weak and illusive reason. So let him think as he pleases.

But this method of fixing belief, which may be called the method of tenacity, will be unable to hold its ground in practice. The social impulse is against it. The man who adopts it will find that other men think differently from him, and it will be apt to occur to him, in some saner moment, that their opinions are quite as good as his own, and this will shake his confidence in his belief. This conception, that another man's thought or sentiment may be equivalent to one's own, is a distinctly new step, and a highly important one. It arises from an impulse too strong in man to be suppressed, without danger of destroying the human species. Unless we make ourselves hermits, we shall necessarily influence each other's opinions; so that the problem becomes how to fix belief, not in the individual merely, but in the community.

Let the will of the state act, then, instead of that of the individual. Let an institution be created which shall have for its object to keep correct doctrines before the attention of the people, to reiterate them perpetually, and to teach them to the young; having at the same time power to prevent contrary doctrines from being taught, advocated, or expressed. Let all possible causes of a change of mind be removed from men's apprehensions. Let them be kept ignorant, lest they should learn of some reason to think otherwise than they do. Let their passions be enlisted, so that they may regard private and unusual opinions with hatred and horror. Then, let all men who reject the established belief be terrified into silence. Let the people turn out and tar-and-feather such men, or let inquisitions be made into the manner of thinking of suspected persons, and when they are found guilty of forbidden beliefs, let them be subjected to some signal punishment. When complete agreement could not otherwise be reached, a general massacre of all who have not thought in a certain way has proved a very effective means of settling opinion in a country. If the power to do this be wanting, let a list of opinions be drawn up, to which no man of the least independence of thought can assent, and let the faithful be required to accept all these propositions, in order to segregate them as radically as possible from the influence of the rest of the world.

This method has, from the earliest times, been one of the chief means of upholding correct theological and political doctrines, and of preserving their universal or catholic character. In Rome, especially, it has been practised from the days of Numa Pompilius to those of Pius Nonus. This is the most perfect example in history; but wherever there is a priest-hood—and no religion has been without one—this method has been more or less made use of. Wherever there is an aristocracy, or a guild, or any association of a class of men whose interests depend, or are supposed to depend, on certain propositions, there will be inevitably found some traces of this natural product of social feeling. Cruelties always accompany this system; and when it is consistently carried out, they become atrocities of the most horrible kind in the eyes of any rational man. Nor should this occasion surprise, for the officer of a society does not feel justified in surrendering the interests of that society for the sake of mercy, as he might his own private interests. It is natural, therefore, that sympathy and fellowship should thus produce a most ruthless power.

In judging this method of fixing belief, which may be called the method of authority, we must, in the first place, allow its immeasurable mental and moral superiority to the method of tenacity. Its success is proportionately greater; and, in fact, it has over and over again worked the most majestic results. The mere structures of stone which it has caused to be put together—in Siam, for example, in Egypt, and in Europe—have many of them a sublimity hardly more than rivaled by the greatest works of Nature. And, except the geological epochs, there are no periods of time so vast as those which are measured by some of these organized faiths. If we scrutinize the matter closely, we shall find that there has not been one of their creeds which has remained always the same; yet the change is so slow as to be imperceptible during one person's life, so that individual belief remains sensibly fixed. For the mass of mankind, then, there is perhaps no better method than this. If it is their highest impulse to be intellectual slaves, then slaves they ought to remain.

But no institution can undertake to regulate opinions upon every subject. Only the most important ones can be attended to, and on the rest men's minds must be left to the action of natural causes. This imperfection will be no source of weakness so long as men are in such a state of culture that one opinion does not influence another—that is, so long as they cannot put two and two together. But in the most priest-ridden states some individuals will be found who are raised above that condition. These men possess a wider sort of social feeling; they see that men in other countries and in other ages have held to very different doctrines from those which they themselves have been brought up to believe; and they cannot help seeing that it is the mere accident of their having been taught as they have, and of their having been surrounded with the manners and associations they have, that has caused them to believe as they do and not far differently. Nor can their candour resist the reflection that there is no reason to rate their own views at a higher value than those of other nations and other centuries; thus giving rise to doubts in their minds.

They will further perceive that such doubts as these must exist in their minds with reference to every belief which seems to be determined by the caprice either of themselves or of those who originated the popular opinions. The willful adherence to a belief, and the arbitrary forcing of it upon others, must, therefore, both be given up. A different new method of settling opinions must be adopted, that shall not only produce an impulse to believe, but shall also decide what proposition it is which is to be believed. Let the action of natural preferences be unimpeded, then, and under their influence let men, conversing together and regarding matters in different lights, gradually develop beliefs in harmony with natural causes. This method resembles that by which conceptions of art have been brought to maturity. The most perfect example of it is to be found in the history of metaphysical philosophy. Systems of this sort have not usually rested upon any observed facts, at least not in any great degree. They have been chiefly adopted because their fundamental propositions seemed "agreeable to reason." This is an apt expression; it does not mean that which agrees with experience, but that which we find ourselves inclined to believe. Plato, for example, finds it agreeable to reason that the distances of the celestial spheres from one another should be proportional to the different lengths of strings which produce harmonious chords. Many philosophers have been led to their main conclusions by considerations like this; but this is the lowest and least developed form which the method takes, for it is clear that another man might find Kepler's theory, that the celestial spheres are proportional to the inscribed and circumscribed spheres of the different regular solids, more agreeable to *his* reason. But the shock of opinions will soon lead men to rest on preferences of a far more universal nature. Take, for example, the doctrine that man only acts selfishly—that is, from the consideration that acting in one way will afford him more pleasure than acting in another. This rests on no fact in the world, but it has had a wide acceptance as being the only reasonable theory.

This method is far more intellectual and respectable from the point of view of reason than either of the others which we have noticed. Indeed, as long as no better method can be applied, it ought to be followed, since it is then the expression of instinct which must be the ultimate cause of belief in all cases. But its failure has been the most manifest. It makes of inquiry something similar to the development of taste; but taste, unfortunately, is always more or less a matter of fashion, and accordingly metaphysicians have never come to any fixed agreement, but the pendulum has swung backward and forward between a more material and a more spiritual philosophy, from the earliest times to the latest. And so from this, which has been called the *a priori* method, we are driven, in Lord Bacon's phrase, to a true induction. We have examined into this *a priori* method as something which promised to deliver our opinions from their accidental and capricious element. But development, while it is a process which eliminates the effect of some casual circumstances, only magnifies that of others. This method, therefore, does not differ in a very essential way from that of authority. The government may not have lifted its finger to influence my convictions; I may have been left outwardly quite free to choose, we will say, between monogamy and polygamy, and, appealing to my conscience only, I may have concluded that the latter practice is in itself licentious. But when I come to see that the chief obstacle to the spread of Christianity among a people of as high culture as the Hindoos has been a conviction of the immorality of our way of treating women, I cannot help seeing that, though governments do not interfere, sentiments in their development will be very greatly determined by accidental causes. Now, there are some people, among whom I must suppose that my reader is to be found, who, when they see that any belief of theirs is determined by any circumstance extraneous to the facts, will from that moment not merely admit in words that that belief is doubtful, but will experience a real doubt of it, so that it ceases in some degree at least to be a belief.

To satisfy our doubts, therefore, it is necessary that a method should be found by which our beliefs may be determined by nothing human, but by some external permanency—by something upon which our thinking has no effect. Some mystics imagine that they have such a method in a private inspiration from on high. But that is only a form of the method of tenacity, in which the conception of truth as something public is not yet developed. Our external permanency would not be external, in our sense, if it was restricted in its influence to one individual. It must be something which affects, or might affect, every man. And, though these affections are necessarily as various as are individual conditions, yet the method must be such that the ultimate conclusion of every man shall be the same. Such is the method of science. Its fundamental hypothesis, restated in more familiar language, is this: There are Real things, whose characters are entirely independent of our opinions about them; those Reals affect our senses according to regular laws, and, though our sensations are as different as are our relations to the objects, yet, by taking advantage of the laws of perception, we can ascertain by reasoning how things really and truly are; and any man, if he have sufficient experience and he reason enough about it, will be led to the one True conclusion. The new conception here involved is that of Reality. It may be asked how I know that there are any Reals. If this hypothesis is the sole support of my method of inquiry, my method of inquiry must not be used to support my hypothesis. The reply is this: 1. If investigation cannot be regarded as proving that there are Real things, it at least does not lead to a contrary conclusion; but the method and the conception on which it is based remain ever in harmony. No doubts of the method, therefore, necessarily arise from its practice, as is the case with all the others. 2. The feeling which gives rise to any method of fixing belief is a dissatisfaction at two repugnant propositions. But here already is a vague concession that there is some *one* thing which a proposition should represent. Nobody, therefore, can really doubt that there are Reals, for, if he did, doubt would not be a source of dissatisfaction. The hypothesis, therefore, is one which every mind admits. So that the social impulse does not cause men to doubt it. 3. Everybody uses the scientific method about a great many things, and only ceases to use it when he does not know how to apply it. 4. Experience of the method has not led us to doubt it, but, on the contrary, scientific investigation has had the most wonderful triumphs in the way of settling opinion. These afford the explanation of my not doubting the method or the hypothesis which it supposes; and not having any doubt, nor believing that anybody else whom I could influence has, it would be the merest babble for me to say more about it. If there be anybody with a living doubt upon the subject, let him consider it.

To describe the method of scientific investigation is the object of this series of papers. At present I have only room to notice some points of contrast between it and other methods of fixing belief.

This is the only one of the four methods which presents any distinction of a right and a wrong way. If I adopt the method of tenacity, and shut myself out from all influences, whatever I think necessary to doing this, is necessary according to that method. So with the method of authority: the state may try to put down heresy by means which, from a scientific point of view, seem very ill-calculated to accomplish its purposes; but the only test *on that method* is what the state thinks; so that it cannot pursue the method wrongly. So with the *a priori* method. The very essence of it is to think as one is inclined to think. . . . But with the scientific method the case is different. I may start with known and observed facts to proceed to the unknown; and yet the rules which I follow in doing so may not be such as investigation would approve. The test of whether I am truly following the method is not an immediate appeal to my feelings and purposes, but, on the contrary, itself involves the application of the method. Hence it is that bad reasoning as well as good reasoning is possible; and this fact is the foundation of the practical side of logic.

It is not to be supposed that the first three methods of settling opinion present no advantage whatever over the scientific method. On the contrary, each has some peculiar convenience of its own. The *a priori* method is distinguished for its comfortable conclusions. It is the nature of the process to adopt whatever belief we are inclined to, and there are certain flatteries to the vanity of man which we all believe by nature, until we are awakened from our pleasing dream by rough facts. The method of authority will always govern the mass of mankind; and those who wield the various forms of organized force in the state will never be convinced that dangerous reasoning ought not to be suppressed in some way. If liberty of speech is to be untrammeled from the grosser forms of constraint, then uniformity of opinion will be secured by a moral terrorism to which the respectability of society will give its thorough approval. Following the method of authority is the path of peace. Certain non-conformities are permitted; certain others (considered unsafe) are forbidden. These are different in different countries and in different ages; but, wherever you are, let it be known that you seriously hold a tabooed belief, and you may be perfectly sure of being treated with a cruelty less brutal but more refined than hunting you like a wolf. Thus, the greatest intellectual benefactors of mankind have never dared, and dare not now, to utter the whole of their thought; and thus a shade of *prima facie* doubt is cast upon every proposition which is considered essential to the security of society. Singularly enough, the persecution does not all come from without; but a man torments himself and is oftentimes most distressed at finding himself believing propositions which he has been brought up to regard with aversion. The peaceful and sympathetic man will, therefore, find it hard to resist the temptation to submit his opinions to authority. But most of

all I admire the method of tenacity for its strength, simplicity, and direct-
ness. Men who pursue it are distinguished for their decision of character,
which becomes very easy with such a mental rule. They do not waste time
in trying to make up their minds what they want, but, fastening like
lightning upon whatever alternative comes first, they hold to it to the end,
whatever happens, without an instant's irresolution. This is one of the
splendid qualities which generally accompany brilliant, unlasting success.
It is impossible not to envy the man who can dismiss reason, although we
know how it must turn out at last.

Such are the advantages which the other methods of settling opinion
have over scientific investigation. A man should consider well of them; and
then he should consider that, after all, he wishes his opinions to coincide
with the fact, and that there is no reason why the results of those three
first methods should do so. To bring about this effect is the prerogative of
the method of science. Upon such considerations he has to make his
choice—a choice which is far more than the adoption of any intellectual
opinion, which is one of the ruling decisions of his life, to which, when
once made, he is bound to adhere. The force of habit will sometimes
cause a man to hold on to old beliefs, after he is in a condition to see that
they have no sound basis. But reflection upon the state of the case will
overcome these habits, and he ought to allow reflection its full weight.
People sometimes shrink from doing this, having an idea that beliefs are
wholesome which they cannot help feeling rest on nothing. But let such
persons suppose an analogous though different case from their own. Let
them ask themselves what they would say to a reformed Mussulman who
should hesitate to give up his old notions in regard to the relations of the
sexes; or to a reformed Catholic who should still shrink from reading the
Bible. Would they not say that these persons ought to consider the matter
fully, and clearly understand the new doctrine, and then ought to embrace
it, in its entirety? But, above all, let it be considered that what is more
wholesome than any particular belief is integrity of belief, and that to
avoid looking into the support of any belief from a fear that it may turn
out rotten is quite as immoral as it is disadvantageous. The person who
confesses that there is such a thing as truth, which is distinguished from
falsehood simply by this, that if acted on it should, on full consideration,
carry us to the point we aim at and not astray, and then, though convinced of this, dares not know the truth and seeks to avoid it, is in a sorry
state of mind indeed.

Yes, the other methods do have their merits: a clear logical conscience
does cost something—just as any virtue, just as all that we cherish, costs
us dear. But we should not desire it to be otherwise. The genius of a

man's logical method should be loved and reverenced as his bride, whom he has chosen from all the world. He need not contemn the others; on the contrary, he may honor them deeply, and in doing so he only honors her the more. But she is the one that he has chosen, and he knows that he was right in making that choice. And having made it, he will work and fight for her, and will not complain that there are blows to take, hoping that there may be as many and as hard to give, and will strive to be the worthy knight and champion of her from the blaze of whose splendors he draws his inspiration and his courage.

*Herbert Feigl is Professor of Philosophy at
the University of Minnesota.*

Herbert Feigl

THE NATURE OF
THE SCIENTIFIC METHOD

What . . . are the basic characteristics of the scientific method? The
often alleged difficulties of an adequate definition of science seem to me
mainly a matter of terminology. We must first distinguish between pure
mathematics as an exclusively formal-conceptual discipline, and the
factual (or empirical, that is, the natural and the social-cultural) sciences.
The certainty, complete exactitude, and necessity of pure mathematics
depends precisely on its detachment from empirical fact. Mathematics as
applied in the factual sciences merely lends its forms and deductive structures to the contents furnished by experience. But no matter how predominant mathematics may be in the formulations and derivations of
empirical facts, factual knowledge cannot attain either the absolute precision or necessity of pure mathematics. The knowledge claimed in the
natural and the social sciences is a matter of successive approximations

Reprinted by permission of the publisher and author from *American Quarterly,
1* (1949), Copyright, 1949, Trustees of the University of Pennsylvania.

and of increasing degrees of confirmation. Warranted assertibility or probability is all that we can conceivably secure in the sciences that deal with the facts of experience. It is empirical science, thus conceived as an unending quest (its truth-claims to be held only "until further notice"), which is under consideration here. Science in this sense differs only in degree from the knowledge accumulated throughout the ages by sound and common sense.

The aims of science are description, explanation, and prediction. The first aim is basic and indispensable, the second and third (closely related to each other) arise as the most desirable fruits of scientific labors whenever inquiry rises beyond the mere fact-gathering stage. History, often and nowadays quite fashionably declared an art, is scientific to the extent that it ascertains its facts concerning past events by a meticulous scrutiny of present evidence. Causal interpretation of these facts (in history, but similarly also in psychology, sociology, cultural anthropology, and economics) is usually much more difficult than, but in principle not logically different from, causal interpretation (that is, explanation) in the natural sciences. The aims of the pure (empirical) sciences are then essentially the same throughout the whole field. What the scientists are seeking are descriptions, explanations, and predictions which are as adequate and accurate as possible in the given context of research.

The quest for scientific knowledge is therefore regulated by certain standards or criteria which may best be formulated in the form of ideals to be approximated, but perhaps never fully attained. The most important of these regulative ideals are:

1. *Intersubjective Testability.* This is only a more adequate formulation of what is generally meant by the "objectivity" of science. What is here involved is not only the freedom from personal or cultural bias or partiality, but—even more fundamentally—the requirement that the knowledge claims of science be in principle capable of test (confirmation or disconfirmation, at the least indirectly and to some degree) on the part of any person properly equipped with intelligence and the technical devices of observation or experimentation. The term *intersubjective* stresses the social nature of the scientific enterprise. If there be any "truths" that are accessible only to privileged individuals, such as mystics or visionaries— that is, knowledge-claims which by their very nature cannot independently be checked by anyone else—then such "truths" are not of the kind that we seek in the sciences. The criterion of intersubjective testability thus delimits the scientific from the nonscientific activities of man.

Religious ecstasy, the elations of love, the inspiration of the artist, yes, even the flash of insight on the part of a scientific genius are not in themselves scientific activities. All these processes may eventually become subject matter for scientific study. But in themselves they do not validate knowledge-claims. They may, as in the case of the scientific intuition (or empathy in the psychological-cultural field) be instrumental in the generation of knowledge claims. But it is these knowledge-claims which have to be, first, formulated in an intersubjectively intelligible (or communicable) manner, and, second, subjected to the appropriate kind of tests in order to ascertain their validity. Beliefs transcending all possible tests by observation, self-observation, experiment, measurement, or statistical analysis are recognized as theological or metaphysical and therefore devoid of the type of meaning that we all associate with the knowledge-claims of common sense or factual science. From the point of view of the scientific outlook in philosophy it may be suggested that the sort of significance with which the in-principle-unconfirmable assertions of transcendent theology and metaphysics impress so many people is largely emotive. The pictorial, emotional, and motivational appeals of language, no matter how indispensable or valuable in the contexts of practical life, art, education, persuasion, and propaganda, must, however, not be confused with the cognitive meanings (purely formal- and/or factual-empirical) that are of the essence of science. Each type of significance has its function, and in most uses of language both are combined or even fused. The only point stressed here is that they must not be *con*fused, that is, mistaken for one another, if we wish to be clear as to what we are about.

2. *Reliability, or a Sufficient Degree of Confirmation.* This second criterion of scientific knowledge enables us to distinguish what is generally called "mere opinion" (or worse still, "superstition") from knowledge (well-substantiated belief). It may be considered as the delimitation of the scientific from the unscientific knowledge-claims. Clearly, in contrast to the first criterion, we face here a distinction of degree. There is no sharp line of demarcation between the well-confirmed laws, theories, or hypotheses of science, and the only poorly substantiated hunches and ideas-on-trial which may ultimately either be included in the corpus of scientific knowledge or else rejected as unconfirmed. Truth-claims which we repudiate as "superstition," and, quite generally, as judgments based upon hasty generalization or weak analogy (if they fulfill the criterion of testability), differ from what we accept as "scientific truth" in the extremely low degree of probability to which they are supported by the available evidence. Astrology or alchemy, for example, are not factually meaningless, but they are considered false to fact in that all available evidence speaks overwhelmingly against them. Modern techniques of

experimentation and of statistical analysis are the most powerful tools we have in the discernment between chance and law and hence the best means of enhancing the reliability of knowledge.

3. *Definiteness and Precision.* This obvious standard of scientific method requires that the concepts used in the formulation of scientific knowledge-claims be as definitely delimited as possible. On the level of the qualitative-classificatory sciences this amounts to the attempt to reduce all border-zone vagueness to a minimum. On the level of quantitative science the exactitude of the concepts is enormously enhanced through the application of the techniques of measurement. The mensurational devices usually also increase the degree of objectivity. This is especially clear when they are contrasted with purely impressionistic ways of estimating magnitudes. Of course, there is no point in sharpening precision to a higher degree than the problem in hand requires. (You need no razor to cut butter.)

4. *Coherence or Systematic Structure.* This is what T. H. Huxley had in mind when he defined science as "organized common-sense." Not a mere collection of miscellaneous items of information, but a well-connected account of the facts is what we seek in science. On the descriptive level this results, for example, in systems of classification or division, in diagrams, statistical charts, and the like. On the explanatory levels of science sets of laws, or theoretical assumptions, are utilized. Explanation in science consists in the hypothetico-deductive procedure. The laws, theories, or hypotheses form the premises from which we derive logically, or logico-mathematically, the observed or observable facts. These facts, often belonging to heterogeneous domains, thus become integrated into a coherent, unifying structure. (Theological and metaphysical systems have, frequently enough, ambitiously tried to imitate this feature of science; but even if they succeeded in proceeding *more geometrico,* the important difference from science remains: they either lack testability or else reliability in the senses specified in our previous points.)

5. *Comprehensiveness or Scope of Knowledge.* This final point in our enumeration of criteria of science also characterizes scientific knowledge as different in degree (often enormously) from common-sense knowledge. Not only through bold and sweeping hypotheses, but especially through the ingenious devices by means of which they are tested, science acquires a reach far beyond the limits of our unaided senses. With telescopes, microscopes, spectroscopes, Geiger Counters, lie detectors, and the thousands of other contrivances of modern science we manage to amplify our senses and thus open up avenues of at least indirect access to the worlds of the very distant, the very large, the extremely small, or the disguised

and concealed. The resulting increase in the completeness of our knowledge is, of course, popularly the most impressive feature of science. It must be kept in mind, however, that the scope thus achieved is a product of hard labor, and not to be confused with the sham completeness metaphysicians procure for their world pictures by verbal magic. Instead of presenting a finished account of the world, the genuine scientist keeps his unifying hypotheses open to revision and is always ready to modify or abandon them if evidence should render them doubtful. This self-corrective aspect of science has rightly been stressed as its most important characteristic and must always be kept in mind when we refer to the comprehensiveness or the unification achieved by the scientific account of the universe. It is a sign of one's maturity to be able to live with an unfinished world view.

The foregoing outline of the criteria of science has been set down in a somewhat dogmatic tone. But this was done only for the sake of brevity.[1] The spirit behind it is that of a humble account of what, I think, an impartial and elaborate study of the history of thought from magic to science would reveal. In any case, these criteria seem unquestionably the guiding ideals of present-day empirical science. They may therefore be used in a definition of science as we understand this term today. It seems rather useless to speculate about just what this term, by a change of meaning, might come to connote in the future.

It should be remembered that the criteria listed characterize the *pure* factual (empirical) sciences. The aims of the *applied* sciences—the technologies, medicine, social and economic planning, and others—are practical control, production, guidance, therapy, reform, and so forth. Responsible activity in the application of science clearly presupposes information which is fairly well substantiated by the methods of the pure sciences. (These remarks intend to draw merely a logically important distinction. The obvious practical interpenetration and important mutual fertilization of the pure and the applied disciplines is of course not denied here.)

CRITIQUE OF MISCONCEPTIONS

Having indicated at least in broad outline the nature of scientific method we may now turn to the critique of some of the misconceptions to which

---

[1] A thorough discussion of the logical, epistemological, methodological, and historical issues connected with the criteria would require a whole book, not just another essay.

it is all too commonly exposed. In what follows, a dozen typical charges against science are stated and answered consecutively.[2]

Science arises exclusively out of practical and social needs and has its only value in serving them in turn. (Dialectical Materialism and Vocationalism)

While this is important it does not tell the whole story. Science has always also been the pursuit of knowledge, the satisfaction of a deep-rooted curiosity. It should be recognized as one of the cultural values along with art, literature, and music. Better teaching of the sciences and their history can redress the balance. Fuller utilization of results and suggestions from the history and the philosophy of science would give the student a deeper appreciation of the evolution of scientific knowledge and of the scientific point of view. Through proper instruction, the student could be led to rediscover some of the important results of science. The intellectual gratification that comes with a grasp of the order of nature, with the understanding of its processes by means of laws and theories, is one of the most powerful incentives in the pursuit of pure knowledge.

Science cannot furnish a secure basis for human affairs since it is unstable. It changes its views continually. (Traditionalism)

While there is constant evolution, and occasionally a revolution, in the scientific outlook, the charge is a superficial (usually journalistic) exaggeration. The typical progress of science reveals that later views often contain much of the earlier views (to the extent that these have stood the test of repeated examination). The more radical or revolutionary changes usually amount to a revision of the conceptual frame of a scientific discipline. The criticism often also presupposes other sources of certainty which will simply not bear critical scrutiny. The quest for absolute certainty is an immature, if not infantile, trait of thinking. The best knowledge we have can be established only by the method of trial and error. It is of the essence of science to make such knowledge as reliable as is humanly and technically possible.

Science rests on uncritical or uncriticized presuppositions. It validates its outlook by its own standards. It therefore begs the question as regards alternative approaches for settling problems of knowledge and action.

---

2 These charges are not straw men. In more than twenty years of reading, listening, teaching, and argument I have encountered them again and again in Europe and just as frequently in this country. If space permitted and time were less valuable, I could quote many well-known writers in connection with each charge.

Science has been clarifying and revising its basic assumptions throughout its development. Particularly since the beginning of the modern age and still more intensively since the beginning of our century, an increasing awareness of, and critical attitude toward, the fundamental presuppositions has been most fruitfully applied in the repudiation of dogmatic prejudices and in the articulation of the conceptual frame of scientific method. It can be shown (through logical analysis) that the procedure of science is the only one we are *certain* will yield the results (reliable knowledge, that is, valid explanation and predictions) *if* such results can at all be achieved. Any alleged rival method—theology, metaphysics, mysticism, intuition, dialectics—if it made any contributions at all could not be examined and appraised on any basis other than the usual inductive criteria of science. Generally, it seems that these alleged alternatives do not even aim primarily at knowledge but, like the arts, at the enrichment of experience. They may therefore more properly be said to be *non*-scientific, rather than *un*scientific.

Science distorts the facts of reality. In its Procrustean manner it introduces discontinuities where there is continuity (and vice versa). The abstractions and idealizations used in science can never do justice to the richness and complexities of experience.

Since the task of science is to discover reliable and precise knowledge of what happens under what conditions, it always tries to approximate the facts as closely as the problem on hand requires and permits. Both continuity and discontinuity can be formulated mathematically and be given an adequate formulation only with the help of modern mathematics.

Science can deal only with the measurable and therefore tends to "explain away" that which it cannot measure.

While measurement is eminently desirable in order to enhance the precision and objectivity of knowledge, it is not indispensable in many branches of science or, at least, on their more qualitative levels of analysis. Science does not explain away the qualities of experience. It aims at, and often succeeds in, making these qualities more predictable.

Science never explains, it merely describes the phenomena of experience. The reality beyond the appearances is also beyond the reach of science.

This is partly a terminological issue and partly a result of the (traditional but most misleading and useless) metaphysical distinction between appearance and reality. In the sense in which the word *explaining* is used in common life, science *does* explain facts—it deduces them from laws or theoretical assumptions. Questions which are in principle incapable of being answered by the scientific method turn out, on closer analysis, not to be questions of knowledge. They are expressions of emotional tensions or of the wish for soothing (or exciting) experience.

Science and the scientific attitude are incompatible with religion and the religious attitude.

If by religion one refers to an explanation of the universe and a derivation of moral norms from theological premises, then indeed there is logical incompatibility with the results, methods, and general outlook of science. But if religion means an attitude of sincere devotion to human values, such as justice, peace, relief from suffering, there is not only no conflict between religion and science but rather a need for mutual supplementation.

Science is responsible for the evils and maladjustments of our civilization. It is creating ever more powerful weapons of destruction. The employment of scientific techniques in the machine age has contributed to the misery, physical and mental, of the multitudes. Moreover, the biological facts of evolution imply the negation of all morality: the law of the jungle.

These are particularly superficial charges. It is the social-political-economic structure of a society that is responsible for these various evils. Scientific knowledge itself is socially and morally neutral. But the manner in which it is applied, whether for the benefit or to the detriment of humanity, depends entirely on ourselves. Scientists are becoming increasingly aware that they, even more than the average citizen, have to work for enlightenment toward the proper use of knowledge. The facts and theories of evolution have been construed in many ways as regards their implications for ethics. Julian Huxley reads them very differently from the way his grandfather Thomas Henry did.[3] It should be easy to see that the forces active on the level of human civilization and intelligent communal life are not completely reducible to those involved in the ruthless struggle for survival.

The ethical neutrality of scientific truth and the ivory tower situation of the pure researcher is apt to generate an attitude of indifference toward the pressing problems of humanity.

3 Compare Julian Huxley, *Touchstone for Ethics* (Harper, 1947); but see also C. D. Broad, "Review of Julian S. Huxley's Evolutionary Ethics" (*Mind, 53,* 1944), reprinted in H. Feigl and W. Sellars, *Readings in Philosophical Analysis* (Appleton-Century-Crofts, 1949).

Only maladjusted individuals are unable to combine the detachment necessary for the pursuit of truth with an ardent interest in the improvement of the condition of humanity.

Scientific method, while eminently successful in the explanation, prediction, and control of physical phenomena, is distinctly less successful in regard to the facts of organic life and almost altogether hopeless in the mental and social realm. The methods of the physical sciences are essentially mechanistic (if not materialistic) and therefore reductionistic; they cannot do justice to the complex organismic, teleological, and emergent features of life and mind.

"Scientism" as a slogan of criticism and reproach is very fashionable these days. It is true that some scientists and especially some of the popularizers of science have indulged in reductive fallacies of various sorts. But the true scientific spirit as exemplified in some of the foremost researchers is free from that impatience and simple-mindedness that tries to finish the unfinished business of science by hasty speculation. Admittedly, there are tremendous problems yet to be solved. On the other hand what method is there but the method of science to solve them? Explanations of the mechanistic type (in *one* sense of the term) have been abandoned even in physics. But mechanistic explanation in the wider sense of a search for law (deterministic or statistical) is still the indispensable procedure of all sciences that have gone beyond the purely classificatory level. Organic wholeness, teleology, and emergence can be understood, if at all, only by causal analysis on the usual empirical basis. Purposiveness and freedom of choice, far from being incompatible with causality, presuppose causal order.

The methods of science can never replace the intuitive insight or empathic understanding of the practical psychologist, psychiatrist, cultural anthropologist, or historian. This claim is made particularly wherever the object of knowledge is the individual, the unique and unrepeatable.

It is only through the scientific method that the validity and reliability of the intuitive approach can be gauged. There is, on this ground, some doubt as to its more exaggerated claims. However, there is nothing in the principles of scientific method that would deny the occasional, or even frequent, efficacy of intuitive judgments based, as they must be, on a rich (but often not articulated) background of experience in the given field. Aside from the mere artistic contemplation of the unique and individual, knowledge, in the proper sense of the word, always means the subsumption of the specific case under general concepts or laws. This holds in the social sciences just as much as in the natural sciences.

Science cannot determine values. Since scientific knowledge can (at best) find out only what is the case, it can, by its very nature, never tell what ought to be.

This final challenge often comes from theology or metaphysics. It usually maintains that questions of aims, goals, and ideals cannot be settled by the methods of science but rather require recourse either to divine revelation, the voice of conscience, or some metaphysical a priori truths. The answer to this in a scientific age would seem to be that a mature mankind should be able to determine its own value standards on the basis of its needs, wants, and the facts of the social condition of man. But it is true that science cannot dictate value standards. It can, as in social psychology, ascertain the actual evaluations of groups and individuals, study their compatibilities and incompatibilities, and recommend (that is *applied* science!) ways and means of harmonizing conflicting evaluations. True enough, in many of the urgent issues that confront us, we do not possess enough scientific knowledge to warrant a course of action. This means that we have to act, as so often in life, on the highest probabilities available even if these probabilities be low in themselves. But such estimates of probabilities will still be made most reliable by the scientific method. Common life experience and wisdom, when freed from its adherence to prescientific thought patterns, is not fundamentally different from scientific knowledge. In both we find the procedure of self-correction, so essentially needed if knowledge is to be a guide for action. There is an important common element in mature thinking (as we find it in science) and mature social action (as we find it in democracy): progress arises out of the peaceful competition of ideas as they are put to intersubjective test. Cooperative planning on the basis of the best and fullest knowledge available is the only path left to an awakened humanity that has embarked on the adventure of science and civilization.

SUGGESTIONS FOR FURTHER READING

BARKER, STEPHEN F., *The Elements of Logic*, New York: McGraw-Hill Book Company, 1965. A clear introduction to the techniques of traditional and modern logic.

DEWEY, JOHN, *The Quest for Certainty*, New York: G. P. Putnam's Sons, 1960. Paperback. A fascinating discussion of the aims and methods of philosophy.

HEMPEL, CARL G., *Philosophy of Natural Science*, Englewood Cliffs, N.J.: Prentice-Hall, Inc., 1966. Paperback. A superb discussion of the nature of scientific method.

PART II

FREE WILL

*Baron d'Holbach (1723–1789) was a leading figure
of the French Enlightenment.*

Baron d'Holbach

DETERMINISM

. . . In whatever manner man is considered, he is connected to universal
nature, and submitted to the necessary and immutable laws that she
imposes on all the beings she contains, according to their peccliar
essences or to the respective properties with which, without consulting
them, she endows each particular species. Man's life is a line that nature
commands him to describe upon the surface of the earth, without his
ever being able to swerve from it, even for an instant. He is born without
his own consent; his organization does in nowise depend upon himself; his
ideas come to him involuntarily; his habits are in the power of those who
cause him to contract them; he is unceasingly modified by causes,
whether visible or concealed, over which he has no control, which necessarily regulate his mode of existence, give the hue to his way of thinking,
and determine his manner of acting. He is good or bad, happy or miserable, wise or foolish, reasonable or irrational, without his will being for

---

Reprinted from *A System of Nature* (1770), trans. H. D. Robinson.

anything in these various states. Nevertheless, in spite of the shackles by which he is bound, it is pretended he is a free agent, or that independent of the causes by which he is moved, he determines his own will, and regulates his own condition.

However slender the foundation of this opinion, of which everything ought to point out to him the error, it is current at this day and passes for an incontestable truth with a great number of people, otherwise extremely enlightened; it is the basis of religion, which, supposing relations between man and the unknown being she has placed above nature, has been incapable of imagining how man could merit reward or deserve punishment from this being, if he was not a free agent. Society has been believed interested in this system; because an idea has gone abroad, that if all the actions of man were to be contemplated as necessary, the right of punishing those who injure their associates would no longer exist. At length human vanity accommodated itself to a hypothesis which, unquestionably, appears to distinguish man from all other physical beings, by assigning to him the special privilege of a total independence of all other causes, but of which a very little reflection would have shown him the impossibility. . . .

The will, as we have elsewhere said, is a modification of the brain, by which it is disposed to action, or prepared to give play to the organs. This will is necessarily determined by the qualities, good or bad, agreeable or painful, of the object or the motive that acts upon his senses, or of which the idea remains with him, and is resuscitated by his memory. In consequence, he acts necessarily, his action is the result of the impulse he receives either from the motive, from the object, or from the idea which has modified his brain, or disposed his will. When he does not act according to this impulse, it is because there comes some new cause, some new motive, some new idea, which modifies his brain in a different manner, gives him a new impulse, determines his will in another way, by which the action of the former impulse is suspended: thus, the sight of an agreeable object, or its idea, determines his will to set him in action to procure it; but if a new object or a new idea more powerfully attracts him, it gives a new direction to his will, annihilates the effect of the former, and prevents the action by which it was to be procured. This is the mode in which reflection, experience, reason, necessarily arrests or suspends the action of man's will: without this he would of necessity have followed the anterior impulse which carried him towards a then desirable object. In all this he always acts according to necessary laws from which he has no means of emancipating himself.

If when tormented with violent thirst, he figures to himself in idea, or really perceives a fountain, whose limpid streams might cool his feverish want, is he sufficient master of himself to desire or not to desire the object competent to satisfy so lively a want? It will no doubt be conceded, that it is impossible he should not be desirous to satisfy it; but it will be said—if at this moment it is announced to him that the water he so ardently desires is poisoned, he will, notwithstanding his vehement thirst, abstain from drinking it: and it has, therefore, been falsely concluded that he is a free agent. The fact, however, is, that the motive in either case is exactly the same: his own conservation. The same necessity that determined him to drink before he knew the water was deleterious upon this new discovery equally determined him not to drink; the desire of conserving himself either annihilates or suspends the former impulse; the second motive becomes stronger than the preceding, that is, the fear of death, or the desire of preserving himself, necessarily prevails over the painful sensation caused by his eagerness to drink: but, it will be said, if the thirst is very parching, an inconsiderate man without regarding the danger will risk swallowing the water. Nothing is gained by this remark: in this case, the anterior impulse only regains the ascendancy; he is persuaded that life may possibly be longer preserved, or that he shall derive a greater good by drinking the poisoned water than by enduring the torment, which, to his mind, threatens instant dissolution: thus the first becomes the strongest and necessarily urges him on to action. Nevertheless, in either case, whether he partakes of the water, or whether he does not, the two actions will be equally necessary; they will be the effect of that motive which finds itself most puissant; which consequently acts in the most coercive manner upon his will.

This example will serve to explain the whole phenomena of the human will. This will, or rather the brain, finds itself in the same situation as a bowl, which, although it has received an impulse that drives it forward in a straight line, is deranged in its course whenever a force superior to the first obliges it to change its direction. The man who drinks the poisoned water appears a madman; but the actions of fools are as necessary as those of the most prudent individuals. The motives that determine the voluptuary and the debauchee to risk their health, are as powerful, and their actions are as necessary, as those which decide the wise man to manage his. But, it will be insisted, the debauchee may be prevailed on to change his conduct: this does not imply that he is a free agent; but that motives may be found sufficiently powerful to annihilate the effect of those that previously acted upon him; then these new motives determine his will to the new mode of conduct he may adopt as necessarily as the former did to the old mode. . . .

The errors of philosophers on the free agency of man, have arisen from their regarding his will as the *primum mobile,* the original motive of his actions; for want of recurring back, they have not perceived the multiplied, the complicated causes which, independently of him, give motion to the will itself; or which dispose and modify his brain, whilst he himself is purely passive in the motion he receives. Is he the master of desiring or not desiring an object that appears desirable to him? Without doubt it will be answered, no: but he is the master of resisting his desire, if he reflects on the consequences. But, I ask, is he capable of reflecting on these consequences, when his soul is hurried along by a very lively passion, which entirely depends upon his natural organization, and the causes by which he is modified? Is it in his power to add to these consequences all the weight necessary to counterbalance his desire? Is he the master of preventing the qualities which render an object desirable from residing in it? I shall be told: he ought to have learned to resist his passions; to contract a habit of putting a curb on his desires. I agree to it without any difficulty. But in reply, I again ask, is his nature susceptible of this modification? Does his boiling blood, his unruly imagination, the igneous fluid that circulates in his veins, permit him to make, enable him to apply true experience in the moment when it is wanted? And even when his temperament has capacitated him, has his education, the examples set before him, the ideas with which he has been inspired in early life, been suitable to make him contract this habit of repressing his desires? Have not all these things rather contributed to induce him to seek with avidity, to make him actually desire those objects which you say he ought to resist?

The *ambitious man* cries out: you will have me resist my passion; but have they not unceasingly repeated to me that rank, honours, power, are the most desirable advantages in life? Have I not seen my fellow citizens envy them, the nobles of my country sacrifice every thing to obtain them? In the society in which I live, am I not obliged to feel, that if I am deprived of these advantages, I must expect to languish in contempt; to cringe under the rod of oppression?

The *miser* says: you forbid me to love money, to seek after the means of acquiring it: alas! does not every thing tell me that, in this world, money is the greatest blessing; that it is amply sufficient to render me happy? In the country I inhabit, do I not see all my fellow citizens covetous of riches? but do I not also witness that they are little scrupulous in the means of obtaining wealth? As soon as they are enriched by the means which you censure, are they not cherished, considered and respected? By what authority, then, do you defend me from amassing treasure? What right have you to prevent my using means, which, although you call them sordid and criminal, I see approved by the sovereign? Will you have me renounce my happiness?

The *voluptuary* argues: you pretend that I should resist my desires; but was I the maker of my own temperament, which unceasingly invites me to pleasure? You call my pleasures disgraceful; but in the country in which I live, do I not witness the most dissipated men enjoying the most distinguished rank? Do I not behold that no one is ashamed of adultery but the husband it has outraged? Do not I see men making trophies of their debaucheries, boasting of their libertinism, rewarded with applause?

The *choleric man* vociferates: you advise me to put a curb on my passions, and to resist the desire of avenging myself: but can I conquer my nature? Can I alter the received opinions of the world? Shall I not be forever disgraced, infallibly dishonoured in society, if I do not wash out in the blood of my fellow creatures the injuries I have received?

The *zealous enthusiast* exclaims: you recommend me mildness; you advise me to be tolerant; to be indulgent to the opinions of my fellow men; but is not my temperament violent? Do I not ardently love my God? Do they not assure me, that zeal is pleasing to him; that sanguinary inhuman persecutors have been his friends? As I wish to render myself acceptable in his sight, I therefore adopt the same means.

In short, the actions of man are never free; they are always the necessary consequence of his temperament, of the received ideas, and of the notions, either true or false, which he has formed to himself of happiness; of his opinions, strengthened by example, by education, and by daily experience. So many crimes are witnessed on the earth only because every thing conspires to render man vicious and criminal; the religion he has adopted, his government, his education, the examples set before him, irresistibly drive him on to evil: under these circumstances, morality preaches virtue to him in vain. In those societies where vice is esteemed, where crime is crowned, where venality is constantly recompensed, where the most dreadful disorders are punished only in those who are too weak to enjoy the privilege of committing them with impunity, the practice of virtue is considered nothing more than a painful sacrifice of happiness. Such societies chastise, in the lower orders, those excesses which they respect in the higher ranks; and frequently have the injustice to condemn those in the penalty of death, whom public prejudices, maintained by constant example, have rendered criminal.

Man, then, is not a free agent in any one instant of his life; he is necessarily guided in each step by those advantages, whether real or fictitious, that he attaches to the objects by which his passions are roused these passions themselves are necessary in a being who unceasingly tends towards his own happiness; their energy is necessary, since that depends on his temperament; his temperament is necessary, because it depends on the physical elements which enter into his composition; the modification of this temperament is necessary, as it is the infallible and inevitable consequence of the impulse he receives from the incessant action of moral and physical beings.

In spite of these proofs of the want of free agency in man, so clear to unprejudiced minds, it will, perhaps be insisted upon with no small feeling of triumph, that if it be proposed to any one, to move or not to move his hand, an action in the number of those called indifferent, he evidently appears to be the master of choosing; from which it is concluded that evidence has been offered of free agency. The reply is, this example is perfectly simple; man in performing some action which he is resolved on doing, does not by any means prove his free agency: the very desire of displaying this quality, excited by the dispute, becomes a necessary motive, which decides his will either for the one or the other of these actions: What deludes him in this instance, or that which persuades him he is a free agent at this moment, is, that he does not discern the true motive which sets him in action, namely, the desire of convincing his opponent: if in the heat of the dispute he insists and asks, "Am I not the master of throwing myself out of the window?" I shall answer him, no; that whilst he preserves his reason there is no probability that the desire of proving his free agency, will become a motive sufficiently powerful to make him sacrifice his life to the attempt: if, notwithstanding this, to prove he is a free agent, he should actually precipitate himself from the window, it would not be a sufficient warranty to conclude he acted freely, but rather that it was the violence of his temperament which spurred him on to this folly. Madness is a state, that depends upon the heat of the blood, not upon the will. A fanatic or a hero braves death as necessarily as a more phlegmatic man or coward flies from it.

There is, in point of fact, no difference between the man that is cast out of the window by another, and the man who throws himself out of it, except that the impulse in the first instance comes immediately from without whilst that which determines the fall in the second case, springs from within his own peculiar machine, having its more remote cause also exterior. When Mutius Scaevola held his hand in the fire, he was as much acting under the influence of necessity (caused by interior motives) that urged him to this strange action, as if his arm had been held by strong men: pride, despair, the desire of braving his enemy, a wish to astonish him, and anxiety to intimidate him, etc., were the invisible chains that held his hand bound to the fire. The love of glory, enthusiasm for their country, in like manner caused Codrus and Decius to devote themselves for their fellow-citizens. The Indian Colanus and the philosopher Peregrinus were equally obliged to burn themselves, by desire of exciting the astonishment of the Grecian assembly.

It is said that free agency is the absence of those obstacles competent to oppose themselves to the actions of man, or to the exercise of his faculties: it is pretended that he is a free agent whenever, making use of these faculties, he produces the effect he has proposed to himself. In reply to this reasoning, it is sufficient to consider that it in nowise depends upon himself to place or remove the obstacles that either determine or resist him; the motive that causes his action is no more in his own power than the obstacle that impedes him, whether this obstacle or motive be within his own machine or exterior of his person: he is not master of the thought presented to his mind, which determines his will; this thought is excited by some cause independent of himself.

To be undeceived on the system of his free agency, man has simply to recur to the motive by which his will is determined; he will always find this motive is out of his own control. It is said: that in consequence of an idea to which the mind gives birth, man acts freely if he encounters no obstacle. But the question is, what gives birth to this idea in his brain? was he the master either to prevent it from presenting itself, or from renewing itself in his brain? Does not this idea depend either upon objects that strike him exteriorly and in despite of himself, or upon causes, that without his knowledge, act within himself and modify his brain? Can he prevent his eyes, cast without design upon any object whatever, from giving him an idea of this object, and from moving his brain? He is not more master of the obstacles; they are the necessary effects of either interior or exterior causes, which always act according to their given properties. A man insults a coward; this necessarily irritates him against his insulter; but his will cannot vanquish the obstacle that cowardice places to the object of his desire, because his natural conformation, which does not depend upon himself, prevents his having courage. In this case, the coward is insulted in spite of himself; and against his will is obliged patiently to brook the insult he has received.

The partisans of the system of free agency appear ever to have confounded constraint with necessity. Man believes he acts as a free agent, every time he does not see any thing that places obstacles to his actions; he does not perceive that the motive which causes him to will, is always necessary and independent of himself. A prisoner loaded with chains is compelled to remain in prison; but he is not a free agent in the desire to emancipate himself; his chains prevent him from acting, but they do not prevent him from willing; he would save himself if they would loose his fetters; but he would not save himself as a free agent; fear or the idea of punishment would be sufficient motives for his action.

Man may, therefore, cease to be restrained, without, for that reason, becoming a free agent: in whatever manner he acts, he will act necessarily, according to motives by which he shall be determined. He may be compared to a heavy body that finds itself arrested in its descent by any obstacle whatever: take away this obstacle, it will gravitate or continue to fall; but who shall say this dense body is free to fall or not? Is not its descent the necessary effect of its own specific gravity? The virtuous Socrates submitted to the laws of his country, although they were unjust; and though the doors of his jail were left open to him, he would not save himself; but in this he did not act as a free agent: the invisible chains of opinion, the secret love of decorum, the inward respect for the laws, even when they were iniquitous, the fear of tarnishing his glory, kept him in his prison; they were motives sufficiently powerful with this enthusiast for virtue, to induce him to wait death with tranquility; it was not in his power to save himself, because he could find no potential motive to bring him to depart, even for an instant, from those principles to which his mind was accustomed.

Man, it is said, frequently acts against his inclination, from whence it is falsely concluded he is a free agent; but when he appears to act contrary to his inclination, he is always determined to it by some motive sufficiently efficacious to vanquish this inclination. A sick man, with a veiw to his cure, arrives at conquering his repugnance to the most disgusting remedies: the fear of pain, or the dread of death, then become necessary motives; consequently this sick man cannot be said to act freely.

When it is said, that man is not a free agent, it is not pretended to compare him to a body moved by a simple impulsive cause: he contains within himself causes inherent to his existence; he is moved by an interior organ, which has its own peculiar laws, and is itself necessarily determined in consequence of ideas formed from perception resulting from sensation which it receives from exterior objects. As the mechanism of these sensations, of these perceptions, and the manner they engrave ideas on the brain of man, are not known to him; because he is unable to unravel all these motions; because he cannot perceive the chain of operations in his soul, or the motive principle that acts within him, he supposes himself a free agent; which literally translated, signifies, that he moves himself by himself; that he determines himself without cause: when he rather ought to say, that he is ignorant how or why he acts in the manner he does. It is true the soul enjoys an activity peculiar to itself: but it is equally certain that this activity would never be displayed, if some motive or some cause did not put it in a condition to exercise itself: at least it will not be pretended that the soul is able either to love or to hate without being moved, without knowing the objects, without having some idea of their qualities. Gunpowder has unquestionably a particular activity, but this activity will never display itself, unless fire be applied to it; this, however, immediately sets it in motion.

It is the great complication of motion in man, it is the variety of his action, it is the multiplicity of causes that move him, whether simultaneously or in continual succession, that persuades him he is a free agent: if all his motions were simple, if the causes that move him did not confound themselves with each other, if they were distinct, if his machine were less complicated, he would perceive that all his actions were necessary, because he would be enabled to recur instantly to the cause that made him act. A man who should be always obliged to go towards the west, would always go on that side; but he would feel that, in so going, he was not a free agent: if he had another sense, as his actions or his motion, augmented by a sixth, would be still more varied and much more complicated, he would believe himself still more a free agent than he does with his five senses.

It is, then, for want of recurring to the causes that move him; for want of being able to analyze, from not being competent to decompose the complicated motion of his machine, that man believes himself a free agent: it is only upon his own ignorance that he founds the profound yet deceitful notion he has of his free agency; that he builds those opinions which he brings forward as a striking proof of his pretended freedom of action. If, for a short time, each man was willing to examine his own peculiar actions, search out their true motives to discover their concatenation, he would remain convinced that the sentiment he has of his natural free agency, is a chimera that must speedily be destroyed by experience.

Nevertheless it must be acknowledged that the multiplicity and diversity of the causes which continually act upon man, frequently without even his knowledge, render it impossible, or at least extremely difficult for him to recur to the true principles of his own peculiar actions, much less the actions of others: they frequently depend upon causes so fugitive, so remote from their effects, and which, superficially examined, appear to have so little analogy, so slender a relation with them, that it requires singular sagacity to bring them into light. This is what renders the study of the moral man a task of such difficulty; this is the reason why his heart is an abyss, of which it is frequently impossible for him to fathom the depth. . . .

If he understood the play of his organs, if he were able to recall to himself all the impulsions they have received, all the modifications they have undergone, all the effects they have produced, he would perceive that all his actions are submitted to that fatality, which regulates his own particular system, as it does the entire system of the universe: no one effect in him, any more than in nature, produces itself by chance; this, as has been before proved, is word void of sense. All that passes in him; all that is done by him; as well as all that happens in nature, or that is attributed to her, is derived from necessary causes, which act according to necessary laws, and which produce necessary effects from whence necessarily flow others.

Fatality is the eternal, the immutable, the necessary order, established in nature; or the indispensable connexion of causes that act, with the effects they operate. Conforming to this order, heavy bodies fall: light bodies rise; that which is analogous in matter reciprocally attracts; that which is heterogeneous mutually repels; man congregates himself in society, modifies each his fellow; becomes either virtuous or wicked; either contributes to his mutual happiness, or reciprocates his misery; either loves his neighbour, or hates his companion necessarily, according to the manner in which the one acts upon the other. From whence it may be seen, that the same necessity which regulates the physical, also regulates the moral world, in which every thing is in consequence submitted to fatality. Man, in running over, frequently without his own knowledge, often in spite of himself, the route which nature has marked out for him, resembles a swimmer who is obliged to follow the current that carries him along: he believes himself a free agent, because he sometimes consents, sometimes does not consent, to glide with the stream, which, notwithstanding, always hurries him forward; he believes himself the master of his condition, because he is obliged to use his arms under the fear of sinking. . . .

A. J. Ayer is Wykeham Professor of
Logic at the University of Oxford.

A. J. Ayer

FREEDOM AND NECESSITY

When I am said to have done something of my own free will it is implied
that I could have acted otherwise; and it is only when it is believed that I
could have acted otherwise that I am held to be morally responsible for
what I have done. For a man is not thought to be morally responsible for
an action that it was not in his power to avoid. But if human behaviour is
entirely governed by causal laws, it is not clear how any action that is
done could ever have been avoided. It may be said of the agent tht he
would have acted otherwise if the causes of his action had been different,
but they being what they were, it seems to follow that he was bound to
act as he did. Now it is commonly assumed both that men are capable of
acting freely, in the sense that is required to make them morally responsible, and that human behaviour is entirely governed by causal laws: and

Reprinted from *Philosophical Essays* (1954) by A. J. Ayer, by permission of
Macmillan & Co., Ltd., London; The Macmillan Company of Canada Limited;
and St. Martin's Press, Inc.

it is the apparent conflict between these two assumptions that gives rise to the philosophical problem of the freedom of the will.

Confronted with this problem, many people will be inclined to agree with Dr. Johnson: 'Sir, we *know* our will is free, and *there's* an end on't'. But, while this does very well for those who accept Dr. Johnson's premiss, it would hardly convince anyone who denied the freedom of the will. Certainly, if we do know that our wills are free, it follows that they are so. But the logical reply to this might be that since our wills are not free, it follows that no one can know that they are: so that if anyone claims, like Dr. Johnson, to know that they are, he must be mistaken. What is evident, indeed, is that people often believe themselves to be acting freely; and it is to this "feeling" of freedom that some philosophers appeal when they wish, in the supposed interests of morality, to prove that not all human action is causally determined. But if these philosophers are right in their assumption that a man cannot be acting freely if his action is causally determined, then the fact that someone feels free to do, or not to do, a certain action does not prove that he really is so. It may prove that the agent does not himself know what it is that makes him act in one way rather than another: but from the fact that a man is unaware of the causes of his action, it does not follow that no such causes exist.

So much may be allowed to the determinist; but his belief that all human actions are subservient to causal laws still remains to be justified. If, indeed, it is necessary that every event should have a cause, then the rule must apply to human behaviour as much as to anything else. But why should it be supposed that every event must have a cause? The contrary is not unthinkable. Nor is the law of universal causation a necessary presupposition of scientific thought. The scientist may try to discover causal laws, and in many cases he succeeds; but sometimes he has to be content with statistical laws, and sometimes he comes upon events which, in the present state of his knowledge, he is not able to subsume under any law at all. In the case of these events he assumes that if he knew more he would be able to discover some law, whether causal or statistical, which would enable him to account for them. And this assumption cannot be disproved. For however far he may have carried his investigation, it is always open to him to carry it further; and it is always conceivable that if he carried it further he would discover the connection which had hitherto escaped him. Nevertheless, it is also conceivable that the events with which he is concerned are not systematically connected with any others: so that the reason why he does not discover the sort of laws that he requires is simply that they do not obtain.

Now in the case of human conduct the search for explanations has not in fact been altogether fruitless. Certain scientific laws have been established; and with the help of these laws we do make a number of successful predictions about the ways in which different people will behave. But these predictions do not always cover every detail. We may be able to predict that in certain circumstances a particular man will be angry, without being able to prescribe the precise form that the expression of his anger will take. We may be reasonably sure that he will shout, but not sure how loud his shout will be, or exactly what words he will use. And it is only a small proportion of human actions that we are able to forecast even so precisely as this. But that, it may be said, is because we have not carried our investigations very far. The science of psychology is still in its infancy and, as it is developed, not only will more human actions be explained, but the explanations will go into greater detail. The ideal of complete explanation may never in fact be attained: but it is theoretically attainable. Well, this may be so: and certainly it is impossible to show *a priori* that it is not so: but equally it cannot be shown that it is. This will not, however, discourage the scientist who, in the field of human behaviour, as elsewhere, will continue to formulate theories and test them by the facts. And in this he is justified. For since he has no reason *a priori* to admit that there is a limit to what he can discover, the fact that he also cannot be sure that there is no limit does not make it unreasonable for him to devise theories, nor, having devised them, to try constantly to improve them.

But now suppose it to be claimed that, so far as men's actions are concerned, there is a limit: and that this limit is set by the fact of human freedom. An obvious objection is that in many cases in which a person feels himself to be free to do, or not to do, a certain action, we are even now able to explain, in causal terms, why it is that he acts as he does. But it might be argued that even if men are sometimes mistaken in believing that they act freely, it does not follow that they are always so mistaken. For it is not always the case that when a man believes that he has acted freely we are in fact able to account for his action in causal terms. A determinist would say that we should be able to account for it if we had more knowledge of the circumstances, and had been able to discover the appropriate natural laws. But until those discoveries have been made, this remains only a pious hope. And may it not be true that, in some cases at least, the reason why we can give no causal explanation is that no causal explanation is available; and that this is because the agent's choice was literally free, as he himself felt it to be?

The answer is that this may indeed be true, inasmuch as it is open to anyone to hold that no explanation is possible until some explanation is actually found. But even so it does not give the moralist what he wants. For he is anxious to show that men are capable of acting freely in order to infer that they can be morally responsible for what they do. But if it is a matter of pure chance that a man should act in one way rather than another, he may be free but he can hardly be responsible. And indeed when a man's actions seem to us quite unpredictable, when, as we say, there is no knowing what he will do, we do not look upon him as a moral agent. We look upon him rather as a lunatic.

To this it may be objected that we are not dealing fairly with the moralist. For when he makes it a condition of my being morally responsible that I should act freely, he does not wish to imply that it is purely a matter of chance that I act as I do. What he wishes to imply is that my actions are the result of my own free choice: and it is because they are the result of my own free choice that I am held to be morally responsible for them.

But now we must ask how it is that I come to make my choice. Either it is an accident that I choose to act as I do or it is not. If it is an accident, then it is merely a matter of chance that I did not choose otherwise; and if it is merely a matter of chance that I did not choose otherwise, it is surely irrational to hold me morally responsible for choosing as I did. But if it is not an accident that I choose to do one thing rather than another, then presumably there is some causal explanation of my choice: and in that case we are led back to determinism.

Again, the objection may be raised that we are not doing justice to the moralist's case. His view is not that it is a matter of chance that I choose to act as I do, but rather that my choice depends upon my character. Nevertheless he holds that I can still be free in the sense that he requires; for it is I who am responsible for my character. But in what way am I responsible for my character? Only, surely, in the sense that there is a causal connection between what I do now and what I have done in the past. It is only this that justifies the statement that I have made myself what I am: and even so this is an over-simplification, since it takes no account of the external influences to which I have been subjected. But, ignoring the external influences, let us assume that it is in fact the case that I have made myself what I am. Then it is still legitimate to ask how it is that I have come to make myself one sort of person rather than another. And if it be answered that it is a matter of my strength of will, we can put the same question in another form by asking how it is that my will has the strength that it has and not some other degree of strength. Once more, either it is an accident or it is not. If it is an accident, then by the same argument as before, I am not morally responsible, and if it is not an accident we are led back to determinism.

Furthermore, to say that my actions proceed from my character or, more colloquially, that I act in character, is to say that my behaviour is consistent and to that extent predictable: and since it is, above all, for the actions that I perform in character that I am held to be morally responsible, it looks as if the admission of moral responsibility, so far from being incompatible with determinism, tends rather to presuppose it. But how can this be so if it is a necessary condition of moral responsibility that the person who is held responsible should have acted freely? It seems that if we are to retain this idea of moral responsibility, we must either show that men can be held responsible for actions which they do not do freely, or else find some way of reconciling determinism with the freedom of the will.

It is no doubt with the object of effecting this reconcilation that some philosophers have defined freedom as the consciousness of necessity. And by so doing they are able to say not only that a man can be acting freely when his action is causally determined, but even that his action must be causally determined for it to be possible for him to be acting freely. Nevertheless this definition has the serious disadvantage that it gives to the word 'freedom' a meaning quite different from any that it ordinarily bears. It is indeed obvious that if we are allowed to give the word 'freedom' any meaning that we please, we can find a meaning that will reconcile it with determinism: but this is no more a solution of our present problem than the fact that the word 'horse' could be arbitrarily used to mean what is ordinarily meant by 'sparrow' is a proof that horses have wings. For suppose that I am compelled by another person to do something 'against my will'. In that case, as the word 'freedom' is ordinarily used, I should not be said to be acting freely: and the fact that I am fully aware of the constraint to which I am subjected makes no difference to the matter. I do not become free by becoming conscious that I am not. It may, indeed, be possible to show that my being aware that my action is causally determined is not incompatible with my acting freely: but it by no means follows that it is in this that my freedom consists. Moreover, I suspect that one of the reasons why people are inclined to define freedom as the consciousness of necessity is that they think that if one is conscious of necessity one may somehow be able to master it. But this is a fallacy. It is like someone's saying that he wishes he could see into the future, because if he did he would know what calamities lay in wait for him and so would be able to avoid them. But if he avoids the calamities then they don't lie in the future and it is not true that he foresees them. And similarly if I am able to master necessity, in the sense of escaping the operation of a necessary law, then the law in question is not necessary. And if the law is not necessary, then neither my freedom nor anything else can consist in my knowing that it is.

Let it be granted, then, that when we speak of reconciling freedom with determinism we are using the word 'freedom' in an ordinary sense. It still remains for us to make this usage clear: and perhaps the best way to make it clear is to show what it is that freedom, in this sense, is contrasted with. Now we began with the assumption that freedom is contrasted with causality: so that a man cannot be said to be acting freely if his action is causally determined. But this assumption has led us into difficulties and I now wish to suggest that it is mistaken. For it is not, I think, causality that freedom is to be contrasted with, but constraint. And while it is true that being constrained to do an action entails being caused to do it, I shall try to show that the converse does not hold. I shall try to show that from the fact that my action is causally determined it does not necessarily follow that I am constrained to do it: and this is equivalent to saying that it does not necessarily follow that I am not free.

If I am constrained, I do not act freely. But in what circumstances can I legitimately be said to be constrained? An obvious instance is the case in which I am compelled by another person to do what he wants. In a case of this sort the compulsion need not be such as to deprive one of the power of choice. It is not required that the other person should have hypnotized me, or that he should make it physically impossible for me to go against his will. It is enough that he should induce me to do what he wants by making it clear to me that, if I do not, he will bring about some situation that I regard as even more undesirable than the consequences of the action that he wishes me to do. Thus, if the man points a pistol at my head I may still choose to disobey him: but this does not prevent its being true that if I do fall in with his wishes he can legitimately be said to have compelled me. And if the circumstances are such that no reasonable person would be expected to choose the other alternative, then the action that I am made to do is not one for which I am held to be morally responsible.

A similar, but still somewhat different, case is that in which another person has obtained an habitual ascendancy over me. Where this is so, there may be no question of my being induced to act as the other person wishes by being confronted with a still more disagreeable alternative: for if I am sufficiently under his influence this special stimulus will not be necessary. Nevertheless I do not act freely, for the reason that I have been deprived of the power of choice. And this means that I have acquired so strong a habit of obedience that I no longer go through any process of deciding whether or not to do what the other person wants. About other matters I may still deliberate; but as regards the fulfilment of this other person's wishes, my own deliberations have ceased to be a causal factor in my behaviour. And it is in this sense that I may be said to be constrained.

It is not, however, necessary that such constraint should take the form of subservience to another person. A kleptomaniac is not a free agent, in respect of his stealing, because he does not go through any process of deciding whether or not to steal. Or rather, if he does go through such a process, it is irrelevant to his behaviour. Whatever he resolved to do, he would steal all the same. And it is this that distinguishes him from the ordinary thief.

But now it may be asked whether there is any essential difference between these cases and those in which the agent is commonly thought to be free. No doubt the ordinary thief does go through a process of deciding whether or not to steal, and no doubt it does affect his behaviour. If he resolved to refrain from stealing, he could carry his resolution out. But if it be allowed that his making or not making this resolution is causally determined, then how can he be any more free than the kleptomaniac? It may be true that unlike the kleptomaniac he could refrain from stealing if he chose: but if there is a cause, or set of causes, which necessitate his choosing as he does, how can he be said to have the powr of choice? Again, it may be true that no one now compels me to get up and walk across the room: but if my doing so can be causally explained in terms of my history or my environment, or whatever it may be, then how am I any more free than if some other person had compelled me? I do not have the feeling of constraint that I have when a pistol is manifestly pointed at my head but the chains of causation by which I am bound are no less effective for being invisible.

The answer to this is that the cases I have mentioned as examples of constraint do differ from the others: and they differ just in the ways that I have tried to bring out. If I suffered from a compulsion neurosis, so that I got up and walked across the room, whether I wanted to or not, or if I did so because somebody else compelled me, then I should not be acting freely. But if I do it now, I shall be acting freely, just because these conditions do not obtain; and the fact that my action may nevertheless have a cause is, from this point of view, irrelevant. For it is not when my action has any cause at all, but only when it has a special sort of cause, that it is reckoned not to be free.

But here it may be objected that, even if this distinction corresponds to ordinary usage, it is still very irrational. For why should we distinguish, with regard to a person's freedom, between the operations of one sort of cause and those of another? Do not all causes equally necessitate? And is it not therefore arbitrary to say that a person is free when he is necessitated in one fashion but not when he is necessitated in another?

That all causes equally necessitate is indeed a tautology, if the word 'necessitate' is taken merely as equivalent to 'cause': but if, as the objection requires, it is taken as equivalent to 'constrain' or 'compel', then I do not think that this proposition is true. For all that is needed for one event to be the cause of another is that, in the given circumstances, the event which is said to be the effect would not have occurred if it had not been for the occurrence of the event which is said to be the cause, or *vice versa,* according as causes are interpreted as necessary, or sufficient, conditions: and this fact is usually deducible from some causal law which states that whenever an event of the one kind occurs then, given suitable conditions, an event of the other kind will occur in a certain temporal or spatio-temporal relationship to it. In short, there is an invariable concomitance between the two classes of events; but there is no compulsion, in any but a metaphorical sense. Suppose, for example, that a psychoanalyst is able to account for some aspect of my behaviour by referring it to some lesion that I suffered in my childhood. In that case, it may be said that my childhood experience, together with certain other events, necessitates my behaving as I do. But all that this involves is that it is found to be true in general that when people have had certain experiences as children, they subsequently behave in certain specifiable ways; and my case is just another instance of this general law. It is in this way indeed that my behaviour is explained. But from the fact that my behaviour is capable of being explained, in the sense that it can be subsumed under some natural law, it does not follow that I am acting under constraint.

If this is correct, to say that I could have acted otherwise is to say, first, that I should have acted otherwise if I had so chosen; secondly, that my action was voluntary in the sense in which the actions, say, of the kleptomaniac are not; and thirdly, that nobody compelled me to choose as I did: and these three conditions may very well be fulfilled. When they are fulfilled, I may be said to have acted freely. But this is not to say that it was a matter of chance that I acted as I did, or, in other words, that my action could not be explained. And that my actions should be capable of being explained is all that is required by the postulate of determinism.

If more than this seems to be required it is, I think, because the use of the very word 'determinism' is in some degree misleading. For it tends to suggest that one event is somehow in the power of another, whereas the truth is merely that they are factually correlated. And the same applies to the use, in this context, of the word 'necessity' and even of the word 'cause' itself. Moreover, there are various reasons for this. One is the tendency to confuse causal with logical necessitation, and so to infer mistakenly that the effect is contained in the cause. Another is the uncritical use of a concept of force which is derived from primitive experiences of pushing and striking. A third is the survival of an animistic conception of causality, in which all causal relationships are modelled on the example of one person's exercising authority over another. As a result we tend to form an imaginative picture of an unhappy effect trying vainly to escape from the clutches of an overmastering cause. But, I repeat, the fact is simply that when an event of one type occurs, an event of another type occurs also, in a certain temporal or spatio-temporal relation to the first. The rest is only metaphor. And it is because of the metaphor, and not because of the fact, that we come to think that there is an antithesis between causality and freedom.

Nevertheless, it may be said, if the postulate of determinism is valid, then the future can be explained in terms of the past: and this means that if one knew enough about the past one would be able to predict the future. But in that case what will happen in the future is already decided. And how then can I be said to be free? What is going to happen is going to happen and nothing that I do can prevent it. If the determinist is right, I am the helpless prisoner of fate.

But what is meant by saying that the future course of events is already decided? If the implication is that some person has arranged it, then the proposition is false. But if all that is meant is that it is possible, in principle, to deduce it from a set of particular facts about the past, together with the appropriate general laws, then, even if this is true, it does not in the least entail that I am the helpless prisoner of fate. It does not even entail that my actions make no difference to the future: for they are causes as well as effects; so that if they were different their consequences would be different also. What it does entail is that my behaviour can be predicted: but to say that my behaviour can be predicted is not to say that I am acting under constraint. It is indeed true that I cannot escape my destiny if this is taken to mean no more than that I shall do what I shall do. But this is a tautology, just as it is a tautology that what is going to happen is going to happen. And such tautologies as these prove nothing whatsoever about the freedom of the will.

*John Hospers is Professor of Philosophy at
the University of Southern California.*

John Hospers

FREE WILL AND
PSYCHOANALYSIS

O Thou, who didst with pitfall and with gin
Beset the Road I was to wander in,
   Thou wilt not with Predestined Evil round
Enmesh, and then impute my Fall to Sin!
     —Edward FitzGerald, *The Rubaiyat of Omar Khayyam.*

. . . It is extremely common for nonprofessional philosophers and
iconoclasts to deny that human freedom exists, but at the same time to
have no clear idea of what it is that they are denying to exist. The first
thing that needs to be said about the free-will issue is that any meaningful
term must have a meaningful opposite: if it is meaningful to assert that
people are not free, it must be equally meaningful to assert that people *are*
free, whether this latter assertion is in fact true or not. Whether it is true,
of course, will depend on the meaning that is given the weasel-word

Reprinted from *Philosophy and Phenomenological Research, 10* (1949), by
permission of *Philosophy and Phenomenological Research* and the author.

"free." For example, if freedom is made dependent on indeterminism, it may well be that human freedom is nonexistent. But there seem to be no good grounds for asserting such a dependence, especially since lack of causation is the furthest thing from people's minds when they call an act free. Doubtless there are other senses that can be given to the word "free"—such as "able to do anything we want to do"—in which no human beings are free. But the first essential point about which the denier of freedom must be clear is *what* it is that he is denying. If one knows what it is like for people not to be free, one must know what it *would* be like for them to *be* free.

Philosophers have advanced numerous senses of "free" in which countless acts performed by human beings can truly be called free acts. The most common conception of a free act is that according to which an act is free if and only if it is a *voluntary* act. But the word "voluntary" does not always carry the same meaning. Sometimes to call an act voluntary means that we can do the act *if* we choose to do it: in other words, that it is physically and psychologically possible for us to do it, so that the occurrence of the act follows upon the decision to do it. (One's decision to raise his arm is in fact followed by the actual raising of his arm, unless he is a paralytic; one's decision to pluck the moon from the sky is not followed by the actual event.) Sometimes a voluntary act is conceived (as by Moore[1]) as an act which would not have occurred if, just beforehand, the agent had chosen not to perform it. But these senses are different from the sense in which a voluntary act is an act resulting from *deliberation,* or perhaps merely from *choice.* For example, there are many acts which we could have avoided, if we had chosen to do so, but which we nevertheless did not *choose* to perform, much less *deliberate* about them. The act of raising one's leg in the process of taking a step while out for a walk, is one which a person could have avoided by choosing to, but which, after one has learned to walk, takes place automatically or semi-automatically through habit, and thus is not the result of choice. (One may have chosen to take the walk, but not to take this or that step while walking.) Such acts are free in Moore's sense but are not free in the sense of being deliberate. Morever, there are classes of acts of the same general character which are not even covered by Moore's sense: sudden outbursts of feeling, in some cases at least, could not have been avoided by an immediately preceding volition, so that if these are to be included under the heading of voluntary acts, the proviso that the act could have been avoided by an immediately preceding volition must be

---

[1] *Ethics,* pp. 15–16.

amended to read "could have been avoided by a volition or series of volitions by the agent *at some time in the past*"—such as the adoption of a different set of habits in the agent's earlier and more formative years.

(Sometimes we call *persons,* rather than their acts, free. Stebbing, for example, declares that one should never call acts free, but only the doers of the acts.[2] But the two do not seem irreconcilable: can we not speak of a *person* as free *with respect to a certain act* (never just free in general) if that *act* is free—whatever we may then go on to mean by saying that an act is free? Any statement about a free act can then be translated into a statement about the doer of the act.)

Now, no matter in which of the above ways we may come to define "voluntary," there are still acts which are voluntary *but which we would be very unlikely to think of as free.* Thus, when a person submits to the command of an armed bandit, he may do so voluntarily in every one of the above senses: he may do so as a result of choice, even of deliberation, and he could have avoided doing it by willing not to—he could, instead, have refused and been shot. The man who reveals a state secret under torture does the same: he could have refused and endured more torture. Yet such acts, and persons in respect of such acts, are not generally called free. We say that they were performed *under compulsion,* and if an act is performed under compulsion we do not call it free. We say, "He wasn't free because he was forced to do as he did," though of course his act was voluntary.

This much departure from the identification of free acts with voluntary acts almost everyone would admit. Sometimes, however, it would be added that this is all the departure that can be admitted. According to Schlick, for example,

> Freedom means the opposite of compulsion; a man is *free* if he does not act under *compulsion,* and he is compelled or unfree when he is hindered from without in the realization of his natural desires. Hence he is unfree when he is locked up, or chained, or when someone forces him at the point of a gun to do what otherwise he would not do. This is quite clear, and everyone will admit that the everyday or legal notion of the lack of freedom is thus correctly interpreted, and that a man will be considered quite free . . . if no such external compulsion is exerted upon him.[3]

Schlick adds that the entire vexed free-will controversy in philosophy is so much wasted ink and paper, because compulsion has been confused with causality and necessity with uniformity. If the question is asked

---

2 *Philosophy and the Physicists,* p. 212.

3 *The Problems of Ethics,* Rynin translation, p. 150.

whether every event is caused, the answer is doubtless yes; but if it is whether every event is compelled, the answer is clearly no. Free acts are uncompelled acts, not uncaused acts. Again, when it is said that some state of affairs (such as water flowing downhill) is necessary, if "necessary" means "compelled," the answer is no; if it means merely that it always happens that way, the answer is yes: universality of application is confused with compulsion. And this, according to Schlick, is the end of the matter.

Schlick's analysis is indeed clarifying and helpful to those who have fallen victim to the confusions he exposes—and this probably includes most persons in their philosophical growing-pains. But *is* this the end of the matter? Is it true that all acts, though caused, are free as long as they are not compelled in the sense which he specifies? May it not be that, while the identification of "free" with "uncompelled" is acceptable, the area of compelled acts is vastly greater than he or most other philosophers have ever suspected? (Moore is more cautious in this respect than Schlick; while for Moore an act is free if it is voluntary in the sense specified above, he thinks there may be another sense in which human beings, and human acts, are not free at all.[4]) We remember statements about human beings being pawns of their early environment, victims of conditions beyond their control, the result of causal influences stemming from their parents, and the like, and we ponder and ask, "Still, are we really free?" Is there not something in what generations of sages have said about man being fettered? Is there not perhaps something too facile, too sleight-of-hand, in Schlick's cutting of the Gordian knot? For example, when a metropolitan newspaper headlines an article with the words "Boy Killer Is Doomed Long Before He Is Born,"[5] and then goes on to describe how a twelve-year-old boy has been sentenced to prison for the murder of a girl, and how his parental background includes records of drunkenness, divorce, social maladjustment, and paresis, are we still to say that his act, though voluntary and assuredly *not* done at the point of a gun, is free? The boy has early displayed a tendency toward sadistic activity to hide an underlying masochism and "prove that he's a man"; being coddled by his mother only worsens this tendency, until, spurned by a girl in his attempt on her, he kills her—not simply in a fit of anger, but calculatingly, deliberately. Is he free in respect of his criminal act, or for that matter in most of the acts of his life? Surely to ask this question is to answer it in the negative. Perhaps I have taken an extreme case; but it is

---

4 *Ethics,* chapter 6, pp. 217 ff.

5 *New York Post,* Tuesday, May 18, 1948, p. 4.

only to show the superficiality of the Schlick analysis the more clearly. Though not everyone has criminotic tendencies, everyone has been moulded by influences which in large measure at least determine his present behavior; he is literally the product of these influences, stemming from periods prior to his "years of discretion," giving him a host of character traits that he cannot change now even if he would. So obviously does what a man is depend upon how a man comes to be, that it is small wonder that philosophers and sages have considered man far indeed from being the master of his fate. It is not as if man's will were standing high and serene above the flux of events that have moulded him; it is itself caught up in this flux, itself carried along on the current. An act is free when it is determined by the man's character, say moralists; but what if the most decisive aspects of his character were already irrevocably acquired before he could do anything to mould them? What if even the degree of will power available to him in shaping his habits and disciplining himself now to overcome the influence of his early environment is a factor over which he has no control? What are we to say of this kind of "freedom"? Is it not rather like the freedom of the machine to stamp labels on cans when it has been devised for just that purpose? Some machines can do so more efficiently than others, but only because they have been better constructed.

It is not my purpose here to establish this thesis in general, but only in one specific respect which has received comparatively little attention, namely, the field referred to by psychiatrists as that of unconscious motivation. In what follows I shall restrict my attention to it because it illustrates as clearly as anything the points I wish to make.

Let me try to summarize very briefly the psychoanalytic doctrine on this point.[6] The conscious life of the human being, including the conscious decisions and volitions, is merely a mouthpiece for the unconscious—not directly for the enactment of unconscious drives, but of the compromise between unconscious drives and unconscious reproaches. There is a Big Three behind the scenes which the automaton called the conscious personality carries out: the id, an "eternal gimme," presents its

---

[6] I am aware that the theory presented below is not accepted by all practicing psychoanalysts. Many non-Freudians would disagree with the conclusions presented below. But I do not believe that this fact affects my argument, as long as the concept of unconscious motivation is accepted. I am aware, too, that much of the language employed in the following descriptions is animistic and metaphorical; but as long as I am presenting a view I would prefer to "go the whole hog" and present it in its most dramatic form. The theory can in any case be made clearest by the use of such language, just as atomic theory can often be made clearest to students with the use of models.

wish and demands its immediate satisfaction; the super-ego says no to the wish immediately upon presentation, and the unconscious ego, the mediator between the two, tries to keep peace by means of compromise.[7]

To go into examples of the functioning of these three "bosses" would be endless; psychoanalytic case books supply hundreds of them. The important point for us to see in the present context is that *it is the unconscious that determines what the conscious impulse and the conscious action shall be.* Hamlet, for example, had a strong Oedipus wish, which was violently counteracted by super-ego reproaches; these early wishes were vividly revived in an unusual adult situation in which his uncle usurped the coveted position from Hamlet's father and won his mother besides. This situation evoked strong strictures on the part of Hamlet's super-ego, and it was this that was responsible for his notorious delay in killing his uncle. A dozen times Hamlet could have killed Claudius easily; but every time Hamlet "decided" not to: a free choice, moralists would say—but no, listen to the super-ego: "What you feel such hatred toward your uncle for, what you are plotting to kill him for, is precisely the crime which you yourself desire to commit: to kill your father and replace him in the affections of your mother. Your fate and your uncle's are bound up together." This paralyzes Hamlet into inaction. Consciously all he knows is that he is unable to act; this conscious inability he rationalizes, giving a different excuse each time.[8]

We have always been conscious of the fact that we are not masters of our fate in every respect—that there are many things which we cannot do, that nature is more powerful than we are, that we cannot disobey laws without danger of reprisals, etc. We have become "officially" conscious, too, though in our private lives we must long have been aware of it, that we are not free with respect to the emotions that we feel—whom we love or hate, what types we admire, and the like. More lately still we have been reminded that there are unconscious motivations for our basic attractions and repulsions, our compulsive actions or inabilities to act. But what is not welcome news is that our very acts of volition, and the entire train of deliberations leading up to them, are but façades for the expression of unconscious wishes, or rather, unconscious compromises and defenses.

A man is faced by a choice: shall he kill another person or not?

---

[7] This view is very clearly developed in Edmund Bergler, *Divorce Won't Help,* especially chapter I.

[8] See *The Basic Writings of Sigmund Freud,* Modern Library Edition, p. 310. (In *The Interpretation of Dreams.*) Cf. also the essay by Ernest Jones, "A Psycho-analytical Study of Hamlet."

Moralists would say, here is a free choice—the result of deliberation, an action consciously entered into. And yet, though the agent himself does not know it, and has no awareness of the forces that are at work within him, his choice is already determined for him: his conscious will is only an instrument, a slave, in the hands of a deep unconscious motivation which determines his action. If he has a great deal of what the analyst calls "free-floating guilt," he will not; but if the guilt is such as to demand immediate absorption in the form of self-damaging behavior, this accumulated guilt will have to be discharged in some criminal action. The man himself does not know what the inner clockwork is; he is like the hands on the clock, thinking they move freely over the face of the clock.

A woman has married and divorced several husbands. Now she is faced with a choice for the next marriage: shall she marry Mr. A, or Mr. B, or nobody at all? She may take considerable time to "decide" this question, and her decision may appear as a final triumph of her free will. Let us assume that A is a normal, well-adjusted, kind, and generous man, while B is a leech, an impostor, one who will become entangled constantly in quarrels with her. If she belongs to a certain classifiable psychological type, she will inevitably choose B, and she will do so even if her previous husbands have resembled B, so that one would think that she "had learned from experience." Consciously, she will of course "give the matter due consideration," etc., etc. To the psychoanalyst all this is irrelevant chaff in the wind—only a camouflage for the inner workings about which she knows nothing consciously. If she is of a certain kind of masochistic strain, as exhibited in her previous set of symptoms, she *must* choose B: her super-ego, always out to maximize the torment in the situation, seeing what dazzling possibilities for self-damaging behavior are promised by the choice of B, compels her to make the choice she does, and even to conceal the real basis of the choice behind an elaborate façade of rationalizations.

A man is addicted to gambling. In the service of his addiction he loses all his money, spends what belongs to his wife, even sells his property and neglects his children. For a time perhaps he stops; then, inevitably, he takes it up again. The man does not know that he is a victim rather than an agent; or, if he sometimes senses that he is in the throes of something-he-knows-not-what, he will have no inkling of its character and will soon relapse into the illusion that he (his conscious self) is freely deciding the course of his own actions. What he does not know, of course, is that he is still taking out on his mother the original lesion to his infantile narcissism, getting back at her for her fancied refusal of his infantile wishes—and this by rejecting everything identified with her, namely education, discipline, logic, common sense, training. At the roulette wheel, almost alone among adult activities, chance—the opposite of all these things—rules supreme; and his addiction represents his continued and emphatic reiteration of his rejection of Mother and all she represents to his unconscious.

This pseudo-aggression of his is of course masochistic in its effects. In the long run he always loses; he can never quit while he is winning. And far from playing in order to win, rather one can say that his losing is a *sine qua non* of his psychic equilibrium (as it was for example with Dostoyevsky): guilt demands punishment, and in the ego's "deal" with the super-ego the super-ego has granted satisfaction of infantile wishes in return for the self-damaging conditions obtaining. Winning would upset the neurotic equilibrium.[9]

A man has wash-compulsion. He must be constantly washing his hands—he uses up perhaps 400 towels a day. Asked why he does this, he says, "I need to, my hands are dirty"; and if it is pointed out to him that they are not really dirty, he says, "They feel dirty anyway, I feel better when I wash them." So once again he washes them. He "freely decides" every time; he feels that he must wash them, he deliberates for a moment perhaps, but always ends by washing them. What he does not see, of course, are the invisible wires inside him pulling him inevitably to do the thing he does: the infantile id-wish concerns preoccupation with dirt, the super-ego charges him with this, and the terrified ego must respond, "No, I don't like dirt, see how clean I like to be, look how I wash my hands!"

Let us see what further "free acts" the same patient engages in (this is an actual case history): he is taken to a concentration camp, and given the worst of treatment by the Nazi guards. In the camp he no longer chooses to be clean, does not even try to be—on the contrary, his choice is now to wallow in filth as much as he can. All he is aware of now is a disinclination to be clean, and every time he must choose he chooses not to be. Behind the scenes, however, another drama is being enacted: the super-ego, perceiving that enough torment is being administered from the outside, can afford to cease pressing its charges in this quarter—the outside world is doing the torturing now, so the super-ego is relieved of the responsibility. Thus the ego is relieved of the agony of constantly making terrified replies in the form of washing to prove that the super-ego

---

9   See Edmund Bergler's article on the pathological gambler in *Diseases of the Nervous System* (1943). Also "Suppositions about the Mechanism of Criminosis," *Journal of Criminal Psychopathology* (1944) and "Clinical Contributions to the Psychogenesis of Alcohol Addiction," *Quarterly Journal of Studies on Alcohol, 5:* 434 (1944).

is wrong. The defense no longer being needed, the person slides back into what is his natural predilection anyway, for filth. This becomes too much even for the Nazi guards: they take hold of him one day, saying, "We'll teach you how to be clean!" drag him into the snow, and pour bucket after bucket of icy water over him until he freezes to death. Such is the end-result of an original id-wish, caught in the machinations of a destroying super-ego.

Let us take, finally, a less colorful, more everyday example. A student at a university, possessing wealth, charm, and all that is usually considered essential to popularity, begins to develop the following personality-pattern: although well taught in the graces of social conversation, he always makes a *faux pas* somewhere, and always in the worse possible situation; to his friends he makes cutting remarks which hurt deeply—and always apparently aimed in such a way as to hurt the most: a remark that would not hurt A but would hurt B he invariably makes to B rather than to A, and so on. None of this is conscious. Ordinarily he is considerate of people, but he contrives always (unconsciously) to impose on just those friends who would resent it most, and at just the times when he should know that he should not impose: at 3 o'clock in the morning, without forewarning, he phones a friend in a near-by city demanding to stay at his apartment for the weekend; naturally the friend is offended, but the person himself is not aware that he has provoked the grievance ("common sense" suffers a temporary eclipse when the neurotic pattern sets in, and one's intelligence, far from being of help in such a situation, is used in the interest of the neurosis), and when the friend is cool to him the next time they meet, he wonders why and feels unjustly treated. Aggressive behavior on his part invites resentment and aggression in turn, but all that he consciously sees is others' behavior towards him—and he considers himself the innocent victim of an unjustified "persecution."

Each of these acts is, from the moralist's point of view, free: he chose to phone his friend at 3 A.M.; he chose to make the cutting remark that he did, etc. What he does not know is that an ineradicable masochistic pattern has set in. His unconscious is far more shrewd and clever than is his conscious intellect; it sees with uncanny accuracy just what kind of behavior will damage him most, and unerringly forces him into that behavior. Consciously, the student "doesn't know why he did it"—he gives different "reasons" at different times, but they are all, once again, rationalizations cloaking the unconscious mechanism which propels him willy-nilly into actions that his "common sense" eschews.

The more of this sort of thing one observes, the more he can see what the psychoanalyst means when he talks about *the illusion of freedom.*

And the more of a psychiatrist one becomes, the more he is overcome with a sense of what an illusion this free-will can be. In some kinds of cases most of us can see it already: it takes no psychiatrist to look at the epileptic and sigh with sadness at the thought that soon this person before you will be as one possessed, not the same thoughtful intelligent person you knew. But people are not aware of this in other contexts, for example when they express surprise at how a person whom they have been so good to could treat them so badly. Let us suppose that you help a person financially or morally or in some other way, so that he is in your debt; suppose further that he is one of the many neurotics who unconsciously identify kindness with weakness and aggression with strength, then he will unconsciously take your kindness to him as weakness and use it as the occasion for enacting some aggression against you. He can't help it, he may regret it himself later; still, he will be driven to do it. If we gain a little knowledge of psychiatry, we can look at him with pity, that a person otherwise so worthy should be so unreliable—but we will exercise realism too, and be aware that there are some types of people that you cannot be good to in "free" acts of their conscious volition, they will use your own goodness against you.

Sometimes the persons themselves will become dimly aware that "something behind the scenes" is determining their behavior. The divorcee will sometimes view herself with detachment, as if she were some machine (and indeed the psychoanalyst does call her a "repeating-machine"): "I know I'm caught in a net, that I'll fall in love with this guy and marry him and the whole ridiculous merry-go-round will start all over again."

We talk about free-will, and we say, for example, the person is free to do so-and-so if he can do so *if* he wants to—and we forget that his wanting to is itself caught up in the stream of determinism, that unconscious forces drive him into the wanting or not wanting to do the thing in question. The analogy of the puppet whose motions are manipulated from behind by invisible wires, or better still, by springs inside, is a telling one at almost every point.

And the glaring fact is that it all started so early, before we new what was happening. The personality-structure is inelastic after the age of five, and comparatively so in most cases after the age of three. Whether one acquires a neurosis or not is determined by that age—and just as involuntarily as if it had been a curse of God. If, for example, a masochistic pattern was set up, under pressure of hyper-narcissism combined with real or fancied infantile deprivation, then the masochistic snowball was on its course downhill long before we or anybody else know what was happening, and long before anyone could do anything about it.

To speak of human beings as "puppets" in such a context is no idle metaphor, but a stark rendering of a literal fact: only the psychiatrist knows what puppets people really are; and it is no wonder that the protestations of philosophers that "the act which is the result of a volition, a deliberation, a conscious decision, is free" leave these persons, to speak mildly, somewhat cold.

But, one may object, all the states thus far described have been abnormal, neurotic ones. The well-adjusted (normal) person at least is free.

Leaving aside the question of how clearly and on what grounds one can distinguish the neurotic from the normal, let me use an illustration of a proclivity that everyone would call normal, namely, the decision of a man to support his wife and possibly a family, and consider briefly its genesis, according to psychoanalytic accounts.[10]

Every baby comes into the world with a full-fledged case of megalomania—interested only in himself, acting as if believing that he is the center of the universe and that others are present only to fulfill his wishes, and furious when his own wants are not satisfied immediately no matter for what reason. Gratitude, even for all the time and worry and care expended on him by the mother, is an emotion entirely foreign to the infant, and as he grows older it is inculcated in him only with the greatest difficulty; his natural tendency is to assume that everything that happens to him is due to himself, except for denials and frustrations, which are due to the "cruel, denying" outer world, in particular the mother; and that he owes nothing to anyone, is dependent on no one. This omnipotence-complex, or illusion of non-dependence, has been called the "autarchic fiction." Such a conception of the world is actually fostered in the child by the conduct of adults, who automatically attempt to fulfill the infant's every wish concerning nourishment, sleep, and attention. The child misconceives causality and sees in these wish-fulfillments not the results of maternal kindness and love, but simply the result of his own omnipotence.

This fiction of omnipotence is gradually destroyed by experience, and its destruction is probably the deepest disappointment of the early years of life. First of all, the infant discovers that he is the victim of organic urges and necessities: hunger, defecation, urination. More important, he discovers that the maternal breast, which he has not previously distinguished from his own body (he has not needed to, since it was available when he wanted it), is not a part of himself after all, but of another creature upon

10   E.g., Edmund Bergler, *The Battle of the Conscience,* chapter I.

whom he is dependent. He is forced to recognize this, e.g., when he wants nourishment and it is at the moment not present; even a small delay is most damaging to the "autarchic fiction." Most painful of all is the experience of weaning, probably the greatest tragedy in every baby's life, when his dependence is most cruelly emphasized; it is a frustrating experience because what he wants is no longer there at all; and if he has been able to some extent to preserve the illusion of non-dependence heretofore, he is not able to do so now—it is plain that the source of his nourishment is not dependent on him, but he on it. The shattering of the autarchic fiction is a great disillusionment to every child, a tremendous blow to his ego which he will, in one way or another, spend the rest of his life trying to repair. How does he do this?

First of all, his reaction to frustration is anger and fury; and he responds by kicking, biting, etc., the only ways he knows. But he is motorically helpless, and these measures are ineffective, and only serve to emphasize his dependence the more. Moreover, against such responses of the child the parental reaction is one of prohibition, often involving deprivation of attention and affection. Generally the child soon learns that this form of rebellion is profitless, and brings him more harm than good. He wants to respond to frustration with violent aggression, and at the same time learns that he will be punished for such aggression, and that in any case the latter is ineffectual. What face-saving solution does he find? Since he must "face facts," since he must in any case "conform" if he is to have any peace at all, he tries to make it seem as if he himself is the source of the commands and prohibitions: the *external* prohibitive force is *internalized*—and here we have the origin of conscience. By making the prohibitive agency seem to come from within himself, the child can "save face"—as if saying, "The prohibition comes from within me, not from outside, so I'm not subservient to external rule. I'm only obeying rules I've set up myself," thus to some extent saving the autarchic fiction, and at the same time avoiding unpleasant consequences directed against himself by complying with parental commands.

Moreover, the boy[11] has unconsciously never forgiven the mother for his dependence on her in early life, for nourishment and all other things. It has upset his illusion of non-dependence. These feelings have been repressed and are not remembered; but they are acted out in later life in many ways—e.g., in the constant deprecation man has for woman's duties

---

11   The girl's development after this point is somewhat different. Society demands more aggressiveness of the adult male, hence there are more super-ego strictures on tendencies toward passivity in the male; accordingly his defenses must be stronger.

such as cooking and housework of all sorts ("All she does is stay home and get together a few meals, and she calls that work"), and especially in the man's identification with the mother in his sex experiences with women. By identifying with someone one cancels out in effect the person with whom he identifies—replacing that person, unconsciously denying his existence, and the man, identifying with his early mother, playing the active rôle in "giving" to his wife as his mother has "given" to him, is in effect the denial of his mother's existence, a fact which is narcissistically embarrassing to his ego because it is chiefly responsible for shattering his autarchic fiction. In supporting his wife, he can unconsciously deny that his mother gave to him, and that he was dependent on her giving. Why is it that the husband plays the provider, and wants his wife to be dependent on no one else, although twenty years before he was nothing but a parasitic baby? This is a face-saving device on his part: he can act out the reasoning "See, I'm not the parasitic baby, on the contrary I'm the provider, the giver." His playing the provider is a constant face-saving device, to deny his early dependence which is so embarrassing to his ego. It is no wonder that men generally dislike to be reminded of their babyhood, when they were dependent on woman.

Thus we have here a perfectly normal adult reaction which is unconsciously motivated. The man "chooses" to support a family—and his choice is as unconsciously motivated as anything could be. (I have described here only the "normal" state of affairs, uncomplicated by the well-nigh infinite number of variations that occur in actual practice.)

Now, what of the notion of responsibility? What happens to it on our analysis?

Let us begin with an example, not a fictitious one. A woman and her two-year-old baby are riding on a train to Montreal in mid-winter. The child ill. The woman wants badly to get to her destination. She is, unknown to herself, the victim of a neurotic conflict whose nature is irrelevant here except for the fact that it forces her to behave aggressively toward the child, partly to spite her husband whom she despises and who loves the child, but chiefly to ward off super-ego charges of masochistic attachment. Consciously she loves the child, and when she says this she says it sincerely, but she must behave aggressively toward it nevertheless, just as many children love their mothers but are nasty to them most of the time in neurotic pseudo-aggression. The child becomes more ill as the train approaches Montreal; the heating system of the train is not working, and the conductor pleads with the woman to get off the train at the next town and get the child to a hospital at once. The woman refuses. Soon after, the child's condition worsens, and the mother does all she can to keep it alive, without, however, leaving the train, for she declares that it is absolutely necessary that she reach her destination. But before she gets there the child is dead. After that, of course, the mother grieves, blames herself, weeps hysterically, and joins the church to gain surcease from the guilt that constantly overwhelms her when she thinks of how her aggressive behavior has killed her child.

Was she responsible for her deed? In ordinary life, after making a mistake, we say, "Chalk it up to experience." Here we should say, "Chalk it up to the neurosis." *She* could not help it if her neurosis forced her to act this way—she didn't even know what was going on behind the scenes, her conscious self merely acted out its assigned part. This is far more true than is generally realized: criminal actions in general are not actions for which their agents are responsible; the agents are passive, not active— they are victims of a neurotic conflict. Their very hyper-activity is unconsciously determined.

To say this is, of course, not to say that we should not punish criminals. Clearly, for our own protection, we must remove them from our midst so that they can no longer molest and endanger organized society. And, of course, if we use the word "responsible" in such a way that justly to hold someone responsible for a deed is by definition identical with being justified in punishing him, then we can and do hold people responsible. But this is like the sense of "free" in which free acts are voluntary ones. It does not go deep enough. In a deeper sense we cannot hold the person responsible: we can hold his neurosis responsible, but *he is not responsible for his neurosis,* particularly since the age at which its onset was inevitable was an age before he could even speak.

The neurosis is responsible—but isn't the neurosis a part of *him?* We have been speaking all the time as if the person and his unconscious were two separate beings; but isn't he one personality, including conscious and unconscious departments together?

I do not wish to deny this. But it hardly helps us here; for what people want when they talk about freedom, and what they hold to when they champion it, is the idea that the *conscious* will is the master of their destiny. "I am the master of my fate, I am the captain of my soul"—and they surely mean their conscious selves, the self that they can recognize and search and introspect. Between an unconscious that willy-nilly determines your actions, and an external force which pushes you, there is little if anything to choose. The unconscious is just *as if* it were an outside force; and indeed, psychiatrists will assert that the inner Hitler (your super-ego) can torment you far more than any external Hitler can. Thus the kind of freedom that people want, the only kind they will settle for, is precisely the kind that psychiatry says that they cannot have.

Heretofore it was pretty generally thought that, while we could not rightly blame a person for the color of his eyes or the morality of his parents, or even for what he did at the age of three, or to a large extent of what impulses he had and whom he fell in love with, one *could* do so for other of his adult activities, particularly the acts he performed voluntarily and with premeditation. Later this attitude was shaken. Many voluntary acts came to be recognized, at least in some circles, as compelled by the unconscious. Some philosophers recognized this too—Ayer[12] talks about the kleptomaniac being unfree, and about a person being unfree when another person exerts a habitual ascendancy over his personality. But this is as far as he goes. The usual examples, such as the kleptomaniac and the schizophrenic, apparently satisfy most philosophers, and with these exceptions removed, the rest of mankind is permitted to wander in the vast and alluring fields of freedom and responsibility. So far, the inroads upon freedom left the vast majority of humanity untouched; they began to hit home when psychiatrists began to realize, though philosophers did not, that the domination of the conscious by the unconscious extended, not merely to a few exceptional individuals, but to all human beings, that the "big three behind the scenes" are not respecters of persons, and dominate us all, even including that *sanctum sanctorum* of freedom, our conscious will. To be sure, the domination by the unconscious in the case of "normal" individuals is somewhat more benevolent than the tyranny and despotism exercised in neurotic cases, and therefore the former have evoked less comment; but the principle remains in all cases the same: the unconscious is the master of every fate and the captain of every soul.

We speak of a machine turning out good products most of the time but every once in a while it turns out a "lemon." We do not, of course, hold the product responsible for this, but the machine, and via the machine, its maker. Is it silly to extend to inanimate objects the idea of responsibility? Of course. But is it any less so to employ the notion in speaking of human creatures? Are not the two kinds of cases analogous in countless important ways? Occasionally a child turns out badly too, even when his environment and training are the same as that of his brothers and sisters who turn out "all right." He is the "bad penny." His acts of rebellion against parental discipline in adult life (such as the case of the gambler, already cited) are traceable to early experiences of real or fancied denial of infantile wishes. Sometimes the denial has been real, though many denials are absolutely necessary if the child is to grow up to observe the common decencies of civilized life; sometimes, if the child has an unusual

---

12 A. J. Ayer, "Freedom and Necessity," *Polemic* (September–October 1946), pp. 40–43. [The article may be found on pp. 205–213 in this book.]

quantity of narcissism, every event that occurs is interpreted by him as a denial of his wishes, and nothing a parent could do, even granting every humanly possible wish, would help. In any event, the later neurosis can be attributed to this. Can the person himself be held responsible? Hardly. If he engages in activities which are a menace to society, he must be put into prison, of course, but responsibility is another matter. The time when the events occurred which rendered his neurotic behavior inevitable was a time long before he was capable of thought and decision. As an adult, he is a victim of a world he never made—only this world is inside him.

What about the children who turn out "all right"? All we can say is that "it's just lucky for them" that what happened to their unfortunate brother didn't happen to them; *through no virtue of their own* they are not doomed to the life of unconscious guilt, expiation, conscious depression, terrified ego-gestures for the appeasement of a tyrannical super-ego, that he is. The machine turned them out with a minimum of damage. But if the brother cannot be blamed for his evils, neither can they be praised for their good; unless, of course, we should blame people for what is not their fault, and praise them for lucky accidents.

We all agree that machines turn out "lemons," we all agree that nature turns out misfits in the realm of biology—the blind, the crippled, the diseased; but we hesitate to include the realm of the personality, for here, it seems, is the last retreat of our dignity as human beings. Our ego can endure anything but this; this island at least must remain above the encroaching flood. But may not precisely the same analysis be made here also? Nature turns out psychological "lemons" too, in far greater quantities than any other kind; and indeed all of us are "lemons" in some respect or other, the difference being one of degree. Some of us are lucky enough not to have a gambling-neurosis or criminotic tendencies or masochistic mother-attachment or overdimensional repetition-compulsion to make our lives miserable, but most of our actions, those usually considered the most important, are unconsciously dominated just the same. And, if a neurosis may be likened to a curse of God, let those of us, the elect, who are enabled to enjoy a measure of life's happiness without the hell-fire of neurotic guilt, take this, not as our own achievement, but simply for what it is—a gift of God.

Let us, however, quit metaphysics and put the situation schematically in the form of a deductive argument.

1. An occurrence over which we had no control is something we cannot be held responsible for.
2. Events E, occurring during our babyhood, were events over which we had no control.

3. Therefore events E were events which we cannot be held responsible for.
4. But if there is something we cannot be held responsible for, neither can we held responsible for something that inevitably results from it.
5. Events E have as inevitable consequence Neurosis N, which in turn has as inevitable consequence Behavior B.
6. Since N is the inevitable consequence of E and B is the inevitable consequence of N, B is the inevitable consequence of E.
7. Hence, not being responsible for E, we cannot be responsible for B.

In Samuel Butler's Utopian satire *Erewhon* there occurs the following passage, in which a judge is passing sentence on a prisoner:

> It is all very well for you to say that you came of unhealthy parents, and had a severe accident in your childhood which permanently undermined your constitution; excuses such as these are the ordinary refuge of the criminal; but they cannot for one moment be listened to by the ear of justice. I am not here to enter upon curious metaphysical questions as to the origin of this or that—questions to which there would be no end were their introduction once tolerated, and which would result in throwing the only guilt on the tissues of the primordial cell, or on the elementary gases. There is no question of how you came to be wicked, but only this—namely, are you wicked or not? This has been decided in the affirmative, neither can I hesitate for a single moment to say that it has been decided justly. You are a bad and dangerous person, and stand branded in the eyes of your fellow countrymen with one of the most heinous known offenses.[13]

As moralists read this passage, they may perhaps nod with approval. But the joke is on them. The sting comes when we realize what the crime is for which the prisoner is being sentenced: namely, consumption. The defendant is reminded that during the previous year he was sentenced for aggravated bronchitis, and is warned that he should profit from experience in the future. Butler is employing here his familiar method of presenting some human tendency (in this case, holding people responsible for what isn't their fault) to a ridiculous extreme and thereby reducing it to absurdity.

Assuming the main conclusions of this paper to be true, is there any room left for freedom?

This, of course, all depends on what we mean by "freedom." In the senses suggested at the beginning of this paper, there are countless free

---

[13] Samuel Butler, *Erewhon* (Modern Library edition), p. 107.

acts, and unfree ones as well. When "free" means "uncompelled," and only external compulsion is admitted, again there are countless free acts. But now we have extended the notion of compulsion to include determination by unconscious forces. With this sense in mind, our question is, "With the concept of compulsion thus extended, and in the light of present psychoanalytic knowledge, is there any freedom left in human behavior?"

If practicing psychoanalysts were asked this question, there is little doubt that their answer would be along the following lines: they would say that they were not accustomed to using the term "free" at all, but that if they had to suggest a criterion for distinguishing the free from the unfree, they would say that a person's freedom is present *in inverse proportion to his neuroticism;* in other words, the more his acts are determined by a *malevolent* unconscious, the less free he is. Thus they would speak of *degrees* of freedom. They would say that as a person is cured of his neurosis, he becomes more free—free to realize capabilities that were blocked by the neurotic affliction. The psychologically well-adjusted individual is in this sense comparatively the most free. Indeed, those who are cured of mental disorders are sometimes said to have *regained their freedoms:* they are freed from the tyranny of a malevolent unconscious which formerly exerted as much of a domination over them as if they had been the abject slaves of a cruel dictator.

But suppose one says that a person is free only to the extent that his acts are *not unconsciously determined at all,* be they unconscious benevolent *or* malevolent? If this is the criterion, psychoanalysts would say, most human behavior cannot be called free at all: our impulses and volitions having to do with our basic attitudes toward life, whether we are optimists of pessimists, tough-minded or tender-minded, whether our tempers are quick or slow, whether we are "naturally self-seeking" or "naturally benevolent" (and *all the acts consequent upon these things*), what things annoy us, whether we take to blondes or brunettes, old or young, whether we become philosophers or artists or businessmen—all this has its basis in the unconscious. If people generally call most acts free, it is not because they believe that compelled acts should be called free, it is rather through not knowing how large a proportion of our acts actually are compelled. Only the comparatively "vanilla-flavored" aspects of our lives—such as our behavior toward people who don't really matter to us—are exempted from this rule.

These, I think, are the two principal criteria for distinguishing freedom from the lack of it which we might set up on the basis of psychoanalytic knowledge. Conceivably we might set up others. In every case, of course, it remains trivially true that "it all depends on how we choose to use the word." The facts are what they are, regardless of what words we choose for labeling them. But if we choose to label them in a way which is not in accord with what human beings, however vaguely, have long had in mind in applying these labels, as we would be doing if we labeled as "free" many acts which we know as much about as we now do through modern psychoanalytic methods, then we shall only be manipulating words to mislead our fellow creatures.

C. A. Campbell is Professor Emeritus at
the University of Glasgow.

C. A. Campbell

HAS THE SELF 'FREE WILL'?

1. . . . . It is something of a truism that in philosophic enquiry the exact formulation of a problem often takes one a long way on the road to its solution. In the case of the Free Will problem I think there is a rather special need of careful formulation. For there are many sorts of human freedom; and it can easily happen that one wastes a great deal of labour in proving or disproving a freedom which has almost nothing to do with the freedom which is at issue in the traditional problem of Free Will. The abortiveness of so much of the argument for and against Free Will in contemporary philosophical literature seems to me due in the main to insufficient pains being taken over the preliminary definition of the problem. There is, indeed, one outstanding exception, Professor Broad's brilliant inaugural lecture entitled, 'Determinism, Indeterminism, and Libertarianism,'[1] in which forty-three pages are devoted to setting out the

---

Reprinted from *On Selfhood and Godhood* (London: George Allen & Unwin Ltd., 1957), by permission of the publisher.
1 Reprinted in *Ethics and the History of Philosophy, Selected Essays.*

problem, as against seven to its solution! I confess that the solution does not seem to myself to follow upon the formulation quite as easily as all that:[2] but Professor Broad's eminent example fortifies me in my decision to give here what may seem at first sight a disproportionate amount of time to the business of determining the essential characteristics of the kind of freedom with which the traditional problem is concerned.

Fortunately we can at least make a beginning with a certain amount of confidence. It is not seriously disputable that the kind of freedom in question is the freedom which is commonly recognised to be in some sense a precondition of moral responsibility. Clearly, it is on account of this integral connection with moral responsibility that such exceptional importance has always been felt to attach to the Free Will problem. But in what precise sense is free will a precondition of moral responsibility, and thus a postulate of the moral life in general? This is an exceedingly troublesome question; but until we have satisfied ourselves about the answer to it, we are not in a position to state, let alone decide, the question whether 'Free Will' in its traditional, ethical, significance is a reality.

Our first business, then, is to ask, exactly what kind of freedom is it which is required for moral responsibility? And as to method of procedure in this inquiry, there seems to me to be no real choice. I know of only one method that carries with it any hope of success; viz. the critical comparison of those acts for which, on due reflection, we deem it proper to attribute moral praise or blame to the agents, with those acts for which, on due reflection, we deem such judgments to be improper. The ultimate touchstone, as I see it, can only be our moral consciousness as it manifests itself in our more critical and considered moral judgments. The 'linguistic' approach by way of the analysis of moral *sentences* seems to me, despite its present popularity, to be an almost infallible method for reaching wrong results in the moral field; but I must reserve what I have to say about this for the next lecture.

2. The first point to note is that the freedom at issue (as indeed the very name 'Free *Will* Problem' indicates) pertains primarily not to overt acts but to inner acts. The nature of things has decreed that, save in the case of one's self, it is only overt acts which one can directly observe. But a very little reflection serves to show that in our moral judgments upon others their overt acts are regarded as significant only in so far as they are

---

[2] I have explained the grounds for my dissent from Broad's final conclusions on pp. 27 ff. of *In Defence of Free Will* (Jackson Son & Co., 1938).

the expression of inner acts. We do not consider the acts of a robot to be morally responsible acts; nor do we consider the acts of a man to be so save in so far as they are distinguishable from those of a robot by reflecting an inner life of choice. Similarly, from the other side, if we are satisfied (as we may on occasion be, at least in the case of ourselves) that a person has definitely elected to follow a course which he believes to be wrong, but has been prevented by external circumstances from translating his inner choice into an overt act, we still regard him as morally blameworthy. Moral freedom, then, pertains to *inner* acts.

The next point seems at first sight equally obvious and uncontroversial; but, as we shall see, it has awkward implications if we are in real earnest with it (as almost nobody is). It is the simple point that the act must be one of which the person judged can be regarded as the *sole* author. It seems plain enough that if there are any *other* determinants of the act, external to the self, to that extent the act is not an act which the *self* determines, and to that extent not an act for which the self can be held morally responsible. The self is only part-author of the act, and his moral responsibility can logically extend only to those elements within the act (assuming for the moment that these can be isolated) of which he is the *sole* author.

The awkward implications of this apparent truism will be readily appreciated. For, if we are mindful of the influences exerted by heredity and environment, we may well feel some doubt whether there is any act of will at all of which one can truly say that the self is sole author, sole determinant. No man has a voice in determining the raw material of impulses and capacities that constitute his hereditary endowment, and no man has more than a very partial control of the material and social environment in which he is destined to live his life. Yet it would be manifestly absurd to deny that these two factors do constantly and profoundly affect the nature of a man's choices. That this is so we all of us recognise in our moral judgments when we 'make allowances', as we say, for a bad heredity or a vicious environment, and acknowledge in the victim of them a diminished moral responsibility for evil courses. Evidently we do *try,* in our moral judgments, however crudely, to praise or blame a man only in respect of that of which we can regard him as *wholly* the author. And evidently we do recognise that, for a man to be the author of an act in the full sense required for moral responsibility, it is not enough merely that he 'wills' or 'chooses' the act: since even the most unfortunate victim of heredity or environment does, as a rule, 'will' what he does. It is significant, however, that the ordinary man, though well enough aware of the influence upon choices of heredity and environment, does not feel obliged thereby to give up his assumption that moral predicates *are* somehow applicable. Plainly he still believes that there is *something* for which a man is morally responsible, something of which we can fairly say that he is the sole author. *What is this something?* To that question common-sense is not ready with an explicit answer—though an answer is, I think, implicit in the line which its moral judgments take. I shall do what I can to give an explicit answer later in this lecture. Meantime it must suffice to observe that, if we are to be true to the deliverances of our moral consciousness, it is very difficult to deny that *sole* authorship is a necessary condition of the morally responsible act.

Thirdly we come to a point over which much recent controversy has raged. We may approach it by raising the following question. Granted an act of which the agent is sole author, does this 'sole authorship' suffice to make the act a morally free act? We may be inclined to think that it does, until we contemplate the possibility that an act of which the agent is sole author might conceivably occur as a necessary expression of the agent's nature; the way in which, e.g. some philosophers have supposed the Divine act of creation to occur. This consideration excites a legitimate doubt; for it is far from easy to see how a person can be regarded as a proper subject for moral praise or blame in respect of an act which he *cannot help* performing—even if it be his own 'nature' which necessitates it. Must we not recognise it as a condition of the morally free act that the agent 'could have acted otherwise' than he in fact did? It is true, indeed, that we sometimes praise or blame a man for an act about which we are prepared to say, in the light of our knowledge of his established character, that he 'could no other.' But I think that a little reflection shows that in such cases we are not praising or blaming the man strictly for what he does *now* (or at any rate we ought not to be), but rather for those past acts of his which have generated the firm habit of mind from which his *present* act follows 'necessarily'. In other words, our praise and blame, so far as justified, are really retrospective, being directed not to the agent *qua* performing *this* act, but to the agent *qua* performing those past acts which have built up his present character, and in respect to which we presume that he *could* have acted otherwise, that there really *were* open possibilities before him. These cases, therefore, seem to me to constitute no valid exception to what I must take to be the rule, viz. that a man can be morally praised or blamed for an act only if he could have acted otherwise.

Now philosophers today are fairly well agreed that it is a postulate of the morally responsible act that the agent 'could have acted otherwise' in *some* sense of that phrase. But sharp differences of opinion have arisen over the way in which the phrase ought to be interpreted. There is a strong disposition to water down its apparent meaning by insisting that it is not (as a postulate of moral responsibility) to be understood as a straightforword categorical proposition, but rather as a disguised hypothetical proposition. All that we really require to be assured of, in order to justify our holding X morally responsible for an act, is, we are told, that X could have acted otherwise *if* he had *chosen* otherwise or perhaps that X could have acted otherwise *if* he had had a different character, or *if* he had been placed in different circumstances.

I think it is easy to understand, and even, in a measure, to sympathise with, the motives which induce philosophers to offer these counter-interpretations. It is not just the fact that 'X could have acted otherwise', as a bald categorical statement, is incompatible with the universal sway of causal law—though this is, to some philosophers, a serious stone of stumbling. The more wide-spread objection is that at least looks as though it were incompatible with that causal continuity of an agent's character with his conduct which is implied when we believe (surely with justice) that we can often tell the sort of thing a man will do from our knowledge of the sort of man he is.

We shall have to make our accounts with that particular difficulty later. At this stage I wish merely to show that neither of the hypothetical propositions suggested—and I think the same could be shown for *any* hypothetical alternative—is an acceptable substitute for the categorical proposition 'X could have acted otherwise' as the presupposition of moral responsibility.

Let us look first at the earlier suggestion—'X could have acted otherwise *if* he had chosen otherwise'. Now clearly there are a great many acts with regard to which we are entirely satisfied that the agent is thus situated. We are often perfectly sure that—for this is all it amounts to—if X had chosen otherwise, the circumstances presented no external obstacle to the translation of that choice into action. For example, we often have no doubt at all that X, who in point of fact told a lie, could have told the truth *if* he had so chosen. But does our confidence on this score allay all legitimate doubts about whether X is really blameworthy? Does it entail that X is free in the sense required for moral responsibility? Surely not. The obvious question immediately arises: 'But *could* X have *chosen* otherwise than he did?' It is doubt about the true answer to *that* question which leads most people to doubt the reality of moral responsibility. Yet on this crucial question the hypothetical proposition which is offered as a sufficient statement of the condition justifying the ascription of moral responsibility gives us no information whatsoever.

Indeed this hypothetical substitute for the categorical 'X could have acted otherwise' seems to me to lack all plausibility unless one contrives to forget why it is, after all, that we ever come to feel fundamental doubts about man's moral responsibility. Such doubts are born, surely, when one becomes aware of certain reputable world-views in religion or philosophy, or of certain reputable scientific beliefs, which in their several ways imply that man's actions are necessitated, and thus could not be otherwise than they in fact are. But clearly a doubt so based is not even touched by the recognition that a man could very often act otherwise *if* he so chose. That proposition is entirely compatible with the necessitarian theories which generate our doubt: indeed it is this very compatibility that has recommended it to some philosophers, who are reluctant to give up either moral responsibility or Determinism. The proposition which we *must* be able to affirm if moral praise or blame of X is to be justified is the categorical proposition that X could have acted otherwise because—not if—he could have chosen otherwise; or, since it is essentially the inner side of the act that matters, the proposition simply that X could have chosen otherwise.

For the second of the alternative formulae suggested we cannot spare more than a few moments. But its inability to meet the demands it is required to meet is almost transparent. 'X could have acted otherwise', as a statement of a precondition of X's moral responsibility, really means (we are told) 'X could have acted otherwise *if* he were differently constituted, or *if* he had been placed in different circumstances'. It seems a sufficient reply to this to point out that the person whose moral responsibility is at issue is X; a specific individual, in a specific set of circumstances. It is totally irrelevant to X's moral responsibility that we should be able to say that some person differently constituted from X, or X in a different set of circumstances, could have done something different from what X did.

3. Let me, then, briefly sum up the answer at which we have arrived to our question about the kind of freedom required to justify moral responsibility. It is that a man can be said to exercise free will in a morally significant sense only in so far as his chosen act is one of which he is the sole cause or author, and only if—in the straightforward, categorical sense of the phrase—he 'could have chosen otherwise'.

I confess that this answer is in some ways a disconcerting one, disconcerting, because most of us, however objective we are in the actual conduct of our thinking, would *like* to be able to believe that moral responsibility is real: whereas the freedom required for moral responsibility, on the analysis we have given, is certainly far more difficult to establish than the freedom required on the analyses we found ourselves obliged to reject. If, e.g. moral freedom entails only that I could have acted otherwise *if* I had chosen otherwise, there is no real 'problem' about it at all. I am 'free' in the normal case where there is no external obstacle to prevent my translating the alternative choice into action, and not free in other cases. Still less is there a problem if all that moral freedom entails is that I could have acted otherwise *if* I had been a differently constituted person, or been in different circumstances. Clearly I am *always* free in *this* sense of freedom. But, as I have argued, these so-called 'freedoms' fail to give us the pre-conditions of moral responsibility, and hence leave the freedom of the traditional free-will problem, the freedom that people are really concerned about, precisely where it was.

4. Another interpretation of freedom which I am bound to reject on the same general ground, i.e. that it is just not the kind of freedom that is relevant to moral responsibility, is the old idealist view which identifies the *free* will with the *rational* will; the rational will in its turn being identified with the will which wills the moral law in whole-hearted, single-minded obedience to it. This view is still worth at least a passing mention, if only because it has recently been resurrected in an interesting work by Professor A. E. Teale.[3] Moreover, I cannot but feel a certain nostalgic tenderness for a view in which I myself was (so to speak) philosophically cradled. The almost apostolic fervour with which my revered nursing-mother, the late Sir Henry Jones, was wont to impart it to his charges, and, hardly less, his ill-concealed scorn for ignoble natures (like my own) which still hankered after a free will in the old 'vulgar' sense, are vividly recalled for me in Professor Teale's stirring pages.

The true interpretation of free will, according to Professor Teale, the interpretation to which Kant, despite occasional back-slidings, adhered in his better moments, is that 'the will is free in the degree that it is informed and disciplined by the moral principle'.[4]

Now this is a perfectly intelligible sense of the word 'free'—or at any rate it can be made so with a little explanatory comment which Professor Teale well supplies but for which there is here no space. But clearly it is a very different sort of freedom from that which is at issue in the traditional problem of free will. This idealist 'freedom' sponsored by Teale belongs, on his own showing, only to the self in respect of its *good* willing. The freedom with which the traditional problem is concerned, inasmuch as it is the freedom presupposed by moral responsibility, must belong to the self in respect of its *bad*, no less than its *good*, willing. It is, in fact, the

3 *Kantian Ethics.*
4 *Op. cit.* p. 261.

freedom to decide between genuinely open alternatives of good and bad willing.

Professor Teale, of course, is not unaware that the freedom he favours differs from freedom as traditionally understood. He recognises the traditional concept under its Kantian title of 'elective' freedom. But he leaves the reader in no kind of doubt about his disbelief in both the reality and the value of this elective freedom to do, or forbear from doing, one's duty.

The question of the reality of elective freedom I shall be dealing with shortly; and it will occupy us to the end of the lecture. At the moment I am concerned only with its value, and with the rival view that all that matters for the moral life is the 'rational' freedom which a man has in the degree that his will is 'informed and disciplined by the moral principle'. I confess that to myself the verdict on the rival view seems plain and inescapable. No amount of verbal ingenuity or argumentative convolutions can obscure the fact that it is in flat contradiction to the implications of moral responsibility. The point at issue is really perfectly straightforward. If, as this idealist theory maintains, my acting in defiance of what I deem to be my duty is not a 'free' act in *any* sense, let alone in the sense that 'I could have acted otherwise', then I cannot be morally blameworthy, and that is all there is to it. Nor, for that matter, is the idealist entitled to say that I am morally praiseworthy if I act dutifully; for although that act *is* a 'free' act in the idealist sense, it is on his own avowal not free in the sense that 'I could have acted otherwise'.

It seems to me idle, therefore, to pretend that if one has to give up freedom in the traditional elective sense one is not giving up anything important. What we are giving up is, quite simply, the reality of the moral life. I recognise that to a certain type of religious nature (as well as, by an odd meeting of extremes, to a certain type of secular nature) that does not appear to matter so very much; but, for myself, I still think it sufficiently important to make it well worth while enquiring seriously into the possibility that the elective freedom upon which it rests may be real after all.

5. That brings me to the second, and more constructive, part of this lecture. From now on I shall be considering whether it is reasonable to believe that man does in fact possess a free will of the kind specified in the first part of the lecture. If so, just how and where within the complex fabric of the volitional life are we to locate it?—for although free will must presumably belong (if anywhere) to the volitional side of human experience, it is pretty clear from the way in which we have been forced to define it that it does not pertain simply to volition as such; not even to

all volitions that are commonly dignified with the name of 'choices'. It has been, I think, one of the more serious impediments to profitable discussion of the Free Will problem that Libertarians and Determinists alike have so often failed to appreciate the comparatively narrow area within which the free will that is necessary to 'save' morality is required to operate. It goes without saying that this failure has been gravely prejudicial to the case for Libertarianism. I attach a good deal of importance, therefore, to the problem of locating free will correctly within the volitional orbit. Its solution forestalls and annuls, I believe, some of the more tiresome clichés of Determinist criticism.

We saw earlier that Common Sense's practice of 'making allowances' in its moral judgments for the influence of heredity and environment indicates Common Sense's conviction, both that a just moral judgment must discount determinants of choice over which the agent has no control, and also (since it still accepts moral judgments as legitimate) that *something* of moral relevance survives which can be regarded as genuinely self-originated. We are now to try to discover what this 'something' is. And I think we may still usefully take Common Sense as our guide. Suppose one asks the ordinary intelligent citizen *why* he deems it proper to make allowances for X, whose heredity and/or environment are unfortunate. He will tend to reply, I think, in some such terms as these: that X has more and stronger temptations to deviate from what is right than Y or Z, who are normally circumstanced, so that he must put forth a *stronger moral effort* if he is to achieve the same level of external conduct. The intended implication seems to be that X is just as morally praiseworthy as Y or Z *if* he exerts an equivalent moral effort, even though he may not thereby achieve an equal success in conforming his will to the 'concrete' demands of duty. And this implies, again, Common Sense's belief that *in moral effort* we have something for which a man is responsible *without qualification,* something that is *not* affected by heredity and environment but depends *solely* upon the self itself.

Now in my opinion Common Sense has here, in principle, hit upon the one and only defensible answer. Here, and here alone, so far as I can see, in the act of deciding whether to put forth or withhold the moral effort required to resist temptation and rise to duty, is to be found an act which is free in the sense required for moral responsibility; an act of which the self is sole author, and of which it is true to say that 'it could be' (or, after the event, 'could have been') 'otherwise'. Such is the thesis which we shall now try to establish.

6. The species of argument appropriate to the establishment of a thesis of this sort should fall, I think, into two phases. First, there should be a

consideration of the evidence of the moral agent's own inner experience. What *is* the act of moral decision, and what does it imply, from the standpoint of the actual participant? Since there is no way of knowing the act of moral decision—or for that matter any other form of activity—except by actual participation in it, the evidence of the subject, or agent, is on an issue of this kind of palmary importance. It can hardly, however, be taken as in itself conclusive. For even if that evidence should be overwhelmingly to the effect that moral decision does have the characteristics required by moral freedom, the question is bound to be raised—and in view of considerations from other quarters pointing in a contrary direction is *rightly* raised—Can we *trust* the evidence of inner experience? That brings us to what will be the second phase of the argument. We shall have to go on to show, if we are to make good our case, that the extraneous considerations so often supposed to be fatal to the belief in moral freedom are in fact innocuous to it.

In the light of what was said in the last lecture about the self's experience of moral decision as a *creative* activity, we may perhaps be absolved from developing the first phase of the argument at any great length. The appeal is throughout to one's own experience in the actual taking of the moral decision in the stiuation of moral temptation. 'Is it possible', we must ask, 'for anyone so circumstanced to *dis*believe that he could be deciding otherwise?' The answer is surely not in doubt. When we decide to exert moral effort to resist a temptation, we feel quite certain that we *could* withhold the effort; just as, if we decide to withhold the effort and yield to our desires, we feel quite certain that we *could* exert it—otherwise we should not blame ourselves afterwards for having succumbed. It may be, indeed, that this conviction is mere self-delusion. But that is not at the moment our concern. It is enough at present to establish that the act of deciding to exert or to withhold moral effort, as we know it from the inside in actual moral living, belongs to the category of acts which 'could have been otherwise'.

Mutatis mutandis, the same reply is forthcoming if we ask, 'Is it possible for the moral agent in the taking of his decision to *dis*believe that he is the *sole* author of that decision?' Clearly he cannot disbelieve that it is *he* who takes the decision. That, however, is not in itself sufficient to enable him, on reflection, to regard himself as *solely* responsible for the act. For his 'character' as so far formed might conceivably be a factor in determining it, and no one can suppose that the constitution of his 'character' is uninfluenced by circumstances of heredity and environment with which *he* has nothing to do. But as we pointed out in the last lecture, the very essence of the moral decision as it is experienced is that it is a decision whether or not to *combat* our strongest desire, and our strongest desire *is* the expression in the situation of our character as so far formed. Now clearly our character cannot be a factor in determining the decision whether or not to *oppose* our character. I think we are entitled to say, therefore, that the act of moral decision is one in which the self is for itself not merely 'author' but 'sole author'.

7. We may pass on, then, to the second phase of our constructive argument; and this will demand more elaborate treatment. Even if a moral agent *qua* making a moral decision in the situation of 'temptation' cannot help believing that he has free will in the sense at issue—a moral freedom between real alternatives, between genuinely open possibilities— are there, nevertheless, objections to a freedom of this kind so cogent that we are bound to distrust the evidence of 'inner experience'?

I begin by drawing attention to a simple point whose significance tends, I think, to be under-estimated. If the phenomenological analysis we have offered is substantially correct, no one while functioning as a moral agent can help believing that he enjoys free will. Theoretically he may be completely convinced by Determinist arguments, but when actually con- fronted with a personal situation of conflict between duty and desire he is quite certain that it lies with him here and now whether or not he will rise to duty. It follows that if Determinists could produce convincing theo- retical arguments against a free will of this kind, the awkward predica- ment would ensure that man has to deny as a theoretical being what he has to assert as a practical being. Now I think the Determinist ought to be a good deal more worried about this then he usually is. He seems to imagine that a strong case on general theoretical grounds is enough to prove that the 'practical' belief in free will, even if inescapable for us as practical beings, is mere illusion. But in fact it proves nothing of the sort. There is no reason whatever why a belief that we find ourselves obliged to hold *qua* practical beings should be required to give way before a belief which we find ourselves obliged to hold *qua* theoretical beings; or, for that matter, *vice versa*. All that the theoretical arguments of Determinism can prove, unless they are reinforced by a refutation of the phenomenological analysis that supports Libertarianism, is that there is a radical conflict between the theoretical and the practical sides of man's nature, an antimony at the very heart of the self. And this is a state of affairs with which no one can easily rest satisfied. I think therefore that the Deter- minist ought to concern himself a great deal more than he does with phenomenological analysis, in order to show, if he can, that the assurance of free will is not really an inexpugnable element in man's practical consciousness. There is just as much obligation upon him, convinced though he may be of the soundness of his theoretical arguments, to expose the errors of the Libertarian's phenomenological analysis, as there is upon us, convinced though we may be of the soundness of the Libertarian's phenomenological analysis, to expose the errors of the Determinist's theoretical arguments.

8. However, we must at once begin the discharge of our own obligation. The rest of this lecture will be devoted to trying to show that the arguments which seem to carry most weight with Determinists are, to say the least of it, very far from compulsive.

Fortunately a good many of the arguments which at an earlier time in the history of philosophy would have been strongly urged against us make almost no appeal to the bulk of philosophers today, and we may here pass them by. That applies to any criticism of 'open possibilities' based on a metaphysical theory about the nature of the universe as a whole. Nobody today *has* a metaphysical theory about the nature of the universe as a whole! It applies also, with almost equal force, to criticisms based upon the universality of causal law as a supposed postulate of science. There have always been, in my opinion, sound philosophic reasons for doubting the validity, as distinct from the convenience, of the causal postulate in its universal form, but at the present time, when scientists themselves are deeply divided about the need for postulating causality even within their own special field, we shall do better to concentrate our attention upon criticisms which are more confidently advanced. I propose to ignore also, on different grounds, the type of criticism of free will that is sometimes advanced from the side of religion, based upon religious postulates of Divine Omnipotence and Omniscience. So far as I can see, a postulate of human freedom is every bit as necessary to meet certain religious demands (e.g. to make sense of the 'conviction of sin'), as postulates of Divine Omniscience and Omnipotence are to meet certain other religious demands. If so, then it can hardly be argued that religious experience as such tells more strongly against than for the position we are defending; and we may be satisfied, in the present context, to leave the matter there. It will be more profitable to discuss certain arguments which contemporary philosophers do think important, and which recur with a somewhat monotonous regularity in the literature of anti-Libertarianism.

These arguments can, I think, be reduced in principle to no more than two: first, the argument from 'predictability'; second, the argument from the alleged meaninglessness of an act supposed to be the self's act and yet not an expression of the self's character. Contemporary criticism of free will seems to me to consist almost exclusively of variations on these two themes. I shall deal with each in turn.

9. On the first we touched in passing at an earlier stage. Surely it is beyond question (the critic urges) that when we know a person intimately we can foretell with a high degree of accuracy how he will respond to at least a large number of practical situations. One feels safe in predicting that one's dog-loving friend will not use his boot to repel the little mongrel that comes yapping at his heels; or again that one's wife will not pass with incurious eyes (or indeed pass at all) the new hat-shop in the city. So to behave would not be (as we say) 'in character'. But, so the criticism runs, you with your doctrine of 'genuinely open possibilities', of a free will by which the self can diverge from its own character, remove all rational basis from such prediction. You require us to make the absurd supposition that the success of countless predictions of the sort in the past has been mere matter of chance. If you *really* believed in your theory, you would not be surprised if tomorrow your friend with the notrious horror of strong drink should suddenly exhibit a passion for whisky and soda, or if your friend whose taste for reading has hitherto been satisfied with the sporting columns of the newspapers should be discovered on a fine Saturday afternoon poring over the works of Hegel. But of course you *would* be surprised. Social life would be sheer chaos if there were not well-grounded social expectations; and social life is not sheer chaos. Your theory is hopelessly wrecked upon obvious facts.

Now whether or not this criticism holds good against some versions of Libertarian theory I need not here discuss. It is sufficient if I can make it clear that against the version advanced in this lecture, according to which free will is localised in a relatively narrow field of operation, the criticism has no relevance whatsoever.

Let us remind ourselves briefly of the setting within which, on our view, free will functions. There is X, the course which we believe we ought to follow, and Y, the course towards which we feel our desire is strongest. The freedom which we ascribe to the agent is the freedom to put forth or refrain from putting forth the moral effort required to resist the pressure of desire and do what he thinks he ought to do.

But then there is surely an immense range of practical situations— covering by far the greater part of life—in which there is no question of a conflict within the self between what he most desires to do and what he thinks he ought to do? Indeed such conflict is a comparatively rare phenomenon for the majority of men. Yet over that whole vast range there is nothing whatever in our version of Libertarianism to prevent our agreeing that character determines conduct. In the absence, real or supposed, of any 'moral' issue, what a man chooses will be simply that course which, after such reflection as seems called for, he deems most likely to bring him what he most strongly desires; and that is the same as to say the course to which his present character inclines him.

Over by far the greater area of human choices, then, our theory offers no more barrier to successful prediction on the basis of character than any other theory. For where there is no clash of strongest desire with duty, the free will we are defending has no business. There is just nothing for it to do.

But what about the situations—rare enough though they may be—in which there *is* this clash and in which free will does therefore operate? Does our theory entail that there at any rate, as the critic seems to suppose, 'anything may happen'?

Not by any manner of means. In the first place, and by the very nature of the case, the range of the agent's possible choices is bounded by what he thinks he ought to do on the one hand, and what he most strongly desires on the other. The freedom claimed for him is a freedom of decision to make or withhold the effort required to do what he thinks he ought to do. There is no question of a freedom to act in some 'wild' fashion, out of all relation to his characteristic beliefs and desires. This so-called 'freedom of caprice', so often charged against the Libertarian, is, to put it bluntly, a sheer figment of the critic's imagination, with no *habitat* in serious Libertarian theory. Even in situations where free will does come into play it is perfectly possible, on a view like ours, given the appropriate knowledge of a man's character, to predict within certain limits how he will respond.

But 'probable' prediction in such situations can, I think, go further than this. It is obvious that where desire and duty are at odds, the felt 'gap' (as it were) between the two may vary enormously in breadth in different cases. The moderate drinker and the chronic tippler may each want another glass, and each deem it his duty to abstain, but the felt gap between desire and duty in the case of the former is trivial beside the great gulf which is felt to separate them in the case of the latter. Hence it will take a far harder moral effort for the tippler than for the moderate drinker to achieve the same external result of abstention. So much is matter of common agreement. And we are entitled, I think, to take it into account in prediction, on the simple principle that the harder the moral effort required to resist desire the less likely it is to occur. Thus in the example taken, most people would predict that the tippler will very probably succumb to his desires, whereas there is a reasonable likelihood that the moderate drinker will make the comparatively slight effort needed to resist them. So long as the prediction does not pretend to more than a measure of probability, there is nothing in our theory which would disallow it.

I claim, therefore, that the view of free will I have been putting forward is consistent with predictability of conduct on the basis of character over a very wide field indeed. And I make the further claim that that field will cover all the situations in life concerning which there is any empirical evidence that successful prediction is possible.

10. Let us pass on to consider the second main line of criticism. This is, I think, much the more illuminating of the two, if only because it compels the Libertarian to make explicit certain concepts which are indispensable to him, but which, being desperately hard to state clearly, are apt not to be stated at all. The critic's fundamental point might be stated somewhat as follows:

'Free will as you describe it is completely unintelligible. On your own showing no *reason* can be given, because there just *is* no reason, why a man decides to exert rather than to withhold moral effort, or *vice versa*. But such an act—or more properly, such an 'occurrence'—it is nonsense to speak of as an act of a *self*. If there is nothing in the self's character to which it is, even in principle, in any way traceable, the self has nothing to do with it. Your so-called 'freedom', therefore, so far from supporting the self's moral responsibility, destroys it as surely as the crudest Determinism could do'.

If we are to discuss this criticism usefully, it is important, I think, to begin by getting clear about two different senses of the word 'intelligible'.

If, in the first place, we mean by an 'intelligible' act one whose occurrence is in principle capable of being inferred, since it follows necessarily from something (though we may not know in fact from what), then it is certainly true that the Libertarian's free will is unintelligible. But that is only saying, is it not, that the Libertarian's 'free' act is not an act which follows necessarily from something! This can hardly rank as a *criticism* of Libertarianism. It is just a description of it. That there can be nothing unintelligible in *this* sense is precisely what the Determinist has got to *prove*.

Yet it is surprising how often the critic of Libertarianism involves himself in this circular mode of argument. Repeatedly it is urged against the Libertarian, with a great air of triumph, that on his view he can't say *why* I now decide to rise to duty, or now decide to follow my strongest desire in defiance of duty. Of course he can't. If he could he wouldn't *be* a

Libertarian. To 'account for' a 'free' act is a contradiction in terms. A free will is *ex hypothesi* the sort of thing of which the request for an *explanation* is absurd. The assumption that an explanation must be in principle possible for the act of moral decision deserves to rank as a classic example of the ancient fallacy of 'begging the question'.

But the critic usually has in mind another sense of the word 'unintelligible'. He is apt to take it for granted that an act which is unintelligible in the *above* sense (as the morally free act of the Libertarian undoubtedly is) is unintelligible in the *further* sense that we can attach no meaning to it. And this is an altogether more serious matter. If it could really be shown that the Libertarian's 'free will' were unintelligible in this sense of being meaningless, that, for myself at any rate, would be the end of the affair. Libertarianism would have been conclusively refuted.

But it seems to me manifest that this can *not* be shown. The critic has allowed himself, I submit, to become the victim of a widely accepted but fundamentally vicious assumption. He has assumed that whatever is meaningful must exhibit its meaningfulness to those who view it from the standpoint of external observation. Now if one chooses thus to limit one's self to the rôle of external observer, it is, I think, perfectly true that one can attach no meaning to an act which is the act of something we call a 'self' and yet follows from nothing in that self's character. But then *why should we* so limit ourselves, when what is under consideration is a subjective activity? For the apprehension of subjective acts there is *another* standpoint available, that of *inner experience,* of the practical consciousness in its actual functioning. If our free will should turn out to be something to which we can attach a meaning from *this* standpoint, no more is required. And no more ought to be expected. For I must repeat that only from the inner standpoint of living experience *could* anything of the nature of 'activity' be directly grasped. Observation from without is in the nature of the case impotent to apprehend the active *qua* active. We can from without observe sequences of states. If into these we read activity (as we sometimes do), this can only be on the basis of what we discern in ourselves from the inner standpoint. It follows that if anyone insists upon taking his criterion of the meaningful simply from the standpoint of external observation, he is really deciding in advance of the evidence that the notion of activity, and *a fortiori* the notion of a free will, is 'meaningless'. He looks for the free act through a medium which is in the nature of the case incapable of revealing it, and then, because inevitably he doesn't find it, he declares that it doesn't exist!

But if, as we surely ought in this context, we adopt the inner standpoint, then (I am suggesting) things appear in a totally different light.

From the inner standpoint, it seems to me plain, there is no difficulty whatever in attaching meaning to an act which is the self's act and which nevertheless does not follow from the self's character. So much I claim has been established by the phenomenological analysis, in this and the previous lecture, of the act of moral decision in face of moral temptation. It is thrown into particularly clear relief where the moral decision is to make the moral effort required to rise to duty. For the very function of moral effort, as it appears to the agent engaged in the act, is to enable the self to act against the line of least resistance, against the line to which his character as so far formed most strongly inclines him. But if the self is thus conscious here of *combating* his formed character, he surely cannot possibly suppose that the act, although his own act, *issues from* his formed character? I submit, therefore, that the self knows very well indeed—from the inner standpoint—what is meant by an act which is the *self's* act and which nevertheless does not follow from the self's *character*.

What this implies—and it seems to me to be an implication of cardinal importance for any theory of the self that aims at being more than superficial—is that the nature of the self is for itself something more than just its character as so far formed. The 'nature' of the self and what we commonly call the 'character' of the self are by no means the same thing, and it is utterly vital that they should not be confused. The 'nature' of the self comprehends, but is not without remainder reducible to, its 'character'; it must, if we are to be true to the testimony of our experience of it, be taken as including *also* the authentic creative power of fashioning and re-fashioning 'character'.

The misguided, and as a rule quite uncritical, belittlement, of the evidence offered by inner experience has, I am convinced, been responsible for more bad argument by the opponents of Free Will than has any other single factor. How often, for example, do we find the Determinist critic saying, in effect, '*Either* the act follows necessarily upon precedent states, *or* it is a mere matter of chance and accordingly of no moral significance'. The disjunction is invalid, for it does not exhaust the possible alternatives. It seems to the critic to do so only because he *will* limit himself to the standpoint which is proper, and indeed alone possible, in dealing with the physical world, the standpoint of the external observer. If only he would allow himself to assume the standpoint which is not merely proper for, but necessary to, the apprehension of subjective activity, the inner standpoint of the practical consciousness in its actual functioning, he would find himself obliged to recognise the falsity of his disjunction. Reflection upon the act of moral decision as apprehended from the inner standpoint would force him to recognise a *third* possibility, as remote from chance as from necessity, that, namely, of *creative activity,* in which (as I have ventured to express it) nothing determines the act save the agent's doing of it.

11. There we must leave the matter. But as this lecture has been, I know, somewhat densely packed, it may be helpful if I conclude by reminding you, in bald summary, of the main things I have been trying to say. Let me set them out in so many successive theses.

1. The freedom which is at issue in the traditional Free Will problem is the freedom which is presupposed in moral responsibility.
2. Critical reflection upon carefully considered attributions of moral responsibility reveals that the only freedom that will do is a freedom which pertains to inner acts of choice, and that these acts must be acts (*a*) of which the self is *sole* author, and (*b*) which the self could have performed otherwise.
3. From phenomenological analysis of the situation of moral temptation we find that the self as engaged in this situation is inescapably convinced that it possesses a freedom of precisely the specified kind, located in the decision to exert or withhold the moral effort needed to rise to duty where the pressure of its desiring nature is felt to urge it in a contrary direction.

    Passing to the question of the *reality* of this moral freedom which the moral agent believes himself to possess, we argued:
4. Of the two types of Determinist criticism which seem to have most influence today, that based on the predictability of much human behaviour fails to touch a Libertarianism which confines the area of free will as above indicated. Libertarianism so understood is compatible with all the predictability that the empirical facts warrant. And:
5. The second main type of criticism, which alleges the 'meaninglessness' of an act which is the self's act and which is yet not determined by the self's character, is based on a failure to appreciate that the standpoint of inner experience is not only legitimate but indispensable where what is at issue is the reality and nature of a subjective activity. The creative act of moral decision is inevitably meaningless to the mere external observer; but from the inner standpoint it is as real, and as significant, as anything in human experience.

Richard Taylor is Professor of Philosophy
at the University of Rochester.

Richard Taylor

FATALISM

A fatalist—if there is any such—thinks he cannot do anything about the future. He thinks it is not up to him what is going to happen next year, tomorrow, or the very next moment. He thinks that even his own behavior is not in the least within his power, any more than the motions of the heavenly bodies, the events of remote history, or the political developments in China. It would, accordingly, be pointless for him to deliberate about what he is going to do, for a man deliberates only about such things as he believes are within his power to do and to forego, or to affect by his doings and foregoings.

A fatalist, in short, thinks of the future in the manner in which we all think of the past. For we do all believe that it is not up to us what happened last year, yesterday, or even a moment ago, that these things are not within our power, any more than are the motions of the heavens, the events of remote history or of China. And we are not, in fact, ever tempted to deliberate about what we have done and left undone. At best we can speculate about these things, rejoice over them or repent, draw

Reprinted from *The Philosophical Review, 71* (1962), by permission of *The Philosophical Review* and the author.

conclusions from such evidence as we have, or perhaps—if we are not fatalists about the future—extract lessons and precepts to apply henceforth. As for what has in fact happened, we must simply take it as given; the possibilities for action, if there are any, do not lie there. We may, indeed, say that some of those past things *were* once within our power, while they were still future—but this expresses our attitude toward the future, not the past.

There are various ways in which a man might get to thinking in this fatalistic way about the future, but they would be most likely to result from ideas derived from theology or physics. Thus, if God is really all-knowing and all-powerful, then, one might suppose, perhaps he has already arranged for everything to happen just as it is going to happen, and there is nothing left for you or me to do about it. Or, without bringing God into the picture, one might suppose that everything happens in accordance with invariable laws, that whatever happens in the world at any future time is the only thing that can then happen, given that certain other things were happening just before, and that these, in turn, are the only things that can happen at that time, given the total state of the world just before then, and so on, so that again, there is nothing left for us to do about it. True, what we do in the meantime will be a factor in determining how some things finally turn out—but these things that we are *going* to do will perhaps be only the causal consequences of what will be going on just before we do them, and so on back to a not distant point at which it seems obvious that we have nothing to do with what happens then. Many philosophers, particularly in the seventeenth and eighteenth centuries, have found this line of thought quite compelling.

I want to show that certain presuppositions made almost universally in contemporary philosophy yield a proof that fatalism is true, without any recourse to theology or physics. If, to be sure, it is assumed that there is an omniscient god, then that assumption can be worked into the argument so as to convey the reasoning more easily to the unphilosophical imagination, but this assumption would add nothing to the force of the argument, and will therefore be omitted here. And similarly, certain views about natural laws could be appended to the argument, perhaps for similar purposes, but they, too, would add nothing to its validity, and will therefore be ignored.

PRESUPPOSITIONS

The only presuppositions we shall need are the six following.

First, we presuppose that any proposition whatever is either true or, if not true, then false. This is simply the standard interpretation, *tertium nondatur,* of the law of excluded middle, usually symbolized $(p \lor -p)$, which is generally admitted to be a necessary truth.

Second, we presuppose that, if any state of affairs is sufficient for, though logically unrelated to, the occurrence of some further condition at the same or any other time, then the former cannot occur without the latter occurring also. This is simply the standard manner in which the concept of *sufficiency* is explicated. Another and perhaps better way of saying the same thing is that, if one state of affairs *ensures* without logically entailing the occurrence of another, then the former cannot occur without the latter occurring. Ingestion of cyanide, for instance, *ensures* death under certain familiar circumstances, though the two states of affairs are not logically related.

Third, we presuppose that, if the occurrence of any condition is necessary for, but logically unrelated to, the occurrence of some other condition at the same or any other time, then the latter cannot occur without the former occurring also. This is simply the standard manner in which the concept of a *necessary condition* is explicated. Another and perhaps better way of saying the same thing is that, if one state of affairs is *essential* for another, then the latter cannot occur without it. Oxygen, for instance, is *essential* to (though it does not by itself ensure) the maintenance of human life—though it is not logically impossible that we should live without it.

Fourth, we presuppose that, if one condition or set of conditions is sufficient for (ensures) another, then that other is necessary (essential) for it, and conversely, if one condition or set of conditions is necessary (essential) for another, then that other is sufficient for (ensures) it. This is but a logical consequence of the second and third presuppositions.

Fifth, we presuppose that no agent can perform any given act if there is lacking, at the same or any other time, some condition necessary for the occurrence of that act. This follows, simply from the idea of anything being essential for the accomplishment of something else. I cannot, for example, live without oxygen, or swim five miles without ever having been in water, or read a given page of print without having learned Russian, or win a certain election without having been nominated, and so on.

And *sixth,* we presuppose that time is not by itself "efficacious"; that is, that the mere passage of time does not augment or diminish the capacities of anything and, in particular, that it does not enhance or decrease an agent's powers or abilities. This means that if any substance or agent gains or loses powers or abilities over the course of time—such as, for instance, the power of a substance to corrode, or a man to do thirty push-ups, and so on—then such gain or loss is always the result of something other than the mere passage of time.

With these presuppositions before us, we now consider two situations in turn, the relations involved in each of them being identical except for certain temporal ones.

THE FIRST SITUATION

We imagine that I am about to open my morning newspaper to glance over the headlines. We assume, further, that conditions are such that only if there was a naval battle yesterday does the newspaper carry a certain kind (shape) of headline—i.e., that such a battle is essential for this kind of headline—whereas if it carries a certain different sort (shape) of headline, this will ensure that there was no such battle. Now, then, I am about to perform one or the other of two acts, namely, one of seeing a headline of the first kind, or one of seeing a headline of the second kind. Call these alternative acts S and S' respectively. And call the propositions, "A naval battle occurred yesterday" and "No naval battle occurred yesterday," P and P' respectively. We can assert, then, that if I perform act S, then my doing such will ensure that there was a naval battle yesterday (i.e., that P is true), whereas if I perform S', then my doing that will ensure that no such battle occurred (or, that P' is true).

With reference to this situation, then, let us now ask whether it is up to me which sort of headline I shall read as I open the newspaper; that is, let us see whether the following proposition is true:

(A) It is within my power to do S, and it is also within my power to do S'.

It seems quite obvious that this is not true. For if both these acts were equally within my power, that is, if it were up to me which one to do, then it would also be up to me whether or not a naval battle has taken place, giving me a power over the past which I plainly do not possess. It will be well, however, to express this point in the form of a proof, as follows:

1. If P is true, then it is not within my power to do S' (for in case P is true, then there is, or was, lacking a condition essential for my doing S', the condition, namely, of there being no naval battle yesterday).

2. But if P' is true, then it is not within my power to do S (for a similar reason).

3. But either P is true, or P' is true.

∴ 4. Either it is not within my power to do S, or it is not within my power to do S';

and (A) is accordingly false. A common-sense way of expressing this is to say that what sort of headline I see depends, among other things, on whether a naval battle took place yesterday, and that, in turn, is not up to me.

Now this conclusion is perfectly in accordance with common sense, for we all are, as noted, fatalists with respect to the past. No one considers past events as being within his power to control; we simply have to take them as they have happened and make the best of them. It is significant to note, however, that, in the hypothetical sense in which statements of human power or ability are usually formulated, one *does* have power over the past. For we can surely assert that, *if* I do *S*, this will ensure that a naval battle occurred yesterday, whereas *if*, alternatively, I do *S'*, this will equally ensure the nonoccurrence of such a battle, since these acts are, in terms of our example, quite sufficient for the truth of *P* and *P'* respectively. Or we can equally say that I can ensure the occurrence of such a battle yesterday simply by doing *S* and that I can ensure its nonoccurrence simply by doing *S'*. Indeed, if I should ask *how* I can go about ensuring that no naval battle occurred yesterday, perfectly straightforward instructions can be given, namely, the instruction to do *S'* and by all means to avoid doing *S*. But of course the hitch is that I cannot do *S'* *unless P'* is true, the occurrence of the battle in question rendering me quite powerless to do it.

The second situation. Let us now imagine that I am a naval commander, about to issue my order of the day to the fleet. We assume, further, that, within the totality of other conditions prevailing, my issuing of a certain kind of order will ensure that a naval battle will occur tomorrow, whereas if I issue another kind of order, this will ensire that no naval battle occurs. Now, then, I am about to perform one or the other of these two acts, namely, one of issuing an order of the first sort or one of the second sort. Call these alternative acts *O* and *O'* respectively. And call the two propositions, "A naval battle will occur tomorrow" and "No naval battle will occur tomorrow," *Q* and *Q'* respectively. We can assert, then, that, if I do act *O*, then my doing such will ensure that there will be a naval battle, whereas if I do *O'*, my doing that will ensure that no naval battle will occur.

With reference to this situation, then, let us now ask whether it is up to me which sort of order I issue; that is, let us see whether the following proposition is true:

(*B*) It is within my power to do *O*, and it is also within my power to do *O'*.

Anyone, except a fatalist, would be inclined to say that, in the situation we have envisaged, this proposition might well be true, that is, that both acts are quite within my power (granting that I cannot do both at once). For in the circumstances we assume to prevail, it is, one would think, up to me as the commander whether the naval battle occurs or not; it depends only on what kind of order I issue, given all the other conditions as they are, and what kind of order is issued is something quite within my power. It is precisely the denial that such propositions are ever true that would render one a fatalist.

But we have, unfortunately, the same formal argument to show that (*B*) is false that we had for proving the falsity of (*A*), namely:

1′. If *Q* is true, then it is not within my power to do *O'* (for in case *Q* is true, then there is, or will be, lacking a condition essential for my doing *O'*, the condition, namely, of there being no naval battle tomorrow).

2′. But if *Q'* is true, then it is not within my power to do *O* (for a similar reason).

3′. But either *Q* is true, or *Q'* is true.

∴ 4′. Either it is not within my power to do *O*, or it is not within my power to do *O'*;

and (*B*) is accordingly false. Another way of expressing this is to say that what sort of order I issue depends, among other things, on whether a naval battle takes place tomorrow—for in this situation a naval battle tomorrow is (by our fourth presupposition) a necessary condition of my doing *O*, whereas no naval battle tomorrow is equally essential for my doing *O'*.

Considerations of time. Here it might be tempting, at first, to say that *time* makes a difference, and that no condition can be necessary for any other *before* that condition exists. But this escape is closed by both our fifth and sixth presuppositions. Surely if some condition, at *any* given time, whether past, present, or future, is necessary for the occurrence of something else, and that condition does not in fact exist *at the time it is needed,* then nothing we do can be of any avail in bringing about that occurrence for which it is necessary. To deny this would be equivalent to saying that I can do something now which is, together with other conditions prevailing, sufficient for, or which ensures, the occurrence of something else in the future, *without* getting that future occurrence as a result. This is absurd in itself and contrary to our second presupposition. And if one should suggest, in spite of all this, that a state of affairs that exists *not yet* cannot, just because of this temporal removal, be a necessary condition of *anything* existing prior to it, this would be logically equivalent to saying that no present state of affairs can ensure another subsequent to it. We could with equal justice say that a state of affairs, such as yesterday's naval battle, which exists *no longer,* cannot be a necessary condition of anything existing subsequently, there being the same temporal interval here; and this would be arbitrary and false. All that is needed, to restrict the powers that I imagine myself to have to do this or that, is that some condition essential to my doing it *does* not, *did* not, or *will* not occur.

Nor can we wriggle out of fatalism by respresenting this sort of situation as one in which there is a simple loss of ability or power resulting from the passage of time. For according to our sixth presupposition, the mere passage of time does not enhance or diminish the powers or abilities of anything. We cannot, therefore, say that I have the power to do O' until, say, tomorrow's naval battle occurs, or the power to do O until tomorrow arrives and we find no naval battle occurring, and so on. What restricts the range of my power to do this thing or that is not the mere *temporal* relations between my acts and certain other states of affairs, but the very existence of those states of affairs themselves; and according to our first presupposition, the fact of tomorrow's containing, or lacking, a naval battle, as the case may be, is no less a fact than yesterday's containing or lacking one. If, at any time, I lack the power to perform a certain act, then it can only be the result of something, other than the passage of time, that has happened, is happening, or will happen. The fact that there *is going* to be a naval battle tomorrow is quite enough to render me unable to do O', just as the fact that there *has been* a naval battle yesterday renders me unable to do S', the nonoccurrence of those conditions being essential, respectively, for my doing those things.

Causation. Again, it does no good here to appeal to any particular analyses of causation, or to the fact, if it is one, that causes only "work" forwards and not backwards, for our problem has been formulated without any reference to causation. It may be, for all we know, that causal relations have an unalterable direction (which is an unclear claim in itself), but it is very certain that the relations of necessity and sufficiency between events or states of affairs have not, and it is in terms of these that our data have been described.

The law of excluded middle. There is, of course, one other way to avoid fatalism, and that is to deny one of the premises used to refute (B). The first two, hypothetical, premises cannot be denied, however, without our having to reject all but the first, and perhaps the last, of our original six presuppositions, and none of these seems the least doubtful. And the third premise—that either Q is true, or Q' is true—can be denied only by rejecting the first of our six presuppositions, that is, by rejecting the standard interpretation, *tertium non datur,* of what is called the law of excluded middle.

This last escape has, however, been attempted, and it apparently involves no absurdity. Aristotle, according to an interpretation that is sometimes rendered of his *De Interpretatione,* rejected it. According to this view, the disjunction $(Q \vee Q')$ or, equivalently, $(Q \vee - Q)$, which is an instance of the law in question, is a necessary truth. Neither of its disjuncts, however—i.e., neither Q, nor Q'—is a necessary truth nor, indeed, even a truth, but is instead a mere "possibility," or "contingency" (whatever that may mean). And there is, it would seem, no obvious absurdity in supposing that two propositions, neither of them true and neither of them false, but each "possible," might nevertheless combine into a disjunction which is a necessary truth—for that disjunction might, as this one plainly does exhaust the possibilities.

Indeed, by assuming the truth of (B)—i.e., the statement that it is within my power to do O and it is also within my power to do O'—and substituting this as our third premise, a formal argument can be rendered to prove that a disjunction of contradictories might disjoin propositions which are neither true nor false. Thus:

1″.   If Q is true, then it is not within my power to do O'.
2″.   But if Q' is true, then it is not within my power to do O.
3″.   But it is within my power to do O, and it is also within my power to do O'.
∴ 4″. Q' is not true, and Q is not true;

and to this we can add that, since Q and Q' are logical contradictories, such that if either is false then the other is true, then Q is not false, and Q' is not false—i.e., that neither of them is true and neither of them false.

There seems to be no good argument against this line of thought which does not presuppose the very thing at issue, that is, which does not presuppose, not just the truth of a disjunction of contradictories, which is here preserved, but one special interpretation of the law thus expressed, namely, that no third value, like "possible," can ever be assigned to any proposition. And that particular interpretation can, perhaps, be regarded as a more or less arbitrary restriction.

We would not, furthermore, be obliged by this line of thought to reject the traditional interpretation of the so-called law of contradiction, which can be expressed by saying that, concerning any proposition, not both it and its contradictory can be true—which is clearly consistent with what is here suggested.

Nor need we suppose that, from a sense of neatness and consistency, we ought to apply the same considerations to our first situation and to proposition (*A*)—that, if we so interpret the law in question as to avoid fatalism with respect to the future, then we ought to retain the same interpretation as it applies to things past. The difference here is that we have not the slightest inclination to suppose that it is at all within our power what happened in the past, or that propositions like (*A*) in situations such as we have described are ever true, whereas we do, if we are not fatalists, believe that it is sometimes within our power what happens in the future, that is, that propositions like (*B*) are sometimes true. And it was only from the desire to preserve the truth of (*B*), but not (*A*), and thus avoid fatalism, that the *tertium non datur* was doubted, using (*B*) as a premise.

Temporal efficacy. It now becomes apparent, however, that if we seek to avoid fatalism by this device, then we shall have to reject not only our first but also our sixth presupposition; for on this view time will by itself have the power to render true or false certain propositions which were hitherto neither, and this is an "efficacy" of sorts. In fact, it is doubtful whether one can in any way avoid fatalism with respect to the future while conceding that things past are, by virtue of their pastness alone, no longer within our power without also conceding an efficacy to time; for *any* such view will entail that future possibilities, at one time within our power to realize or not, cease to be such *merely* as a result of the passage of time—which is precisely what our sixth presupposition denies. Indeed, this is probably the whole point in casting doubt upon the law of excluded middle in the first place, namely, to call attention to the status of some future things as mere possibilities, thus denying both their complete factuality and their complete lack of it. If so, then our first and sixth presuppositions are inseparably linked, standing or falling together.

The assertion of fatalism. Of course one other possibility remains, and that is to assert, out of a respect for the law of excluded middle and a preference for viewing things under the aspect of eternity, that fatalism is indeed a true doctrine, that propositions such as (*B*) are, like (*A*), never true in such situations as we have described, and that the difference in our *attitudes* toward things future and past, which leads us to call some of the former but none of the latter "possibilities," results entirely from epistem- ological and psychological considerations—such as, that we happen to *know* more about what the past contains than about what is contained in the future, that our memory extends to past experiences rather than future ones, and so on. Apart from subjective feelings of our power to control things, there seem to be no good philosophical reasons against this opinion, and very strong ones in its favor.

SUGGESTIONS FOR FURTHER READING

BEROFSKY, BERNARD, ed., *Free Will and Determinism,* New York: Harper & Row, 1966. Paperback. A comprehensive anthology that contains readings representing a variety of approaches to the free-will problem.

CAHN, STEVEN M., *Fate, Logic, and Time,* New Haven, Conn.: Yale University Press, 1967. A detailed discussion of historical and contemporary approaches to the issue of fatalism.

TAYLOR, RICHARD, *Action and Purpose,* Englewood Cliffs, N.J.: Prentice-Hall, Inc., 1966. A challenging study of the nature of human action.

PART III

PHILOSOPHY OF RELIGION

St. Anselm (1033–1109) was Archbishop of Canterbury.

St. Anselm

THE ONTOLOGICAL ARGUMENT

And so, Lord, do thou, who dost give understanding to faith, give me, so far as thou knowest it to be profitable, to understand that thou art as we believe; and that thou art that which we believe. And, indeed, we believe that thou art a being than which nothing greater can be conceived. Or is there no such nature, since the fool hath said in his heart, there is no God? (Psalms xiv. 1). But, at any rate, this very fool, when he hears of this being of which I speak—a being than which nothing greater can be conceived—understands what he hears, and what he understands is in his understanding; although he does not understand it to exist.

For, it is one thing for an object to be in the understanding, and another to understand that the object exists. When a painter first conceives of what he will afterwards perform, he has it in his understanding, but he does not yet understand it to be, because he has not yet performed

Reprinted from *St. Anselm: Basic Writings,* trans. S. N. Deane, with an introduction by Charles Hartshorne, La Salle, Ill.: 1961, by permission of The Open Court Publishing Company.

it. But after he has made the painting, he both has it in his understanding, and he understands that it exists, because he has made it.

Hence, even the fool is convinced that something exists in the understanding, at least, than which nothing greater can be conceived. For, when he hears of this, he understands it. And whatever is understood, exists in the understanding. And assuredly that, than which nothing greater can be conceived, cannot exist in the understanding alone. For, suppose it exists in the understanding alone: then it can be conceived to exist in reality; which is greater.

Therefore, if that, than which nothing greater can be conceived, exists in the understanding alone, the very being, than which nothing greater can be conceived, is one, than which a greater can be conceived. But obviously this is impossible. Hence, there is no doubt that there exists a being, than which nothing greater can be conceived, and it exists both in the understanding and in reality.

And it assuredly exists so truly, that it cannot be conceived not to exist. For, it is possible to conceive of a being which cannot be conceived not to exist; and this is greater than one which can be conceived not to exist. Hence, if that, than which nothing greater can be conceived, can be conceived not to exist, it is not that, than which nothing greater can be conceived. But this is an irreconcilable contradiction. There is, then, so truly a being than which nothing greater can be conceived to exist, that it cannot even be conceived not to exist; and this being thou art, O Lord, our God.

So truly, therefore, dost thou exist, O Lord, my God, that thou canst not be conceived not to exist; and rightly. For, if a mind could conceive of a being better than thee, the creature would rise above the Creator; and this is most absurd. And, indeed, whatever else there is, except thee alone, can be conceived not to exist. To thee alone, therefore, it belongs to exist more truly than all other beings, and hence in a higher degree than all others. For, whatever else exists does not exist so truly, and hence in a less degree it belongs to it to exist. Why, then, has the fool said in his heart, there is no God (Psalms xiv. 1), since it is so evident, to a rational mind, that thou dost exist in the highest degree of all? Why, except that he is dull and a fool?

But how has the fool said in his heart what he could not conceive; or how is it that he could not conceive what he said in his heart? since it is the same to say in the heart, and to conceive.

But, if really, nay, since really, he both conceived, because he said in his heart; and did not say in his heart, because he could not conceive; there is more than one way in which a thing is said in the heart or conceived. For, in one sense, an object is conceived, when the word signifying it is conceived; and in another, when the very entity, which the object is, is understood.

In the former sense, then, God can be conceived not to exist; but in the latter, not at all. For no one who understands what fire and water are can conceive fire to be water, in accordance with the nature of the facts themselves, although this is possible according to the words. So, then, no one who understands what God is can conceive that God does not exist; although he says these words in his heart, either without any, or with some foreign, signification. For, God is that than which a greater cannot be conceived. And he who thoroughly understands this, assuredly understands that this being so truly exists, that not even in concept can it be non-existent. Therefore, he who understands that God so exists, cannot conceive that he does not exist.

I thank thee, gracious Lord, I thank thee; because what I formerly believed by thy bounty, I now so understand by thine illumination, that if I were unwilling to believe that thou dost exist, I should not be able not to understand this to be true.

IN BEHALF OF THE FOOL

AN ANSWER TO THE ARGUMENT OF ANSELM
IN THE PROSLOGIUM.
BY GAUNILON, A MONK OF MARMOUTIER.

If one doubts or denies the existence of a being of such a nature that nothing greater than it can be conceived, he receives this answer:

The existence of this being is proved, in the first place, by the fact that he himself, in his doubt or denial regarding this being, already has it in his understanding; for in hearing it spoken of he understands what is spoken of. It is proved, therefore, by the fact that what he understands must exist not only in his understanding, but in reality also.

And the proof of this is as follows.—It is a greater thing to exist both in the understanding and in reality than to be in the understanding alone. And if this being is in the understanding alone, whatever has even in the past existed in reality will be greater than this being. And so that which was greater than all beings will be less than some being, and will not be greater than all: which is a manifest contradiction.

And hence, that which is greater than all, already proved to be in the understanding, must exist not only in the understanding, but also in reality: for otherwise it will not be greater than all other beings.

The fool might make this reply:

This being is said to be in my understanding already, only because I understand what is said. Now could it not with equal justice be said that I have in my understanding all manner of unreal objects, having absolutely no existence in themselves, because I understand these things if one speaks of them, whatever they may be?

• • •

For example: it is said that somewhere in the ocean is an island, which, because of the difficulty, or rather the impossibility, of discovering what does not exist, is called the lost island. And they say that this island has an inestimable wealth of all manner of riches and delicacies in greater abundance than is told of the Islands of the Blest; and that having no owner or inhabitant, it is more excellent than all other countries, which are inhabited by mankind, in the abundance with which it is stored.

Now if some one should tell me that there is such an island, I should easily understand his words, in which there is no difficulty. But suppose that he went on to say, as if by a logical inference: "You can no longer doubt that this island which is more excellent than all lands exists somewhere, since you have no doubt that it is in your understanding. And since it is more excellent not to be in the understanding alone, but to exist both in the understanding and in reality, for this reason it must exist. For if it does not exist, any land which really exists will be more excellent than it; and so the island already understood by you to be more excellent will not be more excellent."

If a man should try to prove to me by such reasoning that this island truly exists, and that its existence should no longer be doubted, either I should believe that he was jesting, or I know not which I ought to regard as the greater fool: myself, supposing that I should allow this proof; or him, if he should suppose that he had established with any certainty the existence of this island. For he ought to show first that the hypothetical excellence of this island exists as a real and indubitable fact, and in no wise as any unreal object, or one whose existence is uncertain, in my understanding.

This, in the mean time, is the answer the fool could make to the arguments urged against him. When he is assured in the first place that this being is so great that its non-existence is not even conceivable, and that this in turn is proved on no other ground than the fact that otherwise it will not be greater than all things, the fool may make the same answer, and say:

When did I say that any such being exists in reality, that is, a being greater than all others?—that on this ground it should be proved to me that it also exists in reality to such a degree that it cannot even be conceived not to exist? Whereas in the first place it should be in some way proved that a nature which is higher, that is, greater and better, than all other natures, exists; in order that from this we may then be able to prove all attributes which necessarily the being that is greater and better than all possesses.

Moreover, it is said that the non-existence of this being is inconceivable. It might better be said, perhaps, that its non-existence, or the possibility of its non-existence, is unintelligible. For according to the true meaning of the word, unreal objects are unintelligible. Yet their existence is conceivable in the way in which the fool conceived of the non-existence of God. I am most certainly aware of my own existence; but I know, nevertheless, that my non-existence is possible. As to that supreme being, moreover, which God is, I understand without any doubt both his existence, and the impossibility of his non-existence. Whether, however, so long as I am most positively aware of my existence, I can conceive of my non-existence, I am not sure. But if I can, why can I not conceive of the non-existence of whatever else I know with the same certainty? If, however, I cannot, God will not be the only being of which it can be said, it is impossible to conceive of his non-existence.

ANSELM'S APOLOGETIC

IN REPLY TO GAUNILON'S ANSWER IN
BEHALF OF THE FOOL.

. . . But, you say, it is as if one should suppose an island in the ocean, which surpasses all lands in its fertility, and which, because of the difficulty, or rather the impossibility, of discovering what does not exist, is called a lost island; and should say that there can be no doubt that this island truly exists in reality, for this reason, that one who hears it described easily understands what he hears.

Now I promise confidently that if any man shall devise anything existing either in reality or in concept alone (except that than which a greater cannot be conceived) to which he can adapt the sequence of my reasoning, I will discover that thing, and will give him his lost island, not to be lost again.

But it now appears that this being than which a greater is inconceivable cannot be conceived not to be, because it exists on so assured a ground of truth; for otherwise it would not exist at all.

Hence, if any one says that he conceives this being not to exist, I say that at the time when he conceives of this either he conceives of a being than which a greater is inconceivable, or he does not conceive at all. If he does not conceive, he does not conceive of the non-existence of that of which he does not conceive. But if he does conceive, he certainly conceives of a being which cannot be even conceived not to exist. For if it could be conceived not to exist, it could be conceived to have a beginning and an end. But this is impossible.

He, then, who conceives of this being conceives of a being which cannot be even conceived not to exist; but he who conceives of this being does not conceive that it does not exist; else he conceives what is inconceivable. The non-existence, then, of that than which a greater cannot be conceived is inconceivable.

You say, moreover, that whereas I assert that this supreme being cannot be *conceived* not to exist, it might better be said that its non-existence, or even the possibility of its non-existence, cannot be *understood*.

But it was more proper to say, it cannot be conceived. For if I had said that the object itself cannot be understood not to exist, possibly you yourself, who say that in accordance with the true meaning of the term what is unreal cannot be understood, would offer the objection that nothing which is can be understood not to be, for the non-existence of what exists is unreal: hence God would not be the only being of which it could be said, it is impossible to understand its non-existence. For thus one of those beings which most certainly exist can be understood not to exist in the same way in which certain other real objects can be understood not to exist.

But this objection, assuredly, cannot be urged against the term *conception,* if one considers the matter well. For although no objects which exist can be understood not to exist, yet all objects, except that which exists in the highest degree, can be conceived not to exist. For all those objects, and those alone, can be conceived not to exist, which have a beginning or end or composition of parts: also, as I have already said, whatever at any place or at any time does not exist as a whole.

That being alone, on the other hand, cannot be conceived not to exist, in which any conception discovers neither beginning nor end nor composition of parts, and which any conception finds always and everywhere as a whole.

Be assured, then, that you can conceive of your own non-existence, although you are most certain that you exist. I am surprised that you should have admitted that you are ignorant of this. For we conceive of the non-existence of many objects which we know to exist, and of the existence of many which we know not to exist; not by forming the opinion that they so exist, but by imagining that they exist as we conceive of them.

And indeed, we can conceive of the non-existence of an object, although we know it to exist, because at the same time we can conceive of the former and know the latter. And we cannot conceive of the non-existence of an object, so long as we know it to exist, because we cannot conceive at the same time of existence and non-existence.

If, then, one will thus distinguish these two senses of this statement, he will understand that nothing, so long as it is known to exist, can be conceived not to exist; and that whatever exists, except that being than which a greater cannot be conceived, can be conceived not to exist, even when it is known to exist.

So, then, of God alone it can be said that it is impossible to conceive of his non-existence; and yet many objects, so long as they exist, in one sense cannot be conceived not to exist. But in what sense God is to be conceived not to exist, I think has been shown clearly enough in my book.

St. Thomas Aquinas (ca. 1224–1274) was a leading figure
in medieval Christian philosophy.

St. Thomas Aquinas

FIVE PROOFS
FOR THE EXISTENCE OF GOD

The existence of God can be proved in five ways.

The first and more manifest way is the argument from motion. It is certain, and evident to our senses, that in the world some things are in motion. Now whatever is moved is moved by another, for nothing can be moved except it is in potentiality to that towards which it is moved; whereas a thing moves inasmuch as it is in act. For motion is nothing else than the reduction of something from potentiality to actuality. But nothing can be reduced from potentiality to actuality, except by something in a state of actuality. Thus that which is actually hot, as fire, makes wood, which is potentially hot, to be actually hot, and thereby moves and changes it. Now it is not possible that the same thing should be at once in actuality and potentiality in the same respect, but only in different respects. For what is actually hot cannot simultaneously be potentially hot;

Reprinted from *The Basic Writings of St. Thomas Aquinas* (1945), ed. Anton C. Pegis, by permission of the publisher, Random House, Inc.

but it is simultaneously potentially cold. It is therefore impossible that in the same respect and in the same way a thing should be both mover and moved, *i.e.*, that it should move itself. Therefore, whatever is moved must be moved by another. If that by which it is moved be itself moved, then this also must needs be moved by another, and that by another again. But this cannot go on to infinity, because then there would be no first mover, and, consequently, no other mover, seeing that subsequent movers move only inasmuch as they are moved by the first mover; as the staff moves only because it is moved by the hand. Therefore it is necessary to arrive at a first mover, moved by no other; and this everyone understands to be God.

The second way is from the nature of efficient cause. In the world of sensible things we find there is an order of efficient causes. There is no case known (neither is it, indeed, possible) in which a thing is found to be the efficient cause of itself; for so it would be prior to itself, which is impossible. Now in efficient causes it is not possible to go on to infinity, because in all efficient causes following in order, the first is the cause of the intermediate cause, and the intermediate is the cause of the ultimate cause, whether the intermediate cause be several, or one only. Now to take away the cause is to take away the effect. Therefore, if there be no first cause among efficient causes, there will be no ultimate, nor any intermediate, cause. But if in efficient causes it is possible to go on to infinity, there will be no first efficient cause, neither will there be an ultimate effect, nor any intermediate efficient causes; all of which is plainly false. Therefore it is necessary to admit a first efficient cause, to which everyone gives the name of God.

The third way is taken from possibility and necessity, and runs thus. We find in nature things that are possible to be and not to be, since they are found to be generated, and to be corrupted, and consequently, it is possible for them to be and not to be. But it is impossible for these always to exist, for that which can not-be at some time is not. Therefore, if everything can not-be, then at one time there was nothing in existence. Now if this were true, even now there would be nothing in existence, because that which does not exist begins to exist only through something already existing. Therefore, if at one time nothing was in existence, it would have been impossible for anything to have begun to exist; and thus even now nothing would be in existence—which is absurd. Therefore, not all beings are merely possible, but there must exist something the existence of which is necessary. But every necessary thing either has its necessity caused by another, or not. Now it is impossible to go on to infinity in necessary things which have their necessity caused by another, as has been already proved in regard to efficient causes. Therefore we cannot but admit the existence of some being having of itself its own necessity, and not receiving it from another, but rather causing in others their necessity. This all men speak of as God.

The fourth way is taken from the gradation to be found in things. Among beings there are some more and some less good, true, noble, and the like. But *more* and *less* are predicated of different things according as they resemble in their different ways something which is the maximum, as a thing is said to be hotter according as it more nearly resembles that which is hottest; so that there is something which is truest, something best, something noblest, and, consequently, something which is most being, for those things that are greatest in truth are greatest in being, as it is written in *Metaph*.ii. Now the maximum in any genus is the cause of all in that genus, as fire, which is the maximum of heat, is the cause of all hot things, as is said in the same book. Therefore there must also be something which is to all beings the cause of their being, goodness, and every other perfection; and this we call God.

The fifth way is taken from the governance of the world. We see that things which lack knowledge, such as natural bodies, act for an end, and this is evident from their acting always, or nearly always, in the same way, so as to obtain the best result. Hence it is plain that they achieve their end, not fortuitously, but designedly. Now whatever lacks knowledge cannot move towards an end, unless it be directed by some being endowed with knowledge and intelligence; as the arrow is directed by the archer. Therefore some intelligent being exists by whom all natural things are directed to their end; and this being we call God.

Richard Taylor

A DEFENSE OF THEISM

An active, living, and religious belief in the gods has probably never arisen and been maintained on purely metaphysical grounds. Such beliefs are found in every civilized land and time, and are often virtually universal in a particular culture, yet relatively few men have much of a conception of metaphysics. There are in fact entire cultures, such as ancient Israel, to whom metaphysics is quite foreign, though these cultures may nevertheless be religious.

Belief in the gods seems to have its roots in human desires and fears, particularly those associated with self-preservation. Like all other creatures, men have a profound will to live, which is what mainly gives one's existence a meaning from one sunrise to the next. Unlike other creatures, however, men are capable of the full and terrible realization of their own inevitable decay. A man can bring before his mind the image of his own

Richard Taylor, *Metaphysics,* © 1963. Reprinted by permission of Prentice-Hall, Inc., Englewood Cliffs, N.J.

grave, and with it the complete certainty of its ultimate reality, and against this his will naturally recoils. It can hardly seem to him less than an absolute catastrophe, the very end, so far as he is concerned, of everything, though he has no difficulty viewing death, as it touches others more or less remote from himself, as a perhaps puzzling, occasionally distressing, but nonetheless necessary aspect of nature. It is probably partly in response to this fear that he turns to the gods, as those beings of such power that they can overturn this verdict of nature.

The sources of religious belief are doubtless much more complex than this, but they seem to lie in man's will rather than in his speculative intelligence, nevertheless. Men who possess such a belief seldom permit any metaphysical considerations to wrest it from them, while those who lack it are seldom turned toward it by other metaphysical considerations. Still, in every land in which philosophy has flourished, there have been profound thinkers who have sought to discover some metaphysical basis for a rational belief in the existence of some supreme being or beings. Even though religion may properly be a matter of faith rather than reason, still, a philosophical person can hardly help wondering whether it might, at least in part, be also a matter of reason, and whether, in particular, the existence of God might be something that can be not merely believed but shown. It is this question that we want now to consider; that is, we want to see whether there are not strong metaphysical considerations from which the existence of some supreme and supranatural being might reasonably be inferred.

Suppose you were strolling in the woods and, in addition to the sticks, stones, and other accustomed litter of the forest floor, you one day came upon some quite unaccustomed object, something not quite like what you had ever seen before and would never expect to find in such a place. Suppose, for example, that it is a large ball, about your own height, perfectly smooth and translucent. You would deem this puzzling and mysterious, certainly, but if one considers the matter, it is no more inherently mysterious that such a thing should exist than that anything else should exist. If you were quite accustomed to finding such objects of various sizes around you most of the time, but had never seen an ordinary rock, then upon finding a large rock in the woods one day you would be just as puzzled and mystified. This illustrates the fact that something that is mysterious ceases to seem so simply by its accustomed presence. It is strange indeed, for example, that a world such as ours should exist; yet few men are very often struck by this strangeness, but simply take it for granted.

Suppose, then, that you have found this translucent ball and are mysti-

fied by it. Now whatever else you might wonder about it, there is one
thing you would hardly question; namely, that it did not appear there all
by itself, that it owes its existence to something. You might not have the
remotest idea whence and how it came to be there, but you would hardly
doubt that there was an explanation. The idea that it might have come
from nothing at all, that it might exist without there being any explanation of its existence, is one that few people would consider worthy of
entertaining.

This illustrates a metaphysical belief that seems to be almost a part of
reason itself, even though few men ever think upon it; the belief, namely,
that there is some explanation for the existence of anything whatever,
some reason why it should exist rather than not. The sheer nonexistence
of anything, which is not to be confused with the passing out of existence
of something, never requires a reason; but existence does. That there
should never have been any such ball in the forest does not require any
explanation or reason, but that there should ever be such a ball does. If
one were to look upon a barren plain and ask why there is not and never
has been any large translucent ball there, the natural response would be to
ask why there should be; but if one finds such a ball, and wonders why it
is there, it is not quite so natural to ask why it should *not* be, as though
existence should simply be taken for granted. That anything should not
exist, then, and that, for instance, no such ball should exist in the forest,
or that there should be no forest for it to occupy, or no continent containing a forest, or no earth, nor any world at all, do not seem to be
things for which there needs to be any explanation or reason; but that
such things should be, does seem to require a reason.

The principle involved here has been called the principle of sufficient
reason. Actually, it is a very general principle, and is best expressed by
saying that, in the case of any positive truth, there is some sufficient
reason for it, something which, in this sense, makes it true—in short, that
there is some sort of explanation, known or unknown, for everything.

Now some truths depend on something else, and are accordingly called
contingent, while others depend only upon themselves, that is, are true by
their very natures and are accordingly called *necessary*. There is, for
example, a reason why the stone on my window sill is warm; namely, that
the sun is shining upon it. This happens to be true, but not by its very
nature. Hence, it is contingent, and depends upon something other than
itself. It is also true that all the points of a circle are equidistant from the
center, but this truth depends upon nothing but itself. No matter what
happens, nothing can make it false. Similarly, it is a truth, and a necessary one, that if the stone on my window sill is a body, as it is, then it has

a form, since this fact depends upon nothing but itself for its confirmation. Untruths are also, of course, either contingent or necessary, it being contingently false, for example, that the stone on my window sill is cold, and necessarily false that it is both a body and formless, since this is by its very nature impossible.

The principle of sufficient reason can be illustrated in various ways, as we have done, and if one thinks about it, he is apt to find that he presupposes it in his thinking about reality, but it cannot be proved. It does not appear to be itself a necessary truth, and at the same time it would be most odd to say it is contingent. If one were to try proving it, he would sooner or later have to appeal to considerations that are less plausible than the principle itself. Indeed, it is hard to see how one could even make an argument for it, without already assuming it. For this reason it might properly be called a presupposition of reason itself. One can deny that it is true, without embarrassment or fear of refutation, but one is then apt to find that what he is denying is not really what the principle asserts. We shall, then, treat it here as a datum—not something that is provably true, but as something which all men, whether they ever reflect upon it or not, seem more or less to presuppose.

It happens to be true that something exists, that there is, for example, a world, and while no one ever seriously supposes that this might not be so, that there might exist nothing at all, there still seems to be nothing the least necessary in this, considering it just by itself. That no world should ever exist at all is perfectly comprehensible and seems to express not the slightest absurdity. Considering any particular item in the world it seems not at all necessary in itself that it should ever have existed, nor does it appear any more necessary that the totality of these things, or any totality of things, should ever exist.

From the principle of sufficient reason it follows, of course, that there must be a reason, not only for the existence of everything in the world but for the world itself, meaning by "the world" simply everything that ever does exist, except God, in case there is a god. This principle does not imply that there must be some purpose or goal for everything, or for the totality of all things; for explanations need not, and in fact seldom are, teleological or purposeful. All the principle requires is that there be some sort of reason for everything. And it would certainly be odd to maintain that everything in the world owes its existence to something, that nothing in the world is either purely accidental, or such that it just bestows its own being upon itself, and then to deny this of the world itself. One can indeed *say* that the world is in some sense a pure accident, that there simply is no reason at all why this or any world should exist, and one can equally say that the world exists by its very nature, or is an inherently necessary being. But it is at least very odd and arbitrary to deny of this existing world the need for any sufficient reason, whether independent of itself or not, while presupposing that there is a reason for every other thing that ever exists.

Consider again the strange ball that we imagine has been found in the forest. Now we can hardly doubt that there must be an explanation for the existence of such a thing, though we may have no notion what that explanation is. It is not, moreover, the fact of its having been found in the forest rather than elsewhere that renders an explanation necessary. It matters not in the least where it happens to be, for our question is not how it happens to be *there* but how it happens to exist at all. If we in our imagination annihilate the forest, leaving only this ball in an open field, our conviction that it is a contingent thing and owes its existence to something other than itself is not reduced in the least. If we now imagine the field to be annihilated, and in fact everything else as well to vanish into nothingness, leaving only this ball to constitute the entire physical universe, then we cannot for a moment suppose that its existence has thereby been explained, or the need of any explanation eliminated, or that its existence is suddenly rendered self-explanatory. If we now carry this thought one step further and suppose that no other reality ever has existed or ever will exist, that this ball forever constitutes the entire physical universe, then we must still insist on there being some reason independent of itself why it should exist rather than not. If there must be a reason for the existence of any particular thing, then the necessity of such a reason is not eliminated by the mere supposition that certain other things do *not* exist. And again, it matters not at all what the thing in question is, whether it be large and complex, such as the world we actually find ourselves in, or whether it be something small, simple and insignificant, such as a ball, a bacterium, or the merest grain of sand. We do not avoid the necessity of a reason for the existence of something merely by describing it in this way or that. And it would, in any event, seem quite plainly absurd to say that if the world were comprised entirely of a single ball about six feet in diameter, or of a single grain of sand, then it would be contingent and there would have to be some explanation other than itself why such a thing exists, but that, since the actual world is vastly more complex than this, there is no need for an explanation of its existence, independent of itself.

It should now be noted that it is no answer to the question, why a thing exists, to state *how long* it has existed. A geologist does not suppose that he has explained why there should be rivers and mountains merely by pointing out that they are old. Similarly, if one were to ask, concerning the ball of which we have spoken, for some sufficient reason for its being, he would not receive any answer upon being told that it had been there since yesterday. Nor would it be any better answer to say that it had existed since before anyone could remember, or even that it had always existed; for the question was not one concerning its age but its existence. If, to be sure, one were to ask where a given thing came from, or how it came into being, then upon learning that it had always existed he would learn that it never really *came* into being at all; but he could still reasonably wonder why it should exist at all. If, accordingly, the world—that is, the totality of all things excepting God, in case there is a god—had really no beginning at all, but has always existed in some form or other, then there is clearly no answer to the question, where it came from and when; it did not, on this supposition, *come* from anything at all, at any time. But still, it can be asked why there is a world, why indeed there is a beginning-less world, why there should have perhaps always been something rather than nothing. And, if the principle of sufficient reason is a good principle, there must be an answer to that question, an answer that is by no means supplied by giving the world an age, or even an infinite age.

This brings out an important point with respect to the concept of creation that is often misunderstood, particularly by those whose thinking has been influenced by Christian ideas. People tend to think that creation —for example, the creation of the world by God—*means* creation *in time,* from which it of course logically follows that if the world had no beginning in time, then it cannot be the creation of God. This, however, is erroneous, for creation means essentially *dependence,* even in Christian theology. If one thing is the creation of another, then it depends for its existence on that other, and this is perfectly consistent with saying that both are eternal, that neither ever came into being, and hence, that neither was ever created at any point of time. Perhaps an analogy will help convey this point. Consider, then, a flame that is casting beams of light. Now there seems to be a clear sense in which the beams of light are dependent for their existence upon the flame, which is their source, while the flame, on the other hand, is not similarly dependent for its existence upon them. The beams of light arise from the flame, but the flame does not arise from them. In this sense, they are the creation of the flame; they derive their existence from it. And none of this has any reference to time; the relationship of dependence in such a case would not be altered in the slightest if we supposed that the flame, and with it the beams of light, had always existed, that neither had ever *come* into being.

Now if the world is the creation of God, its relationship to God should be thought of in this fashion; namely, that the world depends for its existence upon God, and could not exist independently of God. If God is eternal, as those who believe in God generally assume, then the world may (though it need not) be eternal too, without that altering in the least its dependence upon God for its existence, and hence without altering its being the creation of God. The supposition of God's eternality, on the other hand, does not by itself imply that the world is eternal too; for there is not the least reason why something of finite duration might not depend for its existence upon something of infinite duration—though the reverse is, of course, impossible.

If we think of God as "the creator of heaven and earth," and if we consider heaven and earth to include everything that exists except God, then we appear to have, in the foregoing considerations, fairly strong reasons for asserting that God, as so conceived, exists. Now of course most people have much more in mind than this when they think of God, for religions have ascribed to God ever so many attributes that are not at all implied by describing him merely as the creator of the world; but that is not relevant here. Most religious persons do, in any case, think of God as being at least the creator, as that being upon which everything ultimately depends, no matter what else they may say about him in addition. It is, in fact, the first item in the creeds of Christianity that God is the "creator of heaven and earth." And, it seems, there are good metaphysical reasons, as distinguished from the persuasions of faith, for thinking that such a creative being exists.

If, as seems clearly implied by the principle of sufficient reason, there must be a reason for the existence of heaven and earth—i.e., for the world—then that reason must be found either in the world itself, or outside it, in something that is literally supranatural, or outside heaven and earth. Now if we suppose that the world—i.e., the totality of all things except God—contains within itself the reason for its existence, we are supposing that it exists by its very nature, that is, that it is a necessary being. In that case there would, of course, be no reason for saying that it must depend upon God or anything else for its existence; for if it exists by its very nature, then it depends upon nothing but itself, much as the sun depends upon nothing but itself for its heat. This, however, is implausible, for we find nothing about the world or anything in it to suggest that it exists by its very nature must necessarily be eternal and indestructible. It things to suggest that it does not. For in the first place, anything which exits by its very nature must necessarily be eternal and indestructible. It would be a self-contradiction to say of anything that it exists by its own nature, or is a necessarily existing thing, and at the same time to say that it comes into being or passes away, or that it ever could come into being or pass away. Nothing about the world seems at all like this, for concerning anything in the world, we can perfectly easily think of it as being annihilated, or as never having existed in the first place, without there being the slightest hint of any absurdity in such a supposition. Some of the things in the universe are, to be sure, very old; the moon, for example, or the stars and the planets. It is even possible to imagine that they have always existed. Yet it seems quite impossible to suppose that they owe their existence to nothing but themselves, that they bestow existence upon themselves by their very natures, or that they are in themselves things of such nature that it would be impossible for them not to exist. Even if we suppose that something, such as the sun, for instance, has existed forever, and will never cease, still we cannot conclude just from this that it exists by its own nature. If, as is of course very doubtful, the sun has existed forever and will never cease, then it is possible that its heat and light have also existed forever and will never cease; but that would not show that the heat and light of the sun exist by their own natures. They are obviously contingent and depend on the sun for their existence, whether they are beginningless and everlasting or not.

There seems to be nothing in the world, then, concerning which it is at all plausible to suppose that it exists by its own nature, or contains within itself the reason for its existence. In fact, everything in the world appears to be quite plainly the opposite, namely, something that not only need not exist, but at some time or other, past or future or both, does not in fact exist. Everything in the world seems to have a finite duration, whether long or short. Most things, such as ourselves, exist only for a short while; they come into being, then soon cease. Other things, like the heavenly bodies, last longer, but they are still corruptible, and from all that we can gather about them, they too seem destined eventually to perish. We arrive at the conclusion, then, that while the world may contain some things which have always existed and are destined never to perish, it is nevertheless doubtful that it contains any such thing and, in any case, everything in the world is capable of perishing, and nothing in it, however long it may already have existed and however long it may yet remain, exists by its own nature, but depends instead upon something else.

While this might be true of everything in the world, is it necessarily true of the world itself? That is, if we grant, as we seem forced to, that nothing in the world exists by its own nature, that everything in the world is contingent and perishable, must we also say that the world itself, or the totality of all these perishable things, is also contingent and perishable? Logically, we are not forced to, for it is logically possible that the totality of all perishable things might itself be imperishable, and hence, that the world might exist by its own nature, even though it is comprised exclusively of things which are contingent. It is not logically necessary that a totality should share the defects of its members. For example, even though every man is mortal, it does not follow from this that the human race, or the totality of all men, is also mortal; for it is possible that there will always be human beings, even though there are no human beings which will always exist. Similarly, it is possible that the world is in itself a necessary thing, even though it is comprised entirely of things that are contingent.

This is logically possible, but it is not plausible. For we find nothing whatever about the world, any more than in its parts, to suggest that it exists by its own nature. Concerning anything in the world, we have not the slightest difficulty in supposing that it should perish, or even, that it should never have existed in the first place. We have almost as little difficulty in supposing this of the world itself. It might be somewhat hard to think of everything as utterly perishing and leaving no trace whatever of its ever having been, but there seems to be not the slightest difficulty in imagining that the world should never have existed in the first place. We can, for instance, perfectly easily suppose that nothing in the world had ever existed except, let us suppose, a single grain of sand, and we can thus suppose that this grain of sand has forever constituted the whole universe. Now if we consider just this grain of sand, it is quite impossible for us to suppose that it exists by its very nature, and could never have failed to exist. It clearly depends for its existence upon something other than itself, if it depends on anything at all. The same will be true if we consider the world to consist, not of one grain of sand, but of two, or of a million, or, as we in fact find, of a vast number of stars and planets and all their minuter parts.

It would seem, then, that the world, in case it happens to exist at all—and this is quite beyond doubt—is contingent and thus dependent upon something other than itself for its existence, if it depends upon anything at all. And it must depend upon something, for otherwise there could be no reason why it exists in the first place. Now that upon which the world depends must be something that either exists by its own nature or does not. If it does not exist by its own nature, then it, in turn, depends for its existence upon something else, and so on. Now then, we can say either of two things; namely, (1) that the world depends for its existence upon something else, which in turn depends on still another thing, this depending upon still another, *ad infinitum;* or (2) that the world derives its existence from something that exists by its own nature and which is accordingly eternal and imperishable, and is the creator of heaven and earth. The first of these alternatives, however, is impossible, for it does not render a sufficient reason why anything should exist in the first place. Instead of supplying a reason why any world should exist, it repeatedly begs off giving a reason. It explains what is dependent and perishable in terms of what is itself dependent and perishable, leaving us still without a reason why perishable things should exist at all, which is what we are seeking. Ultimately, then, it would seem that the world, or the totality of contingent or perishable things, in case it exists at all, must depend upon something that is necessary and imperishable, and which accordingly exists, not in dependence upon something else, but by its own nature.

What has been said thus far gives some intimation of what meaning should be attached to the concept of a self-caused being, a concept that is quite generally misunderstood, sometimes even by scholars. To say that something—God, for example—is self-caused, or is the cause of its own existence, does not mean that this being brings itself into existence, which is a perfectly absurd idea. Nothing can *bring* itself into existence. To say that something is self-caused (*causa sui*) means only that it exists, not contingently or in dependence upon something else, but by its own nature, which is only to say that it is a being which is such that it can neither come into being nor perish. Now whether such a being in fact exists or not, there is in any case no absurdity in the idea. We have found, in fact, that the principle of sufficient reason seems to point to the existence of such a being, as upon which the world, with everything in it, must ultimately depend for its existence.

A being that depends for its existence upon nothing but itself, and is in this sense self-caused, can equally be described as a necessary being; that is to say, a being that is not contingent, and hence not perishable. For in the case of anything which exists by its own nature, and is dependent upon nothing else, it is impossible that it should not exist, which is equivalent to saying that it is necessary. Many persons have professed to find the gravest difficulties in this concept, too, but that is partly because it has been confused with other notions. If it makes sense to speak of anything as an *impossible* being, or something which by its very nature does not exist, then it is hard to see why the idea of a necessary being, or something which in its very nature exists, should not be just as comprehensible. And of course, we have not the slightest difficulty in speaking of something, such as a square circle or a formless body, as an impossible being. And if it makes sense to speak of something as being perishable, contingent, and dependent upon something other than itself for its existence, as it surely does, then there seems to be no difficulty in thinking of something as imperishable and dependent upon nothing other than itself for its existence.

From these considerations we can see also what is properly meant by a first cause, an appellative that has often been applied to God by theologians, and which many persons have deemed an absurdity. It is a common criticism of this notion to say that there need not be any first cause, since the series of causes and effects which constitute the history of the universe might be infinite or beginningless and must, in fact, be infinite in case the universe itself had no beginning in time. This criticism, however, reflects a total misconception of what is meant by a first cause. *First* here does not mean first in time, and when God is spoken of as a first cause, he is not being described as a being which, at some time in the remote past, *started* everything. To describe God as a first cause is only to say that he is literally a *primary* rather than a secondary cause, an *ultimate* rather than a derived cause, or a being upon which all other things, heaven and earth, ultimately depend for their existence. It is, in short, only to say that God is the creator, in the sense of creation explained above. Now this, of course, is perfectly consistent with saying that the world is eternal or beginningless. As we have seen, one gives no reason for the existence of a world merely by giving it an age, even if it is supposed to have an infinite age. To use a helpful analogy, we can say that the sun is the first cause of daylight and, for that matter, of the moonlight of the night as well, which means only that daylight and moonlight ultimately depend upon the sun for their existence. The moon, on the other hand, is only a secondary or derivative cause of its light. This light would be no less dependent upon the sun if we affirmed that it had no beginning, for an ageless and beginningless light requires a source no less than an ephemeral one. If we supposed that the sun has always existed, and with it its light, then we would have to say that the sun has always been the first—i.e., the primary or ultimate—cause of its light. Such is precisely the manner in which God should be thought of, and is by theologians often thought of, as the first cause of heaven and earth.

*David Hume (1711–1776), Scottish philosopher and
historian, played a central role in the development
of modern philosophy.*

David Hume

THE TELEOLOGICAL ARGUMENT
AND THE PROBLEM OF EVIL

Not to lose any time in circumlocutions, said Cleanthes, addressing himself to Demea, much less in replying to the pious declamations of Philo, I
shall briefly explain how I conceive this matter. Look round the world,
contemplate the whole and every part of it: you will find it to be nothing
but one great machine, subdivided into an infinite number of lesser
machines, which again admit of subdivisions to a degree beyond what
human senses and faculties can trace and explain. All these various
machines, and even their most minute parts, are adjusted to each other
with an accuracy which ravishes into admiration all men who have ever
contemplated them. The curious adapting of means to ends, throughout
all nature, resembles exactly, though it much exceeds, the productions of
human contrivance—of human design, thought, wisdom, and intelligence.
Since therefore the effects resemble each other, we are led to infer, by all
the rules of analogy, that the causes also resemble, and that the Author of

Reprinted from *Dialogues Concerning Natural Religion* (1779).

nature is somewhat simlar to the mind of man, though possessed of much larger faculties, proportioned to the grandeur of the work which he has executed. By this argument *a posteriori,* and by this argument alone, do we prove at once the existence of a Deity and his similarity to human mind and intelligence.

I shall be so free, Cleanthes, said Demea, as to tell you that from the beginning I could not approve of your conclusion concerning the similarity of the Deity to men, still less can I approve of the mediums by which you endeavour to establish it. What! No demonstration of the Being of God! No abstract arguments! No proofs *a priori!* Are these which have hitherto been so much insisted on by philosophers all fallacy, all sophism? Can we reach 'no farther in this subject than experience and probability? I will not say that this is betraying the cause of a Deity; but surely, by this affected candour, you give advantages to atheists which they never could obtain by the mere dint of argument and reasoning.

What I chiefly scruple in this subject, said Philo, is not so much that all religious arguments are by Cleanthes reduced to experience, as that they appear not to be even the most certain and irrefragable of that inferior kind. That a stone will fall, that fire will burn, that the earth has solidity, we have observed a thousand and a thousand times; and when any new instance of this nature is presented, we draw without hesitation the accustomed inference. The exact similarity of the cases gives us a perfect assurance of a similar event, and a stronger evidence is never desired nor sought after. But wherever you depart, in the least, from the similarity of the cases, you diminish proportionably the evidence, and may at last bring it to a very weak *analogy,* which is confessedly liable to error and uncertainty. After having experienced the circulation of the blood in human creatures, we make no doubt that it takes place in Titius and Maevius; but from its circulation in frogs and fishes it is only a presumption, though a strong one, from analogy that it takes place in men and other animals. The analogical reasoning is much weaker when we infer the circulation of the sap in vegetables from our experience that the blood circulates in animals; and those who hastily followed that imperfect analogy are found, by more accurate experiments, to have been mistaken.

If we see a house, Cleanthes, we conclude, with the greatest certainty, that it had an architect or builder because this is precisely that species of effect which we have experienced to proceed from that species of cause. But surely you will not affirm that the universe bears such a resemblance to a house that we can with the same certainty infer a similar cause, or that the analogy is here entire and perfect. The dissimilitude is so striking that the utmost you can here pretend to is a guess, a conjecture, a presumption concerning a similar cause; and how that pretension will be received in the world, I leave you to consider.

It would surely be very ill received, replied Cleanthes; and I should be deservedly blamed and detested did I allow that the proofs of a Deity amounted to no more than a guess or conjecture. But is the whole adjustment of means to ends in a house and in the universe so slight a resemblance? the economy of final causes? the order, proportion, and arrangement of every part? Steps of a stair are plainly contrived that human legs may use them in mounting; and this inference is certain and infallible. Human legs are also contrived for walking and mounting; and this inference, I allow, is not altogether so certain because of the dissimilarity which you remark; but does it, therefore, deserve the name only of presumption or conjecture?

Good God! cried Demea, interrupting him, where are we? Zealous defenders of religion allow that the proofs of a Deity fall short of perfect evidence! And you, Philo, on whose assistance I depended in proving the adorable mysteriousness of the Divine Nature, do you assent to all these extravagant opinions of Cleanthes? For what other name can I give them? or, why spare my censure when such principles are advanced, supported by such an authority, before so young a man as Pamphilus?

You seem not to apprehend, replied Philo, that I argue with Cleanthes in his own way, and, by showing him the dangerous consequences of his tenets, hope at last to reduce him to our opinion. But what sticks most with you, I observe, is the representation which Cleanthes has made of the argument *a posteriori* and, finding that that argument is likely to escape your hold and vanish into air, you think it so disguised that you can scarcely believe it to be set in its true light. Now, however much I may dissent, in other respects, from the dangerous principle of Cleanthes, I must allow that he has fairly represented that argument, and I shall endeavour so to state the matter to you that you will entertain no further scruples with regard to it.

Were a man to abstract from everything which he knows or has seen, he would be altogether incapable, merely from his own ideas, to determine what kind of scene the universe must be, or to give the preference to one state or situation of things above another. For as nothing which he clearly conceives could be esteemed impossible or implying a contradiction, every chimera of his fancy would be upon an equal footing; nor could he assign any just reason why he adheres to one idea or system, and rejects the others which are equally possible.

Again, after he opens his eyes and contemplates the world as it really is, it would be impossible for him at first to assign the cause of any one event, much less of the whole of things, or of the universe. He might set his fancy a rambling, and she might bring him in an infinite variety of reports and representations. These would all be possible, but, being all equally possible, he would never of himself give a satisfactory account for his preferring one of them to the rest. Experience alone can point out to him the true cause of any phenomenon.

Now, according to this method of reasoning, Demea, it follows (and is, indeed, tacitly allowed by Cleanthes himself) that order, arrangement, or the adjustment of final causes, is not of itself any proof of design, but only so far as it has been experienced to proceed from that principle. For aught we can know *a priori,* matter may contain the source or spring of order originally within itself, as well as mind does; and there is no more difficulty in conceiving that the several elements, from an internal un- known cause, may fall into the most exquisite arrangement, than to conceive that their ideas, in the great universal mind, from a like internal unknown cause, fall into that arrangement. The equal possibility of both these suppositions is allowed. But, by experience, we find (according to Cleanthes) that there is a difference between them. Throw several pieces of steel together, without shape or form, they will never arrange them- selves so as to compose a watch. Stone and mortar and wood, without an architect, never erect a house. But the ideas in a human mind, we see, by an unknown, inexplicable economy, arrange themselves so as to form the plan of a watch or house. Experience, therefore, proves that there is an original principle of order in mind, not in matter. From similar effects we infer similar causes. The adjustment of means to ends is alike in the universe, as in a machine of human contrivance. The causes, therefore, must be resembling.

I was from the beginning scandalized, I must own, with this resem- blance which is asserted between the Deity and human creatures, and must conceive it to imply such a degradation of the Supreme Being as no sound theist could endure. With your assistance, therefore, Demea, I shall endeavour to defend what you justly call the adorable mysteriousness of the Divine Nature, and shall refute this reasoning of Cleanthes, provided he allows that I have made a fair representation of it.

When Cleanthes had assented, Philo, after a short pause, proceeded in the following manner.

That all inferences, Cleanthes, concerning fact are founded on experi- ence, and that all experimental reasonings are founded on the supposition that similar causes prove similar effects, and similar effects similar causes, I shall not at present much dispute with you. But observe, I entreat you, with what extreme caution all just reasoners proceed in the transferring of experiments to similar cases. Unless the cases be exactly similar, they repose no perfect confidence in applying their past observation to any particular phenomenon. Every alteration of circumstances occasions a doubt concerning the event; and it requires new experiments to prove certainly that the new circumstances are of no moment or importance. A change in bulk, situation, arrangement, age, disposition of the air, or surrounding bodies—any of these particulars may be attended with the most unexpected consequences. And unless the objects be quite familiar to us, it is the highest temerity to expect with assurance, after any of these changes, an event similar to that which before fell under our observation. The slow and deliberate steps of philosophers here, if anywhere, are distinguished from the precipate march of the vulgar, who, hurried on by the smallest similitude, are incapable of all discernment or consideration.

But can you think, Cleanthes, that your usual phlegm and philosophy have been preserved in so wide a step as you have taken when you compared to the universe houses, ships, furniture, machines, and, from their similarity in some circumstances, inferred a similarity in their causes? Thought, design, intelligence, such as we discover in men and other animals, is no more than one of the springs and principles of the universe, as well as heat or cold, attraction or repulsion, and a hundred others which fall under daily observation. It is an active cause by which some particular parts of nature, we find, produce alterations on other parts. But can a conclusion, with any propriety, be transferred from parts to the whole? Does not the great disproportion bar all comparison and inference? From observing the growth of a hair, can we learn anything concerning the generation of a man? Would the manner of a leaf's blowing, even though perfectly known, afford us any instruction concerning the vegetation of a tree?

But allowing that we were to take the *operations* of one part of nature upon another for the foundation of our judgment concerning the *origin* of the whole (which never can be admitted), yet why select so minute, so weak, so bounded a principle as the reason and design of animals is found to be upon this planet? What peculiar privilege has this little agitation of the brain which we call *thought,* that we must thus make it the model of the whole universe? Our partiality in our own favour does indeed present it on all occasions, but sound philosophy ought carefully to guard against so natural an illusion.

So far from admitting, continued Philo, that the operations of a part can afford us any just conclusion concerning the origin of the whole, I will not allow any one part to form a rule for another part if the latter be very remote from the former. Is there any reasonable ground to conclude that the inhabitants of other planets possess thought, intelligence, reason, or anything similar to these faculties in men? When nature has so extremely diversified her manner of operation in this small globe, can we imagine that she incessantly copies herself throughout so immense a universe? And if thought, as we may well suppose, be confined merely to this narrow corner and has even there so limited a sphere of action, with what propriety can we assign it for the original cause of all things? The narrow views of a peasant who makes his domestic economy the rule for the government of kingdoms is in comparison a pardonable sophism.

But were we ever so much assured that a thought and reason resembling the human were to be found throughout the whole universe, and were its activity elsewhere vastly greater and more commanding than it appears in this globe, yet I cannot see why the operations of a world constituted, arranged, adjusted, can with any propriety be extended to a world which is in its embryo state, and is advancing towards that constitution and arrangement. By observation we know somewhat of the economy, action, and nourishment of a finished animal, but we must transfer with great caution that observation to the growth of a fœtus in the womb, and still more to the formation of an animalcule in the loins of its male parent. Nature, we find, even from our limited experience, possesses an infinite number of springs and principles which incessantly discover themselves on every change of her position and situation. And what new and unknown principles would actuate her in so new and unknown a situation as that of the formation of a universe, we cannot, without the utmost temerity, pretend to determine.

A very small part of this great system, during a very short time, is very imperfectly discovered to us; and do we thence pronounce decisively concerning the origin of the whole?

Admirable conclusion! Stone, wood, brick, iron, brass, have not, at this time, in this minute globe of earth, an order or arrangement without human art and contrivance; therefore, the universe could not originally attain its order and arrangement without something similar to human art. But is a part of nature a rule for another part very wide of the former? Is it a rule for the whole? Is a very small part a rule for the universe? Is nature in one situation a certain rule for nature in another situation vastly different from the former?

And can you blame me, Cleanthes, if I here imitate the prudent reserve of Simonides, who, according to the noted story, being asked by Hiero, *What God was?* desired a day to think of it, and then two days more; and after that manner continually prolonged the term, without ever bringing in his definition or description? Could you even blame me if I had answered, at first, *that I did not know,* and was sensible that this subject lay vastly beyond the reach of my faculties? You might cry out sceptic and rallier, as much as you pleased; but, having found in so many other subjects much more familiar the imperfections and even contradictions of human reason, I never should expect any success from its feeble conjectures in a subject so sublime and so remote from the sphere of our observation. When two *species* of objects have always been observed to be conjoined together, I can *infer,* by custom, the existence of one wherever I *see* the existence of the other; and this I call an argument from experience. But how this argument can have place where the objects, as in the present case, are single, individual, without parallel or specific resemblance, may be difficult to explain. And will any man tell me with a serious countenance that an orderly universe must arise from some thought and art like the human because we have experience of it? To ascertain this reasoning it were requisite that we had experience of the origin of worlds; and it is not sufficient, surely, that we have seen ships and cities arise from human art and contrivance.

Philo was proceeding in this vehement manner, somewhat between jest and earnest, as it appeared to me, when he observed some signs of impatience in Cleanthes, and then immediately stopped short. What I had to suggest, said Cleanthes, is only that you would not abuse terms, or make use of popular expressions to subvert philosophical reasonings. You know that the vulgar often distinguish reason from experience, even where the question relates only to matter of fact and existence, though it is found, where that *reason* is properly analyzed, that it is nothing but a species of experience. To prove by experience the origin of the universe from mind is not more contrary to common speech than to prove the motion of the earth from the same principle. And a caviller might raise all the same objections to the Copernican system which you have urged against my reasonings. Have you other earths, might he say, which you have seen to move? Have . . .

Yes! cried Philo, interrupting him, we have other earths. Is not the moon another earth, which we see to turn round its centre? Is not Venus another earth, where we observe the same phenomenon? Are not the revolutions of the sun also a confirmation, from analogy, of the same theory? All the planets, are they not earths which revolve about the sun? Are not the satellites moons which move round Jupiter and Saturn, and along with these primary planets round the sun? These analogies and resemblances, with others which I have not mentioned, are the sole proofs of the Copernican system; and to you it belongs to consider whether you have any analogies of the same kind to support your theory.

In reality, Cleanthes, continued he, the modern system of astronomy is now so much received by all inquirers, and has become so essential a part even of our earliest education, that we are not commonly very scrupulous in examining the reasons upon which it is founded. It is now become a matter of mere curiosity to study the first writers on that subject who had the full force of prejudice to encounter, and were obliged to turn their arguments on every side in order to render them popular and convincing. But if we peruse Galileo's famous *Dialogues*[1] concerning the system of the world, we shall find that that great genius, one of the sublimest that ever existed, first bent all his endeavours to prove that there was no foundation for the distinction commonly made between elementary and celestial substances. The schools, proceeding from the illusions of sense, had carried this distinction very far; and had established the latter substances to be ingenerable, incorruptible, unalterable, impassible; and had assigned all the opposite qualities to the former. But Galileo, beginning with the moon, proved its similarity in every particular to the earth: its convex figure, its natural darkness when not illuminated, its density, its distinction into solid and liquid, the variations of its phases, the mutual illuminations of the earth and moon, their mutual eclipses, the inequalities of the lunar surface, etc. After many instances of this kind, with regard to all the planets, men plainly saw that these bodies became proper objects of experience, and that the similarity of their nature? enabled us to extend the same arguments and phenomena from one to the other.

In this cautious proceeding of the astronomers you may read your own condemnation, Cleanthes, or rather may see that the subject in which you are engaged exceeds all human reason and inquiry. Can you pretend to show any such similarity between the fabric of a house and the generation of a universe? Have you ever seen nature in any such situation as resembles the first arrangement of the elements? Have worlds ever been formed under your eye, and have you had leisure to observe the whole progress of the phenomenon, from the first appearance of order to its final consummation? If you have, then cite your experience and deliver your theory.

• • •

But to show you still more inconveniences, continued Philo, in your anthropomorphism, please to take a new survey of your principles. *Like effects prove like causes.* This is the experimental argument; and this, you say too, is the sole theological argument. Now it is certain that the liker

---

1   *Dialogo dei due Massimi Sistemi del Mondo* (1632).

the effects are which are seen and the liker the causes which are inferred, the stronger is the argument. Every departure on either side diminishes the probability and renders the experiment less conclusive. You cannot doubt of the principle; neither ought you to reject its consequences.

All the new discoveries in astronomy which prove the immense grandeur and magnificence of the works of nature are so many additional arguments for a Deity, according to the true system of theism; but, according to your hypothesis of experimental theism, they become so many objections, by removing the effect still farther from all resemblance to the effects of human art and contrivance. . . .

The discoveries by microscopes, as they open a new universe in miniature, are still objections, according to you, arguments, according to me. The further we push our researches of this kind, we are still led to infer the universal cause of all to be vastly different from mankind, or from any object of human experience and observation.

And what say you to the discoveries in anatomy, chemistry, botany? . . . These surely are no objections, replied Cleanthes; they only discover new instances of art and contrivance. It is still the image of mind reflected on us from innumerable objects. Add a mind *like the human,* said Philo. I know of no other, replied Cleanthes. And the liker, the better, insisted Philo. To be sure, said Cleanthes.

Now, Cleanthes, said Philo, with an air of alacrity and triumph, mark the consequences. *First,* by this method of reasoning you renounce all claim to infinity in any of the attributes of the Deity. For, as the cause ought only to be proportioned to the effect, and the effect, so far as it falls under our cognizance, is not infinite, what pretensions have we, upon your suppositions, to ascribe that attribute to the Divine Being? You will still insist that, by removing him so much from all similarity to human creatures, we give in to the most arbitrary hypothesis, and at the same time weaken all proofs of his existence.

Secondly, you have no reason, on your theory, for ascribing perfection to the Deity, even in his finite capacity, or for supposing him free from every error, mistake, or incoherence, in his undertakings. There are many inexplicable difficulties in the works of nature which, if we allow a perfect author to be proved *a priori,* are easily solved, and become only seeming difficulties from the narrow capacity of man, who cannot trace infinite relations. But according to your method of reasoning, these difficulties become all real, and, perhaps, will be insisted on as new instances of likeness to human art and contrivance. At least, you must acknowledge that it is impossible for us to tell, from our limited views, whether this system contains any great faults or deserves any considerable praise if compared to other possible and even real systems. Could a peasant, if the *Æneid* were read to him, pronounce that poem to be absolutely faultless, or even assign to it its proper rank among the productions of human wit, he who had never seen any other production?

But were this world ever so perfect a production, it must still remain uncertain whether all the excellences of the work can justly be ascribed to the workman. If we survey a ship, what an exalted idea must we form of the ingenuity of the carpenter who framed so complicated, useful, and beautiful a machine? And what surprise must we feel when we find him a stupid mechanic who imitated others, and copied an art which, through a long succession of ages, after multiplied trials, mistakes, corrections, deliberations, and controversies, had been gradually improving? Many worlds might have been botched and bungled, throughout an eternity, ere this system was struck out; much labour lost, many fruitless trials made, and a slow but continued improvement carried on during infinite ages in the art of world-making. In such subjects, who can determine where the truth, nay, who can conjecture where the probability lies, amidst a great number of hypotheses which may be proposed, and a still greater which may be imagined?

And what shadow of an argument, continued Philo, can you produce from your hypothesis to prove the unity of the Deity? A great number of men join in building a house or ship, in rearing a city, in framing a commonwealth; why may not several deities combine in contriving and framing a world? This is only so much greater similarity to human affairs. By sharing the work among several, we may so much further limit the attributes of each, and get rid of that extensive power and knowledge which must be supposed in one deity, and which, according to you, can only serve to weaken the proof of his existence. And if such foolish, such vicious creatures as man can yet often unite in framing and executing one plan, how much more those deities or demons, whom we may suppose several degrees more perfect!

To multiply causes without necessity is indeed contrary to true philosophy, but this principle applies not to the present case. Were one deity antecedently proved by your theory who were possessed of every attribute requisite to the production of the universe, it would be needless, I own, (though not absurd) to suppose any other deity existent. But while it is still a question whether all these attributes are united in one subject or dispersed among several independent beings, by what phenomena in nature can we pretend to decide the controversy? Where we see a body raised in a scale, we are sure that there is in the opposite scale, however concealed from sight, some counterpoising weight equal to it; but it is still allowed to doubt whether that weight be an aggregate of several distinct bodies or one uniform united mass. And if the weight requisite very much exceeds anything which we have ever seen conjoined in any single body, the former supposition becomes still more probable and natural. An intelligent being of such vast power and capacity as is necessary to produce the universe, or, to speak in the language of ancient philosophy, so prodigious an animal exceeds all analogy and even comprehension.

But further, Cleanthes: Men are mortal, and renew their species by generation; and this is common to all living creatures. The two great sexes of |male| and female, says Milton, animate the world. Why must this circumstance, so universal, so essential, be excluded from those numerous and limited deities? Behold, then, the theogeny of ancient times brought back upon us.

And why not become a perfect anthropomorphite? Why not assert the deity or deities to be corporeal, and to have eyes, a nose, mouth, ears, etc.? Epicurus maintained that no man had ever seen reason but in a human figure; therefore, the gods must have a human figure. And this argument, which is deservedly so much ridiculed by Cicero, becomes, according to you, solid and philosophical.

In a word, Cleanthes, a man who follows your hypothesis is able, perhaps, to assert or conjecture that the universe sometime arose from something like design; but beyond that position he cannot ascertain one single circumstance, and is left afterwards to fix every point of his theology by the utmost license of fancy and hypothesis. This world, for aught he knows, is very faulty and imperfect, compared to a superior standard, and was only the first rude essay of some infant deity who afterwards abandoned it, ashamed of his lame performance; it is the work only of some dependent, inferior deity, and is the object of derision to his superiors; it is the production of old age and dotage in some superannuated deity, and ever since his death has run on at adventures, from the first impulse and active force which it received from him. You justly give signs of horror, Demea, at these strange suppositions; but these, and a thousand more of the same kind, are Cleanthes' suppositions, not mine. From the moment the attributes of the Deity are supposed finite, all these have place. And I cannot, for my part, think that so wild and unsettled a system of theology is, in any respect, preferable to none at all.

These suppositions I absolutely disown, cried Cleanthes: they strike me, however, with no horror, especially when proposed in that rambling way in which they drop from you. On the contrary, they give me pleasure when I see that, by the utmost indulgence of your imagination, you never get rid of the hypothesis of design in the universe, but are obliged at every turn to have recourse to it. To this concession I adhere steadily; and this I regard as a sufficient foundation for religion.

* * *

It is my opinion, I own, replied Demea, that each man feels, in a manner, the truth of religion within his own breast, and, from a consciousness of his imbecility and misery rather than from any reasoning, is led to seek protection from that Being on whom he and all nature is dependent. So anxious or so tedious are even the best scenes of life that futurity is still the object of all our hopes and fears. We incessantly look forward and endeavour, by prayers, adoration, and sacrifice, to appease those unknown powers whom we find, by experience, so able to afflict and oppress us. Wretched creatures that we are! What resource for us amidst the innumerable ills of life did not religion suggest some methods of atonement, and appease those terrors with which we are incessantly agitated and tormented?

I am indeed persuaded, said Philo, that the best and indeed the only method of bringing everyone to a due sense of religion is by just representations of the misery and wickedness of men. And for that purpose a talent of eloquence and strong imagery is more requisite than that of reasoning and argument. For is it necessary to prove what everyone feels within himself? It is only necessary to make us feel it, if possible, more intimately and sensibly.

The people, indeed, replied Demea, are sufficiently convinced of this great and melancholy truth. The miseries of life, the unhappiness of man, the general corruptions of our nature, the unsatisfactory enjoyment of pleasures, riches, honours—these phrases have become almost proverbial in all languages. And who can doubt of what all men declare from their own immediate feeling and experience?

In this point, said Philo, the learned are perfectly agreed with the vulgar; and in all letters, *sacred* and *profane,* the topic of human misery has been insisted on with the most pathetic eloquence that sorrow and melancholy could inspire. The poets, who speak from sentiment, without a system, and whose testimony has therefore the more authority, abound in images of this nature. From Homer down to Dr. Young, the whole inspired tribe have ever been sensible that no other representation of things would suit the feeling and observation of each individual.

As to authorities, replied Demea, you need not seek them. Look round this library of Cleanthes. I shall venture to affirm that, except authors of particular sciences, such as chemistry or botany, who have no occasion to treat of human life, there is scarce one of those innumerable writers from whom the sense of human misery has not, in some passage or other, extorted a complaint and confession of it. At least, the chance is entirely on that side; and no one author has ever, so far as I can recollect, been so extravagant as to deny it.

There you must excuse me, said Philo: Leibniz has denied it, and is perhaps the first[2] who ventured upon so bold and paradoxical an opinion; at least, the first who made it essential to his philosophical system.

And by being the first, replied Demea, might he not have been sensible of his error? For is this a subject in which philosophers can propose to make discoveries especially in so late an age? And can any man hope by a simple denial (for the subject scarcely admits of reasoning) to bear down the united testimony of mankind, founded on sense and consciousness?

And why should man, added he, pretend to an exemption from the lot of all other animals? The whole earth, believe me, Philo, is cursed and polluted. A perpetual war is kindled amongst all living creatures. Necessity, hunger, want stimulate the strong and courageous; fear, anxiety, terror agitate the weak and infirm. The first entrance into life gives anguish to the new-born infant and to its wretched parent; weakness, impotence, distress attend each stage of that life, and it is, at last, finished in agony and horror.

Observe, too, says Philo, the curious artifices of nature in order to embitter the life of every living being. The stronger prey upon the weaker and keep them in perpetual terror and anxiety. The weaker, too, in their turn, often prey upon the stronger, and vex and molest them without relaxation. Consider that innumerable race of insects, which either are bred on the body of each animal or, flying about, infix their stings in him. These insects have others still less than themselves which torment them. And thus on each hand, before and behind, above and below, every animal is surrounded with enemies which incessantly seek his misery and destruction.

Man alone, said Demea, seems to be, in part, an exception to this rule. For by combination in society he can easily master lions, tigers, and bears, whose greater strength and agility naturally enable them to prey upon him.

On the contrary, it is here chiefly, cried Philo, that the uniform and equal maxims of nature are most apparent. Man, it is true, can, by combination, surmount all his *real* enemies and become master of the whole animal creation; but does he not immediately raise up to himself

---

2   That sentiment had been maintained by Dr. King and some few others before Leibniz, though by none of so great fame as that German philosopher.

imaginary enemies, the demons of his fancy, who haunt him with superstitious terrors and blast every enjoyment of life? His pleasure, as he imagines, becomes in their eyes a crime; his food and repose give them umbrage and offence; his very sleep and dreams furnish new materials to anxious fear; and even death, his refuge from every other ill, presents only the dread of endless and innumerable woes. Nor does the wolf molest more the timid flock than superstition does the anxious breast of wretched mortals.

Besides, consider, Demea: This very society by which we surmount those wild beasts, our natural enemies, what new enemies does it not raise to us? What woe and misery does it not occasion? Man is the greatest enemy of man. Oppression, injustice, contempt, contumely, violence, sedition, war, calumny, treachery, fraud—by these they mutually torment each other, and they would soon dissolve that society which they had formed were it not for the dread of still greater ills which must attend their separation.

But though these external insults, said Demea, from animals, from men, from all the elements, which assault us form a frightful catalogue of woes, they are nothing in comparison of those which arise within ourselves, from the distempered condition of our mind and body. How many lie under the lingering torment of diseases? Hear the pathetic enumeration of the great poet.

> Intestine stone and ulcer, colic-pangs,
> Demoniac frenzy, moping melancholy,
> And moon-struck madness, pining atrophy,
> Marasmus, and wide-wasting pestilence.
> Dire was the tossing, deep the groans: *Despair*
> Tended the sick, busiest from couch to couch.
> And over them triumphant *Death* his dart
> Shook: but delay'd to strike, though oft invok'd
> With vows, as their chief good and final hope.[3]

The disorders of the mind, continued Demea, though more secret, are not perhaps less dismal and vexatious. Remorse, shame, anguish, rage, disappointment, anxiety, fear, dejection, despair—who has ever passed through life without cruel inroads from these tormentors? How many have scarcely ever felt any better sensations? Labour and poverty, so abhorred by everyone, are the certain lot of the far greater number; and those few privileged persons who enjoy ease and opulence never reach contentment or true felicity. All the goods of life united would not make a

---

3 Milton: *Paradise Lost,* Bk. XI.

very happy man, but all the ills united would make a wretch indeed; and any one of them almost (and who can be free from every one?), nay, often the absence of one good (and who can possess all?) is sufficient to render life ineligible.

Were a stranger to drop on a sudden into this world, I would show him, as a specimen of its ills, an hospital full of diseases, a prison crowded with malefactors and debtors, a field of battle strewed with carcases, a fleet foundering in the ocean, a nation languishing under tyranny, famine, or pestilence. To turn the gay side of life to him and give him a notion of its pleasures—whether should I conduct him? To a ball, to an opera, to court? He might justly think that I was only showing him a diversity of distress and sorrow.

There is no evading such striking instances, said Philo, but by apologies which still further aggravate the charge. Why have all men, I ask, in all ages, complained incessantly of the miseries of life? . . . They have no just reason, says one: these complaints proceed only from their discontented, repining, anxious disposition. . . . And can there possibly, I reply, be a more certain foundation of misery than such a wretched temper?

But if they were really as unhappy as they pretend, says my antagonist, why do they remain in life? . . .

Not satisfied with life, afraid of death—

this is the secret chain, say I, that holds us. We are terrified, not bribed to the continuance of our existence.

It is only a false delicacy, he may insist, which a few refined spirits indulge, and which has spread these complains among the whole race of mankind. . . . And what is this delicacy, I ask, which you blame? Is it anything but a greater sensibility to all the pleasures and pains of life? And if the man of a delicate, refined temper, by being so much more alive than the rest of the world, is only so much more unhappy, what judgment must we form in general of human life?

Let men remain at rest, says our adversary, and they will be easy. They are willing artificers of their own misery. . . . No! reply I: an anxious languor follows their repose; disappointment, vexation, trouble, their activity and ambition.

I can observe something like what you mention in some others, replied Cleanthes, but I confess I feel little or nothing of it in myself, and hope that it is not so common as you represent it.

If you feel not human misery yourself, cried Demea, I congratulate you on so happy a singularity. Others, seemingly the most prosperous, have not been ashamed to vent their complaints in the most melancholy strains. Let us attend to the great, the fortunate emperor, Charles V, when, tired with human grandeur, he resigned all his extensive dominions into the hands of his son. In the last harangue which he made on that memorable occasion, he publicly avowed *that the greatest prosperities which he had ever enjoyed had been mixed with so many adversities that he might truly say he had never enjoyed any satisfaction or contentment.* But did the retired life in which he sought for shelter afford him any greater happiness? If we may credit his son's account, his repentance commenced the very day of his resignation.

Cicero's fortune, from small beginnings, rose to the greatest lustre and renown; yet what pathetic complaints of the ills of life do his familiar letters, as well as philosophical discourses, contain? And suitably to his own experience, he introduces Cato, the great, the fortunate Cato protesting in his old age that had he a new life in his offer he would reject the present.

Ask yourself, ask any of your acquaintance, whether they would live over again the last ten or twenty years of their life. No! but the next twenty, they say, will be better:

> And from the dregs of life, hope to receive
> What the first sprightly running could not give.[4]

Thus, at last, they find (such is the greatness of human misery, it reconciles even contradictions) that they complain at once of the shortness of life and of its vanity and sorrow.

And is it possible, Cleanthes, said Philo, that after all these reflections, and infinitely more which might be suggested, you can still persevere in your anthropomorphism, and assert the moral attributes of the Deity, his justice, benevolence, mercy, and rectitude, to be of the same nature with these virtues in human creatures? His power, we allow, is infinite; whatever he wills is executed; but neither man nor any other animal is happy; therefore, he does not will their happiness. His wisdom is infinite; he is never mistaken in choosing the means to any end; but the course of nature tends not to human or animal felicity; therefore, it is not established for that purpose. Through the whole compass of human knowledge there are no inferences more certain and infallible than these. In what respect, then, do his benevolence and mercy resemble the benevolence and mercy of men?

---

4   John Dryden, *Aureng-Zebe,* Act IV, sc. 1.

Epicurus' old questions are yet unanswered.

Is he willing to prevent evil, but not able? then is he impotent. Is he able, but not willing? then is he malevolent. Is he both able and willing? whence then is evil?

You ascribe, Cleanthes, (and I believe justly) a purpose and intention to nature. But what, I beseech you, is the object of that curious artifice and machinery which she has displayed in all animals—the preservation alone of individuals, and propagation of the species? It seems enough for her purpose, if such a rank be barely upheld in the universe, without any care or concern for the happiness of the members that compose it. No resource for this purpose: no machinery in order merely to give pleasure or ease; no fund of pure joy and contentment; no indulgence without some want or necessity accompanying it. At least, the few phenomena of this nature are overbalanced by opposite phenomena of still greater importance.

Our sense of music, harmony, and indeed beauty of all kinds, gives satisfaction, without being absolutely necessary to the preservation and propagation of the species. But what racking pains, on the other hand, arise from gouts, gravels, megrims, toothaches, rheumatisms, where the injury to the animal machinery is either small or incurable? Mirth, laughter, play, frolic seem gratuitous satisfactions which have no further tendency; spleen, melancholy, discontent, superstition are pains of the same nature. How then does the Divine benevolence display itself, in the sense of you anthropomorphites? None but we mystics, as you were pleased to call us, can account for this strange mixture of phenomena, by deriving it from attributes infinitely perfect but incomprehensible.

And have you, at last, said Cleanthes smiling, betrayed your intentions, Philo? Your long agreement with Demea did indeed a little surprise me, but I find you were all the while erecting a concealed battery against me. And I must confess that you have now fallen upon a subject worthy of your noble spirit of opposition and controversy. If you can make out the present point, and prove mankind to be unhappy or corrupted, there is an end at once of all religion. For to what purpose establish the natural attributes of the Deity, while the moral are still doubtful and uncertain?

You take umbrage very easily, replied Demea, at opinions the most innocent and the most generally received, even amongst the religious and devout themselves; and nothing can be more surprising than to find a topic like this—concerning the wickedness and misery of man—charged with no less than atheism and profaneness. Have not all pious divines and preachers who have indulged their rhetoric on so fertile a subject, have they not easily, I say, given a solution of any difficulties which may attend it? This world is but a point in comparison of the universe; this life but a moment in comparison of eternity. The present evil phenomena, therefore, are rectified in other regions, and in some future period of existence. And the eyes of men, being then opened to larger views of things, see the whole connection of general laws, and trace, with adoration, the benevolence and rectitude of the Deity through all the mazes and intricacies of his providence.

No! replied Cleanthes, no! These arbitrary suppositions can never be admitted, contrary to matter of fact, visible and uncontroverted. Whence can any cause be known but from its known effects? Whence can any hypothesis be proved but from the apparent phenomena? To establish one hypothesis upon another is building entirely in the air; and the utmost we ever attain by these conjectures and fictions is to ascertain the bare possibility of our opinion, but never can we, upon such terms, establish its reality.

The only method of supporting Divine benevolence—and it is what I willingly embrace—is to deny absolutely the misery and wickedness of man. Your representations are exaggerated; your melancholy views mostly fictitious; your inferences contrary to fact and experience. Health is more common than sickness; pleasure than pain; happiness than misery. And for one vexation which we meet with, we attain, upon computation, a hundred enjoyments.

Admitting your position, replied Philo, which yet is extremely doubtful, you must at the same time allow that, if pain be less frequent than pleasure, it is infinitely more violent and durable. One hour of it is often able to outweigh a day, a week, a month of our common insipid enjoyments; and how many days, weeks, and months are passed by several in the most acute torments? Pleasure, scarcely in one instance, is ever able to reach ecstasy and rapture; and in no one instance can it continue for any time at its highest pitch and altitude. The spirits evaporate, the nerves relax, the fabric is disordered, and the enjoyment quickly degenerates into fatigue and uneasiness. But pain often, good God, how often! rises to torture and agony; and the longer it continues, it becomes still more genuine agony and torture. Patience is exhausted, courage languishes, melancholy seizes us, and nothing terminates our misery but the removal of its cause or another event which is the sole cure of all evil, but which, from our natural folly, we regard with still greater horror and consternation.

But not to insist upon these topics, continued Philo, though most obvious, certain, and important, I must use the freedom to admonish you, Cleanthes, that you have put the controversy upon a most dangerous issue, and are unawares introducing a total scepticism into the most essential articles of natural and revealed theology. What! no method of fixing a just foundation for religion unless we allow the happiness of human life, and maintain a continued existence even in this world, with all our present pains, infirmities, vexations, and follies, to be eligible and desirable! But this is contrary to everyone's feeling and experience; it is contrary to an authority so established as nothing can subvert. No decisive proofs can ever be produced against this authority; nor is it possible for you to compute, estimate, and compare all the pains and all the pleasures in the lives of all men and of all animals; and thus, by your resting the whole system of religion on a point which, from its very nature, must for ever be uncertain, you tacitly confess that that system is equally uncertain.

But allowing you what never will be believed, at least, what you never possibly can prove, that animal or, at least, human happiness in this life exceeds its misery, you have yet done nothing; for this is not, by any means, what we expect from infinite power, infinite wisdom, and infinite goodness. Why is there any misery at all in the world? Not by chance, surely. From some cause then. Is it from the intention of the Deity? But he is perfectly benevolent. Is it contrary to his intention? But he is almighty. Nothing can shake the solidity of this reasoning, so short, so clear, so decisive, except we assert that these subjects exceed all human capacity, and that our common measures of truth and falsehood are not applicable to them—a topic which I have all along insisted on, but which you have, from the beginning, rejected with scorn and indignation.

But I will be contented to retire still from this intrenchment, for I deny that you can ever force me in it. I will allow that pain or misery in man is *compatible* with infinite power and goodness in the Deity, even in your sense of these attributes: what are you advanced by all these concessions? A mere possible compatibility is not sufficient. You must *prove* these pure, unmixt, and uncontrollable attributes from the present mixed and confused phenomena, and from these alone. A hopeful undertaking! Were the phenomena ever so pure and unmixed, yet, being finite, they would be insufficient for that purpose. How much more, where they are also so jarring and discordant!

Here, Cleanthes, I find myself at ease in my argument. Here I triumph. Formerly, when we argued concerning the natural attributes of intelligence and design, I needed all my sceptical and metaphysical subtilty to elude your grasp. In many views of the universe and of its parts, particularly the latter, the beauty and fitness of final causes strike us with such irresistible force that all objections appear (what I believe they really are) mere cavils and sophisms; nor can we then imagine how it was ever possible for us to repose any weight on them. But there is no view of human life or of the condition of mankind from which, without the greatest violence, we can infer the moral attributes or learn that infinite benevolence, conjoined with infinite power and infinite wisdom, which we must discover by the eyes of faith alone. It is your turn now to tug the labouring oar, and to support your philosophical subtilties against the dictates of plain reason and experience.

· · ·

I scruple not to allow, said Cleanthes, that I have been apt to suspect the frequent repetition of the word *infinite,* which we meet with in all theological writers, to savour more of panegyric than of philosophy, and that any purposes of reasoning, and even of religion, would be better served were we to rest contented with more accurate and more moderate expressions. The terms *admirable, excellent, superlatively great, wise,* and *holy*—these sufficiently fill the imaginations of men, and anything beyond, besides that it leads into absurdities, has no influence on the affections or sentiments. Thus, in the present subject, if we abandon all human analogy, as seems your intention, Demea, I am afraid we abandon all religion and retain no conception of the great object of our adoration. If we preserve human analogy, we must forever find it impossible to reconcile any mixture of evil in the universe with infinite attributes; much less can we ever prove the latter from the former. But supposing the Author of nature to be finitely perfect, though far exceeding mankind, a satisfactory account may then be given of natural and moral evil, and every untoward phenomenon be explained and adjusted. A less evil may then be chosen in order to avoid a greater; inconveniences be submitted to in order to reach a desirable end; and, in a word, benevolence, regulated by wisdom and limited by necessity, may produce just such a world as the present. You, Philo, who are so prompt at starting views and reflections and analogies, I would gladly hear, at length, without interruption, your opinion of this new theory; and if it deserve our attention, we may afterwards, at more leisure, reduce it into form.

My sentiments, replied Philo, are not worth being made a mystery of; and, therefore, without any ceremony, I shall deliver what occurs to me with regard to the present subject. It must, I think, be allowed that, if a very limited intelligence whom we shall suppose utterly unacquainted with the universe were assured that it were the producton of a very good, wise, and powerful Being, however finite, he would, from his conjectures, form *beforehand* a different notion of it from what we find it to be by experience; nor would he ever imagine, merely from these attributes of the cause of which he is informed, that the effect could be so full of vice and misery and disorder, as it appears in this life. Supposing now that this person were brought into the world, still assured that it was the workmanship of such a sublime and benevolent Being, he might, perhaps, be surprised at the disappointment, but would never retract his former belief if founded on any very solid argument, since such a limited intelligence must be sensible of his own blindness and ignorance, and must allow that there may be many solutions of those phenomena which will for ever escape his comprehension. But supposing, which is the real case with regard to man, that this creature is not antecedently convinced of a supreme intelligence, benevolent, and powerful, but is left to gather such a belief from the appearances of things—this entirely alters the case, nor will he ever find any reason for such a conclusion. He may be fully convinced of the narrow limits of his understanding, but this will not help him in forming an inference concerning the goodness of superior powers, since he must form that inference from what he knows, not from what he is ignorant of. The more you exaggerate his weakness and ignorance, the more diffident you render him, and give him the greater suspicion that such subjects are beyond the reach of his faculties. You are obliged, therefore, to reason with him merely from the known phenomena, and to drop every arbitrary supposition or conjecture.

Did I show you a house or palace where there was not one apartment convenient or agreeable, where the windows, doors, fires, passages, stairs, and the whole economy of the building were the source of noise, confusion, fatigue, darkness, and the extremes of heat and cold, you would certainly blame the contrivance, without any further examination. The architect would in vain display his subtilty, and prove to you that, if this door or that window were altered, greater ills would ensue. What he says may be strictly true: the alteration of one particular, while the other parts of the building remain, may only augment the inconveniences. But still you would assert in general that, if the architect had had skill and good intentions, he might have formed such a plan of the whole, and might have adjusted the parts in such a manner as would have remedied all or most of these inconveniences. His ignorance, or even your own ignorance of such a plan, will never convince you of the impossibility of it. If you find any inconveniences and deformities in the building, you will always, without entering into any detail, condemn the architect.

In short, I repeat the question: Is the world, considered in general and as it appears to us in this life, different from what a man or such a limited being would, *beforehand*, expect from a very powerful, wise, and benevolent Deity? It must be strange prejudice to assert the contrary. And from thence I conclude that, however consistent the world may be, allowing certain suppositions and conjectures with the idea of such a Deity, it can never afford us an inference concerning his existence. The consistency is not absolutely denied, only the inference. Conjectures, especially where infinity is excluded from the Divine attributes, may perhaps be sufficient to prove a consistency, but can never be foundations for any inference.

There seem to be *four* circumstances on which depend all or the greatest part of the ills that molest sensible creatures; and it is not impossible but all these circumstances may be necessary and unavoidable. We know so little beyond common life, or even of common life, that, with regard to the economy of a universe, there is no conjecture, however wild, which may not be just, nor any one, however plausible, which may not be erroneous. All that belongs to human understanding, in this deep ignorance and obscurity, is to be sceptical or at least cautious, and not to admit of any hypothesis whatever, much less of any which is supported by no appearance of probability. Now this I assert to be the case with regard to all the causes of evil and the circumstances on which it depends. None of them appear to human reason in the least degree necessary or unavoidable, nor can we suppose them such, without the utmost license of imagination.

The *first* circumstance which introduces evil is that contrivance or economy of the animal creation by which pains, as well as pleasures, are employed to excite all creatures to action, and make them vigilant in the great work of self-preservation. Now pleasure alone, in its various degrees, seems to human understanding sufficient for this purpose. All animals might be constantly in a state of enjoyment; but when urged by any of the necessities of nature, such as thirst, hunger, weariness, instead of pain, they might feel a diminution of pleasure by which they might be prompted to seek that object which is necessary to their subsistence. Men pursue pleasure as eagerly as they avoid pain; at least, they might have been so constituted. It seems, therefore, plainly possible to carry on the business of life without any pain. Why then is any animal ever rendered susceptible of such a sensation? If animals can be free from it an hour, they might enjoy a perpetual exemption from it, and it required as particular a contrivance of their organs to produce that feeling as to endow them with sight, hearing, or any of the senses. Shall we conjecture that such a contrivance was necessary, without any appearance of reason, and shall we build on that conjecture as on the most certain truth?

But a capacity of pain would not alone produce pain were it not for the *second* circumstance, viz., the conducting of the world by general laws;

and this seems nowise necessary to a very perfect Being. It is true, if everything were conducted by particular volitions, the course of nature would be perpetually broken, and no man could employ his reason in the conduct of life. But might not other particular volitions remedy this inconvenience? In short, might not the Deity exterminate all ill, wherever it were to be found, and produce all good, without any preparation or long progress of causes and effects?

Besides, we must consider that, according to the present economy of the world, the course of nature, though supposed exactly regular, yet to us appears not so, and many events are uncertain, and many disappoint our expectations. Health and sickness, calm and tempest, with an infinite number of other accidents whose causes are unknown and variable, have a great influence both on the fortunes of particular persons and on the prosperity of public societies; and indeed all human life, in a manner, depends on such accidents. A being, therefore, who knows the secret springs of the universe might easily, by particular volitions, turn all these accidents to the good of mankind and render the whole world happy, without discovering himself in any operation. A fleet whose purposes were salutary to society might always meet with a fair wind. Good princes enjoy sound health and long life. Persons born to power and authority be framed with good tempers and virtuous dispositions. A few such events as these, regularly and wisely conducted, would change the face of the world, and yet would no more seem to disturb the course of nature or confound human conduct than the present economy of things where the causes are secret and variable and compounded. Some small touches given to Caligula's brain in his infancy might have converted him into a Trajan. One wave, a little higher than the rest, by burying Caesar and his fortune in the bottom of the ocean, might have restored liberty to a considerable part of mankind. There may, for aught we know, be good reasons why Providence interposes not in this manner, but they are unknown to us; and, though the mere supposition that such reasons exist may be sufficient to *save* the conclusion concerning the Divine attributes, yet surely it can never be sufficient to *establish* that conclusion.

If everything in the universe be conducted by general laws, and if animals be rendered susceptible of pain, it scarcely seems possible but some ill must arise in the various shocks of matter and the various concurrence and opposition of general laws; but this ill would be very rare were it not for the *third* circumstance which I proposed to mention, viz., the great frugality with which all powers and faculties are distributed to every particular being. So well adjusted are the organs and capacities of all animals, and so well fitted to their preservation, that, as far as history or tradition reaches, there appears not to be any single species which has yet been extinguished in the universe. Every animal has the requisite endowments, but these endowments are bestowed with so scrupulous an economy that any considerable diminution must entirely destroy the creature. Wherever one power is increased, there is a proportional abatement in the others. Animals which excel in swiftness are commonly defective in force. Those which possess both are either imperfect in some of their senses or are oppressed with the most craving wants. The human species, whose chief excellence is reason and sagacity, is of all others the most necessitous, and the most deficient in bodily advantages, without clothes, without arms, without food, without lodging, without any convenience of life, except what they owe to their own skill and industry. In short, nature seems to have formed an exact calculation of the necessities of her creatures, and, like a *rigid master,* has afforded them little more powers or endowments than what are strictly sufficient to supply those necessities. An *indulgent parent* would have bestowed a large stock in order to guard against accidents, and secure the happiness and welfare of the creature in the most unfortunate concurrence of circumstances. Every course of life would not have been so surrounded with precipices that the least departure from the true path, by mistake or necessity, must involve us in misery and ruin. Some reserve, some fund, would have been provided to ensure happiness, nor would the powers and the necessities have been adjusted with so rigid an economy. The Author of nature is inconceivably powerful; his force is supposed great, if not altogether inexhaustible, nor is there any reason, as far as we can judge, to make him observe this strict frugality in his dealings with his creatures. It would have been better, were his power extremely limited, to have created fewer animals, and to have endowed these with more faculties for their happiness and preservation. A builder is never esteemed prudent who undertakes a plan beyond what his stock will enable him to finish.

In order to cure most of the ills of human life, I require not that man should have the wings of the eagle, the swiftness of the stag, the force of the ox, the arms of the lion, the scales of the crocodile or rhinoceros; much less do I demand the sagacity of an angel or cherubim. I am contented to take an increase in one single power or faculty of his soul. Let him be endowed with a greater propensity to industry and labour, a more vigorous spring and activity of mind, a more constant bent to business and application. Let the whole species possess naturally an equal diligence with that which many individuals are able to attain by habit and reflection, and the most beneficial consequences, without any allay of ill, is the immediate and necessary result of this endowment. Almost all the moral as well as natural evils of human life arise from idleness; and were our species, by the original constitution of their frame, exempt from this vice or infirmity, the perfect cultivation of land, the improvement of arts and manufactures, the exact execution of every office and duty, immediately follow; and men at once may fully reach that state of society which is so imperfectly attained by the best regulated government. But as industry is a power, and the most valuable of any, nature seems determined, suitably to her usual maxims, to bestow it on men with a very sparing hand, and rather to punish him severely for his deficiency in it than to reward him for his attainments. She has so contrived his frame that nothing but the most violent necessity can oblige him to labour; and she employs all his other wants to overcome, at least in part, the want of diligence, and to endow him with some share of a faculty of which she has thought fit naturally to bereave him. Here our demands may be allowed very humble, and therefore the more reasonable. If we required the endowments of superior penetration and judgment, of a more delicate taste of beauty, of a nicer sensibility to benevolence and friendship, we might be told that we impiously pretend to break the order of nature, that we want to exalt ourselves into a higher rank of being, that the presents which we require, not being suitable to our state and condition, would only be pernicious to us. But it is hard, I dare to repeat it, it is hard that, being placed in a world so full of wants and necessities, where almost every being and element is either our foe or refuses its assistance . . . we should also have our own temper to struggle with, and should be deprived of that faculty which can alone fence against these multiplied evils.

The *fourth* circumstance whence arises the misery and ill of the universe is the inaccurate workmanship of all the springs and principles of the great machine of nature. It must be acknowledged that there are few parts of the universe which seem not to serve some purpose, and whose removal would not produce a visible defect and disorder in the whole. The parts hang all together, nor can one be touched without affecting the rest, in a greater or less degree. But at the same time, it must be observed that none of these parts or principles, however useful, are so accurately adjusted as to keep precisely within those bounds in which their utility consists; but they are, all of them, apt, on every occasion, to run into the one extreme or the other. One would imagine that this grand production had not received the last hand of the maker—so little finished is every part, and so coarse are the strokes with which it is executed. Thus the winds are requisite to convey the vapours along the surface of the globe, and to assist men in navigation; but how often, rising up to tempests and hurricanes, do they become pernicious? Rains are necessary to nourish all the plants and animals of the earth; but how often are they defective? how often excessive? Heat is requisite to all life and vegetation, but is not always found in the due proportion. On the mixture and secretion of the humours and juices of the body depend the health and prosperity of the animal; but the parts perform not regularly their proper function. What more useful than all the passions of the mind, ambition, vanity, love, anger? But how often do they break their bounds and cause the greatest convulsions in society? There is nothing so advantageous in the universe but what frequently becomes pernicious, by its excess or defect; nor has nature guarded, with the requisite accuracy, against all disorder or confusion. The irregularity is never perhaps so great as to destroy any species, but is often sufficient to involve the individuals in ruin and misery.

On the concurrence, then, of these *four* circumstances does all or the greatest part of natural evil depend. Were all living creatures incapable of pain, or were the world administered by particular volitions, evil never could have found access into the universe; and were animals endowed with a large stock of powers and faculties, beyond what strict necessity requires, or were the several springs and principles of the universe so accurately framed as to preserve always the just temperament and medium, there must have been very little ill in comparison of what we feel at present. What then shall we pronounce on this occasion? Shall we say that these circumstances are not necessary, and that they might easily have been altered in the contrivance of the universe? This decision seems too presumptuous for creatures so blind and ignorant. Let us be more modest in our conclusions. Let us allow that, if the goodness of the Deity (I mean a goodness like the human) could be established on any tolerable reasons *a priori,* these phenomena, however untoward, would not be sufficient to subvert that principle, but might easily, in some unknown manner, be reconcilable to it. But let us still assert that, as this goodness is not antecedently established but must be inferred from the phenomena, there can be no grounds for such an inference while there are so many ills in the universe, and while these ills might so easily have been remedied, as far as human understanding can be allowed to judge on such a subject. I am sceptic enough to allow that the bad appearances, notwithstanding all my reasonings, may be compatible with such attributes as you suppose, but surely they can never prove these attributes. Such a conclusion cannot result from scepticism, but must arise from the phenomena, and from our confidence in the reasonings which we deduce from these phenomena.

Look round this universe. What an immense profusion of beings, animated and organized, sensible and active! You admire this prodigious variety and fecundity. But inspect a little more narrowly these living existences, the only beings worth regarding. How hostile and destructive to each other! How insufficient all of them for their own happiness! How contemptible or odious to the spectator! The whole presents nothing but the idea of a blind nature, impregnated by a great vivifying principle, and pouring forth from her lap, without discernment or parental care, her maimed and abortive children!

Here the Manichaean system occurs as a proper hypothesis to solve the difficulty; and, no doubt, in some respects it is very specious and has more probability than the common hypothesis, by giving a plausible account of the strange mixture of good and ill which appears in life. But if we consider, on the other hand, the perfect uniformity and agreement of the parts of the universe, we shall not discover in it any marks of the combat of a malevolent with a benevolent being. There is indeed an opposition of pains and pleasures in the feelings of sensible creatures; but are not all the operations of nature carried on by an opposition of principles, of hot and cold, moist and dry, light and heavy? The true conclusion is that the original Source of all things is entirely indifferent to all these principles, and has no more regard to good above ill than to heat above cold, or to drought above moisture, or to light above heavy.

There may *four* hypotheses be framed concerning the first causes of the universe: that they are endowed with perfect goodness; that they have perfect malice; that they are opposite and have both goodness and malice; that they have neither goodness nor malice. Mixed phenomena can never prove the two former unmixed principles; and the uniformity and steadiness of general laws seem to oppose the third. The fourth, therefore, seems by far the most probable.

What I have said concerning natural evil will apply to moral with little or no variation; and we have no more reason to infer that the rectitude of the Supreme Being resembles human rectitude than that his benevolence resembles the human. Nay, it will be thought that we have still greater cause to exclude from him moral sentiments, such as we feel them, since moral evil, in the opinion of many, is much more predominant above moral good than natural evil above natural good.

But even though this should not be allowed, and though the virtue which is in mankind should be acknowledged much superior to the vice, yet, so long as there is any vice at all in the universe, it will very much puzzle you anthropomorphites how to account for it. You must assign a cause for it, without having recourse to the first cause. But as every effect must have a cause, and that cause another, you must either carry on the progression *in infinitum* or rest on that original principle, who is the ultimate cause of all things. . . .

Hold! hold! cried Demea: Whither does your imagination hurry you? I joined in alliance with you in order to prove the incomprehensible nature of the Divine Being, and refute the principles of Cleanthes, who would measure everything by human rule and standard. But I now find you running into all the topics of the greatest libertines and infidels, and betraying that holy cause which you seemingly espoused. Are you secretly, then, a more dangerous enemy than Cleanthes himself?

And are you so late in perceiving it? replied Cleanthes. Believe me, Demea, your friend Philo, from the beginning, has been amusing himself at both our expense; and it must be confessed that the injudicious reasoning of our vulgar theology has given him but too just a handle of ridicule. The total infirmity of human reason, the absolute incomprehensibility of the Divine Nature, the great and universal misery, and still greater wickedness of men—these are strange topics, surely, to be so fondly cherished by orthodox divines and doctors. In ages of stupidity and ignorance, indeed, these principles may safely be espoused; and perhaps no views of things are more proper to promote superstition than such as encourage the blind amazement, the diffidence, and melancholy of mankind. But at present . . .

Blame not so much, interposed Philo, the ignorance of these reverend gentlemen. They know how to change their style with the times. Formerly, it was a most popular theological topic to maintain that human life was vanity and misery, and to exaggerate all the ills and pains which are incident to men. But of late years, divines, we find, begin to retract this position and maintain, though still with some hesitation, that there are more goods than evils, more pleasures than pains, even in this life. When religion stood entirely upon temper and education, it was thought proper to encourage melancholy, as, indeed, mankind never have recourse to superior powers so readily as in that disposition. But as men have now learned to form principles and to draw consequences, it is necessary to change the batteries, and to make use of such arguments as will endure at least some scrutiny and examination. This variation is the same (and from the same causes) with that which I formerly remarked with regard to scepticism.

Thus Philo continued to the last his spirit of opposition, and his censure of established opinions. But I could observe that Demea did not at all relish the latter part of the discourse; and he took occasion soon after, on some pretence or other, to leave the company.

Ernest Nagel

A DEFENSE OF ATHEISM

The essays in this book are devoted in the main to the exposition of the major religious creeds of humanity. It is a natural expectation that this final paper, even though its theme is so radically different from nearly all of the others, will show how atheism belongs to the great tradition of religious thought. Needless to say, this expectation is difficult to satisfy, and did anyone succeed in doing so he would indeed be performing the neatest conjuring trick of the week. But the expectation nevertheless does cause me some embarrassment, which is only slightly relieved by an anecdote Bertrand Russell reports in his recent book, *Portraits from Memory*. Russell was imprisoned during the First World War for pacifistic activities. On entering the prison he was asked a number of customary questions about himself for the prison records. One question was about his religion. Russell explained that he was an agnostic. "Never

Reprinted from *Basic Beliefs* (1959), ed. J. E. Fairchild, by permission of the publisher, Sheridan House, Inc.

heard of it," the warden declared. "How do you spell it?" When Russell told him, the warden observed, "Well, there are many religions, but I suppose they all worship the same God." Russell adds that this remark kept him cheerful for about a week. Perhaps philosophical atheism also is a religion.

1

I must begin by stating what sense I am attaching to the word "atheism," and how I am construing the theme of this paper. I shall understand by "atheism" a critique and a denial of the major claims of all varieties of theism. And by theism I shall mean the view which holds, as one writer has expressed it, "that the heavens and the earth and all that they contain owe their existence and continuance in existence to the wisdom and will of a supreme, self-consistent, omnipotent, omniscient, righteous, and benevolent being, who is distinct from, and independent of, what he has created." Several things immediately follow from these definitions.

In the first place, atheism is not necessarily an irreligious concept, for theism is just one among many views concerning the nature and origin of the world. The denial of theism is logically compatible with a religious outlook upon life, and is in fact characteristic of some of the great historical religions. For as readers of this volume will know, early Buddhism is a religion which does not subscribe to any doctrine about a god; and there are pantheistic religions and philosophies which, because they deny that God is a being separate from and independent of the world, are not theistic in the sense of the word explained above.

The second point to note is that atheism is not to be identified with sheer unbelief, or with disbelief in some particular creed of a religious group. Thus, a child who has received no religious instruction and has never heard about God, is not an atheist—for he is not denying any theistic claims. Similarly in the case of an adult who, if he has withdrawn from the faith of his fathers without reflection or because of frank indifference to any theological issue, is also not an atheist—for such an adult is not challenging theism and is not professing any views on the subject. Moreover, though the term "atheist" has been used historically as an abusive label for those who do not happen to subscribe to some regnant orthodoxy (for example, the ancient Romans called the early Christians atheists, because the latter denied the Roman divinities), or for those who engage in conduct regarded as immoral it is not in this sense that I am discussing atheism.

One final word of preliminary explanation. I propose to examine some *philosophic* concepts of atheism, and I am not interested in the slightest in the many considerations atheists have advanced against the evidences for some particular religious and theological doctrine—for example, against the truth of the Christian story. What I mean by "philosophical" in the present context is that the views I shall consider are directed against any form of theism, and have their origin and basis in a logical analysis of the theistic position, and in a comprehensive account of the world believed to be wholly intelligible without the adoption of a theistic hypothesis.

Theism as I conceive it is a theological proposition, not a statement of a position that belongs primarily to religion. On my view, religion as a historical and social phenomenon is primarily an institutionalized *cultus* or practice, which possesses identifiable social functions and which expresses certain attitudes men take toward their world. Although it is doubtful whether men ever engage in religious practices or assume religious attitudes without some more or less explicit interpretation of their ritual or some rationale for their attitude, it is still the case that it is possible to distinguish religion as a social and personal phenomenon from the theological doctrines which may be developed as justifications for religious practices. Indeed, in some of the great religions of the world the profession of a creed plays a relatively minor role. In short, religion is a form of social communion, a participation in certain kinds of ritual (whether it be a dance, worship, prayer, or the like), and a form of experience (sometimes, though not invariably, directed to a personal confrontation with divine and holy things). Theology is an articulated and, at its best, a rational attempt at understanding these feelings and practices, in the light of their relation to other parts of human experience, and in terms of some hypothesis concerning the nature of things entire.

2

As I see it, atheistic philosophies fall into two major groups: 1) those which hold that the theistic doctrine is meaningful, but reject it either on the ground that, (a) the positive evidence for it is insufficient, or (b) the negative evidence is quite overwhelming; and 2) those who hold that the theistic thesis is not even meaningful, and reject it (a) as just nonsense or (b) as literally meaningless but interpreting it as a symbolic rendering of human ideals, thus reading the theistic thesis in a sense that most believers in theism would disavow. It will not be possible in the limited space at my disposal to discuss the second category of atheistic critiques; and in any event, most of the traditional atheistic critiques of theism belong to the first group.

But before turning to the philosophical examination of the major classical arguments for theism, it is well to note that such philosophical critiques do not quite convey the passion with which atheists have often carried on their analyses of theistic views. For historically, atheism has been, and indeed continues to be, a form of social and political protest, directed as much against institutionalized religion as against theistic doctrine. Atheism has been, in effect, a moral revulsion against the undoubted abuses of the secular power exercised by religious leaders and religious institutions.

Religious authorities have opposed the correction of glaring injustices, and encouraged politically and socially reactionary policies. Religious institutions have been havens of obscurantist thought and centers for the dissemination of intolerance. Religious creeds have been used to set limits to free inquiry, to perpetuate inhumane treatment of the ill and the underprivileged, and to support moral doctrines insensitive to human suffering.

These indictments may not tell the whole story about the historical significance of religion; but they are at least an important part of the story. The refutation of theism has thus seemed to many as an indispensable step not only towards liberating men's minds from superstition, but also towards achieving a more equitable reordering of society. And no account of even the more philosophical aspects of atheistic thought is adequate, which does not give proper recognition to the powerful social motives that actuate many atheistic arguments.

But however this may be, I want now to discuss three classical arguments for the existence of God, arguments which have constituted at least a partial basis for theistic commitments. As long as theism is defended simply as a dogma, asserted as a matter of direct revelation or as the deliverance of authority, belief in the dogma is impregnable to rational argument. In fact, however, reasons are frequently advanced in support of the theistic creed, and these reasons have been the subject of acute philosophical critiques.

One of the oldest intellectual defenses of theism is the cosmological argument, also known as the argument from a first cause. Briefly put, the argument runs as follows. Every event must have a cause. Hence an event A must have as cause some event B, which in turn must have a cause C, and so on. But if there is no end to this backward progression of causes, the progression will be infinite; and in the opinion of those who use this argument, an infinite series of actual events is unintelligible and absurd.

Hence there must be a first cause, and this first cause is God, the initiator of all change in the universe.

The argument is an ancient one, and is especially effective when stated within the framework of assumptions of Aristotelian physics; and it has impressed many generations of exceptionally keen minds. The argument is nonetheless a weak reed on which to rest the theistic thesis. Let us waive any question concerning the validity of the principle that every event has a cause, for though the question is important its discussion would lead us far afield. However, if the principle is assumed, it is surely incongruous to postulate a first cause as a way of escaping from the coils of an infinite series. For if everything must have a cause, why does not God require one for His own existence? The standard answer is that He does not need any, because He is self-caused. But if God can be self-caused, why cannot the world itself be self-caused? Why do we require a God transcending the world to bring the world into existence and to initiate changes in it? On the other hand, the supposed inconceivability and absurdity of an infinite series of regressive causes will be admitted by no one who has competent familiarity with the modern mathematical analysis of infinity. The cosmological argument does not stand up under scrutiny.

The second "proof" of God's existence is usually called the ontological argument. It too has a long history going back to early Christian days, though it acquired great prominence only in medieval times. The argument can be stated in several ways, one of which is the following. Since God is conceived to be omnipotent, he is a perfect being. A perfect being is defined as one whose essence or nature lacks no attributes (or properties) whatsoever, one whose nature is complete in every respect. But it is evident that we have an idea of a perfect being, for we have just defined the idea; and since this is so, the argument continues, God who is the perfect being must exist. Why must he? Because his existence follows from his defined nature. For if God lacked the attribute of existence, he would be lacking at least one attribute, and would therefore not be perfect. To sum up, since we have an idea of God as a perfect being, God must exist.

There are several ways of approaching this argument, but I shall consider only one. The argument was exploded by the 18th century philosopher Immanuel Kant. The substance of Kant's criticism is that it is just a confusion to say that existence is an attribute, and that though the *word* "existence" may occur as the grammatical predicate in a sentence no attribute is being predicated of a thing when we say that the thing exists or has existence. Thus, to use Kant's example, when we think of $100 we are thinking of the nature of this sum of money; but the nature of $100 remains the same whether we have $100 in our pockets or not. Accordingly, we are confounding grammar with logic if we suppose that some characteristic is being attributed to the nature of $100 when we say that a hundred dollar bill exists in someone's pocket.

To make the point clearer, consider another example. When we say that a lion has a tawny color, we are predicating a certain attribute of the animal, and similarly when we say that the lion is fierce or is hungry. But when we say the lion exists, all that we are saying is that something is (or has the nature of) a lion; we are not specifying an attribute which belongs to the nature of anything that is a lion. In short, the word "existence" does not signify any attribute, and in consequence no attribute that belongs to the nature of anything. Accordingly, it does not follow from the assumption that we have an idea of a perfect being that such a being exists. For the idea of a perfect being does not involve the attribute of existence as a constituent of that idea, since there is no such attribute. The ontological argument thus has a serious leak, and it can hold no water.

3

The two arguments discussed thus far are purely dialectical, and attempt to establish God's existence without any appeal to empirical data. The next argument, called the argument from design, is different in character, for it is based on what purports to be empirical evidence. I wish to examine two forms of this argument.

One variant of it calls attention to the remarkable way in which different things and processes in the world are integrated with each other, and concludes that this mutual "fitness" of things can be explained only by the assumption of a divine architect who planned the world and everything in it. For example, living organisms can maintain themselves in a variety of environments, and do so in virtue of their delicate mechanisms which adapt the organisms to all sorts of environmental changes. There is thus an intricate pattern of means and ends throughout the animate world. But the existence of this pattern is unintelliglble, so the argument runs, except on the hypothesis that the pattern has been deliberately instituted by a Supreme Designer. If we find a watch in some deserted spot, we do not think it came into existence by chance, and we do not hesitate to conclude that an intelligent creature designed and made it. But the world and all its contents exhibit mechanisms and mutual adjustments that are far more complicated and subtle than are those of a watch. Must we not therefore conclude that these things too have a Creator?

The conclusion of this argument is based on an inference from analogy: the watch and the world are alike in possessing a congruence of parts and an adjustment of means to ends; the watch has a watch-maker; hence the world has a world-maker. But is the analogy a good one? Let us once more waive some important issues, in particular the issue whether the universe is the unified system such as the watch admittedly is. And let us concentrate on the question what is the ground for our assurance that watches do not come into existence except through the operations of intelligent manufacturers. The answer is plain. We have never run across a watch which has not been deliberately made by someone. But the situation is nothing like this in the case of the innumerable animate and inanimate systems with which we are familiar. Even in the case of living organisms, though they are generated by their parent organisms, the parents do not "make" their progeny in the same sense in which watch-makers make watches. And once this point is clear, the inference from the existence of living organisms to the existence of a supreme designer no longer appears credible.

Moreover, the argument loses all its force if the facts which the hypothesis of a divine designer is supposed to explain can be understood on the basis of a better supported assumption. And indeed, such an alternative explanation is one of the achievements of Darwinian biology. For Darwin showed that one can account for the variety of biological species, as well as for their adaptations to their environments, without invoking a divine creator and acts of special creation. The Darwinian theory explains the diversity of biological species in terms of chance variations in the structure of organisms, and of a mechanism of selection which retains those variant forms that possess some advantages for survival. The evidence for these assumptions is considerable; and developments subsequent to Darwin have only strengthened the case for a thoroughly naturalistic explanation of the facts of biological adaptation. In any event, this version of the argument from design has nothing to recommend it.

A second form of this argument has been recently revived in the speculations of some modern physicists. No one who is familiar with the facts, can fail to be impressed by the success with which the use of mathematical methods has enabled us to obtain intellectual mastery of many parts of nature. But some thinkers have therefore concluded that since the book of nature is ostensibly written in mathematical language, nature must be the creation of a divine mathematician. However, the argument is most dubious. For it rests, among other things, on the assumption that mathematical tools can be successfully used only if the events of nature exhibit some *special* kind of order, and on the further assumption that if the structure of things were different from what they are mathematical language would be inadequate for describing such structure. But it can be shown that no matter what the world were like—even if it impressed us as being utterly chaotic—it would still possess some order, and would in principle be amenable to a mathematical description. In point of fact, it makes no sense to say that there is absolutely *no* pattern in any conceivable subject matter. To be sure, there are differences in complexities of structure, and if the patterns of events were sufficiently complex we might not be able to unravel them. But however that may be, the success of mathematical physics in giving us some understanding of the world around us does not yield the conclusion that only a mathematician could have devised the patterns of order we have discovered in nature.

4

The inconclusiveness of the three classical arguments for the existence of God was already made evident by Kant, in a manner substantially not different from the above discussion. There are, however, other types of arguments for theism that have been influential in the history of thought, two of which I wish to consider, even if only briefly.

Indeed, though Kant destroyed the classical intellectual foundations for theism, he himself invented a fresh argument for it. Kant's attempted proof is not intended to be a purely theoretical demonstration, and is based on the supposed facts of our moral nature. It has exerted an enormous influence on subsequent theological speculation. In barest outline, the argument is as follows. According to Kant, we are subject not only to physical laws like the rest of nature, but also to moral ones. These moral laws are categorical imperatives, which we must heed not because of their utilitarian consequences, but simply because as autonomous mortal agents it is our duty to accept them as binding. However, Kant was keenly aware that though virtue may be its reward, the virtuous man (that is, the man who acts out of a sense of duty and in conformity with the moral law) does not always receive his just desserts in this world; nor did he shut his eyes to the fact that evil men frequently enjoy the best things this world has to offer. In short, virtue does not always reap happiness. Nevertheless, the highest human good is the realization of happiness commensurate with one's virtue; and Kant believed that it is a practical postulate of the moral life to promote this good. But what can guarantee that the highest good is realizable? Such a guarantee can be found only in God, who must therefore exist if the highest good is not to be a fatuous ideal. The existence of an omnipotent, omniscient, and omnibenevolent God is thus postulated as a necessary condition for the possibility of a moral life.

Despite the prestige this argument has acquired, it is difficult to grant it any force. It is easy enough to postulate God's existence. But as Bertrand Russell observed in another connection, postulation has all the advantages of theft over honest toil. No postulation carries with it any assurance that what is postulated is actually the case. And though we may postulate God's existence as a means to guaranteeing the possibility of realizing happiness together with virtue, the postulation establishes neither the actual realizability of this ideal nor the fact of his existence. Moreover, the argument is not made more cogent when we recognize that it is based squarely on the highly dubious conception that considerations of utility and human happiness must not enter into the determination of what is morally obligatory. Having built his moral theory on a radical separation of means from ends, Kant was driven to the desperate postulation of God's existence in order to relate them again. The argument is thus at best a *tour de force,* contrived to remedy a fatal flaw in Kant's initial moral assumptions. It carries no conviction to anyone who does not commit Kant's initial blunder.

One further type of argument, pervasive in much Protestant theological literature, deserves brief mention. Arguments of this type take their point of departure from the psychology of religious and mystical experience. Those who have undergone such experiences, often report that during the experience they feel themselves to be in the presence of the divine and holy, that they loose their sense of self-identity and become merged with some fundamental reality, or that they enjoy a feeling of total dependence upon some ultimate power. The overwhelming sense of transcending one's finitude which characterizes such vivid periods of life, and of coalescing with some ultimate source of all existence, is then taken to be compelling evidence for the existence of a supreme being. In a variant form of this argument, other theologians have identified God as the object which satisfies the commonly experienced need for integrating one's scattered and conflicting impulses into a coherent unity, or as the subject which is of ultimate concern to us. In short, a proof of God's existence is found in the occurrence of certain distinctive experiences.

It would be flying in the face of well-attested facts were one to deny that such experiences frequently occur. But do these facts constitute evidence for the conclusion based on them? Does the fact, for example, that an individual experiences a profound sense of direct contact with an alleged transcendent ground of all reality, constitute competent evidence for the claim that there is such a ground and that it is the immediate cause of the experience? If well-established canons for evaluating evidence are accepted, the answer is surely negative. No one will dispute that many men do have vivid experiences in which such things as ghosts or pink elephants appear before them; but only the hopelessly credulous will without further ado count such experiences as establishing the existence of ghosts and pink elephants. To establish the existence of such things, evidence is required that is obtained under controlled conditions and that can be confirmed by independent inquirers. Again, though a man's report that he is suffering pain may be taken at face value, one cannot take at face value the claim, were he to make it, that it is the food he ate which is the cause (or a contributory cause) of his felt pain—not even if the man were to report a vivid feeling of abdominal disturbance. And similarly, an overwhelming feeling of being in the presence of the Divine is evidence enough for admitting the genuineness of such feeling; it is no evidence for the claim that a supreme being with a substantial existence independent of the experience is the cause of the experience.

5

Thus far the discussion has been concerned with noting inadequacies in various arguments widely used to support theism. However, much atheistic criticism is also directed toward exposing incoherencies in the very thesis of theism. I want therefore to consider this aspect of the atheistic critique, though I will restrict myself to the central difficulty in the theistic position which arises from the simultaneous attribution of omnipotence, omniscience, and omnibenevolence to the Deity. The difficulty is that of reconciling these attributes with the occurrence of evil in the world. Accordingly, the question to which I now turn is whether, despite the existence of evil, it is possible to construct a theodicy which will justify the ways of an infinitely powerful and just God to man.

Two main types of solutions have been proposed for this problem. One way that is frequently used is to maintain that what is commonly called evil is only an illusion, or at worst only the "privation" or absence of good. Accordingly, evil is not "really real," it is only the "negative" side of God's beneficence, it is only the product of our limited intelligence which fails to plumb the true character of God's creative bounty. A sufficient comment on this proposed solution is that facts are not altered or abolished by rebaptizing them. Evil may indeed by only an appearance and not genuine. But this does not eliminate from the realm of appearance the tragedies, the sufferings, and the iniquities which men so frequently endure. And it raises once more, though on another level, the problem of reconciling the fact that there is evil in the realm of appearance with God's alleged omnibenevolence. In any event, it is small comfort to anyone suffering a cruel misfortune for which he is in no way responsible, to be told that what he is undergoing is only the absence of good. It is a gratuitous insult to mankind, a symptom of insensitivity and indifference to human suffering, to be assured that all the miseries and agonies men experience are only illusory.

Another gambit often played in attempting to justify the ways of God to man is to argue that the things called evil are evil only because they are viewed in isolation; they are not evil when viewed in proper perspective and in relation to the rest of creation. Thus, if one attends to but a single instrument in an orchestra, the sounds issuing from it may indeed be harsh and discordant. But if one is placed at a proper distance from the whole orchestra, the sounds of that single instrument will mingle with the sounds issuing from the other players to produce a marvellous bit of symphonic music. Analogously, experiences we call painful undoubtedly occur and are real enough. But the pain is judged to be an evil only because it is experienced in a limited perspective—the pain is there for the sake of a more inclusive good, whose reality eludes us because our intelligences are too weak to apprehend things in their entirety.

It is an appropriate retort to this argument that of course we judge things to be evil in a human perspective, but that since we are not God this is the only proper perspective in which to judge them. It may indeed be the case that what is evil for us is not evil for some other part of creation. However, we are not this other part of creation, and it is irrelevant to argue that were we something other than what we are, our evaluations of what is good and bad would be different. Moreover, the worthlessness of the argument becomes even more evident if we remind ourselves that it is unsupported speculation to suppose that whatever is evil in a finite perspective is good from the purported perspective of the totality of things. For the argument can be turned around: what we judge to be a good is a good only because it is viewed in isolation; when it is viewed in proper perspective, and in relation to the entire scheme of things, it is an evil. This is in fact a standard form of the argument for a universal pessimism. Is it any worse than the similar argument for a universal optimism? The very raising of this question is a *reductio ad absurdum* of the proposed solution to the ancient problem of evil.

I do not believe it is possible to reconcile the alleged omnipotence and omnibenevolence of God with the unvarnished facts of human existence. In point of fact, many theologians have concurred in this conclusion; for in order to escape from the difficulty which the traditional attributes of God present, they have assumed that God is not all powerful, and that there are limits as to what He can do in his efforts to establish a righteous order in the universe. But whether such a modified theology is better off, is doubtful; and in any event, the question still remains whether the facts of human life support the claim that an omnibenevolent Deity, though limited in power, is revealed in the ordering of human history. It is pertinent to note in this connection that though there have been many historians who have made the effort, no historian has yet succeeded in showing to the satisfaction of his professional colleagues that the hypothesis of a Divine Providence is capable of explaining anything which cannot be explained just as well without this hypothesis.

6

This last remark naturally leads to the question whether, apart from their polemics against theism, philosophical atheists have not shared a common set of positive views, a common set of philosophical convictions which set them off from other groups of thinkers. In one very clear sense of this query the answer is indubitably negative. For there never has been what one might call a "school of atheism," in the way in which there has been a Platonic school or even a Kantian school. In point of fact, atheistic critics of theism can be found among many of the conventional groupings of philosophical thinkers—even, I venture to add, among professional theologians in recent years who in effect preach atheism in the guise of language taken bodily from the Christian tradition.

Nevertheless, despite the variety of philosophic positions to which at one time or another in the history of thought atheists have subscribed, it seems to me that atheism is not simply a negative standpoint. At any rate, there is a certain quality of intellectual temper that has characterized, and continues to characterize, many philosophical atheists. (I am excluding from consideration the so-called "village atheist," whose primary concern is to twit and ridicule those who accept some form of theism, or for that matter those who have any religious convictions.) Moreover, their rejection of theism is based not only on the inadequacies they have found in the arguments for theism, but often also on the positive ground that atheism is a corollary to a better supported general outlook upon the nature of things. I want therefore to conclude this discussion with a brief enumeration of some points of positive doctrine to which by and large philosophical atheists seem to me to subscribe. These points fall into three major groups.

In the first place, philosophical atheists reject the assumption that there are disembodied spirits, or that incorporeal entities of any sort can exercise a causal agency. On the contrary, atheists are generally agreed that if we wish to achieve any understanding of what takes place in the universe, we must look to the operations of organized bodies. Accordingly, the various processes taking place in nature, whether animate or inanimate, are to be explained in terms of the properties and structures of identifiable and spatio-temporally located objects. Moreover, the present variety of systems and activities found in the universe is to be accounted for on the basis of the transformations things undergo when they enter into different relations with one another—transformations which often result in the emergence of novel kinds of objects. On the other hand, though things are in flux and undergo alteration, there is no all-encompassing unitary pattern of change. Nature is ineradicably plural, both in respect to the individuals occurring in it as well as in respect to the processes in which things become involved. Accordingly, the human scene and the human perspective are not illusory; and man and his works are no less and no more "real" than are other parts or phases of the cosmos. At the risk of using a possibly misleading characterization, all of this can be summarized by saying that an atheistic view of things is a form of materialism.

In the second place, atheists generally manifest a marked empirical temper, and often take as their ideal the intellectual methods employed in the contemporaneous empirical sciences. Philosophical atheists differ considerably on important points of detail in their account of how responsible claims to knowledge are to be established. But there is substantial agreement among them that controlled sensory observation is the court of final appeal in issues concerning matters of fact. It is indeed this commitment to the use of an empirical method which is the final basis of the atheistic critique of theism. For at bottom this critique seeks to show that we can understand whatever a theistic assumption is alleged to explain, through the use of the proved methods of the positive sciences and without the introduction of empirically unsupported *ad hoc* hypotheses about a Deity. It is pertinent in this connection to recall a familiar legend about the French mathematical physicist Laplace. According to the story, Laplace made a personal presentation of a copy of his now famous book on celestial mechanics to Napoleon. Napoleon glanced through the volume, and finding no reference to the Deity asked Laplace whether God's existence played any role in the analysis. "Sire, I have no need for that hypothesis," Laplace is reported to have replied. The dismissal of sterile hypotheses characterizes not only the work of Laplace; it is the uniform rule in scientific inquiry. The sterility of the theistic assumption is one of the main burdens of the literature of atheism both ancient and modern.

And finally, atheistic thinkers have generally accepted a utilitarian basis for judging moral issues, and they have exhibited a libertarian attitude toward human needs and impulses. The conceptions of the human good they have advocated are conceptions which are commensurate with the actual capacities of mortal men, so that it is the satisfaction of the complex needs of the human creature which is the final standard for evaluating the validity of a moral ideal or moral prescription.

In consequence, the emphasis of atheistic moral reflection has been this-worldly rather than other-worldly, individualistic rather than authoritarian. The stress upon a good life that must be consummated in this world, has made atheists vigorous opponents of moral codes which seek to repress human impulses in the name of some unrealizable other-worldly ideal. The individualism that is so pronounced a strain in many philosophical atheists has made them tolerant of human limitations and sensitive to the plurality of legitimate moral goals. On the other hand, this individualism has certainly not prevented many of them from recognizing the crucial role which institutional arrangements can play in achieving desirable patterns of human living. In consequence, atheists have made important contributions to the development of a climate of opinon favorable to pursuing the values of a liberal civilization and they have played effective roles in attempts to rectify social injustices.

Atheists cannot build their moral outlook on foundations upon which so many men conduct their lives. In particular, atheism cannot offer the incentives to conduct and the consolations for misfortune which theistic religions supply to their adherents. It can offer no hope of personal immortality, no threats of Divine chastisement, no promise of eventual recompense for injustices suffered, no blueprints to sure salvation. For on its view of the place of man in nature, human excellence and human dignity must be achieved within a finite life-span, or not at all, so that the rewards of moral endeavor must come from the quality of civilized living, and not from some source of disbursement that dwells outside of time. Accordingly, atheistic moral reflection at its best does not culminate in a quiescent ideal of human perfection, but is a vigorous call to intelligent activity—activity for the sake of realizing human potentialities and for eliminating whatever stands in the way of such realization. Nevertheless, though slavish resignation to remediable ills is not characteristic of atheistic thought, responsible atheists have never pretended that human effort can invariably achieve the heart's every legitimate desire. A tragic view of life is thus an uneliminable ingredient in atheistic thought. This ingredient does not invite or generally produce lugubrious lamentation. But it does touch the atheist's view of man and his place in nature with an emotion that makes the philosophical atheist a kindred spirit to those who, within the frameworks of various religious traditions, have developed a serenely resigned attitude toward the inevitable tragedies of the human estate.

Bertrand Russell (1872–1970), one of the leading philosophers of the twentieth century, made significant contributions to virtually every area of philosophy.

Bertrand Russell

A FREE MAN'S WORSHIP

To Dr. Faustus in his study Mephistopheles told the history of the Creation, saying,

> The endless praises of the choirs of angels had begun to grow wearisome; for, after all, did he not deserve their praise? Had he not given them endless joy? Would it not be more amusing to obtain undeserved praise, to be worshiped by beings whom he tortured? He smiled inwardly, and resolved that the great drama should be performed.
> For countless ages the hot nebula whirled aimlessly through space. At length it began to take shape, the central mass threw off planets, the planets cooled, boiling seas and burning mountains heaved and tossed, from black masses of cloud hot sheets of rain deluged the barely solid crust. And now the first germ of life grew in the depths of the ocean and developed rapidly in the fructifying warmth into vast forest trees, huge ferns springing from the damp mold, sea

Reprinted from *Why I Am Not a Christian* (1957), by permission of the publisher, George Allen & Unwin Ltd.

monsters breeding, fighting, devouring, and passing away. And from the monsters, as the play unfolded itself, Man was born, with the power of thought, the knowledge of good and evil, and the cruel thirst for worship. And Man saw that all is passing in this mad, monstrous world, that all is struggling to snatch, at any cost, a few brief moments of life before Death's inexorable decree. And Man said, "There is a hidden purpose, could we but fathom it, and the purpose is good; for we must reverence something, and in the visible world there is nothing worthy of reverence." And Man stood aside from the struggle, resolving that God intended harmony to come out of chaos by human efforts. And when he followed the instincts which God had transmitted to him from his ancestry of beasts of prey, he called it Sin, and asked God to forgive him. But he doubted whether he could be justly forgiven, until he invented a divine Plan by which God's wrath was to have been appeased. And seeing the present was bad, he made it yet worse, that thereby the future might be better. And he gave God thanks for the strength that enabled him to forgo even the joys that were possible. And God smiled; and when he saw that Man had become perfect in renunciation and worship, he sent another sun through the sky, which crashed into Man's sun; and all returned again to nebula.

"Yes," he murmured, "it was a good play; I will have it performed again."

Such, in outline, but even more purposeless, more void of meaning, is the world which science presents for our belief. Amid such a world, if anywhere, our ideals henceforward must find a home. That man is the product of causes which had no prevision of the end they were achieving; that his origin, his growth, his hopes and fears, his loves and his beliefs, are but the outcome of accidental collocations of atoms; that no fire, no heroism, no intensity of thought and feeling, can preserve an individual life beyond the grave; that all the labors of the ages, all the devotion, all the inspiration, all the noonday brightness of human genius, are destined to extinction in the vast death of the solar system, and that the whole temple of man's achievement must inevitably be buried beneath the debris of a universe in ruins—all these things, if not quite beyond dispute, are yet so nearly certain that no philosophy which rejects them can hope to stand. Only within the scaffolding of these truths, only on the firm foundation of unyielding despair, can the soul's habitation henceforth be safely built.

How, in such an alien and inhuman world, can so powerless a creature as man preserve his aspirations untarnished? A strange mystery it is that nature, omnipotent but blind, in the revolutions of her secular hurryings through the abysses of space, has brought forth at last a child, subject still to her power, but gifted with sight, with knowledge of good and evil, with the capacity of judging all the works of his unthinking mother. In spite of death, the mark and seal of the parental control, man is yet free, during his brief years, to examine, to criticize, to know, and in imagination to create. To him alone, in the world with which he is acquainted, this freedom belongs; and in this lies his superiority to the resistless forces that control his outward life.

The savage, like ourselves, feels the oppression of his impotence before the powers of nature; but having in himself nothing that he respects more than power, he is willing to prostrate himself before his gods, without inquiring whether they are worthy of his worship. Pathetic and very terrible is the long history of cruelty and torture, of degradation and human sacrifice, endured in the hope of placating the jealous gods: surely, the trembling believer thinks, when what is most precious has been freely given, their lust for blood must be appeased, and more will not be required. The religion of Moloch—as such creeds may be generally called—is in essence the cringing submission of the slave, who dare not, even in his heart, allow the thought that his master deserves no adulation. Since the independence of ideals is not yet acknowledged, power may be freely worshiped and receive an unlimited respect, despite its wanton infliction of pain.

But gradually, as morality grows bolder, the claim of the ideal world begins to be felt; and worship, if it is not to cease, must be given to gods of another kind than those created by the savage. Some, though they feel the demands of the ideal, will still consciously reject them, still urging that naked power is worthy of worship. Such is the attitude inculcated in God's answer to Job out of the whirlwind: the divine power and knowledge are paraded, but of the divine goodness there is no hint. Such also is the attitude of those who, in our own day, base their morality upon the struggle for survival, maintaining that the survivors are necessarily the fittest. But others, not content with an answer so repugnant to the moral sense, will adopt the position which we have become accustomed to regard as specially religious, maintaining that, in some hidden manner, the world of fact is really harmonious with the world of ideals. Thus man created God, all-powerful and all-good, the mystic unity of what is and what should be.

But the world of fact, after all, is not good; and, in submitting our judgment to it, there is an element of slavishness from which our thoughts must be purged. For in all things it is well to exalt the dignity of man, by freeing him as far as possible from the tyranny of nonhuman power. When we have realized that power is largely bad, that man, with his knowledge of good and evil, is but a helpless atom in a world which has no such knowledge, the choice is again presented to us: Shall we worship force, or shall we worship goodness? Shall our God exist and be evil, or shall he be recognized as the creation of our own conscience?

The answer to this question is very momentous and affects profoundly our whole morality. The worship of force, to which Carlyle and Nietzsche and the creed of militarism have accustomed us, is the result of failure to maintain our own ideals against a hostile universe: it is itself a prostrate submission to evil, a sacrifice of our best to Moloch. If strength indeed is to be respected, let us respect rather the strength of those who refuse that false "recognition of facts" which fails to recognize that facts are often bad. Let us admit that, in the world we know, there are many things that would be better otherwise, and that the ideals to which we do and must adhere are not realized in the realm of matter. Let us preserve our respect for truth, for beauty, for the ideal of perfection which life does not permit us to attain, though none of these things meet with the approval of the unconscious universe. If power is bad, as it seems to be, let us reject it from our hearts. In this lies man's true freedom: in determination to worship only the God created by our own love of the good, to respect only the heaven which inspires the insight of our best moments. In action, in desire, we must submit perpetually to the tyranny of outside forces; but in thought, in aspiration, we are free, free from our fellow men, free from the petty planet on which our bodies impotently crawl, free even, while we live, from the tyranny of death. Let us learn, then, that energy of faith which enables us to live constantly in the vision of the good; and let us descend, in action, into the world of fact, with that vision always before us.

When first the opposition of fact and ideal grows fully visible, a spirit of fiery revolt, of fierce hatred of the gods, seems necessary to the assertion of freedom. To defy with Promethean constancy a hostile universe, to keep its evil always in view, always actively hated, to refuse no pain that the malice of power can invent, appears to be the duty of all who will not bow before the inevitable. But indignation is still a bondage, for it compels our thoughts to be occupied with an evil world; and in the fierceness of desire from which rebellion springs there is a kind of self-assertion which it is necessary for the wise to overcome. Indignation is a submission of our thoughts but not of our desires; the Stoic freedom in which wisdom consists is found in the submission of our desires but not of our thoughts. From the submission of our desires springs the virtue of resignation; from the freedom of our thoughts springs the whole world of art and philosophy, and the vision of beauty by which, at last, we half reconquer the reluctant world. But the vision of beauty is possible only to unfettered contemplation, to thoughts not weighted by the load of eager wishes; and thus freedom comes only to those who no longer ask of life that it shall yield them any of those personal goods that are subject to the mutations of time.

Although the necessity of renunciation is evidence of the existence of evil, yet Christianity, in preaching it, has shown a wisdom exceeding that of the Promethean philosophy of rebellion. It must be admitted that, of the things we desire, some, though they prove impossible, are yet real goods; others, however, as ardently longed for, do not form part of a fully purified ideal. The belief that what must be renounced is bad, though sometimes false, is far less often false than untamed passion supposes; and the creed of religion, by providing a reason for proving that it is never false, has been the means of purifying our hopes by the discovery of many austere truths.

But there is in resignation a further good element: even real goods, when they are unattainable, ought not to be fretfully desired. To every man comes, sooner or later, the great renunciation. For the young, there is nothing unattainable; a good thing desired with the whole force of a passionate will, and yet impossible, is to them not credible. Yet, by death, by illness, by poverty, or by the voice of duty, we must learn, each one of us, that the world was not made for us, and that, however beautiful may be the things we crave, Fate may nevertheless forbid them. It is the part of courage, when misfortune comes, to bear without repining the ruin of our hopes, to turn away our thoughts from vain regrets. This degree of submission to power is not only just and right: it is the very gate of wisdom.

But passive renunciation is not the whole of wisdom; for not by renunciation alone can we build a temple for the worship of our own ideals. Haunting foreshadowings of the temple appear in the realm of imagination, in music, in architecture, in the untroubled kingdom of reason, and in the golden sunset magic of lyrics, where beauty shines and glows, remote from the touch of sorrow, remote from the fear of change, remote from the failures and disenchantments of the world of fact. In the contemplation of these things the vision of heaven will shape itself in our hearts, giving at once a touchstone to judge the world about us and an inspiration by which to fashion to our needs whatever is not incapable of serving as a stone in the sacred temple.

Except for those rare spirits that are born without sin, there is a cavern of darkness to be traversed before that temple can be entered. The gate of the cavern is despair, and its floor is paved with the gravestones of abandoned hopes. There self must die; there the eagerness, the greed of

untamed desire, must be slain, for only so can the soul be freed from the
empire of Fate. But out of the cavern, the Gate of Renunciation leads
again to the daylight of wisdom, by whose radiance a new insight, a new
joy, a new tenderness, shine forth to gladden the pilgrim's heart.

When, without the bitterness of impotent rebellion, we have learned
both to resign ourselves to the outward rule of Fate and to recognize that
the nonhuman world is unworthy of our worship, it becomes possible at
last so to transform and refashion the unconscious universe, so to trans-
mute it in the crucible of imagination, that a new image of shining gold
replaces the old idol of clay. In all the multiform facts of the world—in
the visual shapes of trees and mountains and clouds, in the events of the
life of man, even in the very omnipotence of death—the insight of
creative idealism can find the reflection of a beauty which its own
thoughts first made. In this way mind asserts its subtle mastery over the
thoughtless forces of nature. The more evil the material with which it
deals, the more thwarting to untrained desire, the greater is its achievement in inducing the reluctant rock to yield up its hidden treasures, the
prouder its victory in compelling the opposing forces to swell the pageant
of its triumph. Of all the arts, tragedy is the proudest, the most tri-
umphant; for it builds its shining citadel in the very center of the enemy's
country, on the very summit of his highest mountain; from its impregnable watchtowers, his camps and arsenals, his columns and forts, are all
revealed; within its walls the free life continues, while the legions of death
and pain and despair, and all the servile captains of tyrant Fate, afford the
burghers of that dauntless city new spectacles of beauty. Happy those
sacred ramparts, thrice happy the dwellers on that all-seeing eminence.
Honor to those brave warriors who, through countless ages of warfare,
have preserved for us the priceless heritage of liberty and have kept
undefiled by sacrilegious invaders the home of the unsubdued.

But the beauty of tragedy does but make visible a quality which, in
more or less obvious shapes, is present always and everywhere in life. In
the spectacle of death, in the endurance of intolerable pain, and in the
irrevocableness of a vanished past, there is a sacredness, an overpowering
awe, a feeling of the vastness, the depth, the inexhaustible mystery of
existence, in which, as by some strange marriage of pain, the sufferer is
bound to the world by bonds of sorrow. In these moments of insight, we
lose all eagerness of temporary desire, all struggling and striving for petty
ends, all care for the little trivial things that, to a superficial view, make up
the common life of day by day; we see, surrounding the narrow raft
illumined by the flickering light of human comradeship, the dark ocean
on whose rolling waves we toss for a brief hour; from the great night

without, a chill blast breaks in upon our refuge; all the loneliness of humanity amid hostile forces is concentrated upon the individual soul, which must struggle alone, with what of courage it can command, against the whole weight of a universe that cares nothing for its hopes and fears. Victory, in this struggle with the powers of darkness, is the true baptism into the glorious company of heroes, the true initiation into the over-mastering beauty of human existence. From that awful encounter of the soul with the outer world, renunciation, wisdom, and charity are born; and with their birth a new life begins. To take into the inmost shrine of the soul the irresistible forces whose puppets we seem to be—death and change, the irrevocableness of the past, and the powerlessness of man before the blind hurry of the universe from vanity to vanity—to feel these things and know them is to conquer them.

This is the reason why the past has such magical power. The beauty of its motionless and silent pictures is like the enchanted purity of late autumn, when the leaves, though one breath would make them fall, still glow against the sky in golden glory. The past does not change or strive; like Duncan, after life's fitful fever it sleeps well; what was eager and grasping, what was petty and transitory, has faded away; the things that were beautiful and eternal shine out of it like stars in the night. Its beauty, to a soul not worthy of it, is unendurable; but to a soul which has conquered Fate it is the key of religion.

The life of man, viewed outwardly, is but a small thing in comparison with the forces of nature. The slave is doomed to worship Time and Fate and Death, because they are greater than anything he finds in himself, and because all his thoughts are of things which they devour. But, great as they are, to think of them greatly, to feel their passionless splendor, is greater still. And such thought makes us free men; we no longer bow before the inevitable in Oriental subjection, but we absorb it and make it a part of ourselves. To abandon the struggle for private happiness, to expel all eagerness of temporary desire, to burn with passion for eternal things—this is emancipation, and this is the free man's worship. And this liberation is effected by contemplation of Fate; for Fate itself is subdued by the mind which leaves nothing to be purged by the purifying fire of time.

United with his fellow men by the strongest of all ties, the tie of a common doom, the free man finds that a new vision is with him always, shedding over every daily task the light of love. The life of man is a long march through the night, surrounded by invisible foes, tortured by weariness and pain, toward a goal that few can hope to reach, and where none may tarry long. One by one, as they march, our comrades vanish from our sight, seized by the silent orders of omnipotent death. Very brief is the time in which we can help them, in which their happiness or misery is decided. Be it ours to shed sunshine on their path, to lighten their sorrows by the balm of sympathy, to give them the pure joy of a never-tiring affection, to strengthen failing courage, to instill faith in hours of despair. Let us not weigh in grudging scales their merits and demerits, but let us think only of their need—of the sorrows, the difficulties, perhaps the blindnesses, that make the misery of their lives; let us remember that they are fellow sufferers in the same darkness, actors in the same tragedy with ourselves. And so, when their day is over, when their good and their evil have become eternal by the immortality of the past, be it ours to feel that, where they suffered, where they failed, no deed of ours was the cause; but wherever a spark of the divine fire kindled in their hearts, we were ready with encouragement, with sympathy, with brave words in which high courage glowed.

Brief and powerless is man's life; on him and all his race the slow, sure doom falls pitiless and dark. Blind to good and evil, reckless of destruction, omnipotent matter rolls on its relentless way; for man, condemned today to lose his dearest, tomorrow himself to pass through the gate of darkness, it remains only to cherish, ere yet the blow fall, the lofty thoughts that ennoble his little day; disdaining the coward terrors of the slave of Fate, to worship at the shrine that his own hands have built; undismayed by the empire of chance, to preserve a mind free from the wanton tyranny that rules his outward life; proudly defiant of the irresistible forces that tolerate, for a moment, his knowledge and his condemnation, to sustain alone, a weary but unyielding Atlas, the world that his own ideals have fashioned despite the trampling march of unconscious power.

*Antony Flew is Professor of Philosophy at the University of
Keele. R. M. Hare is White's Professor of Moral Philosophy
at the University of Oxford. Basil Mitchell is Nolloth
Professor of the Philosophy of the Christian Religion
at the University of Oxford.*

Antony Flew, R. M. Hare, and Basil Mitchell

THEOLOGY AND FALSIFICATION

ANTONY FLEW

Let us begin with a parable. It is a parable developed from a tale told by
John Wisdom in his haunting and revelatory article 'Gods'.[1] Once upon a
time two explorers came upon a clearing in the jungle. In the clearing
were growing many flowers and many weeds. One explorer says, 'Some
gardener must tend this plot'. The other disagrees, 'There is no gardener'.
So they pitch their tents and set a watch. No gardener is ever seen. 'But
perhaps he is an invisible gardener'. So they set up a barbed-wire fence.

Reprinted with permission of The Macmillan Company (New York) and the
Student Christian Movement Press Limited (London) from *New Essays in
Philosophical Theology* by Antony Flew and Alasdair MacIntyre, eds. First
published in 1955.

[1] *P.A.S.,* 1944–5, reprinted as Ch. X of *Logic and Language,* Vol. I (Blackwell, 1951), and in his *Philosophy and Psychoanalysis* (Blackwell, 1953).

They electrify it. They patrol with bloodhounds. (For they remember how H. G. Wells's *The Invisible Man* could be both smelt and touched though he could not be seen.) But no shrieks ever suggest that some intruder has received a shock. No movements of the wire ever betray an invisible climber. The bloodhounds never give cry. Yet still the Believer is not convinced. 'But there is a gardener, invisible, intangible, insensible to electric shocks, a gardener who has no scent and makes no sound, a gardener who comes secretly to look after the garden which he loves'. At last the Sceptic despairs, 'But what remains of your original assertion? Just how does what you call an invisible, intangible, eternally elusive gardener differ from an imaginary gardener or even from no gardener at all?'

In this parable we can see how what starts as an assertion, that something exists or that there is some analogy between certain complexes of phenomena, may be reduced step by step to an altogether different status, to an expression perhaps of a 'picture preference'.[2] The Sceptic says there is no gardener. The Believer says there is a gardener (but invisible, etc.). One man talks about sexual behaviour. Another man prefers to talk of Aphrodite (but knows that there is not really a superhuman person additional to, and somehow responsible for, all sexual phenomena).[3] The process of qualification may be checked at any point before the original assertion is completely withdrawn and something of that first assertion will remain (Tautology). Mr. Wells's invisible man could not, admittedly, be seen, but in all other respects he was a man like the rest of us. But though the process of qualification may be, and of course usually is, checked in time, it is not always judiciously so halted. Someone may dissipate his assertion completely without noticing that he has done so. A fine brash hypothesis may thus be killed by inches, the death by a thousand qualifications.

And in this, it seems to me, lies the peculiar danger, the endemic evil, of theological utterance. Take such utterances as 'God has a plan', 'God created the world', 'God loves us as a father loves his children'. They look at first sight very much like assertions, vast cosmological assertions. Of

---

2 Cf. J. Wisdom, 'Other Minds', *Mind,* 1940; reprinted in his *Other Minds* (Blackwell, 1952).

3 Cf. Lucretius, *De Rerum Natura,* II, 655–60,
    Hic siquis mare Neptunum Cereremque vocare
    Constituet fruges et Bacchi nomine abuti
    Mavolat quam laticis proprium proferre vocamen
    Concedamus ut hic terrarum dictitet orbem
    Esse deum matrem dum vera re tamen ipse
    Religione animum turpi contingere parcat.

course, this is no sure sign that they either are, or are intended to be, assertions. But let us confine ourselves to the cases where those who utter such sentences intend them to express assertions. (Merely remarking parenthetically that those who intend or interpret such utterances as crypto-commands, expressions of wishes, disguised ejaculations, concealed ethics, or as anything else but assertions, are unlikely to succeed in making them either properly orthodox or practically effective.)

Now to assert that such and such is the case is necessarily equivalent to denying that such and such is not the case.[4] Suppose then that we are in doubt as to what someone who gives vent to an utterance is asserting, or suppose that, more radically, we are sceptical as to whether he is really asserting anything at all, one way of trying to understand (or perhaps it will be to expose) his utterance is to attempt to find what he would regard as counting against, or as being incompatible with, its truth. For if the utterance is indeed an assertion, it will necessarily be equivalent to a denial of the negation of that assertion. And anything which would count against the assertion, or which would induce the speaker to withdraw it and to admit that it had been mistaken, must be part of (or the whole of) the meaning of the negation of that assertion. And to know the meaning of the negation of an assertion, is as near as makes no matter, to know the meaning of that assertion.[5] And if there is nothing which a putative assertion denies then there is nothing which it asserts either: and so it is not really an assertion. When the Sceptic in the parable asked the Believer, 'Just how does what you call an invisible, intangible, eternally elusive gardener differ from an imaginary gardener or even from no gardener at all?' he was suggesting that the Believer's earlier statement had been so eroded by qualification that it was no longer an assertion at all.

Now it often seems to people who are not religious as if there was no conceivable event or series of events the occurrence of which would be admitted by sophisticated religious people to be a sufficient reason for conceding 'There wasn't a God after all' or 'God does not really love us then'. Someone tells us that God loves us as a father loves his children. We are reassured. But then we see a child dying of inoperable cancer of the throat. His earthly father is driven frantic in his efforts to help, but his Heavenly Father reveals no obvious sign of concern. Some qualification is made—God's love is 'not a merely human love' or it is 'an inscrutable love', perhaps—and we realize that such sufferings are quite compatible with the truth of the assertion that 'God loves us as a father (but, of

---

[4] For those who prefer symbolism: $p \equiv \sim \sim p$.

[5] For by simply negating $\sim p$ we get $p: \sim \sim p \equiv p$.

course, . . .)'. We are reassured again. But then perhaps we ask: what is this assurance of God's (appropriately qualified) love worth, what is this apparent guarantee really a guarantee against? Just what would have to happen not merely (morally and wrongly) to tempt but also (logically and rightly) to entitle us to say 'God does not love us' or even 'God does not exist'? I therefore put to the succeeding symposiasts the simple central questions, 'What would have to occur or to have occurred to constitute for you a disproof of the love of, or of the existence of, God?'

R. M. HARE

I wish to make it clear that I shall not try to defend Christianity in particular, but religion in general—not because I do not believe in Christianity, but because you cannot understand what Christianity is, until you have understood what religion is.

I must begin by confessing that, on the ground marked out by Flew, he seems to me to be completely victorious. I therefore shift my ground by relating another parable. A certain lunatic is convinced that all dons want to murder him. His friends introduce him to all the mildest and most respectable dons that they can find, and after each of them has retired, they say, 'You see, he doesn't really want to murder you; he spoke to you in a most cordial manner; surely you are convinced now?' But the lunatic replies, 'Yes, but that was only his diabolical cunning; he's really plotting against me the whole time, like the rest of them; I know it I tell you'. However many kindly dons are produced, the reaction is still the same.

Now we say that such a person is deluded. But what is he deluded about? About the truth or falsity of an assertion? Let us apply Flew's test to him. There is no behaviour of dons that can be enacted which he will accept as counting against his theory; and therefore his theory, on this test, asserts nothing. But it does not follow that there is no difference between what he thinks about dons and what most of us think about them—otherwise we should not call him a lunatic and ourselves sane, and dons would have no reason to feel uneasy about his presence in Oxford.

Let us call that in which we differ from this lunatic, our respective *bliks*. He has an insane *blik* about dons; we have a sane one. It is important to realize that we have a sane one, not no *blik* at all; for there must be two sides to any argument—if he has a wrong *blik,* then those who are right about dons must have a right one. Flew has shown that a *blik* does not consist in an assertion or system of them; but nevertheless it is very important to have the right *blik*.

Let us try to imagine what it would be like to have different *bliks* about other things than dons. When I am driving my car, it sometimes occurs to me to wonder whether my movements of the steering-wheel will always continue to be followed by corresponding alterations in the direction of the car. I have never had a steering failure, though I have had skids, which must be similar. Moreover, I know enough about how the steering of my car is made, to know the sort of thing that would have to go wrong for the steering to fail—steel joints would have to part, or steel rods break, or something—but how do I know that this won't happen? The truth is, I don't know; I just have a *blik* about steel and its properties, so that normally I trust the steering of my car; but I find it not at all difficult to imagine what it would be like to lose this *blik* and acquire the opposite one. People would say I was silly about steel; but there would be no mistaking the reality of the difference between our respective *bliks*—for example, I should never go in a motor-car. Yet I should hesitate to say that the difference between us was the difference between contradictory assertions. No amount of safe arrivals or bench-tests will remove my *blik* and restore the normal one; for my *blik* is compatible with any finite number of such tests.

It was Hume who taught us that our whole commerce with the world depends upon our *blik* about the world; and that differences between *bliks* about the world cannot be settled by observation of what happens in the world. That was why, having performed the interesting experiment of doubting the ordinary man's *blik* about the world, and showing that no proof could be given to make us adopt one *blik* rather than another, he turned to backgammon to take his mind off the problem. It seems, indeed, to be impossible even to formulate as an assertion the normal *blik* about the world which makes me put my confidence in the future reliability of steel joints, in the continued ability of the road to support my car, and not gape beneath it revealing nothing below; in the general non-homicidal tendencies of dons; in my own continued well-being (in some sense of that word that I may not now fully understand) if I continue to do what is right according to my lights; in the general likelihood of people like Hitler coming to a bad end. But perhaps a formulation less inadequate than most is to be found in the Psalms: 'The earth is weak and all the inhabiters thereof: I bear up the pillars of it'.

The mistake of the position which Flew selects for attack is to regard this kind of talk as some sort of *explanation,* as scientists are accustomed to use the word. As such, it would obviously be ludicrous. We no longer believe in God as an Atlas—*nous n'avons pas besoin de cette hypothèse.* But it is nevertheless true to say that, as Hume saw, without a *blik* there can be no explanation; for it is by our *bliks* that we decide what is and what is not an explanation. Suppose we believed that everything that happened, happened by pure chance. This would not of course be an assertion; for it is compatible with anything happening or not happening, and so, incidentally, is its contradictory. But if we had this belief, we should not be able to explain or predict or plan anything. Thus, although we should not be *asserting* anything different from those of a more normal belief, there would be a great difference between us; and this is the sort of difference that there is between those who really believe in God and those who really disbelieve in him.

The word 'really' is important, and may excite suspicion. I put it in, because when people have had a good Christian upbringing, as have most of those who now profess not to believe in any sort of religion, it is very hard to discover what they really believe. The reason why they find it so easy to think that they are not religious, is that they have never got into the frame of mind of one who suffers from the doubts to which religion is the answer. Not for them the terrors of the primitive jungle. Having abandoned some of the more picturesque fringes of religion, they think that they have abandoned the whole thing—whereas in fact they still have got, and could not live without, a religion of a comfortably substantial, albeit highly sophisticated, kind, which differs from that of many 'religious people' in little more than this, that 'religious people' like to sing Psalms about theirs—a very natural and proper thing to do. But nevertheless there may be a big difference lying behind—the difference between two people who, though side by side, are walking in different directions. I do not know in what direction Flew is walking; perhaps he does not know either. But we have had some examples recently of various ways in which one can walk away from Christianity, and there are any number of possibilities. After all, man has not changed biologically since primitive times; it is his religion that has changed, and it can easily change again. And if you do not think that such changes make a difference, get acquainted with some Sikhs and some Mussulmans of the same Punjabi stock; you will find them quite different sorts of people.

There is an important difference between Flew's parable and my own which we have not yet noticed. The explorers do not *mind* about their garden; they discuss it with interest, but not with concern. But my lunatic, poor fellow, minds about dons; and I mind about the steering of my car; it often has people in it that I care for. It is because I mind very much about what does on in the garden in which I find myself, that I am unable to share the explorers' detachment.

BASIL MITCHELL

Flew's article is searching and perceptive, but there is, I think, something odd about his conduct of the theologian's case. The theologian surely would not deny that the fact of pain counts against the assertion that God loves men. This very incompatibility generates the most intractable of theological problems—the problem of evil. So the theologian *does* recognize the fact of pain as counting against Christian doctrine. But it is true that he will not allow it—or anything—to count decisively against it; for he is committed by his faith to trust in God. His attitude is not that of the detached observer, but of the believer.

Perhaps this can be brought out by yet another parable. In time of war in an occupied country, a member of the resistance meets one night a stranger who deeply impresses him. They spend that night together in conversation. The Stranger tells the partisan that he himself is on the side of the resistance—indeed that he is in command of it, and urges the partisan to have faith in him no matter what happens. The partisan is utterly convinced at that meeting of the Stranger's sincerity and constancy and undertakes to trust him.

They never meet in conditions of intimacy again. But sometimes the Stranger is seen helping members of the resistance, and the partisan is grateful and says to his friends, 'He is on our side'.

Sometimes he is seen in the uniform of the police handing over patriots to the occupying power. On these occasions his friends murmur against him: but the partisan still says, 'He is on our side'. He still believes that, in spite of appearances, the Stranger did not deceive him. Sometimes he asks the Stranger for help and receives it. He is then thankful. Sometimes he asks and does not receive it. Then he says, 'The Stranger knows best'. Sometimes his friends, in exasperation, say, 'Well, what *would* he have to do for you to admit that you were wrong and that he is not on our side?' But the partisan refuses to answer. He will not consent to put the Stranger to the test. And sometimes his friends complain, 'Well, if *that's* what you mean by his being on our side, the sooner he goes over to the other side the better'.

The partisan of the parable does not allow anything to count decisively against the proposition 'The Stranger is on our side'. This is because he has committed himself to trust the Stranger. But he of course recognizes that the Stranger's ambiguous behaviour *does* count against what he believes about him. It is precisely this situation which constitutes the trial of his faith.

When the partisan asks for help and doesn't get it, what can he do? He can (*a*) conclude that the stranger is not on our side or; (*b*) maintain that he is on our side, but that he has reasons for withholding help.

The first he will refuse to do. How long can he uphold the second position without its becoming just silly?

I don't think one can say in advance. It will depend on the nature of the impression created by the Stranger in the first place. It will depend, too, on the manner in which he takes the Stranger's behaviour. If he blandly dismisses it as of no consequence, as having no bearing upon his belief, it will be assumed that he is thoughtless or insane. And it quite obviously won't do for him to say easily, 'Oh, when used of the Stranger the phrase "is on our side" *means* ambiguous behaviour of this sort'. In that case he would be like the religious man who says blandly of a terrible disaster 'It is God's will'. No, he will only be regarded as sane and reasonable in his belief, if he experiences in himself the full force of the conflict.

It is here that my parable differs from Hare's. The partisan admits that many things may and do count against his belief: whereas Hare's lunatic who has a *blik* about dons doesn't admit that anything counts against his *blik*. Nothing *can* count against *bliks*. Also the partisan has a reason for having in the first instance committed himself, viz. the character of the Stranger; whereas the lunatic has no reason for his *blik* about dons—because, of course, you can't have reasons for *bliks*.

This means that I agree with Flew that theological utterances must be assertions. The partisan is making an assertion when he says, 'The Stranger is on our side'.

Do I want to say that the partisan's belief about the Stranger is, in any sense, an explanation? I think I do. It explains and makes sense of the Stranger's behaviour: it helps to explain also the resistance movement in the context of which he appears. In each case it differs from the interpretation which the others put upon the same facts.

'God loves men' resembles 'the Stranger is on our side' (and many other significant statements, e.g. historical ones) in not being conclusively falsifiable. They can both be treated in at least three different ways: (1) As provisional hypotheses to be discarded if experience tells against them; (2) As significant articles of faith; (3) As vacuous formulae (expressing, perhaps, a desire for reassurance) to which experience makes no difference and which make no difference to life.

The Christian, once he has committed himself, is precluded by his faith from taking up the first attitude: 'Thou shalt not tempt the Lord thy God'. He is in constant danger, as Flew has observed, of slipping into the third. But he need not; and, if he does, it is a failure in faith as well as in logic.

ANTONY FLEW

It has been a good discussion: and I am glad to have helped to provoke it. But now—at least in *University*—it must come to an end: and the Editors of *University* have asked me to make some concluding remarks. Since it is impossible to deal with all the issues raised or to comment separately upon each contribution, I will concentrate on Mitchell and Hare, as representative of two very different kinds of response to the challenge made in 'Theology and Falsification'.

The challenge, it will be remembered, ran like this. Some theological utterances seem to, and are intended to, provide explanations or express assertions. Now an assertion, to be an assertion at all, must claim that things stand thus and thus; *and not otherwise*. Similarly an explanation, to be an explanation at all, must explain why this particular thing occurs; *and not something else*. Those last clauses are crucial. And yet sophisticated religious people—or so it seemed to me—are apt to overlook this, and tend to refuse to allow, not merely that anything actually does occur, but that anything conceivably could occur, which would count against their theological assertions and explanations. But in so far as they do this their supposed explanations are actually bogus, and their seeming assertions are really vacuous.

Mitchell's response to this challenge is admirably direct, straightforward, and understanding. He agrees 'that theological utterances must be assertions'. He agrees that if they are to be assertions, there must be something that would count against their truth. He agrees, too, that believers are in constant danger of transforming their would-be assertions into 'vacuous formulae'. But he takes me to task for an oddity in my 'conduct of the theologian's case. The theologian surely would not deny that the fact of pain counts against the assertion that God loves men. This very incompatibility generates the most intractable of theological problems, the problem of evil'. I think he is right. I should have made a distinction between two very different ways of dealing with what looks like evidence against the love of God: the way I stressed was the expedient of qualifying the original assertion; the way the theologian usually takes, at first, is to admit that it looks bad but to insist that there is—there must be—some explanation which will show that, in spite of appearances, there really is a God who loves us. His difficulty, it seems to me, is that he has given God attributes which rule out all possible saving explanations. In Mitchell's parable of the Stranger it is easy for the believer to find plausible excuses for ambiguous behaviour: for the Stranger is a man. But suppose the Stranger is God. We cannot say that he would like to help but cannot: God is omnipotent. We cannot say that he would help if he only knew: God is omniscient. We cannot say that he is not responsible for the wickedness of others: God creates those others. Indeed an omnipotent, omniscient God must be an accessory before (and during) the fact to every human misdeed; as well as being responsible for every non-moral defect in the universe. So, though I entirely concede that Mitchell was absolutely right to insist against me that the theologian's first move is to look for an *explanation*, I still think that in the end, if relentlessly pursued, he will have to resort to the avoiding action of *qualification*. And there lies the danger of that death by a thousand qualifications, which would, I agree, constitute 'a failure in faith as well as in logic'.

Hare's approach is fresh and bold. He confesses that 'on the ground marked out by Flew, he seems to me to be completely victorious'. He therefore introduces the concept of *blik*. But while I think that there is room for some such concept in philosophy, and that philosophers should be grateful to Hare for his invention, I nevertheless want to insist that any attempt to analyse Christian religious utterances as expressions or affirmations of a *blik* rather than as (at least would-be) assertions about the cosmos is fundamentally misguided. *First,* because thus interpreted they would be entirely unorthodox. If Hare's religion really is a *blik,* involving no cosmological assertions about the nature and activities of a supposed personal creator, then surely he is not a Christian at all? *Second,* because thus interpreted, they could scarcely do the job they do. If they were not even intended as assertions then many religious activities would become fraudulent, or merely silly. If 'You ought *because* it is God's will' asserts no more than 'You ought', then the person who prefers the former phraseology is not really giving a reason, but a fraudulent substitute for one, a dialectical dud cheque. If 'My soul must be immortal *because* God loves his children, etc.' asserts no more than 'My soul must be immortal', then the man who reassures himself with theological arguments for immortality is being as silly as the man who tries to clear his overdraft by writing his bank a cheque on the same account. (Of course neither of these utterances would be distinctively Christian: but this discussion never pretended to be so confined.) Religious utterances may indeed express false or even bogus assertions: but I simply do not believe that they are not both intended and interpreted to be or at any rate to presuppose assertions, at least in the context of religious practice; whatever shifts may be demanded, in another context, by the exigencies of theological apologetic.

One final suggestion. The philosophers of religion might well draw upon George Orwell's last appalling nightmare *1984* for the concept of *doublethink*. '*Doublethink* means the power of holding two contradictory beliefs simultaneously, and accepting both of them. The party intellectual knows that he is playing tricks with reality, but by the exercise of *doublethink* he also satisfies himself that reality is not violated' (*1984,* p. 220). Perhaps religious intellectuals too are sometimes driven to doublethink in order to retain their faith in a loving God in face of the reality of a heartless and indifferent world. But of this more another time, perhaps.

*Jack J. Cohen is Director of the Hillel Foundation
at the Hebrew University in Jerusalem.*

Jack J. Cohen

THE CASE FOR
RELIGIOUS NATURALISM

1

"Naturalism" and "supernaturalism" are key words in any discussion of religion. They are also among the most difficult concepts to free of semantic confusion. They are overloaded with prejudices. To illustrate, when the Catholic speaks of "natural law," he posits along with it a conception of nature in which the suspension of that law by a supernatural deity is possible. For him, since naturalism cannot possibly mean a renunciation of miracle, there is no clear demarcation between it and supernaturalism. Yet a distinction between naturalism and supernaturalism is essential if rational communication is to be a possibility. Naturalism cannot be made to mean supernaturalism and vice versa. Let us examine some of the ramifications of these terms.

Reprinted from *The Case for Religious Naturalism* (New York: The Reconstructionist Press, 1958), by permission of the Jewish Reconstructionist Foundation, Inc.

2

By naturalism I mean the disposition to believe that any phenomenon can be explained by appeal to general laws confirmable either by observation or by inference from observation. The term disposition is used advisedly, since it is perfectly clear that even the most ardent supporter of the scientific method cannot in any "ultimate" sense disprove "miracles." But it is inherent in the naturalist disposition to accept any discontinuities in the affairs of the physical universe or of man as part of the "natural" scheme of things. This is not to say that everything that happens in the universe is necessarily explainable. Only extreme arrogence would lead men to believe they possessed the potentiality of omniscience. All the naturalist insists upon is that man has only one instrument of knowledge, his reason, and that any knowledge or "vision" purportedly received by man from sources beyond "nature" are products of that same rational faculty operating either in inspired fashion or mistakenly, as the case may be.

The main problem in any definition or description of naturalism is the fog surrounding "nature" itself. This is a concept which appears, in all likelihood, as frequently as any other in the literature of philosophy, science, and religion. It is, therefore, important to realize the great variety of meanings and shades of meanings conferred upon it by the leading thinkers of all ages. Nature is sometimes a designation for the physical universe exclusive of man. It is sometimes held to include man as well. Frequently nature is set off in contrast to man's spiritual qualities, much as the body is contrasted to the spirit. Nature is conceived of as created existence, in contrast to the absolute existence of God. It is the totality of all existence, and it is the orderly process which characterizes that part of reality which man can experience. It is the totality of physical reality, and it is the principle of its operation. Nature is substance, and it is function. And so it goes. Some of these usages contradict one another; some are complementary.

In these pages, nature will be conceived of as the totality of reality—its substance, functioning, and principles of operation—including man and his spiritual qualities. The naturalist thus tends to explore as deeply as possible the pattern of things as they lend themselves to human understanding and to deny the existence of any realm of human knowledge beyond that apprehensible through men's faculties of mind. He would deny that there is a realm of meaning "beyond" the process of life manifest to human investigation.

But to many thinkers human understanding is itself a problem. Are there not methods of arriving at truth, such as intuition and revelation, which are as valid as the scientific method of hypothetical reasoning and experimental verification? Assuming that such methods are different in character from that of science, what are their implications for the meaning of nature? Do they imply a spatial beyondness, such as that pictured in traditional accounts of heaven and hell? In this case would not some form of revelation be essential if man were ever to receive any inkling of that realm? Or is the beyondness an ontological dimension, a principle of explanation, without which nature itself is hardly understandable? If so, revelation might still be considered essential for man's grasp of nature to be more than a tenuous one.

It is a common assumption that there is a sharp cleavage between the methods of science and religion, that there are different roads to truth, and that there are, indeed, different kinds of truth, each apprehended by its own distinctive method. I take the view that all hypothetical thinking is a projection beyond the actually experienced, that all so-called revelations and intuitions are extensions of such imaginative constructions, and that the ultimate test of their validity must lie in experience. The key to the solution of the foregoing questions I find in the concept of transcendence. For this concept opens the door to harmonizing the so-termed scientific and nonscientific methods of arriving at truth.

The problem of thinking deserves the kind of extensive consideration which cannot be given to it here. I shall limit my discussion of thinking primarily to its connection with the idea of transcendence which is basic in religious terminology.

Transcendence is a necessary category of all human thinking; but it in no way requires going beyond nature. Consider, for a moment, scientific method. The scientist, faced with the problem of relating facts of observation in some pattern of cause and effect, or of analyzing the factors entering into a given phenomenon, must necessarily transcend a given situation in order to arrive at a new and more inclusive framework of explanation. Transcendence in this sense actually adds nothing to nature which is not inherently and essentially involved in a particular concatenation of events. In the realm of values, however, it is frequently asserted that transcendence involves an entirely new category of existence, one which is "beyond" nature and which can only be grasped by the human mind through intuition or revelation.

There is really only one method of arriving at knowledge about the universe. What intuitionists and revelationists do is to omit the final step in the process of thought, which is validation. For example, what happens when we try to understand the status of freedom? To say that man is free, in the sense that he *ought* to be free, is to transcend the present state of man and to project for him a new mode of existence. This kind of transcendence seems, on the surface, to add a new dimension to nature, a dimension that has been supplied only by man and that if absent would in no way affect man's understanding of nature. But to conclude that human values are not part of nature is superficial, for it ignores completely man's proneness to transcend his immediate experience. This human characteristic is as much an aspect of nature as an observed fact or the scientific context into which that fact is placed. Furthermore, the fact that man feels he ought to be free is not the final step in the process of value judgment, no matter how dogmatically certain religious theorists insist that we must accept this ideal as moral truth. There are a number of other serious questions that require investigation. What, really, do we mean by human freedom? How does this ideal relate to the other values we hold out for human life? What are the conditions of human intercourse essential to the achievement of freedom? Are not the answers to these questions prerequisites for the acceptance of freedom as an "ought"? And when we have undergone such a process of investigation, have we not at the same time validated our assumption that this "freedom" is part of the very existential framework within which the nature of man becomes more clearly apprehended?

All thinking, in other words, requires acts of imaginative vision about an infinite present and of equally imaginative projection into an always expanding future. The realm of the transcendent is thus the ever-present unknown, the source at one and the same time of intellectual and spiritual challenge and of our future knowledge. But it is all part of nature, for nature, too, has a future, as well as a past and a present.

Some naturalists, on the basis of scientific experience, include in the naturalist disposition a tendency to assume that the universe is an orderly process. But whether or not they make this admittedly unverifiable assumption, all naturalists believe that there is no conscious force outside the universe acting upon it. On the other hand, the assumption that the universe is orderly permits many generalizations about reality that take us far beyond the realm of mere observation. Naturalism is not a commitment to holding as real only those phenomena which are capable of mechanistic determination. Indeed, mechanism is no longer considered to be an adequate explanation of the behavior of even the physical universe. There is too much mystery, creativity, and uncertainty in life for us to countenance mechanism as a satisfactory explanation of reality. But disbelief in mechanism does not warrant belief in arbitrariness. It warrants only reserving judgment about the significance of a particular experience. Man has unraveled the answer to many mysteries, and there is no reason to assume that he will not unravel others. The naturalist believes that solutions can be found to the unsolved mysteries of life, because the still mysterious phenomena are subject to the same natural processes as those already understood.

It should be realized that naturalists do not deny their inability to answer questions like "Was the world created?" and "How was life initiated?" But although they find such questions, at least for the present, unanswerable, they do not posit a cause outside nature; to do this, they assert, would simply add to the mystery.

3

The difficulty with language is that we have to define words with words. I have been using "supernaturalism" in my discussion in connection with naturalism, and I suppose the reader has been wondering if I ever intended to define it. The time has come to do so.

By supernaturalism I mean the belief that there is a power (or powers) operating in the universe not subject to the same restraints as are imposed on natural phenomena. Whatever order does exist is present by virtue of an arbitrary, omnipotent will above nature and is subject to interference at any time. The world, according to this view, exists by the grace of a living God.[1]

Both the assumption of a self-ordered universe, which is the view taken here, and of a God transcending (in the sense of "beyond") nature and capable of overturning it are acts of faith by which man tries to read meaning into his life. From the perspective of human values, there is perhaps as much evidence that the world is chaotic as that it is orderly.

---

[1] Making allowances for the mood of their thinking, we can classify both Reinhold Niebuhr and Paul Tillich in the naturalist camp as described here. However, it seems to me that Niebuhr, in his profound work *The Nature and Destiny of Man,* introduces considerable confusion by setting up an arbitrary and restrictive definition of nature. By denying to nature elements of freedom and spirituality, he is able to refer to the self-transcending aspects of nature, such as freedom and creativity, as "supernatural." Tillich similarly denies to nature the quality of self-transcendence. Supernaturalism for him then becomes the ontological tool by means of which alone man can gain true perspective on himself and on the process of nature. For both these thinkers super-nature is the transcendent aspects of reality, not a realm of space and time beyond nature.

Earthquakes, tornadoes, floods are as real as night and day, summer and winter. Why, then, does not the naturalist posit either chaos or arbitrary rule from above? The answer, which is necessarily psychological rather than ontological, lies in the fact that the assumption of order is at least capable of validation. Every successful experiment points in this direction, and many of the admitted disorders in nature have gradually been explained in terms of natural causes. No such canons of validation have ever been worked out for the existence of an omnipotent God transcending nature.

In the spiritual realm, the struggle between naturalism and supernaturalism is centered in the problem of the source of values. Whence do we derive our ideals of justice, truth, equality? And once derived, how is their fulfillment to be guaranteed? The naturalist would assert, as we have seen, that it is the very nature of man, by virtue of his powers of thinking and willing, to establish values for himself. He would contend further that some values are more worthy than others, in the sense that the attainment of specific objectives is dependent on the integration of certain values rather than others into the life of the individual and society. For example, given the objective of peace, equality of opportunity is more likely than class stratification to lead a society toward this goal. The naturalist would concede also that there are certain values or spiritual objectives which are absolute in a given context. That is to say, while peace may not always be desirable—for instance, where freedom is at stake—this does not gainsay the fact that peace as an objective of mankind is a goal toward which all men should strive. Naturalism would stop at this point in the argument, claiming that the further question "Why is peace more desirable (or more 'good') as a value than war?" can be answered only by locating peace in the scheme of all values, the keystone of which is the affirmation of life itself.

Supernaturalism cannot be satisfied with this self-contained system of values. It seeks to break through the circle and locate the source of values and the guarantee of their fulfillment in a cause beyond man. Therefore God beyond nature is invoked once again, as in the case of the physical world. Otherwise by virtue of what standard, asks the supernaturalist, do democrats struggle for their system against that of the totalitarians? Unless democratic ethics are grounded in the will of God—and God is here interpreted as being a Power who communicates his values to man, who could never be certain of their truth without such revelation—they can make no legitimate claim on the conscience of man. For without such cosmic authority, it is held, one man's claim would be as valid as another's.

Naturalism and supernaturalism agree on the existence of moral order, but they differ in their understanding of that order. Naturalism holds this order, in the form that it is available to human awareness, to be a construct of the human mind, subject to all its weaknesses. The moral law, in other words, is for the naturalist a term applied to *man's* understanding of what is ethically valid. Supernaturalism, equally cognizant of human frailty, asserts the need for an absolute system of morality whose validity is dependent on its being equated with the will of God. Naturalism is satisfied to struggle for human betterment without any guarantee concerning the ultimate triumph of goodness (except the guarantee of potentiality); supernaturalism insists on the existence of God as man's assurance that evil will be banished from the earth (or in the afterlife). In the search for such certainty, supernaturalism has often involved itself in two basic paradoxes: the first, that if God's absolute goodness and omnipotence will necessarily produce an ethical world, then man's conduct is actually of little moment in its achievement; the second, that if God is absolutely good and omnipotent, then evil should be impossible.

Naturalism is not a new approach to reality. But its early formulations lacked the backing of scientific knowledge, which has now been marshaled to support it. Thus, although the Greeks developed a conception of nature and took the first real steps toward the scientific method, their science, being embryonic, scarcely touched the popular religion of the time. Rather was it the dialectician who challenged the traditional beliefs, in much the same way that thinkers and religious geniuses (or virtuosos, to use a term of Max Weber's) had effected changes in other religions in both Eastern and Western Asia. It was not until the cumulative effect of centuries of scientific discovery had swept away the last hope of convincingly explaining the universe by positing a conscious deity that the era of naturalism really arrived.

When religion arose in society, its intellectual foundation was neither supernatural nor natural. Primitive man had only a vague conception of nature as a "self-operative" phenomenon; therefore, he could have no idea of the supernatural, in the refined sense in which we use the term today. Cassirer, in summarizing Renan's views, declares:

> What we today call a miracle, what appears as such to the modern man, can be expressed only through a definite contrast and difference. A miracle is something that falls outside the field of "natural" occurrences which is governed by fixed and universal laws, but for a consciousness that has not yet achieved such a view of nature and its complete subjection to causal order, this contrast has no meaning; the idea of a miracle escapes it. Hence our historical perspective

is false when we transfer to primeval times an antithesis that is valid and decisive for us."[2]

For the ancients, literally everything that happened was caused by the activity of a god or gods. Whether for good or for evil, the final authority was not man's. Man could have a hand in his fate by keeping on good terms with his deity, but it was the deity who managed the world.

Ancient Jewish thinkers made the concept of God's rule more subtle by attributing to man freedom of the will. If everything was in the hands of God, then human behavior could have no independent status. Hence God created man with a peculiar nature of his own, a nature which included freedom. Man's freedom could have meaning only if the world in which he functioned was so orderly as to make sense of his power to choose. Miracles, in turn, were a deliberate and occasional intervention of God in the orderly affairs of His universe in pursuit of some divine purpose. This refinement of the more primitive concept, however, did not eliminate the idea that nature itself was a miracle. This view, as examplified in the prayer "We will give thanks to Thee—for Thy miracles [the ordinary acts of nature] which are daily with us . . ." permeated the tradition.

The following passage from the writings of Joseph Albo, fifteenth-century Jewish philosopher, should counteract any tendency to credit premodern Judaism with a consistent view of an independent natural law: "Now the existence of rain cannot be ascribed to nature, because it is not a thing which occurs every year at the same time in the same way, like the other natural phenomena. Rain comes at different itmes, in different ways, in a wonderful manner, not uniformly and naturally."[3] The tradition, like many modern religionists who delight in the limitations of science, ascribed the slightest discontinuity in nature to the operation of a supernatural force. And since there are always areas of discontinuity, the belief in the supernatural continues to flourish.

During the many centuries of their progressive discovery of the laws of nature, scientists were unaware of the revolution they were helping to foster. Many of them were as devout as their religious leaders, and some of them were churchmen. Today, however, we realize fully what they wrought. They destroyed the entire intellectual foundation of the then existing Western civilization. That civilization rested on the assumption that since all of life depended on the actions of an omnipotent power, it

---

[2] Ernst Cassirer, *The Problem of Knowledge* (New Haven: Yale University Press, 1950), p. 305.

[3] Joseph Albo, *Sefer Ha-'Ikharim* (Philadelphia: Jewish Publication Society, 1946), vol. 4, p. 65.

was necessary for men to abide by the code of behavior which the deity had supposedly revealed to them. It was not only revealed religion that was undermined; every institution which rested on the assumption that the status quo was God-inspired was weakened. Monarchical governments, for example, even after the Reformation and the break-up of the temporal power of the Roman Church, found justification in the assumption that class distinctions were divinely approved.

The foregoing analysis should make it clear why authoritarian religionists insist on the supernaturalist view; it should also help to explain the usefulness of supernaturalism to a diametrically opposed group, the authoritarian antireligionists. The dogmatic religionist knows that to admit the legitimacy in religion of replacing the supernaturalist position by a naturalist one would be to weaken the authority of orthodoxy. The dogmatic antireligionist, of the Marxist type in particular, stands to gain equally from the pinning of the supernaturalist label on all religion. It helps support his own critique of religion as intellectually reactionary and unworthy of serious consideration as an option for intelligent men. For these two types of minds religion, by definition, includes the assumption that there is a conscious Power beyond nature which brought the universe into being and which ultimately determines its fate. No naturalistic belief can be religion in the eyes of the Marxist, any more than it can in the eyes of the fundamentalist.

The fact is that the identity of religion and supernaturalism that some thinkers try to establish is a historical judgment arising from the fact that religion, during a considerable portion of human history, could hardly have been grounded in any other view. Supernaturalism was for centuries convincing to mankind as a whole; the naturalism of the Greeks had its influence and its small following among the intellectuals, but it never came anywhere near achieving the popularity of supernaturalism. Today, however, given the context of scientific knowledge, it can be urgently argued that supernaturalism is a millstone around the neck of religion: with the spread of education supernaturalism becomes less and less appealing even to nonintellectuals.

Moreover, the identity of religion and supernaturalism can stand only when religion is treated without concern for its bearing on human needs. Taken as an institution which has an independent existence, religion could, of course, be defined as the embodiment of supernaturalism. This would be a structural definition. When viewed functionally, however, as an institution capable of fulfilling certain needs of man, religion cannot so easily be limited; it cannot be restricted in definition to one particular method of satisfying those needs. We see, then, that a structural definition of religion associates religion with some specific *Weltanschauung;* it follows that when the *Weltanschauung* changes, the religion is undermined. Indeed tradition religionists, who hold to the structural definition, to this day insist that the future of religion depends entirely on its ability to continue to inspire belief in revelation. Those who define religion functionally, on the other hand, take account of the fact that there are often many answers to a single problem and realize that there are thus many pathways in man's eternal quest for fulfillment.

The distinction between these two concepts of religion, the structural and the functional, also involves a presumption about the nature of religious development. Those who hold to the structural definition conceive of religion statically. The church is an end in itself; all other institutions must adapt themselves to its spiritual hegemony. The church never changes; it is eternal. Those who abandon it are sinners, deliberate or unwitting. The church never errs, since it operates on a mandate from God. Proponents of the structural definition of religion also posit certain basic doctrines that are unchangeable and eternal. Adaptation to new conditions is never necessary because the doctrines are assumed to have anticipated their own evolution and to have embodied a method of interpretation at the time of their revelation.

Those who interpret religion functionally, quite otherwise, discern unending change in the conditions of life, change that necessitates constant revision of the doctrines and institutions of religion. They must, then, find some identifying factor common to religion in all its varying forms. If no common factor could be found, then the term religion could justifiably be used only in the narrowest sense. Indeed, we should have to rewrite almost every book containing the word. For it is apparent that the particular sense in which "religion" is understood varies from author to author. This conclusion should show the absurdity of trying to pin "religion" down to a single theology or a single institutional form. An adequate definition, which would enable normal discourse about religion to continue without the necessity of the invention of a new term for each subtle nuance, must therefore provide a suitable generalization. It will perhaps shed light on the problem to use the concept of government as an analogy.

If we examine governments throughout the ages, we find a wide variety of forms, from the patriarchy of the early Hebrews to the republicanism of the United States. The functions of government as well have varied, beginning, among the primitives, with the rudimentary purposes of protection and the securing of food. These minimal needs obviously cannot account for the pyramiding of structure characteristic of subsequent governments. Initially established to care for the basic physical wants, governments were later called upon to answer additional needs, physical, intellectual, and spiritual, resulting from the growth of civilization—the need for internal law and order, for the development of agriculture and industry, for the maintenance (or eradication) of class distinctions, for education and culture, etc. To identify government with the satisfaction of just one of these needs would be an unwarranted circumscription of its function. If we were to apply to government the logic of those who define religion structurally and identify it with a particular response to a particular human need, we should have to eliminate the term government from our vocabulary as the designation for many of our present-day ruling authorities. In the United States the government was once conceived of as an instrument for ensuring the untrammeled exercise of free private enterprise. For some time now the government has been imposing limits on such freedom, yet no one in his right mind would declare that the term government, as applied to the ruling power of our country, has outlived its function and ought to be superseded by a new designation.

If I seem to labor this point, it is because so many liberal intellectuals try to read "religion" out of existence by denying that it can be legitimately employed as a designation for any other attitude than the supernaturalism of a bygone age.

Doubtless there are religions which originated, at least partially, as responses to fear, and doubtless there are a few religions in which fear still plays a significant role. But some religions today exhibit only normal concern with that emotion. Some orthodox churches seek power in order to force their conceptions of truth and salvation on the world, but there are others, for instance the Quakers, which have traditions of serving mankind. Some religions abound in ritual; others, like Unitarianism and Quakerism, are relatively devoid of it. I need not multiply examples. From the standpoint of specific function, there is as much (or as little) reason to provide a new term for every kind of religion as there is for every kind of government.

4

I have tried by semantic analysis to rescue religion from the vested interests, both intellectual and institutional, which would like to appropriate it for their own purposes. Semantics alone, however, cannot solve the problem. Whatever power religion retains as an institution, as an intellectual or emotional factor in modern society, is a mere vestige of past glory. Like the monarch of England, it reigns but does not rule. It is respectable but not respected. Its restoration to its former position of importance in the thinking and behavior of intelligent men and women depends on whether religious spokesmen will have the courage to abandon outmoded positions and strike out in new directions.

SUGGESTIONS FOR FURTHER READING

ALSTON, WILLIAM P., ed., *Religious Belief and Philosophical Thought,* New York: Harcourt Brace Jovanovich, Inc., 1963. Historical and contemporary readings in philosophy of religion.

CAHN, STEVEN M., ed., *Philosophy of Religion,* New York: Harper & Row, 1970. Paperback. A volume of essays that charts the course of developments in philosophy of religion during the past two decades.

HICK, JOHN, *Philosophy of Religion,* Englewood Cliffs, N.J.: Prentice-Hall, Inc., 1963. Paperback. An excellent introduction to important issues in philosophy of religion.

PART IV

ETHICS

Bertrand Russell

SCIENCE AND ETHICS

Different philosophers have formed different conceptions of the Good. Some hold that it consists in the knowledge and love of God; others in universal love; others in the enjoyment of beauty; and yet others in pleasure. The Good once defined, the rest of ethics follows: we ought to act in the way we believe most likely to create as much good as possible, and as little as possible of its correlative evil. The framing of moral rules, so long as the ultimate Good is supposed known, is matter for science. For example: should capital punishment be inflicted for theft, or only for murder, or not at all? Jeremy Bentham, who considered pleasure to be the Good, devoted himself to working out what criminal code would most promote pleasure, and concluded that it ought to be much less severe than that prevailing in his day. All this, except the proposition that pleasure is the Good, comes within the sphere of science.

Reprinted from Bertrand Russell, *Religion and Science* (1935) by permission of the Clarendon Press, Oxford.

But when we try to be definite as to what we mean when we say that this or that is "the Good," we fine ourselves involved in very great difficulties. Bentham's creed that pleasure is the Good roused furious opposition, and was said to be a pig's philosophy. Neither he nor his opponents could advance any argument. In a scientific question, evidence can be adduced on both sides, and in the end one side is seen to have the better case—or, if this does not happen, the question is left undecided. But in a question as to whether this or that is the ultimate Good, there is no evidence either way; each disputant can only appeal to his own emotions, and employ such rhetorical devices as shall rouse similar emotions in others.

Take, for example, a question which has come to be important in practical politics. Bentham held that one man's pleasure has the same ethical importance as another man's, provided the quantities are equal; and on this ground he was led to advocate democracy. Nietzsche, on the contrary, held that only the great man can be regarded as important on his own account, and that the bulk of mankind are only means to his well-being. He viewed ordinary men as many people view animals: he thought it justifiable to make use of them, not for their own good, but for that of the superman, and this view has since been adopted to justify the abandonment of democracy. We have here a sharp disagreement of great practical importance, but we have absolutely no means, of a scientific or intellectual kind, by which to persuade either party that the other is in the right. There are, it is true, ways of altering men's opinions on such subjects, but they are all emotional, not intellectual.

Questions as to "values"—that is to say, as to what is good or bad on its own account, independently of its effects—lie outside the domain of science, as the defenders of religion emphatically assert. I think that in this they are right, but I draw the further conclusion, which they do not draw, that questions as to "values" lie wholly outside the domain of knowledge. That is to say, when we assert that this or that has "value," we are giving expression to our own emotions, not to a fact which would still be true if our personal feelings were different. To make this clear, we must try to analyse the conception of the Good.

It is obvious, to begin with, that the whole idea of good and bad has some connection with *desire*. *Prima facie*, anything that we all desire is "good," and anything that we all dread is "bad." If we all agreed in our desires, the matter could be left there, but unfortunately our desires conflict. If I say "what I want is good," my neighbour will say "No, what I want." Ethics is an attempt—though not, I think, a successful one—to escape from this subjectivity. I shall naturally try to show, in my dispute with my neighbour, that my desires have some quality which makes them more worthy of respect than his. If I want to preserve a right of way, I shall appeal to the landless inhabitants of the district; but he, on his side, will appeal to the landowners. I shall say: "What use is the beauty of the countryside if no one sees it?" He will retort: "What beauty will be left if trippers are allowed to spread devastation?" Each tries to enlist allies by showing that his own desires harmonize with those of other people. When this is obviously impossible, as in the case of a burglar, the man is condemned by public opinion, and his ethical status is that of a sinner.

Ethics is thus closely related to politics: it is an attempt to bring the collective desires of a group to bear upon individuals; or, conversely, it is an attempt by an individual to cause his desires to become those of his group. This latter is, of course, only possible if his desires are not too obviously opposed to the general interest: the burglar will hardly attempt to persuade people that he is doing them good, though plutocrats make similar attempts, and often succeed. When our desires are for things which all can enjoy in common, it seems not unreasonable to hope that others may concur; thus the philosopher who values Truth, Goodness and Beauty seems, to himself, to be not merely expressing his own desires, but pointing the way to the welfare of all mankind. Unlike the burglar, he is able to believe that his desires are for something that has value in an impersonal sense.

Ethics is an attempt to give universal, and not merely personal, importance to certain of our desires. I say "certain" of our desires, because in regard to some of them this is obviously impossible, as we saw in the case of the burglar. The man who makes money on the Stock Exchange by means of some secret knowledge does not wish others to be equally well informed: Truth (in so far as he values it) is for him a private possession, not the general human good that it is for the philosopher. The philosopher may, it is true, sink to the level of the stock-jobber, as when he claims priority for a discovery. But this is a lapse: in his purely philosophic capacity, he wants only to enjoy the contemplation of Truth, in doing which he in no way interferes with others who wish to do likewise. . . .

. . . Every attempt to persuade people that something is good (or bad) in itself, and not merely in its effects, depends upon the art of rousing feelings, not upon an appeal to evidence. In every case the preacher's skill consists in creating in others emotions similar to his own—or dissimilar, if he is a hypocrite. I am not saying this as a criticism of the preacher, but as an analysis of the essential character of his activity.

When a man says "this is good in itself," he *seems* to be making a statement, just as much as if he said "this is square" or "this is sweet." I believe this to be a mistake. I think that what the man really means is: "I wish everybody to desire this," or rather "Would that everybody desired this." If what he says is interpreted as a statement, it is merely an affirmation of his own personal wish; if, on the other hand, it is interpreted in a general way, it states nothing, but merely desires something. The wish, as an occurrence, is personal, but what it desires is universal. It is, I think, this curious interlocking of the particular and the universal which has caused so much confusion in ethics.

The matter may perhaps become clearer by contrasting an ethical sentence with one which makes a statement. If I say "all Chinese are Buddhists," I can be refuted by the production of a Chinese Christian or Mohammedan. If I say "I believe that all Chinese are Buddhists," I cannot be refuted by any evidence from China, but only by evidence that I do not believe what I say; for what I am asserting is only something about my own state of mind. If, now, a philosopher says "Beauty is good," I may interpret him as meaning either "Would that everybody loved the beautiful" (which corresponds to "all Chinese are Buddhists") or "I wish that everybody loved the beautiful" (which corresponds to "I believe that all Chinese are Buddhists"). The first of these makes no assertion, but expresses a wish; since it affirms nothing, it is logically impossible that there should be evidence for or against it, or for it to possess either truth or falsehood. The second sentence, instead of being merely optative, does make a statement, but it is one about the philosopher's state of mind, and it could only be refuted by evidence that he does not have the wish that he says he has. This second sentence does not belong to ethics, but to psychology or biography. The first sentence, which does belong to ethics, expresses a desire for something, but asserts nothing.

Ethics, if the above analysis is correct, contains no statements, whether true or false, but consists of desires of a certain general kind, namely such as are concerned with the desires of mankind in general—and of gods, angels, and devils, if they exist. Science can discuss the causes of desires, and the means for realizing them, but it cannot contain any genuinely ethical sentences, because it is concerned with what is true or false.

The theory which I have been advocating is a form of the doctrine which is called the "subjectivity" of values. This doctrine consists in maintaining that, if two men differ about values, there is not a disagreement as to any kind of truth, but a difference of taste. If one man says "oysters are good" and another says "*I* think they are bad," we recognize that there is nothing to argue about. The theory in question holds that all differences as to values are of this sort, although we do not naturally think them so when we are dealing with matters that seem to us more exalted than oysters. The chief ground for adopting this view is the complete impossibility of finding any arguments to prove that this or that has intrinsic value. If we all agreed, we might hold that we know values by intuition. We cannot *prove,* to a colour-blind man, that grass is green and not red. But there are various ways of proving to him that he lacks a power of discrimination which most men possess, whereas in the case of values there are no such ways, and disagreements are much more frequent than in the case of colours. Since no way can be even imagined for deciding a difference as to values, the conclusion is forced upon us that the difference is one of tastes, not one as to any objective truth.

The consequences of this doctrine are considerable. In the first place, there can be no such thing as "sin" in any absolute sense; what one man calls "sin" another may call "virtue," and though they may dislike each other on account of this difference, neither can convict the other of intellectual error. Punishment cannot be justified on the ground that the criminal is "wicked," but only on the ground that he has behaved in a way which others wish to discourage. Hell, as a place of punishment for sinners, becomes quite irrational.

In the second place, it is impossible to uphold the way of speaking about values which is common among those who believe in Cosmic Purpose. Their argument is that certain things which have been evolved are "good," and therefore the world must have had a purpose which was ethically admirable. In the language of subjective values, this argument becomes: "Some things in the world are to our liking, and therefore they must have been created by a Being with our tastes, Whom, therefore, we also like, and Who, consequently, is good." Now it seems fairly evident that, if creatures having likes and dislikes were to exist at all, they were pretty sure to like *some* things in their environment, since otherwise they would find life intolerable. Our values have been evolved along with the rest of our constitution, and nothing as to any original purpose can be inferred from the fact that they are what they are.

Those who believe in "objective" values often contend that the view which I have been advocating has immoral consequences. This seems to me to be due to faulty reasoning. There are, as has already been said, certain ethical consequences of the doctrine of subjective values, of which the most important is the rejection of vindictive punishment and the notion of "sin." But the more general consequences which are feared, such as the decay of all sense of moral obligation, are not to be logically deduced. Moral obligation, if it is to influence conduct, must consist not merely of a belief, but of a desire. The desire, I may be told, is the desire to be "good" in a sense which I no longer allow. But when we analyse the desire to be "good" it generally resolves itself into a desire to be approved, or, alternatively, to act so as to bring about certain general consequences which we desire. We have wishes which are not purely personal, and, if we had not, no amount of ethical teaching would influence our conduct except through fear of disapproval. The sort of life that most of us admire is one which is guided by large impersonal desires; now such desires can, no doubt, be encouraged by example, education, and knowledge, but they can hardly be created by the mere abstract belief that they are good, nor discouraged by an analysis of what is meant by the word "good."

When we contemplate the human race, we may desire that it should be happy, or healthy, or intelligent, or warlike, and so on. Any one of these desires, if it is strong, will produce its own morality; but if we have no such general desires, our conduct, whatever our ethic may be, will only serve social purposes in so far as self-interest and the interests of society are in harmony. It is the business of wise institutions to create such harmony as far as possible, and for the rest, whatever may be our theoretical definition of value, we must depend upon the existence of impersonal desires. When you meet a man with whom you have a fundamental ethical disagreement—for example, if you think that all men count equally, while he selects a class as alone important—you will find yourself no better able to cope with him if you believe in objective values than if you do not. In either case, you can only influence his conduct through influencing his desires: if you succeed in that, his ethic will change, and if not, not.

Some people feel that if a general desire, say for the happiness of mankind, has not the sanction of absolute good, it is in some way irrational. This is due to a lingering belief in objective values. A desire cannot, in itself, be either rational or irrational. It may conflict with other desires, and therefore lead to unhappiness; it may rouse opposition in others, and therefore be incapable of gratification. But it cannot be considered "irrational" merely because no reason can be given for feeling it. We may desire A because it is a means to B, but in the end, when we have done with mere means, we must come to something which we desire for no reason, but not on that account "irrationally." All systems of ethics embody the desires of those who advocate them, but this fact is concealed in a mist of words. Our desires are, in fact, more general and less purely selfish than many moralists imagine; if it were not so, no theory of ethics would make moral improvement possible. It is, in fact, not by ethical theory, but by the cultivation of large and generous desires through intelligence, happiness, and freedom from fear, that men can be brought to act more than they do at present in a manner that is consistent with the general happiness of mankind. Whatever our definition of the "Good," and whether we believe it to be subjective or objective, those who do not desire the happiness of mankind will not endeavour to further it, while those who do desire it will do what they can to bring it about.

Brand Blanshard

THE NEW
SUBJECTIVISM IN ETHICS

By the new subjectivism in ethics I mean the view that when anyone says "this is right" or "this is good," he is only expressing his own feeling, he is not asserting anything true or false, because he is not asserting or judging at all; he is really making an exclamation that expresses a favorable feeling.

This view has recently come into much favor. With variations of detail, it has been advocated by Russell, Wittgenstein and Ayer in England, and by Carnap, Stevenson, Feigl, and others, in this country. Why is it that the theory has come into so rapid a popularity? Is it because moralists of insight have been making a fresh and searching examination of moral experience and its expression? No, I think not. A consideration of the names just mentioned suggests a truer reason. All these names belong, roughly speaking, to a single school of thought in the theory of knowl-

Reprinted from *Philosophy and Phenomenological Research, 9* (1949), by permission of *Philosophy and Phenomenological Research* and the author. For this reprinting the author has made a few slight changes in the text.

edge. If the new view has become popular in ethics, it is because certain persons who were at work in the theory of knowledge arrived at a new view *there,* and found, on thinking it out, that it required the new view in ethics; the view comes less from ethical analysis than from logical positivism.

As positivists, these writers held that every judgment belongs to one or other of two types. On the one hand, it may be *a priori* or necessary. But then it is always analytic, i.e., it unpacks in its predicate part or all of its subject. Can we safely say that 7 + 5 make 12? Yes, because 12 is what we mean by "7 + 5." On the other hand, the judgment may be empirical, and then, if we are to verify it, we can no longer look to our meanings only; it refers to sense experience and there we must look for its warrant. Having arrived at this division of judgments, the positivists raised the question where value judgments fall. The judgment that knowledge is good, for example, did not seem to be analytic; the value that knowledge might have did not seem to be part of our concept of knowledge. But neither was the statement empirical, for goodness was not a quality like red or squeaky that could be seen or heard. What were they to do, then, with these awkward judgments of value? To find a place for them in their theory of knowledge would require them to revise the theory radically, and yet that theory was what they regarded as their most important discovery. It appeared that the theory could be saved in one way only. If it could be shown that judgments of good and bad were not judgments at all, that they asserted nothing true or false, but merely expressed emotions like "Hurrah" or "Fiddlesticks," then these wayward judgments would cease from troubling and weary heads could be at rest. This is the course the positivists took. They explained value judgments by explaining them away.

Now I do not think their view will do. But before discussing it, I should like to record one vote of thanks to them for the clarity with which they have stated their case. It has been said of John Stuart Mill that he wrote so clearly that he could be found out. This theory has been put so clearly and precisely that it deserves criticism of the same kind, and this I will do my best to supply. The theory claims to show by analysis that when we say, "That is good," we do not mean to assert a character of the subject of which we are thinking. I shall argue that we do mean to do just that.

Let us work through an example, and the simpler and commoner the better. There is perhaps no value statement on which people would more universally agree than the statement that intense pain is bad. Let us take a set of circumstances in which I happen to be interested on the legislative side and in which I think every one of us might naturally make such a statement. We come upon a rabbit that has been caught in one of the brutal traps in common use. There are signs that it has struggled for days to escape and that in a frenzy of hunger, pain, and fear, it has all but eaten off its own leg. The attempt failed: the animal is now dead. As we think of the long and excruciating pain it must have suffered, we are very likely to say: "It was a bad thing that the little animal should suffer so." The positivist tells us that when we say this we are only expressing our present emotion. I hold, on the contrary, that we mean to assert something of the pain itself, namely, that it was bad, an intrinsic evil, when and as it occurred.

Consider what follows from the positivist view. On that view, nothing good or bad happened in the case until I came on the scene and made my remark. For what I express in my remark is something going on in me at the time, and that of course did not exist until I did come on the scene. The pain of the rabbit was not itself bad; nothing evil was happening when that pain was being endured; badness, in the only sense in which it is involved at all, waited for its appearance till I came and looked and felt. Now that this is at odds with our meaning may be shown as follows. Let us put to ourselves the hypothesis that we had not come on the scene and that the rabbit never was discovered. Are we prepared to say that in that case nothing bad occurred in the sense in which we said it did? Clearly not. Indeed we should say, on the contrary, that the accident of our later discovery made no difference whatever to the badness of the animal's pain, that it would have been every whit as bad whether a chance passer-by happened later to discover the body and feel repugnance or not. If so, then it is clear that in saying the suffering was bad we are not expressing our feelings only. We are saying that the pain was bad when and as it occurred and before anyone took an attitude toward it.

The first argument is thus an ideal experiment in which we use the method of difference. It removes our present expression and shows that the badness we meant would not be affected by this, whereas on positivist grounds it should be. The second argument applies the method in the reverse way. It ideally removes the past event, and shows that this would render false what we mean to say, whereas on positivist grounds it should not. Let us suppose that the animal did not in fact fall into the trap and did not suffer at all, but that we mistakenly believe it did, and say as before that its suffering was an evil thing. On the positivist theory, everything I sought to express by calling it evil in the first case is still present in the second. In the only sense in which badness is involved at all, whatever was bad in the first case is still present in its entirety, since all that is expressed in either case is a state of feeling, and that feeling is still there.

And our question is, is such an implication consistent with what we mean? Clearly it is not. If anyone asked us, after we made the remark that the suffering was a bad thing, whether we should think it relevant to what we said to learn that the incident had never occurred and no pain had been suffered at all, we should say that it made all the difference in the world, that what we were asserting to be bad was precisely the suffering we thought had occurred back there, that if this had not occurred, there was nothing left to be bad, and that our assertion was in that case mistaken. The suggestion that in saying something evil had occurred we were after all making no mistake, because we had never meant anyhow to say anything about the past suffering, seems to me merely frivolous. If we did not mean to say this, why should we be so relieved on finding that the suffering had not occurred? On the theory before us, such relief would be groundless, for in that suffering itself there was nothing bad at all, and hence in its non-occurrence there would be nothing to be relieved about. The positivist theory would here distort our meaning beyond recognition.

So far as I can see, there is only one way out for the positivist. He holds that goodness and badness lie in feelings of approval or disapproval. And there is a way in which he might hold that badness did in this case precede our own feeling of disapproval without belonging to the pain itself. The pain in itself was neutral; but unfortunately the rabbit, on no grounds at all, took up toward this neutral object an attitude of disapproval, and that made it for the first time, and in the only intelligible sense, bad. This way of escape is theoretically possible, but since it has grave difficulties of its own and has not, so far as I know, been urged by positivists, it is perhaps best not to spend time over it.

I come now to a third argument, which again is very simple. When we come upon the rabbit and make our remark about its suffering being a bad thing, we presumably make it with some feeling; the positivists are plainly right in saying that such remarks do usually express feeling. But suppose that a week later we revert to the incident in thought and make our statement again. And suppose that the circumstances have now so changed that the feeling with which we made the remark in the first place has faded. The pathetic evidence is no longer before us; and we are now so fatigued in body and mind that feeling is, as we say, quite dead. In these circumstances, since what was expressed by the remark when first made is, on the theory before us, simply absent, the remark now expresses nothing. It is as empty as the word "Hurrah" would be when there was no enthusiasm behind it. And this seems to me untrue. When we repeat the remark that such suffering was a bad thing, the feeling with which we made it last week may be at or near the vanishing point, but if we were asked whether we meant to say what we did before, we should certainly answer Yes. We should say that we made our point with feeling the first time and little or no feeling the second time, but that it was the same point we were making. And if we can see that what we meant to say remains the same, while the feeling varies from intensity to near zero, it is not the feeling that we primarily meant to express.

I come now to a fourth consideration. We all believe that toward acts or effects of a certain kind one attitude is fitting and another not; but on the theory before us such a belief would not make sense. Broad and Ross have lately contended that this fitness is one of the main facts of ethics, and I suspect they are right. But that is not exactly my point. My point is this: whether there is such fitness or not, we all assume that there is, and if we do, we express in moral judgments more than the subjectivists say we do. Let me illustrate.

In his novel *The House of the Dead*, Dostoevsky tells of his experiences in a Siberian prison camp. Whatever the unhappy inmates of such camps are like today, Dostoevsky's companions were about as grim a lot as can be imagined. "I have heard stories," he writes, "of the most terrible, the most unnatural actions, of the most monstrous murders, told with the most spontaneous, childishly merry laughter." Most of us would say that in this delight at the killing of others or the causing of suffering there is something very unfitting. If we were asked why we thought so, we should say that these things involve great evil and are wrong, and that to take delight in what is evil or wrong is plainly unfitting. Now on the subjectivist view, this answer is ruled out. For before someone takes up an attitude toward death, suffering, or their infliction, they have no moral quality at all. There is therefore nothing about them to which an attitude of approval or condemnation could be fitting. They are in themselves neutral, and, so far as they get a moral quality, they get it only through being invested with it by the attitude of the onlooker. But if that is true, why is any attitude more fitting than any other? Would applause, for example, be fitting if, apart from the applause, there were nothing good to applaud? Would condemnation be fitting if, independently of the condemnation, there were nothing bad to condemn? In such a case, any attitude would be as fitting or unfitting as any other, which means that the notion of fitness has lost all point.

Indeed we are forced to go much farther. If goodness and badness lie in attitudes only and hence are brought into being by them, those men who greeted death and misery with childishly merry laughter are taking the only sensible line. If there is nothing evil in these things, if they get their moral complexion only from our feeling about them, why shouldn't they be greeted with a cheer? To greet them with repulsion would turn what before was neutral into something bad; it would needlessly bring badness into the world; and even on subjectivist assumptions that does not seem very bright. On the other hand, to greet them with delight would convert what before was neutral into something good; it would bring goodness into the world. If I have murdered a man and wish to remove the stain, the way is clear. It is to cry, "Hurrah for murder."

What is the subjectivist to reply? I can only guess. He may point out that the inflicting of death is *not* really neutral before the onlooker takes his attitude, for the man who inflicted the death no doubt himself took an attitude, and thus the act had a moral quality derived from this. But that makes the case more incredible still, for the man who did the act presumably approved it, and if so it was good in the only sense in which anything is good, and then our conviction that the laughter is unfit is more unaccountable still. It may be replied that the victim, too, had his attitude and that since this was unfavorable, the act was not unqualifiedly good. But the answer is plain. Let the killer be expert at his job; let him despatch his victim instantly beofre he has time to take an attitude, and then gloat about his perfect crime without ever telling anyone. Then, so far as I can see, his act will be good without any qualification. It would become bad only if someone found out about it and disliked it. And that would be a curiously irrational procedure, since the man's approving of his own killing is in itself just as neutral as the killing that it approves. Why then should anyone dislike it?

It may be replied that we can defend our dislike on this ground that, if the approval of killing were to go unchecked and spread, most men would have to live in insecurity and fear, and these things are undesirable. But surely this reply is not open; these things are not, on the theory, undesirable, for nothing is; in themselves they are neutral. Why then should I disapprove men's living in this state? The answer may come that if other men live in insecurity and fear, I shall in time be infected myself. But even in my own insecurity and fear there is, on the theory before us, nothing bad whatever, and therefore, if I disapprove them, it is without a shadow of ground and with no more fitness in my attitude than if I cordially cheered them. The theory thus conflicts with our judgments of fitness all along the line.

I come now to a fifth and final difficulty with the theory. It makes mistakes about values impossible. There is a whole nest of inter-connected criticisms here, some of which have been made so often that I shall not develop them again, such as that I can never agree or disagree in opinion with anyone else about an ethical matter, and that in these matters I can never be inconsistent with others or with myself. I am not at all content with the sort of analysis which says that the only contradictions in such cases have regard to facts and that contradictions about value are only differences of feeling. I think that if anyone tells me that having a bicuspid out without an anaesthetic is not a bad experience and I say it is a very nasty experience indeed, I am differing with him in opinion, and differing about the degree of badness of the experience. But without pressing this further, let me apply the argument in what is perhaps a fresh direction.

There is an old and merciful distinction that moralists have made for many centuries about conduct—the distinction between what is subjectively and what is objectively right. They have said that in any given situation there is some act which, in view of all the circumstances, would be the best act to do; and this is what would be objectively right. The notion of an objectively right act is the ground of our notion of duty: our duty is always to find and do this act if we can. But of course we often don't find it. We often hit upon and do acts that we think are the right ones, but we are mistaken; and then our act is only subjectively right. Between these two acts the disparity may be continual; Professor Prichard suggested that probably few of us in the course of our lives ever succeed in doing *the* right act.

Now so far as I can see, the new subjectivism would abolish this difference at a stroke. Let us take a case. A boy abuses his small brother. We should commonly say, "That is wrong, but perhaps he doesn't know any better. By reason of bad teaching and a feeble imagination, he may see nothing wrong in what he is doing, and may even be proud of it. If so, his act may be subjectively right, though it is miles away from what is objectively right." What concerns me about the new subjectivism is that it prohibits this distinction. If the boy feels this way about his act, then it is right in the only sense in which anything is right. The notion of an objective right lying beyond what he has discovered, and which he ought to seek and do is meaningless. There might, to be sure, be an act that would more generally arouse favorable feelings in others, but that would not make it right for him unless he thought of it and approved it, which he doesn't. Even if he did think of it, it would not be obligatory for him to feel about it in any particular way, since there is nothing in any act, as we have seen, which would make any feeling more suitable than any other.

Now if there is no such thing as an objectively right act, what becomes of the idea of duty? I have suggested that the idea of duty rests on the idea of such an act, since it is always our duty to find that act and do it if we can. But if whatever we feel approval for at the time is right, what is the point of doubting and searching further? Like the little girl in Boston who was asked if she would like to travel, we can answer, "Why should I travel when I'm already there?" If I am reconciled in feeling to my present act, no act I could discover by reflection could be better, and therefore why reflect or seek at all? Such a view seems to me to break the mainspring of duty, to destroy the motive for self-improvement, and to remove the ground for self-criticism. It may be replied that by further reflection I can find an act that would satisfy my feelings more widely than the present one, and that this is the act I should seek. But this reply means either that such general satisfaction is objectively better, which would contradict the theory, or else that, if at the time I don't feel it better, it isn't better, in which case I have no motive for seeking it. When certain self-righteous persons took an inflexible line with Oliver Cromwell, his very Cromwellian reply was, "Bethink ye, gentlemen, by the bowels of Christ, that ye may be mistaken." It was good advice. I hope nobody will take from me the privilege of finding myself mistaken. I should be sorry to think that the self of thirty years ago was as far along the path as the self of today, merely because he was a smug young jackanapes, or even that the paragon of today has little room for improvement as would be allowed by his myopic complacency.

One final remark. The great problems of the day are international problems. Has the new subjectivism any bearing upon these problems? I think it has, and a somewhat sinister bearing. I would not suggest, of course, that those who hold the theory are one whit less public-spirited than others; surely there are few who could call themselves citizens of the world with more right (if "rights" have meaning any longer) than Mr. Russell. But Mr. Russell has confessed himself discontented with his ethical theory, and in view of his breadth of concern, one cannot wonder. For its general acceptance would, so far as one can see, be an international disaster. The assumption behind the old League and the new United Nations was that there is such a thing as right and wrong in the conduct of a nation, a right and wrong that do not depend on how it happens to feel at the time. It is implied, for example, that when Japan invaded Manchuria in 1931 she might be wrong, and that by discussion and argument she might be shown to be wrong. It was implied that when the Nazis invaded Poland they might be wrong, even though German public sentiment overwhelmingly approved it. On the theory before us, it would be meaningless to call these nations mistaken; if they felt approval for what they did, then it was right with as complete a justification as could be supplied for the disapproval felt by the rest of the world. In the present dispute between Russia and our own country over southeast Asia or Palestine, it is nonsense to speak of the right or rational course for either of us to take; if with all the facts before the two parties, each feels approval for its own course, both attitudes are equally justified or unjustified; neither is mistaken; there is no common reason to which they can take an appeal; there are no principles by which an international court could pronounce on the matter; nor would there be any obligation to obey the pronouncement if it were made. This cuts the ground from under any attempt to establish one's case as right or anyone else's case as wrong. So if our friends the subjectivists still hold their theory after I have applied my little ruler to their knuckles, which of course they will, I have but one request to make of them: Do keep it from the Kremlin.

*Charles L. Stevenson is Professor of Philosophy
at the University of Michigan.*

Charles L. Stevenson

THE NATURE OF
ETHICAL DISAGREEMENT

1

When people disagree about the value of something—one saying that it is good or right and another that it is bad or wrong—by what methods of argument or inquiry can their disagreement be resolved? Can it be resolved by the methods of science, or does it require methods of some other kind, or is it open to no rational solution at all?

The question must be clarified before it can be answered. And the word that is particularly in need of clarification, as we shall see, is the word "disagreement."

Let us begin by noting that "disagreement" has two broad senses: In the first sense it refers to what I shall call "disagreements in belief." This occurs when Mr. A believes *p,* when Mr. B believes *not-p,* or something

Reprinted from *Facts and Values* (New Haven, Conn.: Yale University Press, 1963), by permission of the author.

incompatible with *p,* and when neither is content to let the belief of the other remain unchallenged. Thus doctors may disagree in belief about the causes of an illness; and friends may disagree in belief about the exact date on which they last met.

In the second sense the word refers to what I shall call "disagreement in attitude." This occurs when Mr. A has a favorable attitude to something, when Mr. B has an unfavorable or less favorable attitude to it, and when neither is content to let the other's attitude remain unchanged. The term "attitude" is here used in much the same sense that R. B. Perry uses "interest"; it designates any psychological disposition of being *for* or *against* something. Hence love and hate are relatively specific kinds of attitudes, as are approval and disapproval, and so on.

This second sense can be illustrated in this way: Two men are planning to have dinner together. One wants to eat at a restaurant that the other doesn't like. Temporarily, then, the men cannot "agree" on where to dine. Their argument may be trivial, and perhaps only half serious; but in any case it represents a disagreement *in attitude*. The men have divergent preferences and each is trying to redirect the preference of the other— though normally, of course, each is willing to revise his own preference in the light of what the other may say.

Further examples are readily found. Mrs. Smith wishes to cultivate only the four hundred; Mr. Smith is loyal to his old poker-playing friends. They accordingly disagree, in attitude, about whom to invite to their party. The progressive mayor wants modern school buildings and large parks; the older citizens are against these "new-fangled" ways; so they disagree on civic policy. These cases differ from the one about the restaurant only in that the clash of attitudes is more serious and may lead to more vigorous argument.

The difference between the two senses of "disagreement" is essentially this: the first involves an opposition of beliefs, both of which cannot be true, and the second involves an opposition of attitudes, both of which cannot be satisfied.

Let us apply this distinction to a case that will sharpen it. Mr. A believes that most voters will favor a proposed tax and Mr. B disagrees with him. The disagreement concerns attitudes—those of the voters—but note that A and B are *not* disagreeing in attitude. Their disagreement is *in belief about* attitudes. It is simply a special kind of disagreement in belief, differing from disagreement in belief about head colds only with regard to subject matter. It implies not an opposition of the actual attitudes of the speakers but only of their beliefs about certain attitudes. Disagreement *in* attitude, on the other hand, implies that the very attitudes of the speakers are opposed. A and B may have opposed beliefs about attitudes without having opposed attitudes, just as they may have opposed beliefs about head colds without having opposed head colds. Hence we must not, from the fact that an argument is concerned with attitudes, infer that it necessarily involves disagreement *in* attitude.

2

We may now turn more directly to disagreement about values, with particular reference to normative ethics. When people argue about what is good, do they disagree in belief, or do they disagree in attitude? A long tradition of ethical theorists strongly suggest, whether they always intend to or not, that the disagreement is one *in belief*. Naturalistic theorists, for instance, identify an ethical judgment with some sort of scientific statement, and so make normative ethics a branch of science. Now a scientific argument typically exemplifies disagreement in belief, and if an ethical argument is simply a scientific one, then it too exemplifies disagreement in belief. The usual naturalistic theories of ethics that stress attitudes—such as those of Hume, Westermarck, Perry, Richards, and so many others—stress disagreement in belief no less than the rest. They imply, of course, that disagreement about what is good is disagreement *in belief* about attitudes; but we have seen that that is simply one sort of disagreement in belief, and by no means the same as disagreement in attitude. Analyses that stress disagreement *in* attitude are extremely rare.

If ethical arguments, as we encounter them in everyday life, involved disagreement in belief exclusively—whether the beliefs were about attitudes or about something else—then I should have no quarrel with the ordinary sort of naturalistic analysis. Normative judgments could be taken as scientific statements and amenable to the usual scientific proof. But a moment's attention will readily show that disagreement in belief has not the exclusive role that theory has so repeatedly ascribed to it. It must be readily granted that ethical arguments usually involve disagreement in belief; but they *also* involve disagreement in attitude. And the conspicuous role of disagreement in attitude is what we usually take, whether we realize it or not, as the distinguishing feature of ethical arguments. For example:

Suppose that the representative of a union urges that the wage level in a given company ought to be higher—that it is only right that the workers receive more pay. The company representative urges in reply that the workers ought to receive no more than they get. Such an argument clearly represents a disagreement in attitude. The union is *for* higher wages; the company is *against* them, and neither is content to let the other's attitude remain unchanged. *In addition* to this disagreement in attitude, of course, the argument may represent no little disagreement in belief. Perhaps the parties disagree about how much the cost of living has risen and how much the workers are suffering under the present wage scale. Or perhaps they disagree about the company's earnings and the extent to which the company could raise wages and still operate at a profit. Like any typical ethical argument, then, this argument involves both disagreement in attitude and disagreement in belief.

It is easy to see, however, that the disagreement in attitude plays a unifying and predominating role in the argument. This is so in two ways:

In the first place, disagreement in attitude determines what beliefs are *relevant* to the argument. Suppose that the company affirms that the wage scale of fifty years ago was far lower than it is now. The union will immediately urge that this contention, even though true, is irrelevant. And it is irrelevant simply because information about the wage level of fifty years ago, maintained under totally different circumstances, is not likely to affect the present attitudes of either party. To be relevant, any belief that is introduced into the argument must be one that is likely to lead one side or the other to have a different attitude, and so reconcile disagreement in attitude. Attitudes are often functions of beliefs. We often change our attitudes to something when we change our beliefs about it; just as a child ceases to *want* to touch a live coal when he comes to *believe* that it will burn him. Thus in the present argument any beliefs that are at all likely to alter attitudes, such as those about the increasing cost of living or the financial state of the company, will be considered by both sides to be relevant to the argument. Agreement in belief on these matters may lead to agreement in attitude toward the wage scale. But beliefs that are likely to alter the attitudes of neither side will be declared irrelevant. They will have no bearing on the disagreement in attitude, with which both parties are primarily concerned.

In the second place, ethical argument usually terminates when disagreement in attitude terminates, even though a certain amount of disagreement in belief remains. Suppose, for instance, that the company and the union continue to disagree in belief about the increasing cost of living, but that the company, even so, ends by favoring the higher wage scale. The union will then be content to end the argument and will cease to press its point about living costs. It may bring up that point again, in some future argument of the same sort, or in urging the righteousness of its victory to the newspaper columnists; but for the moment the fact that the company has agreed in attitude is sufficient to terminate the argument. On the other hand: suppose that both parties agreed on all beliefs that were introduced into the argument, but even so continued to disagree in attitude. In that case neither party would feel that their dispute had been successfully terminated. They might look for other beliefs that could be introduced into the argument. They might use words to play on each other's emotion. They might agree (in attitude) to submit the case to arbitration, both feeling that a decision, even if strongly adverse to one party or the other, would be preferable to a continued impasse. Or, perhaps, they might abandon hope of settling their dispute by any peaceable means.

In many other cases, of course, men discuss ethical topics without having the strong, uncompromising attitudes that the present example has illustrated. They are often as much concerned with redirecting their own attitudes, in the light of greater knowledge, as with redirecting the attitudes of others. And the attitudes involved are often altruistic rather than selfish. Yet the above example will serve, so long as that is understood, to suggest the nature of ethical disagreement. Both disagreement in attitude and disagreement in belief are involved, but the former predominates in that (1) it determines what sort of disagreement in belief is relevantly disputed in a given ethical argument, and (2) it determines by its continued presence or its resolution whether or not the argument has been settled. We may see further how intimately the two sorts of disagreement are related: since attitudes are often functions of beliefs, an agreement in belief may lead people, as a matter of psychological fact, to agree in attitude.

3

Having discussed disagreement, we may turn to the broad question that was first mentioned, namely: By what methods of argument or inquiry may disagreement about matters of value be resolved?

It will be obvious that to whatever extent an argument involves disagreement in belief, it is open to the usual methods of the sciences. If these methods are the *only* rational methods for supporting beliefs—as I believe to be so, but cannot now take time to discuss—then scientific methods are the only rational methods for resolving the disagreement in *belief* that arguments about values may include.

But if science is granted an undisputed sway in reconciling beliefs, it does not thereby acquire, without qualification, an undisputed sway in reconciling attitudes. We have seen that arguments about values include disagreement in attitude, no less than disagreement in belief, and that in certain ways the disagreement in attitude predominates. By what methods shall the latter sort of disagreement be resolved?

The methods of science are still available for that purpose, but only in an indirect way. Initially, these methods have only to do with establishing agreement in belief. If they serve further to establish agreement in attitude, that will be due simply to the psychological fact that altered beliefs may cause altered attitudes. Hence scientific methods are conclusive in ending arguments about values only to the extent that their success in obtaining agreement in belief will in turn lead to agreement in attitude.

In other words: the extent to which scientific methods can bring about agreement on values depends on the extent to which a commonly accepted body of scientific beliefs would cause us to have a commonly accepted set of attitudes.

How much is the development of science likely to achieve, then, with regard to values? To what extent *would* common beliefs lead to common attitudes? It is, perhaps, a pardonable enthusiasm to *hope* that science will do everything—to hope that in some rosy future, when all men know the consequences of their acts, they will all have common aspirations and live peaceably in complete moral accord. But if we speak not from our enthusiastic hopes but from our present knowledge, the answer must be far less exciting. We usually *do not know,* at the beginning of any argument about values, whether an agreement in belief, scientifically established, will lead to an agreement in attitude or not. It is logically possible, at least, that two men should continue to disagree in attitude even though they had all their beliefs in common, and even though neither had made any logical or inductive error, or omitted any relevant evidence. Differences in temperament, or in early training, or in social status, might make the men retain different attitudes even though both were possessed of the complete scientific truth. Whether this logical possibility is an empirical likelihood I shall not presume to say; but it is unquestionably a possibility that must not be left out of account.

To say that science can always settle arguments about value, we have seen, is to make this assumption: Agreement in attitude will always be consequent upon complete agreement in belief, and science can always bring about the latter. Taken as purely heuristic, this assumption has its usefulness. It leads people to discover the discrepancies in their beliefs and to prolong enlightening argument that *may* lead, as a matter of fact, from commonly accepted beliefs to commonly accepted attitudes. It leads people to reconcile their attitudes in a rational, permanent way, rather than by rhapsody or exhortation. But the assumption is *nothing more,* for present knowledge, than a heuristic maxim. It is wholly without any proper foundation of probability. I conclude, therefore, that scientific methods cannot be guaranteed the definite role in the so-called normative sciences that they may have in the natural sciences. Apart from a heuristic assumption to the contrary, it is possible that the growth of scientific knowledge may leave many disputes about values permanently unsolved. Should these disputes persist, there are nonrational methods for dealing with them, of course, such as impassioned, moving oratory. But the purely intellectual methods of science, and, indeed, *all* methods of reasoning, may be insufficient to settle disputes about values even though they may greatly help to do so.

For the same reasons I conclude that normative ethics is not a branch of any science. It deliberately deals with a type of disagreement that science deliberately avoids. Ethics is not psychology, for instance; for although psychologists may, of course, agree or disagree in belief about attitudes, they need not, as psychologists, be concerned with whether they agree or disagree with one another *in* attitude. Insofar as normative ethics draws from the sciences, in order to change attitudes *via* changing people's beliefs, it *draws* from *all* the sciences; but a moralist's peculiar aim—that of *redirecting* attitudes—is a type of activity, rather than knowledge, and falls within no science. Science may study that activity and may help indirectly to forward it; but is not *identical* with that activity.

4

I can take only a brief space to explain why the ethical terms, such as "good," "wrong," "ought," and so on, are so habitually used to deal with disagreement in attitude. On account of their repeated occurrence in emotional situations they have acquired a strong emotive meaning. This emotive meaning makes them serviceable in initiating changes in a hearer's attitudes. Sheer emotive impact is not likely, under many circumstances, to change attitudes in any permanent way; but it *begins* a process that can then be supported by other means.

There is no occasion for saying that the meaning of ethical terms is *purely* emotive, like that of "alas" or "hurrah." We have seen that ethical *arguments* include many expressions of *belief,* and the rough rules of ordinary language permit us to say that some of these beliefs are expressed by an ethical judgment itself. But the beliefs so expressed are by no means always the same. Ethical terms are notable for their ambiguity, and opponents in an argument may use them in different senses. Sometimes this leads to artificial issues, but it usually does not. So long as one person says "this is good" with emotive praise, and another says "no, it is bad," with emotive condemnation, a disagreement in attitude is manifest. Whether or not the beliefs that these statements express are logically incompatible may not be discovered until later in the argument; but even if they are actually compatible, disagreement in attitude will be preserved by emotive meaning; and this disagreement, so central to ethics, may lead to an argument that is certainly not artificial in its issues so long as it is taken for what it is.

The many theorists who have refused to identify ethical statements with scientific ones have much to be said in their favor. They have seen that ethical judgments mold or alter attitudes, rather than describe them, and they have seen that ethical judgments can be guaranteed no definitive scientific support. But one need not on that account provide ethics with any extramundane, sui generis *subject matter*. The distinguishing features of an ethical judgment can be preserved by a recognition of emotive meaning and disagreement in attitude, rather than by some nonnatural quality—and with far greater intelligibility. If a unique subject matter is *postulated*, as it usually is, to preserve the important distinction between normative ethics and science, it serves no purpose that is not served by the very simple analysis I have here suggested. Unless nonnatural qualities can be defended by positive arguments, rather than as an "only resort" from the acknowledged weakness of ordinary forms of naturalism, they would seem nothing more than the invisible shadows cast by emotive meaning.

Immanuel Kant (1726–1806), Professor of Logic and Metaphysics at the University of Königsberg, was a major figure in the history of modern philosophy.

Immanuel Kant

THE SUPREME MORAL PRINCIPLE

. . . Unless we wish to deny all truth to the concept of morality and renounce its application to any possible object, we cannot refuse to admit that the law of this concept is of such broad significance that it holds not merely for men but for all rational beings as such; we must grant that it must be valid with absolute necessity and not merely under contingent conditions and with exceptions. For with what right could we bring into unlimited respect something that might be valid only under contingent human conditions? And how could laws of the determination of our will be held to be laws of the determination of the will of a rational being in general and of ourselves in so far as we are rational beings, if they were merely empirical and did not have their origin completely a priori in pure, but practical, reason?

Nor could one give poorer counsel to morality than to attempt to derive it from examples. For each example of morality which is exhibited to me must itself have been previously judged according to principles of morality to see whether it is worthy to serve as an original example, i.e., as a model. By no means could it authoritatively furnish the concept of morality. Even the Holy One of the Gospel must be compared with our ideal of moral perfection before He is recognized as such; even He says of Himself, "Why call ye Me (whom you see) good? None is good (the archetype of the good) except God only (whom you do not see)." But whence do we have the concept of God as the highest good? Solely from the idea of moral perfection which reason formulates a priori and which it inseparably connects with the concept of a free will. Imitation has no place in moral matters, and examples serve only for encouragement.

. . .

From what has been said it is clear that all moral concepts have their seat and origin entirely a priori in reason. This is just as much the case in the most ordinary reason as in reason which is speculative to the highest degree. It is obvious that they cannot be abstracted from any empirical and hence merely contingent cognitions. In the purity of their origin lies their worthiness to serve us as supreme practical principles, and to the extent that something empirical is added to them just this much is subtracted from their genuine influence and from the unqualified worth of actions. Furthermore, it is evident that it is not only of the greatest necessity in a theoretical point of view when it is a question of speculation but also of the utmost practical importance to derive the concepts and laws of morals from pure reason and to present them pure and unmixed, and to determine the scope of this entire practical but pure rational knowledge (the entire faculty of pure practical reason) without making the principles depend upon the particular nature of human reason as speculative philosophy may permit and even sometimes find necessary. But since moral laws should hold for every rational being as such, the principles must be derived from the universal concept of a rational being generally. In this manner all morals, which need anthropology for their application to men, must be completely developed first as pure philosophy, i.e., metaphysics, independently of anthropology (a thing which is easily done in such distinct fields of knowledge). For we know well that if we are not in possession of such a metaphysics, it is not merely futile to define accurately for the purposes of speculative judgment the moral element of duty in all actions which accord with duty, but impossible to base morals on legitimate principles for merely ordinary and practical use, especially in moral instruction; and it is only in this manner that pure moral dispositions can be produced and engrafted on men's minds for the purpose of the highest good in the world.

In this study we do not advance merely from the common moral judgment (which here is very worthy of respect) to the philosophical . . . but we advance by natural stages from a popular philosophy (which goes no further than it can grope by means of examples) to metaphysics (which is not held back by anything empirical and which, as it must measure out the entire scope of rational knowledge of this kind, reaches even Ideas, where examples fail us). In order to make this advance, we must follow and clearly present the practical faculty of reason from its universal rules of determination to the point where the concept of duty arises from it.

Everything in nature works according to laws. Only a rational being has the capacity of acting according to the conception of laws, i.e., according to principles. This capacity is will. Since reason is required for the derivation of actions from laws, will is nothing else than practical reason. If reason infallibly determines the will, the actions which such a being recognizes as objectively necessary are also subjectively necessary. That is, the will is a faculty of choosing only that which reason, independently of inclination, recognizes as practically necessary, i.e., as good. But if reason of itself does not sufficiently determine the will, and if the will is subjugated to subjective conditions (certain incentives) which do not always agree with objective conditions; in a word, if the will is not of itself in complete accord with reason (the actual case of men), then the actions which are recognized as objectively necessary are subjectively contingent, and the determination of such a will according to objective laws is constraint. That is, the relation of objective laws to a will which is not completely good is conceived as the determination of the will of a rational being by principles of reason to which this will is not by nature necessarily obedient.

The conception of an objective principle so far as it constrains a will, is a command (of reason), and the formula of this command is called an *imperative*.

All imperatives are expressed by an "ought" and thereby indicate the relation of an objective law of reason to a will which is not in its subjective constitution necessarily determined by this law. This relation is that of constraint. Imperatives say that it would be good to do or to refrain from doing something, but they say it to a will which does not always do something simply because it is presented as a good thing to do. . . .

A perfectly good will, therefore, would be equally subject to objective laws (of the good), but it could not be conceived as constrained by them to act in accord with them, because, according to its own subjective constitution, it can be determined to act only through the conception of the good. Thus no imperatives hold for the divine will or, more generally, for a holy will. The "ought" is here out of place, for the volition of itself is necessarily in unison with the law. Therefore imperatives are only formulas expressing the relation of objective laws of volition in general to the subjective imperfection of the will of this or that rational being, e.g., the human will.

All imperatives command either hypothetically or categorically. The former present the practical necessity of a possible action as a means to achieving something else which one desires (or which one may possibly desire). The categorical imperative would be one which presented an action as of itself objectively necessary, without regard to any other end. . . .

If the action is good only as a means to something else, the imperative is hypothetical; but if it is thought of as good in itself, and hence as necessary in a will which of itself conforms to reason as the principle of this will, the imperative is categorical.

The imperative thus says what action possible to me would be good, and it presents the practical rule in relation to a will which does not forthwith perform an action simply because it is good, in part because the subject does not always know that the action is good and in part (when he does know it) because his maxims can still be opposed to the objective principles of practical reason.

The hypothetical imperative, therefore, says only that the action is good to some purpose, possible or actual. In the former case it is a problematical, in the latter an assertorical, practical principle. The categorical imperative, which declares the action to be of itself objectively necessary without making any reference to a purpose, i.e., without having any other end, holds as an apodictical (practical) principle.

. . . All sciences have some practical part which consists of problems of some end which is possible for us and of imperatives as to how it can be reached. These can therefore generally be called imperatives of skill. Whether the end is reasonable and good is not in question at all, for the question is only of what must be done in order to attain it. The precepts to be followed by a physician in order to cure his patient and by a poisoner in order to bring about certain death are of equal value in so far as each does that which will perfectly accomplish his purpose. Since in early youth we do not know what ends may occur to us in the course of life, parents seek to let their children learn a great many things and provide for skill in the use of means to all sorts of arbitrary ends among which they cannot determine whether any one of them may later become an actual purpose of their pupil, though it is possible that he may some day have it as his actual purpose. And this anxiety is so great that they commonly neglect to form and correct their judgment on the worth of things which they may make their ends.

There is one end, however, which we may presuppose as actual in all rational beings so far as imperatives apply to them, i.e., so far as they are dependent beings; there is one purpose not only which they *can* have but which we can presuppose that they all *do* have by a necessity of nature. This purpose is happiness. The hypothetical imperative which represents the practical necessity of action as means to the promotion of happiness is an assertorical imperative. We may not expound it as merely necessary to an uncertain and a merely possible purpose, but as necessary to a purpose which we can a priori and with assurance assume for everyone because it belongs to his essence. Skill in the choice of means to one's own highest welfare can be called prudence in the narrowest sense. Thus the imperative which refers to the choice of means to one's own happiness, i.e., the precept of prudence, is still only hypothetical; the action is not absolutely commanded but commanded only as a means to another end.

Finally, there is one imperative which directly commands a certain conduct without making its condition some purpose to be reached by it. This imperative is categorical. It concerns not the material of the action and its intended result but the form and the principle from which it results. What is essentially good in it consists in the intention, the result being what it may. This imperative may be called the imperative of morality. . . .

The question now arises: how are all these imperatives possible? This question does not require an answer as to how the action which the imperative commands can be performed but merely as to how the constraint of the will, which the imperative expresses in the problem, can be conceived. How an imperative of skill is possible requires no particular discussion. Whoever wills the end, so far as reason has decisive influence on his action, wills also the indispensably necessary means to it that lie in his power. This proposition, in what concerns the will, is analytical; for, in willing an object as my effect, my causality as an acting cause, i.e., the use of the means, is already thought, and the imperative derives the concept of necessary actions to this end from the concept of willing this end. Synthetical propositions undoubtedly are necessary in determining the means to a proposed end, but they do not concern the ground, the act of the will, but only the way to make the object real. Mathematics teaches, by synthetical propositions only, that in order to bisect a line according to an infallible principle I must make two intersecting arcs from each of its extremities; but if I know the proposed result can be obtained only by such an action, then it is an analytical proposition that, if I fully will the effect, I must also will the action necessary to produce it. For it is one and the same thing to conceive of something as an effect which is in a certain way possible through me and to conceive of myself as acting in this way.

• • •

[I]n the case of the categorical imperative or law of morality, the cause of difficulty in discerning its possibility is very weighty. This imperative is an a priori synthetical practical proposition,[1] and, since to discern the possibility of propositions of this sort is so difficult in theoretical knowledge, it may well be gathered that it will be no less difficult in the practical.

In attacking this problem, we will first inquire whether the mere concept of a categorical imperative does not also furnish the formula containing the proposition which alone can be a categorical imperative. For even when we know the formula of the imperative, to learn how such an absolute law is possible will require difficult and special labors which we shall postpone to the last section.

If I think of a hypothetical imperative as such, I do not know what it will contain until the condition is stated [under which it is an imperative]. But if I think of a categorical imperative, I know immediately what it contains. For since the imperative contains besides the law only the necessity that the maxim[2] should accord with this law, while the law contains no condition to which it is restricted, there is nothing remaining

---

1 I connect a priori, and hence necessarily, the action with the will without supposing as a condition that there is any inclination [to the action] (though I do so only objectively, i.e., under the idea of a reason which would have complete power over all subjective motives). This is, therefore, a practical proposition which does not analytically derive the willing of an action from some other volition already presupposed (for we do not have such a perfect will); it rather connects it directly with the concept of the will of a rational being as something which is not contained within it.

2 A maxim is the subjective principle of acting and must be distinguished from the objective principle, i.e., the practical law. The former contains the practical rule which reason determines according to the conditions of the subject (often its ignorance or inclinations) and is thus the principle according to which the subject acts. The law, on the other hand, is the objective principle valid for every rational being, and the principle by which it ought to act, i.e., an imperative.

in it except the universality of law as such to which the maxim of the action should conform; and in effect this conformity alone is represented as necessary by the imperative.

There is, therefore, only one categorical imperative. It is: Act only according to that maxim by which you can at the same time will that it should become a universal law.

Now if all imperatives of duty can be derived from this one imperative as a principle, we can at least show what we understand by the concept of duty and what it means, even though it remain undecided whether that which is called duty is an empty concept or not.

The universality of law according to which effects are produced constitutes what is properly called nature in the most general sense (as to form), i.e., the existence of things so far as it is determined by universal laws. [By analogy], then, the universal imperative of duty can be expressed as follows: Act as though the maxim of your action were by your will to become a universal law of nature.

We shall now enumerate some duties, adopting the usual division of them into duties to ourselves and to others and into perfect and imperfect duties.

1. A man who is reduced to despair by a series of evils feels a weariness with life but is still in possession of his reason sufficiently to ask whether it would not be contrary to his duty to himself to take his own life. Now he asks whether the maxim of his action could become a universal law of nature. His maxim, however, is: For love of myself, I make it my principle to shorten my life when by a longer duration it threatens more evil than satisfaction. But it is questionable whether this principle of self-love could become a universal law of nature. One immediately sees a contradiction in a system of nature whose law would be to destroy life by the feeling whose special office is to impel the improvement of life. In this case it would not exist as nature; hence that maxim cannot obtain as a law of nature, and thus it wholly contradicts the supreme principle of all duty.

2. Another man finds himself forced by need to borrow money. He well knows that he will not be able to repay it, but he also sees that nothing will be loaned him if he does not firmly promise to repay it at a certain time. He desires to make such a promise, but he has enough conscience to ask himself whether it is not improper and opposed to duty to relieve his distress in such a way. Now, assuming he does decide to do so, the maxim of his action would be as follows: When I believe myself to be in need of money, I will borrow money and promise to repay it, although I know I shall never do so. Now this principle of self-love or of

his own benefit may very well be compatible with his whole future welfare, but the question is whether it is right. He changes the pretension of self-love into a universal law and then puts the question: How would it be if my maxim became a universal law? He immediately sees that it could never hold as a universal law of nature and be consistent with itself; rather it must necessarily contradict itself. For the universality of a law which says that anyone who believes himself to be in need could promise what he pleased with the intention of not fulfilling it would make the promise itself and the end to be accomplished by it impossible; no one would believe what was promised to him but would only laugh at any such assertion as vain pretense.

3. A third finds in himself a talent which could, by means of some cultivation, make him in many respects a useful man. But he finds himself in comfortable circumstances and prefers indulgence in pleasure to troubling himself with broadening and improving his fortunate natural gifts. Now, however, let him ask whether his maxim of neglecting his gifts, besides agreeing with his propensity to idle amusement, agrees also with what is called duty. He sees that a system of nature could indeed exist in accordance with such a law, even though man (like the inhabitants of the South Sea Islands) should let his talents rust and resolve to devote his life merely to idleness, indulgence, and propagation—in a word, to pleasure. But he cannot possibly will that this should become a universal law of nature or that it should be implanted in us by a natural instinct. For, as a rational being, he necessarily wills that all his faculties should be developed, inasmuch as they are given to him for all sorts of possible purposes.

4. A fourth man, for whom things are going well, sees that others (whom he could help) have to struggle with great hardships, and he asks, "What concern of mine is it? Let each one be as happy as heaven wills, or as he can make himself; I will not take anything from him or even envy him; but to his welfare or to his assistance in time of need I have no desire to contribute." If such a way of thinking were a universal law of nature, certainly the human race could exist, and without doubt even better than in a state where everyone talks of sympathy and good will, or even exerts himself occasionally to practice them while, on the other hand, he cheats when he can and betrays or otherwise violates the rights of man. Now although it is possible that a universal law of nature according to that maxim could exist, it is nevertheless impossible to will that such a principle should hold everywhere as a law of nature. For a will which resolved this would conflict with itself, since instances can often arise in which he would need the love and sympathy of others, and in

which he would have robbed himself, by such a law of nature springing from his own will, of all hope of the aid he desires.

The foregoing are a few of the many actual duties, or at least of duties we hold to be actual, whose derivation from the one stated principle is clear. We must be able to will that a maxim of our action become a universal law; this is the canon of the moral estimation of our action generally. Some actions are of such a nature that their maxim cannot even be *thought* as a universal law of nature without contradiction, far from it being possible that one could will that it should be such. In others this internal impossibility is not found, though it is still impossible to *will* that their maxim should be raised to the universality of a law of nature, because such a will would contradict itself. We easily see that the former maxim conflicts with the stricter or narrower (imprescriptible) duty, the latter with broader (meritorious) duty. Thus all duties, so far as the kind of obligation (not the object of their action) is concerned, have been completely exhibited by these examples in their dependence on the one principle.

When we observe ourselves in any transgression of a duty, we find that we do not actually will that our maxim should become a universal law. That is impossible for us; rather, the contrary of this maxim should remain as a law generally, and we only take the liberty of making an exception to it for ourselves or for the sake of our inclination, and for this one occasion. . . .

We have thus at least established that if duty is a concept which is to have significance and actual legislation for our actions, it can be expressed only in categorical imperatives and not at all in hypothetical ones. For every application of it we have also clearly exhibited the content of the categorical imperative which must contain the principle of all duty (if there is such). This is itself very much. But we are not yet advanced far enough to prove a priori that that kind of imperative really exists, that there is a practical law which of itself commands absolutely and without any incentives, and that obedience to this law is duty. . . .

The question then is: Is it a necessary law for all rational beings that they should always judge their actions by such maxims as they themselves could will to serve as universal laws? If it is such a law, it must be connected (wholly a priori) with the concept of the will of a rational being as such. But in order to discover this connection we must, however reluctantly, take a step into metaphysics, although into a region of it different from speculative philosophy, i.e., into metaphysics of morals. . . . [H]ere it is a question of objectively practical laws and thus of the relation of a will to itself so far as it determines itself only by reason; for everything which has a relation to the empirical automatically falls away, because if reason of itself alone determines conduct it must necessarily do so a priori. The possibility of reason thus determining conduct must now be investigated.

The will is thought of as a faculty of determining itself to action in accordance with the conception of certain laws. Such a faculty can be found only in rational beings. That which serves the will as the objective ground of its self-determination is an end, and, if it is given by reason alone, it must hold alike for all rational beings. On the other hand, that which contains the ground of the possibility of the action, whose result is an end, is called the means. The subjective ground of desire is the incentive, while the objective ground of volition is the motive. Thus arises the distinction between subjective ends, which rest on incentives, and objective ends, which depend on motives valid for every rational being. Practical principles are formal when they disregard all subjective ends; they are material when they have subjective ends, and thus certain incentives, as their basis. The ends which a rational being arbitrarily proposes to himself as consequences of his action are material ends and are without exception only relative, for only their relation to a particularly constituted faculty of desire in the subject gives them their worth. And this worth cannot, therefore, afford any universal principles for all rational beings or valid and necessary principles for every volition. That is, they cannot give rise to any practical laws. All these relative ends, therefore, are grounds for hypothetical imperatives only.

But suppose that there were something the existence of which in itself had absolute worth, something which, as an end in itself, could be a ground of definite laws. In it and only in it could lie the ground of a possible categorical imperative, i.e., of a practical law.

Now, I say, man and, in general, every rational being exists as an end in himself and not merely as a means to be arbitrarily used by this or that will. In all his actions, whether they are directed to himself or to other rational beings, he must always be regarded at the same time as an end. All objects of inclinations have only a conditional worth, for if the inclinations and the needs founded on them did not exist, their object would be without worth. The inclinations themselves as the sources of needs, however, are so lacking in absolute worth that the universal wish of every rational being must be indeed to free himself completely from them. Therefore, the worth of any objects to be obtained by our actions is at all times conditional. Beings whose existence does not depend on our will but on nature, if they are not rational beings, have only a relative worth as means and are therefore called "things"; on the other hand, rational beings are designated "persons" because their nature indicates that they are ends in themselves, i.e., things which may not be used merely as means. Such a being is thus an object of respect and, so far, restricts all [arbitrary] choice. Such beings are not merely subjective ends whose existence as a result of our action has a worth for us, but are objective ends, i.e., beings whose existence in itself is an end. Such an end is one for which no other end can be substituted, to which these beings should serve merely as means. For, without them, nothing of absolute worth could be found, and if all worth is conditional and thus contingent, no supreme practical principle for reason could be found anywhere.

Thus if there is to be a supreme practical principle and a categorical imperative for the human will, it must be one that forms an objective principle of the will from the conception of that which is necessarily an end for everyone because it is an end in itself. Hence this objective principle can serve as a universal practical law. The ground of this principle is: rational nature exists as an end in itself. Man necessarily thinks of his own existence in this way; thus far it is a subjective principle of human actions. Also every other rational being thinks of his existence by means of the same rational ground which holds also for myself; thus it is at the same time an objective principle from which, as a supreme practical ground, it must be possible to derive all laws of the will. The practical imperative, therefore, is the following: Act so that you treat humanity, whether in your own person or in that of another, always as an end and never as a means only. Let us now see whether this can be achieved.

To return to our previous examples:

First, according to the concept of necessary duty to one's self, he who contemplates suicide will ask himself whether his action can be consistent with the idea of humanity as an end in itself. If, in order to escape from burdensome circumstances, he destroys himself, he uses a person merely as a means to maintain a tolerable condition up to the end of life. Man, however, is not a thing, and thus not something to be used merely as a means; he must always be regarded in all his actions as an end in himself. Therefore, I cannot dispose of man in my own person so as to mutilate, corrupt, or kill him. (It belongs to ethics proper to define more accurately this basic principle so as to avoid all misunderstanding, e.g., as to the amputation of limbs in order to preserve myself, or to exposing my life to danger in order to save it; I must, therefore, omit them here.)

Second, as concerns necessary or obligatory duties to others, he who intends a deceitful promise to others sees immediately that he intends to use another man merely as a means, without the latter containing the end in himself at the same time. For he whom I want to use for my own purposes by means of such a promise cannot possibly assent to my mode of acting against him and cannot contain the end of this action in himself. This conflict against the principle of other men is even clearer if we cite examples of attacks on their freedom and property. For then it is clear that he who transgresses the rights of men intends to make use of the persons of others merely as a means, without considering that, as rational beings, they must always be esteemed at the same time as ends, i.e., only as beings who must be able to contain in themselves the end of the very same action.[3]

Third, with regard to contingent (meritorious) duty to one's self, it is not sufficient that the action not conflict with humanity in our person as an end in itself; it must also harmonize with it. Now in humanity there are capacities for greater perfection which belong to the end of nature with respect to humanity in our own person; to neglect these might perhaps be consistent with the preservation of humanity as an end in itself but not with the furtherance of that end.

Fourth, with regard to meritorious duty to others, the natural end which all men have is their own happiness. Humanity might indeed exist if no one contributed to the happiness of others, provided he did not intentionally detract from it; but this harmony with humanity as an end in itself is only negative rather than positive if everyone does not also endeavor, so far as he can, to further the ends of others. For the ends of any person, who is an end in himself, must as far as possible also be my end, if that conception of an end in itself is to have its full effect on me.

---

[3] Let it not be thought that the banal *quod tibi non vis fieri,* etc., could here serve as guide or principle, for it is only derived from the principle and is restricted by various limitations. It cannot be a universal law, because it contains the ground neither of duties to one's self nor of the benevolent duties to others (for many a man would gladly consent that others should not benefit him, provided only that he might be excused from showing benevolence to them). Nor does it contain the ground of obligatory duties to another, for the criminal would argue on this ground against the judge who sentences him. And so on.

John Stuart Mill (1806–1873), philosopher, economist, and member of the House of Commons, was a leading spokesman for the liberal tradition.

John Stuart Mill

UTILITARIANISM

WHAT UTILITARIANISM IS

. . . The creed which accepts as the foundation of morals, Utility, or the Greatest Happiness Principle, holds that actions are right in proportion as they tend to promote happiness, wrong as they tend to produce the reverse of happiness. By happiness is intended pleasure, and the absence of pain; by unhappiness, pain, and the privation of pleasure. To give a clear view of the moral standard set up by the theory, much more requires to be said; in particular, what things it includes in the ideas of pain and pleasure; and to what extent this is left an open question. But these supplementary explanations do not affect the theory of life on which this theory of morality is grounded—namely, that pleasure, and freedom from pain, are the only things desirable as ends; and that all desirable things (which are as numerous in the utilitarian as in any other scheme) are

Reprinted from *Utilitarianism* (1863).

desirable either for the pleasure inherent in themselves, or as means to the promotion of pleasure and the prevention of pain.

Now, such a theory of life excites in many minds, and among them in some of the most estimable in feeling and purpose, inveterate dislike. To suppose that life has (as they express it) no higher end than pleasure—no better and nobler object of desire and pursuit—they designate as utterly mean and grovelling; as a doctrine worthy only of swine, to whom the followers of Epicurus were, at a very early period, contemptuously likened; and modern holders of the doctrine are occasionally made the subject of equally polite comparisons by its German, French, and English assailants.

When thus attacked, the Epicureans have always answered, that it is not they, but their accusers, who represent human nature in a degrading light; since the accusation supposes human beings to be capable of no pleasures except those of which swine are capable. If this supposition were true, the charge could not be gainsaid, but would then be no longer an imputation; for if the sources of pleasure were precisely the same to human beings and to swine, the rule of life which is good enough for the one would be good enough for the other. The comparison of the Epicurean life to that of beasts is felt as degrading, precisely because a beast's pleasures do not satisfy a human being's conceptions of happiness. Human beings have faculties more elevated than the animal appetites, and when once made conscious of them, do not regard anything as happiness which does not include their gratification. I do not, indeed, consider the Epicureans to have been by any means faultless in drawing out their scheme of consequences from the utilitarian principle. To do this in any sufficient manner, many Stoic, as well as Christian elements require to be included. But there is no known Epicurean theory of life which does not assign to the pleasures of the intellect, of the feelings and imagination, and of the moral sentiments, a much higher value as pleasures than to those of mere sensation. It must be admitted, however, that utilitarian writers in general have placed the superiority of mental over bodily pleasures chiefly in the greater permanency, safety, uncostliness, etc., of the former—that is, in their circumstantial advantages rather than in their intrinsic nature. And on all these points utilitarians have fully proved their case; but they might have taken the other, and, as it may be called, higher ground, with entire consistency. It is quite compatible with the principle of utility to recognise the fact, that some *kinds* of pleasure are more desirable and more valuable than others. It would be absurd that while, in estimating all other things, quality is considered as well as quantity, the estimation of pleasures should be supposed to depend on quantity alone.

If I am asked, what I mean by difference of quality in pleasures, or what makes one pleasure more valuable than another, merely as a pleasure, except its being greater in amount, there is but one possible answer. Of two pleasures, if there be one to which all or almost all who have experience of both give a decided preference, irrespective of any feeling of moral obligation to prefer it, that is the more desirable pleasure. If one of the two is, by those who are competently acquainted with both, placed so far above the other that they prefer it, even though knowing it to be attended with a greater amount of discontent, and would not resign it for any quantity of the other pleasure which their nature is capable of, we are justified in ascribing to the preferred enjoyment a superiority in quality, so far outweighing quantity as to render it, in comparison, of small account.

Now it is an unquestionable fact that those who are equally acquainted with, and equally capable of appreciating and enjoying, both, do give a most marked preference to the manner of existence which employs their higher faculties. Few human creatures would consent to be changed into any of the lower animals, for a promise of the fullest allowance of a beast's pleasures; no intelligent human being would consent to be a fool, no instructed person would be an ignoramus, no person of feeling and conscience would be selfish and base, even though they should be persuaded that the fool, the dunce, or the rascal is better satisfied with his lot than they are with theirs. They would not resign what they possess more than he for the most complete satisfaction of all the desires which they have in common with him. If they ever fancy they would, it is only in cases of unhappiness so extreme, that to escape from it they would exchange their lot for almost any other, however undesirable in their own eyes. A being of higher faculties requires more to make him happy, is capable probably of more acute suffering, and certainly accessible to it at more points, than one of an inferior type; but in spite of these liabilities, he can never really wish to sink into what he feels to be a lower grade of existence. We may give what explanation we please of this unwillingness; we may attribute it to pride, a name which is given indiscriminately to some of the most and to some of the least estimable feelings of which mankind are capable: we may refer it to the love of liberty and personal independence, an appeal to which was with the Stoics one of the most effective means for the inculcation of it; to the love of power, or to the love of excitement, both of which do really enter into and contribute to it: but its most appropriate appellation is a sense of dignity, which all human beings possess in one form or other, and in some, though by no means in exact, proportion to their higher faculties, and which is so essential a part of the happiness of those in whom it is strong, that nothing which conflicts with it could be, otherwise than momentarily, an object of desire to them. Whoever supposes that this preference takes place at a sacrifice of happiness—that the superior being, in anything like equal circumstances, is not happier than the inferior—confounds the two very different ideas, of happiness, and content. It is indisputable that the being whose capacities of enjoyment are low, has the greatest chance of having them fully satisfied; and a highly endowed being will always feel that any happiness which he can look for, as the world is constituted, is imperfect. But he can learn to bear its imperfections, if they are at all bearable; and they will not make him envy the being who is indeed unconscious of the imperfections, but only because he feels not at all the good which those imperfections qualify. It is better to be a human being dissatisfied than a pig satisfied; better to be Socrates dissatisfied than a fool satisfied. And if the fool, or the pig, are of a different opinion, it is because they only know their own side of the question. The other party to the comparison knows both sides.

It may be objected, that many who are capable of the higher pleasures, occasionally, under the influence of temptation, postpone them to the lower. But this is quite compatible with a full appreciation of the intrinsic superiority of the higher. Men often, from infirmity of character, make their election for the nearer good, though they know it to be the less valuable; and this no less when the choice is between two bodily pleasures, than when it is between bodily and mental. They pursue sensual indulgences to the injury of health, though perfectly aware that health is the greater good. It may be further objected, that many who begin with youthful enthusiasm for everything noble, as they advance in years sink into indolence and selfishness. But I do not believe that those who undergo this very common change, voluntarily choose the lower description of pleasures in preference to the higher. I believe that before they devote themselves exclusively to the one, they have already become incapable of the other. Capacity for the nobler feelings is in most natures a very tender plant, easily killed, not only by hostile influences, but by mere want of sustenance; and in the majority of young persons it speedily dies away if the occupations to which their position in life has devoted them, and the society into which it has thrown them, are not favourable to keeping that higher capacity in exercise. Men lose their high aspirations as they lose their intellectual tastes, because they have not time or opportunity for indulging them; and they addict themselves to inferior pleasures, not because they deliberately prefer them, but because they are either the only ones to which they have access, or the only ones which they are any longer capable of enjoying. It may be questioned whether any one who has remained equally susceptible to both classes of pleasures, ever knowingly and calmly preferred the lower; though many, in all ages, have broken down in an ineffectual attempt to combine both.

From this verdict of the only competent judges, I apprehend there can be no appeal. On a question which is the best worth having of two pleasures, or which of two modes of existence is the most grateful to the feelings, apart from its moral attributes and from its consequences, the judgment of those who are qualified by knowledge of both, or, if they differ, that of the majority among them, must be admitted as final. And there needs be the less hesitation to accept this judgment respecting the quality of pleasures, since there is no other tribunal to be referred to even on the question of quantity. What means are there of determining which is the acutest of two pains, or the intensest of two pleasurable sensations, except the general suffrage of those who are familiar with both? Neither pains nor pleasures are homogeneous, and pain is always heterogeneous with pleasure. What is there to decide whether a particular pleasure is worth purchasing at the cost of a particular pain, except the feelings and judgment of the experienced? When, therefore, those feelings and judgment declare the pleasures derived from the higher faculties to be preferable *in kind,* apart from the question of intensity, to those of which the animal nature, disjoined from the higher faculties, is suspectible, they are entitled on this subject to the same regard.

I have dwelt on this point, as being a necessary part of a perfectly just conception of Utility or Happiness, considered as the directive rule of human conduct. But it is by no means an indispensable conditon to the acceptance of the utilitarian standard; for that standard is not the agent's own greatest happiness, but the greatest amount of happiness altogether; and if it may possibly be doubted whether a noble character is always the happier for its nobleness, there can be no doubt that it makes other people happier, and that the world in general is immensely a gainer by it. Utilitarianism, therefore, could only attain its end by the general cultivation of nobleness of character, even if each individual were only benefited by the nobleness of others, and his own, so far as happiness is concerned, were a sheer deduction from the benefit. But the bare enunciation of such an absurdity as this last, renders refutation superfluous.

According to the Greatest Happiness Principle, as above explained, the ultimate end, with reference to and for the sake of which all other things are desirable (whether we are considering our own good or that of other people), is an existence exempt as far as possible from pain, and as rich as possible in enjoyments, both in point of quantity and quality; the test of quality, and the rule for measuring it against quantity, being the preference felt by those who in their opportunities of experience, to which must be added their habits of self-consciousness and self-observation, are best furnished with the means of comparison. This, being, according to the utilitarian opinion, the end of human action, is necessarily also the standard of morality; which may accordingly be defined, the rules and precepts for human conduct, by the observance of which an existence such as has been described might be, to the greatest extent possible, secured to all mankind; and not to them only, but, so far as the nature of things admits, to the whole sentient creation.

• • •

The utilitarian morality does recognise in human beings the power of sacrificing their own greatest good for the good of others. It only refuses to admit that the sacrifice is itself a good. A sacrifice which does not increase, or tend to increase, the sum total of happiness, it considers as wasted. The only self-renunciation which it applauds, is devotion to the happiness, or to some of the means of happiness, of others; either of mankind collectively, or of individuals within the limits imposed by the collective interests of mankind.

I must again repeat, what the assailants of utilitarianism seldom have the justice to acknowledge, that the happiness which forms the utilitarian standard of what is right in conduct, is not the agent's own happiness, but that of all concerned. As between his own happiness and that of others, utilitarianism requires him to be as strictly impartial as a disinterested and benevolent spectator. In the golden rule of Jesus of Nazareth, we read the complete spirit of the ethics of utility. To do as you would be done by, and to love your nieghbour as yourself, constitute the ideal perfection of utilitarian morality. As the means of making the nearest approach to this ideal, utility would enjoin, first, that laws and social arrangements should place the happiness, or (as speaking practically it may be called) the interest, of every individual, as nearly as possible in harmony with the interest of the whole; and secondly, that education and opinion, which have so vast a power over human character, should so use that power as to establish in the mind of every individual an indissoluble association between his own happiness and the good of the whole; especially between his own happiness and the practice of such modes of conduct, negative and positive, as regard for the universeal happiness prescribes; so that not only he may be unable to conceive the possibility of happiness to himself, consistently with conduct opposed to the general good, but also that a direct impulse to promote the general good may be in every individual one of the habitual motives of action, and the sentiments connected therewith may fill a large and prominent place in every human being's sentient existence. If the impugners of the utilitarian morality represented it to their own minds in this its true character, I know not what recommendation possessed by any other morality they could possibly affirm to be wanting to it; what more beautiful or more exalted developments of human nature any other ethical system can be supposed to foster, or what springs of action, not accessible to the utilitarian, such systems rely on for giving effect to their mandates.

The objectors to utilitarianism cannot always be charged with representing it in a discreditable light. On the contrary, those among them who entertain anything like a just idea of its disinterested character, sometimes find fault with its standard as being too high for humanity. They say it is exacting too much to require that people shall always act from the inducement of promoting the general interests of society. But this is to mistake the very meaning of a standard of morals, and confound the rule of action with the motive of it. It is the business of ethics to tell us what are our duties, or by what test we may know them; but no system of ethics requires that the sole motive of all we do shall be a feeling of duty; on the contrary, ninety-nine hundredths of all our actions are done from other motives, and rightly so done, if the rule of duty does not condemn them. It is the more unjust to utilitarianism that this particular misappreciation should be made a ground of objection to it, inasmuch as utilitarian moralists have gone beyond almost all others in affirming that the motive has nothing to do with the morality of the action, though much with the worth of the agent. He who saves a fellow creature from drowning does what is morally right, whether his motive be duty, or the hope of being paid for his trouble; he who betrays the friend that trusts him, is guilty of a crime, even if his object be to serve another friend to whom he is under greater obligations. But to speak only of actions done from the motive of duty, and in direct obedience to principle: it is a misapprehension of the utilitarian mode of thought, to conceive it as implying that people should fix their minds upon so wide a generality as the world, or society at large. The great majority of good actions are intended not for the benefit of the world, but for that of individuals, of which the good of the world is made up; and the thoughts of the most virtuous man need not on these occasions travel beyond the particular persons concerned, except so far as is necessary to assure himself that in benefiting them he is not violating the rights, that is, the legitimate and authorised expectations, of any one else. The multiplication of happiness is, according to the utilitarian ethics, the object of virtue: the occasions on which any person (except one in a thousand) has it in his power to do this on an extended scale, in other words to be a public benefactor, are but exceptional; and on these occasions alone is he called on to consider public utility; in every other case, private utility, the interest or happiness of some few persons, is all he has to attend to. Those alone the influence of whose actions extends to society in general, need concern themselves habitually about so large an object. In the case of abstinences indeed—of things which people forbear to do from moral considerations, though the consequences in the particular case might be beneficial—it would be unworthy of an intelligent agent not to be consciously aware that the action is of a class which, if practised generally, would be generally injurious, and that this is the ground of the obligation to abstain from it. The amount of regard for the public interest implied in this recognition, is no greater than is demanded by every system of morals, for they all enjoin to abstain from whatever is manifestly pernicious to society.

The same considerations dispose of another reproach against the doctrine of utility, founded on a still grosser misconception of the purpose of a standard of morality, and of the very meaning of the words right and wrong. It is often affirmed that utilitarianism renders men cold and unsympathising; that it chills their moral feelings towards individuals; that it makes them regard only the dry and hard consideration of the consequences of actions, not taking into their moral estimate the qualities from which those actions emanate. If the assertion means that they do not allow their judgment respecting the rightness or wrongness of an action to be influenced by their opinion of the qualities of the person who does it, this is a complaint not against utilitarianism, but against having any standard of morality at all; for certainly no known ethical standard decides an action to be good or bad because it is done by a good or a bad man, still less because done by an amiable, a brave, or a benevolent man, or the contrary. These considerations are relevant, not to the estimation of actions, but of persons; and there is nothing in the utilitarian theory inconsistent with the fact that there are other things which interest us in persons besides the rightness and wrongness of their actions. The Stoics, indeed, with the paradoxical misuse of language which was part of their system, and by which they strove to raise themselves above all concern about anything but virtue, were fond of saying that he who has that has everything; that he, and only he, is rich, is beautiful, is a king. But no claim of this description is made for the virtuous man by the utilitarian doctrine. Utilitarians are quite aware that there are other desirable possessions and qualities besides virtue, and are perfectly willing to allow to all of them their full worth. They are also aware that a right action does not necessarily indicate a virtuous character, and that actions which are blamable, often proceed from qualities entitled to praise. When this is apparent in any particular case, it modifies their estimation, not certainly of the act, but of the agent. I grant that they are, notwithstanding, of opinion, that in the long run the best proof of a good character is good actions; and resolutely refuse to consider any mental dispositon as good, of which the predominant tendency is to produce bad conduct. This makes them unpopular with many people; but it is an unpopularity which they must share with every one who regards the distinction between right and wrong in a serious light; and the reproach is not one which a conscientious utilitarian need be anxious to repel.

. . .

Again, Utility is often summarily stigmatised as an immoral doctrine by giving it the name of Expediency, and taking advantage of the popular use of that term to contrast it with Principle. But the Expedient, in the sense in which it is opposed to the Right, generally means that which is expedient for the particular interest of the agent himself; as when a minister sacrifices the interests of his country to keep himself in place. When it means anything better than this, it means that which is expedient for some immediate object, some temporary purpose, but which violates a rule whose observance is expedient in a much higher degree. The Expedient, in this sense, instead of being the same thing with the useful, is a branch of the hurtful. Thus, it would often be expedient, for the purpose of getting over some momentary embarrassment, or attaining some object immediately useful to ourselves or others, to tell a lie. But inasmuch as the cultivation in ourselves of a sensitive feeling on the subject of veracity, is one of the most useful, and the enfeeblement of that feeling one of the most hurtful, things to which our conduct can be instrumental; and inasmuch as any, even unintentional, deviation from truth, does that much towards weakening the trustworthiness of human assertion, which is not only the principal support of all present social well-being, but the insufficiency of which does more than any one thing that can be named to keep back civilisation, virtue, everything on which human happiness on the largest scale depends; we feel that the violation, for a present advantage, of a rule of such transcendant expediency, is not expedient, and that he who, for the sake of a convenience to himself or to some other individual, does what depends on him to deprive mankind of the good, and inflict upon them the evil, involved in the greater or less reliance which they can place in each other's word, acts the part of one of their worst enemies. Yet that even this rule, sacred as it is, admits of possible exceptions, is acknowledged by all moralists; the chief of which is when the withholding of some fact (as of information from a malefactor, or of bad news from a person dangerously ill) would save an individual (especially an individual other than oneself) from great and unmerited evil, and when the withholding can only be effected by denial. But in order that the exception may not extend itself beyond the need, and may have the least possible effect in weakening reliance on veracity, it ought to be recognised, and, if possible, its limits defined; and if the principle of utility is good for anything, it must be good for weighing these conflicting utilities against one another, and marking out the region within which one or the other preponderates.

• • •

[Q]uestions of ultimate ends do not admit of proof, in the ordinary acceptation of the term. To be incapable of proof by reasoning is common to all first principles; to the first premises of our knowledge, as well as to those of our conduct. But the former, being matters of fact, may be the subject of a direct appeal to the faculties which judge of fact—namely, our senses, and our internal consciousness. Can an appeal be made to the same faculties on questions of practical ends? Or by what other faculty is cognisance taken of them?

Questions about ends are, in other words, questions what things are desirable. The utilitarian doctrine is, that happiness is desirable, and the only thing desirable, as an end; all other things being only desirable as means to that end. What ought to be required of this doctrine—what conditions is it requisite that the doctrine should fulfil—to make good its claim to be believed?

The only proof capable of being given that an object is visible, is that people actually see it. The only proof that a sound is audible, is that people hear it: and so of the other sources of our experience. In like manner, I apprehend, the sole evidence it is possible to produce that anything is desirable, is that people do actually desire it. If the end which the utilitarian doctrine proposes to itself were not, in theory and in practice, acknowledged to be an end, nothing could ever convince any person that it was so. No reason can be given why the general happiness is desirable, except that each person, so far as he believes when considered as swelling an aggregate. The principle of utility does not mean that any given pleasure, as music, for instance, or any given exemption from pain, as for example health, is to be looked upon as means to a collective something termed happiness, and to be desired on that account. They are desired and desirable in and for themselves; besides being means, they are a part of the end. Virtue, according to the utilitarian doctrine, is not naturally and originally part of the end, but it is capable of becoming so;

and in those who love it disinterestedly it has become so, and is desired and cherished, not as a means to happiness, but as a part of their happiness.

To illustrate this farther, we may remember that virtue is not the only thing, originally a means, and which if it were not a means to anything else, would be and remain indifferent, but which by association with what it is a means to, comes to be desired for itself, and that too with the utmost intensity. What, for example, shall we say of the love of money? There is nothing originally more desirable about money than about any heap of glittering pebbles. Its worth is solely that of the things which it will buy; the desires for other things than itself, which it is a means of gratifying. Yet the love of money is not only one of the strongest moving forces of human life, but money is, in many cases, desired in and for itself; the desire to possess it is often stronger than the desire to use it, and goes on increasing when all the desires which point to ends beyond it, to be compassed by it, are falling off. It may, then, be said truly, that money is desired not for the sake of an end, but as part of the end. From being a means to happiness, it has come to be itself a principal ingredient of the individual's conception of happiness. The same may be said of the majority of the great objects of human life—power, for example, or fame; except that to each of these there is a certain amount of immediate pleasure annexed, which has at least the semblance of being naturally inherent in them; a thing which cannot be said of money. Still, however, the strongest natural attraction, both of power and of fame, is the immense aid they give to the attainment of our other wishes; and it is the strong association thus generated between them and all our objects of desire, which gives to the direct desire of them the intensity it often assumes, so as in some characters to surpass in strength all other desires. In these cases the means have become a part of the end, and a more important part of it than any of the things which they are means to. What was once desired as an instrument for the attainment of happiness, has come to be desired for its own sake. In being desired for its own sake it is, however, desired as *part* of happiness. The person is made, or thinks he would be made, happy by its mere possession; and is made unhappy by failure to obtain it. The desire of it is not a different thing from the desire of happiness, any more than the love of music, or the desire of health. They are included in happiness. They are some of the elements of which the desire of happiness is made up. Happiness is not an abstract idea, but a concrete whole; and these are some of its parts. And the utilitarian standard sanctions and approves their being so. Life would be a poor thing, very ill provided with sources of happiness, if there were not this provision of nature, by which things originally indifferent, but conducive to, or otherwise associated with, the satisfaction of our primitive desires, become in themselves sources of pleasure more valuable than the primitive pleasures, both in permanency, in the space of human existence that they are capable of covering, and even in intensity.

Virtue, according to the utilitarian conception, is a good of this description. There was no original desire of it, or motive to it, save its conduciveness to pleasure, and especially to protection from pain. But through the association thus formed, it may be felt a good in itself, and desired as such with as great intensity as any other good; and with this difference between it and the love of money, of power, or of fame, that all of these may, and often do, render the individual noxious to the other members of the society to which he belongs, whereas there is nothing which makes him so much a blessing to them as the cultivation of the disinterested love of virtue. And consequently, the utilitarian standard, while it tolerates and approves those other acquired desires, up to the point beyond which they would be more injurious to the general happiness than promotive of it, enjoins and requires the cultivation of the love of virtue up to the greatest strength possible, as being above all things important to the general happiness.

It results from the preceding considerations, that there is in reality nothing desired except happiness. Whatever is desired otherwise than as a means to some end beyond itself, and ultimately to happiness, is desired as itself a part of happiness, and is not desired for itself until it has become so. Those who desire virtue for its own sake, desire it either because the consciousness of it is a pleasure, or because the consciousness of being without it is a pain, or for both reasons united; as in truth the pleasure and pain seldom exist separately, but almost always together, the same person feeling pleasure in the degree of virtue attained, and pain in not having attained more. If one of these gave him no pleasure, and the other no pain, he would not love or desire virtue, or would desire it only for the other benefits which it might produce to himself or to persons whom he cared for.

We have now, then, an answer to the question, of what sort of proof the principle of utility is susceptible. If the opinion which I have now stated is psychologically true—if human nature is so constituted as to desire nothing which is not either a part of happiness or a means of happiness, we can have no other proof, and we require no other, that these are the only things desirable. If so, happiness is the sole end of human action, and the promotion of it the test by which to judge of all human conduct; from whence it necessarily follows that it must be the criterion of morality, since a part is included in the whole.

And now to decide whether this is really so; whether mankind do desire nothing for itself but that which is a pleasure to them, or of which the absence is a pain; we have evidently arrived at a question of fact and experience, dependent, like all similar questions, upon evidence. It can only be determined by practised self-consciousness and self-observation, assisted by observation of others. I believe that these sources of evidence, impartially consulted, will declare that desiring a thing and finding it pleasant, aversion to it and thinking of it as painful, are phenomena entirely inseparable, or rather two parts of the same phenomenon; in strictness of language, two different modes of naming the same psychological fact: that to think of an object as desirable (unless for the sake of its consequences), and to think of it as pleasant, are one and the same thing; and that to desire anything, except in proportion as the idea of it is pleasant, is a physical and metaphysical impossibility.

So obvious does this appear to me, that I expect it will hardly be disputed: and the objection made will be, not that desire can possibly be directed to anything ultimately except pleasure and exemption from pain, but that the will is a different thing from desire; that a person of confirmed virtue, or any other person whose purposes are fixed, carries out his purposes without any thought of the pleasure he has in contemplating them, or expects to derive from their fulfilment; and persists in acting on them, even though these pleasures are much diminished, by changes in his character or decay of his passive sensibilities, or are outweighed by the pains which the pursuit of the purposes may bring upon him. All this I fully admit, and have stated it elsewhere, as positively and emphatically as any one. Will, the active phenomenon, is a different thing from desire, the state of passive sensibility, and though originally an offshoot from it, may in time take root and detach itself from the parent stock; so much so, that in the case of an habitual purpose, instead of willing the thing because we desire it, we often desire it only because we will it. This, however, is but an instance of that familiar fact, the power of habit, and is nowise confined to the case of virtuous actions. Many indifferent things, which men originally did from a motive of some sort, they continue to do from habit. Sometimes this is done unconsciously, the consciousness coming only after the action: at other times with conscious volition, but volition which has become habitual, and is put in operation by the force of habit, in opposition perhaps to the deliberate preference, as often happens with those who have contracted habits of vicious or hurtful indulgence. Third and last comes the case in which the habitual act of will in the individual instance is not in contradiction to the general intention prevailing at other times, but in fulfilment of it; as in the case of the person of confirmed virtue, and of all who pursue deliberately and consistently any determinate end. The distinction between will and desire thus understood is an authentic and highly important psychological fact; but the fact consists solely in this—that will, like all other parts of our constitution, is amenable to habit, and that we may will from habit what we no longer desire for itself, or desire only because we will it. It is not the less true that will, in the beginning, is entirely produced by desire; including in that term the repelling influence of pain as well as the attractive one of pleasure. Let us take into consideration, no longer the person who has a confirmed will to do right, but him in whom that virtuous will is still feeble, conquerable by temptation, and not to be fully relied on; by what means can it be strengthened? How can the will to be virtuous, where it does not exist in sufficient force, be implanted or awakened? Only by making the person *desire* virtue—by making him think of it in a pleasurable light, or of its absence in a painful one. It is by associating the doing right with pleasure, or the doing wrong with pain, or by eliciting and impressing and bringing home to the person's experience the pleasure naturally involved in the one or the pain in the other, that it is possible to call forth that will to be virtuous, which, when confirmed, acts without any thought of either pleasure or pain. Will is the child of desire, and passes out of the dominion of its parent only to come under that of habit. That which is the result of habit affords no presumption of being intrinsically good; and there would be no reason for wishing that the purpose of virtue should become independent of pleasure and pain, were it not that the influence of the pleasurable and painful associations which prompt to virtue is not sufficiently to be depended on for unerring constancy of action until it has acquired the support of habit. Both in feeling and in conduct, habit is the only thing which imparts certainty; and it is because of the importance to others of being able to rely absolutely on one's feelings and conduct, and to oneself of being able to rely on one's own, that the will to do right ought to be cultivated into this habitual independence. In other words, this state of the will is a means to good, not intrinsically a good; and does not contradict the doctrine that nothing is a good to human beings but in so far as it is either itself pleasurable, or a means of attaining pleasure or averting pain.

But if this doctrine be true, the principle of utility is proved. Whether it is so or not, must now be left to the consideration of the thoughtful reader.

William James (1842–1910), American philosopher and psychologist, was Professor of Philosophy at Harvard University.

William James

THE MORAL PHILOSOPHER AND THE MORAL LIFE

I

There are three questions in ethics which must be kept apart. Let them be called respectively the *psychological* question, the *metaphysical* question, and the *casuistic* question. The psychological question asks after the historical *origin* of our moral ideas and judgments; the metaphysical question asks what the very *meaning* of the words 'good,' 'ill,' and 'obligation' are; the casuistic question asks what is the *measure* of the various goods and ills which men recognize, so that the philosopher may settle the true order of human obligations.

●　●　●

The next one in order is the metaphysical question, of what we mean by the words 'obligation,' 'good,' and 'ill.'

Reprinted from *The Will to Believe* (1896).

II

First of all, it appears that such words can have no application or relevancy in a world in which no sentient life exists. Imagine an absolutely material world, containing only physical and chemical facts, and existing from eternity without a God, without even an interested spectator: would there be any sense in saying of that world that one of its states is better than another? Or if there were two such worlds possible, would there be any rhyme or reason in calling one good and the other bad,—good or bad positively, I mean, and apart from the fact that one might relate itself better than the other to the philosopher's private interests? But we must leave these private interests out of the account, for the philosopher is a mental fact, and we are asking whether goods and evils and obligations exist in physical facts *per se*. Surely there is no *status* for good and evil to exist in, in a purely insentient world. How can one physical fact, considered simply as a physical fact, be 'better' than another? Betterness is not a physical relation. In its mere material capacity, a thing can no more be good or bad than it can be pleasant or painful. Good for what? Good for the production of another physical fact, do you say? But what in a purely physical universe demands the production of that other fact? Physical facts simply *are* or are *not;* and neither when present or absent, can they be supposed to make demands. If they do, they can only do so by having desires; and then they have ceased to be purely physical facts, and have become facts of conscious sensibility. Goodness, badness, and obligation must be *realized* somewhere in order really to exist; and the first step in ethical philosophy is to see that no merely inorganic 'nature of things' can realize them. Neither moral relations nor the moral law can swing *in vacuo*. Their only habitat can be a mind which feels them; and no world composed of merely physical facts can possibly be a world to which ethical propositions apply.

The moment one sentient being, however, is made a part of the universe, there is a chance for goods and evils really to exist. Moral relations now have their *status,* in that being's consciousness. So far as he feels anything to be good, he *makes* it good. It *is* good, for him; and being good for him, is absolutely good, for he is the sole creator of values in that universe, and outside of his opinion things have no moral character at all.

In such a universe as that it would of course be absurd to raise the question of whether the solitary thinker's judgments of good and ill are true or not. Truth supposes a standard outside of the thinker to which he must conform; but here the thinker is a sort of divinity, subject to no higher judge. Let us call the supposed universe which he inhabits a *moral solitude*. In such a moral solitude it is clear that there can be no outward obligation, and that the only trouble the god-like thinker is liable to have will be over the consistency of his own several ideals with one another. Some of these will no doubt be more pungent and appealing than the rest, their goodness will have a profounder, more penetrating taste; they will return to haunt him with more obstinate regrets if violated. So the thinker will have to order his life with them as its chief determinants, or else remain inwardly discordant and unhappy. Into whatever equilibrium he may settle, though, and however he may straighten out his system, it will be a right system; for beyond the facts of his own subjectivity there is nothing moral in the world.

If now we introduce a second thinker with his likes and dislikes into the universe, the ethical stiuation becomes much more complex, and several possibilities are immediately seen to obtain.

One of these is that the thinkers may ignore each other's attitude about good and evil altogether, and each continue to indulge his own preferences, indifferent to what the other may feel or do. In such a case we have a world with twice as much of the ethical quality in it as our moral solitude, only it is without ethical unity. The same object is good or bad there, according as you measure it by the view which this one or that one of the thinkers takes. Nor can you find any possible ground in such a world for saying that one thinker's opinion is more correct than the other's, or that either has the truer moral sense. Such a world, in short, is not a moral universe but a moral dualism. Not only is there no single point of view within it from which the values of things can be un-equivocally judged, but there is not even a demand for such a point of view, since the two thinkers are supposed to be indifferent to each other's thoughts and acts. Multiply the thinkers into a pluralism, and we find realized for us in the ethical sphere something like that world which the antique sceptics conceived of,—in which individual minds are the mea-sures of all things, and in which no one 'objective' truth, but only a multitude of 'subjective' opinions, can be found.

But this is the kind of world with which the philosopher, so long as he holds to the hope of a philosophy, will not put up. Among the various ideals represented, there must be, he thinks, some which have the more truth or authority; and to these the others *ought* to yield, so that system and subordination may reign. Here in the word 'ought' the notion of *obligation* comes emphatically into view, and the next thing in order must be to make its meaning clear.

Since the outcome of the discussion so far has been to show us that nothing can be good or right except so far as some consciousness feels it to be good or thinks it to be right, we perceive on the very threshold that the real superiority and authority which are postulated by the philosopher to reside in some of the opinions, and the really inferior character which he supposes must belong to others, cannot be explained by any abstract moral 'nature of things' existing antecedently to the concrete thinkers themselves with their ideals. Like the positive attributes good and bad, the comparative ones better and worse must be *realized* in order to be real. If one ideal judgment be objectively better than another, the betterness must be made flesh by being lodged concretely in some one's actual perception. It cannot float in the atmosphere, for it is not a sort of meteorological phenomenon, like the aurora borealis or the zodiacal light. Its *esse* is *percipi*, like the *esse* of the ideals themselves between which it obtains. The philosopher, therefore, who seeks to know which ideal ought to have supreme weight and which one ought to be subordinated, must trace the *ought* itself to the *de facto* constitution of some existing consciousness, behind which, as one of the data of the universe, he as a purely ethical philosopher is unable to go. This consciousness must make the one ideal right by feeling it to be right, the other wrong by feeling it to be wrong. But now what particular consciousness in the universe *can* enjoy this prerogative of obliging others to conform to a rule which it lays down?

If one of the thinkers were obviously divine, while all the rest were human, there would probably be no practical dispute about the matter. The divine thought would be the model, to which the others should conform. But still the theoretic question would remain, What is the ground of the obligation, even here?

In our first essays at answering this question, there is an inevitable tendency to slip into an assumption which ordinary men follow when they are disputing with one another about questions of good and bad. They imagine an abstract moral order in which the objective truth resides; and each tries to prove that this pre-existing order is more accurately reflected in his own ideas than in those of his adversary. It is because one disputant is backed by this overarching abstract order that we think the other should submit. Even so, when it is a question no longer of two finite thinkers, but of God and ourselves,—we follow our usual habit, and imagine a sort of *de jure* relation, which antedates and overarches the mere facts, and would make it right that we should conform our thoughts to God's thoughts, even though he made no claim to that effect, and though we preferred *de facto* to go on thinking for ourselves.

But the moment we take a steady look at the question, *we see not only that without a claim actually made by some concrete person there can be no obligation, but that there is some obligation wherever there is a claim.* Claim and obligation are, in fact, coextensive terms; they cover each other exactly. Our ordinary attitude of regarding ourselves as subject to an overarching system of moral relations, true 'in themselves,' is therefore either an out-and-out superstition, or else it must be treated as a merely provisional abstraction from that real Thinker in whose actual demand upon us to think as he does our obligation must be ultimately based. In a theistic-ethical philosophy that thinker in question is, of course, the Deity to whom the existence of the universe is due.

I know well how hard it is for those who are accustomed to what I have called the superstitious view, to realize that every *de facto* claim creates in so far forth an obligation. We inveterately think that something which we call the 'validity' of the claim is what gives to it its obligatory character, and that this validity is something outside of the claim's mere existence as a matter of fact. It rains down upon the claim, we think, from some sublime dimension of being, which the moral law inhabits, much as upon the steel of the compass-needle the influence of the Pole rains down from out of the starry heavens. But again, how can such an inorganic abstract character of imperativeness, additional to the imperativeness which is in the concrete claim itself, *exist?* Take any demand, however slight, which any creature, however weak, may make. Ought it not, for its own sole sake, to be satisfied? If not, prove why not. The only possible kind of proof you could adduce would be the exhibition of another creature who should make a demand that ran the other way. The only possible reason there can be why any phenomenon ought to exist is that such a phenomenon actually is desired. Any desire is imperative to the extent of its amount; it *makes* itself valid by the fact that it exists at all. Some desires, truly enough, are small desires; they are put forward by insignificant persons, and we customarily make light of the obligations which they bring. But the fact that such personal demands as these impose small obligations does not keep the largest obligations from being personal demands.

If we must talk impersonally, to be sure we can say that 'the universe' requires, exacts, or makes obligatory such or such an action, whenever it expresses itself through the desires of such or such a creature. But it is better not to talk about the universe in this personified way, unless we believe in a universal or divine consciousness which actually exists. If there be such a consciousness, then its demands carry the most of obligation simply because they are the greatest in amount. But it is even then not *abstractly* right that we should respect them. It is only *concretely* right,—or right after the fact, and by virtue of the fact, that they are actually made. Suppose we do not respect them, as seems largely to be the case in this queer world. That ought not to be, we say; that is wrong. But in what way is this fact of wrongness made more acceptable or intelligible when we imagine it to consist rather in the laceration of an *a priori* ideal order than in the disappointment of a living personal God? Do we, perhaps, think that we cover God and protect him and make his impotence over us less ultimate, when we back him up with this *a priori* blanket from which he may draw some warmth of further appeal? But the only force of appeal to *us,* which either a living God or an abstract ideal order can wield, is found in the 'everlasting ruby vaults' of our own human hearts, as they happen to beat responsive and not irresponsive to the claim. So far as they do feel it when made by a living consciousness, it is life answering to life. A claim thus livingly acknowledged is acknowledged with a solidity and fulness which no thought of an 'ideal' backing can render more complete; while if, on the other hand, the heart's response is withheld, the stubborn phenomenon is there of an impotence in the claims which the universe embodies, which no talk about an eternal nature of things can gloze over or dispel. An ineffective *a priori* order is as impotent a thing as an ineffective God; and in the eye of philosophy, it is as hard a thing to explain.

We may now consider that what we distinguished as the metaphysical question in ethical philosophy is sufficiently answered, and that we have learned what the words 'good,' 'bad,' and 'obligation' severally mean. They mean no absolute natures, independent of personal support. They are objects of feeling and desire, which have no foothold or anchorage in Being, apart from the existence of actually living minds.

Wherever such minds exist, with judgments of good and ill, and demands upon one another, there is an ethical world in its essential features. Were all other things, gods and men and starry heavens, blotted out from this universe, and were there left but one rock with two loving souls upon it, that rock would have as thoroughly moral a constitution as any possible world which the eternities and immensities could harbor. It would be a tragic constitution, because the rock's inhabitants would die. But while they lived, there would be real good things and real bad things in the universe; there would be obligations, claims, and expectations; obediences, refusals, and disappointments; compunctions and longings for harmony to come again, and inward peace of conscience when it was restored; there would, in short, be a moral life, whose active energy would have no limit but the intensity of interest in each other with which the hero and heroine might be endowed.

We, on this terrestrial globe, so far as the visible facts go, are just like the inhabitants of such a rock. Whether a God exist, or whether no God exist, in yon blue heaven above us bent, we form at any rate an ethical republic here below. And the first reflection which this leads to is that ethics have as genuine and real a foothold in a universe where the highest consciousness is human, as in a universe where there is a God as well. 'The religion of humanity' affords a basis for ethics as well as theism does. Whether the purely human system can gratify the philosopher's demand as well as the other is a different question, which we ourselves must answer ere we close.

III

The last fundamental question in Ethics was, it will be remembered, the *casuistic* question. Here we are, in a world where the existence of a divine thinker has been and perhaps always will be doubted by some of the lookers-on, and where, in spite of the presence of a large number of ideals in which human beings agree, there are a mass of others about which no general consensus obtains. It is hardly necessary to present a literary picture of this, for the facts are too well known. The wars of the flesh and the spirit in each man, the concupiscences of different individuals pursuing the same unshareable material or social prizes, the ideals which contrast so according to races, circumstances, temperaments, philosophical beliefs, etc.,—all form a maze of apparently inextricable confusion with no obvious Ariadne's thread to lead one out. Yet the philosopher, just because he is a philosopher, adds his own peculiar ideal to the confusion (with which if he were willing to be a sceptic he would be passably content), and insists that over all these individual opinions there is a *system of truth* which he can discover if he only takes sufficient pains.

We stand ourselves at present in the place of that philosopher, and must not fail to realize all the features that the situation comports. In the first place we will not be sceptics; we hold to it that there is a truth to be ascertained. But in the second place we have just gained the insight that that truth cannot be a self-proclaiming set of laws, or an abstract 'moral reason,' but can only exist in act, or in the shape of an opinion held by some thinker really to be found. There is, however, no visible thinker invested with authority. Shall we then simply proclaim our own ideals as the lawgiving ones? No; for if we are true philosophers we must throw our own spontaneous ideals, even the dearest, impartially in with that total mass of ideals which are fairly to be judged. But how then can we as philosophers ever find a test; how avoid complete moral scepticism on the one hand, and on the other escape bringing a wayward personal standard of our own along with us, on which we simply pin our faith?

The dilemma is a hard one, nor does it grow a bit more easy as we revolve it in our minds. The entire undertaking of the philosopher obliges him to seek an impartial test. That test, however, must be incarnated in the demand of some actually existent person; and how can he pick out the person save by an act in which his own sympathies and prepossessions are implied?

One method indeed presents itself, and has as a matter of history been taken by the more serious ethical schools. If the heap of things demanded proved on inspection less chaotic than at first they seemed, if they furnished their own relative test and measure, then the casuistic problem would be solved. If it were found that all goods *qua* goods contained a common essence, then the amount of this essence involved in any one good would show its rank in the scale of goodness, and order could be quickly made; for this essence would be *the* good upon which all thinkers were agreed, the relatively objective and universal good that the philosopher seeks. Even his own private ideals would be measured by their share of it, and find their rightful place among the rest.

Various essences of good have thus been found and proposed as bases of the ethical system. Thus, to be a mean between two extremes; to be recognized by a special intuitive faculty; to make the agent happy for the moment; to make others as well as him happy in the long run; to add to his perfection or dignity; to harm no one; to follow from reason or flow from universal law; to be in accordance with the will of God; to promote the survival of the human species on this planet,—are so many tests, each of which has been maintained by somebody to constitute the essence of all good things or actions so far as they are good.

No one of the measures that have been actually proposed has, however, given general satisfaction. Some are obviously not universally present in all cases,—*e.g.*, the character of harming no one, or that of following a universal law; for the best course is often cruel; and many acts are reckoned good on the sole condition that they be exceptions, and serve not as examples of a universal law. Other characters, such as following the will of God, are unascertainable and vague. Others again, like survival, are quite indeterminate in their consequences, and leave us in the lurch where we most need their help: a philosopher of the Sioux Nation, for example, will be certain to use the survival-criterion in a very different way from ourselves. The best, on the whole, of these marks and measures of goodness seems to be the capacity to bring happiness. But in order not to break down fatally, this test must be taken to cover innumerable acts and impulses that never *aim* at happiness; so that, after all, in seeking for a universal principle we inevitably are carried onward to the *most* universal principle,—that *the essence of good is simply to satisfy demand.* The demand may be for anything under the sun. There is really no more ground for supposing that all our demands can be accounted for by one universal underlying kind of motive than there is ground for supposing that all physical phenomena are cases of a single law. The elementary forces in ethics are probably as plural as those of physics are. The various ideals have no common character apart from the fact that they are ideals. No single abstract principle can be so used as to yield to the philosopher anything like a scientifically accurate and genuinely useful casuistic scale.

A look at another peculiarity of the ethical universe, as we find it, will still further show us the philosopher's perplexities. As a purely theoretic problem, namely, the casuistic question would hardly ever come up at all. If the ethical philosopher were only asking after the best *imaginable* system of goods he would indeed have an easy task; for all demands as such are *prima facie* respectable, and the best simply imaginary world would be one in which *every* demand was gratified as soon as made. Such a world would, however, have to have a physical constitution entirely different from that of the one which we inhabit. It would need not only a space, but a time, of *n*-dimensions, to include all the acts and experiences incompatible with one another here below, which would then go on in conjunction,—such as spending our money, yet growing rich; taking our holiday, yet getting ahead with our work; shooting and fishing, yet doing no hurt to the beasts; gaining no end of experience, yet keeping our youthful freshness of heart; and the like. There can be no question that such a system of things, however brought about, would be the absolutely ideal system; and that if a philosopher could create universes *a priori,* and provide all the mechanical conditions, that is the sort of universe which he should unhesitatingly create.

But this world of ours is made on an entirely different pattern, and the casuistic question here is most tragically practical. The actually possible in this world is vastly narrower than all that is demanded; and there is always a *pinch* between the ideal and the actual which can only be got through by leaving part of the ideal behind. There is hardly a good which we can imagine except as competing for the possession of the same bit of space and time with some other imagined good. Every end of desire that presents itself appears exclusive of some other end of desire. Shall a man drink and smoke, *or* keep his nerves in condition?—he cannot do both. Shall he follow his fancy for Amelia, *or* for Henrietta?—both cannot be the choice of his heart. Shall he have the dear old Republican party, *or* a spirit of unsophistication in public affairs?—he cannot have both, etc. So that the ethical philosopher's demand for the right scale of subordination in ideals is the fruit of an altogether practical need. Some part of the ideal must be butchered, and he needs to know which part. It is a tragic situation, and no mere speculative conundrum, with which he has to deal.

•   •   •

What can he do, then, it will now be asked, except to fall back on scepticism and give up the notion of being a philosopher at all?

But do we not already see a perfectly definite path of escape which is open to him just because he is a philosopher, and not the champion of one particular ideal? Since everything which is demanded is by that fact a good, must not the guiding principle for ethical philosophy (since all demands conjointly cannot be satisfied in this poor world) be simply to satisfy at all times *as many demands as we can?* That act must be the best act, accordingly, which makes for the *best whole,* in the sense of awakening the least sum of dissatisfactions. In the casuistic scale, therefore, those ideals must be written highest which *prevail at the least cost,* or by whose realization the least possible number of other ideals are destroyed. Since victory and defeat there must be, the victory to be philosophically prayed for is that of the more inclusive side,—of the side which even in the hour of triumph will to some degree do justice to the ideals in which the vanquished party's interests lay. The course of history is nothing but the story of men's struggles from generation to generation to find the more and more inclusive order. *Invent some manner* of realizing your own ideals which will also satisfy the alien demands,—that and that only is the path of peace! Following this path, society has shaken itself into one sort of relative equilibrium after another by a series of social discoveries quite analogous to those of science. Polyandry and polygamy and slavery, private warfare and liberty to kill, judicial torture and arbitrary royal power have slowly succumbed to actually aroused complaints; and though some one's ideals are unquestionably the worse off for each improvement, yet a vastly greater total number of them find shelter in our civilized society than in the older savage ways. So far then, and up to date, the casuistic scale is made for the philosopher already far better than he can ever make it for himself. An experiment of the most searching kind has proved that the laws and usages of the land are what yield the maximum of satisfaction to the thinkers taken all together. The presumption in cases of conflict must always be in favor of the conventionally recognized good. The philosopher must be a conservative, and in the construction of his casuistic scale must put the things most in accordance with the customs of the community on top.

And yet if he be a true philosopher he must see that there is nothing final in any actually given equilibrium of human ideals, but that, as our present laws and customs have fought and conquered other past ones, so they will in their turn be overthrown by any newly discovered order which will hush up the complaints that they still give rise to, without producing others louder still. "Rules are made for man, not man for rules,"—that one sentence is enough to immortalize Green's Prolegomena to Ethics. And although a man always risks much when he breaks away from established rules and strives to realize a larger ideal whole than they permit, yet the philosopher must allow that it is at all times open to any one to make the experiment, provided he fear not to stake his life and character upon the throw. The pinch is always here. Pent in under every system of moral rules are innumerable persons whom it weighs upon, and goods which it represses; and these are always rumbling and grumbling in the background, and ready for any issue by which they may get free. See the abuses which the institution of private property covers, so that even to-day it is shamelessly asserted among us that one of the prime functions of the national government is to help the adroiter citizens to grow rich. See the unnamed and unnamable sorrows which the tyranny, on the whole so beneficent, of the marriage-institution brings to so many, both of the married and the unwed. See the wholesale loss of opportunity under our *régime* of so-called equality and industrialism, with the drummer and the counter-jumper in the saddle, for so many faculties and graces which could flourish in the feudal world. See our kindliness for the humble and the outcast, how it wars with that stern weeding-out which until now has been the condition of every perfection in the breed. See everywhere the struggle and the squeeze; and everlastingly the problem how to make them less. The anarchists, nihilists, and free-lovers; the free-silverites, socialists, and single-tax men; the free-traders and civil-service reformers; the prohibitionists and anti-vivisectionists; the radical darwinians with their idea of the suppression of the weak,—these and all the conservative sentiments of society arrayed against them, are simply deciding through actual experiment by what sort of conduct the maximum amount of good can be gained and kept in this world. These experiments are to be judged, not *a priori,* but by actual finding, after the fact of their making, how much more outcry or how much appeasement comes about. What closet-solutions can possibly anticipate the result of trials made on such a scale? Or what can any superficial theorist's judgment be worth, in a world where every one of hundreds of ideals has its special champion already provided in the shape of some genius expressly born to feel it, and to fight to death in its behalf? The pure philosopher can only follow the windings of the spectacle, confident that the line of least resistance will always be towards the richer and the more inclusive arrangement, and that by one tack after another some approach to the kingdom of heaven is incessantly made.

IV

All this amounts to saying that, so far as the casuistic question goes, ethical science is just like physical science, and instead of being deducible all at once from abstract principles, must simply bide its time, and be ready to revise its conclusions from day to day. The presumption of course, in both sciences, always is that the vulgarly accepted opinions are true, and the right casuistic order that which public opinion believes in; and surely it would be folly quite as great, in most of us, to strike out independently and to aim at originality in ethics as in physics. Every now and then, however, some one is born with the right to be original, and his revolutionary thought or action may bear prosperous fruit. He may replace old 'laws of nature' by better ones; he may, by breaking old moral rules in a certain place, bring in a total condition of things more ideal than would have followed had the rules been kept.

*James Rachels is Assistant Professor of Philosophy at
New York University.*

James Rachels

EGOISM AND MORAL SCEPTICISM

1. Our ordinary thinking about morality is full of assumptions that we almost never question. We assume, for example, that we have an obligation to consider the welfare of other people when we decide what actions to perform or what rules to obey; we think that we must refrain from acting in ways harmful to others, and that we must respect their rights and interests as well as our own. We also assume that people are in fact capable of being motivated by such considerations, that is, that people are not wholly selfish and that they do sometimes act in the interests of others.

Both of these assumptions have come under attack by moral sceptics, as long ago as by Glaucon in Book II of Plato's *Republic*. Glaucon recalls the legend of Gyges, a shepherd who was said to have found a magic ring in a fissure opened by an earthquake. The ring would make its wearer invisible and thus would enable him to go anywhere and do anything undetected. Gyges used the power of the ring to gain entry to the Royal

---

Published here for the first time.

Palace where he seduced the Queen, murdered the King, and subsequently seized the throne. Now Glaucon asks us to determine that there are two such rings, one given to a man of virtue and one given to a rogue. The rogue, of course, will use his ring unscrupulously and do anything necessary to increase his own wealth and power. He will recognize no moral constraints on his conduct, and, since the cloak of invisibility will protect him from discovery, he can do anything he pleases without fear of reprisal. So, there will be no end to the mischief he will do. But how will the so-called virtuous man behave? Glaucon suggests that he will behave no better than the rogue: "No one, it is commonly believed, would have such iron strength of mind as to stand fast in doing right or keep his hands off other men's goods, when he could go to the market-place and fearlessly help himself to anything he wanted, enter houses and sleep with any woman he chose, set prisoners free and kill men at his pleasure, and in a word go about among men with the powers of a god. He would behave no better than the other; both would take the same course."[1] Moreover, why shouldn't he? Once he is freed from the fear of reprisal, why shouldn't a man simply do what he pleases, or what he thinks is best for himself? What reason is there for him to continue being "moral" when it is clearly not to his own advantage to do so?

These sceptical views suggested by Glaucon have come to be known as *psychological egoism* and *ethical egoism* respectively. Psychological egoism is the view that all men are selfish in everything that they do, that is, that the only motive from which anyone ever acts is self-interest. On this view, even when men are acting in ways apparently calculated to benefit others, they are actually motivated by the belief that acting in this way is to their own advantage, and if they did not believe this, they would not be doing that action. Ethical egoism is, by contrast, a normative view about how men *ought* to act. It is the view that, regardless of how men do in fact behave, they have no obligation to do anything except what is in their own interests. According to the ethical egoist, a person is always justified in doing whatever is in his own interests, regardless of the effect on others.

Clearly, if either of these views is correct, then "the moral institution of life" (to use Butler's well-turned phrase) is very different than what we normally think. The majority of mankind is grossly deceived about what is, or ought to be, the case, where morals are concerned.

2. Psychological egoism seems to fly in the face of the facts. We are tempted to say: "Of course people act unselfishly all the time. For ex-

---

[1] *The Republic of Plato,* translated by F. M. Cornford (Oxford, 1941), p. 45.

ample, Smith gives up a trip to the country, which he would have enjoyed very much, in order to stay behind and help a friend with his studies, which is a miserable way to pass the time. This is a perfectly clear case of unselfish behavior, and if the psychological egoist thinks that such cases do not occur, then he is just mistaken." Given such obvious instances of "unselfish behavior," what reply can the egoist make? There are two general arguments by which he might try to show that all actions, including those such as the one just outlined, are in fact motivated by self-interest. Let us examine these in turn:

A. The first argument goes as follows. If we describe one person's action as selfish, and another person's action as unselfish, we are over-looking the crucial fact that in both cases, assuming that the action is done voluntarily, *the agent is merely doing what he most wants to do.* If Smith stays behind to help his friend, that only shows that he wanted to help his friend more than he wanted to go to the country. And why should he be praised for his "unselfishness" when he is only doing what he most wants to do? So, since Smith is only doing what he wants to do, he cannot be said to be acting unselfishly.

This argument is so bad that it would not deserve to be taken seriously except for the fact that so many otherwise intelligent people have been taken in by it. First, the argument rests on the premise that people never voluntarily do anything except what they want to do. But this is patently false; there are at least two classes of actions that are exceptions to this generalization. One is the set of actions which we may not want to do, but which we do anyway as a means to an end which we want to achieve; for example, going to the dentist in order to stop a toothache, or going to work every day in order to be able to draw our pay at the end of the month. These cases may be regarded as consistent with the spirit of the egoist argument, however, since the ends mentioned are wanted by the agent. But the other set of actions are those which we do, not because we want to, nor even because there is an end which we want to achieve, but because we feel ourselves *under an obligation* to do them. For example, someone may do something because he has promised to do it, and thus feels obligated, even though he does not want to do it. It is sometimes suggested that in such cases we do the action because, after all, we want to keep our promises; so, even here, we are doing what we want. How-ever, this dodge will not work: if I have promised to do something, and if I do not want to do it, then it is simply false to say that I want to keep my promise. In such cases we feel a conflict precisely because we do *not* want to do what we feel obligated to do. It is reasonable to think that Smith's action falls roughly into this second category: he might stay behind, not because he wants to, but because he feels that his friend needs help.

But suppose we were to concede, for the sake of the argument, that all voluntary action is motivated by the agent's wants, or at least that Smith is so motivated. Even if this were granted, it would not follow that Smith is acting selfishly or from self-interest. For if Smith wants to do something that will help his friend, even when it means forgoing his own enjoyments, that is precisely what makes him *unselfish*. What else could unselfishness be, if not wanting to help others? Another way to put the same point is to say that it is the *object* of a want that determines whether it is selfish or not. The mere fact that I am acting on *my* wants does not mean that I am acting selfishly; that depends on *what it is* that I want. If I want only my own good, and care nothing for others, then I am selfish; but if I also want other people to be well-off and happy, and if I act on *that* desire, then my action is not selfish. So much for this argument.

B. The second argument for psychological egoism is this. Since so-called unselfish actions always produce a sense of self-satisfaction in the agent,[2] and since this sense of satisfaction is a pleasant state of consciousness, it follows that the point of the action is really to achieve a pleasant state of consciousness, rather than to bring about any good for others. Therefore, the action is "unselfish" only at a superficial level of analysis. Smith will feel much better with himself for having stayed to help his friend—if he had gone to the country, he would have felt terrible about it—and that is the real point of the action. According to a well-known story, this argument was once expressed by Abraham Lincoln:

> Mr. Lincoln once remarked to a fellow-passenger on an old-time mud-coach that all men were prompted by selfishness in doing good. His fellow-passenger was antagonizing this position when they were passing over a corduroy bridge that spanned a slough. As they crossed this bridge they espied an old razor-backed sow on the bank making a terrible noise because her pigs had got into the slough and were in danger of drowning. As the old coach began to climb the hill, Mr. Lincoln called out, "Driver, can't you stop just a moment?" Then Mr. Lincoln jumped out, ran back, and lifted the little pigs out of the mud and water and placed them on the bank. When he returned, his companion remarked: "Now, Abe, where does selfishness come in on this little episode?" "Why, bless your soul, Ed, that was the very essence of selfishness. I should have had no peace of mind all day had I gone on and left that suffering old sow worrying over those pigs. I did it to get peace of mind, don't you see?"[3]

[2] Or, as it is sometimes said, "It gives him a clear conscience," or "He couldn't sleep at night if he had done otherwise," or "He would have been ashamed of himself for not doing it," and so on.

[3] Frank C. Sharp, *Ethics* (New York, 1928), pp. 74–75. Quoted from the Springfield (Ill.) *Monitor* in the *Outlook,* vol. 56, p. 1059.

This argument suffers from defects similar to the previous one. Why should we think that merely because someone derives satisfaction from helping others this makes him selfish? Isn't the unselfish man precisely the one who *does* derive satisfaction from helping others, while the selfish man does not? If Lincoln "got peace of mind" from rescuing the piglets, does this show him to be selfish, or, on the contrary, doesn't it show him to be compassionate and good-hearted? (If a man were truly selfish, why should it bother his conscience that *others* suffer—much less pigs?) Similarly, it is nothing more than shabby sophistry to say, because Smith takes satisfaction in helping his friend, that he is behaving selfishly. If we say this rapidly, while thinking about something else, perhaps it will sound all right; but if we speak slowly, and pay attention to what we are saying, it sounds plain silly.

Moreover, suppose we ask *why* Smith derives satisfaction from helping his friend. The answer will be, it is because Smith cares for him and wants him to succeed. If Smith did not have these concerns, then he would take no pleasure in assisting him; and these concerns, as we have already seen, are the marks of unselfishness, not selfishness. To put the point more generally: if we have a positive attitude toward the attainment of some goal, then we may derive satisfaction from attaining that goal. But the *object* of our attitude is *the attainment of that goal;* and we must want to attain the goal *before* we can find any satisfaction in it. We do not, in other words, desire some sort of "pleasurable consciousness" and then try to figure out how to achieve it; rather, we desire all sorts of different things—money, a new fishing-boat, to be a better chess-player, to get a promotion in our work, etc.—and because we desire these things, we derive satisfaction from attaining them. And so, if someone desires the welfare and happiness of another person, he will derive satisfaction from that; but this does not mean that this satisfaction is the object of his desire, or that he is in any way selfish on account of it.

It is a measure of the weakness of psychological egoism that these insupportable arguments are the ones most often advanced in its favor. Why, then, should anyone ever have thought it a true view? Perhaps because of a desire for theoretical simplicity: In thinking about human conduct, it would be nice if there were some simple formula that would unite the diverse phenomena of human behavior under a single explanatory principle, just as simple formulae in physics bring together a great many apparently different phenomena. And since it is obvious that self-regard is an overwhelmingly important factor in motivation, it is only natural to wonder whether all motivation might not be explained in these terms. But the answer is clearly No; while a great many human actions are motivated entirely or in part by self-interest, only by a deliberate distortion of the facts can we say that all conduct is so motivated. This will be clear, I think, if we correct three confusions which are commonplace. The exposure of these confusions will remove the last traces of plausibility from the psychological egoist thesis.

The first is the confusion of selfishness with self-interest. The two are clearly not the same. If I see a physician when I am feeling poorly, I am acting in my own interest but no one would think of calling me "selfish" on account of it. Similarly, brushing my teeth, working hard at my job, and obeying the law are all in my self-interest but none of these are examples of selfish conduct. This is because selfish behavior is behavior that ignores the interests of others, in circumstances in which their interests ought not to be ignored. This concept has a definite evaluative flavor; to call someone "selfish" is not just to describe his action but to condemn it. Thus, you would not call me selfish for eating a normal meal in normal circumstances (although it may surely be in my self-interest); but you would call me selfish for hoarding food while others about are starving.

The second confusion is the assumption that every action is done *either* from self-interest or from other-regarding motives. Thus, the egoist concludes that if there is no such thing as genuine altruism then all actions must be done from self-interest. But this is certainly a false dichotomy. The man who continues to smoke cigarettes, even after learning about the connection between smoking and cancer, is surely not acting from self-interest, not even by his own standards—self-interest would dictate that he quit smoking at once—and he is not acting altruistically either. He *is,* no doubt, smoking for the pleasure of it, but all that this shows is that undisciplined pleasure-seeking and acting from self-interest are very different. This is what led Butler to remark that "The thing to be lamented is, not that men have so great regard to their own good or interest in the present world, for they have not enough."[4]

The last two paragraphs show (*a*) that it is false that all actions are selfish, and (*b*) that it is false that all actions are done out of self-interest. And it should be noted that these two points can be made, and were, without any appeal to putative examples of altruism.

The third confusion is the common but false assumption that a concern for one's own welfare is incompatible with any genuine concern for the welfare of others. Thus, since it is obvious that everyone (or very nearly

---

[4] *The Works of Joseph Butler,* edited by W. E. Gladstone (Oxford, 1896), vol. II, p. 26. It should be noted that most of the points I am making against psychological egoism were first made by Butler. Butler made all the important points; all that is left for us is to remember them.

everyone) does desire his own well-being, it might be thought that no one can really be concerned with others. But again, this is false. There is no inconsistency in desiring that everyone, including oneself *and* others, be well-off and happy. To be sure, it may happen on occasion that our own interests conflict with the interests of others, and in these cases we will have to make hard choices. But even in these cases we might sometimes opt for the interests of others, especially when the others involved are our family or friends. But more importantly, not all cases are like this: sometimes we are able to promote the welfare of others when our own interests are not involved at all. In these cases not even the strongest self-regard need prevent us from acting considerately toward others.

Once these confusions are cleared away, it seems to me obvious enough that there is no reason whatever to accept psychological egoism. On the contrary, if we simply observe people's behavior with an open mind, we may find that a great deal of it is motivated by self-regard, but by no means all of it; and that there is no reason to deny that "the moral institution of life" can include a place for the virtue of beneficence.[5]

3. The ethical egoist would say at this point, "Of course it is possible for people to act altruistically, and perhaps many people do act that way—but there is no reason why they *should* do so. A person is under no obligation to do anything except what is in his own interests."[6] This is really quite a radical doctrine. Suppose I have an urge to set fire to some public building (say, a department store) just for the fascination of watching the spectacular blaze: according to this view, the fact that several people might be burned to death provides no reason whatever why I should not do it. After all, this only concerns *their* welfare, not my own, and according to the ethical egoist the only person I need think of is myself.

Some might deny that ethical egoism has any such monstrous consequences. They would point out that it is really to my own advantage not to set the fire—for, if I do that I may be caught and put into prison (unlike Gyges, I have no magic ring for protection). Moreover, even if I

---

[5] The capacity for altruistic behavior is not unique to human beings. Some interesting experiments with rhesus monkeys have shown that these animals will refrain from operating a device for securing food if this causes other animals to suffer pain. See Masserman, Wechkin, and Terris, " 'Altruistic' Behavior in Rhesus Monkeys," *The American Journal of Psychiatry,* vol. 121 (1964), 584–585.

[6] I take this to be the view of Ayn Rand, in so far as I understand her confusing doctrine.

could avoid being caught it is still to my advantage to respect the rights and interests of others, for it is to my advantage to live in a society in which people's rights and interests are respected. Only in such a society can I live a happy and secure life; so, in acting kindly toward others, I would merely be doing my part to create and maintain the sort of society which it is to my advantage to have.[7] Therefore, it is said, the egoist would not be such a bad man; he would be as kindly and considerate as anyone else, because he would see that it is to his own advantage to be kindly and considerate.

This is a seductive line of thought, but it seems to me mistaken. Certainly it is to everyone's advantage (including the egoist's) to preserve a stable society where people's interests are generally protected. But there is no reason for the egoist to think that merely because *he* will not honor the rules of the social game, decent society will collapse. For the vast majority of people are not egoists, and there is no reason to think that they will be converted by his example—especially if he is discreet and does not unduly flaunt his style of life. What this line of reasoning shows is not that the egoist himself must act benevolently, but that he must encourage *others* to do so. He must take care to conceal from public view his own self-centered method of decision-making, and urge others to act on precepts very different from those on which he is willing to act.

The rational egoist, then, cannot advocate that egoism be universally adopted by everyone. For he wants a world in which his own interests are maximized; and if other people adopted the egoistic policy of pursuing their own interests to the exclusion of his interests, as he pursues his interests to the exclusion of theirs, then such a world would be impossible. So he himself will be an egoist, but he will want others to be altruists.

This brings us to what is perhaps the most popular "refutation" of ethical egoism current among philosophical writers—the argument that ethical egoism is at bottom inconsistent because it cannot be universalized.[8] The argument goes like this:

To say that any action or policy of action is *right* (or that it *ought* to be adopted) entails that it is right for *anyone* in the same sort of circumstances. I cannot, for example, say that it is right for me to lie to you, and yet object when you lie to me (provided, of course, that the circumstances are the same). I cannot hold that it is all right for me to drink your beer

---

[7] Cf. Thomas Hobbes, *Leviathan* (London, 1651), chap. 17.

[8] See, for example, Brian Medlin, "Ultimate Principles and Ethical Egoism," *Australasian Journal of Philosophy*, vol. 35 (1957), 111–118; and D. H. Monro, *Empiricism and Ethics* (Cambridge, 1967), chap. 16.

and then complain when you drink mine. This is just the requirement that we be consistent in our evaluations; it is a requirement of logic. Now it is said that ethical egoism cannot meet this requirement because, as we have already seen, the egoist would not want others to act in the same way that he acts. Moreover, suppose he *did* advocate the universal adoption of egoistic policies: he would be saying to Peter, "You ought to pursue your own interests even if it means destroying Paul"; and he would be saying to Paul, "You ought to pursue your own interests even if it means destroying Peter." The attitudes expressed in these two recommendations seem clearly inconsistent—he is urging the advancement of Peter's interest at one moment, and countenancing their defeat at the next. Therefore, the argument goes, there is no way to maintain the doctrine of ethical egoism as a consistent view about how we ought to act. We will fall into inconsistency whenever we try.

What are we to make of this argument? Are we to conclude that ethical egoism has been refuted? Such a conclusion, I think, would be unwarranted; for I think that we can show, contrary to this argument, how ethical egoism can be maintained consistently. We need only to interpret the egoist's position in a sympathetic way: we should say that he has in mind a certain kind of world which he would prefer over all others; it would be a world in which his own interests were maximized, regardless of the effects on other people. The egoist's primary policy of action, then, would be to act in such a way as to bring about, as nearly as possible, this sort of world. Regardless of however morally reprehensible we might find it, there is nothing *inconsistent* in someone's adopting this as his ideal and acting in a way calculated to bring it about. And if someone did adopt this as his ideal, then he would not advocate universal egoism; as we have already seen, he would want other people to be altruists. So, if he advocates any principles of conduct for the general public, they will be altruistic principles. This would not be inconsistent; on the contrary, it would be perfectly consistent with his goal of creating a world in which his own interests are maximized. To be sure, he would have to be deceitful; in order to secure the good will of others, and a favorable hearing for his exhortations to altruism, he would have to pretend that he was himself prepared to accept altruistic principles. But again, that would be all right; from the egoist's point of view, this would merely be a matter of adopting the necessary means to the achievement of his goal—and while we might not approve of this, there is nothing inconsistent about it. Again, it might be said: "He advocates one thing, but does another. Surely *that's* inconsistent." But it is not; for what he advocates and what he does are both calculated as means to an end (the *same* end, we might note); and as such, he is doing what is rationally required in each case. Therefore, contrary to the previous argument, there is nothing inconsistent in the ethical egoist's view. He cannot be refuted by the claim that he contradicts himself.

Is there, then, no way to refute the ethical egoist? If by "refute" we mean show that he has made some *logical* error, the answer is that there is not. However, there is something more that can be said. The egoist challenge to our ordinary moral convictions amounts to a demand for an explanation of why we should adopt certain policies of action, namely policies in which the good of others is given importance. We can give an answer to this demand, albeit an indirect one. The reason one ought not to do actions that would hurt other people is: other people would be hurt. The reason one ought to do actions that would benefit other people is: other people would be benefited. This may at first seem like a piece of philosophical sleight-of-hand, but it is not. The point is that the welfare of human beings is something that most of us value *for its own sake,* and not merely for the sake of something else. Therefore, when *further* reasons are demanded for valuing the welfare of human beings, we cannot point to anything further to satisfy this demand. It is not that we have no reason for pursuing these policies, but that our reason *is* that these policies are for the good of human beings.

So: if we are asked "Why shouldn't I set fire to this department store?" one answer would be "Because if you do, people may be burned to death." This is a complete, sufficient reason which does not require qualification or supplementation of any sort. If someone seriously wants to know why this action shouldn't be done, that's the reason. If we are pressed further and asked the sceptical question "But why shouldn't I do actions that will harm others?" we may not know what to say—but this is because the questioner has included in his question the very answer we would like to give: "Why shouldn't you do actions that will harm others? Because, doing those actions would harm others."

The egoist, no doubt, will not be happy with this. He will protest that *we* may accept this as a reason, but *he* does not. And here the argument stops: there are limits to what can be accomplished by argument, and if the egoist really doesn't care about other people—if he honestly doesn't care whether they are helped or hurt by his actions—then we have reached those limits. If we want to persuade him to act decently toward his fellow humans, we will have to make our appeal to such other attitudes as he does possess, by threats, bribes, or other cajolery. That is all that we can do.

Though some may find this situation distressing (we would like to be able to show that the egoist is just *wrong*), it holds no embarrassment for common morality. What we have come up against is simply a fundamental requirement of rational action, namely, that the existence of reasons for action always depends on the prior existence of certain attitudes in the agent. For example, the fact that a certain course of action would make the agent a lot of money is a reason for doing it only if the agent wants to make money; the fact that practicing at chess makes one a better player is a reason for practicing only if one wants to be a better player; and so on. Similarly, the fact that a certain action would help the agent is a reason for doing the action only if the agent cares about his own welfare, and the fact that an action would help others is a reason for doing it only if the agent cares about others. In this respect ethical egoism and what we might call ethical altruism are in exactly the same fix: both require that the agent *care* about himself, or about other people, before they can get started.

So a nonegoist will accept "It would harm another person" as a reason not to do an action simply because he cares about what happens to that other person. When the egoist says that he does *not* accept that as a reason, he is saying something quite extraordinary. He is saying that he has no affection for friends or family, that he never feels pity or compassion, that he is the sort of person who can look on scenes of human misery with complete indifference, so long as he is not the one suffering. Genuine egoists, people who really don't care at all about anyone other than themselves, are rare. It is important to keep this in mind when thinking about ethical egoism; it is easy to forget just how fundamental to human psychological makeup the feeling of sympathy is. Indeed, a man without any sympathy at all would scarcely be recognizable as a man; and that is what makes ethical egoism such a disturbing doctrine in the first place.

4. There are, of course, many different ways in which the sceptic might challenge the assumptions underlying our moral practice. In this essay I have discussed only two of them, the two put forward by Glaucon in the passage that I cited from Plato's *Republic*. It is important that the assumptions underlying our moral practice should not be confused with particular judgments made within that practice. To defend one is not to defend the other. We may assume—quite properly, if my analysis has been correct—that the virtue of beneficence does, and indeed should, occupy an important place in "the moral institution of life"; and yet we may make constant and miserable errors when it comes to judging when and in what ways this virtue is to be exercised. Even worse, we may often

be able to make accurate moral judgments, and know what we ought to do, but not do it. For these ills, philosophy alone is not the cure.

SUGGESTIONS FOR FURTHER READING

BRANDT, RICHARD B., ed., *Value and Obligation: Systematic Readings in Ethics,* New York: Harcourt Brace Jovanovich, Inc., 1961. Historical and contemporary readings in ethics.

EDWARDS, PAUL, *The Logic of Moral Discourse,* New York: The Free Press, 1955. Paperback. An interesting discussion of the nature of moral disagreement.

TAYLOR, RICHARD, *Good and Evil: A New Direction,* New York: The Macmillan Company, 1970. Paperback. An intriguing discussion of a wide variety of moral issues.

PART V

SOCIAL PHILOSOPHY

Thomas Hobbes (1588–1679) was a leading figure in the development of English philosophy.

Thomas Hobbes

THE ORIGINS OF GOVERNMENT

Nature hath made men so equal, in the faculties of the body, and mind; as that though there be found one man sometimes manifestly stronger in body, or of quicker mind than another; yet when all is reckoned together, the difference between man, and man, is not so considerable, as that one man can thereupon claim to himself any benefit, to which another may not pretend, as well as he. For as to the strength of body, the weakest has strength enough to kill the strongest, either by secret machination, or by confederacy with others, that are in the same danger with himself.

And as to the faculties of the mind, setting aside the arts grounded upon words, and especially that skill of proceeding upon general, and infallible rules, called science; which very few have, and but in few things; as being not a native faculty, born with us; nor attained, as prudence, while we look after somewhat else, I find yet a greater equality amongst men, than that of strength. For prudence, is but experience; which equal

Reprinted from *Leviathan* (1651).

time, equally bestows on all men, in those things they equally apply themselves unto. That which may perhaps make such equality incredible, is but a vain conceit of one's own wisdom, which almost all men think they have in a greater degree, than the vulgar; that is, than all men but themselves, and a few others, whom by fame, or for concurring with themselves, they approve. For such is the nature of men, that howsoever they may acknowledge many others to be more witty, or more eloquent, or more learned; yet they will hardly believe there be many so wise as themselves; for they see their own wit at hand, and other men's at a distance. But this proveth rather that men are in that point equal, than unequal. For there is not ordinarily a greater sign of the equal distribution of any thing, than that every man is contented with his share.

From this equality of ability, ariseth equality of hope in the attaining of our ends. And therefore if any two men desire the same thing, which nevertheless they cannot both enjoy, they become enemies; and in the way to their end, which is principally their own conservation, and sometimes their delectation only, endeavour to destroy, or subdue one another. And from hence it comes to pass, that where an invader hath no more to fear, than another man's single power; if one plant, sow, build, or possess a convenient seat, others may probably be expected to come prepared with forces united, to dispossess, and deprive him, not only of the fruit of his labour, but also of his life, or liberty. And the invader again is in the like danger of another.

And from this diffidence of one another, there is no way for any man to secure himself, so reasonable, as anticipation; that is, by force, or wiles, to master the persons of all men he can, so long, till he see no other power great enough to endanger him: and this is no more than his own conservation requireth, and is generally allowed. Also because there be some, that taking pleasure in contemplating their own power in the acts of conquest, which they pursue farther than their security requires; if others, that otherwise would be glad to be at ease within modest bounds, should not by invasion increase their power, they would not be able, long time, by standing only on their defence, to subsist. And by consequence, such augmentation of dominion over men being necessary to a man's conservation, it ought to be allowed him.

Again, men have no pleasure, but on the contrary a great deal of grief, in keeping company, where there is no power able to over-awe them all. For every man looketh that his companion should value him, at the same rate he sets upon himself: and upon all signs of contempt, or undervaluing, naturally endeavours, as far as he dares, (which amongst them that have no common power to keep them in quiet, is far enough to make them destroy each other), to extort a greater value from his contemners, by damage; and from others, by the example.

So that in the nature of man, we find three principal causes of quarrel. First, competition; secondly, diffidence; thirdly, glory.

The first, maketh men invade for gain; the second, for safety; and the third, for reputation. The first use violence, to make themselves masters of other men's persons, wives, children, and cattle; the second, to defend them; the third, for trifles, as a word, a smile, a different opinion, and any other sign of undervalue, either direct in their persons, or by reflection in their kindred, their friends, their nation, their profession, or their name.

Hereby it is manifest, that during the time men live without a common power to keep them all in awe, they are in that condition which is called war; and such a war, as is of every man, against every man. For WAR, consisteth not in battle only, or the act of fighting; but in a tract of time, wherein the will to contend by battle is sufficiently known: and therefore the notion of *time,* is to be considered in the nature of war; as it is in the nature of weather. For as the nature of foul weather, lieth not in a shower or two of rain; but in an inclination thereto of many days together: so the nature of war, consisteth not in actual fighting; but in the known disposition thereto, during all the time there is no assurance to the contrary. All other time is PEACE.

Whatsoever therefore is consequent to a time of war, where every man is enemy to every man; the same is consequent to the time, wherein men live without other security, than what their own strength, and their own invention shall furnish them withal. In such condition, there is no place for industry; because the fruit thereof is uncertain: and consequently no culture of the earth; no navigation, nor use of the commodities that may be imported by sea; no commodious building; no instruments of moving, and removing, such things as require much force; no knowledge of the face of the earth; no account of time; no arts; no letters; no society; and which is worst of all, continual fear, and danger of violent death; and the life of man, solitary, poor, nasty, brutish, and short.

It may seem strange to some man, that has not well weighed these things; that nature should thus dissociate, and render men apt to invade, and destroy one another: and he may therefore, not trusting to this inference, made from the passions, desire perhaps to have the same confirmed by experience. Let him therefore consider with himself, when taking a journey, he arms himself, and seeks to go well accompanied; when going to sleep, he locks his doors; when even in his house he locks his chests; and this when he knows there be laws, and public officers, armed, to revenge all injuries shall be done him; what opinion he has of his fellow-subjects, when he rides armed; of his fellow citizens, when he locks his doors; and of his children, and servants, when he locks his chests. Does he not there as much accuse mankind by his actions, as I do by my words? But neither of us accuse man's nature in it. The desires, and other passions of man, are in themselves no sin. No more are the actions, that proceed from those passions, till they know a law that forbids them: which till laws be made they cannot know: nor can any law be made, till they have agreed upon the person that shall make it.

It may peradventure be thought, there was never such a time, nor condition of war as this; and I believe it was never generally so, over all the world: but there are many places, where they live so now. For the savage people in many places of America, except the government of small families, the concord whereof dependeth on natural lust, have no government at all; and live at this day in that brutish manner, as I said before. Howsoever, it may be perceived what manner of life there would be, where there were no common power to fear, by the manner of life, which men that have formerly lived under a peaceful government, use to degenerate into, in a civil war.

But though there had never been any time, wherein particular men were in a condition of war one against another; yet in all times, kings, and persons of sovereign authority, because of their independency, are in continual jealousies, and in the state and posture of gladiators; having their weapons pointing, and their eyes fixed on one another; that is, their forts, garrisons, and guns upon the frontiers of their kingdoms; and continual spies upon their neighbours; which is a posture of war. But because they uphold thereby, the industry of their subjects; there does not follow from it, that misery, which accompanies the liberty of particular men.

To this war of every man, against every man, this also is consequent; that nothing can be unjust. The notions of right and wrong, justice and injustice have there no place. Where there is no common power, there is no law: where no law, no injustice. Force, and fraud, are in war the two cardinal virtues. Justice, and injustice are none of the faculties neither of the body, nor mind. If they were, they might be in a man that were alone in the world, as well as his senses, and passions. They are qualities, that relate to men in society, not in solitude. It is consequent also to the same condition, that there be no propriety, no dominion, no *mine* and *thine* distinct; but only that to be every man's, that he can get: and for so long, as he can keep it. And thus much for the ill condition, which man by mere nature is actually placed in; though with a possibility to come out of it, consisting partly in the passions, partly in his reason.

The passions that incline men to peace, are fear of death; desire of such things as are necessary to commodious living; and a hope by their industry to obtain them. And reason suggesteth convenient articles of peace, upon which men may be drawn to agreement. These articles, are they, which otherwise are called the Laws of Nature. . . .

THE RIGHT OF NATURE, which writers commonly call *jus naturale,* is the liberty each man hath, to use his own power, as he will himself, for the preservation of his own nature; that is to say, of his own life; and consequently, of doing any thing, which in his own judgment, and reason, he shall conceive to be the aptest means thereunto.

BY LIBERTY, is understood, according to the proper signification of the word, the absence of external impediments: which impediments, may oft take away part of a man's power to do what he would; but cannot hinder him from using the power left him, according as his judgment, and reason shall dictate to him.

A LAW OF NATURE, *lex naturalis,* is a precept or general rule, found out by reason, by which a man is forbidden to do that, which is destructive of his life, or taketh away the means of preserving the same; and to omit that, by which he thinketh it may be best preserved. For though they that speak of this subject, use to confound *jus,* and *lex, right* and *law:* yet they ought to be distinguished; because RIGHT, consisteth in liberty to do, or to forbear: whereas LAW, determineth, and bindeth to one of them: so that law, and right, differ as much, as obligation, and liberty; which in one and the same matter are inconsistent.

And because the condition of man . . . is a condition of war of every one against every one; in which case every one is governed by his own reason; and there is nothing he can make use of, that may not be a help unto him, in preserving his life against his enemies; it followeth, that in such a condition, every man has a right to every thing; even to one another's body. And therefore, as long as this natural right of every man to every thing endureth, there can be no security to any man, how strong or wise soever he be, of living out the time, which nature ordinarily alloweth men to live. And consequently it is a precept, or general rule of reason, *that every man, ought to endeavour peace, as far as he has hope of obtaining it; and when he cannot obtain it, that he may seek, and use, all helps, and advantages of war.* The first branch of which rule, containeth the first, and fundamental law of nature; which is, *to seek peace, and follow it.* The second, the sum of the right of nature; which is, *by all means we can, to defend ourselves.*

From this fundamental law of nature, by which men are commanded to endeavour peace, is derived this second law; *that a man be willing, when*

*others are so too, as far-forth, as for peace, and defence of himself he
shall think it necessary, to lay down this right to all things; and be
contented with so much liberty against other men, as he would allow
other men against himself.* For as long as every man holdeth this right, of
doing any thing he liketh; so long are all men in the condition of war. But
if other men will not lay down their right, as well as he; then there is no
reason for any one, to divest himself of his: for that were to expose
himself to prey, which no man is bound to, rather than to dispose himself
to peace. This is that law of the Gospel; *whatsoever you require that
others should do to you, that do ye to them.* And that law of all men,
quod tibi fieri non vis, alteri ne feceris.

To *lay down* a man's *right* to any thing, is to *divest* himself of the
liberty, of hindering another of the benefit of his own right to the same.
For he that renounceth, or passeth away his right, giveth not to any other
man a right which he had not before; because there is nothing to which
every man had not right by nature: but only standeth out of his way, that
he may enjoy his own original right, without hindrance from him; not
without hindrance from another. So that the effect which redoundeth to
one man, by another man's defect of right, is but so much diminution of
impediments to the use of his own right original. Right is laid aside, either
by simply renouncing it; or by transferring it to another. By *simply*
RENOUNCING; when he cares not to whom the benefit thereof redoundeth.
By TRANSFERRING; when he intendeth the benefit thereof to some certain
person, or persons. And when a man hath in either manner abandoned, or
granted away his right; then he is said to be OBLIGED, or BOUND, not to
hinder those, to whom such right is granted, or abandoned, from the
benefit of it: and that he *ought,* and it is his DUTY, not to make void that
voluntary act of his own: and that such hindrance is INJUSTICE, and
INJURY, as being *sine jure;* the right being before renounced, or transferred. So that *injury,* or *injustice,* in the controversies of the world, is
somewhat like to that, which in the disputations of scholars is called
absurdity. For as it is there called an absurdity, to contradict what one
maintained in the beginning: so in the world, it is called injustice, and
injury, voluntarily to undo that, which from the beginning he had
voluntarily done. The way by which a man either simply renounceth, or
transferreth his right, is a declaration, or signification, by some voluntary
and sufficient sign, or signs, that he doth so renounce, or transfer; or hath
so renounced, or transferred the same, to him that accepteth it. And these
signs are either words only, or actions only; or, as it happeneth most
often, both words, and actions. And the same are the BONDS, by which
men are bound, and obliged: bonds, that have their strength, not from

their own nature, for nothing is more easily broken than a man's word, but from fear of some evil consequence upon the rupture.

Whensoever a man transferreth his right, or renounceth it; it is either in consideration of some right reciprocally transferred to himself; or for some other good he hopeth for thereby. For it is a voluntary act: and of the voluntary acts of every man, the object is some *good to himself*. And therefore there be some rights, which no man can be understood by any words, or other signs, to have abandoned, or transferred. As first a man cannot lay down the right of resisting them, that assault him by force, to take away his life; because he cannot be understood to aim thereby, at any good to himself. The same may be said of wounds, and chains, and imprisonment; both because there is no benefit consequent to such patience; as there is to the patience of suffering another to be wounded, or imprisoned: as also because a man cannot tell, when he seeth men proceed against him by violence, whether they intend his death or not. And lastly the motive, and end for which this renouncing, and transfer-ring of right is introduced, is nothing else but the security of a man's person, in his life, and in the means of so preserving life, as not to be weary of it. And therefore if a man by words, or other signs, seem to despoil himself of the end, for which those signs were intended; he is not to be understood as if he meant it, or that it was his will; but that he was ignorant of how such words and actions were to be interpreted.

The mutual transferring of right, is that which men call CONTRACT.

•   •   •

The final cause, end, or design of men, who naturally love liberty, and dominion over others, in the introduction of that restraint upon them-selves, in which we see them live in commonwealths, is the foresight of their own preservation, and of a more contented life thereby; that is to say, of getting themselves out from that miserable condition of war, which is necessarily consequent . . . to the natural passions of men, when there is no visible power to keep them in awe, and tie them by fear of punishment to the performance of their covenants, and observation of [the] laws of nature. . . .

For the laws of nature, as *justice, equity, modesty, mercy,* and, in sum, *doing to others, as we would be done to,* of themselves, without the terror of some power, to cause them to be observed, are contrary to our natural passions, that carry us to partiality, pride, revenge, and the like. And covenants, without the sword, are but words, and of no strength to secure a man at all. Therefore notwithstanding the laws of nature (which every one hath then kept, when he has the will to keep them, when he can do it safely) if there be no power erected, or not great enough for our security; every man will, and may lawfully rely on his own strength and art, for caution against all other men.

. . .

It is true, that certain living creatures, as bees, and ants, live sociably one with another, which are therefore by Aristotle numbered amongst political creatures; and yet have no other direction, than their particular judgments and appetites; nor speech, whereby one of them can signify to another, what he thinks expedient for the common benefit: and therefore some man may perhaps desire to know, why mankind cannot do the same. To which I answer,

First, that men are continually in competition for honour and dignity, which these creatures are not; and consequently amongst men there ariseth on that ground, envy and hatred, and finally war; but amongst these not so.

Secondly, that amongst these creatures, the common good differeth not from the private; and being by nature inclined to their private, they procure thereby the common benefit. But man, whose joy consisteth in comparing himself with other men, can relish nothing but what is eminent.

Thirdly, that these creatures, having not, as man, the use of reason, do not see, nor think they see any fault, in the administration of their common business; whereas amongst men, there are very many, that think themselves wiser, and abler to govern the public, better than the rest; and these strive to reform and innovate, one this way, another that way; and thereby bring it into distraction and civil war.

Fourthly, that these creatures, though they have some use of voice, in making known to one another their desires, and other affections; yet they want that art of words, by which some men can represent to others, that which is good, in the likeness of evil; and evil, in the likeness of good; and augment, or diminish the apparent greatness of good and evil; discontenting men, and troubling their peace at their pleasure.

Fifthly, irrational creatures cannot distinguish between *injury,* and *damage;* and therefore as long as they be at ease, they are not offended with their fellows; whereas man is then most troublesome, when he is most at ease: for then it is that he loves to shew his wisdom, and control the actions of them that govern the commonwealth.

Lastly, the agreement of these creatures is natural; that of men, is by covenant only, which is artificial: and therefore it is no wonder if there be somewhat else required, besides covenant, to make their agreement constant and lasting; which is a common power, to keep them in awe, and to direct their actions to the common benefit.

The only way to erect such a common power, as may be able to defend them from the invasion of foreigners, and the injuries of one another, and thereby to secure them in such sort, as that by their own industry, and by the fruits of the earth, they may nourish themselves and live contentedly; is, to confer all their power and strength upon one man, or upon one assembly of men, that may reduce all their wills, by plurality of voices, unto one will: which is as much as to say, to appoint one man, or assembly of men, to bear their person; and every one to own, and acknowledge himself to be author of whatsoever he that so beareth their person, shall act, or cause to be acted, in those things which concern the common peace and safety; and therein to submit their wills, every one to his will, and their judgments, to his judgment. This is more than consent, or concord; it is a real unity of them all, in one and the same person, made by covenant of every man with every man, in such manner, as if every man should say to every man, *I authorize and give up my right of governing myself, to this man, or to this assembly of men, on this condition, that thou give up thy right to him, and authorize all his actions in like manner.* This done, the multitude so united in one person, is called a COMMONWEALTH, in Latin CIVITAS. This is the generation of that great LEVIATHAN, or rather, to speak more reverently, of that *mortal god,* to which we owe under the *immortal God,* our peace and defence. For by this authority, given him by every particular man in the commonwealth, he hath the use of so much power and strength conferred on him, that by terror thereof, he is enabled to form the wills of them all, to peace at home, and mutual aid against their enemies abroad. And in him consisteth the essence of the commonwealth; which, to define it, is *one person, of whose acts a great multitude, by mutual covenants one with another, have made themselves every one the author, to the end he may use the strength and means of them all, as he shall think expedient, for their peace and common defence.*

And he that carrieth this person, is called SOVEREIGN, and said to have *sovereign power;* and every one besides, his SUBJECT. . . .

Charles Frankel is Professor of Philosophy
at Columbia University.

Charles Frankel

WHY CHOOSE DEMOCRACY?

We have been overexposed to ideologies and political abstractions in this century, and have seen how much men are willing to sacrifice for the sake of ideological certainty. It is not surprising that sensitive men have developed something close to an ideology of uncertainty, and should look with a jaundiced eye on all questions about the justification of political systems. Why choose democracy? Trained in a hard school that has taught us the perils of belief, can we say anything more than that fanaticism is odious and that democracy should be chosen because it asks us to believe in very little?

On the contrary, it asks us to believe in a great deal. I do not believe we can show that the inside truth about the universe, human history, or the human psyche commands us to adopt democratic ideals. Choosing a political ideal is not like demonstrating the truth of a theorem in some geometry, and those who think that democracy needs that kind of justification are indirectly responsible for the uncertainty about it. Despite

Reprinted from *The Democratic Prospect* (New York: Harper & Row, 1962).

the semantic inflation from which the current discussion of political ideals suffers, the reasons for choosing democracy are neither mysterious nor difficult. But they are unsettling reasons, and they ask those who accept them to bet a great deal on their capacity to live with what they have chosen.

THE SIGNIFICANCE OF THE DEMOCRATIC POLITICAL METHOD

In an area so full of grandiose claims, it is safest to begin by using the word "democracy" in its narrowest sense. So conceived, democracy is the method of choosing a government through competitive elections in which people who are not members of the governing groups participate. Whatever may be said for or against democracy so conceived, it is surely not a supreme ideal of life. It is doubtful that anyone has ever treated the right to cast a ballot once every year or so as an end in itself. A society in which the democratic political method has been consolidated, to be sure, has a tremendous source of reassurance. It possesses a peaceful method for determining who shall hold power and for effecting changes in the structure of power. Yet even peace is only one value among others. It is worth something to have security and order, but how much it is worth depends on the kind of security and order it is. The importance of the democratic political method lies mainly in its nonpolitical by-products. It is important because a society in which it is well established will probably be different in at least four respects—in the conditions that protect its liberties, in the kind of consensus that prevails, in the character of the conflicts that go on within it, and in the manner in which it educates its rulers and citizens.

First, liberties. Construed strictly as a method for choosing governments, democracy does not guarantee the citizen's personal liberties. Democratic governments have attacked personal liberties, as in colonial New England, and undemocratic governments have often protected them, as in Vienna before World War I. Yet competitive elections have their points, and it is only one of their points that they allow a society to choose its government. For in order to maintain competitive elections, it is necessary to have an opposition, the opposition must have some independent rights and powers of its own, the good opinion of some people outside government must be sought, and at least some members of the society must have protections against the vengefulness of the powers that be. And this carries a whole train of institutions behind it—courts, a press not wholly devoted to promoting the interests of those in power, and independent agencies for social inquiry and criticism.

It is these necessitating conditions for elections that give elections their long-range significance. So far as political democracy is concerned, these conditions are only means to ends: they make competitive elections possible. But it is because a system of competitive elections requires and fosters such conditions that it justifies itself. The conditions required for maintaining an honest electoral system are the best reasons for wishing to maintain it. Indeed, a man might value such a system even though he thought all elections frivolous and foolish. He would have as good a reason to do so, and perhaps a better reason, than the man who always finds himself voting happily for the winning side. The outsider and the loser are the peculiar beneficiaries of a political system that creates institutions with a vested interest in liberty.

The democratic political method, furthermore, helps to foster a different kind of social consensus. There have been many kinds of political arrangement that have allowed men to feel that the government under which they live is *their* government. There is no clear evidence that democracy is necessarily superior to other systems in promoting a sense of oneness between rulers and ruled. But the special virtue of a democratic political system is that it permits men to feel at home within it who do not regard their political leaders as their own kind, and who would lose their self-respect, indeed, if they gave their unprovisional loyalty to any human institution. Despite all that is said about democratic pressures towards conformity—and a little of what is said is true—the democratic political system ceremonializes the fact of disagreement and the virtue of independent judgment. If it is to work, it requires an extraordinarily sophisticated human attitude—loyal opposition. The mark of a civilized man, in Justice Holmes' famous maxim, is that he can act with conviction while questioning his first principles. The ultimate claim of a democratic government to authority is that it permits dissent and survives it. In this respect, it dwells on the same moral landscape as the civilized man.

The democratic political method also changes the character of the conflicts that take place in a society. The perennial problem of politics is to manage conflict. And what happens in a conflict depends in part on who the onlookers are, how they react, and what powers they have. A significant fact about political democracy is that it immensely expands the audience that looks on and that feels itself affected and involved. This is why democratic citizens so often find democracy tiring and feel that their societies are peculiarly fragile. Hobbes, who said that he and fear were born as twins, recommended despotism in the interests of psychological security as well as physical safety.

But to say that democracy expands the scope of a conflict is also to say that democracy is a technique for the socialization of conflict. It brings a wider variety of pressures to bear on those who are quarreling and extends public control over private fights and private arrangements. And it does so whether these private fights are inside the government or outside. The association of democracy with the conception of private enterprise has something paradoxical about it. In one sense, there is more important enterprise that is private—free from outside discussion and surveillance—in totalitarian systems than in democratic systems. The persistent problem in a democratic system, indeed, is to know where to draw the line, where to say that outside surveillance is out of place. That line is drawn very firmly by those who make the important decisions in totalitarian societies.

But the final contribution that the democratic political method makes to the character of the society in which it is practiced is its contribution to education. Begin with the impact of political democracy on its leaders. The democratic method, like any other political method, is a system of rules for governing political competition. And such rules have both a selective and an educational force. They favor certain kinds of men, and make certain kinds of virtue more profitable and certain kinds of vice more possible. From this point of view, the significant characteristic of democratic rules of competition is that the loser is allowed to lose with honor, and permitted to live and try again if he wants. The stakes are heavy but limited. Such a system of competition gives men with sporting moral instincts a somewhat better chance to succeed. Even its typical kind of corruption has something to be said in its favor. The greased palm is bad but it is preferable to the mailed fist.

The democratic political method, furthermore, rests on methods of mutual consultation between leaders and followers. There are various ways in which support for the policies of political leaders is obtained in a democracy, but one of the most important is that of giving men the sense that they have been asked for their opinions and that their views have been taken into account. This makes leadership in a democracy a nerve-racking affair. One of the great dangers in a democratic political system, in fact, is simply that leaders will not have the privacy and quiet necessary for serene long-range decisions. But this is the defect of a virtue. In general, power insulates. The democratic system is a calculated effort to break in on such insulation. The conditions under which democratic leaders hold power are conditions for educating them in the complexity and subtlety of the problems for which they are responsible.

And the coin has its other side. "We Athenians," said Pericles, "are able to judge policy even if we cannot originate it, and instead of looking on discussion as a stumbling-block in the way of action, we think it an indispensable preliminary to any wise action at all." But the fruits of free discussion do not show themselves only in public policy. They show themselves in the attitudes and capacities of the discussants. Democratic political arrangements are among the factors that have produced one of the painful and more promising characteristics of modern existence—men's sense that their education is inadequate, men's assertion that they have a right to be educated. And democratic politics help to promote a classic conception of education—it must be social as well as technical, general as well as special, free and not doctrinaire. We can reverse the classic conception of the relation of education to democracy and not be any further from the truth: education is not simply a prerequisite for democracy; democracy is a contribution to education.

USES OF DEMOCRACY

But enough of political systems. In any liberal view of men's business, politics is a subordinate enterprise. It has its soul-testing challenges and pleasures, and its great work to do. But like the work of commerce and industry, the work of politics is essentially servile labor. The State is not the place to turn if you want a free commentary on human experience, and governments do not produce science, philosophy, music, literature, or children—or at any rate they do not produce very convincing specimens of any of these things. Politics may achieve its own forms of excellence, but the more important human excellences are achieved elsewhere. And it is from this point of view, I think, that democracy should in the end be considered.

For the democratic idea is based on the assumption that the important ends of life are defined by private individuals in their own voluntary pursuits. Politics, for liberal democracy, is only one aspect of a civilization, a condition for civilization but not its total environment. That is probably why the air seems lighter as one travels from controlled societies to free ones. One receives an impression of vitality, the vitality of people who are going about their own business and generating their own momentum. They may be going off in more different directions than the members of a centrally organized society, but the directions are their own. The best reasons for choosing democracy lie in the qualities it is capable of bringing to our daily lives, in the ways in which it can furnish our minds, imaginations, and consciences. These qualities, I would say, are freedom, variety, self-consciousness, and the democratic attitude itself.

That democracy is hostile to distinction and prefers mediocrity is not a recent view. And there is an obvious sense in which it is true that democracy makes for homogeneity. Democracy erodes the clear distinctions between classes. It destroys ready-made status-symbols so rapidly that the manufacture of new ones becomes the occupation of a major industry. Most obvious of all, democracy increases the demand for a great many good things, from shoes to education. By increasing the demand, it also puts itself under pressure to cheapen the supply.

Yet certain pertinent facts must be set against these tendencies. First, more good things *are* more generally available in democracies. Second, egalitarianism's twin is the morality of achievement. There is a tension between the democratic suspicion of the man who sets himself apart and the democratic admiration for the man who stands out, but the egalitarian hostility towards ostentatious social distinctions is normally rooted in the belief that each man should be given a chance on his own to show what he can do. And finally, pressures towards uniformity are great in all societies. Is suspicion of the eccentric in egalitarian metropolitan America greater than in an eighteenth-century village? It is difficult to think so. "The fallacy of the aristocrat," Bertrand Russell has remarked, "consists in judging a society by the kind of life it affords a privileged few." Standing alone takes courage anywhere. Usually it also takes money; almost invariably it requires the guarantee that the individual will still retain his basic rights. In these respects modern liberal democracy, despite all the complaints about conformity, has made it easier for the ordinary unprivileged man to stand alone, if he has the will to do so, than any other kind of society known in history.

For however ambiguous some of the facts may be, the official commitment of liberal democracy is to the view that each man has his idiosyncrasies, that these idiosyncrasies deserve respect, and that if the individual does not know what is good for him, it is highly unlikely that a self-perpetuating elite will know better. And this is not just an official commitment. The institutions of liberal democracy go very far in giving it concrete embodiment. Assuming that the members of a democratic society have minimal economic securities, there is a flexibility in their situation which not many ordinary men have enjoyed in the past. If they fall out of favor with one set of authorities, they have a chance to turn around and look elsewhere.

It is unquestionable that there are great constellations of concentrated power in contemporary democratic societies; it is equally unquestionable that there is some freedom in any society. For in dealing with power, bright men learn how to work the angles. But in a democratic society there are more angles to work. Individual freedom of choice is not an absolute value. Any society must limit it; indeed, one man's freedom often rests on restricting the next man's. But while freedom of choice is not an absolute value, the democratic doctrine that each man has certain fundamental rights assigns an intrinsic value to his freedom of choice. If it has to be limited, it is recognized that something of value has been sacrificed. Social planning in a democracy is for this reason fundamentally different from social planning in undemocratic environments. The vague phrase "social utility," in a democratic setting, implicitly includes as one of its elements the value of freedom of choice.

What difference does this make? One difference is that variety is promoted; a second is that individuals are educated in self-consciousness. Needless to say, variety, too, has its limits. We do not have to protect dope peddlers in its name. But the full import of variety, of the mere existence of differences and alternatives, is frequently overlooked. It does not merely give us more choices, or offer us a break in the routine. It affects the immediate quality of our experience; it changes our relation to whatever it is that we choose to have or do or be. This is what is forgotten when freedom is defined simply as the absence of felt frustrations, or when it is said that if a man has just what he wants, it makes little difference whether he has any choice or not. A good that is voluntarily chosen, a good which a man is always free to reconsider, belongs to him in a way that a passively accepted good does not. It is his responsibility.

And this means that democratic variety has another use as well. No one can say with assurance that democracy makes people wiser or more virtuous. But political democracy invites men to think that there may be alternatives to the way they are governed. And social democracy, in reducing the barriers of class, caste, and inherited privilege that stand between men, adds to the variety of people and occasions the individual meets and puts greater pressure on his capacity to adapt to the new and different. Political democracy and a socially mobile society thus invite the individual to a greater degree of consciousness about the relativity of his own ways and a greater degree of self-consciousness in the choice of the standards by which he lives. These are conditions for intensified personal experience. The role of democracy in the extension of these attitudes represents one of its principal contributions to the progress of liberal civilization.

The extension of such attitudes, to be sure, has its risks, which explains much of our uneasiness about what the democratic revolution means. Fads and fashions engage and distract larger groups in modern democratic societies. And social mobility, though it gives breadth and variety to men's experience, may well foreshorten their sense of time. Cut loose from fixed ranks and stations, each with its legends, rationale, and sense of historic vocation, the citizens of a modern democracy face a peculiar temptation to live experimentally, with the help of the latest book, as though no one had ever lived before. But these are the risks not simply of democracy but of modernity, and they can be controlled. The courts, the organized professions, the churches, and the universities are storehouses of funded experience. In a society in which they are given independence from the political urgencies of the moment, they can serve as protections against the dictatorship of the specious present. Modernity implies a revolution in human consciousness. Democratic social arrangements reflect that revolution and accept it; but they also provide instruments for guiding and controlling it. None of democracy's contemporary rivals possess these two qualities to the same extent.

In the end, indeed, the risks of democracy are simply the risks implicit in suggesting to men that the answers are not all in. Democracy gives political form to the principle that also regulates the scientific community—the principle that inquiry must be kept open, that there are no sacred books, that no conclusion that men have ever reached can be taken to be the necessary final word. Cant, obscurantism, and lies are of course a good part of the diet of most democracies. Man is a truth-fearing animal, and it would be a miracle if any social system could quickly change this fact. But the institutions of liberal democracy are unique in that they require men to hold no irreversible beliefs in anything except in the method of free criticism and peaceful change itself, and in the ethic on which this method rests. Such a social system permits men to give their highest loyalty, not to temporary human beliefs or institutions, but to the continuing pursuit after truth, whatever it may be. The intellectual rationale of democracy is precisely that it does not need to make the foolish and arrogant claim that it rests on infallible truths. Men can believe in it and still believe that the truth is larger than anything they may think they know.

Yet the question that probably gnaws at us most deeply still remains. Freedom, variety, self-consciousness, a sane awareness of human fallibility, and loyalty to the principle that inquiry must be kept open—obviously, these have much in their favor. But they are refined values. Has liberal democracy priced itself out of the competition? Does it have anything to say, not to those who already know and enjoy it, but to the many more who must come to want it if human liberties are to be a little more secure in the world than they now are?

One of the debilitating illusions of many Western liberals is that the values of liberal culture are only our own values, that they have little point for those who look at the world differently, and no point at all for those whose lives are poor, mean, brutish, and short. Although colonialists used this view for different purposes, they shared it, and it betrays an inexact understanding of the nature of liberal values. Freedom, variety, self-consciousness, and the chance to seek the truth are all taxing experiences. Their virtues may be hard to conceive by those who have never enjoyed them. Yet in spite of the discomforts these values bring, the evidence indicates, I think, that most men would be happy to have them, and would think their lives enhanced. The difficulty with the most characteristic liberal values is not that they are parochial values. The difficulty is that men have other more imperious wants, like the need for medicines, schooling, bread, release from usurers, or a chance to get out from under corrupt and exploitative regimes. Illiberal programs promise these substantial material improvements and frequently deliver. And liberal programs, if they speak of freedom and leave out the usury and corruption, do not generally bring freedom either.

But let us assume, as there is every reason to assume, that liberal programs, if they are willing to recognize that they, too, must make a revolution, can also improve men's material condition. What can be said to the young man or the young—or old—nation in a hurry? What good reasons can we give, reasons that take account of their present condition and justified impatience, when we try to explain to them—and to ourselves—why the liberal path, despite its meanderings, is preferable to the authoritarian path?

One thing that can be said, quite simply, is that the authoritarian path closes up behind the traveler as he moves. The virtue of liberal democracy is that it permits second thoughts. To choose an authoritarian regime is to bet everything on a single throw of the dice; if the bet is bad, there is no way out save through violence, and not much hope in that direction. To choose a liberal approach, while it does not guarantee against errors, guarantees against the error so fatal that there is no peaceful way out or back. But there is another reason as well. The reason for choosing democracy is that it makes democrats.

Imagine a regime wholly committed to the welfare of those it rules. Imagine, against all the practical difficulties, that it is intelligent, honest, courageous, and that it does not have to enter into any deals with any of the international blocs that dominate the modern scene. And imagine, too, that this regime aims, in the end, to bring democracy and liberal values to the country it rules. But assume only that it claims, for the present, to be the one true spokesman for the public interest, the only group in the society that knows what truth and justice mean. What is the consequence? The consequence is that a democratic attitude is impossible. That attitude has been described in various ways—as a love for liberty, equality, and fraternity, as respect for the dignity of the individual, as a consistent regard for individual rights. The descriptions are not wrong, but they overintellectualize the attitude. At bottom, the democratic attitude is simply an attitude of good faith plus a working belief in the probable rationality of others. And that is what political authoritarianism destroys. Once a society is governed by the doctrine that some one group monopolizes all wisdom, it is divided into the Enlightened and the Unenlightened, and the Enlightened determine who shall be accorded membership in the club. In a modern State this makes almost impossible the growth of that mutual trust between opposing groups which is a fundamental condition for the growth of a strong political community that is also free.

The competition that takes place in a democracy is an instance of cooperative competition. It is a struggle in which both sides work to maintain the conditions necessary for a decent struggle. Accordingly, it rests on the assumption that there are no irreconcilable conflicts, that differences can be negotiated or compromised, if men have good will. Such a system requires men to deal with one another honestly, to make a serious effort to reach agreements, and to keep them after they have been made. It requires them to recognize, therefore, that the other side has its interests and to be prepared to make concessions to these interests when such concessions are not inconsistent with fundamental principles. A democratic ethic does not ask men to be fools. They do not have to assume that their opponents have put all their cards on the table. But democratic competition is impossible if the parties to the competition cannot assume that their opponents will recognize their victory if they win and will cooperate with them afterwards. The intention to annihilate the opposition or to win at all costs destroys the possibility of a regulated struggle. In this sense democracy is an exercise in the ethic of good faith. It is a system that makes it possible for men, not to love their enemies, but at least to live without fearing them. That kind of mutual trust between enemies is what authoritarianism destroys.

No doubt, such an argument may seem pathetically beside the point to men who live in societies that have been torn by distrust for centuries and that have known government only as a name for cruelty and dishonesty. If such men succeed in installing democratic regimes in their countries, they will do so by recognizing their enemies and distrusting them. But the harshness that goes with any deep social revolution is one thing if it is recognized as a bitter and dangerous necessity and is kept within limits. It is another if the violence is doctrinal, and the assumption is made that men can never cooperate unless they have the same interests and ideas. Such an assumption, as all the evidence suggests, encourages the adoption of terror as an official policy and condemns a society to an indefinite period in which power will be monopolistically controlled. In a diversified modern society, indeed in any society that has even begun the movement towards modernity, the doctrine of governmental infallibility trains men in suspiciousness and conspiracy. Perhaps other objectives will be achieved, but under such circumstances their taste will be sour.

Nor does the doctrine of infallibility destroy only good faith. It is also incompatible with a belief in the probable rationality of others. To hold a democratic attitude is to proceed on the assumption that other men may have their own persuasive reasons for thinking as they do. If they disagree with you, this does not necessarily make them candidates for correction and cure. This is the homely meaning of the oft-repeated assertion that democracy has faith in the reasonableness and equality of human beings. The faith does not assert that all men are in fact reasonable, or that they are equal in the capacity to think well or live sensibly. The faith is pragmatic: it expresses a policy. And the policy is simply to credit others with minds of their own, and to hold them responsible for their actions, until there are strong and quite specific reasons for thinking otherwise. Such a policy allows room for the idiosyncrasies of men and permits the varieties of human intelligence to be recognized and used.

In the end, the man who asks himself why he should choose democracy is asking himself to decide with which of two policies he would rather live. One is the policy of normally thinking that his fellows are dangerous to him and to themselves. The other is the policy of thinking that they are reasonable until they show themselves dangerous. To act on either policy has its risks. Why should a man choose one rather than the other? One reason can be found if he asks himself about the consequences the policy he adopts will have for the elementary feelings he will entertain towards his fellows, not in some transfigured world to come, but here and now. The point of the democratic policy is that it makes for democratic feelings. Those who do not wish to see human society divided into exploiters and exploited, those who wish to see each man come into his own free estate, believe that in that ultimate condition men will treat each other with the respect and fellow-feeling that equals show to equals. It is in the name of such moral attitudes that they seek democracy. The final reason for choosing the democratic method is that it provides a training ground, here and now, in just these attitudes.

John Stuart Mill

ON LIBERTY

I

The subject of this Essay is not the so-called Liberty of the Will, so unfortunately opposed to the misnamed doctrine of Philosophical Necessity; but Civil, or Social Liberty: the nature and limits of the power which can be legitimately exercised by society over the individual. A question seldom stated, and hardly ever discussed, in general terms, but which profoundly influences the practical controversies of the age by its latent presence, and is likely soon to make itself recognized as the vital question of the future. It is so far from being new, that, in a certain sense, it has divided mankind, almost from the remotest ages; but in the stage of progress into which the more civilized portions of the species have now entered, it presents itself under new conditions, and requires a different and more fundamental treatment.

Reprinted from *On Liberty* (1859).

The struggle between Liberty and Authority is the most conspicuous feature in the portions of history with which we are earliest familiar, particularly in that of Greece, Rome, and England. But in old times this contest was between subjects, or some classes of subjects, and the Government. By liberty, was meant protection against the tyranny of the political rulers. The rulers were conceived (except in some of the popular governments of Greece) as in a necessarily antagonistic position to the people whom they ruled. They consisted of a governing One, or a governing tribe or caste, who derived their authority from inheritance or conquest, who, at all events, did not hold it at the pleasure of the governed, and whose supremacy men did not venture, perhaps did not desire, to contest, whatever precautions might be taken against its oppressive exercise. Their power was regarded as necessary, but also as highly dangerous; as a weapon which they would attempt to use against their subjects, no less than against external enemies. To prevent the weaker members of the community from being preyed upon by innumerable vultures, it was needful that there should be an animal of prey stronger than the rest, commissioned to keep them down. But as the king of the vultures would be no less bent upon preying on the flock than any of the minor harpies, it was indispensable to be in a perpetual attitude of defence against his beak and claws. The aim, therefore, of patriots was to set limits to the power which the ruler should be suffered to exercise over the community; and this limitation was what they meant by liberty. It was attempted in two ways. First, by obtaining a recognition of certain immunities, called political liberties or rights, which it was to be regarded as a breach of duty in the ruler to infringe, and which, if he did infringe, specific resistance, or general rebellion, was held to be justifiable. A second, and generally a later expedient, was the establishment of constitutional checks, by which the consent of the community, or of a body of some sort, supposed to represent its interests, was made a necessary condition to some of the more important acts of the governing power. To the first of these modes of limitation, the ruling power, in most European countries, was compelled, more or less, to submit. It was not so with the second; and, to attain this, or when already in some degree possessed, to attain it more completely, became everywhere the principal object of the lovers of liberty. And so long as mankind were content to combat one enemy by another, and to be ruled by a master, on condition of being guaranteed more or less efficaciously against his tyranny, they did not carry their aspirations beyond this point.

A time, however, came, in the progress of human affairs, when men ceased to think it a necessity of nature that their governors should be an independent power, opposed in interest to themselves. It appeared to them much better that the various magistrates of the State should be their tenants or delegates, revocable at their pleasure. In that way alone, it seemed, could they have complete security that the powers of government would never be abused to their disadvantage. By degrees this new demand for elective and temporary rulers became the prominent object of the exertions of the popular party, wherever any such party existed; and superseded, to a considerable extent, the previous efforts to limit the power of rulers. As the struggle proceeded for making the ruling power emanate from the periodical choice of the ruled, some persons began to think that too much importance had been attached to the limitation of the power itself. *That* (it might seem) was a resource against rulers whose interests were habitually opposed to those of the people. What was now wanted was, that the rulers should be identified with the people; that their interest and will should be the interest and will of the nation. The nation did not need to be protected against its own will. There was no fear of its tyrannizing over itself. Let the rulers be effectually responsible to it, promptly removable by it, and it could afford to trust them with power of which it could itself dictate the use to be made. Their power was but the nation's own power, concentrated, and in a form convenient for exercise. This mode of thought, or rather perhaps of feeling, was common among the last generation of European liberalism, in the Continental section of which it still apparently predominates. Those who admit any limit to what a government may do, except in the case of such governments as they think ought not to exist, stand out as brilliant exceptions among the political thinkers of the Continent. A similar tone of sentiment might by this time have been prevalent in our own country, if the circumstances which for a time encouraged it, had continued unaltered.

But, in political and philosophical theories, as well as in persons, success discloses faults and infirmities which failure might have concealed from observation. The notion, that the people have no need to limit their power over themselves, might seem axiomatic, when popular government was a thing only dreamed about, or read of as having existed at some distant period of the past. Neither was that notion necessarily disturbed by such temporary aberrations as those of the French Revolution, the worst of which were the work of an usurping few, and which, in any case, belonged, not to the permanent working of popular institutions, but to a sudden and convulsive outbreak against monarchical and aristocratic despotism. In time, however, a democratic republic came to occupy a large portion of the earth's surface, and made itself felt as one of the most powerful members of the community of nations; and elective and responsible government became subject to the observations and criticisms which wait upon a great existing fact. It was now perceived that such phrases as "self-government," and "the power of the people over themselves," do not express the true state of the case. The "people" who exercise the power are not always the same people with those over whom it is exercised; and the "self-government" spoken of is not the government of each by himself, but of each by all the rest. The will of the people, moreover, practically means the will of the most numerous or the most active *part* of the people; the majority, or those who succeed in making themselves accepted as the majority; the people, consequently, *may* desire to oppress a part of their number; and precautions are as much needed against this as against any other abuse of power. The limitation, therefore, of the power of government over individuals loses none of its importance when the holders of power are regularly accountable to the community, that is, to the strongest party therein. This view of things, recommending itself equally to the intelligence of thinkers and to the inclination of those important classes in European society to whose real or supposed interests democracy is adverse, has had no difficulty in establishing itself; and in political speculations "the tyranny of the majority" is now generally included among the evils against which society requires to be on its guard.

Like other tyrannies, the tyranny of the majority was at first, and is still vulgarly, held in dread, chiefly as operating through the acts of the public authorities. But reflecting persons perceived that when society is itself the tyrant—society collectively, over the separate individuals who compose it—its means of tyrannizing are not restricted to the acts which it may do by the hands of its political functionaries. Society can and does execute its own mandates: and if it issues wrong mandates instead of right, or any mandates at all in things with which it ought not to meddle, it practises a social tyranny more formidable than many kinds of political oppression, since, though not usually upheld by such extreme penalties, it leaves fewer means of escape, penetrating much more deeply into the details of life, and enslaving the soul itself. Protection, therefore, against the tyranny of the magistrate is not enough: there needs protection also against the tyranny of the prevailing opinion and feeling; against the tendency of society to impose, by other means than civil penalties, its own ideas and practices as rules of conduct on those who dissent from them; to fetter the development, and, if possible, prevent the formation, of any individuality not in harmony with its ways, and compel all characters to fashion themselves upon the model of its own. There is a limit to the legitimate interference of collective opinion with individual independence: and to find that limit, and maintain it against encroachment, is as indispensable to a good condition of human affairs, as protection against political despotism.

* * *

The object of this Essay is to assert one very simple principle, as entitled to govern absolutely the dealings of society with the individual in the way of compulsion and control, whether the means used be physical force in the form of legal penalties, or the moral coercion of public opinion. That principle is, that the sole end for which mankind are warranted, individually or collectively, in interfering with the liberty of action of any of their number, is self-protection. That the only purpose for which power can be rightfully exercised over any member of a civilized community, against his will, is to prevent harm to others. His own good, either physical or moral, is not a sufficient warrant. He cannot rightfully be compelled to do or forbear because it will be better for him to do so, because it will make him happier, because, in the opinions of others, to do so would be wise, or even right. These are good reasons for remonstrating with him, or reasoning with him, or persuading him, or entreating him, but not for compelling him, or visiting him with any evil in case he do otherwise. To justify that, the conduct from which it is desired to deter him, must be calculated to produce evil to some one else. The only part of the conduct of any one, for which he is amenable to society, is that which concerns others. In the part which merely concerns himself, his independence is, of right, absolute. Over himself, over his own body and mind, the individual is sovereign.

It is, perhaps, hardly necessary to say that this doctrine is meant to apply only to human beings in the maturity of their faculties. We are not speaking of children, or of young persons below the age which the law may fix as that of manhood or womanhood. Those who are still in a state to require being taken care of by others, must be protected against their own actions as well as against external injury. For the same reason, we may leave out of consideration those backward states of society in which the race itself may be considered as in its nonage. The early difficulties in the way of spontaneous progress are so great, that there is seldom any choice of means for overcoming them; and a ruler full of the spirit of improvement is warranted in the use of any expedients that will attain an end, perhaps otherwise unattainable. Despotism is a legitimate mode of government in dealing with barbarians, provided the end be their improvement, and the means justified by actually effecting that end. Liberty, as a principle, has no application to any state of things anterior to the time when mankind have become capable of being improved by free and equal discussion. Until then, there is nothing for them but implicit obedience to an Akbar or a Charlemagne, if they are so fortunate as to find one. But as soon as mankind have attained the capacity of being guided to their own improvement by conviction or persuasion (a period long since reached in all nations with whom we need here concern ourselves), compulsion, either in the direct form or in that of pains and penalties for non-compliance, is no longer admissible as a means to their own good, and justifiable only for the security of others.

It is proper to state that I forgo any advantage which could be derived to my argument from the idea of abstract right, as a thing independent of utility. I regard utility as the ultimate appeal on all ethical questions; but it must be utility in the largest sense, grounded on the permanent interests of man as a progressive being. Those interests, I contend, authorize the subjection of individual spontaneity to external control, only in respect to those actions of each, which concern the interest of other people. If any one does an act hurtful to others, there is a prima facie case for punishing him, by law, or, where legal penalties are not safely applicable, by general disapprobation. There are also many positive acts for the benefit of others, which he may rightfully be compelled to perform; such as, to give evidence in a court of justice; to bear his fair share in the common defence, or in any other joint work necessary to the interest of the society of which he enjoys the protection; and to perform certain acts of individual beneficence, such as saving a fellow creature's life, or interposing to protect the defenceless against ill-usage, things which whenever it is obviously a man's duty to do, he may rightfully be made responsible to society for not doing. A person may cause evil to others not only by his actions but by his inaction, and in either case he is justly accountable to them for the injury. The latter case, it is true, requires a much more cautious exercise of compulsion than the former. To make any one answerable for doing evil to others, is the rule; to make him answerable for not preventing evil, is, comparatively speaking, the exception. Yet there are many cases clear enough and grave enough to justify that exception. In all things which regard the external relations of the individual, he is *de jure* amenable to those whose interests are concerned, and if need be, to society as their protector. There are often good reasons for not holding him to the responsibility; but these reasons must arise from the special expediencies of the case: either because it is a kind of case in which he is on the whole likely to act better, when left to his own discretion, than when controlled in any way in which society have it in their power to control him; or because the attempt to exercise control would produce other evils, greater than those which it would prevent. When such reasons as these preclude the enforcement of responsibility, the conscience of the agent himself should step into the vacant judgement-seat, and protect those interests of others which have no external protection; judging himself all the more rigidly, because the case does not admit of his being made accountable to the judgement of his fellow creatures.

But there is a sphere of action in which society, as distinguished from the individual, has, if any, only an indirect interest; comprehending all that portion of a person's life and conduct which affects only himself, or if it also affects others, only with their free, voluntary, and undeceived consent and participation. When I say only himself, I mean directly, and in the first instance: for whatever affects himself, may affect others through himself; and the objection which may be grounded on this contingency will receive consideration in the sequel. This, then, is the appropriate region of human liberty. It comprises, first, the inward domain of consciousness; demanding liberty of conscience, in the most comprehensive sense; liberty of thought and feeling; absolute freedom of opinion and sentiment on all subjects, practical or speculative, scientific, moral, or theological. The liberty of expressing and publishing opinions may seem to fall under a different principle, since it belongs to that part of the conduct of an individual which concerns other people; but, being almost of as much importance as the liberty of thought itself, and resting in great part on the same reasons, is practically inseparable from it. Secondly, the principle requires liberty of tastes and pursuits; of framing the plan of our life to suit our own character; of doing as we like, subject to such consequences as may follow: without impediment from our fellow creatures, so long as what we do does not harm them, even though they should think our conduct foolish, perverse, or wrong. Thirdly, from this liberty of each individual, follows the liberty, within the same limits, of combination among individuals; freedom to unite, for any purpose not involving harm to others: the persons combining being supposed to be of full age, and not forced or deceived.

No society in which these liberties are not, on the whole, respected, is free, whatever may be its form of government; and none is completely free in which they do not exist absolute and unqualified. The only freedom which deserves the name, is that of pursuing our own good in our own way, so long as we do not attempt to deprive others of theirs, or impede their efforts to obtain it. Each is the proper guardian of his own health, whether bodily, or mental and spiritual. Mankind are greater gainers by suffering each other to live as seems good to themselves, than by compelling each to live as seems good to the rest.

• • •

II

The time, it is to be hoped, is gone by, when any defence would be necessary of the "liberty of the press" as one of the securities against corrupt or tyrannical government. No argument, we may suppose, can now be needed, against permitting a legislature or an executive, not identified in interest with the people, to prescribe opinions to them, and determine what doctrines or what arguments they shall be allowed to hear. This aspect of the question, besides, has been so often and so triumphantly enforced by preceding writers, that it needs not be specially insisted on in this place. Though the law of England, on the subject of the press, is as servile to this day as it was in the time of the Tudors, there is little danger of its being actually put in force against political discussion, except during some temporary panic, when fear of insurrection drives ministers and judges from their propriety; and, speaking generally, it is not, in constitutional countries, to be apprehended, that the government, whether completely responsible to the people or not, will often attempt to control the expression of opinion, except when in doing so it makes itself the organ of the general intolerance of the public. Let us suppose, therefore, that the government is entirely at one with the people, and never thinks of exerting any power of coercion unless in agreement with what it conceives to be their voice. But I deny the right of the people to exercise such coercion, either by themselves or by their government. The power itself is illegitimate. The best government has no more title to it than the worst. It is as noxious, or more noxious, when exerted in accordance with public opinion, than when in opposition to it. If all mankind minus one, were of one opinion, and only one person were of the contrary opinion, mankind would be no more justified in silencing that one person, than he, if he had the power, would be justified in silencing mankind. Were an opinion a personal possession of no value except to the owner; if to be obstructed in the enjoyment of it were simply a private injury, it would make some difference whether the injury was inflicted only on a few persons or on many. But the peculiar evil of silencing the expression of an opinion is, that it is robbing the human race; posterity as well as the existing generation; those who dissent from the opinion, still more than those who hold it. If the opinion is right, they are deprived of the opportunity of exchanging error for truth: if wrong, they lose, what is almost as great a benefit, the clearer perception and livelier impression of truth, produced by its collision with error.

It is necessary to consider separately these two hypotheses, each of which has a distinct branch of the argument corresponding to it. We can never be sure that the opinion we are endeavouring to stifle is a false opinion; and if we were sure, stifling it would be an evil still.

First: the opinion which it is attempted to suppress by authority may possibly be true. Those who desire to suppress it, of course deny its truth; but they are not infallible. They have no authority to decide the question for all mankind, and exclude every other person from the means of judging. To refuse a hearing to an opinion, because they are sure that it is false, is to assume that *their* certainty is the same thing as *absolute* certainty. All silencing of discussion is an assumption of infallibility. Its condemnation may be allowed to rest on this common argument, not the worse for being common.

Unfortunately for the good sense of mankind, the fact of their fallibility is far from carrying the weight in their practical judgment, which is always allowed to it in theory; for while every one well knows himself to be fallible, few think it necessary to take any precautions against their own fallibility, or admit the supposition that any opinion, of which they feel very certain, may be one of the examples of the error to which they acknowledge themselves to be liable. Absolute princes, or others who are accustomed to unlimited deference, usually feel this complete confidence in their own opinions on nearly all subjects. People more happily situated, who sometimes hear their opinions disputed, and are not wholly unused to be set right when they are wrong, place the same unbounded reliance only on such of their opinions as are shared by all who surround them, or to whom they habitually defer: for in proportion to a man's want of confidence in his own solitary judgement, does he usually repose, with implicit trust, on the infallibility of "the world" in general. And the world, to each individual, means the part of it with which he comes in contact; his party, his sect, his church, his class of society: the man may be called, by comparison, almost liberal and large-minded to whom it means anything so comprehensive as his own country or his own age. Nor is his faith in this collective authority at all shaken by his being aware that other ages, countries, sects, churches, classes, and parties have thought, and even now think, the exact reverse. He devolves upon his own world the responsibility of being in the right against the dissentient worlds of other people; and it never troubles him that mere accident has decided which of these numerous worlds is the object of his reliance, and that the same causes which make him a Churchman in London, would have made him a Buddhist or a Confucian in Pekin. Yet it is as evident in itself, as any amount of argument can make it, that ages are no more infallible than individuals; every age having held many opinions which subsequent ages have deemed not only false but absurd; and it is as certain that many opinions, now general, will be rejected by future ages, as it is that many, once general, are rejected by the present.

The objection likely to be made to this argument would probably take some such form as the following. There is no greater assumption of infallibility in forbidding the propagation of error, than in any other thing which is done by public authority on its own judgement and responsibility. Judgement is given to men that they may use it. Because it may be used erroneously, are men to be told that they ought not to use it at all? To prohibit what they think pernicious, is not claiming exemption from error, but fulfilling the duty incumbent on them, although fallible, of acting on their conscientious conviction. If we were never to act on our opinions, because those opinions may be wrong, we should leave all our interests uncared for, and all our duties unperformed. An objection which applies to all conduct, can be no valid objection to any conduct in particular. It is the duty of governments, and of individuals, to form the truest opinions they can; to form them carefully, and never impose them upon others unless they are quite sure of being right. But when they are sure (such reasoners may say), it is not conscientiousness but cowardice to shrink from acting on their opinions, and allow doctrines which they honestly think dangerous to the welfare of mankind, either in this life or in another, to be scattered abroad without restraint, because other people, in less enlightened times, have persecuted opinions now believed to be true. Let us take care, it may be said, not to make the same mistake: but governments and nations have made mistakes in other things, which are not denied to be fit subjects for the exercise of authority: they have laid on bad taxes, made unjust wars. Ought we therefore to lay on no taxes, and, under whatever provocation, make no wars? Men, and governments, must act to the best of their ability. There is no such thing as absolute certainty, but there is assurance sufficient for the purposes of human life. We may, and must, assume our opinion to be true for the guidance of our own conduct: and it is assuming no more when we forbid bad men to pervert society by the propagation of opinions which we regard as false and pernicious.

I answer, that it is assuming very much more. There is the greatest difference between presuming an opinion to be true, because, with every opportunity for contesting it, it has not been refuted, and assuming its truth for the purpose of not permitting its refutation. Complete liberty of contradicting and disproving our opinion, is the very condition which justifies us in assuming its truth for purposes of action; and on no other terms can a being with human faculties have any rational assurance of being right.

When we consider either the history of opinion, or the ordinary conduct of human life, to what is it to be ascribed that the one and the other are no worse than they are? Not certainly to the inherent force of the human understanding; for, on any matter not self-evident, there are ninety-nine persons totally incapable of judging of it, for one who is capable; and the capacity of the hundredth person is only comparative; for the majority of the eminent men of every past generation held many opinions now known to be erroneous, and did or approved numerous things which no one will now justify. Why is it, then, that there is on the whole a preponderance among mankind of rational opinions and rational conduct? If there really is this preponderance—which there must be unless human affairs are, and have always been, in an almost desperate state—it is owing to a quality of the human mind, the source of everything respectable in man either as an intellectual or as a moral being, namely, that his errors are corrigible. He is capable of rectifying his mistakes, by discussion and experience. Not by experience alone. There must be discussion, to show how experience is to be interpreted. Wrong opinions and practices gradually yield to fact and argument: but facts and arguments, to produce any effect on the mind, must be brought before it. Very few facts are able to tell their own story, without comments to bring out their meaning. The whole strength and value, then, of human judgement, depending on the wrong property, that it can be set right when it is wrong, reliance can be placed on it only when the means of setting it right are kept constantly at hand. In the case of any person whose judgement is really deserving of confidence, how has it become so? Because he has kept his mind open to criticism of his opinions and conduct. Because it has been his practice to listen to all that could be said against him; to profit by as much of it as was just, and expound to himself, and upon occasion to others, the fallacy of what was fallacious. Because he has felt, that the only way in which a human being can make some approach to knowing the whole of a subject, is by hearing what can be said about it by persons of every variety of opinion, and studying all modes in which it can be looked at by every character of mind. No wise man ever acquired his wisdom in any mode but this; nor is it in the nature of human intellect to become wise in any other manner. The steady habit of correcting and completing his own opinion by collating it with those of others, so far from causing doubt and hesitation in carrying it into practice, is the only stable foundation for a just reliance on it: for, being cognisant of all that can, at least obviously, he said against him, and having taken up his position against all gainsayers—knowing that he has sought for objections and difficulties, instead of avoiding them, and has shut out no light which can be thrown upon the subject from any quarter—he has a right to think his judgement better than that of any person, or any multitude, who have not gone through a similar process.

• • •

Let us now pass to the second division of the argument, and dismissing the supposition that any of the received opinions may be false, let us assume them to be true, and examine into the worth of the manner in which they are likely to be held, when their truth is not freely and openly canvassed. However unwillingly a person who has a strong opinion may admit the possibility that his opinion may be false, he ought to be moved by the consideration that however true it may be, if it is not fully, frequently, and fearlessly discussed, it will be held as a dead dogma, not a living truth.

There is a class of persons (happily not quite so numerous as formerly) who think it enough if a person assents undoubtingly to what they think true, though he has no knowledge whatever of the grounds of the opinion, and could not make a tenable defence of it against the most superficial objections. Such persons, if they can once get their creed taught from authority, naturally think that no good, and some harm, comes of its being allowed to be questioned. Where their influence prevails, they make it nearly impossible for the received opinion to be rejected wisely and considerately, though it may still be rejected rashly and ignorantly; for to shut out discussion entirely is seldom possible, and when it once gets in, beliefs not grounded on conviction are apt to give way before the slightest semblance of an argument. Waiving, however, this possibility—assuming that the true opinion abides in the mind, but abides as a prejudice, a belief independent of, and proof against, argument—this is not the way in which truth ought to be held by a rational being. This is not knowing the truth. Truth, thus held, is but one superstition the more, accidentally clinging to the words which enunciate a truth.

If the intellect and judgement of mankind ought to be cultivated . . . on what can these faculties be more appropriately exercised by any one, than on the things which concern him so much that it is considered necessary for him to hold opinions on them? If the cultivation of the understanding consists in one thing more than in another, it is surely in learning the grounds of one's own opinions. Whatever people believe, on subjects on which it is of the first importance to believe rightly, they ought to be able to defend against at least the common objections. But, some one may say, "Let them be *taught* the grounds of their opinions. It does not follow that opinions must be merely parroted because they are never heard controverted. Persons who learn geometry do not simply commit the theorems to memory, but understand and learn likewise the demonstrations; and it would be absurd to say that they remain ignorant of the grounds of geometrical truths, because they never hear any one deny, and attempt to disprove them." Undoubtedly: and such teaching suffices on a subject like mathematics, where there is nothing at all to be said on the wrong side of the question. The peculiarity of the evidence of mathematical truths is, that all the argument is on one side. There are no objections, and no answers to objections. But on every subject on which difference of opinion is possible, the truth depends on a balance to be struck between two sets of conflicting reasons. Even in natural philosophy, there is always some other explanation possible of the same facts; some geocentric theory instead of heliocentric, some phlogiston instead of oxygen; and it has to be shown why that other theory cannot be the true one: and until this is shown, and until we know how it is shown, we do not understand the grounds of our opinion. But when we turn to subjects infinitely more complicated, to morals, religion, politics, social relations, and the business of life, three-fourths of the arguments for every disputed opinion consist in dispelling the appearances which favour some opinion different from it. The greatest orator, save one, of antiquity, has left it on record that he always studied his adversary's case with as great, if not with still greater, intensity than even his own. What Cicero practised as the means of forensic success, requires to be imitated by all who study any subject in order to arrive at the truth. He who knows only his own side of the case, knows little of that. His reasons may be good, and no one may have been able to refute them. But if he is equally unable to refute the reasons on the opposite side; if he does not so much as know what they are, he has no ground for preferring either opinion. The rational position for him would be suspension of judgement, and unless he contents himself with that, he is either led by authority, or adopts, like the generality of the world, the side to which he feels most inclination. Nor is it enough that he should hear the arguments of adversaries from his own teachers, presented as they state them, and accompanied by what they offer as refutations. That is not the way to do justice to the arguments, or bring them into real contact with his own mind. He must be able to hear them from persons who actually believe them; who defend them in earnest, and do their very utmost for them. He must know them in their most plausible and persuasive form; he must feel the whole force of the

difficulty which the true view of the subject has to encounter and dispose
of; else he will never really possess himself of the portion of truth which
meets and removes that difficulty. Ninety-nine in a hundred of what are
called educated men are in this condition; even of those who can argue
fluently for their opinions. Their conclusion may be true, but it might be
false for anything they know: they have never thrown themselves into the
mental position of these who think differently from them, and considered
what such persons may have to say; and consequently they do not, in any
proper sense of the word, know the doctrine which they themselves profess. They do not know those parts of it which explain and justify the
remainder; the considerations which show that a fact which seemingly
conflicts with another is reconcilable with it, or that, of two apparently
strong reasons, one and not the other ought to be preferred. All that part
of the truth which turns the scale, and decides the judgement of a completely informed mind, they are strangers to; nor is it ever really known,
but to those who have attended equally and impartially to both sides, and
endeavoured to see the reasons of both in the strongest light. So essential
is this discipline to a real understanding of moral and human subjects,
that if opponents of all important truths do not exist, it is indispensable to
imagine them, and supply them with the strongest arguments which the
most skilful devil's advocate can conjure up.

• • •

I do not pretend that the most unlimited use of the freedom of enunciat-
ing all possible opinions would put an end to the evils of religious or philosophical sectarianism. Every truth which men of narrow capacity or in
earnest about, is sure to be asserted, inculcated, and in many ways even
acted on, as if no other truth existed in the world, or at all events none that
could limit or qualify the first. I acknowledge that the tendency of all opinions to become sectarian is not cured by the freest discussion, but is often
heightened and exacerbated thereby; the truth which ought to have been,
but was not, seen, being rejected all the more violently because pro-
claimed by persons regarded as opponents. But it is not on the impassioned partisan, it is on the calmer and more disinterested bystander, that
this collision of opinions works its salutary effect. Not the violent conflict
between parts of the truth, but the quiet suppression of half of it, is the
formidable evil; there is always hope when people are forced to listen to
both sides; it is when they attend only to one that errors harden into
prejudices, and truth itself ceases to have the effect of truth, by being
exaggerated into falsehood. And since there are few mental attributes
more rare than that judicial faculty which can sit in intelligent judgement

between two sides of a question, of which only one is represented by an advocate before it, truth has no chance but in proportion as every side of it, every opinion which embodies any fraction of the truth, not only finds advocates, but is so advocated as to be listened to.

We have now recognized the necessity to the mental well-being of mankind (on which all their other well-being depends) of freedom of opinion, and freedom of the expression of opinion, on four distinct grounds; which we will now briefly recapitulate.

First, if any opinion is compelled to silence, that opinion may, for aught we can certainly know, be true. To deny this is to assume our own infallibility.

Secondly, though the silenced opinion be an error, it may, and very commonly does, contain a portion of truth; and since the general or prevailing opinion on any subject is rarely or never the whole truth, it is only by the collision of adverse opinions that the remainder of the truth has any chance of being supplied.

Thirdly, even if the received opinion be not only true, but the whole truth; unless it is suffered to be, and actually is, vigorously and earnestly contested, it will, by most of those who receive it, be held in the manner of a prejudice, with little comprehension or feeling of its rational grounds. And not only this, but, fourthly, the meaning of the doctrine itself will be in danger of being lost, or enfeebled, and deprived of its vital effect on the character and conduct: the dogma becoming a mere formal profession, inefficacious for good, but cumbering the ground, and preventing the growth of any real and heartfelt conviction, from reason or personal experience.

Plato (ca. 427–347 B.C.) was the Athenian philosopher whose writings are among the foundations of Western thought.

Plato

CRITO

CHARACTERS
Socrates
Crito

Scene—The Prison of Socrates
[Socrates has been sentenced to death on the charge of impiety.—Ed.]

Socr: Why have you come at this hour, Crito? Is it not still early?
Crito: Yes, very early.
Socr: About what time is it?
Crito: It is just daybreak.
Socr: I wonder that the jailer was willing to let you in.

From Plato: *Euthyphro, Apology, Crito,* translated by F. J. Church, revised by Robert D. Cumming, copyright © 1948, 1956, by The Liberal Arts Press, Inc., reprinted by permission of the Liberal Arts Press Division of The Bobbs-Merrill Company, Inc.

Crito: He knows me now, Socrates; I come here so often, and besides, I have given him a tip.

Socr: Have you been here long?

Crito: Yes, some time.

Socr: Then why did you sit down without speaking? Why did you not wake me at once?

Crito: Indeed, Socrates, I wish that I myself were not so sleepless and sorrowful. But I have been wondering to see how soundly you sleep. And I purposely did not wake you, for I was anxious not to disturb your repose. Often before, all through your life, I have thought that your temperament was a happy one; and I think so more than ever now when I see how easily and calmly you bear the calamity that has come to you.

Socr: Nay, Crito, it would be absurd if at my age I were disturbed at having to die.

Crito: Other men as old are overtaken by similar calamities, Socrates; but their age does not save them from being disturbed by their fate.

Socr: That is so; but tell me why are you here so early?

Crito: I am the bearer of sad news, Socrates; not sad, it seems, for you, but for me and for all your friends, both sad and hard to bear; and for none of them, I think, is it as hard to bear as it is for me.

Socr: What is it? Has the ship come from Delos, at the arrival of which I am to die?

Crito: No, It has not actually arrived, but I think that it will be here today, from the news which certain persons have brought from Sunium, who left it there. It is clear from their report that it will be here today; and so, Socrates, tomorrow your life will have to end.

Socr: Well, Crito, may it end well. Be it so, if so the gods will. But I do not think that the ship will be here today.

Crito: Why do you suppose not?

Socr: I will tell you. I am to die on the day after the ship arrives, am I not?[1]

Crito: That is what the authorities say.

Socr: Then I do not think that it will come today, but tomorrow. I am counting on a dream I had a little while ago in the night, so it seems to be fortunate that you did not wake me.

Crito: And what was this dream?

---

[1] Criminals could not be put to death while the sacred ship was away on its voyage.—Ed.

Socr: A fair and beautiful woman, clad in white, seemed to come to me, and call me and say, "O Socrates—

On the third day shall you fertile Phthia reach."[2]

Crito: What a strange dream, Socrates!

Socr: But its meaning is clear, at least to me, Crito.

Crito: Yes, too clear, it seems. But, O my good Socrates, I beg you for the last time to listen to me and save yourself. For to me your death will be more than a single disaster; not only shall I lose a friend the like of whom I shall never find again, but many persons who do not know you and me well will think that I might have saved you if I had been willing to spend money, but that I neglected to do so. And what reputation could be more disgraceful than the reputation of caring more for money than for one's friends? The public will never believe that we were anxious to save you, but that you yourself refused to escape.

Socr: But, my dear Crito, why should we care so much about public opinion? Reasonable men, of whose opinion it is worth our while to think, will believe that we acted as we really did.

Crito: But you see, Socrates, that it is necessary to care about public opinion, too. This very thing that has happened to you proves that the multitude can do a man not the least, but almost the greatest harm, if he is falsely accused to them.

Socr: I wish that the multitude were able to do a man the greatest harm, Crito, for then they would be able to do him the greatest good, too. That would have been fine. But, as it is, they can do neither. They cannot make a man either wise or foolish: they act wholly at random.

Crito: Well, as you wish. But tell me this, Socrates. You surely are not anxious about me and your other friends, and afraid lest, if you escape, the informers would say that we stole you away, and get us into trouble, and involve us in a great deal of expense, or perhaps in the loss of all our property, and, it may be, bring some other punishment upon us besides? If you have any fear of that kind, dismiss it. For of course we are bound to run these risks, and still greater risks than these, if necessary, in saving you. So do not, I beg you, refuse to listen to me.

Socr: I am anxious about that, Crito, and about much besides.

---

2 Homer, *Iliad,* ix, 363.

Crito: Then have no fear on that score. There are men who, for no very large sum, are ready to bring you out of prison into safety. And then, you know, these informers are cheaply bought, and there would be no need to spend much upon them. My fortune is at your service, and I think that it is adequate; and if you have any feeling about making use of my money, there are strangers in Athens whom you know, ready to use theirs; and one of them, Simmias of Thebes, has actually brought enough for this very purpose. And Cebes and many others are ready, too. And therefore, I repeat, do not shrink from saving yourself on that ground. And do not let what you said in the court—that if you went into exile you would not know what to do with yourself—stand in your way; for there are many places for you to go to, where you will be welcomed. If you choose to go to Thessaly, I have friends there who will make much of you and protect you from any annoyance from the people of Thessaly.

And besides, Socrates, I think that you will be doing what is unjust if you abandon your life when you might preserve it. You are simply playing into your enemies' hands; it is exactly what they wanted—to destroy you. And what is more, to me you seem to be abandoning your children, too. You will leave them to take their chance in life, as far as you are concerned, when you might bring them up and educate them. Most likely their fate will be the usual fate of children who are left orphans. But you ought not to bring children into the world unless you mean to take the trouble of bringing them up and educating them. It seems to me that you are choosing the easy way, and not the way of a good and brave man, as you ought, when you have been talking all your life long of the value that you set upon human excellence. For my part, I feel ashamed both for you and for us who are your friends. Men will think that the whole thing which has happened to you—your appearance in court to face trial, when you need not have appeared at all; the very way in which the trial was conducted; and then last of all this, the crowning absurdity of the whole affair—is due to our cowardice. It will look as if we had shirked the danger out of miserable cowardice; for we did not save you, and you did not save yourself, when it was quite possible to do so if we had been good for anything at all. Take care, Socrates, lest these things be not evil only, but also dishonorable to you and to us. Reflect, then, or rather the time for reflection is past; we must make up our minds. And there is only one plan possible. Everything must be done tonight.

If we delay any longer, we are lost. Socrates, I implore you not to refuse to listen to me.

Socr: My dear Crito, if your anxiety to save me be right, it is most valuable; but if not, the greater it is the harder it will be to cope with. We must reflect, then, whether we are to do as you say or not; for I am still what I always have been—a man who will accept no argument but that which on reflection I find to be truest. I cannot cast aside my former arguments because this misfortune has come to me. They seem to me to be as true as ever they were, and I respect and honor the same ones as I used to. And if we have no better argument to substitute for them, I certainly shall not agree to your proposal, not even though the power of the multitude should scare us with fresh terrors, as children are scared with hobgoblins, and inflict upon us new fines and imprisonments, and deaths. What is the most appropriate way of examining the question? Shall we go back first to what you say about opinions, and ask if we used to be right in thinking that we ought to pay attention to some opinions, and not to others? Were we right in saying so before I was condemned to die, and has it now become apparent that we were talking at random and arguing for the sake of argument, and that it was really nothing but playful nonsense? I am anxious, Crito, to examine our former argument with your help, and to see whether my present circumstance will appear to me to have affected its truth in any way or not; and whether we are to set it aside, or to yield assent to it. Those of us who thought at all seriously always used to say, I think, exactly what I said just now, namely, that we ought to respect some of the opinions which men form, and not others. Tell me, Crito, I beg you, do you not think that they were right? For you in all probability will not have to die tomorrow, and your judgment will not be biased by that circumstance. Reflect, then, do you not think it reasonable to say that we should not respect all the opinions of men but only some, nor the opinions of all men but only of some men? What do you think? Is not this true?

Crito: It is.

Socr: And we should respect the good opinions, and not the worthless ones?

Crito: Yes.

Socr: But the good opinions are those of the wise, and the worthless ones those of the foolish?

Crito: Of course.

Socr: And what did we say about this? Does a man who is in training, and who is serious about it, pay attention to the praise and blame and opinion of all men, or only of the one man who is a doctor or a trainer?

Crito: He pays attention only to the opinion of the one man.

Socr: Then he ought to fear the blame and welcome the praise of this one man, not of the multitude?

Crito: Clearly.

Socr: Then he must act and exercise, and eat and drink in whatever way the one man who is his director, and who understands the matter, tells him; not as others tell him?

Crito: That is so.

Socr: Good. But if he disobeys this one man, and disregards his opinion and his praise, and respects instead what the many say, who understand nothing of the matter, will he not suffer for it?

Crito: Of course he will.

Socr: And how will he suffer? In what way and in what part of himself?

Crito: Of course in his body. That is disabled.

Socr: You are right. And, Crito, to be brief, is it not the same in everything? And, therefore, in questions of justice and injustice, and of the base and the honorable, and of good and evil, which we are now examining, ought we to follow the opinion of the many and fear that, or the opinion of the one man who understands these matters (if we can find him), and feel more shame and fear before him than before all other men? For if we do not follow him, we shall corrupt and maim that part of us which, we used to say, is improved by justice and disabled by injustice. Or is this not so?

Crito: No, Socrates, I agree with you.

Socr: Now, if, by listening to the opinions of those who do not understand, we disable that part of us which is improved by health and corrupted by disease, is our life worth living when it is corrupt? It is the body, is it not?

Crito: Yes.

Socr: Is life worth living with the body corrupted and crippled?

Crito: No, certainly not.

Socr: Then is life worth living when that part of us which is maimed by injustice and benefited by justice is corrupt? Or do we consider that part of us, whatever it is, which has to do with justice and injustice to be of less consequence than our body?

Crito: No, certainly not.

Socr: But more valuable?

Crito: Yes, much more so.

Socr: Then, my good friend, we must not think so much of what the many will say of us; we must think of what the one man who understands justice and injustice, and of what truth herself will say of us. And so you are mistaken, to begin with, when you invite us to regard the opinion of the multitude concerning the just and the honorable and the good, and their opposites. But, it may be said, the multitude can put us to death?

Crito: Yes, that is evident. That may be said, Socrates.

Socr: True. But, my good friend, to me it appears that the conclusion which we have just reached is the same as our conclusion of former times. Now consider whether we still hold to the belief that we should set the highest value, not on living, but on living well?

Crito: Yes, we do.

Socr: And living well and honorably and justly mean the same thing: do we hold to that or not?

Crito: We do.

Socr: Then, starting from these premises, we have to consider whether it is just or not for me to try to escape from prison, without the consent of the Athenians. If we find that it is just, we will try; if not, we will give up the idea. I am afraid that considerations of expense, and of reputation, and of bringing up my children, of which you talk, Crito, are only the opinions of the many, who casually put men to death, and who would, if they could, as casually bring them to life again, without a thought. But reason, which is our guide, shows us that we can have nothing to consider but the question which I asked just now—namely, shall we be acting justly if we give money and thanks to the men who are to aid me in escaping, and if we ourselves take our respective parts in my escape? Or shall we in truth be acting unjustly if we do all this? And if we find that we should be acting unjustly, then we must not take any account either of death, or of any other evil that may be the consequence of remaining here, where we are, but only of acting unjustly.

Crito: I think that you are right, Socrates. But what are we to do?

Socr: Let us examine this question together, my friend, and if you can contradict anything that I say, do so, and I shall be persuaded. But if you cannot, do not go on repeating to me any longer, my dear friend, that I should escape without the consent of the Athenians. I am very anxious to act with your approval and consent. I do not want you to think me mistaken. But now tell me if you agree with the premise from which I start, and try to answer my questions as you think best.

Crito: I will try.

Socr: Ought we never to act unjustly voluntarily? Or may we act unjustly in some ways, and not in others? Is it the case, as we have often agreed in former times, that it is never either good or honorable to act unjustly? Or have all our former conclusions been overturned in these few days; and did we at our age fail to recognize all along, when we were seriously conversing with each other, that we were no better than children? Is not what we used to say most certainly the truth, whether the multitude agrees with us or not? Is not acting unjustly evil and shameful in every case, whether we incur a heavier or a lighter punishment as the consequence? Do we believe that?

Crito: We do.

Socr: Then we ought never to act unjustly?

Crito: Certainly not.

Socr: If we ought never to act unjustly at all, ought we to repay injustice with injustice, as the multitude thinks we may?

Crito: Clearly not.

Socr: Well, then, Crito, ought we to do evil to anyone?

Crito: Certainly I think not, Socrates.

Socr: And is it just to repay evil with evil, as the multitude thinks, or unjust?

Crito: Certainly it is unjust.

Socr: For there is no difference, is there, between doing evil to a man and acting unjustly?

Crito: True.

Socr: Then we ought not to repay injustice with injustice or to do harm to any man, no matter what we may have suffered from him. And in conceding this, Crito, be careful that you do not concede more than you mean. For I know that only a few men hold, or ever will hold, this opinion. And so those who hold it and those who do not have no common ground of argument; they can of necessity only look with contempt on each other's belief. Do you therefore consider very carefully whether or not you agree with me and share my opinion. Are we to start in our inquiry from the premise that it is never right either to act unjustly, or to repay injustice with injustice, or to avenge ourselves on any man who harms us, by harming him in return? Or do you disagree with me and dissent from my premise? I myself have believed in it for a long time, and I believe in it still. But if you differ in any way, explain to me how. If you still hold to our former opinion, listen to my next point.

Crito: Yes, I hold to it, and I agree with you. Go on.

Socr: Then, my next point, or rather my next question, is this: Ought a man to carry out his just agreements, or may he shuffle out of them?

Crito: He ought to carry them out.

Socr: Then consider. If I escape without the state's consent, shall I be injuring those whom I ought least to injure, or not? Shall I be abiding by my just agreements or not?

Crito: I cannot answer your question, Socrates. I do not understand it.

Socr: Consider it in this way. Suppose the laws and the commonwealth were to come and appear to me as I was preparing to run away (if that is the right phrase to describe my escape) and were to ask, "Tell us, Socrates, what have you in your mind to do? What do you mean by trying to escape but to destroy us, the laws and the whole state, so far as you are able? Do you think that a state can exist and not be overthrown, in which the decisions of law are of no force, and are disregarded and undermined by private individuals?" How shall we answer questions like that, Crito? Much might be said, especially by an orator, in defense of the law which makes judicial decisions supreme. Shall I reply, "But the state has injured me by judging my case unjustly?" Shall we say that?

Crito: Certainly we will, Socrates.

Socr: And suppose the laws were to reply, "Was that our agreement? Or was it that you would abide by whatever judgments the state should pronounce?" And if we were surprised by their words, perhaps they would say, "Socrates, don't be surprised by our words, but answer us; you yourself are accustomed to ask questions and to answer them. What complaint have you against us and the state, that you are trying to destroy us? Are we not, first of all, your parents? Through us your father took your mother and brought you into the world. Tell us, have you any fault to find with those of us that are the laws of marriage?" "I have none," I should reply. "Or have you any fault to find with those of us that regulate the raising of the child and the education which you, like others, received? Did we not do well in telling your father to educate you in music and athletics?" "You did," I should say. "Well, then, since you were brought into the world and raised and educated by us, how, in the first place, can you deny that you are our child and our slave, as your fathers were before you? And if this be so, do you think that your rights are on a level with ours? Do you think that you have a right to retaliate if we should try to do anything to you? You had not the same rights that your father had, or that your master would have had if you had been a slave. You had no right to retaliate if they ill-treated you, or to answer them if they scolded you, or to strike them back if they struck you, or to repay them evil with evil in any way. And do you think that you may retaliate in the case of your country and its laws? If we try to destroy you, because we think it just, will you in return do all that you can to destroy us, the laws, and your country, and say that in so doing you are acting justly—you, the man who really thinks so much of excellence? Or are you too wise to see that your country is worthier, more to be revered, more sacred, and held in higher honor both by the gods and by all men of understanding, than your father and your mother and all your other ancestors; and that you ought to reverence it, and to submit to it, and to approach it more humbly when it is angry with you than you would approach your father; and either to do whatever it tells you to do or to persuade it to excuse you; and to obey in silence if it orders you to endure flogging or imprisonment, or if it sends you to battle to be wounded or to die? That is just. You must not give way, nor retreat, nor desert your station. In war, and in the court of justice, and everywhere, you must do whatever your state and your country tell you to do, or you must persuade them that their commands are unjust. But it is impious to use violence against your father or your mother; and much more impious to use violence against your country." What answer shall we make, Crito? Shall we say that the laws speak the truth, or not?

Crito: I think that they do.

Socr: "Then consider, Socrates," perhaps they would say, "if we are right in saying that by attempting to escape you are attempting an injustice. We brought you into the world, we raised you, we educated you, we gave you and every other citizen a share of all the good things we could. Yet we proclaim that if any man of the Athenians is dissatisfied with us, he may take his goods and go away wherever he pleases; we give that privilege to every man who chooses to avail himself of it, so soon as he has reached manhood, and sees us, the laws, and the administration of our state. No one of us stands in his way or forbids him to take his goods and go wherever he likes, whether it be to an Athenian colony or to any foreign country, if he is dissatisfied with us and with the state. But we say that every man of you who remains here, seeing how we administer justice, and how we govern the state in other matters, has agreed, by the very fact of remaining here, to do whatsoever we tell him. And, we say, he who disobeys us acts unjustly on three counts: he disobeys us who are his parents, and he disobeys us who reared him, and he disobeys us after he has agreed to obey us, without persuading us that we are wrong. Yet we did not tell him sternly to do whatever we told him. We offered him an alternative; we gave him his choice either to obey us or to convince us that we were wrong; but he does neither.

"These are the charges, Socrates, to which we say that you will expose yourself if you do what you intend; and you are more exposed to these charges than other Athenians." And if I were to ask, "Why?" they might retort with justice that I have bound myself by the agreement with them more than other Athenians. They would say, "Socrates, we have very strong evidence that you were satisfied with us and with the state. You would not have been content to stay at home in it more than other Athenians unless you had been satisfied with it more than they. You never went away from Athens to the festivals, nor elsewhere except on military service; you never made other journeys like other men; you had no desire to see other states or other laws; you were contented with us and our state; so strongly did you prefer us, and agree to be governed by us. And what is more, you had children in this city, you found it so satisfactory. Besides, if you had wished, you might at your trial have offered to go into exile. At that time you could have done with the state's consent what you are trying now to do without it. But then you gloried in being willing to die. You said that you preferred death to exile. And now you do not honor those words: you do not respect us, the laws, for you are trying to destroy us; and you are acting just as a miserable slave would act, trying to run away, and breaking the contracts and agreement which you made to live as our citizen. First, therefore, answer this question. Are we right, or are we wrong, in saying that you have agreed not in mere words, but in your actions, to live under our government?" What are we to say, Crito? Must we not admit that it is true?

Crito: We must, Socrates.

Socr: Then they would say, "Are you not breaking your contracts and agreements with us? And you were not led to make them by force or by fraud. You did not have to make up your mind in a hurry. You had seventy years in which you might have gone away if you had been dissatisfied with us, or if the agreement had seemed to you unjust. But you preferred neither Sparta nor Crete, though you are fond of saying that they are well governed, nor any other state, either of the Greeks or the Barbarians. You went away from Athens less than the lame and the blind and the crippled. Clearly you, far more than other Athenians, were satisfied with the state, and also with us who are its laws; for who would be satisfied with a state which had no laws? And now will you not abide by your agreement? If you take our advice, you will, Socrates; then you will not make yourself ridiculous by going away from Athens.

"Reflect now. What good will you do yourself or your friends by thus transgressing and breaking your agreement? It is tolerably certain that they, on their part, will at least run the risk of exile, and of losing their civil rights, or of forfeiting their property. You yourself might go to one of the neighboring states, to Thebes or to Megara, for instance—for both of them are well governed—but, Socrates, you will come as an enemy to these governments, and all who care for their city will look askance at you, and think that you are a subverter of law. You will confirm the judges in their opinion, and make it seem that their verdict was a just one. For a man who is a subverter of law may well be supposed to be a corrupter of the young and thoughtless. Then will you avoid well-governed states and civilized men? Will life be worth having, if you do? Will you associate with such men, and converse without shame—about what, Socrates? About the things which you talk of here? Will you tell them that excellence and justice and institutions and law are the most valuable things that men can have? And do you not think that that will be a disgraceful thing for Socrates? You ought to think so. But you will leave these places; you will go to the friends of Crito in Thessaly. For there is found the greatest disorder and license, and very likely they will be delighted to hear of the ludicrous way in which you escaped from prison, dressed up in peasant's clothes, or in some other disguise which people put on when they are running away, and with your appearance altered. But will no one say how you, an old man, with probably only a few more years to live, clung so greedily to life that you dared to break the highest laws? Perhaps not, if you do not annoy them. But if you do, Socrates, you will hear much that will make you blush. You will pass your life as the flatterer and the slave of all men; and what will you be doing but feasting in Thessaly?[3] It will be as if you had made a journey to Thessaly for a banquet. And where will be

---

[3] The Athenians disdained the Thessalians as heavy eaters and drinkers.—Ed.

all our old arguments about justice and excellence then? But you wish to live for the sake of your children? You want to bring them up and educate them? What? Will you take them with you to Thessaly, and bring them up and educate them there? Will you make them strangers to their own country, that you may bestow this benefit of exile on them too? Or supposing that you leave them in Athens, will they be brought up and educated better if you are alive, though you are not with them? Yes, your friends will take care of them. Will your friends take care of them if you make a journey to Thessaly, and not if you make a journey to Hades? You ought not to think that, at least if those who call themselves your friends are worth anything at all.

"No, Socrates, be persuaded by us who have reared you. Think neither of children nor of life, nor of any other thing before justice, so that when you come to the other world you may be able to make your defense before the rulers who sit in judgment there. It is clear that neither you nor any of your friends will be happier, or juster, or more pious in this life, if you do this thing, nor will you be happier after you are dead. Now you will go away a victim of the injustice, not of the laws, but of men. But if you repay evil with evil, and injustice with injustice in this shameful way, and break your agreements and covenants with us, and injure those whom you should least injure, yourself and your friends and your country and us, and so escape, then we shall be angry with you while you live, and when you die our brothers, the laws in Hades, will not receive you kindly; for they will know that on earth you did all that you could to destroy us. Listen then to us, and let not Crito persuade you to do as he says."

Be sure, my dear friend Crito, that this is what I seem to hear, as the worshippers of Cybele seem, in their passion, to hear the music of flutes; and the sound of these arguments rings so loudly in my ears, that I cannot hear any other arguments. And I feel sure that if you try to change my mind you will speak in vain. Nevertheless, if you think that you will succeed, speak.

Crito: I have nothing more to say, Socrates.

Socr: Then let it be, Crito, and let us do as I say, since the god is our guide.

John Rawls is Professor of Philosophy
at Harvard University.

John Rawls

THE JUSTIFICATION OF CIVIL DISOBEDIENCE

I. INTRODUCTION

I should like to discuss briefly, and in an informal way, the grounds of civil disobedience in a constitutional democracy. Thus, I shall limit my remarks to the conditions under which we may, by civil disobedience, properly oppose legally established democratic authority; I am not concerned with the situation under other kinds of government nor, except incidentally, with other forms of resistance. My thought is that in a reasonably just (though of course not perfectly just) democratic regime, civil disobedience, when it is justified, is normally to be understood as a political action which addresses the sense of justice of the majority in order to urge reconsideration of the measures protested and to warn that in the firm opinion of the dissenters the conditions of social cooperation are not being honored. This characterization of civil disobedience is

Reprinted from *Civil Disobedience: Theory and Practice,* ed. Hugo Adam Bedau (New York: Pegasus, 1969), by permission of the author.

intended to apply to dissent on fundamental questions of internal policy, a limitation which I shall follow to simplify our question.

II. THE SOCIAL CONTRACT DOCTRINE

It is obvious that the justification of civil disobedience depends upon the theory of political obligation in general, and so we may appropriately begin with a few comments on this question. The two chief virtues of social institutions are justice and efficiency, where by the efficiency of institutions I understand their effectiveness for certain social conditions and ends the fulfillment of which is to everyone's advantage. We should comply with and do our part in just and efficient social arrangements for at least two reasons: first of all, we have a natural duty not to oppose the establishment of just and efficient institutions (when they do not yet exist) and to uphold and comply with them (when they do exist); and second, assuming that we have knowingly accepted the benefits of these institutions and plan to continue to do so, and that we have encouraged and expect others to do their part, we also have an obligation to do our share when, as the arrangement requires, it comes our turn. Thus, we often have both a natural duty as well as an obligation to support just and efficient institutions, the obligation arising from our voluntary acts while the duty does not.

Now all this is perhaps obvious enough, but it does not take us very far. Any more particular conclusions depend upon the conception of justice which is the basis of a theory of political obligation. I believe that the appropriate conception, at least for an account of political obligation in a constitutional democracy, is that of the social contract theory from which so much of our political thought derives. If we are careful to interpret it in a suitably general way, I hold that this doctrine provides a satisfactory basis for political theory, indeed even for ethical theory itself, but this is beyond our present concern.[1] The interpretation I suggest is the following: that the principles to which social arrangements must conform, and in particular the principles of justice, are those which free and rational men would agree to in an original position of equal liberty; and similarly,

---

[1] By the social contract theory I have in mind the doctrine found in Locke, Rousseau, and Kant. I have attempted to give an interpretation of this view in: "Justice as Fairness," *Philosophical Review* (April, 1958); "Justice and Constitutional Liberty," *Nomos,* VI (1963); "The Sense of Justice," *Philosophical Review* (July 1963). [Ed. note. See also "Distributive Justice," in Peter Laslett and W. G. Runciman, eds., *Philosophy, Politics and Society* (1967).]

the principles which govern men's relations to institutions and define their natural duties and obligations are the principles to which they would consent when so situated. It should be noted straightway that in this interpretation of the contract theory the principles of justice are understood as the outcome of a hypothetical agreement. They are principles which would be agreed to if the situation of the original position were to arise. There is no mention of an actual agreement nor need such an agreement ever be made. Social arrangements are just or unjust according to whether they accord with the principles for assigning and securing fundamental rights and liberties which would be chosen in the original position. This position is, to be sure, the analytic analogue of the traditional notion of the state of nature, but it must not be mistaken for a historical occasion. Rather it is a hypothetical situation which embodies the basic ideas of the contract doctrine; the description of this situation enables us to work out which principles would be adopted. I must now say something about these matters.

The contract doctrine has always supposed that the persons in the original position have equal powers and rights, that is, that they are symmetrically situated with respect to any arrangements for reaching agreement, and that coalitions and the like are excluded. But it is an essential element (which has not been sufficiently observed although it is implicit in Kant's version of the theory) that there are very strong restrictions on what the contracting parties are presumed to know. In particular, I interpret the theory to hold that the parties do not know their position in society, past, present, or future; nor do they know which institutions exist. Again, they do not know their own place in the distribution of natural talents and abilities, whether they are intelligent or strong, man or woman, and so on. Finally, they do not know their own particular interests and preferences or the system of ends which they wish to advance: they do not know their conception of the good. In all these respects the parties are confronted with a veil of ignorance which prevents any one from being able to take advantage of his good fortune or particular interests or from being disadvantaged by them. What the parties do know (or assume) is that Hume's circumstances of justice obtain: namely, that the bounty of nature is not so generous as to render cooperative schemes superfluous nor so harsh as to make them impossible. Moreover, they assume that the extent of their altruism is limited and that, in general, they do not take an interest in one another's interests. Thus, given the special features of the original position, each man tries to do the best he can for himself by insisting on principles calculated to protect and advance his system of ends whatever it turns out to be.

I believe that as a consequence of the peculiar nature of the original position there would be an agreement on the following two principles for assigning rights and duties and for regulating distributive shares as these are determined by the fundamental institutions of society: first, each person is to have an equal right to the most extensive liberty compatible with a like liberty for all; second, social and economic inequalities (as defined by the institutional structure or fostered by it) are to be arranged so that they are both to everyone's advantage and attached to positions and offices open to all. In view of the content of these two principles and their application to the main institutions of society, and therefore to the social system as a whole, we may regard them as the two principles of justice. Basic social arrangements are just insofar as they conform to these principles, and we can, if we like, discuss questions of justice directly by reference to them. But a deeper understanding of the justification of civil disobedience requires, I think, an account of the derivation of these principles provided by the doctrine of the social contract. Part of our task is to show why this is so.

III. THE GROUNDS OF COMPLIANCE WITH AN UNJUST LAW

If we assume that in the original position men would agree both to the principle of doing their part when they have accepted and plan to continue to accept the benefits of just institutions (the principle of fairness), and also to the principle of not preventing the establishment of just institutions and of upholding and complying with them when they do exist, then the contract doctrine easily accounts for our having to conform to just institutions. But how does it account for the fact that we are normally required to comply with unjust laws as well? The injustice of a law is not a sufficient ground for not complying with it any more than the legal validity of legislation is always sufficient to require obedience to it. Sometimes one hears these extremes asserted, but I think that we need not take them seriously.

An answer to our question can be given by elaborating the social contract theory in the following way. I interpret it to hold that one is to envisage a series of agreements as follows: first, men are to agree upon the principles of justice in the original position. Then they are to move to a constitutional convention in which they choose a constitution that satisfies the principles of justice already chosen. Finally they assume the role of a legislative body and guided by the principles of justice enact laws subject to the constraints and procedures of the just constitution. The decisions reached in any stage are binding in all subsequent stages. Now whereas in the original position the contracting parties have no knowledge of their society or of their own position in it, in both a constitutional convention and a legislature, they do know certain general facts about their institutions, for example, the statistics regarding employment and output required for fiscal and economic policy. But no one knows particular facts about his own social class or his place in the distribution of natural assets. On each occasion the contracting parties have the knowledge required to make their agreement rational from the appropriate point of view, but not so much as to make them prejudiced. They are unable to tailor principles and legislation to take advantage of their social or natural positions; a veil of ignorance prevents their knowing what this position is. With this series of agreements in mind, we can characterize just laws and policies as those which would be enacted were this whole process correctly carried out.

In choosing a constitution the aim is to find among the just constitutions the one which is most likely, given the general facts about the society in question, to lead to just and effective legislation. The principles of justice provide a criterion for the laws desired; the problem is to find a set of political procedures that will give this outcome. I shall assume that, at least under the normal conditions of a modern state, the best constitution is some form of democratic regime affirming equal political liberty and using some sort of majority (or other plurality) rule. Thus it follows that on the contract theory a constitutional democracy of some sort is required by the principles of justice. At the same time it is essential to observe that the constitutional process is always a case of what we may call imperfect procedural justice: that is, there is no feasible political procedure which guarantees that the enacted legislation is just even though we have (let us suppose) a standard for just legislation. In simple cases, such as games of fair division, there are procedures which always lead to the right outcome (assume that equal shares is fair and let the man who cuts the cake take the last piece). These situations are those of perfect procedural justice. In other cases it does not matter what the outcome is as long as the fair procedure is followed: fairness of the process is transferred to the result (fair gambling is an instance of this). These situations are those of pure procedural justice. The constitutional process, like a criminal trial, resembles neither of these; the result matters and we have a standard for it. The difficulty is that we cannot frame a procedure which guarantees that only just and effective legislation is enacted. Thus even under a just constitution unjust laws may be passed and unjust policies enforced. Some form of the majority principle is necessary but the majority may be mistaken, more or less willfully, in what it legislates. In agreeing to a democratic constitution (as an instance of imperfect procedural justice) one accepts at the same time the principle of majority rule. Assuming that the constitution is just and that we have accepted and plan to continue to accept its benefits, we then have both an obligation and a natural duty (and in any case the duty) to comply with what the majority enacts even though it may be unjust. In this way we become bound to follow unjust laws, not always, of course, but provided the injustice does not exceed certain limits. We recognize that we must run the risk of suffering from the defects of one another's sense of justice; this burden we are prepared to carry as long as it is more or less evenly distributed or does not weigh too heavily. Justice binds us to a just constitution and to the unjust laws which may be enacted under it in precisely the same way that it binds us to any other social arrangement. Once we take the sequence of stages into account, there is nothing unusual in our being required to comply with unjust laws.

It should be observed that the majority principle has a secondary place as a rule of procedure which is perhaps the most efficient one under usual circumstances for working a democratic constitution. The basis for it rests essentially upon the principles of justice and therefore we may, when conditions allow, appeal to these principles against unjust legislation. The justice of the constitution does not insure the justice of laws enacted under it; and while we often have both an obligation and a duty to comply with what the majority legislates (as long as it does not exceed certain limits), there is, of course, no corresponding obligation or duty to regard what the majority enacts as itself just. The right to make law does not guarantee that the decision is rightly made; and while the citizen submits in his conduct to the judgment of democratic authority, he does not submit his judgment to it.[2] And if in his judgment the enactments of the majority exceed certain bounds of injustice, the citizen may consider civil disobedience. For we are not required to accept the majority's acts unconditionally and to acquiesce in the denial of our and others' liberties; rather we submit our conduct to democratic authority to the extent necessary to share the burden of working a constitutional regime, distorted as it must inevitably be by men's lack of wisdom and the defects of their sense of justice.

---

[2]   On this point see A. E. Murphy's review of Yves Simon's *The Philosophy of Democratic Government* (1951) in the *Philosophical Review* (April, 1952).

IV. THE PLACE OF CIVIL DISOBEDIENCE
IN A CONSTITUTIONAL DEMOCRACY

We are now in a position to say a few things about civil disobedience. I shall understand it to be a public, nonviolent, and conscientious act contrary to law usually done with the intent to bring about a change in the policies or laws of the government.[3] Civil disobedience is a political act in the sense that it is an act justified by moral principles which define a conception of civil society and the public good. It rests, then, on political conviction as opposed to a search for self or group interest; and in the case of a constitutional democracy, we may assume that this conviction involves the conception of justice (say that expressed by the contract doctrine) which underlies the constitution itself. That is, in a viable democratic regime there is a common conception of justice by reference to which its citizens regulate their political affairs and interpret the constitution. Civil disobedience is a public act which the dissenter believes to be justified by this conception of justice and for this reason it may be understood as addressing the sense of justice of the majority in order to urge reconsideration of the measures protested and to warn that, in the sincere opinion of the dissenters, the conditions of social cooperation are not being honored. For the principles of justice express precisely such conditions, and their persistent and deliberate violation in regard to basic liberties over any extended period of time cuts the ties of community and invites either submission or forceful resistance. By engaging in civil disobedience a minority leads the majority to consider whether it wants to have its acts taken in this way, or whether, in view of the common sense of justice, it wishes to acknowledge the claims of the minority.

Civil disobedience is also civil in another sense. Not only is it the outcome of a sincere conviction based on principles which regulate civic life, but it is public and nonviolent, that is, it is done in a situation where arrest and punishment are expected and accepted without resistance. In this way it manifests a respect for legal procedures. Civil disobedience expresses disobedience to law within the limits of fidelity to law, and this feature of it helps to establish in the eyes of the majority that it is indeed conscientious and sincere, that it really is meant to address their sense of

---

[3] Here I follow H. A. Bedau's definition of civil disobedience. See his "On Civil Disobedience," *Journal of Philosophy* (October, 1961).

justice.[4] Being completely open about one's acts and being willing to accept the legal consequences of one's conduct is a bond given to make good one's sincerity, for that one's deeds are conscientious is not easy to demonstrate to another or even before oneself. No doubt it is possible to imagine a legal system in which conscientious belief that the law is unjust is accepted as a defense for noncompliance, and men of great honesty who are confident in one another might make such a system work. But as things are such a scheme would be unstable; we must pay a price in order to establish that we believe our actions have a moral basis in the convictions of the community.

The nonviolent nature of civil disobedience refers to the fact that it is intended to address the sense of justice of the majority and as such it is a form of speech, an expression of conviction. To engage in violent acts likely to injure and to hurt is incompatible with civil disobedience as a mode of address. Indeed, an interference with the basic rights of others tends to obscure the civilly disobedient quality of one's act. Civil disobedience is nonviolent in the further sense that the legal penalty for one's action is accepted and that resistance is not (at least for the moment) contemplated. Nonviolence in this sense is to be distinguished from nonviolence as a religious or pacifist principle. While those engaging in civil disobedience have often held some such principle, there is no necessary connection between it and civil disobedience. For on the interpretation suggested, civil disobedience in a democratic society is best understood as an appeal to the principles of justice, the fundamental conditions of willing social cooperation among free men, which in the view of the community as a whole are expressed in the constitution and guide its interpretation. Being an appeal to the moral basis of public life, civil disobedience is a political and not primarily a religious act. It addresses itself to the common principles of justice which men can require one another to follow and not to the aspirations of love which they cannot. Moreover by taking part in civilly disobedient acts one does not foreswear indefinitely the idea of forceful resistance; for if the appeal against injustice is repeatedly denied, then the majority has declared its intention to invite submission or resistance and the latter may conceivably be justified even in a democratic regime. We are not required to acquiesce in the crushing of fundamental liberties by democratic majorities which have shown themselves blind to the principles of justice upon which justification of the constitution depends.

---

[4] For a fuller discussion of this point to which I am indebted, see Charles Fried, "Moral Causation," *Harvard Law Review* (1964).

V. THE JUSTIFICATION OF CIVIL DISOBEDIENCE

So far we have said nothing about the justification of civil disobedience, that is, the conditions under which civil disobedience may be engaged in consistent with the principles of justice that support a democratic regime. Our task is to see how the characterization of civil disobedience as addressed to the sense of justice of the majority (or to the citizens as a body) determines when such action is justified.

First of all, we may suppose that the normal political appeals to the majority have already been made in good faith and have been rejected, and that the standard means of redress have been tried. Thus, for example, existing political parties are indifferent to the claims of the minority and attempts to repeal the laws protested have been met with further repression since legal institutions are in the control of the majority. While civil disobedience should be recognized, I think, as a form of political action within the limits of fidelity to the rule of law, at the same time it is a rather desperate act just within these limits, and therefore it should, in general, be undertaken as a last resort when standard democratic processes have failed. In this sense it is not a normal political action. When it is justified there has been a serious breakdown; not only is there grave injustice in the law but a refusal more or less deliberate to correct it.

Second, since civil disobedience is a political act addressed to the sense of justice of the majority, it should usually be limited to substantial and clear violations of justice and preferably to those which, if rectified, will establish a basis for doing away with remaining injustices. For this reason there is a presumption in favor of restricting civil disobedience to violations of the first principle of justice, the principle of equal liberty, and to barriers which contravene the second principle, the principle of open offices which protects equality of opportunity. It is not, of course, always easy to tell whether these principles are satisfied. But if we think of them as guaranteeing the fundamental equal political and civil liberties (including freedom of conscience and liberty of thought) and equality of opportunity, then it is often relatively clear whether their principles are being honored. After all, the equal liberties are defined by the visible structure of social institutions; they are to be incorporated into the recognized practice, if not the letter, of social arrangements. When minorities are denied the right to vote or to hold certain political offices, when certain religious groups are repressed and others denied equality of opportunity in the economy, this is often obvious and there is no doubt that justice is not being given. However, the first part of the second principle which requires that inequalities be to everyone's advantage is a much more imprecise and controversial matter. Not only is there a problem of assigning it a determinate and precise sense, but even if we do so and agree on what it should be, there is often a wide variety of reasonable opinion as to whether the principle is satisfied. The reason for this is that the principle applies primarily to fundamental economic and social policies. The choice of these depends upon theoretical and speculative beliefs as well as upon a wealth of concrete information, and all of this mixed with judgment and plain hunch, not to mention in actual cases prejudice and self-interest. Thus unless the laws of taxation are clearly designed to attack a basic equal liberty, they should not be protested by civil disobedience; the appeal to justice is not sufficiently clear and its resolution is best left to the political process. But violations of the equal liberties that define the common status of citizenship are another matter. The deliberate denial of these more or less over any extended period of time in the face of normal political protest is, in general, an appropriate object of civil disobedience. We may think of the social system as divided roughly into two parts, one which incorporates the fundamental equal liberties (including equality of opportunity) and another which embodies social and economic policies properly aimed at promoting the advantage of everyone. As a rule civil disobedience is best limited to the former where the appeal to justice is not only more definite and precise, but where, if it is effective, it tends to correct the injustices in the latter.

Third, civil disobedience should be restricted to those cases where the dissenter is willing to affirm that everyone else similarly subjected to the same degree of injustice has the right to protest in a similar way. That is, we must be prepared to authorize others to dissent in similar situations and in the same way, and to accept the consequences of their doing so. Thus, we may hold, for example, that the widespread disposition to disobey civilly clear violations of fundamental liberties more or less deliberate over an extended period of time would raise the degree of justice throughout society and would insure men's self-esteem as well as their respect for one another. Indeed, I believe this to be true, though certainly it is partly a matter of conjecture. As the contract doctrine emphasizes, since the principles of justice are principles which we would agree to in an original position of equality when we do not know our social position and the like, the refusal to grant justice is either the denial of the other as an equal (as one in regard to whom we are prepared to constrain our actions by principles which we would consent to) or the manifestation of a willingness to take advantage of natural contingencies and social fortune at his expense. In either case, injustice invites submission or resistance; but submission arouses the contempt of the oppressor and confirms him in his intention. If straightway, after a decent period of time to make reasonable political appeals in the normal way, men were in general to dissent by civil disobedience from infractions of the fundamental equal liberties, these liberties would, I believe, be more rather than less secure. Legitimate civil disobedience properly exercised is a stabilizing device in a constitutional regime, tending to make it more firmly just.

Sometimes, however, there may be a complication in connection with this third condition. It is possible, although perhaps unlikely, that there are so many persons or groups with a sound case for resorting to civil disobedience (as judged by the foregoing criteria) that disorder would follow if they all did so. There might be serious injury to the just constitution. Or again, a group might be so large that some extra precaution is necessary in the extent to which its members organize and engage in civil disobedience. Theoretically the case is one in which a number of persons or groups are equally entitled to and all want to resort to civil disobedience, yet if they all do this, grave consequences for everyone may result. The question, then, is who among them may exercise their right, and it falls under the general problem of fairness. I cannot discuss the complexities of the matter here. Often a lottery or a rationing system can be set up to handle the case; but unfortunately the circumstances of civil disobedience rule out this solution. It suffices to note that a problem of fairness may arise and that those who contemplate civil disobedience should take it into account. They may have to reach an understanding as to who can exercise their right in the immediate situation and to recognize the need for special constraint.

The final condition, of a different nature, is the following. We have been considering when one has a right to engage in civil disobedience, and our conclusion is that one has this right should three conditions hold: when one is subject to injustice more or less deliberate over an extended period of time in the face of normal political protests; where the injustice is a clear violation of the liberties of equal citizenship; and provided that the general disposition to protest similarly in similar cases would have acceptable consequences. These conditions are not, I think, exhaustive but they seem to cover the more obvious points; yet even when they are satisfied and one has the right to engage in civil disobedience, there is still the different question of whether one should exercise this right, that is, whether by doing so one is likely to further one's ends. Having established one's right to protest one is then free to consider these tactical questions. We may be acting within our rights but still foolishly if our action only serves to provoke the harsh retaliation of the majority; and it is likely to do so if the majority lacks a sense of justice, or if the action is poorly timed or not well designed to make the appeal to the sense of justice effective. It is easy to think of instances of this sort, and in each case these practical questions have to be faced. From the standpoint of the theory of political obligation we can only say that the exercise of the right should be rational and reasonably designed to advance the protester's aims, and that weighing tactical questions presupposes that one has already established one's right, since tactical advantages in themselves do not support it.

VI. CONCLUSION: SEVERAL OBJECTIONS CONSIDERED

In a reasonably affluent democratic society justice becomes the first virtue of institutions. Social arrangements irrespective of their efficiency must be reformed if they are significantly unjust. No increase in efficiency in the form of greater advantages for many justifies the loss of liberty of a few. That we believe this is shown by the fact that in a democracy the fundamental liberties of citizenship are not understood as the outcome of political bargaining nor are they subject to the calculus of social interests. Rather these liberties are fixed points which serve to limit political transactions and which determine the scope of calculations of social advantage. It is this fundamental place of the equal liberties which makes their systematic violation over any extended period of time a proper object of civil disobedience. For to deny men these rights is to infringe the conditions of social cooperation among free and rational persons, a fact which is evident to the citizens of a constitutional regime since it follows from the principles of justice which underlie their institutions. The justification of civil disobedience rests on the priority of justice and the equal liberties which it guarantees.

It is natural to object to this view of civil disobedience that it relies too heavily upon the existence of a sense of justice. Some may hold that the feeling for justice is not a vital political force, and that what moves men are various other interests, the desire for wealth, power, prestige, and so on. Now this is a large question the answer to which is highly conjectural and each tends to have his own opinion. But there are two remarks which may clarify what I have said: first, I have assumed that there is in a constitutional regime a common sense of justice the principles of which are recognized to support the constitution and to guide its interpretation. In any given situation particular men may be tempted to violate these principles, but the collective force in their behalf is usually effective since they are seen as the necessary terms of cooperation among free men; and presumably the citizens of a democracy (or sufficiently many of them) want to see justice done. Where these assumptions fail, the justifying conditions for civil disobedience (the first three) are not affected, but the rationality of engaging in it certainly is. In this case, unless the costs of repressing civil dissent injures the economic self-interest (or whatever) of the majority, protest may simply make the position of the minority worse. No doubt as a tactical matter civil disobedience is more effective when its appeal coincides with other interests, but a constitutional regime is not viable in the long run without an attachment to the principles of justice of the sort which we have assumed.

Then, further, there may be a misapprehension about the manner in which a sense of justice manifests itself. There is a tendency to think that it is shown by professions of the relevant principles together with actions of an altruistic nature requiring a considerable degree of self-sacrifice. But these conditions are obviously too strong, for the majority's sense of justice may show itself simply in its being unable to undertake the measures required to suppress the minority and to punish as the law requires the various acts of civil disobedience. The sense of justice undermines the will to uphold unjust institutions, and so a majority despite its superior power may give way. It is unprepared to force the minority to be subject to injustice. Thus, although the majority's action is reluctant and grudging, the role of the sense of justice is nevertheless essential, for without it the majority would have been willing to enforce the law and to defend its position. Once we see the sense of justice as working in this negative way to make established injustices indefensible, then it is recognized as a central element of democratic politics.

Finally, it may be objected against this account that it does not settle the question of who is to say when the situation is such as to justify civil disobedience. And because it does not answer this question, it invites anarchy by encouraging every man to decide the matter for himself. Now the reply to this is that each man must indeed settle this question for himself, although he may, of course, decide wrongly. This is true on any theory of political duty and obligation, at least on any theory compatible with the principles of a democratic constitution. The citizen is responsible for what he does. If we usually think that we should comply with the law, this is because our political principles normally lead to this conclusion. There is a presumption in favor of compliance in the absence of good reasons to the contrary. But because each man is responsible and must decide for himself as best he can whether the circumstances justify civil disobedience, it does not follow that he may decide as he pleases. It is not by looking to our personal interests or to political allegiances narrowly construed, that we should make up our mind. The citizen must decide on the basis of the principles of justice that underlie and guide the interpretation of the constitution and in the light of his sincere conviction as to how these principles should be applied in the circumstances. If he concludes that conditions obtain which justify civil disobedience and conducts himself accordingly, he has acted conscientiously and perhaps mistakenly, but not in any case at his convenience.

In a democratic society each man must act as he thinks the principles of political right require him to. We are to follow our understanding of these principles, and we cannot do otherwise. There can be no morally binding legal interpretation of these principles, not even by a supreme court or legislature. Nor is there any infallible procedure for determining what or who is right. In our system the Supreme Court, Congress, and the President often put forward rival interpretations of the Constitution. Although the Court has the final say in settling any particular case, it is not immune from powerful political influence that may change its reading of the law of the land. The Court presents its point of view by reason and argument; its conception of the Constitution must, if it is to endure, persuade men of its soundness. The final court of appeal is not the Court, or Congress, or the President, but the electorate as a whole.[5] The civilly disobedient appeal in effect to this body. There is no danger of anarchy as long as there is a sufficient working agreement in men's conceptions of political justice and what it requires. That men can achieve such an understanding when the essential political liberties are maintained is the assumption implicit in democratic institutions. There is no way to avoid entirely the risk of divisive strife. But if legitimate civil disobedience seems to threaten civil peace, the responsibility falls not so much on those who protest as upon those whose abuse of authority and power justifies such opposition.

---

[5] For a presentation of this view to which I am indebted, see A. M. Bickel, *The Least Dangerous Branch* (Indianapolis, 1962), especially Chapters 5 and 6.

*Sidney Hook is Professor of Philosophy
at New York University.*

Sidney Hook

THE CONTENT OF A LIBERAL EDUCATION

What, concretely, should the modern man know in order to live intelligently in the world today? What should we require that he learn of subject matters and skills in his educational career in order that he may acquire maturity in feeling, in judgment, in action? Can we indicate the minimum indispensables of a liberal education in the modern world? This approach recognizes that no subject per se is inherently liberal at all times and places. But it also recognizes that within a given age in a given culture, the enlightenment and maturity, the freedom and power, which liberal education aims to impart, is more likely to be achieved by mastery of some subject matters and skills than by others. In short, principles must bear fruit in specific programs in specific times. In what follows I shall speak of studies rather than of conventional courses.

(1) The liberally educated person should be intellectually at home in

the world of physical nature. He should know something about the earth he inhabits and its place in the solar system, about the solar system and its relation to the cosmos. He should know something about mechanics, heat, light, electricity, and magnetism as the universal forces that condition anything he is or may become. He should be just as intimately acquainted with the nature of man as a biological species, his evolution, and the discoveries of experimental genetics. He should know something about the structure of his own body and mind, and the cycle of birth, growth, learning, and decline. To have even a glimmer of understanding of these things, he must go beyond the level of primary description and acquire some grasp of the principles that explain what he observes. Where an intelligent grasp of principles requires a knowledge of mathematics, its fundamental ideas should be presented in such a way that students carry away the sense of mathematics not only as a tool for the solution of problems but as a study of types of order, system, and language.

Such knowledge is important to the individual *not* merely because of its intrinsic fascination. Every subject from numismatics to Sanskrit possesses an intrinsic interest to those who are curious about it. It is important because it helps make everyday experience more intelligible; because it furnishes a continuous exemplification of scientific method in action; because our world is literally being remade by the consequences and applications of science; because the fate of nations and the vocations of men depend upon the use of this knowledge; and because it provides the instruments to reduce our vast helplessness and dependence in an uncertain world.

Such knowledge is no less important because it bears upon the formation of *rational belief* about the place of man in the universe. Whatever views a man professes today about God, human freedom, Cosmic Purpose, and personal survival, he cannot reasonably hold them in ignorance of the scientific account of the world and man.

These are some of the reasons why the study of the natural sciences, and the elementary mathematical notions they involve, should be *required* of everyone. Making such study required imposes a heavy obligation and a difficult task of pedagogical discovery upon those who teach it. It is commonly recognized that the sciences today are taught as if all students enrolled in science courses were preparing to be professional scientists. Most of them are not. Naturally they seek to escape a study whose wider and larger uses they do not see because many of their teachers do not see it. Here is not the place to canvass and evaluate the attempts being made to organize instruction in the sciences. The best experience seems to show that one science should not be taken as the exemplar of all, but that the basic subject matter of astronomy, physics, chemistry, geology, in one group, and biology and psychology in another, should be covered. For when only one science is taught it tends to be treated professionally. Similarly, the best experience indicates that instruction should be inter-departmental—any competent teacher from one of these fields in either group should be able to teach all of them in the group, instead of having a succession of different teachers each representing his own field. This usually destroys both the continuity and the cumulative effect of the teaching as a whole.

(2) Every student should be required to become intelligently aware of how the society in which he lives functions, of the great forces molding contemporary civilization, and of the crucial problems of our age which await decision. The studies most appropriate to this awareness have been conventionally separated into history, economics, government, sociology, social psychology, and anthropology. This separation is an intellectual scandal. For it is impossible to have an adequate grasp of the problems of government without a knowledge of economics, and vice versa. Except for some special domains of professional interest, the same is true for the other subjects as well.

The place of the social studies, properly integrated around problems and issues, is fundamental in the curriculum of modern education. It is one of the dividing points between the major conflicting schools of educational thought. The question of its justification must be sharply distinguished from discussion of the relative merits of this or that mode of approach to the social studies.

The knowledge and insight that the social studies can give are necessary for every student because no matter what his specialized pursuits may later be, the extent to which he can follow them, and the "contextual" developments within these fields, depend upon the total social situation of which they are in some sense a part. An engineer today whose knowledge is restricted only to technical matters of engineering, or a physician whose competence extends only to the subject matter of traditional medical training, is ill-prepared to plan intelligently for a life-career or to understand the basic problems that face his profession. He is often unable to cope adequately with those specific problems in his own domain that involve, as so many problems of social and personal health do, economic and psychological difficulties. No matter what an individual's vocation, the conditions of his effective functioning depend upon pervasive social tendencies which set the occasions for the application of knowledge, provide the opportunities of employment, and not seldom determine even the direction of research.

More important, the whole presuppositon of the theory of democracy is that the electorate will be able to make intelligent decisions on the issues before it. These issues are basically political, social, and economic. Their specific character changes from year to year. But their generic form, and the character of the basic problems, do not. Nor, most essential of all, do the proper intellectual habits of meeting them change. It is undeniably true that the world we live in is one marked by greater changes, because of the impact of technology, than ever before. This does not necessitate changing the curriculum daily to catch up with today's newspapers, nor does it justify a concentration on presumably eternal problems as if these problems had significance independent of cultural place-time. The fact that we are living in a world where the rate of cultural change is greater than at any time in the past, together with its ramifications, may itself become a central consideration for analysis.

The construction of a social studies curriculum is a task of the greatest difficulty even after the artificiality of departmental lines of division has been recognized. For the integration of the material demands a historical approach, set not by bare chronology, but by the problems themselves. It must incorporate large amounts of philosophy and the scientific disciplines of evaluating judgments of fact and value. It must abandon misconceived interpretations of the "institutional approach" which describe social practices without confronting the challenge of theories and problems. It must not shrink from considering "solutions," and at the same time must guard against indoctrination of conclusions. It must learn how to use our life in cities, factories, and fields as a kind of "laboratory," not as occasions for sight-seeing excursions of dubious educational significance.

Properly organized studies of this kind are not something which already exist. They are something to be achieved. Their content must be definite and yet not fixed in detail. They do not exclude treatment of historical background but relate it to something of momentous issue in the present. They do not exclude great books of the past and present, nor bad books, nor material not found in books.

One of the reasons for the low estate in which the social studies are held is the failure to recognize the distinction between the general pattern of inquiry, whose logic holds for all fields in which truth is sought, and the specific criteria of validity, which are appropriate to special domains. We are all familiar with the type of historian who thinks "geometrically," i.e., who believes he can reach conclusions about human beings in historical situations with almost the same degree of rigor he uses to reach conclusions about triangles and circles. The warning against taking certain standards of precision as a model for all fields is at least as old as Aristotle.

> "Discussion," he says, "will be adequate if it has as much clearness as the subject-matter admits of, for precision is not to be sought for alike in all discussions . . . it is the mark of an educated man to look for precision in each class of things just so far as the nature of the subject admits; it is evidently equally foolish to accept probable reasoning from a mathematician and to demand from a rhetorician scientific proofs."[1]

Nonetheless, most discussions of the content of a liberal education which are heavily accented with a bias towards classic studies sin against this wisdom. In such accounts, mathematics and physics are justified as models of precise thought on which the social sciences are to pattern themselves. It is overlooked that the "logic" of mathematics and physics is a specific application of the general pattern of inquiry. Its precision reflects the nature of the subject matter considered. A physician, an economist, an anthropologist—even a biologist—who sought to carry into his domain the same standards would get grotesque results. *The models of correct thinking in each field must be the best illustrations of thinking in that field, not the pattern of another field.* "The type of exercise in consistent thinking" in mathematics is one thing, in the field of psychosomatic medicine it is quite another; "fidelity to empirical data" in astronomy is something else again from "fidelity to empirical data" in linguistics. This is blurred over in passages like the following from books on liberal education which, even when they give the social studies a place in the liberal arts curriculum, do so in a grudging and suspicious way:

> . . . The social studies cannot compete with pure mathematics and the natural sciences in exhaustive analysis, rigorous inference, or verifiable interpretations. Their methods are by nature such as to forbid the substitution of these studies for the more precise and established disciplines. The latter must continue to supply a distinctive and fundamental type of exercise in consistent reasoning and fidelity to empirical data.[2]

Literally read, this may seem to provide for the independence of social studies: but it is obvious from its overtones that an invidious distinction is

---

[1] Aristotle: *Nicomachean Ethics* (tr. Ross; Oxford: Oxford University Press; 1942), 1094b 12–14, 24–27.

[2] Greene, *et al.: Liberal Education Re-Examined,* pp. 56–7.

being drawn between the mathematical-physical sciences on the one hand, and the social sciences on the other.

(3) Everyone recognizes a distinction between knowledge and wisdom. This distinction is not clarified by making a mystery of wisdom and speaking of it as if it were begotten by divine inspiration while knowledge had a more lowly source. Wisdom is a kind of knowledge. It is knowledge of the nature, career, and consequences of *human values*. Since these cannot be separated from the human organism and the social scene, the moral ways of man cannot be understood without knowledge of the ways of things and institutions.

To study social affairs without an analysis of policies is to lose oneself in factual minutiae that lack interest and relevance. But knowledge of values is a prerequisite of the intelligent determination of policy. Philosophy, most broadly viewed, is the critical survey of existence from the standpoint of value. This points to the twofold role of philosophy in the curriculum of the college.

The world of physical nature may be studied without reference to human values. But history, art, literature, and particularly the social studies involve problems of value at every turn. A social philosophy whose implications are worked out is a series of proposals that something be *done* in the world. It includes a set of *plans* to conserve or change aspects of social life. Today the community is arrayed under different banners without a clear understanding of the basic issues involved. In the press of controversy, the ideals and values at the heart of every social philosophy are widely affirmed as articles of blind faith. They are partisan commitments justified only by the emotional security they give to believers. They spread by contagion, unchecked by critical safeguards; yet the future of civilization largely depends upon them and how they are held. It is therefore requisite that their study be made an integral part of the liberal arts curriculum. Systematic and critical instruction should be given in the great maps of life—the ways to heaven, hell, and earth— which are being unrolled in the world today.

Ideals and philosophies of life are not parts of the world of nature; but it is a pernicious illusion to imagine that they cannot be studied "scientifically." Their historical origins, their concatenation of doctrine, their controlling assumptions, their means, methods, and consequences in practice, can and should be investigated in a scientific spirit. There are certain social philosophies that would forbid such an investigation for fear of not being able to survive it; but it is one of the great merits of the democratic way of life and one of its strongest claims for acceptance that it can withstand analysis of this sort. It is incumbent upon the liberal arts college to provide for close study of the dominant social and political philosophies, ranging from one end of the color-spectrum to the other. Proper study will disclose that these philosophies cannot be narrowly considered in their own terms. They involve an examination of the great ways of life—of the great visions of philosophy which come into play whenever we try to arrange our values in a preference scale in order to choose the better between conflicting goods. Philosophy is best taught when the issues of moral choice arise naturally out of the problems of social life. The effective integration of concrete materials from history, literature, and social studies can easily be achieved within a philosophical perspective.

(4) Instruction in the natural, social, and technological forces shaping the world, and in the dominant conflicting ideals is behalf of which these forces are to be controlled, goes a long way. But not far enough. Far more important than knowledge is the method by which it is reached, and the ability to recognize when it constitutes *evidence* and when not; and more important than any particular ideal is the way in which it is held, and the capacity to evaluate it in relation to other ideals. From first to last, in season and out, our educational institutions, especially on the college level, must emphasize *methods* of analysis. They must build up in students a critical sense of evidence, relevance, and validity against which the multitudinous seas of propaganda will wash in vain. They must strengthen the powers of independent reflection, which will enable students to confront the claims of ideals and values by their alternatives and the relative costs of achieving them. . . .

It is taken for granted that every subject taught will be taught in a fashion that will bring home the ways in which warranted conclusions are reached. But it is well known that the habits of correct thinking are not carried over from one field to another unless the second field is similar in nature to the first. We do not need to wait for the results of experiments on transference of training to realize that a great many able scientists who pontificate on matters outside their fields display not only ignorance but utter inability to grasp essential points at issue or to make valid elementary inferences. More and more, thinking is becoming thinking in specialized domains, largely professional, accompanied by the feeling that outside that domain it is unimportant what conclusions are reached, or by the feeling that any conclusion is as valid as any other.

Those who believe that this state of affairs can be rectified by giving a course in some special subject matter like mathematics or Latin have never confronted the challenge to provide evidence for their claim. To teach something else in order to teach *how to think* is not a short cut to logic but a circuitous way to nowhere.

There are some who deny that there is a power of general thought, that thinking is a habit that always has a specific locus in a definite field, and that there is no carry-over from one field to a widely dissimilar one. In a certain sense, this is true. But we certainly can distinguish between domains or fields of interest which are broad and those that are narrow; and between those domains in which everyone has an interest because it affects him as a human being and citizen, and those domains that are more specialized.

The field of language, of inference and argument, is a broad field but a definite one in which specific training can be given to all students. How to read intelligently, how to recognize good from bad reasoning, how to evaluate evidence, how to distinguish between a definition and a hypothesis and between a hypothesis and a resolution, can be taught in such a way as to build up permanent habits of logic in action. The result of thorough training in "semantic" analysis—using that term in its broadest sense without invidious distinctions between different schools—is an intellectual sophistication without which a man may be learned but not intelligent.

Judging by past and present curricular achievements in developing students with intellectual sophistication and maturity, our colleges must be pronounced in the main, dismal failures. The main reason for the failure is the absence of serious effort, except in a few institutions, to realize this goal. The necessity of the task is not even recognized. This failure is not only intellectually reprehensible; it is socially dangerous. For the natural susceptibility of youth to enthusiasms, its tendency to glorify action, and its limited experience make it easy recruiting material for all sorts of demagogic movements which flatter its strength and impatience. Recent history furnishes many illustrations of how, in the absence of strong critical sense, youthful strength can lead to cruelty, and youthful impatience to folly. It is true that people who are incapable of thinking cannot be taught how to think, and that the incapacity for thought is not restricted to those who learn. But the first cannot be judged without being exposed to the processes of critical instruction, and the second should be eliminated from the ranks of the teachers. There is considerable evidence to show that students who are capable of completing high school can be so taught that they are aware of *whether* they are thinking or not. There is hope that, with better pedagogic skill and inspiration, they may become capable of grasping the main thought of *what* they are reading or hearing in non-technical fields—of developing a sense of *what validly follows from what,* an accompanying sensitiveness to the dominant types of fallacies, and a habit of weighing evidence for conclusions advanced.

My own experience has led me to the conclusion that this is *not* accomplished by courses in formal logic which, when given in a rigorous and elegant way, accomplish little more than courses in pure mathematics. There is an approach to the study of logic that on an elementary level is much more successful in achieving the ends described above than the traditional course in formal logic. This plunges the student into an analysis of language material around him. By constant use of concrete illustrations drawn from all fields, but especially the fields of politics and social study, insight is developed into the logical principles of definition, the structure of analogies, dilemmas, types of fallacies and the reasons *why* they are fallacies, the criteria of good hypotheses, and related topics. Such training may legitimately be required of all students. Although philosophers are usually best able to give it, any teacher who combines logical capacity with pedagogic skill can make this study a stimulating experience.

(5) There is less controversy about the desirability of the study of composition and literature than about any other subject in the traditional or modern curriculum. It is appreciated that among the essentials of clear thought are good language habits and that, except in the higher strata of philosophic discourse, tortuous obscurities of expression are more likely to be an indication of plain confusion than of stuttering profundity. It is also widely recognized that nothing can take the place of liberature in developing the imagination, and in imparting a sense of the inexhaustible richness of human personality. The questions that arise at this point are not of justification, but of method, technique, and scope of comprehensiveness.

If good language habits are to be acquired *only* in order to acquire facility in thinking, little can be said for the conventional courses in English composition. Students cannot acquire facility in clear expression in the space of a year, by developing sundry themes from varied sources, under the tutelage of instructors whose training and interest may not qualify them for sustained critical thought. Clear thinking is best controlled by those who are at home in the field in which thinking is done. If language instruction is to be motivated only by the desire to strengthen the power of organizing ideas in written discourse, it should be left to properly trained instructors in other disciplines.

But there are other justifications for teaching students English composition. The first is that there are certain rules of intelligent reading that are essential to—if they do not constitute—understanding. These rules are very elementary. By themselves they do not tell us how to understand a poem, a mathematical demonstration, a scientific text, or a religious prayer—all of which require special skills. But they make it easier for the student to uncover the nature of the "argument"—what is being said, what is being assumed, what is being presented as evidence—in any piece of prose that is not a narrative or simply informational in content. In a sense these rules are integral to the study of logic in action, but in such an introductory way that they are usually not considered part of logical study which begins its work after basic meanings have been established, or in independence of the meaning of logical symbols.

Another reason for teaching English composition independently is its uses in learning how to write. "Effective writing" is not necessarily the same thing as logical writing. The purpose for which we write determines whether our writing is effective. And there are many situations in which we write not to convince or to prove but to explain, arouse, confess, challenge, or assuage. To write *interestingly* may sometimes be just as important as to write soundly because getting a hearing and keeping attention may depend upon it. How much of the skills of writing can be taught is difficult to say. That it is worth making the effort to teach these skills is indisputable.

The place of language in the curriculum involves not merely our native language but *foreign* languages. Vocational considerations aside, should knowledge of a foreign language be required, and why?

Here again the discussion reveals great confusion. Most of the reasons advanced for making knowledge of a foreign language required are either demonstrably false or question-begging. There is a valid reason for making such study prescribed, but it is rarely stated.

It is sometimes asserted that no one can understand the structure of his own language unless he understands the structure of another. By "structure" is usually meant the grammar of the language.

> The study of Greek and Latin has a special value in increasing an American student's understanding of his own language. . . . The study of Greek and Latin provides one of the best introductions to the role of inflection in our grammatical methods and, by contrast, to an understanding of the function of other devices we now use in place of inflections.[3]
>
> . . . One's own language should be known as well as possible in terms of its peculiar genius; and at least one other language—Greek

---

[3] Ibid., p. 58.

> is still the best one for the purpose, and indeed for any purpose [*sic!*]—should be equally known. The lines of any two languages converge in the structure of language itself.[4]

The assumption behind these passages is that mastery of the intricacies of English grammar makes for greater ability in writing, reading, and understanding modern English prose. No evidence has ever been offered for this statement and many intelligent teachers of English deny it. The best grammarians are conspicuously not the best speakers and writers of English. It is one thing to have grammar "in the bones" as a consequence of acquiring good habits of speech and writing. It is quite another to learn grammar as a means of acquiring those habits. There are better and more direct ways to that goal. But let us grant the questionable assumption. The recommendations in the quoted passages would still be a horrendous *non sequitur*. For there is every reason to believe that if the time spent on learning the grammar of foreign languages were devoted to more intensive and prolonged study of English, the result would be far greater proficiency in English than if the available time were divided between the two languages.

A second reason often advanced for making the study of foreign languages mandatory, especially Greek and Latin, is that it contributes to the enrichment of the English vocabulary of students, and gives them a sense for shades of meaning in use which is necessary for even a fair degree of mastery of our language. The following is representative of claims of this character:

> Although many of these words have now certain semantic values that were foreign to their use in their original settings, still an experience of these words in contexts of Greek and Latin provides an insight into their functioning in English *which no other experience can give*.[5]

What a breath-taking piece of dogmatism! All the evidence is begged. Once more, the obvious advantage of devoting the time spent on foreign language to additional study of English words in use is evaded. It is further assumed that Greek and Latin must be systematically studied in order to learn the historical derivation of the English words we owe these languages. Courses have been devised in which Greek and Latin words in current English use are studied without intensive study of these languages. It is still an open question whether an intensive study of the English language helps students understand the meanings of the words they

---

[4] Mark van Doren: *Liberal Education* (New York: Henry Holt & Company; 1943), pp. 131–132.

[5] Greene, *et al.: Liberal Education Re-Examined*, p. 59. My italics.

encounter in the study of Greek and Latin rather than vice versa. It has often been observed that in sight reading of Greek and Latin, when students cannot consult dictionaries, those who are already most proficient in English do much better than those whose English vocabularies are limited.

The main reason why students should be requested to learn another language is that it is the most effective medium by which, when properly taught, they can acquire a sensitivity to language, to the subtle tones, undertones, and overtones of words, and to the licit ambiguities of imaginative discourse. No one who has not translated prose or poetry from one language to another can appreciate both the unique richness and the unique limitations of his own language. This is particularly true where the life of the emotions is concerned; and it is particularly important that it should be realized. For the appreciation of emotions, perhaps even their recognition in certain cases, depends upon their linguistic identification. The spectrum of human emotions is much more dense than the words by which we render them. Knowledge of different languages, and the attempts made to communicate back and forth between them in our own minds, broaden and diversify our own feelings. They multiply points of view, and liberate us from the prejudice that words—*our* words—are the natural signs of things and events. The genius of a culture is exemplified in a pre-eminent way in the characteristic idioms of its language. In learning another language we enable ourselves to appreciate both the cultural similarities and differences of the Western world.

So far as I know, this argument for the teaching of foreign languages was first advanced by Warner Fite.[6] But it is allied with a disparagement of "abstract thinking" on the ground that, since symbolic or conceptual thought strives to dissociate itself from the particularities of images and qualities, in the nature of the case it must falsify the fluidities of experience. This is a very serious error. Two things do not have to be identical in order to be characterized by identical relationships. And it is the relationships between things which are expressed in the symbols of abstract thinking. There is no opposition between "abstract thinking" and "concrete" or "qualitative" thinking. They involve differences in emphasis, subject matter, and interest, not different logics or formal criteria of validity.

The place of literature in the curriculum is justified by so many considerations that it is secure against all criticism. Here, too, what is at issue

---

[6] Warner Fite: "The Philosopher and His Words," *Philosophical Review,* Vol. 44, No. 2 (March 1935), p. 120.

is not whether literature—Greek, Latin, English, European, American—should be read and studied in the schools but what should be read, when, and by what methods. These are details, important details—but outside the scope of our inquiry.

Something should be said about the unique opportunity which the teaching of literature provides, not only in giving delight by heightening perception of the formal values of literary craftsmanship, but in giving insight into people. The opposite of a liberal education, William James somewhere suggests, is a literal education. A literal education is one which equips a person to read formulas and equations, straightforward prose, doggerel verse, and advertising signs. It does not equip one to read the language of metaphor, of paradox, of indirect analogy, of serious fancy in which the emotions and passions and half-believed ideas of human beings express themselves. To read great literature is to read men—their fears and motives, their needs and hopes. Every great novelist is a *menschenkenner* who opens the hearts of others to us and helps us to read our own hearts as well. The intelligent study of literature should never directly aim to strengthen morals and improve manners. For its natural consequences are a delicacy of perception and an emotional tact that are defeated by preaching and didactic teaching.

A liberal education will impart an awareness of the amazing and precious complexity of human relationships. Since those relationships are violated more often out of insensitiveness than out of deliberate intent, whatever increases sensitiveness of perception and understanding humanizes life. Literature in all its forms is the great humanizing medium of life. It must therefore be representative of life; not only of past life but of our own; not only of our own culture but of different cultures.

(6) An unfailing mark of philistinism in education is reference to the study of art and music as "the frills and fads" of schooling. Insofar as those who speak this way are not tone-deaf or color-blind, they are themselves products of a narrow education, unaware of the profound experiences which are uniquely bound up with the trained perception of color and form. There is no reason to believe that the capacity for the appreciation of art and music shows a markedly different curve of distribution from what is observable in the measurement of capacity of drawing inferences or recalling relevant information. A sufficient justification for making some study of art and music required in modern education is that it provides an unfailing source of delight in personal experience, a certain grace in living, and a variety of dimensions of meaning by which to interpret the world around us. This is a sufficient

justification: there are others, quite subsidiary, related to the themes, the occasions, the history and backgrounds of the works studied. Perhaps one should add—although this expresses only a reasonable hope—that a community whose citizens have developed tastes would not tolerate the stridency, the ugliness and squalor which assault us in our factories, our cities, and our countryside.

One of the reasons why the study of art and music has not received as much attention as it should by educators, particularly on the college level, is that instruction in these subjects often suffers from two opposite defects. Sometimes courses in art and music are given as if all students enrolled in them were planning a career as practicing artists or as professional *teachers* of the arts. Sometimes they are given as hours for passive enjoyment or relaxation in which the teacher does the performing or talking and in which there is no call upon the students to make an intelligent response.

The key-stress in courses in art and music should be *discrimination* and *interpretation,* rather than appreciation and cultivation. The latter can take care of themselves, when the student has learned to discriminate and interpret intelligently.

Briefly summarized: the answer to the question *What should we teach?* is selected materials from the fields of mathematics and the natural sciences; social studies, including history; language and literature; philosophy and logic; art and music. The knowledge imparted by such study should be acquired in such a way as to strengthen the skills of reading and writing, of thinking and imaginative interpretation, of criticism and evaluation.

John Dewey (1859–1952), Professor of Philosophy at Columbia University and one of the leading philosophers of the twentieth century, made important contributions to all areas of philosophy.

John Dewey

EXPERIENCE AND EDUCATION

I
TRADITIONAL *VS.* PROGRESSIVE EDUCATION

Mankind likes to think in terms of extreme opposites. It is given to formulating its beliefs in terms of *Either-Ors,* between which it recognizes no intermediate possibilities. When forced to recognize that the extremes cannot be acted upon, it is still inclined to hold that they are all right in theory but that when it comes to practical matters circumstances compel us to compromise. Educational philosophy is no exception. The history of educational theory is marked by opposition between the idea that education is development from within and that it is formation from without; that it is based upon natural endowments and that education is a process of overcoming natural inclination and substituting in its place habits acquired under external pressure.

Reprinted from *Experience and Education* (1938), by permission of Kappa Delta Pi, An Honor Society in Education, owners of the copyright.

At present, the opposition, so far as practical affairs of the school are concerned, tends to take the form of contrast between traditional and progressive education. If the underlying ideas of the former are formulated broadly, without the qualifications required for accurate statement, they are found to be about as follows: The subject-matter of education consists of bodies of information and of skills that have been worked out in the past; therefore, the chief business of the school is to transmit them to the new generation. In the past, there have also been developed standards and rules of conduct; moral training consists in forming habits of action in conformity with these rules and standards. Finally, the general pattern of school organization (by which I mean the relations of pupils to one another and to the teachers) constitutes the school a kind of institution sharply marked off from other social institutions. Call up in imagination the ordinary schoolroom, its time-schedules, schemes of classification, of examination and promotion, of rules of order, and I think you will grasp what is meant by "pattern of organization." If then you contrast this scene with what goes on in the family, for example, you will appreciate what is meant by the school being a kind of institution sharply marked off from any other form of social organization.

The three characteristics just mentioned fix the aims and methods of instruction and discipline. The main purpose or objective is to prepare the young for future responsibilities and for success in life, by means of acquisition of the organized bodies of information and prepared forms of skill which comprehend the material of instruction. Since the subject-matter as well as standards of proper conduct are handed down from the past, the attitude of pupils must, upon the whole, be one of docility, receptivity, and obedience. Books, especially textbooks, are the chief representatives of the lore and wisdom of the past, while teachers are the organs through which pupils are brought into effective connection with the material. Teachers are the agents through which knowledge and skills are communicated and rules of conduct enforced.

I have not made this brief summary for the purpose of criticizing the underlying philosophy. The rise of what is called new education and progressive schools is of itself a product of discontent with traditional education. In effect it is a criticism of the latter. When the implied criticism is made explicit it reads somewhat as follows: The traditional scheme is, in essence, one of imposition from above and from outside. It imposes adult standards, subject-matter, and methods upon those who are only growing slowly toward maturity. The gap is so great that the required subject-matter, the methods of learning and of behaving are foreign to the existing capacities of the young. They are beyond the reach of the experience the young learners already possess. Consequently, they must be imposed; even though good teachers will use devices of art to cover up the imposition so as to relieve it of obviously brutal features.

But the gulf between the mature or adult products and the experience and abilities of the young is so wide that the very situation forbids much active participation by pupils in the development of what is taught. Theirs is to do—and learn, as it was the part of the six hundred to do and die. Learning here means acquisition of what already is incorporated in books and in the heads of the elders. Moreover, that which is taught is thought of as essentially static. It is taught as a finished product, with little regard either to the ways in which it was originally built up or to changes that will surely occur in the future. It is to a large extent the cultural product of societies that assumed the future would be much like the past, and yet it is used as educational food in a society where change is the rule, not the exception.

If one attempts to formulate the philosophy of education implicit in the practices of the newer education, we may, I think, discover certain common principles amid the variety of progressive schools now existing. To imposition from above is opposed expression and cultivation of individuality; to external discipline is opposed free activity; to learning from texts and teachers, learning through experience; to acquisition of isolated skills and techniques by drill, is opposed acquisition of them as means of attaining ends which make direct vital appeal; to preparation for a more or less remote future is opposed making the most of the opportunities of present life; to static aims and materials is opposed acquaintance with a changing world.

Now, all principles by themselves are abstract. They become concrete only in the consequences which result from their application. Just because the principles set forth are so fundamental and far-reaching, everything depends upon the interpretation given them as they are put into practice in the school and the home. It is at this point that the reference made earlier to *Either-Or* philosophies becomes peculiarly pertinent. The general philosophy of the new education may be sound, and yet the difference in abstract principles will not decide the way in which the moral and intellectual preference involved shall be worked out in practice. There is always the danger in a new movement that in rejecting the aims and methods of that which it would supplant, it may develop its principles negatively rather than positively and constructively. Then it takes its clew in practice from that which is rejected instead of from the constructive development of its own philosophy.

I take it that the fundamental unity of the newer philosophy is found in the idea that there is an intimate and necessary relation between the processes of actual experience and education. If this be true, then a positive and constructive development of its own basic idea depends upon having a correct idea of experience. Take, for example, the question of organized subject-matter—which will be discussed in some detail later. The problem for progressive education is: What is the place and meaning of subject-matter and of organization *within* experience? How does subject-matter function? Is there anything inherent in experience which tends towards progressive organization of its contents? What results follow when the materials of experience are not progressively organized? A philosophy which proceeds on the basis of rejection, of sheer opposition, will neglect these questions. It will tend to suppose that because the old education was based on ready-made organization, therefore it suffices to reject the principle of organization *in toto,* instead of striving to discover what it means and how it is to be attained on the basis of experience. We might go through all the points of difference between the new and the old education and reach similar conclusions. When external control is rejected, the problem becomes that of finding the factors of control that are inherent within experience. When external authority is rejected, it does not follow that all authority should be rejected, but rather that there is need to search for a more effective source of authority. Because the older education imposed the knowledge, methods, and the rules of conduct of the mature person upon the young, it does not follow, except upon the basis of the extreme *Either-Or* philosophy, that the knowledge and skill of the mature person has no directive value for the experience of the immature. On the contrary, basing education upon personal experience may mean more multiplied and more intimate contacts between the mature and the immature than ever existed in the traditional school, and consequently more, rather than less, guidance by others. The problem, then, is: how these contacts can be established without violating the principle of learning through personal experience. The solution of this problem requires a well thought-out philosophy of the social factors that operate in the constitution of individual experience.

What is indicated in the foregoing remarks is that the general principles of the new education do not of themselves solve any of the problems of the actual or practical conduct and management of progressive schools. Rather, they set new problems which have to be worked out on the basis of a new philosophy of experience. The problems are not even recognized, to say nothing of being solved, when it is assumed that it suffices to reject the ideas and practices of the old education and then go to the opposite extreme. Yet I am sure that you will appreciate what is meant when I say that many of the newer schools tend to make little or nothing of organized subject-matter of study; to proceed as if any form of direction and guidance by adults were an invasion of individual freedom, and as if the idea that education should be concerned with the present and future meant that acquaintance with the past has little or no role to play in education. Without pressing these defects to the point of exaggeration, they at least illustrate what is meant by a theory and practice of education which proceeds negatively or by reaction against what has been current in education rather than by a positive and constructive development of purposes, methods, and subject-matter on the foundation of a theory of experience and its educational potentialities.

It is not too much to say that an educational philosophy which professes to be based on the idea of freedom may become as dogmatic as ever was the traditional education which is reacted against. For any theory and set of practices is dogmatic which is not based upon critical examination of its own underlying principles. Let us say that the new education emphasizes the freedom of the learner. Very well. A problem is now set. What does freedom mean and what are the conditions under which it is capable of realization? Let us say that the kind of external imposition which was so common in the traditional school limited rather than promoted the intellectual and moral development of the young. Again, very well. Recognition of this serious defect sets a problem. Just what is the role of the teacher and of books in promoting the educational development of the immature? Admit that traditional education employed as the subject-matter for study facts and ideas so bound up with the past as to give little help in dealing with the issues of the present and future. Very well. Now we have the problem of discovering the connection which actually exsts *within* experience between the achievements of the past and the issues of the present. We have the problem of ascertaining how acquaintance with the past may be translated into a potent instrumentality for dealing effectively with the future. We may reject knowledge of the past as the *end* of education and thereby only emphasize its importance as a *means*. When we do that we have a problem that is new in the story of education: How shall the young become acquainted with the past in such a way that the acquaintance is a potent agent in appreciation of the living present?

II
THE NEED OF A THEORY OF EXPERIENCE

In short, the point I am making is that rejection of the philosophy and practice of traditional education sets a new type of difficult educational problem for those who believe in the new type of education. We shall operate blindly and in confusion until we recognize this fact; until we thoroughly appreciate that departure from the old solves no problems. What is said in the following pages is, accordingly, intended to indicate some of the main problems with which the newer education is confronted and to suggest the main lines along which their solution is to be sought. I assume that amid all uncertainties there is one permanent frame of reference: namely, the organic connection between education and personal experience; or, that the new philosophy of education is committed to some kind of empirical and experimental philosophy. But experience and experiment are not self-explanatory ideas. Rather, their meaning is part of the problem to be explored. To know the meaning of empiricism we need to understand what experience is.

The belief that all genuine education comes about through experience does not mean that all experiences are genuinely or equally educative. Experience and education cannot be directly equated to each other. For some experiences are mis-educative. Any experience is mis-educative that has the effect of arresting or distorting the growth of further experience. An experience may be such as to engender callousness; it may produce lack of sensitivity and of responsiveness. Then the possibilities of having richer experience in the future are restricted. Again, a given experience may increase a person's automatic skill in a particular direction and yet tend to land him in a groove or rut; the effect again is to narrow the field of further experience. An experience may be immediately enjoyable and yet promote the formation of a slack and careless attitude; this attitude then operates to modify the quality of subsequent experiences so as to prevent a person from getting out of them what they have to give. Again, experiences may be so disconnected from one another that, while each is agreeable or even exciting in itself, they are not linked cumulatively to one another. Energy is then dissipated and a person becomes scatter-brained. Each experience may be lively, vivid, and "interesting," and yet their disconnectedness may artificially generate dispersive, disintegrated, centrifugal habits. The consequence of formation of such habits is inability to control future experiences. They are then taken, either by way of enjoyment or of discontent and revolt, just as they come. Under such circumstances, it is idle to talk of self-control.

Traditional education offers a plethora of examples of experiences of the kinds just mentioned. It is a great mistake to suppose, even tacitly, that the traditional schoolroom was not a place in which pupils had experiences. Yet this is tacitly assumed when progressive education as a plan of learning by experience is placed in sharp opposition to the old.

The proper line of attack is that the experiences which were had, by pupils and teachers alike, were largely of a wrong kind. How many students, for example, were rendered callous to ideas, and how many lost the impetus to learn because of the way in which learning was experienced by them? How many acquired special skills by means of automatic drill so that their power of judgment and capacity to act intelligently in new situations was limited? How many came to associate the learning process with ennui and boredom? How many found what they did learn so foreign to the situations of life outside the school as to give them no power of control over the latter? How many came to associate books with dull drudgery, so that they were "conditioned" to all but flashy reading matter?

If I ask these questions, it is not for the sake of wholesale condemnation of the old education. It is for quite another purpose. It is to emphasize the fact, first, that young people in traditional schools do have experiences; and, secondly, that the trouble is not the absence of experiences, but their defective and wrong character—wrong and defective from the standpoint of connection with further experience. The positive side of this point is even more important in connection with progressive education. It is not enough to insist upon the necessity of experience, nor even of activity in experience. Everything depends upon the *quality* of the experience which is had. The quality of any experience has two aspects. There is an immediate aspect of agreeableness or disagreeableness, and there is its influence upon later experiences. The first is obvious and easy to judge. The *effect* of an experience is not borne on its face. It sets a problem to the educator. It is his business to arrange for the kind of experiences which, while they do not repel the student, but rather engage his activities are, nevertheless, more than immediately enjoyable since they promote having desirable future experiences. Just as no man lives or dies to himself, so no experience lives and dies to itself. Wholly independent of desire or intent, every experience lives on in further experiences. Hence the central problem of an education based upon experience is to select the kind of present experiences that live fruitfully and creatively in subsequent experiences.

Later, I shall discuss in more detail the principle of the continuity of experience or what may be called the experiential continuum. Here I wish simply to emphasize the importance of this principle for the philosophy of educative experience. A philosophy of education, like any theory, has to be stated in words, in symbols. But so far as it is more than verbal it is a plan for conducting education. Like any plan, it must be framed with reference to what is to be done and how it is to be done. The more definitely and sincerely it is held that education is a development within, by, and for experience, the more important it is that there shall be clear conceptions of what experience is. Unless experience is so conceived that the result is a plan for deciding upon subject-matter, upon methods of instruction and discipline, and upon material equipment and social organization of the school, it is wholly in the air. It is reduced to a form of words which may be emotionally stirring but for which any other set of words might equally well be substituted unless they indicate operations to be initiated and executed. Just because traditional education was a matter of routine in which the plans and programs were handed down from the past, it does not follow that progressive education is a matter of planless improvisation.

The traditional school could get along without any consistently developed philosophy of education. About all it required in that line was a set of abstract words like culture, discipline, our great cultural heritage, etc., actual guidance being derived not from them but from custom and established routines. Just because progressive schools cannot rely upon established traditions and institutional habits, they must either proceed more or less haphazardly or be directed by ideas which, when they are made articulate and coherent, form a philosophy of education. Revolt against the kind of organization characteristic of the traditional school constitutes a demand for a kind of organization based upon ideas. I think that only slight acquaintance with the history of education is needed to prove that educational reformers and innovators alone have felt the need for a philosophy of education. Those who adhered to the established system needed merely a few fine-sounding words to justify existing practices. The real work was done by habits which were so fixed as to be institutional. The lesson for progressive education is that it requires in an urgent degree, a degree more pressing than was incumbent upon former innovators, a philosophy of education based upon a philosophy of experience.

I remarked incidentally that the philosophy in question is, to paraphrase the saying of Lincoln about democracy, one of education of, by, and for experience. No one of these words, *of, by,* or *for,* names anything which is self-evident. Each of them is a challenge to discover and put into operation a principle of order and organization which follows from understanding what educative experience signifies.

It is, accordingly, a much more difficult task to work out the kinds of materials, of methods, and of social relationships that are appropriate to the new education than is the case with traditional education. I think many of the difficulties experienced in the conduct of progressive schools and many of the criticisms leveled against them arise from this source. The difficulties are aggravated and the criticisms are increased when it is supposed that the new education is somehow easier than the old. This belief is, I imagine, more or less current. Perhaps it illustrates again the *Either-Or* philosophy, springing from the idea that about all which is required is *not* to do what is done in traditional schools.

I admit gladly that the new education is *simpler* in principle than the old. It is in harmony with principles of growth, while there is very much which is artificial in the old selection and arrangement of subjects and methods, and artificiality always leads to unnecessary complexity. But the easy and the simple are not identical. To discover what is really simple and to act upon the discovery is an exceedingly difficult task. After the artificial and complex is once institutionally established and ingrained in custom and routine, it is easier to walk in the paths that have been beaten than it is, after taking a new point of view, to work out what is practically involved in the new point of view. The old Ptolemaic astronomical system was more complicated with its cycles and epicycles than the Copernican system. But until organization of actual astronomical phenomena on the ground of the latter principle had been effected the easiest course was to follow the line of least resistance provided by the old intellectual habit. So we come back to the idea that a coherent *theory* of experience, affording positive direction to selection and organization of appropriate educational methods and materials, is required by the attempt to give new direction to the work of the schools. The process is a slow and arduous one. It is a matter of growth, and there are many obstacles which tend to obstruct growth and to deflect it into wrong lines.

I shall have something to say later about organization. All that is needed, perhaps, at this point is to say that we must escape from the tendency to think of organization in terms of the *kind* of organization, whether of content (or subject-matter), or of methods and social relations, that mark traditional education. I think that a good deal of the current opposition to the idea of organization is due to the fact that it is so hard to get away from the picture of the studies of the old school. The moment "organization" is mentioned imagination goes almost automatically to the kind of organization that is familiar, and in revolting against that we are led to shrink from the very idea of any organization. On the other hand, educational reactionaries, who are now gathering force, use the absence of adequate intellectual and moral organization in the newer type of school as proof not only of the need of organization, but to identify any and every kind of organization with that instituted before the rise of experimental science. Failure to develop a conception of organization upon the empirical and experimental basis gives reactionaries a too easy victory. But the fact that the empirical sciences now offer the best type of intellectual organization which can be found in any field shows that there is no reason why we, who call ourselves empiricists, should be "pushovers" in the matter of order and organization.

III
CRITERIA OF EXPERIENCE

If there is any truth in what has been said about the need of forming a theory of experience in order that education may be intelligently conducted upon the basis of experience, it is clear that the next thing in order in this discussion is to present the principles that are most significant in framing this theory. I shall not, therefore, apologize for engaging in a certain amount of philosophical analysis, which otherwise might be out of place. I may, however, reassure you to some degree by saying that this analysis is not an end in itself but is engaged in for the sake of obtaining criteria to be applied later in discussion of a number of concrete and, to most persons, more interesting issues.

I have already mentioned what I called the category of continuity, or the experiential continuum. This principle is involved, as I pointed out, in every attempt to discriminate between experiences that are worth while educationally and those that are not. It may seem superfluous to argue that this discrimination is necessary not only in criticizing the traditional type of education but also in initiating and conducting a different type. Nevertheless, it is advisable to pursue for a little while the idea that it is necessary. One may safely assume, I suppose, that one thing which has recommended the progressive movement is that it seems more in accord with the democratic ideal to which our people is committed than do the procedures of the traditional school, since the latter have so much of the autocratic about them. Another thing which has contributed to its favorable reception is that its methods are humane in comparison with the harshness so often attending the policies of the traditional school.

The question I would raise concerns why we prefer democratic and humane arrangements to those which are autocratic and harsh. And by "why," I mean the *reason* for preferring them, not just the *causes* which lead us to the preference. One *cause* may be that we have been taught not only in the schools but by the press, the pulpit, the platform, and our laws and law-making bodies that democracy is the best of all social institutions.

We may have so assimilated this idea from our surroundings that it has become an habitual part of our mental and moral make-up. But similar causes have led other persons in different surroundings to widely varying conclusions—to prefer fascism, for example. The cause for our preference is not the same thing as the reason why we *should* prefer it.

It is not my purpose here to go in detail into the reason. But I would ask a single question: Can we find any reason that does not ultimately come down to the belief that democratic social arrangements promote a better quality of human experience, one which is more widely accessible and enjoyed, than do non-democratic and anti-democratic forms of social life? Does not the principle of regard for individual freedom and for decency and kindliness of human relations come back in the end to the conviction that these things are tributary to a higher quality of experience on the part of a greater number than are methods of repression and coercion or force? Is it not the reason for our preference that we believe that mutual consultation and convictions reached through persuasion, make possible a better quality of experience than can otherwise be provided on any wide scale?

If the answer to these questions is in the affirmative (and personally I do not see how we can justify our preference for democracy and humanity on any other ground), the ultimate reason for hospitality to progressive education, because of its reliance upon and use of humane methods and its kinship to democracy, goes back to the fact that discrimination is made between the inherent values of different experiences. So I come back to the principle of continuity of experience as a criterion of discrimination.

At bottom, this principle rests upon the fact of habit, when *habit* is interpreted biologically. The basic characteristic of habit is that every experience enacted and undergone modifies the one who acts and undergoes, while this modification affects, whether we wish it or not, the quality of subsequent experiences. For it is a somewhat different person who enters into them. The principle of habit so understood obviously goes deeper than the ordinary conception of *a* habit as a more or less fixed way of doing things, although it includes the latter as one of its special cases. It covers the formation of attitudes, attitudes that are emotional and intellectual; it covers our basic sensitivities and ways of meeting and responding to all the conditions which we meet in living. From this point of view, the principle of continuity of experience means that every experience both takes up something from those which have gone before and modifies in some way the quality of those which come after. As the poet states it,

. . . all experience is an arch wherethro'
Gleams that untraveled world, whose margin fades
For ever and for ever when I move.

So far, however, we have no ground for discrimination among experiences. For the principle is of universal application. There is *some* kind of continuity in every case. It is when we note the different forms in which continuity of experience operates that we get the basis of discriminating among experiences. I may illustrate what is meant by an objection which has been brought against an idea which I once put forth—namely, that the educative process can be identified with growth when that is understood in terms of the active participle, *growing*.

Growth, or growing as developing, not only physically but intellectually and morally, is one exemplification of the principle of continuity. The objection made is that growth might take many different directions: a man, for example, who starts out on a career of burglary may grow in that direction, and by practice may grow into a highly expert burglar. Hence it is argued that "growth" is not enough; we must also specify the direction in which growth takes place, the end towards which it tends. Before, however, we decide that the objection is conclusive we must analyze the case a little further.

That a man may grow in efficiency as a burglar, as a gangster, or as a corrupt politician, cannot be doubted. But from the standpoint of growth as education and education as growth the question is whether growth in this direction promotes or retards growth in general. Does this form of growth create conditions for further growth, or does it set up conditions that shut off the person who has grown in this particular direction from the occasions, stimuli, and opportunities for continuing growth in new directions? What is the effect of growth in a special direction upon the attitudes and habits which alone open up avenues for development in other lines? I shall leave you to answer these questions, saying simply that when and *only* when development in a particular line conduces to continuing growth does it answer to the criterion of education as growing. For the conception is one that must find universal and not specialized limited application.

I return now to the question of continuity as a criterion by which to discriminate between experiences which are educative and those which are mis-educative. As we have seen, there is some kind of continuity in any case since every experience affects for better or worse the attitudes which help decide the quality of further experiences, by setting up certain preference and aversion, and making it easier or harder to act for this or that end. Moreover, every experience influences in some degree the objective conditions under which further experiences are had. For example, a child who learns to speak has a new facility and new desire. But he has also widened the external conditions of subsequent learning. When he learns to read, he similarly opens up a new environment. If a person decides to become a teacher, lawyer, physician, or stockbroker, when he executes his intention he thereby necessarily determines to some extent the environment in which he will act in the future. He has rendered himself more sensitive and responsive to certain conditions, and relatively immune to those things about him that would have been stimuli if he had made another choice.

But, while the principle of continuity applies in some way in every case, the quality of the present experience influences the *way* in which the principle applies. We speak of spoiling a child and of the spoilt child. The effect of over-indulging a child is a continuing one. It sets up an attitude which operates as an automatic demand that persons and objects cater to his desires and caprices in the future. It makes him seek the kind of situation that will enable him to do what he feels like doing at the time. It renders him averse to and comparatively incompetent in situations which require effort and perseverance in overcoming obstacles. There is no paradox in the fact that the principle of the continuity of experience may operate so as to leave a person arrested on a low plane of development, in a way which limits later capacity for growth.

On the other hand, if an experience arouses curiosity, strengthens initiative, and sets up desires and purposes that are sufficiently intense to carry a person over dead places in the future, continuity works in a very different way. Every experience is a moving force. Its value can be judged only on the ground of what it moves toward and into. The greater maturity of experience which should belong to the adult as educator puts him in a position to evaluate each experience of the young in a way in which the one having the less mature experience cannot do. It is then the business of the educator to see in what direction an experience is heading. There is no point in his being more mature if, instead of using his greater insight to help organize the conditions of the experience of the immature, he throws away his insight. Failure to take the moving force of an experience into account so as to judge and direct it on the ground of what it is moving into means disloyalty to the principle of experience itself. The disloyalty operates in two directions. The educator is false to the understanding that he should have obtained from his own past experience. He is also unfaithful to the fact that all human experience is ultimately social: that it involves contact and communication. That mature person, to put it in moral terms, has no right to withhold from the young on given occasions whatever capacity for sympathetic understanding his own experience has given him.

No sooner, however, are such things said than there is a tendency to react to the other extreme and take what has been said as a plea for some sort of disguised imposition from outside. It is worth while, accordingly, to say something about the way in which the adult can exercise the wisdom his own wider experience gives him without imposing a merely external control. On one side, it is his business to be on the alert to see what attitudes and habitual tendencies are being created. In this direction he must, if he is an educator, be able to judge what attitudes are actually conducive to continued growth and what are detrimental. He must, in addition, have that sympathetic understanding of individuals as individuals which gives him an idea of what is actually going on in the minds of those who are learning. It is, among other things, the need for these abilities on the part of the parent and teacher which makes a system of education based upon living experience a more difficult affair to conduct successfully than it is to follow the patterns of traditional education.

But there is another aspect of the matter. Experience does not go on simply inside a person. It does go on there, for it influences the formation of attitudes of desire and purpose. But this is not the whole of the story. Every genuine experience has an active side which changes in some degree the objective conditions under which experiences are had. The difference between civilization and savagery, to take an example on a large scale, is found in the degree in which previous experiences have changed the objective conditions under which subsequent experiences take place. The existence of roads, of means of rapid movement and transportation, tools, implements, furniture, electric light and power, are illustrations. Destroy the external conditions of present civilized experience, and for a time our experience would relapse into that of barbaric peoples.

In a word, we live from birth to death in a world of persons and things which in large measure is what it is because of what has been done and transmitted from previous human activities. When this fact is ignored, experience is treated as if it were something which goes on exclusively inside an individual's body and mind. It ought not to be necessary to say that experience does not occur in a vacuum. There are sources outside an individual which give rise to experience. It is constantly fed from these springs. No one would question that a child in a slum tenement has a different experience from that of a child in a cultured home; that the country lad has a different kind of experience from the city boy, or a boy on the seashore one different from the lad who is brought up on inland prairies. Ordinarily we take such facts for granted as too commonplace to record. But when their educational import is recognized, they indicate the second way in which the educator can direct the experience of the young without engaging in imposition. A primary responsibility of educators is that they not only be aware of the general principle of the shaping of actual experience by environing conditions, but that they also recognize in the concrete what surroundings are conducive to having experiences that lead to growth. Above all, they should know how to utilize the surroundings, physical and social, that exist so as to extract from them all that they have to contribute to building up experiences that are worth while.

Traditional education did not have to face this problem; it could systematically dodge this responsibility. The school environment of desks, blackboards, a small school yard, was supposed to suffice. There was no demand that the teacher should become intimately acquainted with the conditions of the local community, physical, historical, economic, occupational, etc., in order to utilize them as educational resources. A system of education based upon the necessary connection of education with experience must, on the contrary, if faithful to its principle, take these things constantly into account. This tax upon the educator is another reason why progressive education is more difficult to carry on than was ever the traditional system.

It is possible to frame schemes of education that pretty systematically subordinate objective conditions to those which reside in the individuals being educated. This happens whenever the place and function of the teacher, of books, of apparatus and equipment, of everything which represents the products of the more mature experience of elders, is systematically subordinated to the immediate inclinations and feelings of the young. Every theory which assumes that importance can be attached to these objective factors only at the expense of imposing external control and of limiting the freedom of individuals rests finally upon the notion that experience is truly experience only when objective conditions are subordinated to what goes on within the individuals having the experience.

I do not mean that it is supposed that objective conditions can be shut out. It is recognized that they must enter in: so much concession is made to the inescapable fact that we live in a world of things and persons. But I think that observation of what goes on in some families and some schools would disclose that some parents and some teachers are acting upon the idea of *subordinating* objective conditions to internal ones. In that case, it is assumed not only that the latter are primary, which in one sense they are, but that just as they temporarily exist they fix the whole educational process.

Let me illustrate from the case of an infant. The needs of a baby for food, rest, and activity are certainly primary and decisive in one respect. Nourishment must be provided; provision must be made for comfortable sleep, and so on. But these facts do not mean that a parent shall feed the baby at any time when the baby is cross or irritable, that there shall not be a program of regular hours of feeding and sleeping, etc. The wise mother takes account of the needs of the infant but not in a way which dispenses with her own responsibility for regulating the objective conditions under which the needs are satisfied. And if she is a wise mother in this respect, she draws upon past experiences of experts as well as her own for the light that these shed upon what experiences are in general most conducive to the normal development of infants. Instead of these conditions being subordinated to the immediate internal condition of the baby, they are definitely ordered so that a particular kind of *interaction* with these immediate internal states may be brought about.

The word "interaction," which has just been used, expresses the second chief principle for interpreting an experience in its educational function and force. It assigns equal rights to both factors in experience—objective and internal conditions. Any normal experience is an interplay of these two sets of conditions. Taken together, or in their interaction, they form what we call a *situation*. The trouble with traditional education was not that it emphasized the external conditions that enter into the control of the experiences but that it paid so little attention to the internal factors which also decide what kind of experience is had. It violated the principle of interaction from one side. But this violation is no reason why the new education should violate the principle from the other side—except upon the basis of the extreme *Either-Or* educational philosophy which has been mentioned.

The illustration drawn from the need for regulation of the objective conditions of a baby's development indicates, first, that the parent has responsibility for arranging the conditions under which an infant's experience of food, sleep, etc., occurs, and, secondly, that the responsibility is fulfilled by utilizing the funded experience of the past, as this is represented, say, by the advice of competent physicians and others who have made a special study of normal physical growth. Does it limit the freedom of the mother when she uses the body of knowledge thus provided to regulate the objective conditions of nourishment and sleep? Or does the enlargement of her intelligence in fulfilling her parental function widen her freedom? Doubtless if a fetish were made of the advice and directions so that they came to be inflexible dictates to be followed under every possible condition, then restriction of freedom of both parent and child would occur. But this restriction would also be a limitation of the intelligence that is exercised in personal judgment.

In what respect does regulation of objective conditions limit the freedom of the baby? Some limitation is certainly placed upon its immediate movements and inclinations when it is put in its crib, at a time when it wants to continue playing, or does not get food at the moment it would like it, or when it isn't picked up and dandled when it cries for attention. Restriction also occurs when mother or nurse snatches a child away from an open fire into which it is about to fall. I shall have more to say later about freedom. Here it is enough to ask whether freedom is to be thought of and adjudged on the basis of relatively momentary incidents or whether its meaning is found in the continuity of developing experience.

The statement that individuals live in a world means, in the concrete, that they live in a series of situations. And when it is said that they live *in* these situations, the meaning of the word "in" is different from its meaning when it is said that pennies are "in" a pocket or paint is "in" a can. It means, once more, that interaction is going on between an individual and objects and other persons. The conceptions of *situation* and of *interaction* are inseparable from each other. An experience is always what it is because of a transaction taking place between an individual and what, at the time, constitutes his environment, whether the latter consists of persons with whom he is talking about some topic or event, the subject talked about being also a part of the situation; or the toys with which he is playing; the book he is reading (in which his environing conditions at the time may be England or ancient Greece or an imaginary region); or the materials of an experiment he is performing. The environment, in other words, is whatever conditions interact with personal needs, desires, purposes, and capacities to create the experience which is had. Even when a person builds a castle in the air he is interacting with the objects which he constructs in fancy.

The two principles of continuity and interaction are not separate from each other. They intercept and unite. They are, so to speak, the longitudinal and lateral aspects of experience. Different situations succeed one another. But because of the principle of continuity something is carried over from the earlier to the later ones. As an individual passes from one situation to another, his world, his environment, expands or contracts. He does not find himself living in another world but in a different part or aspect of one and the same world. What he has learned in the way of knowledge and skill in one situation becomes an instrument of understanding and dealing effectively with the situations which follow. The process goes on as long as life and learning continue. Otherwise the course of experience is disorderly, since the individual factor that enters into making an experience is split. A divided world, a world whose parts and aspects do not hang together, is at once a sign and a cause of a divided personality. When the splitting-up reaches a certain point we call the person insane. A fully integrated personality, on the other hand, exists only when successive experiences are integrated with one another. It can be built up only as a world of related objects is constructed.

Continuity and interaction in their active union with each other provide the measure of the educative significance and value of an experience. The immediate and direct concern of an educator is then with the situations in which interaction takes place. The individual, who enters as a factor into it, is what he is at a given time. It is the other factor, that of objective conditions, which lies to some extent within the possibility of regulation by the educator. As has already been noted, the phrase "objective conditions" covers a wide range. It includes what is done by the educator and the way in which it is done, not only words spoken but the tone of voice in which they are spoken. It includes equipment, books, apparatus, toys, games played. It includes the materials with which an individual interacts, and, most important of all, the total *social* set-up of the situations in which a person is engaged.

When it is said that the objective conditions are those which are within the power of the educator to regulate, it is meant, of course, that his ability to influence directly the experience of others and thereby the education that obtain places upon him the duty of determining that environment which will interact with the existing capacities and needs of those taught to create a worth-while experience. The trouble with traditional education was not that educators took upon themselves the responsibility for providing an environment. The trouble was that they did not consider the other factor in creating an experience; namely, the powers and purposes of those taught. It was assumed that a certain set of conditions was intrinsically desirable, apart from its ability to evoke a certain quality of response in individuals. This lack of mutual adaptation made the process of teaching and learning accidental. Those to whom the provided conditions were suitable managed to learn. Others got on as best they could. Responsibility for selecting objective conditions carries with it, then, the responsibility for understanding the needs and capacities of the individuals who are learning at a given time. It is not enough that certain materials and methods have proved effective with other individuals at other times. There must be a reason for thinking that they will function in generating an experience that has educative quality with particular individuals at a particular time.

It is no reflection upon the nutritive quality of beefsteak that it is not fed to infants. It is not an invidious reflection upon trigonometry that we do not teach it in the first or fifth grade of school. It is not the subject *per se* that is educative or that is conducive to growth. There is no subject that is in and of itself, or without regard to the stage of growth attained by the learner, such that inherent educational value can be attributed to it. Failure to take into account adaptation to the needs and capacities of individuals was the source of the idea that certain subjects and certain methods are intrinsically cultural or intrinsically good for mental discipline. There is no such thing as educational value in the abstract. The notion that some subjects and methods and that acquaintance with certain facts and truths possess educational value in and of themselves is the reason why traditional education reduced the material of education so largely to a diet of predigested materials. According to this notion, it was enough to regulate the quantity and difficulty of the material provided, in a scheme of quantitative grading, from month to month and from year to year. Otherwise a pupil was expected to take it in the doses that were prescribed from without. If the pupil left it instead of taking it, if he engaged in physical truancy, or in the mental truancy of mind-wandering and finally built up an emotional revulsion against the subject, he was held to be at fault. No question was raised as to whether the trouble might not lie in the subject-matter or in the way in which it was offered. The principle of interaction makes it clear that failure of adaptation of material to needs and capacities of individuals may cause an experience to be non-educative quite as much as failure of an individual to adapt himself to the material.

The principle of continuity in its educational application means, nevertheless, that the future has to be taken into account at every stage of the educational process. This idea is easily misunderstood and is badly distorted in traditional education. Its assumption is, that by acquiring certain skills and by learning certain subjects which would be needed later (perhaps in college or perhaps in adult life) pupils are as a matter of course made ready for the needs and circumstances of the future. Now "preparation" is a treacherous idea. In a certain sense every experience should do something to prepare a person for later experiences of a deeper and more expansive quality. That is the very meaning of growth, continuity, reconstruction of experience. But it is a mistake to suppose that the mere acquisition of a certain amount of arithmetic, geography, history, etc., which is taught and studied because it may be useful at some time in the future, has this effect, and it is a mistake to suppose that acquisition of skills in reading and figuring will automatically constitute preparation for their right and effective use under conditions very unlike those in which they were acquired.

Almost everyone has had occasion to look back upon his school days and wonder what has become of the knowledge he was supposed to have amassed during his years of schooling, and why it is that the technical skills he acquired have to be learned over again in changed form in order to stand him in good stead. Indeed, he is lucky who does not find that in order to make progress, in order to go ahead intellectually, he does not have to unlearn much of what he learned in school. These questions cannot be disposed of by saying that the subjects were not actually learned, for they were learned at least sufficiently to enable a pupil to pass examinations in them. One trouble is that the subject-matter in question was learned in isolation; it was put, as it were, in a water-tight compartment. When the question is asked, then, what has become of it, where has it gone to, the right answer is that it is still there in the special compartment in which it was originally stowed away. If exactly the same conditions recurred as those under which it was acquired, it would also recur and be available. But it was segregated when it was acquired and hence is so disconnected from the rest of experience that it is not available under the actual conditions of life. It is contrary to the laws of experience that learning of this kind, no matter how thoroughly engrained at the time, should give genuine preparation.

Nor does failure in preparation end at this point. Perhaps the greatest of all pedagogical fallacies is the notion that a person learns only the particular thing he is studying at the time. Collateral learning in the way of formation of enduring attitudes, of likes and dislikes, may be and often is much more important than the spelling lesson or lesson in geography or history that is learned. For these attitudes are fundamentally what count in the future. The most important attitude that can be formed is that of desire to go on learning. If impetus in this direction is weakened instead of being intensified, something much more than mere lack of preparation takes place. The pupil is actually robbed of native capacities which otherwise would enable him to cope with the circumstances that he meets in the course of his life. We often see persons who have had little schooling and in whose case the absence of set schooling proves to be a positive asset. They have at least retained their native common sense and power of judgment, and its exercise in the actual conditions of living has given them the precious gift of ability to learn from the experiences they have. What avail is it to win prescribed amounts of information about geography and history, to win ability to read and write, if in the process the individual loses his own soul: loses his appreciation of things worth while, of the values to which these things are relative; if he loses desire to apply what he has learned and, above all, loses the ability to extract meaning from his future experiences as they occur?

What, then, is the true meaning of preparation in the educational scheme? In the first place, it means that a person, young or old, gets out of his present experience all that there is in it for him at the time in which he has it. When preparation is made the controlling end, then the potentialities of the present are sacrificed to a suppositious future. When this happens, the actual preparation for the future is missed or distorted. The ideal of using the present simply to get ready for the future contradicts itself. It omits, and even shuts out, the very conditions by which a person can be prepared for his future. We always live at the time we live and not at some other time, and only by extracting at each present time the full meaning of each present experience are we prepared for doing the same thing in the future. This is the only preparation which in the long run amounts to anything.

All this means that attentive care must be devoted to the conditions which give each present experience a worth-while meaning. Instead of inferring that it doesn't make much difference what the present experience is as long as it is enjoyed, the conclusion is the exact opposite. Here is another matter where it is easy to react from one extreme to the other. Because traditional schools tended to sacrifice the present to a remote and more or less unknown future, therefore it comes to be believed that the educator has little responsibility for the kind of present experiences the young undergo. But the relation of the present and the future is not an *Either-Or* affair. The present affects the future anyway. The persons who should have some idea of the connection between the two are those who have achieved maturity. Accordingly, upon them devolves the responsibility for instituting the conditions for the kind of present experience which has a favorable effect upon the future. Education as growth or maturity should be an ever-present process.

SUGGESTIONS FOR FURTHER READING

CAHN, STEVEN M., ed., *The Philosophical Foundations of Education,* New York: Harper & Row, 1970. Paperback. Historical and contemporary readings in philosophy of education.

HOOK, SIDNEY, *The Paradoxes of Freedom,* Berkeley and Los Angeles: University of California Press, 1962. Paperback. A provocative discussion of the nature and justification of human rights.

LASLETT, PETER, and RUNCIMAN, W. G., eds., *Philosophy, Politics and Society,* First, Second, and Third Series, Oxford: Basil Blackwell, 1956, 1962, 1967. Interesting, recent essays on various issues in political philosophy.

INDEX

(CHAPTERS 1–10)

71 72 73 74   7 6 5 4 3 2 1